Real and Per Capita Data

Total	Personal consumption expenditures	Personal saving	Current prices	1958 prices	Current prices	1958 prices	
Percent			Per capita dollars	Billions of dollars	Per capita dollars	Billions of dollars	
95.0	92.7	5.0	846	204	683	150	1929
95.4	93.8	4.6	734	184	605	138	1930
95.9	94.4	4.1	610	169	516	134	1931
101.3	99.8	−1.3	464	144	390	114	1932
102.0	100.6	−2.0	442	142	362	112	1933
99.3	98.0	.7	514	154	414	120	1934
96.3	95.2	3.7	566	170	459	132	1935
94.6	93.3	5.4	644	193	518	148	1936
94.7	93.4	5.3	700	203	552	153	1937
98.9	97.6	1.1	652	192	504	144	1938
96.3	95.0	3.7	690	209	537	156	1939
94.9	93.6	5.1	754	227	573	166	1940
88.2	86.9	11.8	933	264	695	190	1941
76.4	75.7	23.6	1170	298	867	213	1942
75.0	74.4	25.0	1402	337	976	223	1943
74.5	74.0	25.5	1518	361	1057	232	1944
80.3	79.7	19.7	1514	355	1074	230	1945
90.5	89.6	9.5	1474	312	1132	227	1946
95.7	94.6	4.3	1605	310	1178	218	1947
92.9	91.8	7.1	1757	324	1290	230	1948
95.0	93.8	5.0	1719	324	1264	231	1949
93.7	92.3	6.3	1877	355	1364	250	1950
92.4	91.0	7.6	2128	383	1469	256	1951
92.4	90.9	7.6	2200	395	1518	263	1952
92.8	91.1	7.2	2284	413	1583	275	1953
93.6	91.9	6.4	2246	407	1585	278	1954
94.3	92.4	5.7	2408	438	1666	297	1955
93.0	91.0	7.0	2492	446	1743	309	1956
93.3	91.2	6.7	2575	452	1801	316	1957
93.0	91.0	7.0	2569	447	1831	319	1958
94.4	92.3	5.6	2731	476	1905	333	1959
95.1	92.9	4.9	2788	488	1937	340	1960
94.2	92.0	5.8	2830	497	1984	351	1961
94.4	92.2	5.6	3001	530	2065	367	1962
95.1	92.7	4.9	3118	551	2133	381	1963
94.0	91.6	6.0	3292	581	2283	408	1964
94.0	91.5	6.0	3520	618	2436	435	1965
93.6	91.1	6.4	3806	658	2604	459	1966
92.6	90.1	7.4	3985	675	2749	478	1967
93.3	90.7	6.7	4295	707	2945	499	1968
94.0	91.3	6.0	4590	726	3130	514	1969
91.9	89.3	8.1	4769	723	3376	535	1970
91.9	89.4	8.1	5099	745	3603	555	1971
93.4	90.8	6.6	5544	792	3843	580	1972
91.8	89.1	8.2	6154	839	4295	619	1973
92.1	89.4	7.9	6592	821	4623	602	1974

Table headers: PERCENT OF DISPOSABLE PERSONAL INCOME — Personal outlays (Total, Personal consumption expenditures), Personal saving. Gross national product (Current prices, 1958 prices). Disposable personal income (Current prices, 1958 prices).

ECONOMICS

PRIVATE AND PUBLIC CHOICE

ECONOMICS
PRIVATE AND PUBLIC CHOICE

JAMES D. GWARTNEY
Florida State University

ACADEMIC PRESS   New York / San Francisco / London
A Subsidiary of Harcourt Brace Jovanovich, Publishers

ACADEMIC PRESS, INC.
111 Fifth Avenue, New York, New York 10003

United Kingdom Edition published by
ACADEMIC PRESS, INC. (LONDON) LTD.
24/28 Oval Road, London NW1

Library of Congress Cataloging in Publication Data

Gwartney, James D
    Economics, private and public choice.

    Bibliography: p.
    Includes index.
    1.   Economics.   I.   Title.
HB171.5.G96   1976   330   75-13099
ISBN 0–12–311050–5

PRINTED IN THE UNITED STATES OF AMERICA

Cover painting *Estate* by Robert Rauschenberg, courtesy of the Philadelphia
Museum of Art: Given by the Friends of the Philadelphia Museum of Art.

CONTENTS

Suggested Outlines for One-Semester Courses / xv

Preface / xvii

Acknowledgments / xxi

I   THE ECONOMIC WAY OF THINKING—AN INTRODUCTION

1   The Economic Approach   **3**

What Is Economics About? / 3   Man's Losing Struggle with Scarcity / 4   The Economic Way of Thinking / 5   Normative and Positive Economics / 10   Looking for Action?—Try Economics / 11

Myths of Economics: "Economics rejects the humanitarian side of man." / 9

Perspectives in Economics: Do Material Goods Bring Happiness? / 12

2   Some Tools of the Economist   **16**

Opportunity Cost Is the Highest Valued Opportunity Lost / 16   The Production Possibilities Curve / 18   Trade Tips and Comparative Advantage / 20   Dependence, Specialization, and Exchange / 25   Three Economizing Decisions Facing All Nations: What, How, and for Whom / 27   Two Methods of Making Decisions—The Market and Government Planning / 28

Myths of Economics: "In exchange, if someone gains, someone else must lose. Trading is a zero-sum game." / 26

3   Market Decisions and the Market Process   **32**

Scarcity Necessitates Rationing / 32   Consumer Choice and the Law of Demand / 33 Producer's Choice and the Law of Supply / 36   Price and Market Equilibrium / 37   Shifts in Demand and Advice on How to Pass Your First Economics Exam / 38   Shifts in Supply / 40   Time and the Adjustment Process / 42   Supply and Demand in Action / 44   Repealing the Laws of Supply and Demand / 46   Rationing and Motivating, the Two Great Attributes of the Market / 47

Myths of Economics: "Rent controls are an effective method of assuring adequate housing at a price the poor can afford." / 48

4   A Bird's-Eye View of the Public Sector   **52**

Ideal Economic Efficiency / 52   Why Might the Invisible Hand Fail? / 54 Government—A Potential Vehicle for Gain / 58   Redistribution—Dividing the Economic

Pie / 59   The Market and the Public Sector—Two Methods of Economic
Organization / 60   Conflicts between Good Economics and Good Politics / 64
Outstanding Economist: James Buchanan / 65

5   Taxes and Government Spending   70

What Do Federal, State, and Local Governments Buy? / 71   Sources of Tax Revenues / 74
The Concept of Incidence / 75   Who Pays the Tax Bill? / 79   The Taxes Others Paid / 80
Myths of Economics: "The growth of the federal government has been the major source of
government expansion." / 73
Controversies in Economics: Is There an Energy Crisis or a Policy Crisis? / 81

II   MACROECONOMICS

6   Taking the Nation's Economic Pulse   91

The Concept of the GNP / 91   Two Ways of Measuring GNP / 94   Gross National
Product or Gross National Cost? / 98   Five Problems with GNP as a Measuring Rod / 98
What the GNP Does *Not* Measure / 104   The Great Contribution of GNP / 104   Other
Related Income Measures / 104
Outstanding Economist: Simon Kuznets / 105

7   Unemployment, Inflation, and Business Cycles   110

Swings in the Economic Pendulum / 111   A Hypothetical Business Cycle / 112   Three
Different Views of the Business Cycle / 113   The Normal Rate of Unemployment / 116
Cyclical Unemployment / 119   Actual and Potential GNP / 120   Questions and Answers
about Inflation / 122
Myths of Economics: "Unemployed resources would not exist if the economy were operating
efficiently." / 121

8   Aggregate Equilibrium and a Simple Keynesian Model   131

Keynes and the Views of Classical Economists / 131   Tools of Modern Keynesian
Analysis / 134   Equilibrium and the Keynesian Model / 140   Adding Government
Demand / 145   Leakages and Injections—Another Way of Looking at Equilibrium / 146
Pulling It Together / 147
Outstanding Economist: John Maynard Keynes / 135

**9   The Multiplier, Accelerator, and a Keynesian View of the
      Business Cycle   151**

The Multiplier Principle / 151   Business Pessimism—A Self-Fulfilling Prophecy / 157
Investment Instability and the Accelerator / 158   A Keynesian View of the Business
Cycle / 160   Investment and the Cycle / 161

10   Fiscal Policy   165

Public Policy to Deal with a Recession / 165   Fiscal Policy to Deal with Inflation / 170
The Central Idea of Fiscal Policy / 171   The Full-Employment Budget Concept / 173   Has
Real World Fiscal Policy Been Stabilizing? / 173   Automatic Stabilizers / 175   Spending
versus Taxing Alternatives / 176

Outstanding Economist: Walter Heller / 169

Perspectives in Economics: Fact and Fiction about the National Debt / 177

11   Money and the Banking System   184

What Is Money? / 184   The Business of Banking / 187   Fractional Reserve
Goldsmithing / 188   Fractional Reserve Banking / 189   The Federal Reserve
System / 192   How the Fed Controls Our Money Supply / 194   The Fed and the
Treasury / 199   Dynamics of Monetary Policy / 200

Outstanding Economist: Arthur Burns / 193

12   Money, Employment, Inflation, and a More Complete
Keynesian Model   203

The Demand and Supply of Money / 203   Interest Rates and Investment / 205
Expansionary and Restrictive Monetary Policy / 206   How Monetary Policy Works—The
Keynesian View / 207   Combining Monetary and Fiscal Policy / 208   Did Macropolicy
Cause the Inflation of the 1970s? / 209   Will Monetary Policy Always Stimulate
Demand? / 210   Full Employment and Inflation in the Real World / 214

Outstanding Economist: Paul Samuelson / 211

Controversies in Economics: Will There Ever Be Another Great Depression? / 217

13   The Business Cycle and Inflation—The Monetarist View   224

The Equation of Exchange / 224   The Classical View—Money Does Not Matter / 225
The Early Keynesians—Money Still Does Not Matter Much / 225   The Modern
Monetarist—Money Matters Most / 226   The Impact of Money—The Monetarist
View / 230   Money and Business Cycles / 233   Money, Recessions, and Inflation—The
Record / 234   Money and Inflation in Other Countries / 240

Outstanding Economist: Milton Friedman / 227

Myths of Economics: "Inflation is caused by greedy businessmen and union leaders." / 238

Perspectives in Economics: Inflation: Its Cause and Cure—A Monetarist's View / 241

14   Proper Macropolicy—The Monetarist View   247

Two Things That Monetary Policy Cannot Do—The Monetarist View / 247   Limited
Effectiveness of Monetary Policy—The Monetarist View / 253   Three Things Monetary
Policy Can Do—The Monetarist View / 254   Why Macroplanners May Do the Wrong
Thing / 255   Constant Rate of Monetary Growth—The Monetarist View of Proper
Policy / 259   The Monetarist View of Fiscal Policy / 260

Myths of Economics: "The high interest rates of the 1970s resulted because the Fed was
reducing the rate of monetary expansion." / 250

Perspectives in Economics: Why Fiscal Policy Is Impotent—An Interview with a
Monetarist / 260

15   Dealing with Unemployment and Inflation   266

Can Wage-Price Controls Make Macro-"Solutions" More Effective? / 266   Public
Employment / 271   Dealing with Youth Unemployment / 272   Could We Better Target
Government Spending? / 274   Do Unemployment Compensation and Welfare Benefits
Increase the Unemployment Rate? / 274   Indexing—Learning to Live with
Inflation / 276   Pulling It All Together / 278

Controversies in Economics: Keynesians, Monetarists, and Middle-of-the-Roaders on Macroeconomics / 279

III   MICROECONOMICS

16   Demand and Consumer Choice   289

Consumer Decision-Making—Deciding What to Buy / 289   Individual Demand / 291
Consumer Choice and Market Demand / 293   What Will Cause the Demand Curve to
Shift? / 293   Time Cost and Consumer Choice / 296   Elasticity of Demand / 296   How
Does Income Influence Demand? / 302   Why Do Consumers Buy That? / 302
Outstanding Economist: John Kenneth Galbraith / 301
Controversies in Economics: Advertising—The Views of Its Critics and Defenders / 303

17   Costs and Producer Decisions   310

The Business Firm / 310   Calculating Economic Costs and Profits / 312   Total Costs,
Average Costs, and Marginal Costs / 313   Rate of Output and the Firm's Cost in the Short
Run / 314   Costs in the Long Run / 318   What Factors Will Cause the Firm's Cost
Curves to Shift? / 322   Costs and the Economic Way of Thinking / 323
Myths of Economics: "A good business decision-maker will never sell a product for less than
its production cost." / 325

18   The Firm under Pure Competition   329

Two Meanings of Competition / 329   The Assumptions of the Purely Competitive
Model / 330   Why Is Pure Competition Important? / 330   The Workings of the
Competitive Model / 331   The Firm and Competitive Markets / 335   The Role of
Profits in the Competitive Model / 339   Supply Elasticity and the Role of Time / 339
Market Adjustments to Changing Production Costs / 340   Efficiency and the Competitive
Model / 341

19   Monopolistic Competition, Product Differentiation,
        and Low Barriers to Entry   345

Product Differentiation / 345   The Hypothetical Model of Monopolistic
Competition / 346   Price and Output under Monopolistic Competition / 346   Real
World Monopolistic Competitors / 349   Price Discrimination / 349   Competition and
the Economic Way of Thinking / 350   Contrasting Pure and Monopolistic
Competition / 352
Outstanding Economist: Joan Robinson / 351
Controversies in Economics: Is Monopolistic Competition Inefficient? / 353
Perspectives in Economics: Is Planned Obsolescence Good Business? / 355

20   Monopoly and High Barriers to Entry   360

Competition is Great, But . . . / 360   What Is a Monopoly? / 362   The Hypothetical
Model of Monopoly / 362   Why Monopoly Is Bad / 365   When Can a Monopolized
Industry Be Competitive? / 366   Economies of Scale and Natural Monopoly / 367
Regulating the Monopolist / 369   The Government Operated Firm / 373   There Are No
Ideal Solutions / 374

Perspectives in Economics: How the Regulators Promote Inefficiency and Protect You from Low Prices—The Case of Transportation / 375

21 Oligopoly and the World of Big Business   382

Characteristics of Oligopoly / 382   Price and Output Determination / 383   It Pays to Collude . . . and to Cheat / 385   The Kinked Demand Curve / 387   Monopoly Power and Profit—The Early Bird Gets the Worm / 388   Real World Oligopolists / 390

Outstanding Economist: George Stigler / 389

Perspectives in Economics: Profits and Other Four-Letter Words / 394

22 Business Structure, Competition, and Public Policy   400

The Two Faces of Business Power / 400   How Much of Our Economy Is Competitive? / 401   Does Big Business Dominate the U.S. Economy? / 402   Antitrust Legislation—The Policy Objectives / 405   Major Antitrust Legislation / 406   Alternative Views on Antitrust Policy / 409

Perspectives in Economics: A Program to Promote Competitive Markets / 410

Perspectives in Economics: A Galbraithian View of a Modern Industrial Economy / 413

IV FACTOR MARKETS AND INCOME DISTRIBUTION

23 The Supply and Demand of Productive Resources   421

Human and Nonhuman Resources / 421   The Demand for Resources / 423   The Firm's Hiring Decision / 425   The Supply of Resources in the Short Run / 427   The Supply of Resources in the Long Run / 428   Supply, Demand, and Resource Prices / 430

Outstanding Economist: Gary Becker / 431

24 Earnings and the Job Market   435

Why Do Earnings Differ? / 435   Productivity and the General Level of Wages / 440   How Is the Economic Pie Divided between Physical and Human Capital? / 444   Can Higher Wages Be Legislated? / 445

Myths of Economics: "Automation is the major cause of unemployment." / 443

25 Union Power—A Shield or a Threat?   450

What Is a Collective Bargaining Contract? / 450   The Strike—A "Big Stick" of the Union / 452   The Strike and Serious Bargaining / 453   How Does the "Big Stick" Affect the Public? / 454   Getting More for Union Members / 455   What Gives the Union Muscle? / 457   How Much More Do Union Members Get? / 459   Unions and Inflation / 463   The Power of Big Labor / 463

Myths of Economics: "Unions have increased the share of income going to labor." / 461

Perspectives in Economics: What Can We Expect from the Rapid Growth of Public Sector Unionism? / 466

26 Inequality, Income Mobility, and Poverty   470

Income Inequality in the United States / 470   Income Inequality in Other Countries / 473   Inequality and Income Inequality / 474   Intergenerational Income

Mobility / 475   Poverty in the United States / 477   Three Approaches to Poverty / 481
Controversies in Economics: The Cases for and against the Negative Income Tax / 484

27 Employment Discrimination and the Earnings of Blacks and Women   490

What Is Employment Discrimination? / 490   How Does Discrimination Influence
Earnings? / 491   Does It Pay to Discriminate? / 493   The Cost of Discrimination—The
Case of Baseball / 494   Employment Discrimination and the Earnings of Blacks / 496
Are Things Improving? / 497   Everything You Always Wanted to Know about Female
Earnings—But Were Afraid to Ask / 500   The Future Status of Minorities and Women / 505
Outstanding Economist: Juanita Kreps / 501

V PUBLIC CHOICE

28 Problem Areas for the Market   511

Market Failure: External Cost / 512   Market Failure: External Benefits and Opportunities
Missed / 517   Market Failure: Public Goods / 519   Market Failure: Poor
Information / 522
Outstanding Economist: Allen Kneese / 521
Perspectives in Economics: An Emissions Charge Strategy to Control Pollution / 524

29 Public Choice and Gaining from Government   531

Voters and the Demand for Political Action / 531   Supply, Profits, and the Political
Entrepreneur / 533   Money, Political Advertising, and the Successful Politician / 534
The Opportunity Cost of Government / 536   Market Failure and Gaining from
Government / 536   Can Income Redistribution Promote Social Gain? / 540   Actual
Income Redistribution—Winners and Losers / 542
Perspectives in Economics: Externalities, No-Fault Insurance, and Government Action to
Improve on the Market / 544

30 The Economics of Government Failure   548

Government Failure: Voter Ignorance and Inefficient Public Policy / 549   Government
Failure: The Special Interest Effect / 550   Government Failure: The Shortsightedness
Effect / 553   Government Failure: Little Entrepreneurial Incentive for Internal
Efficiency / 555   Government Failure: Imprecise Reflection of Consumer
Preferences / 558   Is an Economic Analysis of the Public Sector Too Cynical? / 559
Public Sector and the Market—Revisited / 559
Outstanding Economist: Kenneth Arrow / 557
Perspectives in Economics: Dealing with Special Interests / 561

VI INTERNATIONAL ECONOMICS

31 Gaining from International Trade   567

The Size of the International Sector / 567   Why Do Nations Trade? / 570   Supply,
Demand, and International Trade / 571   Tariffs and Quotas / 573   Why Industries Are
on the Dole / 576   International Trade and the Great Oil Cartel / 578

Myths of Economics: "Free trade with low-wage countries such as China and India would cause the wages of U.S. workers to fall." / 575

32 International Finance and Balance of Payments   581

Foreign Exchange Markets / 581   Balance of Payments and Exchange Markets / 584
Deficits, Surpluses, and Balance of Payments / 587   Trading with Flexible Exchange
Rates / 588   Trading with Fixed Exchange Rates / 591   Fixed versus Flexible Exchange
Rates / 592

33 Comparative Economic Systems   597

Comparing Capitalism and Socialism / 597   Common Constraints and the Universality of
Economic Tools / 600   The Soviet Economy / 601   Yugoslavia—Socialism or the
Market? / 608   Socialism or Capitalism? / 611
Outstanding Economist: Wassily Leontief / 607

Appendix A   A Graphic Look at Economics   615

Appendix B   Analyzing the Equilibrium Level of Income with Equations   619

Appendix C   Analyzing Aggregate Equilibrium with the IS–LM Model   624

Suggestions for Additional Reading   631

Hints for Answering Discussion Questions   639

Index / 649

MYTHS OF ECONOMICS

Chapter	Number	Subject	Page
1	1	"Economics rejects the humanitarian side of man."	9
2	2	"In exchange, if someone gains, someone else must lose. Trading is a zero-sum game."	26
3	3	"Rent controls are an effective method of assuring adequate housing at a price the poor can afford."	48
5	4	"The growth of the federal government has been the major source of government expansion."	73
7	5	"Unemployed resources would not exist if the economy were operating efficiently."	121
13	6	"Inflation is caused by greedy businessmen and union leaders."	238
14	7	"The high interest rates of the 1970s resulted because the Fed was reducing the rate of monetary expansion."	250
17	8	"A good business decision-maker will never sell a product for less than its production cost."	325
24	9	"Automation is the major cause of unemployment."	443
25	10	"Unions have increased the share of income going to labor."	461
31	11	"Free trade with low-wage countries such as China and India would cause the wages of U.S. workers to fall."	575

OUTSTANDING ECONOMISTS

Chapter	Economists	Page
30	Kenneth Arrow	557
23	Gary Becker	431
4	James Buchanan	65
11	Arthur Burns	193
13	Milton Friedman	227
16	John Kenneth Galbraith	301
10	Walter Heller	169
8	John Maynard Keynes	135
28	Allen Kneese	521
27	Juanita Kreps	501
6	Simon Kuznets	105
33	Wassily Leontief	607
19	Joan Robinson	351
12	Paul Samuelson	211
21	George Stigler	389

PERSPECTIVES IN ECONOMICS

Chapter	Number	Subject	Page
1	1	Do Material Goods Bring Happiness?	12
10	2	Fact and Fiction about the National Debt	177
13	3	Inflation: Its Cause and Cure—A Monetarist's View	241
14	4	Why Fiscal Policy Is Impotent—An Interview with a Monetarist	260
19	5	Is Planned Obsolescence Good Business?	355
20	6	How the Regulators Promote Inefficiency and Protect You from Low Prices—The Case of Transportation	375
21	7	Profits and Other Four-Letter Words	394
22	8	A Program to Promote Competitive Markets	410
22	9	A Galbraithian View of a Modern Industrial Economy	413
25	10	What Can We Expect from the Rapid Growth of Public Sector Unionism?	466
28	11	An Emissions Charge Strategy to Control Pollution	524
29	12	Externalities, No-Fault Insurance, and Government Action to Improve on the Market	544
30	13	Dealing with Special Interests	561

CONTROVERSIES IN ECONOMICS

Chapter	Number	Subject	Page
5	1	Is There an Energy Crisis or Policy Crisis?	81
12	2	Will There Ever Be Another Great Depression?	217
15	3	Keynesians, Monetarists, and Middle-of-the-Roaders on Macroeconomics	279
16	4	Advertising—The Views of Its Critics and Defenders	303
19	5	Is Monopolistic Competition Inefficient?	353
26	6	The Cases for and against the Negative Income Tax	484

Suggested Outlines for One-Semester Courses

Chapter Number and Topic	Macro-economic Emphasis	Micro-economic Emphasis	Balanced Course—Policy Emphasis
1 The Economic Approach	☐	☐	☐
2 Some Tools of the Economist	☐	☐	☐
3 Market Decisions and the Market Process	☐	☐	☐
4 Bird's-Eye View of the Public Sector	☐	☐	☐
5 Taxes and Government Spending	☐		
6 Taking the Nation's Economic Pulse	☐		☐
7 Unemployment, Inflation, and Business Cycles	☐		☐
8 Aggregate Equilibrium—A Simple Keynesian Model	☐		☐
9 A Keynesian View of the Business Cycle	☐		☐
10 Fiscal Policy	☐		☐
11 Money and the Banking System	☐		
12 Money and a More Complete Keynesian Model	☐		☐
13 The Business Cycle—The Monetarist View	☐		☐
14 Proper Macropolicy—The Monetarist View	☐		☐
15 Dealing with Unemployment and Inflation	☐		☐
16 Demand and Consumer Choice		☐	
17 Costs and Producer Decisions		☐	
18 The Firm under Pure Competition		☐	
19 Monopolistic Competition		☐	
20 Monopoly and High Barriers to Entry		☐	
21 Oligopoly and Big Business		☐	
22 Competition and Public Policy		☐	☐
23 Supply and Demand of Resources		☐	☐
24 Earnings and the Job Market		☐	☐
25 Union Power—A Shield or a Threat?		☐	☐
26 Inequality, Income Mobility, and Poverty		☐	☐
27 Employment Discrimination		☐	
28 Problem Areas for the Market		☐	☐
29 Public Choice		☐	☐
30 The Economics of Government Failure		☐	☐
31 Gaining from International Trade	☐		
32 International Finance	☐		
33 Comparative Economic Systems	☐		☐

Of course these outlines are merely recommendations. The book is flexible. Several other combinations are possible so that each instructor can obtain the desired emphasis. In addition, the perspectives and controversies can be used independently of the chapters in which they are contained. Some instructors may want to utilize specific perspectives or controversies (even though they do not assign the text of the chapter) as supplementary readings.

PREFACE

Economics is on the front page of our current day newspapers. Economic issues usually occupy the center stage of our political campaigns. Knowledge of economics is essential to the understanding of social problems such as poverty, discrimination, pollution, unemployment, and the power of special interest groups. Despite its importance, objectivity forces one to admit that economic literacy in the United States is low. The analysis of our political entrepreneurs, editorial writers, and news commentators often contains elementary economic fallacies. These fallacies usually go unnoticed and unchallenged.

The purpose of this book is to help the reader develop sound economic reasoning. Economics, of course, has a reputation for being rather dull, mathematical, quite difficult, and highly abstract. In my judgment, these charges stem from the short-comings of economists, not the nature of economics. This book paints a different picture. It is application-oriented, designed to promote a better understanding of the real world and the forces that are shaping it. Mathematics is used sparingly. Abstract, mechanical concepts are avoided unless they are going to be applied to real world decision-making. The emphasis is on the economic way of thinking, a tool that will help the reader to both pinpoint economic fallacies and develop sound economic logic.

Both the power and simplicity of economic concepts are highlighted. However, simplicity is not substituted for depth. While the book is written for the student, it incorporates solid, modern analysis in a manner that will sometimes challenge the thinking of even professional economists. Solid economic analysis can be both exciting and applicable to the real world, while it is still comprehensible to the student and professional alike.

Distinguishing Features of Content

Since I am seeking to illustrate that economics is powerful, highly relevant, and readily understandable, the thrust of this book differs slightly from the traditional approach. In this regard, four specific points are worth noting.

1. *Economic reasoning and its applications are emphasized.* Models, theories, and mechanical exercises are important, but they are only tools to help us better develop the economic way of thinking. We must not emphasize abstractions and mechanics to the point where the student feels that they are an end, rather than a means to an end. In order to avoid this pitfall, I have continually stressed the basics and their application. Specific issues such as pollution, energy, inflation, unemployment, auto-

mation, and union power have been dealt with in depth in order to illustrate the power of basic tools and economic reasoning. Real world data are liberally utilized as economic concepts are developed.

2. *Economic tools are applied to both the market and political process.*   Most textbooks currently do three things. They tell students how an *ideal* market economy would work, why real world markets differ from the hypothetical ideal, and how *ideal* public policy could correct the failures of the market. In addition to these three basic areas of study, this book analyzes what real world public policy *is likely to do*. This important step drives home both the power and relevance of modern economics. Building on the pioneering work of Kenneth Arrow, Duncan Black, James Buchanan, Anthony Downs, Gordon Tullock, and others, the economic analysis of public, as well as private, choice helps to bring the subject matter alive to the student. Students are often puzzled by the gulf between the ideal theoretical "solutions" of economists and the events of the real world. The economics of public choice explains this gulf. Economic tools can illustrate why "good politics" sometimes conflicts with "good economics" (that is, economic efficiency). It is important that we explain what government can do to promote a more efficient use of our resources. But the tools of economics permit us to do more. They permit us to explain why there is good reason to expect that public sector action will be counterproductive for certain classes of issues.

3. *The role of the human decision-maker is stressed.*   To the student, it often appears as if economists have eliminated human beings from the economic process. The businessman of most economics texts has perfect knowledge of demand and cost. Like a computer, he simply grinds out the maximum-profit solution. Government planners, having perfect knowledge of the deficiency in aggregate demand and the size of the multiplier, simply increase government spending by the right amount to restore full employment. The employer, knowing the marginal productivity of each resource, utilizes each of them in exactly the proper proportion. All of the really interesting questions are assumed away. Decision-makers are robots. Is it any wonder that students have trouble identifying these mechanical exercises with real world decision-making? Throughout, I have attempted to stress the importance of information, uncertainty, trial-and-error decision-making, future expectations, and other factors that will influence real world choices. Economics should be more than guidelines for robots. If we are to convince students of its applicability, we must emphasize factors that influence and motivate human beings.

4. *Microeconomics reasoning is integrated in the macro section.*   The last decade has been a humbling experience for most macroeconomists. Many older textbooks, arguing that we can have a 3 percent unemployment rate if we are just willing to accept an inflation rate of 5 or 10 percent, are not very convincing any more. In my view many macroeconomists went wrong because they forgot about basic micro concepts such as opportunity cost, expectations, information and search theory, and the passage of time necessary for markets to adjust. These concepts are integrated into the macro section of this book.

Distinguishing Features of Presentation

Several organizational and design features have been incorporated that should make the book both more functional and more interesting to students.

1. *Myths of Economics.* This series contains an explanation of the fallacious reasoning involved in 11 commonly held economic myths. A statement of each myth is followed by a concise explanation of why it is incorrect. Each myth is incorporated into a chapter that contains closely related material.

2. *Perspectives and Controversies in Economics.* The "perspectives" analyze current economic issues in detail. The major purpose of this series is to demonstrate the applications of economics. The writing style is a bit lighter than in the text. Sometimes there are solid, well-founded economic arguments on both sides of an issue. When this is the case, the "controversies" are used to present and contrast alternative viewpoints. Sometimes the controversies are presented in debate format. In other cases, a hypothetical interview is used to present differing perspectives. Class testing of this material has shown that it helps to stimulate interest and discussion, while encouraging the student to develop the economic way of thinking. All 19 perspectives and controversies, which are set off with a light tint, are incorporated into related chapters within the text.

3. *Outstanding Economists.* Students are more likely to maintain a lasting interest in economics if they know something about the economists who are contributing to the field and who are making today's newspaper headlines. This series will familiarize the reader with several such personalities. The series is not intended to be a list of the 15 best economists. Many of those featured would qualify for such honor, but others were chosen because of their outstanding contribution to important related material contained in the text.

4. *Terms and Chapter Summaries.* Each chapter concludes with a statement of learning objectives and a set of definitions for the important terms that have been introduced in the chapter. Students are encouraged to study the learning objectives both before and after they read the chapter. Past experience indicates that many students have trouble with the terminology of economics. When important terms are initially introduced they will appear in boldface. This will alert the reader to their importance and the definitions at the end of the chapter will present the reader with an opportunity to clear up any misapprehensions about the new terms.

5. *Questions and Hints on Answering Them.* Several questions are presented at the end of each chapter. Some of them are primarily for discussion. But others test technical materials and concepts. Sample answers to many questions of the latter variety are contained at the end of the book. These questions and answers will present the student with an opportunity to pretest and review important material. They will permit the student to increase the rate of return from his study time.

Supplementary Materials

The text is accompanied by a *Coursebook*. We call it a *Coursebook* because it is more than just a study guide to the textbook. Of course, numerous true–false, multiple choice, and discussion questions are contained therein. Problems and projects are also included. But the *Coursebook* also contains news articles, short readings, and the views of several outstanding economists. Contrasting positions are often presented and questions are asked, challenging the student to illustrate his understanding of the material and ability to separate a sound argument from economic nonsense. As in the textbook, the emphasis is on helping the student develop the economic way of thinking.

An *Instructor's Manual and Test Bank* is also available. Most of the questions contained in the test bank have been class tested. Information as to their difficulty and their ability to discriminate between the knowledgeable and uninformed student is included for each question that has been class tested.

Adaptability

Course organization and the order in which topics are covered often differ from instructor to instructor. This textbook will provide the instructor with maximum flexibility. The core of the micro material (Parts III and IV) could be covered before the macro section (Part II) if instructors so wish. The book can also be adapted easily to a single semester course of varying emphasis. Suggested outlines are presented on page xv for single-semester courses with a micro, macro, and policy emphasis.

ACKNOWLEDGMENTS

This project owes a debt to several people. Without their assistance, it could not have been completed. My debt to Richard Stroup (Montana State University) and A. H. Studenmund (Occidental College) is particularly large. They are my coauthors for the *Coursebook*. In addition, Professor Stroup authored the initial draft of the perspectives on the energy crisis (Chapter 5) and pollution control (Chapter 28). Professor Studenmund authored the initial draft of Chapter 32, plus Appendixes B and C. Both Stroup and Studenmund made valuable comments on the entire manuscript.

My colleague Ephraim Asher wrote an initial draft of Chapter 33 and provided comments on the micro material. The macro section was greatly strengthened by the comprehensive review supplied by Larry Steinhauer (Albion College). Karl Shell (University of Pennsylvania) acted as an advisor to the entire project and provided helpful suggestions in several areas. Philip W. Perry (Occidental College) helped with the first draft of Appendix C. In addition, various sections of the book were altered in response to the insights provided by Mohmoud Arya (Edison Community College), Conrad Caligaris (Northeastern University), James Long (Auburn University), Michael McBrayer (Pensacola Junior College), Richard Sherman (Ohio State University), Gordon Tullock (Virginia Polytechnic Institute), and Norman Van Cott (West Georgia College). I also benefitted from both discussions and reviews from Marshall Colberg, Sydney Hicks, William Laird, Charles Rockwood, and Irv Sobel, all of whom are my colleagues at Florida State University.

Ann Fountain and Mary Harvey did most of the typing for the project. Lloys Grace read every chapter, cleaning up the author's messy sentence structure and providing enlightened editorial suggestions. Tevfik Nas acted as a research assistant and constructed the index for the text. My greatest debt is to my wife Amy, who offered numerous suggestions that improved the clarity of the manuscript, strengthened me during times of depression, and tolerated my sometime disagreeable disposition, while providing for the every need of her husband and family. Superlative words are inadequate to describe her contribution so I will simply dedicate the book to her.

I
THE ECONOMIC WAY OF THINKING– AN INTRODUCTION

1
THE ECONOMIC APPROACH

*It (economics) is a method rather than a doctrine,
an apparatus of the mind, a technique of thinking
which helps its possessor to draw correct conclusions.
[J. M. Keynes]*

When most people think of economics, they think of employment, national income, wealth, material goods, and the stock market. The study of economics does, of course, deal with all of these topics. But economics also deals with topics that are much closer to the lives of the typical American.

WHAT IS ECONOMICS ABOUT?

The two basic ingredients for an economic topic are scarcity and choice. **Scarcity** is the term used by economists to indicate that man's desire for a "thing" exceeds the amount of it that is freely available from Nature. Since the Garden of Eden, Nature has dealt grudgingly with man. Nature provides far less of many, many things than man would like to have.

A good that is scarce is called an **economic good.** Exhibit 1-1, column 1, presents a partial listing of scarce or economic goods. The list includes food, clothing, and many of the items that all of us commonly recognize as material goods. But it also includes some items that may surprise you. Is leisure a good? Would you like to have more leisure time than is currently available to you? Most of us would. Therefore, leisure is a scarce good. What about clean air? A few years ago many economics texts classified clean air as a free good, a good that Nature had made available in such an abundant supply that everybody could have as much of it as they wanted. This is no longer true. Our utilization of air for the purpose of eliminating waste has created a scarcity of clean air. Many of the residents of Los Angeles, New York, Chicago, and other large cities would like to have more clean air.

Few of us usually think of environmental conditions as economic goods. However, if you know someone who would like more open spaces, green areas, or dogwood trees, you will recognize that these things are scarce. They too are economic goods.

Exhibit 1-1   A General Listing of Desired Scarce Economic Goods and Limited Resources

Economic goods (1)	Limited resources (2)
Food (bread, milk, meat, eggs, vegetables, coffee, etc.)	Land (various degrees of fertility)
Clothing (shirts, pants, blouses, shoes, socks, coats, sweaters, etc.)	Natural resources (rivers, trees, minerals, oceans, etc.)
Household goods (tables, chairs, rugs, beds, dressers, television, etc.)	Machines and other man-made physical resources
Space exploration	Nonhuman animal resources (cattle, horses, buffalo, etc.)
Education	Technology (physical and scientific "recipes" of history)
National defense	Manpower (various skills and talents)
Recreation	
Time	
Entertainment	
Clean air	
Pleasant environment (trees, lakes, rivers, open spaces, etc.)	
Pleasant working conditions	
More productive resources	
Leisure	

The history of man is a record of his struggle to transform available, but limited, resources into things that he would like to have—economic goods.

Time is also an economic good. Most of us would like to have more time to watch TV, take a walk in the woods, do our school work or sleep. But we each have only 24 hours in a day. The scarcity of time imposes a definite limitation on our ability to do many of the things that we would like to do.

Because of this scarcity we must make choices. We cannot have everything we would like to have. **Choice** is the act of selecting among scarce alternatives. Since your time is scarce, your alternatives for an evening's activities are limited. You cannot stay home and study economics, go to a movie, attend a football game, *and* play bridge with friends. You must choose among the available alternatives because your time is scarce. You cannot have your cake and eat it too.

Each day, we all make hundreds of economic choices, although we do not normally think of them as being so. The choice of when to get up in the morning, what to eat for breakfast, how to travel to work, what television program to watch—all of these decisions are economic. They are economic because they involve the utilization of scarce resources (for example, time and income). We all are constantly involved in making choices that relate to the subject matter of economics.

MAN'S LOSING STRUGGLE WITH SCARCITY

Scarcity constrains us. How can we overcome it? **Resources,** including man's own skills, can be used to produce economic goods. Human effort and ingenuity can be combined with machines, land, natural resources, and other productive factors (see

Exhibit 1-1, column 2) to increase the availability of economic goods. These are man's "tools" in his struggle with scarcity. It is important to note that most economic goods are not like manna from heaven. Human energy is nearly always an ingredient in the production of economic goods.

The lessons of past history confirm that man's desire for economic goods far outstrips his resources to produce them. Is man destined to live a hopeless life of misery and drudgery because he is involved in a losing battle with scarcity? Some might answer this question in the affirmative, pointing out that two-thirds of the world's population goes to bed hungry each night. The annual income of a typical worker in countries like China and India is less than $100. And the population in these and other areas is increasing more rapidly than their output of material goods.

Yet the ropes of scarcity have been loosened in most of North America, Western Europe, Japan, and the Soviet Union. Most Americans, Japanese and Europeans have an adequate calorie intake, and sufficient housing and clothing. Many own luxuries like automatic can openers, color television sets, and electric carving knives. From a material point of view life is certainly more pleasant for these people than it was for their forefathers 250 years ago. Despite this, scarcity is still a fact of life, even in relatively affluent countries.

Scarcity and Poverty Are Not the Same Thing

It should be noted that scarcity and poverty are not the same thing. Poverty implies some basic level of need, either in absolute or relative terms. Absence of poverty means that the basic level has been attained. By contrast, absence of scarcity would mean that we have attained, not just some basic level, but as much of all goods as we desire. While the battle against poverty may perhaps be won, the outcome of the battle against scarcity is already painfully obvious. Man's productive capabilities and material desires are such that goods and services will always be scarce.

THE ECONOMIC WAY OF THINKING

Reflecting upon a television appearance with Paul Samuelson and other social scientists (noneconomists), Milton Friedman stated that he was amazed to find that economists, though differing in their ideological viewpoints, usually find themselves as allies in discussions with other social scientists.[1] One does not have to spend much time around economists to recognize that there is "an economic way of thinking." Admittedly, economists, like others, differ widely in their ideological views. A news commentator once remarked that "any half-dozen economists will normally come up with about six different policy prescriptions." Yet, in spite of their philosophical differences, there is a common ground to the approach of economists. They share certain presuppositions

---

[1] The philosophical views of Professor Friedman and Professor Samuelson differ considerably. They are often on opposite sides of economic policy issues.

about the state of the world and how to evaluate efforts to change it. What is this common ground? How does the approach of economists differ from other social scientists? What are the guidelines of the economic way of thinking?

Six Guideposts to Economic Thinking

Economics is not a particularly difficult subject. In fact, once one incorporates certain guidelines in his thought process, economics is a relatively simple subject. Some would say that it is just good common sense.

Students who have difficulty with economics almost always do so because they fail to develop the economic way of thinking. Their thought process is not consistently directed by a few simple economic concepts or guideposts. Students who do well in economics learn to utilize these basic concepts and allow their thought process to be directed by them. Because they are so important, we will discuss six principles that are characteristics of economic thinking—that are essential to the understanding of the economic approach.

1. *Scarce Goods Have a Cost—There Are No Free Lunches.*   The benefits of scarce goods can be obtained only if someone is willing to exert personal effort or give something up. Using the terms of economics, scarce goods cost someone something. The cost of many scarce goods is obvious. A new car costs $4000. The purchaser must give up $4000 of purchasing power over other goods if he is to own the car. Similarly, the cost to the purchaser of a delightful meal, new clothes, or a Las Vegas caper is obvious. But what about a good like public elementary education? Even though the education is usually free to students, it is not free to the community. Buildings, books, and teachers' salaries must be paid for from tax revenues. The taxpayer incurs the cost. If these scarce resources were not used to produce elementary education, they could be used to produce more recreation, entertainment, houses, and other goods. Providing for public education means that we must now forego some of these other scarce goods. Similarly, provision of free medical service, recreation areas, tennis courts, and parking lots involves the use of scarce resources. Again, something must be given up if we are to produce these goods. Taxpayers usually bear the cost of "free" medical services and tennis courts. Consumers often bear the cost of "free" parking lots in the form of higher prices in areas that provide this service. By now the central point should be obvious. Economic thinking recognizes that the provision of a scarce good, any scarce good, involves a cost. We must give up other things if we are to have more of a scarce good. Economic goods are not free.

2. *Decision-Makers Choose Purposefully. Therefore, They Will Economize.*   Since resources are scarce, it is all the more important that decisions are made in a purposeful manner. Decision-makers do not deliberately make choices in a manner that wastes and squanders valuable resources. Recognizing the constraint of their limited resources (income, time, talent, etc.), they seek to choose wisely, trying to select the options that best advance their own personal objectives. In turn, the objectives or preferences of individuals are revealed by the choices that they make.

Economizing behavior results directly from purposeful decision-making. Economizing individuals will seek to accomplish an objective at the least possible cost. When choosing among things that yield equal benefit, an economizer will select the cheapest option. For example, if a hamburger, a fish dinner, and a New York steak are expected to yield identical benefits, economizing behavior implies that the cheapest of the three alternatives, probably the hamburger, will be chosen. Correspondingly, when choosing among alternatives of equal cost, economizing decision-makers will select the option that yields the greatest benefit (that is, utility or satisfaction). Purposeful decision-makers will not deliberately pay more for something than is necessary.

Purposeful choosing implies that decision-makers have some knowledge on which to base their evaluation of potential alternatives. Economists refer to this evaluation as utility. **Utility** is the subjective benefit or satisfaction that an individual expects from the choice of a specific alternative.

3. *Incentives Matter—Human Choice Is Influenced in a Predictable Way by Changes in Economic Incentives.*   This guidepost to clear economic thinking might be called the basic postulate of all economics. As the personal benefits from choosing an option increase, other things constant, a human decision-maker will be more likely to choose the option. In contrast, as the costs associated with the choice of an item increase, a person will be less likely to choose the option. Applying this basic economic postulate to a group of individuals suggests that as an option is made more attractive, more people will choose it. By contrast, as the cost of a selection to the members of a group increases, fewer of them will make this selection.

This basic economic concept provides a powerful tool with which to analyze various types of human behavior. According to this postulate, what would happen to the birthrate if the U.S. government (a) removed the income tax deduction for dependents, (b) imposed a $1500 "birth tax" on parents, and (c) made "the pill" available free to all? The birthrate would fall—that is what. What would happen if the government imposed a $5000 tax on smokestacks, required automobile owners to pay a license fee that was directly related to the exhaust level of the car, and gave a 10 percent corporate tax reduction to all firms that did not utilize the air for disposal purposes? Answer: There would be a decline in air pollution. In both of these hypothetical examples, the policy increased the cost and/or reduced the benefits of conducting a specific activity. Economics suggests that the level of the activities will be reduced because of the "predictable" impact that changes in personal benefits and costs have on human actions.

Our analysis suggests that an instructor could influence the degree of cheating on an examination by merely changing the student payoffs. There would be little cheating on a closely monitored, individualized, essay examination. Why? Because it is difficult (that is, costly) to cheat on such an exam. But suppose that an instructor gives an objective "take home" exam, basing the student's course grade entirely on his performance. Many students would cheat because the benefits of doing so are great and the risk (cost) is nominal. The economic way of thinking never loses sight of the fact that changes in incentives exert a powerful and predictable influence on human decisions.

4. *Information, Like Other Resources, Is Scarce. Therefore, Even Purposeful Decision-Makers Will Not Have Perfect Knowledge about the Future When They Choose.* Rational decision-makers recognize that it is costly to obtain information and make complex calculations. While additional information and techniques that improve one's decision-making capabilities are valuable, often this potential benefit is less than its expected cost. Therefore, the sensible consumer will conserve on these limited resources, just as he conserves on other scarce resources.

5. *Remember the Secondary Effects. Economic Actions Often Have* **Secondary Effects** *in Addition to Their Immediate Direct Effects.*   An economy is a little bit like a balloon. You push it in in one place, and people make adjustments that generate secondary bulges in other places. Frederic Bastiat, a nineteenth century French economist, stated that the difference between a good and a bad economist is that the bad economist would only consider the immediate, visible effects. But the good economist, in addition to the direct impact of a policy, would also have an awareness of secondary effects that were indirectly related to the initial policy and often exerted their influence only with the passage of time.

Secondary effects are important in areas outside of economics. The immediate effect of an aspirin is a bitter taste in one's mouth. The indirect effect, which is not immediately observable, is relief from a headache. The immediate effect of six quarts of beer might be a warm, jolly feeling. The indirect effect, for many, would be a pounding headache the next morning. In economics, too, the secondary effects may be quite different than the initial impact of an action. The economic way of thinking asks, "In addition to the initial result of this policy, what other factors have now changed? How will future actions be influenced by the changes in economic incentives that resulted from policy A?"

Straight economic thinking demands that we recognize the longer range secondary effects as well as the immediate, readily identifiable consequences of economic change. For example, an increase in the earnings of dentists may result in few additional dentists tomorrow. But the higher earnings will make dentistry more attractive. Two years from now, or five years from now, many more people will be attracted to the profession by the higher earnings. The adjustment process requires time. It is important that we incorporate the time dimension that is necessary for secondary effects to fully exert their impact, into our economic way of thinking.

6. *Economic Thinking Is* **Scientific Thinking.** *The Test of a Theory Is Its Ability to Predict.*   The proof of the pudding is in the eating. The usefulness of an economic theory is revealed by its ability to predict the future consequences of economic action. Economists develop economic theory from the analysis of how incentives will affect decision-makers. The theory is then tested against the reality of the real world. It is through testing that we either confirm the theory or recognize the need for amending or rejecting it. If the events of the real world are consistent with a theory, we say that it predicts. In contrast, theories that are inconsistent with real world data must be rejected.

If it is impossible to test the theoretical relationships of a discipline, then the discipline does not qualify as a science. Since economics deals with human beings

—human beings who can think and respond in a variety of ways—can economic theories really be tested? The answer to this question is yes, if, *on the average*, human beings will respond in a predictable way to a change in economic conditions. The economist believes that this is the case. Note that this does not necessarily imply that *all* individuals will respond in a specified manner. Economics usually does not seek to predict the behavior of a specific individual, but rather it focuses on the general behavior of a large number of individuals.

How can one test economic theory since, for the most part, controlled experiments are not feasible? While this does impose limitations, economics is no different than astronomy in this respect. The astronomer also must deal with the world as it is. He cannot change the course of the stars or planets to see what impact the changes would have on the gravitational pull of the earth.

MYTHS OF ECONOMICS
"Economic analysis assumes that people act only because of selfish motives. It rejects the humanitarian side of man."

Probably because economics focuses on the efforts of man to satisfy his material desires, many casual observers of the subject argue that its relevance hinges on the selfish nature of man. Some have even charged that economists, and the study of economics, encourages man to be materialistic rather than humanitarian.

This point of view stems from a fundamental misunderstanding of personal decision-making. Obviously, people act for a variety of reasons, some selfish and some humanitarian. The economist merely assumes that actions will be influenced by costs and benefits, as viewed by the decision-maker. As an activity becomes more costly, it is less likely that a decision-maker will choose it. As it becomes more attractive, it is more likely that the event will be chosen.

The choices of both the humanitarian and the self-centered egocentric will be influenced by changes in personal costs and benefits. For example, both will be more likely to try to save the life of a small child in a three foot swimming pool than in the rapid currents approaching Niagara Falls. Both will be more likely to give a needy person their hand-me-down clothes rather than their best Sunday suit. Why? Because in both cases, the latter alternative is more costly than the former.

Observation would suggest that the right to control one's own destiny is an "economic" good for most persons. Most of us would prefer to make our own choices rather than have someone else decide for us. But is this always greedy and selfish? If so, why do people often make choices in a way that is charitable toward others? After all, many persons freely choose to give a portion of their wealth to the sick, the needy, the less fortunate, religious organizations, and charitable institutions. Economics does not imply that these choices are irrational. It does imply that if you make it more (less) costly to act charitably, fewer (more) persons would do so.

Economics deals with man as he is—not how we would like to remake him. Should persons act more charitably? Perhaps so. But this is not the subject matter of economics.

So it is with the economist. He cannot arbitrarily institute changes in the price of cars or unskilled labor services just to see the effect on quantity purchased or level of employment. But this does not mean economic theory cannot be tested. Economic conditions (for example, prices, production costs, technology, transportation cost, etc.), like the location of the planets, do change from time to time. As conditions change, economic theory can be tested by analyzing its consistency with the actual conditions of the real world. The real world is the laboratory of the economist, just as the universe is the laboratory of the astronomer.

In some cases, observations from the real world may be consistent with two (or more) economic theories. Given the state of our knowledge, currently we will sometimes be unable to distinguish between competitive theories. Much of the work of economists remains undone. But in many areas substantial empirical work has been completed. Throughout this book we will refer to this evidence in an effort to provide the reader information with which to judge the validity of various economic theories. We must not lose sight of the scientific method of thinking because it is a necessary requisite for sound economic thinking.

NORMATIVE AND POSITIVE ECONOMICS

Economics as a social science is concerned with predicting or determining the impact of changes in economic variables on the actions of human beings. Scientific economics, commonly referred to as **positive economics,** attempts to determine "what is." Positive economic statements postulate a relationship that is potentially verifiable. "If the price of butter were higher, people would buy less." "As the money supply increases, the price level will go up." These are positive statements. We can statistically investigate (and estimate) the relationship between butter prices and sales, or the supply of money and the general price level. We can resort to the facts to determine the correctness of a statement about positive economics.

It is not always easy to isolate the impact of economic variables. Differences about positive economics may result because we do not have perfect information about how the economy actually operates. Because our economic knowledge is imperfect, two people may differ on policy matters because of differences about positive economic issues.

Value judgments may also cause differences of opinion about policy issues. Two persons may differ because one is a socialist and the other a libertarian, one a liberal and the other a conservative, or one a traditionalist and the other a radical. They may agree about the results of an economic policy, but because of their philosophical differences, one favors and the other opposes the expected results of the policy. Such disagreements are termed **normative** because they stem from value judgments about "what ought to be." Since normative differences are philosophical they cannot be "proven" by scientific testing.

Normative economic statements are evangelic—they tell us what we should be doing, according to the economic evangelist. The government *should* reduce defense expenditures. Businessmen *should* not maximize profits. Unions *should* be prohibited.

These statements all rest on value judgments. They can be proved neither true nor false.

Positive economics may influence one's normative position on policy matters. For example, suppose one wanted to help people in low income brackets and therefore favored increasing the minimum wage as one instrument to increase their earnings. But suppose he is confronted with evidence of positive economics that suggested minimum wage legislation causes many low wage recipients to lose their jobs and therefore become even worse off. If this were the case, the individual's normative view concerning the desirability of minimum wage legislation might well be changed because of the evidence of positive economics. Therefore, while normative conclusions are influenced by one's philosophical views, positive economics, by providing a greater understanding of the actual (as opposed to the expected) impact of a policy, will also influence one's evaluation of a policy alternative.

Students should be alert (a normative statement) to differentiate between positive and normative economics. Positive economics does not tell us which policy is best. The purpose of positive economics is to increase our knowledge of all policy alternatives, thereby eliminating a potential source of disagreement about policy matters. Better knowledge of positive economics would also serve to reduce a potential source of disappointment with policy. If one does not really understand how the economy operates, he may advocate policies that are inconsistent with his philosophical views. Sometimes what one thinks will happen if a policy is instituted may be a very unlikely result in the real world. The promises of a policy often exceed the results. Positive economics can be a valuable tool to help each of us distinguish between "wishful thinking" and the "real thing."

LOOKING FOR ACTION?—TRY ECONOMICS

What are you looking for when you choose an area of study? If you are seeking relevance, knowledge of social issues, principles that can be applied to your personal life, and a better understanding of both yesterday's history and today's news, economics is where the action is.

Knowledge of economics will help you become a better citizen. It will help you better utilize your time, your personal talents, and creative energy. It will give you a different and fascinating perspective about what motivates people; why they act the way they do; and why their actions sometimes run counter to the best interest of the entire community or nation. It will also give you some valuable insight into how the actions of people can be rechanneled for your personal gain and/or the gain of the community at large.

Would you like to know more about—

(a) why today's environment is deteriorating and what can be done about it,

(b) why it is sometimes good politics to follow policies that will cause future inflation and unemployment,

(c) why there is an energy crisis and what can be done to alleviate it,

(d) why the unregulated market sector will sometimes lead to waste and inefficiency and why government efforts to correct these shortcomings will often become part of the problem rather than the solution,

(e) whether greedy businessmen and labor leaders are the major cause of inflation, and

(f) whether automation is eliminating jobs, making the unemployment problem more and more serious?

Economics is about all of these topics. This book will help you better understand each of them. More than any other science, economics deals with subjects that are of interest to today's typical students. But has it not been referred to as the "dismal science?" Does it not have a reputation of being both dull and difficult?

The author of this book believes that these opinions are the result of the way economics has usually been taught in the past. They are the result of the failings of economists, rather than the shortcomings of economics. Economists are notorious for their efforts to make the simple seem complex, for their focus on the trivial, for their emphasis on theory while ignoring the many interesting applications of the theory. The goal of this book is to avoid these pitfalls.

Economics is difficult for many students because they never develop the economic way of thinking. A primary goal of this book from the first chapter to the last will be to guide—even force—the reader to develop the economic way of thinking. Questions will be asked and materials organized in a manner that constantly emphasizes this approach.

Once you develop the economic way of thinking, economics is easy. At least it need not be difficult. This way of thinking is the key that unlocks the door to the mastery of economics.[2]

Perspectives in Economics

Do Material Goods Bring Happiness?

Every economics text, and this one is no exception, notes that people want more material goods than are available. We all want more "things." Why? How important are "things"? Do they satisfy the needs of man and lead to greater personal happiness? Students usually worry more about these questions than do professional economists.

Certainly factors other than material goods, narrowly defined, are important to the happiness of most. Friends, relatives, spouse, children, religious beliefs, health, achievement, power, recognition, social status—all these factors exert an influence on human happiness, *independent of material goods*. Economics does not deny the contribution of nonmaterial goods as a source of human satisfaction. But people do have a desire for material goods. A hungry man can think of little else other than his desire for food. Appropriate clothing and shelter are desired for protection from the elements. But what of the desires of affluent Americans for a third car, a weekend home, and a heated swimming pool? Are they less urgent? Will the affluent be "happier" because of their possessions? These are difficult questions to answer objectively.

---

[2]Students who have some difficulty understanding graphs and charts may want to study Appendix A at this time.

Economics suggests that additional material goods will improve the well-being of even the affluent, *if their preferences* (desires for other material goods) remain unchanged. But they may not. Wealth may spoil one's appreciation for material things while further increasing his desire for still greater wealth. Consumption of fancy sports cars and filet mignon may whet one's appetite for island vacations and exotic foods. Economics does not deny this possibility.

While satisfaction or happiness is difficult to measure, there does appear to be some relationship between income and self-designated happiness. The American Institute of Public Opinion, in December 1970, asked Americans if they were "very happy," "fairly happy," or "not very happy." Fifty-six percent of persons with incomes of $15000 or more indicated they were "very happy," while only 29 percent of those with incomes of less than $3000 placed themselves in this category. There was a steady positive relationship between income and the percentage of persons indicating they were "very happy." While this association lends some support to the view that wealth or material things increase the likelihood that one will be happy, it may be misleading. Psychologists tell us that self-satisfaction with one's achievements is an important determinant of happiness. Persons with high incomes are more likely to be high achievers. Therefore, the relationship between happiness and income may merely reflect that self-satisfied high achievers also have high incomes.

If self-evaluated achievement is an important determinant of happiness, this suggests a loose relationship between material wealth and happiness. A person who achieved success (and wealth) from a starting point of modest means is likely to be happier than one who inherited great wealth, but has few achievements to show for his own life. Success relative to one's peer group and initial station in life is likely to be an important determinant of happiness.

One thing is certain. Material goods are not the sole determinant of happiness. We observe many persons of modest means who are happy and many others with great wealth who are miserable. The relationship between wealth and happiness is far from precise. The importance of material goods as a determinant of happiness should be kept in perspective. Man has a seemingly insatiable desire for goods. But wealth (goods), even great wealth, assures only the opportunity for an easy life. Happiness is more elusive. It is multidimensional and material goods are only one of the dimensions.

CHAPTER LEARNING OBJECTIVES

1. Scarcity and choice compose the two essential ingredients of an economic topic. Goods are scarce because man's desire for them far outstrips their availability from Nature. Since scarcity prevents us from having as much of everything as we would like, we must choose or select from among the scarce alternatives that are available to us.

2. Scarcity and poverty are not the same thing. Absence of poverty implies that some basic level of need has been met. Absence of scarcity would mean that all of man's desires for goods have been met. We might be able to eliminate poverty, but scarcity will always be with us.

3. Economics is a method of approach, a way of thinking. The economic way of thinking emphasizes that—

(a) Among economic goods, there are no free lunches. Someone must give something up if we are to have more scarce goods.

(b) Individuals make decisions purposefully, always seeking to choose the option that they expect to be most consistent with their personal goals. Purposeful decision-making leads to economizing behavior.

(c) Incentives matter—people will be more likely to choose an option as the benefits expected from that alternative increase. In contrast, higher costs will make an alternative less attractive, reducing the likelihood that it will be chosen.

(d) Since information is scarce, uncertainty will be present when decisions are made.

(e) In addition to their initial impact, economic events often change personal incentives, thereby generating important secondary effects that may be felt only with the passage of time.

(f) The test of an economic theory is its ability to predict, to explain the actual happenings of the real world.

4. Economic science is positive. It attempts to explain the actual consequences of economic actions and alternative policies. Positive economics alone does not say one policy is superior to another. Normative economics is advocative. Using value judgments, normative economics does make suggestions about "what ought to be."

5. Since any choice involving the use of scarce resources is an economic decision, economics has wide applicability. Knowledge of economics will help one better understand the "how" and "why" of decisions that are made by consumers, producers, voters, and politicians.

IMPORTANT TERMS TO REMEMBER

Scarcity: Fundamental concept of economics which indicates that less of a good is freely available than consumers would like.

Economic good: A good that is scarce. The desire for economic goods exceeds the amount that is freely available from Nature.

Choice: The act of choosing among alternatives.

Resource: An input used to produce economic goods. Land, labor skills, natural resources, and capital are examples.

Economizing behavior: Choosing with the objective of gaining a specific benefit at the least possible cost. A corollary of economizing behavior implies that when choosing among items of equal cost, individuals will choose the option that yields the greatest benefit.

Utility: The benefit or satisfaction expected from a choice or course of action.

Secondary effects: Economic consequences that are related to an initial economic change, even though they are not immediately identifiable. The impact of secondary effects will be felt only after a passage of time.

Scientific thinking: Development of theory from basic postulates and the testing of the implications of that theory as to their consistency with real world events. Good theories will be consistent with and help explain real world events. Theories that are inconsistent with the real world are invalid and must be rejected.

Positive economics: The study of "what is," among economic relationships.

Normative economics: Judgments about "what ought to be" in economic matters. Normative economic views cannot be proven false because they are based on value judgments.

THE ECONOMIC WAY OF THINKING—DISCUSSION QUESTIONS

1. Indicate how each of the following changes would influence the incentive of a decision-maker to undertake the action:

(a) a reduction in the temperature from 80° to 50° on one's decision to go swimming;

(b) a change in the meeting time of the introductory economics course from 11:00A.M. to 7:30 A.M. on one's decision to attend the lectures;

(c) a reduction in the number of exam questions that relate to the text on the student's decision to read the text;

(d) an increase in the price of beef on one's decision to have steak every night this week;

(e) an increase in the rental price of apartments on one's decision to build additional housing units.

2. What does it mean to say that a person economizes? Do you attempt to economize? Why or why not?

3. Write a couple of paragraphs, explaining in your own words the meaning and essential ingredients of the economic way of thinking.

4. What's Wrong with This Economic Experiment?

A researcher hypothesizes that the medical service received by U.S. citizens is inadequate because many people cannot afford medical care. He interviews 100 randomly selected individuals and asks them, "Would you use physician services or hospital and nursing home medical facilities more if they were not so expensive?" Ninety six of the one hundred answer in the affirmative. The researcher concludes that there is a critical need to allocate more resources to the provision of free medical service for all citizens.

5. "Reasonable rental housing could be brought within the economic means of all. Adequate housing could be made available to all if the government would prevent landlords from charging more than $100 per month rent for a quality three-bedroom house." Use the economic way of thinking to evaluate this view.

6. SENATOR DOGOODER: I favor an increase in the minimum wage because it would help the unskilled worker.

SENATOR DONOTHING: I oppose an increase in the minimum wage because it would cause the unemployment rate among the young and the unskilled to rise.

Is the disagreement between Senators Dogooder and Donothing positive or normative? Explain.

2
SOME TOOLS OF THE ECONOMIST

In the last chapter you were introduced to the economic approach. In this chapter, we discuss a few important tools that will help you to develop the economic way of thinking.

What Shall We Give Up?

Scarcity calls the tune in economics. We cannot have as much of everything as we would like. Most of us would like to have more time for leisure, recreation, vacations, hobbies, education, and skill development. We would also like to have more wealth, a larger savings account, and accumulate more material things. But these things are all either scarce or require the use of scarce resources. They are in conflict with each other. How can I have more leisure time and simultaneously accumulate more wealth? How can I acquire more material things and simultaneously increase my savings account? The answer is, "I can't." The choice of one requires me to give up something of the other.

OPPORTUNITY COST IS THE HIGHEST VALUED OPPORTUNITY LOST

An unpleasant fact of economics is that the choice to do one thing is, at the same time, a choice *not* to do something else. Your choice to spend time reading this book is a choice *not* to play tennis, date your favorite member of the opposite sex, listen to a math lecture, or attend a party (at least not a very exciting one). This latter set of things must be given up because of your decision to read. The highest valued alternative that must be sacrificed because one chooses an option is the **opportunity cost** of the choice.

Note that the cost of an event is *not* the drudgery and undesirable aspects of the option. The distinction between (a) the undesirable attributes associated with an option and (b) the highest valued opportunity foregone in order to realize the option, is a fundamental distinction because only the latter is considered a cost by the economist.[1]

[1]For an excellent in-depth discussion of this subject, see A. A. Alchian, "Cost," in *International Encyclopedia of the Social Sciences*, Vol. 3 (New York: Macmillan, 1969), pp. 404–415.

Cost is subjective; it exists in the mind of the decision-maker. It is based on expectations—the expectation of how one would evaluate the alternative given up. Cost can never be directly measured by someone other than the decision-maker because only the decision-maker can place an evaluation on what is foregone.[2]

But cost will often have a monetary component that will sometimes allow us to approximate its value. For example, the cost of attending a movie is the highest valued opportunity that is given up because of (a) the time necessary to attend and (b) the purchasing power (that is, money) necessary to obtain a ticket. The monetary component is, of course, objective and can be measured. When there is good reason to expect that nonmonetary considerations are relatively unimportant, then the monetary component will approximate the total cost of an option.

Opportunity Cost and the Real World

Is real world decision-making influenced by opportunity cost? Remember, the basic economic postulate states that the likelihood that an option will be chosen will vary indirectly with its cost to the decision-maker. So economic theory does imply that differences (or changes) in opportunity cost will influence how decisions are made.

Let us consider several examples that demonstrate the real world application of the opportunity cost concept. Poor people are more likely to travel long distances by bus, while the wealthy are more likely to travel by airplane. Why? A simple answer would be that the bus is cheaper. Therefore, the poor will be more likely to purchase the cheaper good. But is the bus cheaper for a high income recipient whose opportunity cost of travel time is expensive? Suppose that a round trip airline ticket from Kansas City to Denver costs $50, while a bus ticket costs only $25. But the bus requires 10 hours of travel time, and the airplane only two hours. Which would be cheaper? It depends on one's opportunity cost of time. If one evaluates his opportunity cost at $2 per hour, the bus is cheapest. But if one values his time at $5 per hour, the airplane is clearly the cheaper option. Since the opportunity cost of the travel time will usually be greater for the wealthy than the poor, the airplane is more likely to be cheaper for high income recipients.

Elderly retirees watch considerably more television than high income lawyers, accountants, and other professionals. Why? Is it because the elderly can better afford the money cost of a TV? Clearly this is not the case. This phenomenon is straightforward when one considers the differences in the opportunity cost of time between the retirees and the professionals. In terms of earnings foregone, watching television costs the professional a lot more than the elderly. The professional watches less TV because it is an expensive good for him in terms of time.

Why do physicians seldom personally care for their own yard? Again opportunity cost explains the happenings of the real world. Since an hour tied up mowing grass would probably mean the sacrifice of a $200 fee for delivering a baby or removing somebody's tonsils, it would be expensive for a physician to care for his own yard.

[2] See James M. Buchanan, *Cost and Choice* (Chicago: Markham, 1969), for an analysis of the relationship between cost and choice.

Why do students watch less television and spend less time at the movies or beach during final exam week? It is more costly, that is why. Using valuable study time to go to the beach would most likely mean foregoing a passing grade in history, though your grade in economics would probably be unaffected if you kept up during the semester and developed the economic way of thinking.

By now you should have the idea. Choosing one thing means giving up others that might have been chosen. Opportunity cost is the highest valued option sacrificed as the result of choosing an alternative.

THE PRODUCTION POSSIBILITIES CURVE *or TRANSformation curve*

The resources of every individual are limited. Purposeful decision-making and economizing behavior imply that individuals seek to get the most out of their limited resources. They do not deliberately waste resources.

The nature of the economizing problem can be brought into clearer focus by the use of a production possibilities diagram. A **production possibilities curve** reveals the maximum amount of any two products that can be produced from a fixed quantity of resources.

Exhibit 2-1 illustrates the production possibilities curve for Susan Smart, an intelligent economics major. It indicates her possible grade combinations for two alternative amounts of study time—six and eight hours. If she uses her six hours of study time efficiently she can choose any grade combination along the six hour production

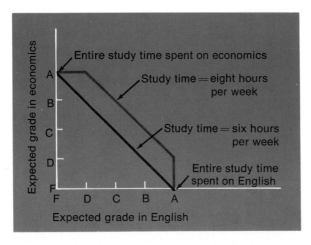

Exhibit 2-1   The Production Possibilities Curve for Grades in English and Economics

The production possibilities, in terms of grades, for Susan Smart, are illustrated for two alternative quantities of total study time. If she studies six hours per week, concentrating entirely on economics, she would expect an A, but would flunk English, because she spent all of her time studying economics. On the other hand, studying six hours per week, she could attain (a) a D in English and B in economics, (b) a C in both, (c) a B in English and D in economics, or (d) an F in economics but an A in English. The black line pictures her production possibilities curve for six hours of studying.

A higher grade in one subject costs a grade reduction in the other. Could she make higher grades in both? Yes, if she is willing to apply more resources, thereby giving up some leisure. The red line indicates her production possibilities curve if she studies eight hours per week.

possibility curve. However, when study time is limited to six hours per week, Susan is able to raise her grade in one of the subjects, only by accepting a lower grade in the other. If she wants to improve her overall performance—raise at least one grade without lowering the other—she will have to apply more time to academic endeavors. For example, she might increase her weekly study time from six to eight hours. Of course, this would require her to give up something else—leisure.

Can the production possibilities concept be applied to the entire economy? The answer is yes. You cannot have both guns and butter as the old saying goes. Increasing military expenditures will use up resources that could otherwise be applied to the production of nonmilitary goods. If scarce resources are being used efficiently, more of one thing will require the sacrifice of others. Exhibit 2-2 illustrates the concept of the production possibility curve for an economy producing only two goods, food and clothing.

What constrains the ability of an economy to produce more of everything? The same thing that constrained Susan from making a higher grade in *both* English and economics—lack of resources. There will be various maximum combinations of goods that an economy will be able to produce when—

(a) it uses some fixed quantity of resources,
(b) the resource inputs are not wasted or used inefficiently, and
(c) the level of technology is constant.

When these three conditions are met, the economy will be at the perimeter of its production possibility frontier (points such as *A*, *B*, and *C*, Exhibit 2-2). Production of

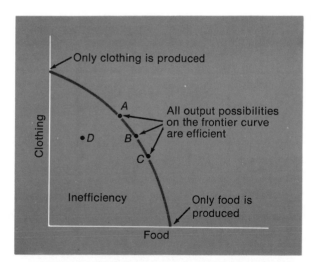

Exhibit 2-2 The Concept of the Production Possibilities Curve for an Economy

When an economy is using its limited resources efficiently, it will be at the edge of its production possibilities frontier (for example, points like *A*, *B*, or *C*). Thus, production of more clothing requires the economy to give up some other goods—food in this simple example. *With time* a technological discovery or expansion of the economy's resource base could make it possible to produce more of both, shifting the production possibilities curve outward. Or the citizens of the economy might decide to give up some leisure for more of both goods. But, these factors aside, limited resources will constrain the production possibilities of an economy.

more of one good, clothing for example, would necessitate less production of other goods (for example, food).

When the resources of an economy are used wastefully and inefficiently, the economy is operating at a point inside of the production possibilities curve—point D for example. Why might this happen? It happens when the economy is not properly solving the economizing problem. A major purpose of economics is to assure that we are getting the most out of the resources available—that we move to the perimeter of the production possibilities curve. We will return to this problem again and again.

Shifting the Production Possibility Curve Outward

Could an economy ever have more of all goods? Could the production possibilities curve be shifted outward? Yes, under certain circumstances. There are three major methods.

1. With time, human knowledge and the available technology may change. **Technology** defines the relationship between resource inputs and the output of goods and services. Technological improvements make it possible for us to generate a larger output from the same base of resources. For example, discoveries of drought-resistant hybrid seeds have led to vast expansions in the output of corn per acre (and per man-hour of labor). A technological improvement will shift the production possibilities curve outward.

2. Many productive resources are man-made. With the passage of time, we can invest in the production of more machines, education, and development of human skills. Expanding the availability of resources in the future will shift *tomorrow's* production possibilities curve outward. But not without a cost. The more of today's resources that are used to produce "tools" that will make man more productive tomorrow, the fewer will be the resources available to produce current consumer goods. More investment in machines and human skills will necessitate less current consumption.

3. The third way the production possibility curve for *material* goods can be increased is the same way that Susan increased her personal possibilities curve, by working harder and giving up current leisure. Strictly speaking, this is not an expansion in the production frontier because leisure is also a good. We are giving up some of that good to have more of other things.

Consideration of this factor does point out that the production possibilities curve for material things is not strictly fixed. It is partly a matter of preferences. We will discuss this topic more thoroughly when we present methods of measuring the output of an economy.

TRADE TIPS AND COMPARATIVE ADVANTAGE

Economizing means getting the most out of the resources available. How can this be accomplished? How can we move the perimeter of the economy's production possibilities curve? In answering these questions, we must not move too rapidly over these important principles.

First, let us consider the economizing problem of just two individuals, Carl Competent and Sam Slow. Exhibit 2-3 presents certain facts about the abilities of Carl and Sam. Carl is highly skilled, fast, and reliable. When constructing frame houses he can build one every week, four per month. Building brick houses, Carl can build one house in two weeks or two per month.

Compared to Carl, poor Sam is really out of it. He works as if all his fingers were left thumbs. It takes Sam an entire month to build either a frame house or a brick one. In absolute terms Sam is less skilled than Carl at building both types of houses. Last year both builders worked the entire 12 months. Carl spent eight months producing 16 brick houses and the other four months producing 16 frame houses. Sam was able to produce only six frame and six brick houses during the year.

One day when Sam and Carl were having coffee together, Carl stated, "I sure would like to take a vacation this year, but I just can't afford to lose the time off. My annual production would really take a nosedive if I took a vacation."

Sam replied sympathetically, "Same here, we're just getting by as it is, but I sure would like a little trip."

Carl thought to himself, "If Sam weren't so dumb and uncoordinated, he would be able to afford a vacation."

About that time an idea hit Sam. He knew how Carl could really build those frame houses. He was the best frame house builder that Sam had ever seen. Carl was good at building brick houses too, but not as good as he was at building those frame ones. Sam

Exhibit 2-3 Comparative Advantage and Producing a Much-Needed Vacation

The monthly production possibilities of Carl Competent and Sam Slow are

Frame houses per month		Brick houses per month	
Carl	Sam	Carl	Sam
4	1	2	1

Initially, they worked all year, each of them producing both frame and brick houses. Annually Carl was able to produce 16 of each and Sam only 6 of each. Thus, their beginning total output was 22 frame and 22 brick units.

After each specialized in his area of greatest comparative advantage, Sam produced only brick houses. During the first 11 months, he produced 11 brick houses. Carl worked $5\frac{1}{2}$ months producing 22 frame houses, and another $5\frac{1}{2}$ months producing 11 brick houses. As the chart shows, after specialization, Carl and Sam were able to match last year's joint output in just 11 months. The law of comparative advantage made it possible for them to maintain their previous output level, and still take that much-needed vacation.

	ANNUAL OUTPUT BEFORE SPECIALIZATION		11 MONTH OUTPUT AFTER SPECIALIZATION	
	Frame houses	Brick houses	Frame houses	Brick houses
Carl	16	16	22	11
Sam	6	6	0	11
Total	22	22	22	22

said, "Look Carl, I think I know how we can both get a vacation this year and still build as many houses as last year. Why don't I spend all of my time producing brick houses, and during the year I will trade you five brick houses for six frame ones."

Sam realized that in 11 months he could produce 11 brick houses. If he could trade five to Carl in exchange for six frame ones, he would have six frame and six brick for 11 months' work!

Carl again thought to himself. "It would take me 10 weeks to produce five brick houses, but I can produce six frame ones for Sam in only six weeks. What a steal! Boy, this Sam must not be any too bright to give me a deal like that. I'm saving myself four weeks' working time. I can take that vacation after all."

"Sam, you've got yourself a deal." Carl blurted out.

After their bargain, Carl Competent and Sam Slow were able to produce, in 11 months, what it would otherwise have taken them the entire year to do. If they had wanted to work all 12 months, they could have even expanded their annual output.

Despite the fact that Carl was better than Sam at producing both frame and brick houses, the two were able to gain from the trade and specialization.[3] Was it magic? What is happening here? Our old friend, opportunity cost, will help us unravel this seemingly paradoxical result. In what sense is Carl better at producing brick houses than Sam? True, in a month, Carl can produce twice as many brick houses as Sam. But what is Carl's opportunity cost of producing a brick house? Two frame ones, right? With the same time required to produce a single brick house, Carl can produce two frame houses.

Consider Sam's opportunity cost of producing a brick house. It is only one frame house. So who is the cheaper producer of brick houses? Sam is, because his opportunity cost of producing a brick house is one frame house, compared to Carl's opportunity cost of two frame houses.

The reason why Carl and Sam could both gain is that their exchange allowed each of them to specialize in the production of the product that, *comparatively* speaking, they could produce cheapest. Sam was the cheaper producer of brick houses. Carl was the cheaper producer of the frame ones. They were able to economize—get more out of their resources—by trading and specializing in the thing that each did comparatively better.

This simple example demonstrates a basic truth known as the law of comparative advantage, that lies at the heart of economizing behavior for any economy. The **law of comparative advantage** states that the total output of a group, an entire economy, or a group of nations will be greatest when the output of each good is produced by the person (or firm) with the lowest opportunity cost.

If output of a product, any product, is produced by one producer when it could have been produced by another with a lower opportunity cost, the economy gives up (after all that is what opportunity cost tells us) more than is necessary. It is not economizing. Economizing, or maximum economic efficiency, requires that output is always generated by the producer who has the lower opportunity cost.

---

[3]Throughout this section we will assume that individuals are equally content to produce either product. Dropping this assumption would add to the complexity of the analysis, but it would not change the basic principle.

Comparative Advantage and Regional Specialization

Why are bananas not raised in Nebraska? Why do not more of those Southern California orange growers raise wheat? Comparative advantage explains a lot about regional specialization that we often take for granted. Different areas of the United States tend to specialize in different products. In the East and Upper Midwest the transportation network is highly developed. Raw materials are either readily accessible or easily transportable, and energy sources are relatively cheap. Manufacturing and trade are the dominant industries of the region.

In the open spaces of the Great Plains, fertile land is cheap. Thus, this region tends to specialize in feed grains, beef, and dairy products. Florida, with its mild winter climate and scenic wonders, specializes in citrus crops and tourism. Since the endowments of land, labor skills, and capital differ among these regions, so too will the opportunity cost of producing different products.

Exhibit 2-4 illustrates why regional differences in comparative advantage will create the potential for gains from regional specialization and trade. The potential output combinations of wheat and cotton are indicated for a Michigan and a Texas farmer.

Exhibit 2-4 Producing Cotton in Michigan

The chart indicates the production possibilities for cotton and wheat for two farmers, one in Michigan and the other in Texas. Their farms are of equal size.

	TEXAS FARMER		MICHIGAN FARMER		
	Cotton (bales)	Wheat (bushels)	Cotton (bales)	Wheat (bushels)	
	0	800	0	400	New output
	100	600	10	300	
	200	400	20	200	Initial output
New Output	220	360	30	100	
	300	200	40	0	
	400	0			

Initially, the Texas farmer was producing 400 bushels of wheat and 200 bales of cotton. Not knowing about the law of comparative advantage, the Michigan farmer was raising 200 bushels of wheat and 20 bales of cotton. The Texas farmer, being a clever businessman, runs an ad in the Michigan newspapers, offering to trade a bale of cotton for five bushels of wheat. With the knowledge that the cotton is available from the Texan, the Michigan farmer specializes in wheat. He raises 400 bushels of wheat, keeps 300 bushels, and trades 100 bushels to the Texan for 20 bales of cotton. He now has 300 bushels of wheat and 20 bales of cotton, *a net gain of 100 bushels of wheat.* The Texas farmer increases his cotton production to 220 bales, which brings a reduction in his wheat production to 360 bushels. But after he has traded 20 bales of cotton to the Michigan farmer for 100 bushels of wheat, he is left with 200 bales of cotton and 460 bushels of wheat *a net gain of 60 bushels of wheat.* What has happened to total output? As the result of specialization and trade, wheat output increased by 160 bushels without any reduction in the output of cotton. Both farmers gain from the specialization and exchange. The law of comparative advantage suggests that the easiest way to produce cotton in Michigan is to produce something else (wheat) and exchange it for the cotton.

The Texan can raise both more wheat and more cotton on his farm than his Michigan counterpart. Does this factor eliminate the possibility of gains from trade between the two? By now the answer should be obvious. Clearly, it does not. It is a *comparative*, not *absolute*, advantage that makes gains from specialization and trade possible.

In terms of opportunities foregone the Michigan farmer is the cheaper producer of wheat and the Texas farmer is the lower cost producer of cotton. Both can gain from the trade of Michigan wheat for Texas cotton.

Comparative Advantage and Trade between Nations

The principle of comparative advantage applies to trade between nations, just as well as to trade between individuals. Whenever natural endowments, labor skills, or other factors result in differences in the opportunity cost of producing goods, nations can gain by specializing in the production of products for which they are best equipped (that is, the low opportunity cost producer), exporting these goods in exchange for those products which the country is least able to produce. Countries like Canada, Australia, Argentina, and even the United States, with an abundance of rich farmland, export feed grains, beef, and other agricultural products. A country like Switzerland, with a labor force that has passed precision skills down from generation to generation, exports watches and scientific instruments. When highly skilled Jewish diamond cutters migrated to Israel, this small nation without a single diamond mine utilized this comparative advantage to become the world's largest exporter of cut diamonds.

The list is seemingly endless. Japan, with few material resources but a highly efficient labor force, imports many raw materials and exports radios, small appliances, cameras, and small manufactured goods. Countries like India and Korea, with an abundance of labor relative to land, export products such as textiles, which use large amounts of labor. All of these countries gain by selling products that they can produce at a low opportunity cost and buying products for which their production opportunity cost would be high.

The Common Sense of Comparative Advantage

When one begins to think about the principle, the law of comparative advantage is almost common sense. Stated in layman's terms, it merely means that if we want to accomplish a task with the least effort, each of us should specialize in that component of the task that we do best.

Square pegs should not be placed in round holes. Small men should become jockeys rather than football players. Persons who learn economics easily, but cannot understand physics, would be more successful as economists than physicists. All of these actions simply reflect potential gains from using one's comparative advantage.

The principle of comparative advantage is perfectly equitable. It is just as valid in socialist countries as it is for capitalists. If the socialist planner is interested in getting the most out of the available resources, he too should apply the principle of comparative advantage.

DEPENDENCE, SPECIALIZATION, AND EXCHANGE

Specialization and mutual interdependence are directly related. If the United States specializes in the production of agricultural products and Middle East countries specialize in the production of oil, the two countries become mutually interdependent. Similarly, if Texas specializes in cotton, and Michigan in wheat, mutual interdependence results. In some cases this dependence could have serious consequences for one or both of the parties. These possible consequences should be weighed against the potential gains, when evaluating the merits of specialization.

Specialization and Work Alienation

Specialization clearly makes it possible to produce more goods. But it also may result in many workers performing simple, boring, and monotonous functions. Our friend Carl may get tired of building just frame houses and Sam's life may lose a certain zest because he does nothing but produce brick ones. At a more practical level specialization will often result in assembly line production techniques. Workers may become quite skilled because they perform identical tasks over and over again. But they may also become bored, because the work is personally unrewarding. Thus, strictly speaking, some of the gains associated with the expansion of physical output may result in worker dissatisfaction.

About now the reader is probably thinking that economists consider nothing but material goods and ignore the importance of human beings. It may seem that they do not care if a worker absolutely hates his job, because he does the same thing over and over and over again. Our initial approach to the topic of specialization is vulnerable to this charge. We stressed only physical production because it makes the principle simpler to communicate. However, it could be considered strictly from the viewpoint of utility, where individuals consider both output and job satisfaction. After all, job satisfaction is an economic good.

An individual's opportunity cost of producing a good (or performing a service) includes the sacrifice of both physical production of other goods and any reduction (or improvement) in the desirability of one's working conditions. This approach does consider both material goods for man's satisfaction and the job satisfaction that is important to any human being. But it does not alter the basic principle. Individuals could still gain by producing and selling those things for which they have a comparatively low opportunity cost, including the job satisfaction component, while buying other things for which their opportunity cost is high. They would tend to specialize in the provision of those things they *both* do well and enjoy most. Persons with a strong aversion to monotonous work would be less likely to choose such work even though they might be skilled at it. A person with less of a comparative advantage, measured strictly in terms of physical goods, might have a lower opportunity cost because he personally finds the work more rewarding.

The introduction of working conditions and job preferences does not invalidate the basic concept. It is still true that maximum economic efficiency, in the utility sense, would require that each productive activity be performed by those persons with the lowest opportunity cost—including costs associated with their personal evaluation of other jobs.

Personal Motivation and Gain from Specialization and Exchange

What motivates people to action? How does the purposeful decision-maker choose? Economic thinking implies that one will choose an option only if he expects the

---

MYTHS OF ECONOMICS
"In exchange, if someone gains, someone else must lose. Trading is a zero-sum game."

People tend to think of making, building, and creating something as productive activities. Agriculture and manufacturing are like this. They create something genuinely new, something that was not there before. But trade is only the exchange of one thing for another. Nothing is created. Therefore, it must be a zero-sum game where one man's gain is necessarily a loss to another. So goes a popular myth.

Voluntary exchange is productive for two reasons. First, it channels goods and services to those who value them most. People have fallen into the habit of thinking of material things as wealth. But material things are not wealth until they are in the hands of someone who values them. A highly technical mathematics book is not wealth to a longshoreman with a sixth grade education. It becomes wealth only after it is guided into the hands of a mathematician. A master painting may be wealth to the art connoisseur, but of little value to a cowboy. Wealth is created by the act of channeling goods to persons who value them highly.

When a good is exchanged for money, it is being channeled toward the person who has the greater evaluation of it. When you pay $200 per month for the services of an apartment, rented by the owner for that amount, a good is channeled toward the party who values it most. You value the apartment more than $200 or you would not have agreed to the transaction. Thus, you gain. The apartment owner places the greater value on the $200, otherwise he would not rent to you. He too gains. The trade makes both you and your landlord better off.

Second, exchange can be advantageous to trading partners because it permits each to specialize in areas for which they have a comparative advantage. For example, exchange permits a skilled carpenter to concentrate on building house frames, while contracting for electrical and plumbing services from others who have comparative advantages in those areas. Similarly, trade permits a country such as Canada to specialize in the production of wheat, while Brazil specializes in coffee. Such specialization would enlarge joint output and permit both to gain from the exchange of Canadian wheat for Brazilian coffee.

The motivating force behind exchange is the pursuit of personal gain. Unless *both* parties expect to gain from an exchange, it will not take place. Mutual gain forms the foundation for voluntary exchange. Trade is a positive-sum game.

---

benefits (utility) of the choice to exceed its opportunity cost. Purposeful decision-makers will be motivated by the pursuit of personal gain. They will never knowingly choose an alternative for which they expect the opportunity cost to exceed the expected benefits from the choice. To do so would be to make a choice with the full awareness that it meant the sacrifice of another, more preferred course of action. That would simply not make sense. To say that people are motivated by personal gain does not, of course, mean that they are inconsiderate of others. Other people's feelings will often affect the personal benefit received by a decision-maker.

When an individual's interests, aptitudes, abilities, and skills make it possible to gain by exchanging low opportunity cost goods for those things for which he is a high opportunity cost producer, pursuit of the potential gain will motivate him to trade precisely in this manner. It will not be necessary for someone to assign him to the "right" job, or tell him that, comparatively speaking, he should trade A for B because he is good at producing A, but not so good at producing B. Individuals seeking personal gain will voluntarily so specialize. Thus, when people simply follow their own personal interests, the goods (or resources) that they sell will be composed primarily of those skills with which they are gifted. Similarly, the decision-maker seeking personal gain will tend to buy those things which are made with skills that he does not possess and productive activities that he finds unrewarding.

THREE ECONOMIZING DECISIONS FACING ALL NATIONS: WHAT, HOW, AND FOR WHOM

We have outlined several basic concepts that are important if one is to understand the economizing problem. In this section we want to outline three general economizing questions that every economy, regardless of its organizational structure, must answer.

1. *What Will Be Produced?* All of the desired goods cannot be produced. What goods should we produce and in what quantities? Should we produce more food and less clothing, more consumer durables and less clean air, more national defense and less leisure? Or should we use up some of our productive resources, producing more goods today even though it will mean less goods in the future? If fewer resources are used to produce food, more resources will be available to produce clothing and other products. If our economy is operating efficiently (that is, on its production possibilities curve), the choice to produce more of one commodity will reduce our ability to produce others. Sometimes the impact may be more direct. Production of some goods will not only require productive resources, but their production may, as a by-product, reduce the amount of other goods that are available. For example, production of warmer houses and more automobile travel may, as a by-product, increase air pollution, reducing the availability of clean air (another desired good). Use of natural resources (water, minerals, trees, etc.) to produce some goods may simultaneously reduce the quality of our environment. Every economy must answer these and similar questions about what should be produced.

2. *How Will Goods Be Produced?* Usually, different combinations of productive resources can be utilized to produce a good. Education could be produced with less

labor by using more television lectures, recording devices, and books. Wheat could be raised with less land and more fertilizer. Chairs could be constructed with more labor and fewer machines. What combinations of the alternative productive resources will be used to produce the goods of an economy?

The decision to produce does not accomplish the task. Resources must be organized and motivated if the task is to be accomplished. How can the resources of an economy be transformed into final output of goods and services? Economies may differ as to the combination of economic incentives, threat of force, and types of competitive behavior that are permissible. But all will still face the problem of how their limited resources can be utilized to produce goods.

3. *For Whom Will Goods Be Produced?* Who will actually consume the products available? This economic question is often referred to as the distribution problem. Property rights for resources, including labor skills, might be established and resource owners permitted to sell their services to the highest bidder. Prices and private ownership of resources that are productive would then determine the share of total output allocated to each person. Alternatively, goods might be split on a strict per capita basis, with each person getting an equal share of the pie. Or, they might be divided according to the relative political influences of citizens, with larger shares going to persons who are more persuasive and skillful than others at organizing and attaining political power. They could be divided according to need, with a dictator or an all-powerful, democratically elected legislature deciding the various "needs" of the citizens.

The Three Decisions Are Interrelated

One thing is obvious. These three questions are highly interrelated. How goods are distributed will exert considerable influence on the "voluntary" availability of productive resources, including human resources. The choice of what to produce will influence how and what resources are used. In reality they all must be resolved simultaneously. But this does not detract from the fact that all economies, whatever their other differences, must somehow answer these three basic economic questions.

TWO METHODS OF MAKING DECISIONS—THE MARKET AND GOVERNMENT PLANNING

In general there are two methods of organizing economic activity—a **market mechanism** and **collective decision-making.** There is, of course, some variation within these two classifications. The rules and guidelines for a market economy will be established by the public decision-making process. The accepted forms of competition may vary slightly between market economies. There may be some variation in how the rights and responsibilities of property owners are defined. But once the rules of the game are established, a market economy will rely on the unregulated pricing mechanism to direct the decisions of consumers, producers, and owners of productive resources. The government will not act to prevent a seller from using price reductions and quality improvements as a method of competing with other sellers. Neither will the government prevent a buyer from using price as a method of bidding a product or productive resource away from another potential buyer. Legal restraints (for example, government licensing) will not be utilized to limit the entry of potential buyers or sellers from producing, selling, or buying in the marketplace. The free interplay and bargaining of buyers and sellers will establish the conditions of trade and answer these three basic economic questions. The government's role is secondary—only that of the referee and rulemaker.

As an alternative to the market organization, economic decisions can be made by collective decision-making—by elected representatives, direct referendum, or some other governmental mechanism (for example, military force). Central planning and political factors replace market forces. The decision to expand or contract the output of education, medical services, automobiles, electricity, steel, consumer durables, and thousands of other commodities is made by government officials and planning boards. This is not to say that the preferences of individuals are of no importance. If the government officials and central planners are influenced by the democratic process, they will have to consider how their actions will influence their election prospects. If they do not, like the firm that produces a product that consumers do not want, their tenure of service is likely to be a short one.

◻ LOOKING AHEAD

In most economies, including the United States, a large number of decisions are made both through the decentralized pricing system and public sector decision-making. Both exert a considerable influence on how we answer fundamental economic problems. While the two arrangements are different, in each case, the choices of individuals acting as decision-makers are important. Economics is about how people make decisions, so the tools of economics can be applied to both market and public sector action. When decisions are made in the public sector, the constraints faced by individuals will be different. The incentive to pursue various types of action will differ. But people are still people. Changes in personal costs and benefits will still influence their choices. In turn the acts of political participants—voters, lobbyists, and politicians—will influence public policy and its economic consequences.

The following chapter is designed to present an overview of the market sector. Chapter 4 focuses on how the public sector, the democratic collective decision-making process, functions. It is not enough merely to study how the pricing system works. If we are to understand fully the forces that exert a powerful influence on the allocation of economic resources in a country like the United States, we must apply the tools of economics to both market and public sector choices.

We think this approach is important, fruitful, and exciting. How does the market sector really work? What does economics say about what activities should be handled by government. What types of economic policies are politically attractive to democractically elected officials? Is there sometimes a conflict between sound economic policy and good politics? Economics has a great deal to say about these questions.

CHAPTER LEARNING OBJECTIVES

1. Because of scarcity, when an individual chooses to do, to make, or to buy something, he must simultaneously give up something else that he might otherwise have chosen. The highest valued activity sacrificed is the opportunity cost of the choice.

2. A production possibilities curve reveals the maximum combination of any two products that could be produced with a fixed quantity of resources, assuming that the level of technology is constant. When an individual or an economy is operating at maximum efficiency, it will be on the production possibilities curve. In such cases, greater production of one good would necessitate a reduction in the output of other goods.

3. Opportunity cost is subjective. It is a utility concept. Maximum efficiency will result when each productive activity is performed by those persons with the lowest opportunity cost, including cost associated with one's personal evaluation of undesirable (or desirable) working conditions.

4. Pursuit of personal gain will motivate people to specialize in those things that they do best (that is, they are low opportunity cost producers) and sell them for goods for which they are high opportunity cost producers.

5. Exchange is productive. It channels **(a)** goods into the hands of people who value them most and **(b)** resources into areas of their greatest comparative advantage. Both trading partners must expect to gain before a voluntary exchange can take place. Trade is a positive-sum game that improves the economic well-being of each voluntary participant.

6. Every economy must answer three basic questions: **(a)** What will be produced? **(b)** How will goods be produced? **(c)** How will the goods be distributed? These three questions are highly interrelated.

7. There are two basic methods of making economic decisions: the market mechanism and public sector decision-making. The decisions of individuals will influence the result in both cases. The tools of economics are general. They are applicable to choices that influence both market and public sector decisions.

IMPORTANT TERMS TO REMEMBER

Opportunity cost: The highest valued benefit that must be sacrificed (foregone) as the result of choosing an option.

Law of comparative advantage: Principle which states that individuals, firms, regions, or nations can gain by specializing in the production of goods that they produce cheaply (that is, at a low opportunity cost) and exchanging them for other desired goods for which they are high opportunity cost producers.

Production possibilities curve: A curve that outlines all possible combinations of total output that could be produced, assuming (a) the utilization of a fixed amount of productive resources, (b) full and efficient use of those resources, and (c) a specific state of technical knowledge.

Technology: The body of know-how and technical knowledge available at any point in time. The level of technology establishes the relationship between inputs and the output they can generate.

Market mechanism: A method of organization that allows unregulated prices and the decentralized decisions of private property owners to resolve the basic economic problems of consumption, production, and distribution.

Collective decision-making mechanism: A method of organization that relies on public sector decision-making (that is, voting, political bargaining, lobbying, etc.). It could be used to resolve the basic economic problems of an economy.

THE ECONOMIC WAY OF THINKING—DISCUSSION QUESTIONS

1. "The principle of comparative advantage gives individuals an incentive to specialize in those things which they do best." Explain in your own words why this is true.

2. Economists often argue that wage rates reflect productivity. Yet the wages of housepainters have increased nearly as rapidly as the national average even though they use approximately the same methods that were applied 50 years ago. Can you explain why the wages of painters have risen substantially even though their productivity has changed little?

3. It takes two hours to travel from New York City to Washington by air, but eight hours by bus. If the airfare is $44 and the bus fare $20, which would be cheaper for someone whose opportunity cost of travel time was $2 per hour? Someone whose opportunity cost was $4 per hour? $6 per hour?

4. Explain why the percentage of college-educated women employed outside of the home exceeds the percentage of women with eight years of schooling who are engaged in outside employment.

5. Explain why parking lots in downtown areas of large cities are often several decks, while lots of equal size in suburban areas usually cover only the ground level.

6. Is exchange productive? If so, what does it produce? Who gains, when goods are voluntarily exchanged?

7. When the government, through the Medicare program, subsidized the purchase of medical service for the elderly in the mid-1960s, did this action have a beneficial or harmful effect on nonsubsidized medical service consumers? Explain.

3
MARKET DECISIONS AND
THE MARKET PROCESS

Every individual necessarily labours to render the annual revenue of the society as great as he can. He generally, indeed neither intends to promote the public interest, nor knows how much he is promoting it . . . he intends only his own gain, and he is in this, as in many other cases, led by an invisible hand to promote an end which was no part of his attention.
[*Adam Smith* (1776)]

In this chapter we analyze the operation of a pricing or market system. For a market economy the basic economic decisions are solved by the independent choices of individual consumers, producers, and factor suppliers. The economic role of government is limited to defining property rights, enforcing contracts, protecting people from fraud, and similar activities that establish the rules of the game. The government neither interferes with the prices established by market forces nor protects existing firms from the pressure of competitors. Markets are free, some would say competitive, in the sense that there are no legal restrictions limiting the market entry of either buyers or sellers. In the real world even strongly market-oriented economies such as the United States use a combination of markets and public sector allocation to answer the basic economic questions. All economies are mixed, part market sector and part government allocation. Nevertheless, it is still quite useful to understand how the free market pricing system functions, how it motivates people, and how it allocates goods and resources.

SCARCITY NECESSITATES RATIONING

When a good is scarce, some criterion must be set up to ration it, to decide who will receive the good and who will do without it. Scarcity makes rationing a necessity.

There are several possible criteria that could be used to ration a limited amount of a good among citizens who would like to have more of it. "First come, first served" could be used. This method would allocate goods to those who were fastest at getting in line or to those who were most willing to wait in line. Beauty could be used, allocating goods to those who were thought to be most beautiful. The political process might be utilized, allocating goods on the basis of need, or ability to manipulate the political process to personal advantage. But one thing is certain, scarcity will require that some method be established to decide who gets the limited available amount of goods and resources.

Competition Is the Result of Rationing

Competition is not unique to a market system. Rather it is a natural outgrowth of scarcity and the necessity of adopting a rationing mechanism. Competition will exist in both capitalist and socialist societies. It will exist when goods are allocated by price and when they are allocated by other means—collective decision-making, for example.

Certainly the rationing criterion adopted will influence the competitive techniques utilized. When the rationing criterion is price, people will devote much of their resourcefulness to the task of making money so they can pay the price. When beauty is the criterion, as it is in the Miss America pageant, people will seek to make themselves attractive. When the appearance of sincerity, broad knowledge, fairness, good judgment, and a positive TV image are important, as they are in the rationing of political positions, people will dedicate their resources to the projection of these qualities. But changing how competition manifests itself and how it is displayed, is not the same thing as eliminating competition. No society has been able to eliminate competition, because no society has been able to eliminate the necessity of rationing. When people who want more scarce goods seek to meet the criteria established to ration those goods, competition occurs.

The market is one method of rationing and allocating scarce goods and resources. Let us investigate how it works.

CONSUMER CHOICE AND THE LAW OF DEMAND

The income of consumer units is almost always substantially less than their wants. I have a desire for a backyard swimming pool, European vacation, and a summer home in the mountains, but I have not purchased any of them. Why? Because given the restriction of my limited income, my desire for other goods is even more urgent. My income would allow me to purchase a backyard swimming pool, but only if I spent less on food, trips to the beach, housing, books, clothes, and other forms of recreation. I have a choice, and have chosen to forego the pool instead of the other goods.

How does a consumer decide which things to buy and which things to forego? Sensibly, he wants to get the most satisfaction from the spending of his money. Economizing behavior suggests that the rational consumer will spend his limited income on the bundle of things that he expects will yield him the most satisfaction. Given his personal tastes, he will choose the best alternative that his limited income will permit. Prices will influence consumer decisions. An increase in the price of a good will increase the consumer's opportunity cost of consuming it. More of other things must now be given up if the consumer chooses the higher priced commodity.

According to the basic postulate of economics, an increase in the cost of an alternative will reduce the likelihood that it will be chosen. This basic postulate implies that higher prices will discourage consumption. Lower prices will reduce the cost of choosing a good, stimulating consumption of it. This negative relationship between the price of a good and the amount of it that will be consumed is called the **law of demand.**

The availability of substitutes—goods that perform similar functions—helps to explain the logic of the law of demand. No good is absolutely essential. Margarine can be substituted for butter. Wood, aluminum, bricks, and glass can be substituted for steel. Insulation, car pools, driving slower, bicycling, and small cars are substitute products that will allow households to reduce their gasoline consumption. As the price (and therefore the consumer's opportunity cost) of a good increases, people have a greater incentive to turn to substitute products and economize on their use of the more expensive good. Prices really do matter.

Exhibit 3-1 is a graphic presentation of the law of demand. In constructing a demand curve, economists measure price on the vertical or y axis and amount demanded on the horizontal or x axis. The demand curve will slope downward to the right, indicating that the amount demanded of a good, beef in this example, will increase as price declines. During 1973 there was a rapid increase in the price of beef. Consumers responded, admittedly with a loud cry, by using less of it. In early 1973 when the price of beef was $1.00 per pound, the average American family consumed 2.3 pounds per week. During the summer of 1973, as beef prices rose to $1.50 per pound, weekly consumption declined to 1.8 pounds, as consumers substituted other goods for beef. At still higher prices, the average weekly consumption of beef would have been even smaller.

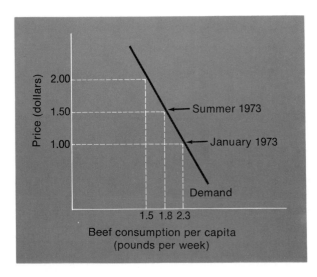

Exhibit 3-1   The Demand for Beef

As beef prices rose in 1973, consumers substituted pork, poultry, vegetables, venison, and even horsemeat for the more expensive beef. The consumption level of beef (and other products) is negatively related to its price.

Some commodities may be much more responsive to a change in price than others. Consider a good for which there are several good substitutes—a Florida vacation, for example. If the price of a Florida vacation increases, perhaps because of higher gasoline prices, consumers will substitute more movies, local family camping trips, baseball games, TV programs, and other recreation activities for the vacation. As illustrated by Exhibit 3-2, since good substitutes are available, an increase in the price of Florida vacations will cause a sharp reduction in quantity demanded. Economists would say that demand for Florida vacations was *elastic*,[1] the term used to indicate that quantity demanded is quite responsive to a change in price.

Other goods may be much less responsive to a change in price. Suppose there was a 15 percent rise in the price of physician services, as indicated by Exhibit 3-2. What impact would this price increase have on quantity demanded? The higher prices would cause some people to prescribe their own medication for colds, flu, and minor illness. Others might turn to chiropractors, osteopaths, and faith healers for even major medical problems. But most consumers would consider these to be poor substitutes for the services of a physician. Thus, higher medical prices would cause a relatively small reduction in their quantity demanded. The demand for medical service is thus *inelastic*, the term used to indicate that the amount demanded is *relatively* unresponsive to a change in price.

However, despite differences in the degree of responsiveness, the fundamental law of demand will hold for all goods. A price increase will induce consumers to turn to substitutes, leading to a reduction in the amount purchased. A price reduction will make a commodity relatively cheaper, inducing consumers to purchase more of it as they substitute it for other goods.

Exhibit 3-2   Responsiveness of Demand to a Price Change

A 15 percent increase in the price of Florida vacations (D_1) caused the quantity demanded to decline from Q_0 to Q_2, a 50 percent reduction. In contrast, a 15 percent increase in the price of physician services (D_2) results in only a 5 percent reduction in quantity demanded (from Q_0 to Q_1). Economists would say that the demand for Florida vacations is elastic, but the demand for physician services is inelastic.

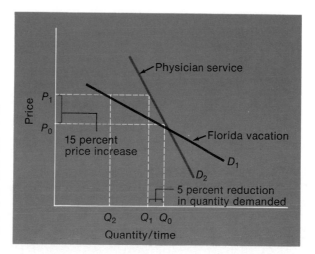

---

[1]The mathematical formula for price elasticity of demand is (a) percent change in quantity demanded divided by (b) the percent change in price. If the absolute value of this expression exceeds one, demand is elastic. If it is less than one, demand is inelastic. This topic is dealt with in more detail in Chapter 16.

PRODUCER'S CHOICE AND THE LAW OF SUPPLY

How does the market process determine the amount of each product that will be produced? Answering this question requires knowledge of factors that influence the choices of producers in a market economy. Producers of goods and services, often utilizing the business firm—

(a) organize productive inputs such as labor, land, natural resources, and intermediate goods,

(b) transform and combine these factors of production into goods desired by households, and

(c) sell the final products to consumers for a price.

The producer pays the owners of the inputs (land, labor, machines, etc.) for their services and seeks to use these inputs to create a product that he can sell for a profit. These payments for the use of inputs are a cost to the producer. The sales of his product to consumers generate revenue. In a market economy alert businessmen and entrepreneurs will be constantly searching for opportunities to undertake projects that yield a profit—an excess of sales revenues over production costs.

How will producers respond to a change in product price? Other things constant, a higher price will increase the producer's incentive to supply the good. New entrepreneurs, seeking personal gain, will enter the market and begin supplying the product. Established producers will expand the scale of their operation, leading to an additional expansion in output. Higher prices will induce producers to supply a greater amount.

The positive relationship between the price of a product and the amount of it that will be supplied is termed the **law of supply.** Exhibit 3-3 presents a graphic picture of the law.

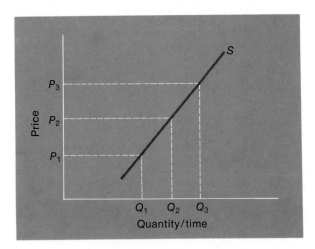

Exhibit 3-3   The Supply Curve

As the price of a product increases, *other things constant*, producers will expand the amount supplied of the product.

PRICE AND MARKET EQUILIBRIUM

Equilibrium is a state where forces are in balance. When there is a balance—an equilibrium—between two conflicting forces, the tendency for continual change is absent. Market prices will coordinate the forces of supply and demand, bringing them into balance. In equilibrium, the amount demanded will just equal the amount supplied. The decisions of consumers will be perfectly consistent with the decisions of producers.

How do prices balance the conflicting forces of supply and demand? Exhibit 3-4 demonstrates the forces that are operating to bring about an equilibrium. Suppose that price was temporarily above equilibrium—P_1, for example. At P_1, the amount supplied by producers would exceed the amount that consumers desired to purchase. An excess supply (CE) would result as producers would be unable to sell all of their produce. Their inventories would accumulate. In order to reduce their inventories, some of the firms would reduce price and cut production. The fall in price would make the activity less attractive to producers. Some of the marginal producers would go out of business and other firms would reduce their current output. By contrast consumers would increase their purchases in response to the lower prices. Eventually, the price reduction would bring the production plans of suppliers into harmony with the consumption plans of consumers. The amount supplied would just equal the amount demanded and equilibrium price P_0 would prevail.

What would happen if the price was below equilibrium—P_2 for example? Then the amount of the good demanded by consumers would exceed the quantity that producers were willing to supply. An excess demand (AB) would be present. Some consumers, who would like to purchase the commodity at P_2, would be unable to do so because of the inadequate supply or shortage of the good. Rather than going without the good, many consumers would be willing to pay higher prices. Recognizing this fact, producers will raise their price toward P_0. As the price increases from P_2 to P_0, producers will

Exhibit 3-4   Market Equilibrium

At an above-equilibrium price, P_1 for example, an excess supply would result, causing the price to decline. When the price is below equilibrium, P_2 for example, an excess demand would be present, causing the price to rise. Thus, market forces would lead to an equilibrium price P_0, where the purchasing decisions of buyers harmonize with the selling decisions of suppliers.

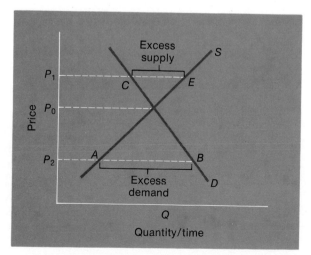

expand their output and consumers will cut down on their consumption. Eventually at P_0 an equilibrium price will again be established. Only at P_0 would the forces of supply and demand be in equilibrium.

Shortages, Surpluses, and Scarcity

Students sometimes mistakenly believe that shortage and scarcity mean the same thing. Misuse of these two terms by the popular media is the major source of this confusion. Scarcity is inescapable. Any time that people want more of a good than Nature has provided, scarcity will result. Almost everything is scarce, but shortages are avoidable. A **shortage** is a situation in which the quantity demanded is greater than the quantity supplied, *at the existing price*. The shortage could be avoided if price were permitted to rise. The higher price would (a) stimulate additional production and (b) discourage consumption while rationing the available supply to those willing to give up the most of other things, that is, pay the highest prices. These forces, expansion in output and a reduction in consumption, would eliminate the shortage.

A **surplus** is a situation in which the quantity supplied is in excess of the quantity demanded. It results because the price is above equilibrium. A reduction in the price of the good would both encourage consumers to purchase more and discourage businessmen from producing so much. The surplus could thus be eliminated by a decline in price. Note that goods that are in surplus will still be scarce. There is nothing inconsistent about people wanting more of a good than Nature has made freely available, while at the same time wanting less than the amount offered by producers *at the current price.*

SHIFTS IN DEMAND AND ADVICE ON HOW TO PASS YOUR FIRST ECONOMICS EXAM

A demand curve isolates the impact that price has on the amount of a product purchased. Of course, factors other than price—for example, consumer income, tastes, prices of related goods, and expectations as to the future price of a product—will also influence the decisions of consumers. If any of these factors should change, the entire demand curve would shift. Economists refer to such shifts in the demand curve as a *change in demand.*

Let us take a closer look at some of the factors that would cause the demand for a product to change. Expansion in income makes it possible for consumers to purchase more goods. They usually respond by increasing their spending on a wide cross section of products. Changes in prices of closely related products will also influence the choices of consumers. If the price of butter fell, many consumers would substitute it for margarine. The demand for margarine would decline (shift to the left) as a result. Our expectations about the future price of a product will also influence our current decisions. For example, if you think that the price of automobiles is going to rise by 20 percent next month, this would increase your incentive to buy now, before the price rises. In contrast, if you thought the price of a product was going to decline, you would demand less *now*, as you attempt to extend your purchasing decision into the future when prices are expected to be lower.

Failure to distinguish between a *change in demand* and a *change in quantity demanded* is one of the most common mistakes of introductory economics students.[2] A change in demand is a shift in the entire demand curve. A change in quantity demanded is a movement along the same demand curve. Exhibit 3-5 clearly demonstrates the difference between the two. The demand curve D_1 indicates the initial demand (the entire curve) for doorknobs. At a price of $3, consumers would purchase Q_1. If the price declined to $1, there would be an increase in quantity demanded from Q_1 to Q_3. Arrow A indicates the change in *quantity demanded*—a movement along demand curve D_1. Now suppose that there is a 20 percent increase in income, causing a housing boom. The *demand* for doorknobs would increase from D_1 to D_2. As indicated by the B arrows, the entire demand curve would shift. At the higher income level, consumers would be willing to purchase more doorknobs at $3, at $2, at $1, and at other prices for which they might sell, than was previously true. The increase in income leads to an *increase in demand*—a shift in the entire curve.

How does the market react to a change in demand? What will happen to price and the amount supplied of a good, if demand increases? Exhibit 3-6 will help answer these questions, while yielding insight into real world past events. In the mid-1970s there was a sharp rise in the price of gasoline. Many car owners attempted to economize on their use of the more expensive fuel by substituting smaller cars for their gas-guzzling heavier models. There was an *increase in demand* for compact cars. The demand curve for such cars shifted to the right (from D_1 to D_2). At the original equilibrium price, $2500, there was an excess demand for compact cars. The excess demand would cause the price of compact cars to rise. Market forces would eventually bring about a new balance between supply and demand, establishing a new equilibrium price ($2800 for example)

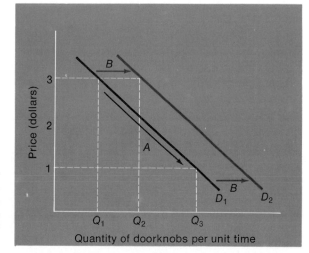

Exhibit 3-5   The Difference between a Change in Demand and a Change in Quantity Demanded

Arrow *A* indicates a change in *quantity demanded*, a movement along the demand curve *D*₁ in response to a change in the price of doorknobs. The *B* arrows illustrate a change in *demand*, a shift of the entire curve.

---

[2]Questions designed to test the ability of students to make this distinction are favorites of many economics instructors. A word to the wise should be sufficient.

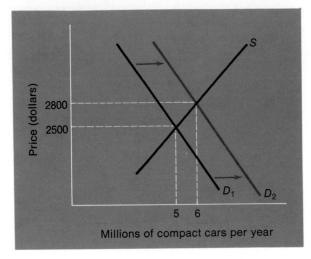

Exhibit 3-6   A Shift in Demand

As conditions change over time, the entire demand curve for a product may shift. Facing higher gasoline prices, many consumers decided to purchase compact cars in the mid-1970s. The *demand* for compact cars increased, causing both an increase in price and greater sales.

at a higher sales level. The pricing system responded to the increase in demand by granting (a) producers a stronger incentive to supply more compact cars and (b) consumers an incentive to search for still other substitute methods of conserving gasoline.

SHIFTS IN SUPPLY

The decisions of producers lie behind the supply curve. Holding other things constant, the supply curve summarizes the willingness of producers to offer a product at alternative prices. But price is not the only factor that producers will consider. Costs are also important. Production requires the use of valuable resources—labor, machines, land, buildings, and raw materials. Use of these resources will be costly to suppliers.

Entrepreneurs will supply only those products for which they expect benefits (primarily sales revenues) to exceed their production cost. Factors that reduce the producer's opportunity cost of production—lower resource prices or a technological improvement, for example—would increase his incentive to supply of product. Cost reductions would cause supply to increase (shift to the right). In contrast, higher input prices and changes that increase the producer's opportunity cost would cause supply to decline (shift to the left).

As for demand, it is important to note the difference between (a) a change in quantity supplied and (b) a change in supply. A change in quantity supplied is a movement along the same supply curve in response to a change in price. A change in supply indicates a shift in the entire supply curve.

How does the market react to a change in supply? Exhibit 3-7 illustrates the impact of a technological improvement that reduced the cost of producing electronic desk calculators in the 1970s. The reduction in cost made it more attractive for entrepreneurs to produce these calculators. Several new firms began production. Old firms also expanded their production, contributing to the expansion of supply. At the old

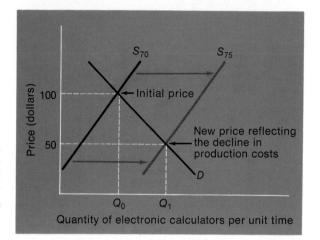

Exhibit 3-7   Improved Technology and a Shift in the Supply Curve

In 1970, small eight-digit electronic calculators were selling for $100 each. Improved technology substantially reduced their production cost in the 1970s, shifting the supply curve to the right (from S_{70} to S_{75}). Price declined, inducing consumers to purchase a larger quantity.

$100 price, consumers would not buy the larger supply of electronic calculators. A reduction in price was necessary to bring the wishes of producers and consumers back into balance. By 1974, the price of the electronic calculators had fallen to $50.

Sometimes the removal or erection of market restrictions will cause the supply curve to shift. During the 1973 Middle East crisis, Arab oil-producing countries used political action to stop the flow of crude oil to Western nations. Temporarily, the United States was completely cut off from this source of petroleum. The reduction in supply led to a shortage of gasoline *at the original price*. In a market economy, the shortage is eliminated by allowing the price to rise, rationing the smaller supply to those willing to pay higher prices (see Exhibit 3-8). The price rise would give consumers incentive to use less gas. Sunday leisure trips become more expensive. Unnecessary travel is curtailed. A new higher equilibrium price P_2 would result and the quantity demanded

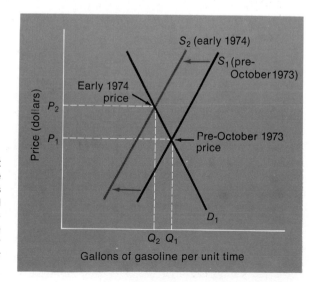

Exhibit 3-8   A Decrease in Supply

During the October 1973 Middle East conflict the Arab countries reduced the supply of crude oil to the United States and other nations. This action reduced the supply of gasoline. In a market economy such action would cause the price of gasoline to rise, rationing the smaller supply to buyers willing to pay the higher prices.

(a movement along the demand curve) is reduced at the now higher price. At this new higher equilibrium price, the consumption decisions of consumers have again been brought into equality with the quantity supplied by producers.

Everything Influences Everything Else

Markets are highly interrelated. Changes in one market will influence supply, demand, and price in related product and input markets. Consider the number of markets that are influenced by a seemingly insignificant increase in the price of a productive resource, lumber. Higher lumber prices will increase the cost of producing houses, furniture, some TV sets, office buildings, and many other products that utilize the resource. The supply of these goods will be reduced by varying amounts, causing their prices to rise. Producers will search out substitutes for the more expensive lumber. The demand for plastics, aluminum, brick, cement, and other substitute inputs will expand, causing their prices to rise. Since less lumber will be used at the higher price, the demand for cabinetmakers and carpenters will decline. Do not forget other secondary effects. The higher lumber prices will give entrepreneurs a greater incentive to develop new substitutes and come up with techniques that would reduce the cost of lumber. Such a simple change will exert an impact on many seemingly unrelated markets.

An increase (or decrease) in consumer demand for a product would set off a similar chain reaction. At the higher demand level, both the product price and output would increase. The demand for inputs used to produce the product would rise, as producers seek to expand the quantity supplied. At the higher product price, some consumers would turn to substitutes, causing their demand to increase and prices to rise. The markets for resources used to produce these substitute goods would also be influenced. Numerous markets will be affected by changes in the demand or supply in a single market.

Visualizing the interrelations between markets is important to understanding the workings of supply and demand. How can one keep all of these changes straight? It is not easy, but you will learn as we go along.

TIME AND THE ADJUSTMENT PROCESS

The signals that the pricing system sends to consumers and producers will change with market conditions. But the market computer does not act instantaneously. Various signals are sent out only with the passage of time.

Suppose that there is an increase in the demand for radios. How would this change be reflected in the market? Initially, retailers note that radios move off their shelves more rapidly. Their inventories decline. But during the first few weeks, individual radio retailers will be unsure whether the increase in demand is a random temporary phenomenon or a permanent change. Therefore, they will most likely increase their wholesale orders, while leaving the retail price constant. Since all retailers are now placing larger orders, the inventories of radio manufacturers will also decline. As these conditions persist, time will convince individual manufacturers that the demand for radios is quite strong. At that point they will raise their prices and expand their rate of output in order to build their inventories back to the normal level. Retailers will soon

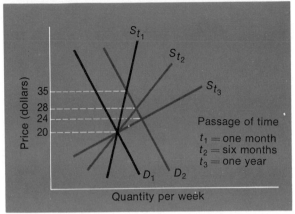

Exhibit 3-9 An Expansion in Demand and Price

As the demand for radios increases from D_1 to D_2, initially the quantity supplied will expand very little. Prices will rise sharply to $35. *With the passage of time* established producers will expand output and new firms will enter the market. The initial sharp rise in radio prices will be moderated (decline to $24 after one year).

pass the higher prices along to consumers. As Exhibit 3-9 shows, radio prices are likely to rise more in the short run than over a longer period of time. At the higher prices, radio manufacturers will do quite well. Profits will exist in the industry. But it will be costly to expand the output of radios rapidly. For most firms, a rapid increase in output would necessitate overtime payments, air shipments of raw materials, and/or the employment of inexperienced workers. With the passage of time, output can be expanded more orderly and at a lower cost. Pursuit of profits will attract new producers to the industry. The supply of radios will expand, moderating the initial increase in their price. All of these responses will take time, even though we economists sometimes act as if the process operates instantaneously.

Consumers, like producers, will be able to adjust more fully to changing market conditions with the passage of time. How did consumers respond to higher prices and the gasoline shortages of 1973–1974? Initially, they cut out some unnecessary trips and leisure driving. Some drove slower in order to get better gas mileage. Many motorists chose smaller cars which used less gas. But the full impact of this latter response took time, as people usually had to wait for their current gas guzzler to wear out. Thus, as illustrated by Exhibit 3-10, the reduction in gas consumption (quantity demanded)

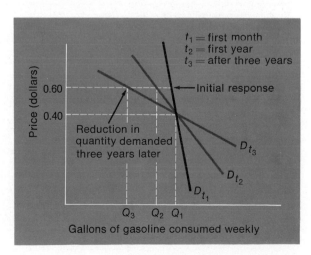

Exhibit 3-10 Time and the Buyer Response to a Price Change

Demand is usually less responsive to a change in price the shorter the time period. Thus, an increase in the price of a gallon of gasoline from 40 to 60 cents will initially induce only a small reduction in gasoline consumption. But as the consumer has a longer time period to adopt gas-saving measures, quantity demanded will fall by a greater amount.

because of a price increase was not immediately discernible. But after one year, as more and more motorists turned to smaller cars, there was an obvious reduction in weekly consumption. The short-run demand response to a price change will usually be less than over a longer period of time.

SUPPLY AND DEMAND IN ACTION

Does supply and demand really help explain the real world? It is often difficult to isolate the impact of a single economic change, particularly a minor change, because so many other things will be going on simultaneously. Failure of "other things to remain constant" makes it difficult to test economic theory.

In July of 1972 the Soviet Union and the United States announced a trade agreement that eventually resulted in the sale of approximately one-fourth of the 1972 U.S. wheat crop to the Soviets. The sheer magnitude of this transaction, one of the largest in history, would suggest that it would have substantial impact in several markets. Thus, it presents a unique opportunity, allowing us to test the predictions of supply and demand analysis against the actual events of the real world.

Exhibits 3-11 to 3-13, utilizing actual real world data, outline the impact of the Russian wheat deal on several markets. What impact would the transaction have on the

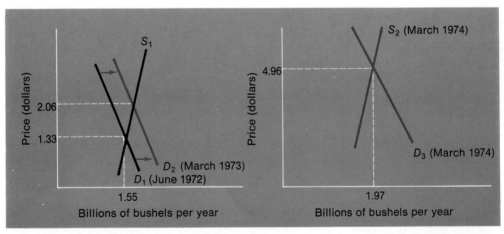

(a)
Pre- and Post-Soviet Wheat Deal

(b)
Strong World Demand (March 1974)

Exhibit 3-11   Wheat Prices and Trading with the Russians

In 1972 the U.S. government relaxed trade restriction toward the Soviet Union. Subsequently, nearly 25 percent of the U.S. wheat crop was exported. Counting the Soviet demand, there was a sharp increase in the demand for U.S. wheat [shift from D_1 to D_2, frame (a)]. Since the 1972 crop was already being harvested at the time of the transaction, the immediate increase in the U.S. output was small. Wheat available for domestic consumption declined and prices increased from $1.33 per bushel in June 1972 to $2.06 per bushel in March 1973. Soviet crop failures and expanding world demand caused the demand of U.S. wheat to continue to expand in 1973–1974 [frame (b)]. A still larger share of our domestic crop was exported in 1973. Thus, even though the 1973 domestic output of wheat was 1.97 billion bushels compared to only 1.55 billion bushels for 1972, the price of wheat rose to $4.96 per bushel in March 1974 [frame (b)].

demand for U.S. wheat (including the demand of the Russians)? It would increase it, right? The price of wheat should rise. As illustrated by Exhibit 3-11, this is precisely what happened. In 1973 continued Soviet purchases, plus an additional increase in world demand, led to a further rise in the price of wheat. These higher prices should induce producers to expand output, right? Again, the real world was consistent with the theory. Both 1973 and 1974 were record years for U.S. production of wheat.

What impact would the higher wheat prices have on the demand for corn and soybeans, two related substitute products? Do you think higher prices really cause the buyer to turn to substitutes? Again this proved true. As illustrated by Exhibit 3-12, the demand for corn and soybeans increased, and with time, the output of these products was also expanded.

But corn and soybeans are not only substitutes for wheat, they are also inputs used in the feeding and production of beef cattle. What impact will these higher resource prices have on the beef market? Higher input prices will increase the opportunity cost of

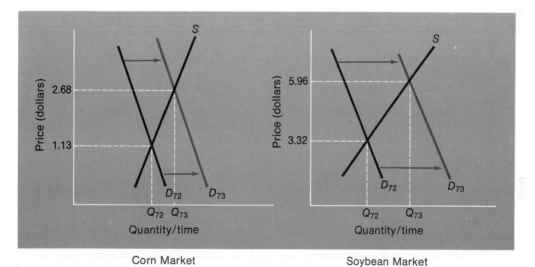

Corn Market   Soybean Market

Exhibit 3-12 Substituting Corn and Soybeans for Wheat

The higher wheat prices caused consumers to substitute corn and soybeans (among other things) for wheat. The chart below presents the before and after price and supply conditions for these two commodities:

	PRICES		SUPPLY	
Crop	June 1972	March 1974	1972 Crop (millions of bushels)	1973 Crop (millions of bushels)
Corn	$1.13	$2.68	5573	5643
Soybeans	3.32	5.96	1270	1566

As pictured by the graph, there was a substantial increase in demand for the two commodities between 1972 and 1974. The price of both rose. The higher prices caused farmers to expand their production, a movement along a long-run supply curve. Thus, output was greater in 1973 than in 1972. What impact would the higher corn and soybean prices have on the cost of producing beef? See Exhibit 3-13.

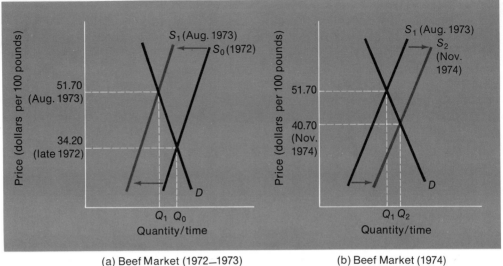

(a) Beef Market (1972–1973)   (b) Beef Market (1974)

Exhibit 3-13   Beef and Feedgrain Prices

The higher prices for corn and soybeans made it expensive to feed these commodities to beef cattle. So farmers reduced the size of their cattle herds so they could sell more grain crops at the high market prices. The supply of beef cattle declined [shifted from S_0 to S_1, frame (a)], leading to the higher beef prices of 1973. The per capita U.S. consumption of beef declined, as households economized on the use of the more expensive good. But, with time what impact would the higher beef prices have on the farmer's incentive to supply it? Increase it, right. Thus, the 1974 supply of beef expanded [S_2, frame (b)], and beef prices declined.

producing beef. Thus, production of beef will be less attractive to entrepreneurs at the old prices. Beef supply will decline. Again the real world is consistent with the theory. For nearly 18 months after the Russian wheat deal, beef prices soared. Housewives boycotted and complained. Americans reduced their consumption of the more expensive beef. But as grain prices began to stabilize, what happened to the quantity supplied (or short-term supply curve) of beef? At $50 per hundred, farmers were happy to supply beef in late 1973. So the short-term supply curve for beef began shifting to the left in late 1973 and early 1974. What happened to beef prices? Sure enough, they began to fall, although they did not decline all the way back to their pre-1972 levels. Are supply and demand applicable to real world markets? What do you think?

REPEALING THE LAWS OF SUPPLY AND DEMAND

Price controls are often suggested as a tool to deal with rising prices or prices that are thought to be excessively high. If prices are too high, by some external standard, why not lower them? Fixing prices seems like a simple, straightforward solution. But "simple, straightforward solutions" often have unanticipated repercussions. Do not forget the secondary effects.

Suppose that, as pictured by Exhibit 3-14, the equilibrium price of a good is P_0. But legislators decide that P_0 is too high. They legislate a **price ceiling,** a requirement that a product cannot be sold for more than a designated price. Price is fixed at P_1,

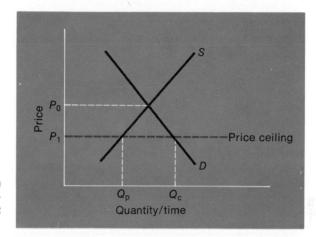

Exhibit 3-14   The Impact of a Price Ceiling

When price is fixed below the equilibrium level, shortages will develop and non-price factors will become more important in the rationing process.

below the equilibrium level. What will be the result of this action? Admittedly, the price of the good will be reduced, but that will not be the end of the story. At the below-equilibrium price, producers are unwilling to supply as much as consumers would like to purchase. A shortage ($Q_c - Q_p$, Exhibit 3-14) of the good will result. How will the Q_p units offered by producers be allocated to consumers who want to buy a larger amount, Q_c? Fixing the price did not eliminate the rationing problem. Nonprice factors will now become more important in the rationing process. Producers will be more discriminating in their sales to eager buyers. Sellers will favor friends, buyers who do them favors, even buyers who are willing to make illegal blackmarket payments. All of these factors will now be more important.

What has happened to the seller's incentive to expand the future supply and eliminate the shortage? It has declined. The below-equilibrium price will make it less attractive to produce this good. Higher profits will be possible elsewhere. Thus, with time the shortage conditions will get even worse if the below-equilibrium price is maintained.

What other secondary effects can we expect? Since buyers will want more of the good than is available at the fixed price, what would happen if sellers allowed the quality of the good to deteriorate? Some buyers, rather than do without, would be willing to purchase a lower quality good. Sellers can gain by pursuing such a policy. In the real world there are two ways that a seller can raise prices. First, he can raise his money price, holding quality constant. But second, money price can be held constant, while reducing the quality of the good. Confronting a price ceiling, sellers will rely on the latter method of raising prices, thereby rationing the goods to those willing to accept the lower quality. It is not easy to repeal the laws of supply and demand (see Myth, page 48).

RATIONING AND MOTIVATING, THE TWO GREAT ATTRIBUTES OF THE MARKET

We have stressed the role of price as a method of rationing goods and resources. The laws of supply and demand ration goods to consumers who are willing to pay the highest prices. Given the income distribution, there is a tendency for units of each

MYTHS OF ECONOMICS
"Rent controls are an effective method of assuring adequate housing at a price the poor can afford."

When rents (a price) are set below the equilibrium level, the amount of housing demanded by consumers will exceed the amount that landlords will make available. An excess demand or shortage will exist. Will this shortage lead to an expansion in the future supply of housing? The answer is clearly No. The below-equilibrium rent controls will discourage entrepreneurs from constructing additional housing units. Fewer housing units will be built because of the controls and the shortage situation will continue.

Since price no longer plays its normal function, nonprice methods of rationing will become more important. Landlords will be more discriminating. They will favor friends, persons of influence, persons willing to lease furniture for the housing at exorbitant prices, and those willing to make illegal bribe payments. In contrast applicants with long hair, unconventional lifestyles, lots of children, and dark skin will find fewer landlords who cater to their personal characteristics. Since the landlord's cost of discriminating against those with characteristics that he does not like has been reduced, such discrimination will become more important in the rationing process.

Quality deterioration will be another secondary effect of the rent controls. Economic thinking suggests that there are two ways to raise prices. The nominal price can be increased, holding quality constant. Or, alternatively, quality can be reduced, while maintaining the same nominal price. When landlords are prohibited from adopting the former, they will utilize the latter. They will paint rental units less often. They will require larger damage deposits and prepaid rent. Normal maintenance and repair service will deteriorate. Eventually, the quality of the rental housing will reflect the controlled price. Cheap housing will be of cheap quality.

Is the real world consistent with economic theory? New York City is the only major city in the United States with a system of rent controls. There are an unusually large number of furniture and housing "package rentals" in New York, as both landlords and renters seek to avoid the impact of the rent controls. Complaints about the failure of landlords to undertake repairs, properly maintain rental units, and provide complimentary services such as garbage pickup and rat control efforts are far more common in New York City than any other place in the United States. Economic theory helps explain why this is the case.

product to be guided to the person willing to give up the most of other things. The rich and the poor bid side by side for goods. The rich, of course, are able to obtain more goods because of their greater wealth. But goods are also rationed to the poor, as they sometimes outbid even the rich. Similarly, productive inputs are rationed among firms by dollar bids. These payments to resource owners generate the income used to purchase products. Some inputs are rationed to large firms and others to small, depending on which offers the most preferred combination of working conditions and wages. There is a tendency for each resource to be rationed to the firm that evaluates it most highly (that is, is willing to pay the most for the services of the productive input).

In addition to performing these rationing functions, the market system also motivates and directs people into the productive process. Entrepreneurs and businessmen are motivated to undertake a project because they believe consumers will evaluate the results so highly that they will pay an amount in excess of the production costs. Profit-seeking businessmen will be constantly searching for opportunities to combine resources so that the value of the final product, as viewed by the consumer, will be greater than the value of the resources used to produce it. Pursuit of personal self-interest motivates the sellers to act in a way that also benefits the consumer. As Adam Smith noted long ago, the butcher provides one with meat, not because of his benevolence, but rather out of regard for his own self-interest,

A major advantage of the pricing system is its capability of motivating productive activity and allocating goods with a minimum of centralized government control. No central authority orders or forces the milkman to deliver milk, the construction firm to produce houses, the farmer to produce wheat, or the baker to produce bread. Producers choose to undertake these and millions of other productive activities because they regard them to be in their self-interest.

Similarly, resource suppliers, motivated by the pursuit of gain, have a strong incentive to acquire, develop, and supply productive inputs. Why are many young people willing to undertake the necessary work, stress, late hours of study, and financial cost to acquire a medical or law degree, a doctoral degree in economics or physics, or an MBA degree? Why will others seek to master a skill requiring an apprentice program and still others seek out self-study and experience as alternative methods of developing skills? Why do individuals save to buy a business, capital equipment, or other assets? While many factors undoubtedly influence decisions to acquire skills and capital assets, the expectation of financial reward offers an important stimulus. Without this stimulus, the motivation to work, create, develop skills, and supply capital assets would be sorely missing. An essential ingredient of the productive process would be lacking. But wage, profit, interest, and rent payments can supply the necessary incentive to motivate individuals to contribute to the productive process. The ability to motivate people into the productive process is one of the strong positive attributes of the market system.

But if the system is to work as we have described, there must be competition between buyers and sellers. Competition is the regulator, capable of protecting both buyer and seller. The existence of alternative competitive firms is a protection to the consumer against a seller charging prices substantially above production cost. The existence of alternative input suppliers protects the producer against a supplier who might be tempted to withhold a vital input unless he is granted exorbitant compensation. The existence of alternative employment opportunities protects the employee from the power of any single employer. Competition is the ingredient that can equalize the bargaining power between buyers and sellers.

☐ LOOKING AHEAD

In this chapter we focused on how a free market pricing system would allocate goods and resources and motivate people. The operation of a market system is sorely dependent on (a) competitive markets and (b) well-defined property rights for resources and products. In the following chapter, we will look at some of the shortcomings of the market mechanism. In addition, we will take a glimpse at the operation of the public sector, the major alternative form of economic organization.

CHAPTER LEARNING OBJECTIVES

1. Since people want more of scarce goods than Nature has made freely available, a rationing mechanism is necessitated. Competition is the natural outgrowth of the necessity to ration scarce goods. The rationing mechanism utilized will alter the forms of competition, but it will not eliminate competitive tactics.

2. The law of demand holds that there will be a negative relationship between price and amount of a good purchased. A rise in price will cause consumers to purchase less because they now have a greater incentive to use substitutes. On the other hand, a reduction in price will induce consumers to buy more as they will substitute the cheaper good for other commodities.

3. The law of supply states that there will be a positive relationship between the price of a product and the amount supplied. Other things constant, an increase in the price of product would induce the established firms to expand their output and new firms to enter the market. The quantity supplied would expand.

4. Market forces will tend to establish an equilibrium price—a price where the quantity demanded by consumers is just equal to the quantity supplied by producers. An above-equilibrium price would result in an excess supply, causing suppliers to reduce prices. A below-equilibrium price will result in an excess demand, causing prices to rise.

5. Changes in consumer income, prices of closely related goods, preferences, expectation as to future prices, and other nonprice factors that influence the choices of consumers will cause the entire demand curve to shift. An increase (decrease) in demand would cause prices to rise (fall) and quantity supplied to increase (decline).

6. Changes in input prices, technology, and other factors that influence the producer's costs of production will cause the entire supply curve to shift. An increase (decrease) in supply would cause prices to fall (increase) and quantity demanded to expand (decline).

7. Markets are highly interrelated. An increase (decrease) in the demand for a product will cause the demand for resources utilized to produce the product to expand (decline). Similarly, changes in a resource market will have indirect effects. An increase (decrease) in the price of a resource will cause the supply of products that are utilizing that input to decline (expand) and the demand for substitute productive inputs to increase (decline).

8. The constraint of time limits the ability of consumers to adjust to changes in prices. A price increase will usually elicit a larger reduction in quantity demanded with the passage of time. Similarly, the market supply curve is usually more elastic in the long run than for the short-term time period.

9. When a price is fixed below the market equilibrium, buyers will want to purchase more than sellers are willing to offer. Shortages will be present. Nonprice factors will become more important in the rationing process. Quality deterioration will be used as a method of raising price (and rationing the good) even though the nominal price remains unchanged. With time, the shortage conditions will tend to worsen, because the below-equilibrium price has reduced the incentive for producers to expand the future supply.

10. The market is both a rationing and motivating system. Goods and productive inputs are rationed to those willing to pay the highest prices. The system of rewards (payments to resource suppliers) motivates individuals into the productive process. A major advantage of a decentralized pricing system is its capability of motivating productive activity and allocating goods with a minimum of centralized government control.

IMPORTANT TERMS TO REMEMBER

Law of demand: Postulate that there will be a negative relationship between the price of a thing and the amount of it purchased by buyers.

Law of supply: Postulate that there will be a positive relationship between the price of a thing and the amount of it offered for sale by sellers.

Equilibrium: State of balance between conflicting forces such as supply and demand.

Shortage: Condition where the amount of a good offered by sellers is less than the amount demanded by buyers at the existing price. An increase in price would eliminate the shortage.

Surplus: Condition where the amount of a good that sellers would be willing to offer for sale is greater than the amount that buyers will purchase at the existing price. A decline in price would eliminate the surplus.

Price ceiling: A legally established maximum price that sellers may charge.

THE ECONOMIC WAY OF THINKING—DISCUSSION QUESTIONS

1. What is the purpose of prices? Do prices do anything other than ration goods to those with the most dollar votes? Why? What factors determine the price of a good?

2. How many of the following "goods" do you think conform to the general law of supply: **(a)** gasoline, **(b)** cheating on exams, **(c)** political favors from legislators, **(d)** the services of heart specialists, **(e)** children, **(f)** legal divorces, **(g)** the services of a minister? Explain your answer in each case.

3. Which of the following do you think would lead to an increase in the current demand for beef: **(a)** higher pork prices, **(b)** higher incomes, **(c)** higher feed grain prices, **(d)** a banner year corn crop, **(e)** an increase in the price of beef?

4. **(a)** "The motivating force behind a market economy is individual self-interest."

   (b) "Cooperation between individuals is the keystone of a market system. Without cooperation there would be no exchange and economic welfare would suffer drastically."

   Are the statements just given true or false? Explain your answer.

5. "We cannot allow the price of gasoline to go any higher because it is as essential to the poor man as to the rich. We cannot allow the rich to bid gasoline away from the poor. I would prefer to ration 10 gallons of gas to each driver—both rich and poor." (Overheard during the gasoline shortage of the 1970s.)

   (a) Do you agree with this quote? Why?

   (b) Do you think gasoline is more essential than food? Should the rich be allowed "to bid food away from the poor"? Should food be rationed —granting equal portions to both rich and poor? Why or why not?

   (c) Was your answer to both (a) and (b) consistent? Explain.

6. What's Wrong with This Way of Thinking?

"Economists argue that lower prices will necessarily result in less supply. But there are exceptions to this rule. For example, in 1970 10-digit electronic calculators sold for $150. By 1975 the price of the same type of calculator had declined to less than $50. Yet, business firms produced and sold three times as many calculators in 1975 as in 1970. Lower prices did *not* result in less production and a decline in the number of calculators supplied."

4

A BIRD'S-EYE VIEW OF
THE PUBLIC SECTOR

The economic role of government is of vital importance. The government sets the rules of the game. It establishes and defines property rights which are necessary to the smooth operation of markets. As we shall soon see, public policy is an important determinant of economic stability. In addition, the government sometimes uses subsidies to encourage the production of some goods while applying special taxes to reduce the availability of others. In a few cases—education, the mail service, and local electric power, for example—the government becomes directly involved in the production process.

Because of government's broad economic role, it is vital that we understand how it works and when it contributes to the efficient allocation of resources. What functions does government perform best? Why does it sometimes fail to perform as we would like? What activities might best be left to the market? These are questions of political economy. Some of them are as old, even older, than the discipline of economics. But recent work in economics, particularly in the area of public choice, is relevant if we are seeking intelligent answers to these age-old questions.

In this chapter, we focus on the shortcomings of the market and the potential of government as an alternate means to resolve economic problems. Issues involving market and public sector organization will come up repeatedly throughout this book. Political economy—how the public sector works in comparison with the market—is an integral and exciting part of economic analysis.

IDEAL ECONOMIC EFFICIENCY

We need a criterion by which to judge market and public sector action. Economists use the standard of economic efficiency. What is **economic efficiency?** The central idea is straightforward. It simply means that *for any given level of effort* (cost), we want to obtain the largest possible benefit. A corollary is that we would want to obtain any specific level of benefits *with the least possible effort.* Economic efficiency is simply getting the most out of the available resources.

But what does this mean when applied to the entire economy? Individuals are the final decision-makers of an economy. Individuals will bear the costs and reap the benefits of economic activity. When applied to the entire economy, two conditions are necessary for ideal economic efficiency to exist:

RULE (1)   An economic action should be undertaken if it will produce more benefits than costs for the individuals of the economy. Such actions result in gains, improvement in the well-being of at least some individuals without offsetting welfare losses to others. Failure to undertake such activities means that potential gain has been foregone.

RULE (2)   No economic action should be undertaken if it will produce more costs to the individuals than they reap in benefits. When an action results in greater total costs than benefits, somebody must be harmed. The benefits that accrue to those who gain are insufficient to compensate for the losses imposed on others. Therefore, when all persons are considered, the net impact of the action is counterproductive.

When either Rule (1) or Rule (2) is violated, economic inefficiency results. There is some spinning of the wheels so to speak. Note that economic efficiency is defined for a specific income distribution. For each income distribution, there will be an ideal resource allocation that will be most efficient. Positive economics does not tell us how income should be distributed. Of course, we all have ideas on the subject. Most of us would like to see more income distributed our way. But the concept of efficiency applies to all possible distributions of income.

A closer look at supply and demand when competitive pressures are present will help the reader better understand the concept of efficiency. The supply curve reflects the producer's opportunity costs. Each point along the supply curve indicates the *minimum* price for which the units could be produced without a loss to the seller. Each point along the demand curve indicates the *maximum* evaluation of the unit by its consumer. Any time the consumer's evaluation exceeds the producer's cost—his minimum supply price—production and sale of the good can generate mutual gain.

Look at Exhibit 4-1. As output is expanded toward Q, consumer evaluation of each cheeseburger always exceeds the producer's opportunity cost. It is always possible for

Exhibit 4-1   What Is Good about Idealized Market Exchange?

When competitive forces are present, price will tend toward the supply–demand intersection *P*. At that price, the seller's opportunity cost of producing the last unit will just equal the buyer's evaluation of that unit. All gains from production and exchange are realized.

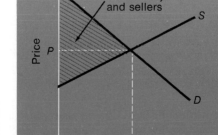

units to be produced and sold at a price that will improve the well-being of both buyer and seller. But this will not be true for units beyond Q. When more than Q cheeseburgers are produced, consumers value the *additional* units less than their costs. Production beyond Q would violate Rule (2). Inefficiency would result.

When only the buyer and seller are affected by the action, supply and demand under competitive conditions would be efficient. Suppliers seeking gain would produce additional units of each good so long as the market price exceeded their production costs. Similarly, consumers would gain from the purchase of additional units so long as their benefits, revealed by the height of the demand curve, exceeded the market price. Market forces would result in an equilibrium output level such as Q. In equilibrium, all units for which the benefits to consumers exceeded the costs to suppliers would be produced. All potential gains from trade between consumers and producers would be fully realized. Rule (1) is met. Neither would output be expanded beyond Q, as suppliers would find it unprofitable to produce such units. Therefore, Rule (2) would not be violated.

Thus, both consumers and producers would be guided by the pricing system to output level Q, just the right amount. The market works beautifully. Individuals, pursuing their own self-interest, are guided as if by an invisible hand to promote the general welfare. This was the message of Adam Smith, the Father of Economics, 200 years ago.

WHY MIGHT THE INVISIBLE HAND FAIL?

Is the invisible hand still working today? Why might it fail? There are four important factors that can limit the ability of the invisible hand to perform its magic.

1. *Lack of Competition and Why That Is Bad.*   Competition is vital to the proper operation of the pricing mechanism. It is competition that drives the prices for consumer goods down to the level of their cost. Similarly, competition in factor markets prevents both (a) sellers from charging exorbitantly high prices to producers and (b) buyers from taking advantage of the owners of productive resources. The existence of competitors reduces the power of both buyers and sellers to rig the market in their favor.

Modern mass production techniques often make it possible for a large-scale producer to gain a cost advantage over smaller competitors. In several industries—automobiles, steel, aircraft, and aluminum, for example—a few large firms produce the entire output. Because an enormous amount of capital investment is required to enter these industries, existing large-scale producers may be partially insulated from the competitive pressure of new rivals.

Since competition is the enemy of high prices, sellers have a strong incentive to escape from its pressures by colluding rather than competing. Competition is something that is good for the other guy. Individually, each of us would prefer to be loosened from its grip. Students do not like stiff competitors at exam time, when seeking entry to graduate school, or for Saturday night dates. Similarly, a seller would prefer few real competitors.

Exhibit 4-2 illustrates how sellers can gain from collusive action. If a group of sellers

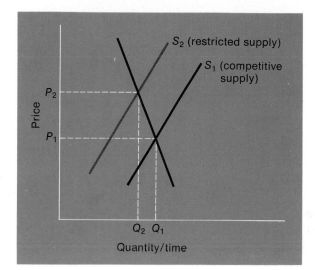

Exhibit 4-2   Rigging the Market

If a group of sellers can restrict the entry of competitors and connive to reduce their own output, they can sometimes get more for selling less. Note, the total sales revenue P_2Q_2 for the restricted supply exceeds the sales revenue P_1Q_1 for the competitive supply.

could eliminate the competition from new entrants to the market, they would be able to raise their prices. The total revenue of sellers is simply the market price multiplied by the quantity sold. The sellers' revenues would be greater when only the restricted output Q_2 is sold rather than the competitive output Q_1. The artificially high price P_2 is in excess of the competitive opportunity cost of supplying the good. The price of the good does not reflect its actual scarcity.

It is in the interest of consumers and the community that output be expanded to Q_1 the output consistent with economic efficiency. But it is in the interests of the sellers to make the good artificially scarce and raise its price. If the sellers can use collusion, government action, or other means of restricting supply, they can gain. But the restricted output level would violate Rule (2). Inefficiency would result. There is a conflict between the self-interest of the seller and what is best for the entire community.

When there are only a few firms in the industry and competition from new entrants can be restrained, the sellers may be able to rig the market in their favor. Through collusion, either tacit or overt, suppliers may be able to escape competitive pressures. What can the government do to preserve competition? Congress has enacted a series of antitrust laws, most notably the Sherman Antitrust Act and the Clayton Act, making it illegal for firms to collude or attempt to monopolize a product. It established the Federal Trade Commission that prohibits "certain methods of competition in commerce" such as false advertising, improper grading of materials, and deceptive business practices.

For the most part, economists favor the principle of government action to assure and promote competitive markets. But there is considerable debate about the effectiveness of past public policy in this area. Few economists are satisfied with the government's role as a promoter of competition.

Two general criticisms are voiced. First, many suggest that the government should pursue a more vigorous antitrust policy. They believe that antitrust action should be taken to expand the number of rivals in several industries—automobiles and steel, for example—that are currently dominated by a few firms. On the other hand, other critics argue that antitrust policy and business regulation, both past and present, have often restricted competition. Consumers have been "protected" against *low* prices and producers from new rivals. These critics argue that government regulatory policy has been part of the problem, rather than the solution. They believe this results from an inherent flaw in the political process—the disproportionate power of special interests. Chapters 20–22 deal with this debate in more detail.

2. *Externalities—What Have You Been Doing to Your Neighbor?* Production and consumption of some goods will result in spillover effects that the market will fail to register. These spillover effects, called **externalities,** are present when the actions of one individual or group affect the welfare of others without their consent.

Examples of externalities abound. If you live in an apartment house, and the noisy stereo of your next door neighbor keeps you from studying economics, he is creating an externality. His actions are imposing an unwanted cost on you. Driving one's car during rush hour increases the level of congestion, thereby imposing a cost on other motorists. If an examination is graded on the curve, cheating creates an externality inasmuch as it raises the class average.

Not all externalities result in the imposition of a cost. Sometimes human actions generate benefits for nonparticipating third parties. The homeowner who keeps his house in good condition and maintains a neatly kept lawn improves the beauty of the entire community, thereby benefiting his neighbors. A flood control project that benefits the upstream residents, will also generate gain for those who live downstream. Scientific theories benefit their authors, but the knowledge also contributes to the welfare of others.

Why do externalities create problems for the market mechanism? Examination of Exhibit 4-3 can help us answer this question. With competitive markets in equilibrium,

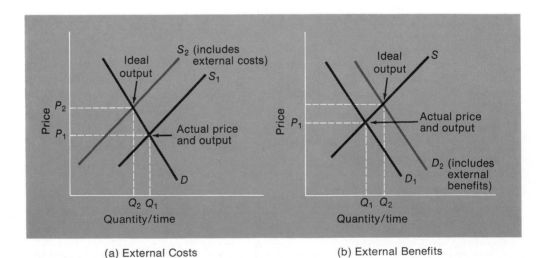

(a) External Costs   (b) External Benefits

Exhibit 4-3   Externalities and Problems for the Market

When external costs are present [frame (a)], the output level of a product will exceed the desired amount. In contrast, market output of goods that generate external benefits [frame (b)] will be less than the ideal level.

the cost of a good (including a normal profit for the producer) will be paid by consumers. Unless consumer benefits exceed the opportunity cost of production, the good will not be produced. But what happens when externalities are present?

Suppose that a firm discharges smoke into the air or sewage into a river. Valuable resources, clean air and pure water, are utilized but neither the firm nor the consumers of their products will pay for these costs. As Exhibit 4-3a shows, the supply curve will understate the opportunity cost of production when external costs are present. Since the producer will consider only his private cost, ignoring the cost imposed on secondary parties, supply curve S_1 will result. If all costs were considered, supply would be S_2. The actual supply curve S_1 will not reflect the loss of the clean air and pure water. Thus, the market price will not fully reflect the opportunity cost of producing the good. Output will be expanded beyond Q_2 (to Q_1) even though the community's evaluation of the additional units is less than their cost. The second efficiency condition, Rule (2), is violated. Inefficiency in the form of excessive air and water pollution results.

As Exhibit 4-3b shows, external benefits can also create problems. When they are present, the market demand curve D_1 will not fully reflect the total benefits, including those that accrue to secondary parties. Output Q_1 will result. Could the community gain from a larger output of the product? Yes. The demand curve D_2 reflects both the direct benefits of consumers and the secondary benefits bestowed upon secondary parties. Expansion of output beyond Q_1 to Q_2 would result in net gain to the community. However, since neither consumers nor producers can capture the secondary benefits, consumption level Q_1 will result. The potential net gain from the larger output level Q_2 will be lost. Rule (1) of our hypothetical efficiency criterion is violated.

Competitive markets will fail to give consumers and producers the right signals when externalities are present. The market will tend to underallocate resources into the production of goods with external benefits, and overallocate them into the production of goods that impose external costs on nonconsenting parties.

3. *Public Goods—More Problems for the Market.* Some goods cannot be provided through the marketplace because there is no way of excluding nonpaying customers. Goods that must be consumed jointly by all are called **public goods.** National defense, the judicial and legal system, and the monetary system are examples of public goods. The national defense that defends you also equally defends others. There is no feasible way that national defense could be provided to some citizens, but not to others. Similarly, the monetary system that influences the prices of things that you buy, also influences the prices and incomes of others. One monetary system cannot be provided for you and another for me.

Why are public goods troublesome for the market? Typically in the marketplace, there will be a direct link between consumption and payment. If you do not pay, you do not consume. Similarly, the payments of consumers provide the incentive to supply products. But public goods are consumed jointly. If a public good is made available to one person, it is simultaneously made available to others. Since people cannot be excluded, their incentive to reveal their true evaluation of the good is destroyed. Why would you voluntarily pay your "fair share" for national defense, the courts, or police protection if these goods were provided in the market? If others contribute a lot, the public good will be provided pretty much regardless of what you do. If others do not pay, your actions will not make much difference anyway. So everyone has an incentive to opt out, to refuse to help pay voluntarily for the public good.

But when everybody opts out, what happens? Not very much of the public good is produced. This is precisely why the market cannot handle public goods very well. Resources will be underallocated to the production of public goods because most people, following their own self-interest, will refuse to pay for them.

4. *Economic Instability.*   If markets are to function well, a stable monetary exchange system must be provided. Many market exchanges involve a time dimension. Houses, cars, consumer durables, land, buildings, equipment, and many other items are paid for over a period of months or even years. Union wage contracts are usually for two or three years. If the purchasing power of the monetary unit, the dollar in the United States, gyrated wildly, few would want to make long-term transactions because of the uncertainty. The smooth functioning of the market would be retarded.

The government's spending and monetary policies exert a powerful influence on economic stability. If properly conducted, they can contribute to economic stability, full and efficient utilization of resources, and stable prices. But, improper stabilization policy can cause massive unemployment, rapidly rising prices, or perhaps both.

Economists are not in complete agreement on the extent to which public policy can stabilize the economy and promote full employment. They often debate the impact of various policy tools. But all agree that a stable economic environment is vitally important to a market economy. We will investigate both the potential and limitations of government action as a stabilizing force on the economy in subsequent chapters.

GOVERNMENT—A POTENTIAL VEHICLE FOR GAIN

The pricing system will fail to meet our ideal efficiency standards if (a) markets are not competitive, (b) externalities are present, (c) public goods necessitate joint consumption, or (d) the aggregate economy is characterized by instability and the uncertainty that it breeds. If public sector action can correct these deficiencies, net gains for the community are possible. Public policy does not have to be a zero-sum game.

The intent of public policy is often to correct the shortcomings of the markets. Antitrust action is designed to promote competition. Government provision of national defense, crime prevention, a legal system, and flood control projects is related to the public good nature of these activities. Similarly, externalities account for public sector action in such areas as pollution control, education, pure research, and no-fault insurance.[1] Clearly, the tax, spending, and monetary policies of the government are utilized to influence the level of economic activity in most Western nations.

But public sector action is merely an extension of individual behavior. The actions of individuals, no doubt primarily concerned with their personal well-being, will combine to shape public policy. There is no reason to expect that government action will always correct the shortcomings of the market, and improve economic efficiency. It may. But it may also reflect the efforts of individuals and organized groups to manipulate public policy for personal gain, even if the policy promotes inefficiency.

[1]See pages 544–545 for a detailed analysis of externalities, no-fault insurance, and public policy.

REDISTRIBUTION—DIVIDING THE ECONOMIC PIE

Since more than one-third of the national income in the United States is channeled through the public sector, government exerts a vast influence on the distribution of income. Many of the demands for public policy stem from a desire to change the income distribution. There is no reason to presume that the unhampered market will lead to the most desirable distribution of income. In fact, the ideal distribution of income is largely a matter of personal preference. There is nothing in positive economics that tells us that one distribution of income is better than another.

Nevertheless, three economic arguments for public policy action to redistribute income are often heard.

First, some economists have suggested that the law of diminishing marginal utility argues for greater equality. The rich man's loss of satisfaction from a redistribution of income to the poor would be less than the poor man's gain.[2] Thus, public sector redistribution from the rich to the poor could expand the general welfare.

The argument has intrinsic appeal, but scientifically it has a major flaw. There is no presumption that the rich man's satisfaction from additional income is less than that of the poor man. The law of diminishing marginal utility applies to additional income earned by the *same* person. It says nothing about the capacity of *different* individuals to gain satisfaction from additional income.[3] This argument for greater equality rests on ethical, not scientific, grounds.

Second, government may redistribute income because of concern for low income citizens. The most common scientific argument for redistribution to the poor is based on the "public good" nature of poverty. Alleviation of poverty may help not only the poor, but also those who are well off. Middle and upper income recipients, for example, may benefit if the less fortunate members of the community enjoy better food, clothing, housing, and health care. If the rich gain, why will they not voluntarily give to the poor? Answer: For the same reason that individuals will do little to provide national defense voluntarily. The antipoverty efforts of any single individual will exert little impact on the total amount of poverty in the community. Because individual action is so insignificant, each has an incentive to opt out. But when everybody opts out, the market provides less than the desired amount of antipoverty action.

Third, a redistribution policy may be based on the community's desire for equality of opportunity regardless of one's social status, race, sex, or religious background. The welfare of each citizen may be improved if *others* have equal opportunity. But equal opportunity is also a public good. An opportunity that is equal to that of all others cannot be provided to one without simultaneously being provided to others. Because of its public good characteristics, market action alone may result in less equality of opportunity than the community desires. Corrective public sector action might re-

---

[2]The eminent economist A. C. Pigou put it this way: "It is evident that any transference of income from a relatively rich man to a relatively poor man of similar temperament, since it enables more intense wants to be satisfied at the expense of less intense wants, must increase the aggregate sum of satisfactions." [A. C. Pigou, *Economics of Welfare*, 4th ed., London: Macmillan, 1948, p. 89.]

[3]The astute reader might argue that, on the average, the additional income would yield more satisfaction to the poor than the rich. If individuals acquired wealth randomly, this view would be correct. But individual preferences, including one's desire for monetary income, will affect one's willingness to do the things that result in high income. Thus, a priori, there can be no presumption that the poor derive more (or less) satisfaction from additional income than the rich.

structure educational opportunities, utilize taxes to reduce the role of inherited wealth, and seek an equalization of training and employment opportunities, regardless of race or sex. The *chance* to enjoy an unequal future income would thereby be equalized.

We have emphasized redistribution objectives that, considering both the donors and recipients, expand the total welfare of the community. Of course, much of the pressure for redistribution will not be motivated by this objective. It will stem from personal self-interest, narrowly defined. How can I use the public sector to get more for me? How can the tax structure and income transfer mechanism be changed to my advantage? As we learn more about how the public sector works, we will take a closer look at the structure of redistribution that we would *expect* (in contrast to that ideally preferred) to result from public sector action.

One final word of caution—income is not like manna from heaven. Actions that change the distribution of income will usually change individual incentives. Substantial redistribution from high earners to low income recipients could adversely affect the incentive to produce, causing the level of income to decline.

THE MARKET AND THE PUBLIC SECTOR—TWO METHODS OF ECONOMIC ORGANIZATION

It is important to understand that ideal government action can promote a net gain for the individuals of a community (or nation). We will emphasize the limitations of the market and the nature of ideal government policy that would improve economic efficiency. However, it is also important to understand that the public sector is merely an alternative form of economic organization. There is nothing magical about it. It, too, has shortcomings.

When making policy choices, scholarship demands that we compare the advantages and disadvantages of all available alternatives. It is not enough to point out that the market has some shortcomings relative to a hypothetical "ideal." Rather, the relevant question should be "How does the market compare with other available alternatives?" Government action is one of the available alternatives. But comparison of these two major alternatives requires knowledge of the "real world" operation of the public sector, as well as that of the market.

Economic Theory and Public Sector Decisions

In analyzing man's behavior in the marketplace, economists develop a logically consistent theory of behavior that can be tested against reality. Through theory and empirical testing we seek to explain various economic actions of decision-makers and, in general, how the market operates.

In the public sphere our purpose should be the same: To explain how the collective decision-making process really operates. This means developing a logically consistent theory linking individual behavior to collective action, analyzing the implications of that theory, and testing these implications against the events of the real world. Just as economists have traditionally sought to explain how the pricing mechanism works, so too should we seek to explain how public choices are made.

Individual Decisions and Public Policy

Public choices will be determined by the behavior of individuals acting in a political context. In a democratic setting individual preferences and expectations will influence the outcome of collective decisions, even as they influence outcomes in the market. The government is *not* a supraindividual that will always make decisions in the "public interest," however that nebulous term might be defined. It is merely an institution through which individuals make collective decisions and through which they carry out activities collectively.

The basic postulate of all economics is that changes in expected costs and benefits will cause decision-makers to alter their actions in a predictable way. Specifically, as the personal costs of an event increase (and/or the benefits decline), decision-makers will be less likely to choose the event. As costs decline and benefits increase, the opposite tendency will be true. This postulate will be maintained throughout our analysis of market behavior. Similarly, it will be utilized to yield insight on the organization and functioning of the public sector.

Since the theory of collective decision-making is not as well developed as our theory of market behavior, our conclusions will, of course, be less definitive. But in the last 25 years, social scientists have made great strides, strides that have improved our understanding of resource allocation through the public sector.[4] Currently, this subject is often dealt with at a more advanced level. Economic tools can be utilized to shed light on how the public sector handles economic activities.

Differences and Similarities Between Market and Collective Action

Market organization is fundamentally different from political allocation. Voluntary exchange is the dominant characteristic of a market economy, although as we have already noted, with the presence of externalities, involuntary exchange may also result. Democratic collective decision-making is characterized by majority rule, either directly or indirectly through legislative procedures. Let us take a closer look at both the differences and similarities between market and public sector allocation.

1. *Breaking the Individual Consumption–Payment Link.* In the market if a consumer is to obtain a commodity, he must be willing to pay the price. For each person there is a one-to-one correspondence between consuming the commodity and payment of the purchase price. In this respect, there is a fundamental difference between market and collective action. The government usually does not establish a one-to-one relationship between the tax bill of a consumer and the amount of political goods that he consumes.

Your tax bill will be the same, whether you like or dislike the national defense, agriculture, or antipoverty policies of the government. You will be taxed for subsidies to higher education, sugarbeet growers, airlines, cultural centers, and many other **political goods,**[5] regardless of whether or not you consume them. In some cases you may

---

[4] The contributions of Kenneth Arrow, James Buchanan, Duncan Black, Anthony Downs, Mancur Olson, and Gordon Tullock have been particularly important.

[5] The term "political good" is a broad term used to designate any action supplied through the public sector. Note that political goods may be either private goods or public goods as far as the nature of the goods is concerned.

even be made worse off by a government program, but this fact will not change your payment (taxes) for political goods. In other cases you may receive very large benefits (either monetary and/or subjective) from a governmental action without any significant impact on your tax bill. The direct link between individual consumption of the good and individual payment for the good is not required in the public sector.

2. *The Reality of the Aggregate Consumption–Payment Link.*   While the government can break the link between payment for the good and the right to consume the good for an *individual*, the reality of the *aggregate consumption–aggregate payment* will remain. Provision of scarce goods requires the foregoing of alternatives. Someone must cover the cost of providing scarce goods regardless of the sector utilized to produce (or distribute) them. There are no free lunches in either the private or the public sector. Free goods provided in the public sector are "free" only to individuals. They are most certainly not free from the viewpoint of society.

Taxpayers must pay for goods that the government might choose to distribute freely to consumers. For example, the government usually provides elementary education free of charge. But this does not mean that such education is not scarce. The cost of producing the education is simply being charged to someone (taxpayers) other than those who directly consume the commodity.

An increase in the amount of goods provided in the public sector will mean an increase in the total costs of government. More political goods will means more taxes. Given scarcity, the link between aggregate consumption and aggregate costs of production cannot be broken by the utilization of the public sector.

3. *The Element of Compulsion.*   In the market sector, goods are traded from producers to consumers so long as mutual opportunity for gain is possible. In the absence of externalities, trade neither affects the welfare of others nor is dependent on the consent of others. There is a direct link between choosing to buy a commodity and receiving it. Similarly, rejection of a good means one will neither receive the good nor have to pay for it. The views of the majority, even an overwhelming majority, do not prevent a consumer from buying a good. Neither do they require that one buy the goods preferred by the majority.

On the other hand, in the political sphere, no means is allowed for the views of both the majority and the minority to prevail. In a democracy the views of the majority of referendum voters will prevail on an issue. Or, if the matter is decided legislatively, the majority of voting legislators will prevail. The minority must accept a policy and help pay for its cost, even if they strongly disagree. If representative legislative policy edicts $10 billion for the development of a superweapon system, the dissenting minority is required to pay taxes that will help finance the project. Other dissenting minorities will be compelled to pay taxes for the support of welfare programs, farm subsides, foreign aid, or hundreds of other projects on which reasonable men will surely differ. When issues are decided in the public sector, dissidents must, at least temporarily, yield to the current dominant view.

4. *Candidates and "Bundles" of Political Goods.*   When decisions are made legislatively, the voter must either support or reject candidates that represent a "bundle" of

positions of issues. The legislative voter cannot choose the views of Senator Free Lunch on poverty and business welfare, but the views of challenger Mr. Austerity on national defense and tariffs. Inability to separate a candidate's views on one issue from his views on another greatly reduces the voter's power to register his preferences on specific issues, particularly issues of minor consequences.

5. *The Political Power Distribution.*   In the marketplace, individuals with more dollar votes obviously have more economic power. Dollar votes call the tune. The number of dollar votes available to an individual will reflect his abilities, ambitions, skills, inheritance, and good fortune, among other things. An unequal distribution of consumer power will result.

In the public sector, ballot votes call the tune when decisions are made democractically. One man, one vote is the rule. But one needs to be careful not to press this point too far. While each citizen has one and only one vote, it does not follow that political power is equally divided. Some citizens are much more astute than others at using the political process to their personal advantage.

One man may be an effective lobbyist, persuasive speaker, or a clever public relations expert. Another may have few talents that exert an effective influence on the outcome of political events. Thus, while each of the men has only one vote, the two have an unequal amount of political power. In addition, dollar votes exert an impact on the outcome of political events. Financing is necesary to communicate one's position, lobby effectively, and organize politically. In general, persons with more dollar votes are likely to possess more political power than those with low incomes.

Is political power more equally distributed than market power? Probably so, because each of us can directly cast only one vote. But it is clear that neither market power nor political power is distributed according to anything near perfect equality.

The Supply and Demand of Public Sector Action

In the marketplace consumers demand goods with their dollar votes. Producers supply goods. The actions of both are influenced by their personal self-interest. Under a democratic political setting, voters and legislators are counterparts to consumers and producers. Voters will demand political goods with their political resources—votes, lobbying, contributions, and organizational abilities. Vote-conscious legislators are suppliers of political goods.

How does a voter decide which political supplier to support? Many things undoubtedly influence his decision, but personal self interest will surely be high on the list. Will the policies of Senator Snodgrass or his challenger, Mr. Good Deal, help *me* most? Where do they stand on the major issues? What are their views on those issues that may seem unimportant to others, but are of vital importance to *me*? Are they likely to raise or lower *my* taxes? All of these factors will influence the voter's personal benefits and costs from public sector action. Economic theory suggests they will influence his choice among the candidates.

Other things constant, a voter will support those candidates that he expects to provide him with the most benefits, net of costs. The greater the expected gains from a candidate's election, the more a voter will do to assure his success. A voter, like the consumer in the marketplace, will ask the supplier, "What can you do for me and how much will it cost me?"

The goal of the political supplier is to put together a majority coalition—to win the election. Vote-seeking politicians, like profit-conscious businessmen, will have a strong incentive to cater to the views of their constituents. The easiest way to win their votes, both politically and financially, is to give them, or at least appear to give them, what they want. The politician who pays no heed to the view of his constituents is as rare as the businessman selling castor oil at a football game.

What type of issues will be most attractive to a political supplier—those that have a high benefit/cost ratio for one's constituents, right? The greater the net benefits from public sector action, the more popular the issue with the voters. Public sector action that corrects, or appears to correct, the shortcomings of the market would be attractive. If properly conducted, it would generate more benefits to the community than costs. Much public policy originates for just this reason. The community's interest and the self-interest of political suppliers would harmonize.

CONFLICTS BETWEEN GOOD ECONOMICS AND GOOD POLITICS

Is there ever reason to believe that political action will result in economic inefficiency? Current economic and political research is continually yielding knowledge that will help us better answer this question. We will deal with it in more detail in a later chapter. But three important characteristics of the political process are introduced at this time.

1. *The Rationally Ignorant Voter.*   Most citizens recognize that their vote is unlikely to determine the outcome of an election. Since their action will not resolve the issue, there is little incentive to seek out costly information in order to cast an intelligent vote. So what if one casts an uninformed vote, it will not be decisive anyway.

Voters have a strong incentive to rely on information that is supplied to them freely by candidates and the mass media. Conversations with friends, information acquired at work, newspapers, the TV news media, and political advertising all take on additional importance because the voter has so little incentive to incur any personal information gathering cost. Some economists have referred to this lack of incentive to cast an intelligent vote as the **rational ignorance effect.** Since the average voter stands to gain little from information about a wide range of issues that are decided in the political arena, we should expect that he will remain uninformed.[6] It is, of course, well documented that few voters can name their congressman, much less indicate his position on very many issues. Certainly, very few voters could accurately indicate the consequences of, say, raising tariffs on automobiles or abolishing the farm price support program. This should not surprise us. They are merely responding to economic incentives.

[6]Anthony Downs in *An Economic Theory of Democracy* (New York: Harper, 1958) and Gordon Tulluck in *Toward a Mathematics of Politics* (Ann Arbor: Univ. of Michigan Press, 1967) have, among others, emphasized this point.

OUTSTANDING ECONOMIST: James Buchanan

Fifteen years ago most economists were content to concentrate on the workings of the marketplace, its shortcomings, and what government action might do to correct these deficiencies. Both political scientists and economists envisioned the public sector as a type of supraindividual, a creature making decisions in the public interest. James Buchanan set out to change all this. He, perhaps more than anyone else, is responsible for what some have called the "public choice revolution."

Buchanan perceives of government as an outgrowth of individual behavior. Human beings are the ultimate choicemakers, shaping and molding group action as well as private affairs. Using the tools of economics, theories are developed about how the political process works. Real world data are used to test the theories. Buchanan's approach is that of scientific politics.

In their widely acclaimed book, *The Calculus of Consent*,[7] Buchanan and Gordon Tullock develop a theory of constitutions and analyze political behavior under alternative decision rules (for example, simple majority, legislative procedure, etc.). Always using the individual as the foundation of the analysis, theories are developed concerning special interests, logrolling, and the types of activities that are most likely to be provided through the public sector. Empirical work, testing many implications of the book, continues today. In a recent book, *The Limits of Liberty*,[8] which he calls a complement to the earlier book with Tullock, Buchanan applies his individualistic perspective to explain the emergence of property rights, law, and of government itself, with a view toward explaining some of the problems of the 1970s.

A past president of the Southern Economic Association, Buchanan has also written widely on externalities, public goods, and public finance. His doctoral degree is from the University of Chicago and he is a member of the Mont Pelerin Society. He taught at Florida State, Virginia, and UCLA before accepting his current position as the General Director of the Center for the Study of Public Choice at Virginia Polytechnic Institute. A favorite expression of his is that to get ahead "you must apply the seat to the chair." His accomplishments verify that he pursues his own advice.

2. *The Problem of Special Interests.* A **special interest issue** is one that yields substantial personal benefits to a small number of constituents, while imposing a small individual cost on a large number of other voters. A few gain a lot, *individually*, while a large number lose little, *individually*.

Special interest issues will be very attractive to vote-conscious politicians (that is most of them, right?). Voters that have a small cost imposed on them will not care much about the issue, particularly if it is fairly complex so that the imposition of the cost is difficult to identify. Because of the cost of information, most of those harmed by such issues will not even be aware of the legislator's views. They will ignore the issue. But the special interests will be vitally concerned. They will let the candidate (or

[7]J. M. Buchanan and G. Tullock, *The Calculus of Consent.* Ann Arbor: Univ. of Michigan Press, 1962.
[8]J. M. Buchanan, *The Limits of Liberty.* Chicago: Univ. of Chicago Press, 1975.

legislator) know how important the issue is to them. They will help, both financially and otherwise, politicians who favor their position and oppose those who do not.

What would you do if you wanted to win an election? Support the special interest. Milk them for financial resources. Use those resources to "educate" the uninformed majority of voters about how you support policies that are in their interest. You would have an incentive to follow this path even though the total community benefits from the support of the special interest might be less than the cost. The policy might cause economic inefficiency, but it could still be a political winner.

Why stand up for a large majority that individually bears a small cost (do not forget, this cost may be large overall)? Most of them are uninformed on the issue. They do not care much about it. They will do little to help you get elected even if you support their best interests on this issue. The astute politician will go with the special interest group if he plans to be around very long.

The political process will tend to be biased in favor of special interest groups. This is the way we should expect it to work. There will sometimes be a conflict between good politics and ideal public policy. Throughout, as we consider public policy alternatives, we will remind the reader to consider how public policy is likely to operate when special interest influence is strong.

Kelly by Jack Moore; © 1974 Universal Press Syndicate

3. *Political Gains from Shortsighted Policies.*   The complexity of many issues makes it difficult for voters to identify the future benefits and costs. Will a tax cut reduce the long-run rate of unemployment? Are wage–price controls an efficient means to deal with inflation? Can pro-union legislation raise the real wages of workers? These questions are complex. Few voters will be able to understand the short-run and long-run implications of policy in these areas. Thus, voters will have a tendency to rely on current conditions. To the voter the best indicator of the success of a policy is "How are things now?"

Political entrepreneurs seeking to win the current election, have a strong incentive to support policies that generate current benefits at the expense of future cost, particularly if the future costs will be difficult to identify on election day. Shortsighted policies can be politically attractive, even when they promote economic inefficiency.

What if the policy leads to serious problems after the election? This is a problem. But is it not better to be an *officeholder* explaining why things are in a mess, than a *defeated candidate* trying to convince nonlisteners why you were right all the time? The political entrepreneur has a strong incentive to win the next election, and worry about what is right later.

▭ LOOKING AHEAD

In the following chapter we will take a look at the government's actual spending and tax policies. In subsequent chapters the significance of economic organization and issues of political economy will be highlighted. The tools of economics are used with a dual objective. We will attempt to point out, *ideally*, what government *should do*. But we will also focus on what we would *expect government to do*. Unsurprisingly, these two are not always identical. Political economy—use of economic tools to help one better understand how both the market and the public sectors actually work—is a fascinating subject.[9] It helps us better understand the why behind many of today's current events. Who said economics is the dismal science?

CHAPTER LEARNING OBJECTIVES

1. Lack of competition may make it possible for a group of sellers to gain by restricting output and raising prices. There is a conflict between **(a)** the self-interest of sellers to collude, restrict output, and raise product prices above their production costs and **(b)** economic efficiency. Public sector action—promoting competition or regulating private firms—may be able to improve economic efficiency in industries where competitive pressures are lacking.

2. The market will tend to underallocate resources to the production of goods with external benefits, and overallocate resources to those products that generate external costs.

3. Public goods are troublesome for the market to handle because nonpaying customers cannot easily be excluded. Since the amount of a public good that each individual receives is largely unaffected by whether he helps pay for it, most individuals will contribute little. Thus, the market will tend to undersupply public goods.

[9]Part V deals with public choice in detail.

4. The public sector can improve the operation of markets by providing a stable economic environment.

5. Concern for the poor, desire for more equality, and equality of opportunity may result in governmental action to redistribute income. Redistribution may also stem from the desire of organized interests to use the public sector to their advantage.

6. The public sector is an alternate method of organizing economic activity. Public sector action may sometimes improve on the market and lead to an increase in the community's welfare, all individuals considered.

7. The direction of public sector actions will be shaped by individuals (that is, legislators, voters, lobbyists, and financial contributors). Successful political candidates will seek to offer voters a program that they favor. Voters will be attracted to candidates who reflect their personal view and self-interest.

8. The political process may conflict with economic efficiency when **(a)** voters have little knowledge of an issue, **(b)** special interests are strong, or **(c)** political figures can gain from following shortsighted policies.

IMPORTANT TERMS TO REMEMBER

Economic efficiency: Economizing behavior—when applied to a community it implies that (a) an activity should be undertaken if the sum of the benefits to the individuals exceeds the sum of their cost and (b) no activity should be undertaken if the costs borne by the individuals exceed their benefits.

Externality: The side effects of an action which influence the well-being of nonconsenting parties. The secondary parties may be either helped (external benefits) or harmed (external costs).

Public goods: Jointly consumed goods—when consumed by one they are also made available to others. National defense, poetry, and scientific theories are examples.

Political good: Any good (or policy) supplied by the political process.

Special interest issue: A policy that results in substantial *individual* benefits to a small minority while imposing a small *individual* cost on other voters. In total, the net cost to the majority might either exceed or fall short of the net benefits to the special interest group.

Rational ignorance effect: Voters, recognizing that their vote is unlikely to be decisive, rationally have little incentive to inform themselves so that they might cast an intelligent vote.

THE ECONOMIC WAY OF THINKING—DISCUSSION QUESTIONS

1. Explain in your own words what is meant by external costs and external benefits. Why may market allocations be less than ideal when they are present?

2. If producers are going to be provided with an incentive to produce a good, why is it important for them to be able to prevent nonpaying customers from receiving the good?

3. Do you think real world politicians adopt political positions because they will help their election prospects? Can you name a current political figure who consistently puts "principles above politics." If so, check with three of your classmates and see if they agree.

4. Do you think special interest groups exert much influence on local government? Why or why not? As a test, check the composition of the local zoning board in your community. How many real estate agents, contractors, developers, and apartment house owners are on the board? How many citizens without any real estate interests?

5. "Economics is a positive science. Government by its very nature is influenced by philosophical considerations. Therefore, the tools of economics cannot tell us much about how the public sector works." Do you agree or disagree? Why?

6. Which of the following are public goods: **(a)** an antimissile system surrounding Washington, D.C., **(b)** a fire department, **(c)** tennis courts, **(d)** Yellowstone National Park, **(e)** elementary schools?

5
TAXES AND GOVERNMENT SPENDING

For half a century, the trend among Western nations has been toward bigger government. Some believe that the emerging problems of today will require a still greater governmental role. Others believe that the guiding hand of government has already gone too far in attempting to replace the market's invisible hand.

The types of things that the government should undertake constitute a highly debatable topic. We will often discuss the pros and cons of government action in various areas. But there can be no debate about the growth of the public sector. Exhibit 5-1 shows that state, local, and federal government expenditures account for almost one-third of the total spending in the 1970s, compared to 23 percent in 1949, and only 10 percent in 1929. In 1974 total government expenditures, including transfer payments, but excluding intergovernmental transfers, were approximately $5600 per household.

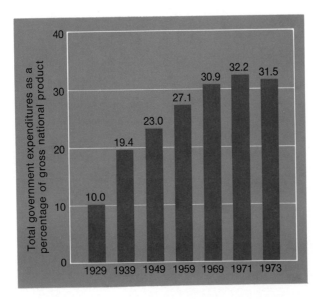

Exhibit 5-1 Growth in the Size of the Public Sector

The share of total spending channeled through the public sector in the United States has been increasing.

Source: Tax Foundation, Inc., *Facts and Figures on Government Finance—1975*, Tables 6 and 20.

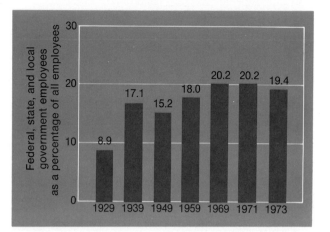

Exhibit 5-2   Public Sector Employment as a Share of the Total

Federal, state, and local governments comprise an expanding share of total employment.

SOURCE: Tax Foundation, Inc., *Facts and Figures on Government Finance—1975*, Table 12. The employment data were measured in terms of full-time equivalent units.

Exhibit 5-2, using employment as the criterion, also illustrates both the size and growth of government. In 1929 state, local, and federal employment comprised 8.9 percent of the total. By 1971, the comparable figure was 20.2 percent. In the early 1970s, approximately one out of every five Americans worked for the government. More than one out of six were involved in nonmilitary employment.

WHAT DO FEDERAL, STATE, AND LOCAL GOVERNMENTS BUY?

There are three levels of government in the United States. The major responsibilities of the three levels differ considerably. A breakdown of expenditures and taxes will highlight some of these differences. The federal government spends the most, approximately three-fifths of the total government expenditures. However, during the last two decades the expenditures of state and local units have grown rapidly, more rapidly than the federal government (see Myth, page 73).

Exhibit 5-3 shows the broad categories of federal expenditures for 1975. The federal government is solely responsible for national defense. Just under one-third of all federal expenditures went for defense and related areas (space and foreign affairs) in 1975. The largest item in the federal budget was *cash income maintenance*—Social Security, unemployment payments, and public assistance to the poor and disabled. Recipients of these income transfers may spend them as they choose. Programs to *help people buy essentials* (medical care, housing, food, etc.) now comprise approximately 11 percent of all federal spending. This category differs from cash income maintenance in that persons must purchase specific goods in order to qualify for the assistance.

Exhibit 5-4 presents a picture of state and local government expenditures. In the United States education has traditionally been the responsibility of state and local governments. More than one-third of their expenditures are allocated for this item. Public welfare, hospitals, highways, and operation of public utilities form other major expenditure items for state and local governments.

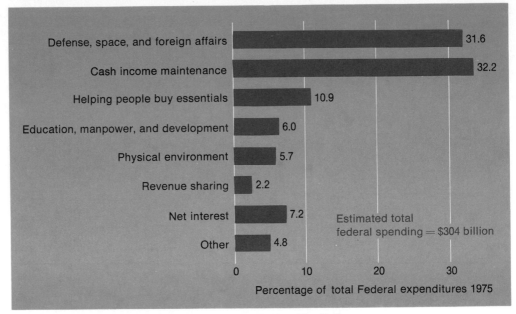

Exhibit 5-3 How the Federal Government Spends Your Tax Dollar

The breakdown of the 1974–1975 fiscal year federal budget is presented here. Defense accounted for 31.6 percent of federal spending. Approximately 50 percent of the federal tax dollar was spent on cash income maintenance, helping people buy essentials, and manpower development.

SOURCE: Barry M. Blechman, Edward M. Gramlich, and R. W. Hartman, *Setting National Priorities—The 1975 Budget.* Washington, D.C.: The Brookings Institution, 1974.

Allocation of state and local spending 1971-1974

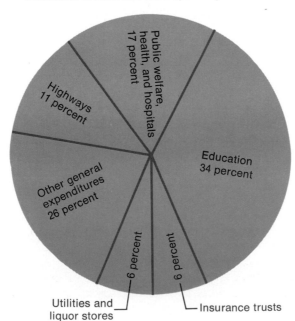

Exhibit 5-4 What State and Local Governments Buy

Education, public welfare, and general administrative expenditures comprise the major budget items of state and local governments.

SOURCE: U.S. Department of Commerce.

MYTHS OF ECONOMICS
"The growth of the federal government has been the major source of government expansion."

This statement was true during the Great Depression of the 1930s, World War II, and into the 1950s. But since 1952, the growth rate of state and local government expenditures has been nearly double the rate for the federal sector. The accompanying chart presents data on the *rate of change* in government expenditures by unit. During the 1952–1972 period, state and local government expenditures increased by 475 percent—almost fivefold.

	PERCENT INCREASE IN GOVERNMENT EXPENDITURES	
	Federal	*State and local*
1927–1940	184.8	34.7
1941–1952	611.3	173.1
1953–1960	35.9	90.2
1961–1972	154.7	201.1
1952–1972	246.6	475.0

SOURCE: Tax Foundation, Inc., *Facts and Figures on Government Finance—1973*, Table 5.

Federal expenditures increased 246.6 percent during the same period. In 1952 federal expenditures accounted for 72 percent of all government expenditures, compared to only 28 percent for state and local units. By the mid-1970s the federal share of government expenditures had declined to 60 percent. State and local expenditures now account for two-fifths of all government expenditures. Since the Korean War, state and local government expenditures have provided the major impetus for government expansion.

The Expanding Nondefense Sector

In recent years there has been a significant change in the composition of public sector expenditures. Income transfer programs have increased in importance. The government's role in providing (or subsidizing) medical care, housing, food, and school lunches has been expanded. Education, training, and development expenditures designed to upgrade the quality of the work force and improve the employment opportunities of disadvantaged groups have also grown rapidly. Exhibit 5-5 summarizes the changing nature of public expenditures. Between 1960 and 1971 the share of total government expenditures—Federal, state, and local—on nondefense functions expanded from 64 percent to 73 percent. As a percentage of the gross national product (GNP), nondefense public sector spending jumped from 17 percent to 23 percent. During this same period, expenditures on defense, space, and international affairs were declining both as a share of the gross national product and all government expendi-

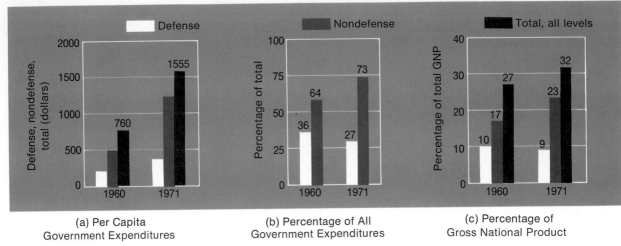

Exhibit 5-5   The Changing Nature of Public Expenditures

Nondefense government expenditures have been increasing both as a percentage of all government expenditures [frame (b)] and as a percentage of GNP [frame (c)]. The corresponding percentages for defense expenditures have declined. Total per capita government expenditures (state, local, and federal) were $1555 in 1971—$429 for defense and $1135 for nondefense [frame (a)]. Intergovernment transfers are not double counted as part of government expenditures.

SOURCE: Tax Foundation, Inc., *Facts and Figures on Government Finance—1975* and *The American Almanac.*

tures. As of 1971, total per capita public expenditures, excluding intergovernmental transfers, were $1555, of which $1135 was for nondefense items.

Have the expanded nondefense expenditures accomplished their objectives? Have they primarily benefited the poor or the well-to-do? As we progress, we will be able to shed some light on each of these questions.

SOURCES OF TAX REVENUES

How does the government raise revenues to finance its expenditures? We all know the answer—taxes. Exhibit 5-6 illustrates the share of total government revenues by type of taxes. The personal income tax accounts for nearly one-third of the total tax dollar, 44 percent of the federal budget receipts. Payroll taxes constitute the most rapidly expanding source of tax revenues. In 1960 the corporate income tax was the second largest source of public sector revenue. By the mid-1970s, payroll taxes, primarily Social Security and unemployment compensation contributions, raised 21 percent of all governmental revenue, twice as much as the corporate income tax.

The sales tax generates 15 percent of all tax revenue. Sales and excise taxes are far and away the largest source of state revenues, although state personal income taxes are of increasing importance. At the local level, the property tax produces nearly 85 percent of all revenues. Despite their declining importance, property taxes still constitute 12 percent of all public sector revenues, a larger share than even the corporate income tax.

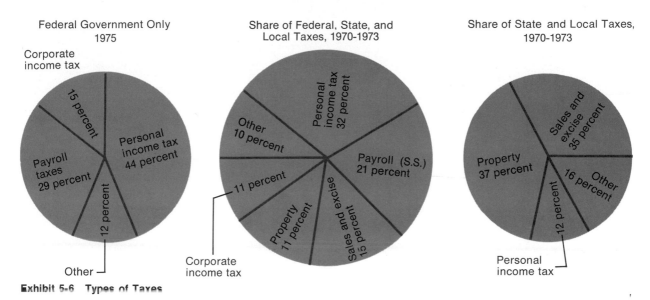

Exhibit 5-6   Types of Taxes

(a) Personal income, payroll, and corporate income taxes are the major source of tax revenues for the federal government. (b) Sales and property taxes are the major source of state and local revenues.
SOURCE: Barry M. Blechman, Edward M. Gramlich, and R. W. Hartman, *Setting National Priorities—The 1975 Budget* (Washington, D.C.: The Brookings Institution, 1974) and *Facts and Figures on Government Finance—1975,* Tax Foundation, Inc.

THE CONCEPT OF INCIDENCE

Sometimes the **incidence** or burden of a tax can be shifted to someone other than the person who writes out the check to the IRS. The tax may cause persons to alter their action so as to push all or most of the tax burden on to others. Let us consider the incidence on four important taxes.

1. *Sales and Excise Taxes.*   These taxes are usually passed along to the consumer. If a 4 percent sales tax is imposed on the seller, the tax increases the seller's cost of providing his product to customers. The price of the product must at least cover the seller's cost, including his tax liability. Otherwise, he will not continue to offer the good. Thus, since sales taxes (and excise taxes on specific products) increase the seller's costs, higher prices will result. When you buy a dollar's worth of merchandise, you will pay $1.04—one dollar for the seller and 4 cents for the tax collector. The incidence of sales and excise taxes will lie primarily on the backs of consumers.

2. *Income Taxes.*   Most economists believe that the incidence of this tax falls on the individual taxpayer. The tax certainly does not affect the demand for the services of resource suppliers. It could affect the supply, but the empirical evidence suggests that it does not, at least for labor services. Even though the income tax takes a share of one's earnings, higher earnings will still lead to more aftertax income. Therefore, people do

*"How old does a country have to be before
it's self-supporting?"*

Reproduced by permission from *Changing Times*.

not work less because of the income tax. Since neither demand nor supply of labor is appreciably affected, individuals will be unable to raise the price of their services in order to cover the tax. The individual taxpayers will feel the pinch of the income tax.

3. *Payroll Taxes.* Social Security, unemployment compensation, and other payroll taxes are now the second largest source of tax revenues. When levied, they are often split between the employee and his employer. The burden of the payroll tax is thought to reside primarily with employees, regardless of how they are levied. The supply of labor will tend to be unresponsive to a payroll tax for the same reasons that it is unresponsive to the income tax. Therefore, when a payroll tax is levied on employees, its major impact is to reduce their after-tax wages. An employer will continue hiring employees so long as the additional employee adds more to revenues than cost. When a payroll tax is levied on the employee, the wage rate will reflect the marginal contribution of an employee to the firm. Alternatively, when the payroll tax is levied on the employer the wage rate *plus the tax* must reflect the value of the marginal labor services to the firm. Since the payroll tax makes it more costly to hire labor, the demand for labor will decline, pushing the burden of the payroll tax on to the employee even when it is levied on the employer.

The employee–employer splitting of a payroll tax will exert little impact on its incidence. Exhibit 5-7 illustrates why. If the tax is levied entirely on employees, market forces, reflecting supply S_1 and demand D_1 will establish an equilibrium wage W_1. After an employee pays the payroll tax T, he is left with an after-tax wage of W_2 (W_1 minus

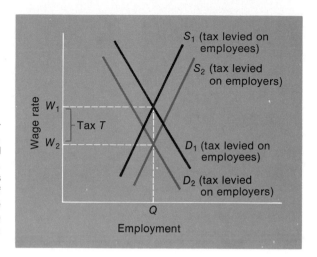

Exhibit 5-7   Sharing the Payroll Tax

When a payroll tax T is levied on employees, a before-tax wage rate of W_1 results. Alternatively, if tax T were levied on employers rather than employees, both the labor supply and demand curves would shift downward by the amount of the tax to S_2 and D_2, respectively. Wage rate W_2, the same as the *after-tax* wage rate when the payroll tax was levied on employees, would result.

T). What would happen if the payroll tax were levied on the employer rather than employees? Unless an employee's productivity is sufficient to cover both his own wage rate *plus the tax T*, he will not be hired. Since the tax would not change employee productivity, the demand for labor will decrease (shift to the left) by the amount of the tax. However, since the tax is no longer levied on employee earnings, the labor supply will increase (shift to the right) by the amount of the tax. Supply curve S_2 (with the tax levied on the employers) is identical to supply curve S_1 when the payroll tax was levied on employees. When the employer pays the tax, the wage rate will be W_2 the exact same *after-tax* wage rate as when the payroll tax was levied on the employee.

Clearly, from the viewpoint of economics, the employer–employee splitting of the tax makes no difference. The employer's cost of hiring the employee, including the payroll tax when it is levied on him, will be identical regardless of whether the tax is levied on the employer or the employee. The employee's after-tax income will also be the same in both cases.

Why then does Congress often spend many hours debating the employer–employee sharing on payroll taxes? Political entrepreneurs have a strong incentive to hide the burden of a tax. Levying a larger share on the employer makes it more difficult for employees to figure out their real tax burden. Increasing the employer's share is good politics (even if it is deceptive), although it fails to lessen the employee's tax.

4. *Corporate Income Tax.*   The incidence of the corporate income tax is debatable. Some economists argue that a firm that is currently charging the profit-maximizing price, will have no reason to change merely because the government takes a share of its profits. If this is the case, then the incidence of the corporate income tax would fall on stockholders. But closer scrutiny suggests this view is only partially correct. If the tax reduces the stockholder's rate of return, financial assets will flow away from stocks and into other forms of savings. Since stockholders have alternatives, corporations will have to raise their temporarily lower after-tax rate of return in order to continue to attract investment funds.

But this will increase corporate costs (including the tax). The higher costs will push the prices of corporate products upward, thereby partially shifting the burden of the tax on to consumers.

While the burden of taxes is sometimes difficult to isolate, one thing is clear. Taxes will be paid by people. It makes good political rhetoric to talk about "businesses" paying taxes. But the hard facts are that individuals—consumers, employees, or stockholders —provide all tax revenues.

Proportional, Progressive, and Regressive Taxes

How is the tax burden related to one's income? A **proportional tax** is one that takes the same *percentage* of one's income, regardless of income level. If the income tax were proportional at a 10 percent rate, a family whose income was $5000 would have a tax bill of $500. Those with $10,000 of income would owe $1000, and so on. As Exhibit 5-8 illustrates, the percentage of income paid to the government is constant for a proportional tax.

A **progressive tax** takes a larger percentage from high income recipients. Additional income is taxed at an increasing rate. Thus, the average percentage of income paid in taxes rises with income level (see Exhibit 5-8). The personal income tax has a progressive rate structure. But exemptions and differential treatment of incomes, tax loopholes if the reader will permit a philosophical bias, distort and sometimes completely negate the progressive principle over the full range of incomes.

A **regressive tax** takes a larger percentage of income from the poor than from those with higher incomes. The tax rate declines with income. Because there is a cutoff point above which income is not taxed, payroll taxes tend to be regressive. Currently, Social Security taxes are levied on only the first $13,200 of income. This would mean that a recipient making $26,400 would pay a rate only half as great as families with incomes of $13,200 or less. In 1975, payroll taxes comprised 29 percent of all federal revenues, compared to 16 percent in 1960.[1] This trend toward increased reliance on payroll taxes tends to reduce the progressivity of the federal tax structure.

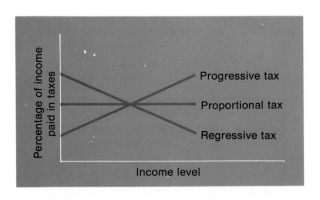

Exhibit 5-8   Proportional, Progressive, and Regressive Taxes

If the *percentage* of income paid in tax increases as income rises, the tax is progressive. If it falls, the tax is regressive. The *percentage* of tax take remains the same across income classes for a proportional tax.

[1] See Barry M. Bleckman, Edward M. Gramlich, and Robert W. Hartman, *Setting National Priorities—The 1975 Budget.* Washington, D.C.: The Brookings Institution, 1974.

WHO PAYS THE TAX BILL?

Considering the incidence of sales, corporate, property, income, and other taxes, who actually pays the bills of government—state, local, and federal? This is a difficult question to answer because of the uncertainty about the incidence of some taxes. But economists have tackled the problem, making estimates under varying assumptions of tax incidence.[2] Their findings support two broad conclusions—

1. Both those with very low incomes (less than $3000) and those with high incomes (more than $50,000) pay a higher tax rate than others. Excluding these two extremes, the average tax rate, including all levels of government, for units with incomes between $5000 and $50,000 is remarkably proportional (see Exhibit 5-9). Taxes take, on average, approximately 30 percent of the income for each income grouping in this range.

2. The income of most taxpayers lies between $5000 and $25,000. This group of middle income recipients accounted for 70 percent of *all* tax revenues in 1968. They contributed two-thirds of the income tax revenues in 1972. On the average, 30 percent of their income goes to taxes. Taxpayers with incomes in excess of $25,000, 4 percent of the total in 1972, received 19 percent of the total income and paid 21.5 percent of the total tax bill (1968 data).

Exhibit 5-9   Who Pays the Tax Bill?

On average, the federal income tax is progressive (column 3). But when all taxes—state, local, and federal—are considered, both low and high income recipients pay a slightly higher tax rate than those in middle income tax brackets (column 5).

Adjusted gross income class	FEDERAL INCOME TAX ONLY—1972			ALL TAXES—1968	
	Share of returns (percent) (1)	Share of income tax (percent) (2)	Effective tax rate (percent) (3)	Share of all taxes (percent) (4)	Overall effective tax rate (percent) (5)
Under $2999	5	0.2	2.6	2.8	42
$3000–$4999	13	2.0	5.8	4.5	32
$5000–$9999	34	14.2	8.9	22.9	30
$10,000–$14,999	25	21.5	10.6	25.8	30
$15,000–$24,999	18	28.4	13.2	22.5	30
Over $25,000	5	33.7	17.8[a]	21.5	33[a]
			(31.1)[b]		(45)[b]
Total	100.0	100.0	13.0	100.0	30

SOURCE: *The Statistical Abstract—1975*, Tables No. 370 and 372, and Roger A. Herriot and Herman P. Miller, "The Taxes We Pay," *The Conference Board Record*, May 1971.

[a] $25,000 to $50,000.
[b] Income greater than $50,000.

[2] Studies conducted by the Tax Foundation, Inc. and M. B. McElray, "Capital Gains and the Concept of Measurement of Purchasing Power," *Business and Economics Statistical Section Proceedings* of the American Statistical Association, 1970, are highly consistent with the findings of Exhibit 5-9.

How should the tax burden be allocated? This is a normative question and economics cannot answer it. Many feel that the rich should shoulder a larger share of the load. Several news items have highlighted cases of extremely wealthy people who paid little or no taxes during specific years. But one must not forget that the rich are a small minority. The opportunity of reducing the overall tax burden by imposing higher taxes on high income recipients is limited. For example, in 1972 if all income of persons making $1 million or more had been confiscated, the yield would have been only $2.1 billion in additional tax revenues, a drop in the bucket compared to the $350 billion tax bill for the year. A 100 percent tax on all income above $50,000 would have yielded $35 billion, about 10 percent of the total tax revenues.[3] Of course, we may want to close specific loopholes that are attractive to many of the wealthy. But clearly such changes will not generate large amounts of tax revenue, thereby significantly reducing the tax burden of others.

THE TAXES OTHERS PAID

How do the tax burden and the accompanying size of the public sector in the United States compare with other countries? Exhibit 5-10 helps answer that question. Taxes are usually higher in Western European countries—West Germany, United Kingdom, Sweden, and France, for example—than in the United States. These higher tax rates

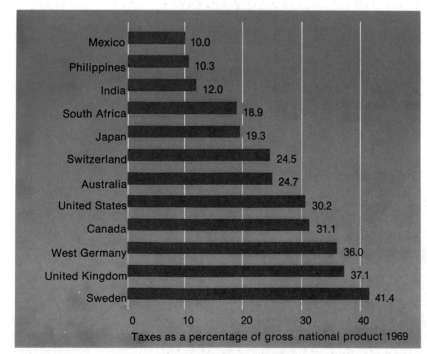

Mexico 10.0
Philippines 10.3
India 12.0
South Africa 18.9
Japan 19.3
Switzerland 24.5
Australia 24.7
United States 30.2
Canada 31.1
West Germany 36.0
United Kingdom 37.1
Sweden 41.4

Taxes as a percentage of gross national product 1969

Exhibit 5-10   The Size of Government—An International Comparison

SOURCE: Tax Foundation, Inc., *Facts and Figures on Government Finance—1973*, Table 22.

[3] Of course, such a policy would affect the incentive to earn, further reducing the tax yield.

reflect great public sector involvement in the provision of housing, health care, retirement insurance, and aid to the poor. The size of the public sector, as measured by the share of income going to taxes, is smaller in Australia, Switzerland, Japan, and South Africa than in the United States. The figure for Japan partially reflects their lack of defense expenditures. Taxes are also much lower in less developed countries, such as India, Philippines, and Mexico, than for industrial nations.

☐☐☐ LOOKING AHEAD

In the first five chapters we have developed several basic economic tools and utilized them to present an overview of both market and public sector action. We would like to conclude this introductory section with a debate on an issue of vital concern to each of us—the "energy crisis." Many of the tools that we have discussed—opportunity cost, supply and demand, externalities, and the theory of public sector action—are applied to this issue. They will help us better understand some of the subtleties involved in the energy crisis.

Is There an Energy Crisis or a Policy Crisis—Two Views

Controversies in Economics

QUESTION: Is the energy crisis real, and if so, what impact will it have on our lives?

PROFESSOR DOOMSDAY: Indeed the energy crisis is real and we are just now beginning to feel its impact. Moreover, it is going to get worse, particularly if we do not change our habits and lifestyles.

The United States, with only 6 percent of the world's population, consumes about 33 percent of the world's energy. Energy consumption in the rest of the world is increasing even faster than consumption here. Energy supplies, at least from conventional sources, are finite and inexorably moving toward exhaustion. In the case of petroleum, *additions* to U.S. proved reserves (in the 48 adjacent states) were 3.9 billion barrels in 1965, and only 3.4 billion in 1970, while consumption jumped from 8.9 billion barrels in 1965 to 10.9 billions in 1970. In the case of natural gas, additions to proved reserves dropped from 21.2 trillion cubic feet in 1965 to 11.1 in 1970.[4] Obviously we cannot continue to increase consumption indefinitely, in the face of declining reserves. Already, costs are increasing as we use up the easily available supplies. Continuing to gobble up what is left of the rest of the world's reserves is risky in the short run, due to uncertainties of supply. It is impossible as a permanent solution, since the rest of the world has finite reserves also.

QUESTION: Professor Optimist, what's your view of the energy crisis?

PROFESSOR OPTIMIST: The rapid increases in energy prices and spot shortages of certain fuels are the result of a combination of unfavorable events and counterproductive policies. First, for almost two decades, the price of energy, relative to other products, has declined (see Exhibit 5-11). Between 1950 and 1970, the price of fuel and related products rose 15.8 percent, compared to a 51.4 percent rise in the consumer price

[4]See Policy Study Group of M.I.T. Energy Laboratory, "Energy Self-Sufficiency: An Economic Evaluation," *Technology Review*, May 1974.

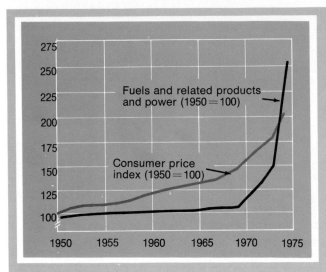

Exhibit 5-11   Changes in Energy Prices and Consumer Prices, 1950–1974

SOURCE: U.S. Department of Commerce.

index.[5] These low prices reflected both market conditions and regulatory policies. In any case, the rapid growth in energy utilization, to which pessimists always refer, was, to a large extent, a response to low prices. With the higher prices of the mid-1970s, our growth rate of energy consumption will decline, particularly as time permits a more complete adjustment.

Second, the Federal Power Commission has fixed the wellhead price of natural gas at approximately one-third the energy equivalent of crude oil. This below-equilibrium price encourages consumers to use more natural gas and at the same time removes the incentive of producers to discover more of it. Needless to say, encouraging consumption while discouraging production provides the perfect formula for shortages. The natural gas shortage, in turn, increased the demand pressure on other fuels, particularly oil.

Third, this extra pressure on the demand for oil would not have been noticeable, except that it came at a time when we were increasingly concerned about environmental conditions. In the early 1970s we began reducing an implicit subsidy to oil refineries, the right to use and pollute our water and air resources without paying for them. The way we removed this implicit subsidy aggravated the situation more than was necessary. Instead of using emission charges or some other strategy that would have brought the benefits of waste elimination procedures into line with their cost, political authorities in many places simply refused permission for the building of added refinery capacity. In addition, the incentive to expand our refinery capacity was further reduced by the uncertainty associated with the import quotas that was present in the early 1970s. Since changes in the import quota legislation could dramatically effect the supply cost of oil, oil companies were reluctant to build facilities costing millions of dollars in locations which five years later might be far from the cheapest sources of crude oil.

All of these factors combined to increase cost and reduce supply. Then, to top things off, the oil embargo and the price-fixing arrangements of OPEC (Organization of Petroleum Exporting Countries) caused the price of imported oil to rise fourfold. The

[5] These data are derived from the detailed consumer and wholesale price indexes.

impact of every one of these factors was either temporary or capable of being reversed with proper public policy. Thus, the short-run conditions were not a reliable indicator of the longer run situation.

PROFESSOR DOOMSDAY: I reject the view that we can go on, business as usual, in the face of finite resources. The insanity of a nation as large and as rich as the United States, doubling its energy consumption every 16 or 17 years has to end soon. The alternative is a country soon crushed under the weight of pollution problems gone wild (many environmental controls would have to be largely scrapped), staggering balance of payments problems (increasing amounts of expensive oil would have to be imported), and inflation (all energy sources have rising prices). The only realistic answer to these problems is for us collectively, governmentally, to turn ourselves around and take a more sensible path, a path leading to a much slower, but sustainable, rate of energy use.

PROFESSOR OPTIMIST: Everybody has different estimates as to the ultimate quantity of oil, natural gas, and resources that the earth contains. For years people have been saying that we are going to run out of this or that. These forecasts have been consistently wrong because they have failed to take note of (a) the size of proven reserves that producers will seek to hold and (b) changes in technology and prices. Edward Mitchell puts it aptly:

> There is the popular tendency to focus on proved reserves, which always appear frighteningly small. Proved reserves in the oil- and gas-producing industry are essentially the same as what are called inventories in other businesses. The fact that oil men hold only ten or fifteen years' supply of oil under the ground should be of as much conern to us as the fact that shoe stores keep only thirty days' supply of shoes on the shelf. To hold more would be unprofitable for the businessman and uneconomical for society. When we do find places, such as the Middle East and North Africa, holding fifty years' supply we are witnessing an error in business judgment, or an expectation of enormous growth of deliveries, or an extremely low cost of holding inventories, or some combination of the three.
>
> When policy makers go beyond proved reserves to estimates of potentially recoverable reserves they often misinterpret the figures. When geologists say that the United States has 300 or 400 billion barrels of potentially recoverable crude oil—about fifty to seventy years' consumption at current rates—they are assuming present technology and present price levels. These quantities, as rough as they are, have meaning only if they have a price tag placed on them. But one of the few certainties in an uncertain world is that future technology and future prices will be different. The ultimate quantity of oil under the ground is (as Professor M. A. Adelman tells us) unknown, unknowable, and, most important, uninteresting. The pertinent questions are, How much do we have to give up to get an extra barrel (or billion barrels) of oil? How much is that barrel worth to us? If it is worth more than it costs, and it costs less than alternative energy sources, we should use it; if not, we should leave it in the ground. When we decide to stop using oil it makes no difference whether we have left in the ground an infinite amount, a trillion barrels, or a barrel and a half.[6]

[6]Edward J. Mitchell, *U.S. Energy Policy: A Primer.* Washington, D.C.: American Enterprise Institute, 1974.

QUESTION: What can be done to deal with the current situation?

PROFESSOR DOOMSDAY: Fundamentally, there are two ways to approach the problem of turning around our rush toward the wasteful exhaustion of our world's limited supply of conventional energy sources. One way, obviously, is to develop nonconventional energy sources. It seems only reasonable that we should greatly expand our efforts to develop economical conversion of solar energy, or its derivative, wind energy. These sources are truly inexhaustible, and they are clean. In some areas, geothermal energy seems promising. There are some concrete indications that the federal government finally is beginning to move in this direction. The fiscal 1976 budget for solar research of the Energy Research and Development Administration was raised to $57.1 million, from $8.8 million the previous year. Yet even if we do apply our research and development resources sufficiently to be successful in these endeavors, it is likely that the second fundamental approach, that of properly moderating economic and population growth trends, also must be employed.

Even large clean sources of energy take space and fail to handle the long-term problem of waste heat disposal. Land, among other finite natural resources, cannot sustain unending growth. Population growth, along with growth in per capita rates of economic output, simply must be controlled. The last several decades of U.S. history show a roughly parallel path for rates of increase in economic output on the one hand, and energy inputs on the other. For example, between 1950 and 1973, real GNP rose by 136 percent, while energy consumption rose 121 percent. Only when our governmental policies reflect the need to contain growth will we be able to move toward a sensible and sustainable lifestyle. The energy crisis, after all, is but one symptom of the general problem of unconstrained growth in a finite world.

Of equal importance is the fact that voluntary or free market discipline simply has not functioned acceptably. It is imperative that we allocate the energy that we do use in a more equitable manner. Some form of collective allocation—nonprice rationing—could ensure that our increasingly scarce and valuable energy sources are used for maximum social benefit. There is a good deal of opposition in the United States to the notion of nonprice rationing for any sort of good or service. Yet nonprice rationing not only allows socially responsible rates of energy use to be imposed, it also avoids the sharp inequities associated with high prices. Most Americans are repelled by the idea of oil-well owners getting richer while poor people pay more and more for fuel oil and gasoline. Both equity and social efficiency are served by policies that keep prices reasonable, while reducing consumption.

Summing up, we must take collective, governmental action rapidly, if we are to avoid the rapidly approaching disaster of drastic energy shortages faced by an economic system addicted to massive doses of energy. To rely upon voluntary action would be inefficient and inequitable, and it would ultimately destroy our economic system.

QUESTION: What policy approach would you suggest Professor Optimist?

PROFESSOR OPTIMIST: Analysis of our energy situation reveals two significant facts. First, both producers and consumers respond to price changes in the energy sector, just as they do in other sectors. Second, most of the "crisis" elements in the current situation are the direct result of a public policy that has prevented the market mechanism from sending decision-makers the proper signals. The solution is less government regulations. In the immediate short run this will mean higher prices. But decision-makers will respond—consumption will be curtailed in an orderly manner, supply will increase, and soon the temporarily higher prices will tumble.

The pricing system does not work instantaneously. It cannot immediately undo the past. As the relative price of energy fell during the 1950s and 1960s, the cars we purchased, the homes and office buildings that we constructed, even our recreation patterns reflected bargain energy prices. In contrast, high energy prices will now induce us to purchase smaller cars, use less glass in construction, better insulate our homes, and make hundreds of other adjustments that will reduce energy consumption. As time and the constant incentive of relative prices permit these adjustments, energy utilization will tumble without any bureaucrat turning down our thermostats. In 1974 the real price (actual price change adjusted for inflation) of fuels and related products rose by more than 30 percent. Economists have estimated that, with time, a 10 percent rise in energy prices will lead to a decline in energy consumption of between 1.5 and 5.0 percent.[7] Therefore, the higher prices of 1974 will lead to a reduction in consumption of between 5 and 15 percent (the energy equivalent of 1.5 to 4.5 billion barrels of oil). This process has already begun. In 1974 energy use in the United States fell by 2.7 percent. Other important factors, including a recession helped cause this reduction. Still, much of the price impact has yet to be felt and it is unlikely (unless energy prices fall again due to technological change) that the U.S. will ever again experience rapidly rising rates in energy use.

Higher prices will, if allowed, correct current shortages. The natural gas shortage is an excellent example. If we deregulate the wellhead price of natural gas, supply will increase. Under current (early 1975) regulations we can expect a natural gas shortage of 10 trillion cubic feet by 1980. Mitchell estimates that a price rise of $0.35 per thousand cubic feet would equate supply and demand.[8] Based on January 1974 prices, this would, if passed straight through to the consumer, amount to about an 18 percent price increase to firm industrial users in Boston, 12 percent in Chicago, and as much as a 76 percent increase for industrial users in Denver. Small users would experience a lesser percentage increase. Even after deregulation gas would be cheaper (and cleaner) than fuels now in use by many, if not most, buyers. The prediction that allowing prices to rise from regulated levels would lead to roughly an extra 10 trillion cubic feet (the energy equivalent of approximately 4.9 million barrels of oil per day) of domestic supplies per year is consistent with several independent studies. The increased output of natural gas would, of course, relieve some of the pressure on other energy sources.

Naturally higher energy prices will also encourage production of nuclear power plants, coal, hydroelectric, and other sources of energy. In the next 10 years the number of nuclear plants is expected to increase fourfold from 50 to nearly 200. Approximately one-sixth of our energy in the 1980s will stem from this source.

Unless we forget that the pricing mechanism works, the energy sector need not cause radical changes and major inconvenience for Americans. In the absence of government intervention, the energy prices of the mid-1970s (adjusted for inflation) will almost surely lead to an excess supply of energy by 1980. Prices for some forms of energy, including crude oil, will begin to fall slightly by that time, although without major technological change, energy will never again be as cheap as it was in the late 1960s.

On the other hand, we can virtually guarantee a crisis of some sort by any one of many well-intended governmental actions now being called for. The adjustment mechanism can be foiled, our energy costs greatly increased, and much uncertainty

---

[7] See Nathan Edmonson, "Real Price and the Consumption of Mineral Energy in the United States, 1901–1968," *Journal of Industrial Economics*, March 1975.

[8] Mitchell, *U.S. Energy Policy.*

introduced if we adopt any combination of the following governmental policies: import quotas, import tariffs, energy rationing, massive subsidies to support or guarantee markets for expensive energy sources, or further energy price controls. Governmental action was necessary to get us into our current mess, and a lack of further governmental action will be sufficient, gradually, to get us out.

Discussion

1. Do you think the energy crisis is real? Explain.
2. Has public policy helped to solve the energy crisis? Why or why not?
3. Would the market mechanism solve the energy crisis? Why or why not?
4. What policy would you favor as a means of dealing with the energy crisis? Why do you think your policy recommendation is better than the alternatives?

CHAPTER LEARNING OBJECTIVES

1. The size of government, particularly state and local government, has been increasing. The expenditures and taxes of federal, state, and local governments comprise nearly one-third of our total income. One out of every five employees works for the government.

2. Nondefense expenditures, particularly for income maintenance, aid to purchase essentials, and manpower development, have increased rapidly since 1960. Nondefense expenditures, including all levels of government, now compose 73 percent of the total.

3. Personal income, payroll, and corporate income taxes are the major source of federal revenues. Sales and property taxes are the major sources of state and local revenues. The poor and the rich pay a greater *percentage* of their income in taxes. In aggregate, taxes are approximately proportional for incomes between $5000 and $50,000.

4. The incidence of a tax is not always easy to determine. The burden of the income tax falls on the individual taxpayer. Most economists believe that payroll taxes are shifted back to employees. Sales and excise taxes are usually shifted forward to consumers.

5. The public sector, as a share of the total economy, is larger in industrial Western European countries and smaller in Australia, Switzerland, Japan, and most less developed nations than in the United States.

IMPORTANT TERMS TO REMEMBER

Tax incidence: The economic unit—consumers, employees, employers, etc.—that bears the burden of the tax. The tax burden may not always fall upon those who pay the tax.

Proportional tax: A tax for which individuals pay the same *percentage* of their income (or other tax base) in taxes, regardless of their income level.

Progressive tax: A tax that takes a higher *percentage* of one's income as his income level increases. Progressive taxes force the rich to pay a greater *percentage* of their income to the government than the poor.

Regressive tax: A tax that takes a smaller *percentage* of one's income as his income level increases. Thus, the proportion of income allocated to taxes would be higher for the poor than the rich.

THE ECONOMIC WAY OF THINKING—DISCUSSION QUESTIONS

1. The major categories of government spending are **(a)** national defense, **(b)** education, and **(c)** income transfers and antipoverty expenditures. Why do you think the public sector has become involved in these activities? Why not leave them to the market?

2. Do you think the tax burden in the United States is too large or too small? Explain. What policies, if any, would you advocate to change the tax burden and its distribution? Be specific and defend your position.

3. What is tax incidence? Why is it important? Who bears the burden of a generalized sales tax? Explain.

4. Why do you think that the federal government breaks payroll taxes into an employee's share and employer's share? Do you think this is a good idea? Why or why not?

5. Outline the major components of the "energy problem." What policies would you advocate to help alleviate the situation? Explain why you believe that your policy would work. Be specific.

---

6. What's Wrong with This Economic Logic?

In the next 30 years our consumption of oil will increase fourfold. Yet in the last 30 years, our supply has only doubled. Production is unable to keep up with demand. Unless the government imposes a quota system, we will most assuredly run out of oil by the year 2000.

---

7. What's Wrong with This Way of Thinking?

"Antiunion Congressmen argue that the Social Security payroll tax should continue to be divided equally between the employer and his employees. My bill would levy five-sixths of the tax on employers, while the employee would pay only one-sixth. This approach would take some of the tax burden off the backs of employees and allocate it to their employers who can better afford to pay it." Senator Friend of the Workingman.

MACROECONOMICS

II

6
TAKING THE NATION'S ECONOMIC PULSE

The Gross National Product is one of the great inventions of the twentieth century, probably almost as significant as the automobile and not quite so significant as TV. The effect of physical inventions is obvious, but social inventions like the GNP change the world almost as much.[1] [Professor Kenneth Boulding]

Ours is a society that is infatuated with measurement. We seek to measure everything from the figure of Miss America to the speed of Nolan Ryan's fast ball. Therefore, the fact that we have devised methods to measure something as important as the performance of our economy is not surprising. However, it is surprising that we waited so long. Beginning in the early 1930s, the Department of Commerce systematically developed and published data on the performance of the economy for the first time. Before that, there were no widely accepted methods or procedures for taking "the pulse of our economy."

As Professor Boulding's statement introducing this chapter indicates, the development of an economic measuring rod was an extremely important "invention." If the performance of an economy could not be identified and measured, it would be difficult to apply public policy.

THE CONCEPT OF THE GNP

The gross national product (GNP) is the most widely used measure of economic performance. Newspaper writers and television commentators give the latest GNP

[1] Kenneth Boulding, "Fun and Games with the Gross National Product—The Role of Misleading Indicators in Social Policy," in *The Environmental Crisis*, edited by Harold W. Helfrich, Jr. New Haven, Connecticut: Yale Univ. Press, 1970.

statistics as proudly as they announce the latest baseball scores. GNP is almost a household expression. What does it indicate? Why is it important?

The **gross national product** is a measure of the market value of goods and services that were produced during a specific time period. GNP is a "flow" concept. It is typically measured in terms of an annual rate. By analogy, a water gauge is a device designed to measure the amount of water that "flows" through a pipe each hour. Similarly, the GNP is a device designed to measure the market value of production that "flows" through the economy's factories and shops each year.

What Counts Toward GNP?

Since GNP seeks to measure only *current production*, it cannot be arrived at merely by summing up the totals on all of the nation's cash registers. Many transactions have to be excluded. What does GNP include and what does it exclude?

1. *Only Final Goods Are Counted.* A "final good" is a good in the hands of its ultimate user or consumer. Goods go through many stages of production. But GNP counts only the dollar market value of all final goods and services produced during a year.

Exhibit 6-1 will help clarify this important point. Before the final good, bread, is in the hands of the consumer, it will go through several stages of production. The farmer produces a pound of wheat and sells it to the miller for 15 cents. The miller grinds the wheat into flour and sells it to the baker for 25 cents. The miller's actions *added 10 cents* to the value of the wheat. The baker combines the flour with other ingredients, makes a loaf of bread, and sells it to the grocer for 45 cents. He *added 20 cents* to the value of the bread. The grocer stocks the bread on his shelves and provides a convenient location for consumers to shop. He sells the loaf of bread for 49 cents, *adding 4*

Exhibit 6-1   GNP and Stages of Production

Most goods go through several stages of production. This chart illustrates both the market value of a loaf of bread as it passes through the various stages of production (column 1) and the amount *added* to the value of the bread by each intermediate producer (column 2). GNP counts only the market value of the final product. Of course, the amount added by each intermediate producer (column 2) sums to the market value of the final product.

Stages of production	Market value of the product (dollars) (1)	Amount added to the value of the product (dollars) (2)
Stage 1: farmer's wheat	0.15	0.15
Stage 2: miller's flour	0.25	0.10
Stage 3: baker's bread (wholesale)	0.45	0.20
Stage 4: grocer's bread (retail)	0.49	0.04
Amount added to GNP		0.49

cents to the value of the final product. Only the market value of the final product—49 cents for the loaf of bread—is counted by GNP. The market value of the final product comprises the amount *added* to the value of the good at each stage of production—the 15 cents added by the farmer, the 10 cents by the miller, the 20 cents by the baker, and the 4 cents by the grocer.

If the market value of the product at each intermediate stage of production (for example, the sum of column 1) were added to GNP, double counting would result. GNP would overstate the value of the final products available to consumers. To avoid this problem, GNP includes only the value of final goods and services.

2. *Only Goods Produced during the Period Count.* Keep in mind that GNP is a measure of current production. Therefore, exchanges of goods or assets produced during a preceding period do not contribute to current GNP.

The purchase of a used car *produced* last year will not enhance current GNP. Neither will the sale of a "used" home, constructed five years ago. Production of these goods was counted at the time they were produced. Current sales and purchases of such items merely involve the exchange of existing goods. They do not involve current production of additional goods. Therefore, they are not counted.

Since GNP counts long-lasting goods like automobiles and houses when they are produced, it is not always an accurate gauge of what is currently being consumed. During an economic slowdown, few new durable assets will be produced. But the consumption services of durable goods produced and counted during another period will continue. During good times, there will be a rapid expansion in the production of durable assets, but their consumption services will be extended over a longer time period. Because of this cycle GNP tends to understate consumption services during a recession and overstate it during an economic boom.

Pure financial transactions are not counted toward GNP since they do not involve current production. Purchase or sale of stocks, bonds, and U.S. securities does not count. They represent exchange of current assets, not production of additional goods. Similarly, private gifts are excluded, as are government transfer payments such as welfare and Social Security payments. They do not enhance current production. Thus, it would be inappropriate to add them to GNP.

Dollars as the Common Denominator of GNP

In grammar school each of us was instructed about the difficulties of adding apples and oranges. Yet, this is precisely the nature of the aggregate measurement problem. Literally millions of different commodities and services are produced each year. How can the production of houses, movies, legal services, education, automobiles, dresses, heart transplants, astrological services, and many other items be added together?

These vastly different commodities and services have only one thing in common. Someone pays for each of them in terms of dollars. Dollars act as a common denominator, establishing a weighting scheme that makes it possible to add these different items. Production of an automobile adds 500 times as much to GNP as production of a briefcase because the new automobile sold for $5000, compared to $10 for the new briefcase. A heart transplant adds 50 times as much to GNP as an appendectomy because the heart transplant sold for $10,000 and the appendectomy for only $200. A fifth of whiskey adds more than a week's supply of household water because the purchaser paid more for the whiskey than the water.

Units of each good are weighted according to their selling price in terms of dollars. The total spending on all final goods produced during the year is then summed, *in dollar terms*, to obtain the annual GNP.

TWO WAYS OF MEASURING GNP

There are really two ways of measuring GNP. GNP can be calculated by adding up the total expenditures on final goods. In a sense, this method of calculating GNP focuses on the buyer's evaluation of the goods produced during the year. Purchasers buy particular goods because they value them more than the alternatives that are available. From the purchaser's viewpoint each product bought is expected to yield a benefit greater than its purchase price. Otherwise, the consumer would not have bought it. GNP, the sum of all of these expenditures on final products, will clearly understate the sum of the purchaser's evaluation of the goods.

GNP can also be calculated by adding up all the costs incurred in the production of final goods during the year. Goods, unlike manna, do not come from heaven. Production of goods involves human toil, wear and tear on machines, foregoing current consumption, risk, uncertainty, managerial responsibilities, and other of life's unpleasantries. In a market economy, resource owners voluntarily supply productive services in exchange for income. As seen through the eyes of resource owners, these income payments (for example, wages, interest, profits, etc.) must be in excess of the disutility associated with the production of the final goods and services. Otherwise, the resource owners would have been unwilling to supply their services. Thus, when GNP is calculated by adding up all the income payments to resource suppliers, it clearly overstates the disutility incurred in the production of final goods and services.

In the accounting sense the total payments to the factors of production, *including the producer's profit or loss,* must be equal to the sales price generated by the good. This is true for each good or service produced and it is also true for the aggregate economy. It is a fundamental accounting identity.

$$\begin{matrix} \text{Dollar flow of expenditures on} \\ \text{final goods} \end{matrix} = \textbf{GNP} = \begin{matrix} \text{dollar flow of the producer's costs} \\ \text{on final goods} \end{matrix}$$

Thus, GNP obtained by adding up the dollar value of final goods and services purchased will equal GNP obtained by adding up the total of all "cost" items, including producer's profits, associated with the production of final goods.

The Expenditure Approach

When the "expenditure" or "purchasing" approach is used to calculate GNP, there are four components of final goods purchased. The left side of Exhibit 6-2 indicates these four components of GNP in 1974.

Exhibit 6-2   Two Ways of Measuring GNP—1974 Data, Billions of Dollars

The left side shows the flow of purchase expenditures and the right side the flow of resource costs. Both of the procedures yield GNP.

Expenditure approach		Resource cost–income approach	
Personal consumption	877	Employee compensation	856
Durable goods	128	Proprietors' income	93
Nondurable goods	380		
Services	369	Rents	27
Gross private		Corporate profits	106
investment	209		
		Interest income	62
Fixed investment	195		
Inventories	14	Indirect business taxes (~~includes~~	133
		transfers)	
Government purchases	309		
		Depreciation (capital consumption)	120
Federal	117		
State and local	192		
Net exports	2		
Gross national product	1397	Gross national product	1397

SOURCE: U.S. Department of Commerce. These data are also available in the *Federal Reserve Bulletin*, which is published monthly.

1. *Consumption Purchases.* Personal consumption purchases are the largest component of GNP. Most consumption expenditures are for nondurable goods or services. Food, clothing, recreation, medical and legal services, education, and fuel would be included in this category. These items are used up or consumed in a relatively short time period. Durable goods, appliances and automobiles for example, comprise approximately one-sixth of all consumer purchases. These products will be enjoyed over a longer period even though they are fully counted at the time they are purchased.

2. *Investment Purchases.* Investment or capital goods provide a "flow" of future consumption or production service. They are not immediately "used" like food or medical services. A house is an investment good because it will provide a stream of services long into the future. Business plants and equipment are, of course, investment goods because they too will provide productive services in the future. Changes in business inventories are also classed as an investment good, since they will provide future consumer benefits.

Many goods possess both consumer and investment good characteristics. There is not always a clear distinction between the two. National accounting procedures have rather arbitrarily classed business purchases of final goods as investment and household purchases, except for housing, as consumption.

In 1974, total investment expenditures were $209 billion, including a $14 billion addition to inventory stock. The inventory component of investment fluctuates substantially. When business conditions are good, inventories are often low. On the other hand, during a recession inventories are sometimes high because firms are unable to sell all of their current production. Later, we will take a closer look at the role of inventory fluctuations, as many economists believe that they play an important role in the determination of economic instability.

3. *Government Purchases.* In 1974, federal, state, and local government purchases were $309 billion or 22 percent of total GNP. The purchases of state and local governments exceeded those of the federal government by a wide margin. The government component would include both investment and consumption services. Education, police protection, missiles, buildings, generation of electric power, as well as medical, legal, and accounting services would be included in the government component. Since transfer payments are excluded, government purchases will be substantially less than the size of the public sector.

4. *Net Exports.* Exports are domestic goods and services purchased by foreigners. Imports are foreign goods and services purchased domestically. We want GNP to measure only domestic production. Therefore, measuring GNP in terms of total purchases requires that we (a) add the dollar value of domestic goods purchased by foreigners and (b) subtract the dollar value of foreign goods purchased by Americans. For national accounting purposes we can then combine these two factors into a single entry *net exports*, where

$$\text{Net exports} = \text{total exports} - \text{total imports}$$

The net impact of the international sector is small. In 1974 the net exports of the United States were $2 billion.

The Relative Size of the Components

Of course, the components of GNP change in their relative importance from time to time. Exhibit 6-3 shows the average proportion of GNP accounted for by each of its

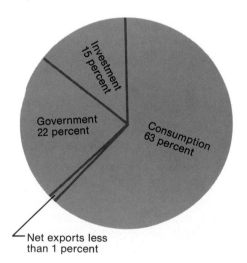

Exhibit 6-3   Major Components of GNP in the United States—1970–1974

The major components of GNP fluctuate annually, but the average proportion of each component in the early 1970s is indicated.

components in recent years. Personal consumption is, by far, the largest and most stable component of GNP. Historically, both private investment and government expenditures have fluctuated with business conditions, war, and international affairs. For the United States, the foreign sector is quite small.

The Resource Cost–Income Approach

As Exhibit 6-2 shows, rather than adding up the flow of expenditures on final goods and services, we could alternatively add up the flow of costs incurred in their production. Labor services play a very important role in the productive process. Thus it is unsurprising that employee compensation is the largest cost incurred in the production of goods and services.

Self-employed proprietors undertake the risk of owning their own business and simultaneously provide their own labor services to the firm. Their earnings in 1974 comprised 6.7 percent of GNP. Together, employees and self-employed proprietors accounted for two-thirds of GNP.

Machines, buildings, land, and other physical assets also contribute to the production process. Rents, corporate profits, and interest are payments to persons who either provided physical resources or the financial resources with which to purchase physical assets. Rents are a return to resource owners who permit another to utilize their assets during a time period. Corporate profits are compensation earned by stockholders, who both bear the risk of the business undertaking and provide the financial resources with which the firm purchases resources. Interest is a payment to parties who extend loans to producers.

Not all cost components of GNP result in an income payment to a resource supplier. There are two major indirect costs.

1. *Indirect Business Taxes.* These taxes are imposed on the sale of many goods and they are clearly passed on to the ultimate consumer. The sales tax is a clear example. When you make a $1 purchase in a state with a 5 percent sales tax, the purchase actually costs you $1.05. The $1 goes to the seller to pay his wage, rent, interest, and managerial costs. The 5 cents goes to the government. Indirect business taxes are directly included in the price of goods when GNP is calculated by the expenditure approach. They are a cost of doing business when looked at from the factor cost viewpoint.

2. *Depreciation.* Utilizing machines to produce goods causes them to wear out. Capital is "used up" in the production process. Depreciation of capital is a cost of producing current goods. In 1974 depreciation (sometimes called capital consumption allowance) amounted to $120 billion, almost 9 percent of GNP.

Depreciation and Net National Product

The inclusion of depreciation in GNP points out that it is indeed a "gross" rather than "net" measure of economic production. Since GNP fails to make an allowance for capital goods that wear out during the year, it overstates the net output of an economy.

The **net national product** (NNP) is a concept designed to correct this defi-ciency. NNP is the total market value of the goods and services available for society's consumption plus any net additions to the nation's capital stock. In accounting terms, net national product is simply GNP minus depreciation.

Since NNP counts only the net additions to the nation's capital stock, it will be less than GNP. Net investment—the additions to capital stock during the period—is always equal to gross investment minus depreciation. NNP counts only net investment.

GROSS NATIONAL PRODUCT OR GROSS NATIONAL COST?

As indicated by Exhibit 6-2, both the cost and the expenditure approach lead to the same estimate of GNP. They are simply two ways of calculating the same thing. Considering the two approaches together helps to keep the GNP in perspective. Looked at from the purchaser's viewpoint, it is indeed a gross national product. "Good things," as seen through the eyes of a purchaser, were produced and either households, investors, foreigners, or the government paid for them. But production also involves costs. Owners of labor services, capital goods, and managerial skills made the sacrifices necessary to bring the final products into existence. Looked at from the producer's viewpoint, GNP might better be termed a gross national cost because resource owners had to forego things in order to produce goods and services.

As we will emphasize below, GNP is not a measure of how much "better off" we are. There is both a positive and a negative side to it. Perhaps it might best be thought of as an index of current productive activity—activity that results in goods and services that we desire, but at an expense of work, waiting, risk, and depreciation that we do not desire.

FIVE PROBLEMS WITH GNP AS A MEASURING ROD

The GNP is not a perfect device for measuring current production and income. Some items are excluded, even though they would be properly classed as "current produc-tion." Sometimes production results in harmful "side effects" that are not fully accounted for. Comparison of GNP between two time periods raises additional prob-lems. In this section we will focus on some of the limitations and shortcomings of GNP as a measure of economic performance.

Watch Out for Price Changes

Were more goods and services produced in 1975 than 1970? How many more? We often like to compare GNP during two different years in order to answer such questions. But price changes make such comparisons more complex. GNP will increase if either (a) more goods and services are produced or (b) prices rise. Often both (a) and (b) will contribute to an increase in GNP. Since we are usually interested in comparing only the output or actual production during two different time intervals, money GNP must be adjusted for the change in prices.

How can we determine the magnitude of a general rise in prices during a period? The **consumer price index** (CPI), calculated monthly by the Bureau of Labor Statistics, is an estimate of how much it costs to buy the typical marketbasket purchased by middle income families in comparison to an earlier base year. This representative marketbasket includes eggs, bread, hamburger, housing, entertainment, medical services, and other goods, in the amounts that they are purchased by most middle income families. As prices rise, the cost of purchasing this representative market basket will go up, reflecting the higher prices.[2]

A base year is chosen and the CPI for that year is arbitrarily assigned a value of 100. For example, the base year is currently 1967. Thus the current cost of purchasing the typical marketbasket is compared to its cost in 1967. If it now costs $750 to purchase the same marketbasket that could have been purchased for $500 in the base year, the price index would be 150. A price index of 150 indicates that prices are now 50 percent higher than during the base year.

A price index is designed to reveal how rapidly prices, in general, are rising (or falling). The price index that is most often used to adjust GNP for price changes is called the **GNP deflator.** This price index contains a market basket of goods that is typical of the products that comprised the GNP during the base year. We can use the GNP deflator to measure GNP in dollars of constant purchasing power. If prices are rising, we simply deflate the **money GNP** during the latter period to account for the effects of the inflation. When GNP is stated in terms of constant dollars economists call it **real GNP.**

Exhibit 6-4 illustrates how real GNP is measured and why it is important to adjust for price changes. Money GNP increased 121 percent between 1964 and 1974. Does this mean that output more than doubled? Indeed not. The GNP deflator in 1974 was 170.2, compared to 108.8 in 1964. Prices rose by 56.4 percent during the decade. In deriving the real GNP for 1974 in terms of 1964 dollars, we deflate the 1974 money GNP for the rise in prices:

$$\text{Real GNP}_{74} = \text{money GNP}_{74} \times \frac{\text{price index}_{64}}{\text{price index}_{74}}$$

Exhibit 6-4   Changes in Prices and the Real GNP

Between 1964 and 1974, GNP more than doubled. But when the 1974 GNP was deflated to account for price increases, real GNP increased by only 41.3 percent.

	GNP (billions of dollars)	Price index (CPI)	Real GNP (1964 dollars)
1964	632	108.8	632
1974	1397	170.2	893
Percent increase	121.0	56.4	41.3

SOURCE: U.S. Department of Commerce. The GNP deflator was the price index used to adjust the money GNP to real dollars.

[2] While the CPI is the most widely used index of prices, another price index, "the GNP deflator," is most appropriate when adjusting GNP for price changes.

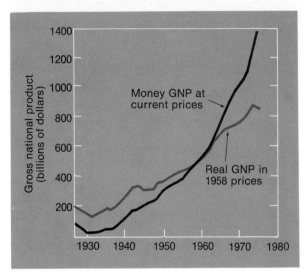

Exhibit 6-5 Price Changes and GNP

Because of inflation, money GNP reflecting current prices has grown more rapidly than GNP in constant (1958) dollars.
SOURCE: U.S. Department of Commerce.

Since prices were rising, the latter fraction was less than one. In terms of 1964 dollars, the real GNP in 1974 was $893 billion, 41.3 percent more than in 1964. Thus, while money GNP more than doubled, real GNP increased by only 41.3 percent.

Exhibit 6-5 shows both money and real GNP since 1929. Money GNP, reflecting rising prices, has increased more rapidly than real GNP. But only the latter reflects changes in the actual production of goods and services.

A change in money GNP tells us nothing about what happened to the rate of real production unless we also know what happened to prices. Money income could double, while production actually declined, if prices more than doubled. Money income could remain constant, while real GNP increases, if prices fall during a time period. Data on both money GNP and price changes are essential for a meaningful comparison of real income between two time periods.

Sins of Omission—Nonmarket Production

The GNP fails to count household production because it does not involve a market transaction. The household and child-rearing services of 50 million housewives are excluded. If the man of the house mows the yard, repairs the car, or paints his home, these labor services are excluded. Such nonmarket productive activities are sizable—10 or 15 percent of total GNP, perhaps more. Their exclusion results in some oddities of national income accounting.

For example, if a man marries his housekeeper, GNP will decline because the services of the housekeeper–wife will now be excluded. There is no longer a market transaction. If a wife hires a babysitter and enters the labor force, her actions have a double-barreled impact on GNP. GNP will rise because of (a) the amount she pays her babysitter plus (b) her on-the-job earnings.

The omission of many nonmarket productive activities makes comparisons over time and between countries at various stages of market development less meaningful. For example, more women are currently involved in *market* work than was true 30 years ago. There is widespread use of appliances today to perform functions previously performed by household labor. This fact, along with increasing market specialization, indicates that excluded household activities are less important today than 30 years ago. This means that our current GNP, even in real dollars, is overstated relative to the earlier period since a larger share of total production was previously excluded.

Similarly, GNP comparisons overstate the output of developed countries in contrast to underdeveloped ones. A larger share of the total production of underdeveloped countries originates in the household sector. For example, Mexican families are more likely than their U.S. counterparts to make their own clothing, raise and prepare their own food, provide their own child-rearing services, and even build their own homes. These productive labor services, originating in the household sector, will be excluded from GNP. Therefore, GNP in Mexico will be understated when compared to the United States.

More Sins of Omission—Production of "Bads"

Production and consumption of some economic goods also have harmful side effects that detract from the total availability of goods. GNP counts only work that was paid for or goods that were purchased. It does not count goods that were used up, destroyed, or diminished in value *if there is not a market transaction.* Junkpiles, garbage, cancer created by consumption of cigarettes, deterioration of minds and bodies because of the consumption of harmful drugs and alcohol, air and water pollution—all of these "disproducts" associated with current consumption are excluded because they did not go through the market. These and other undesirable items are clear deductions from our total available goods and resources. Their total might be called the gross national disproduct.

In order to balance the productive accounts properly, the unaccounted for disproduct should be subtracted from the total product. Net national product does make an allowance for the reduction in capital stock associated with this year's production. But what of the reduction in other assets and goods associated with current production? Both GNP and NNP exclude many of these items. Current depletion of natural resources, like depreciation of capital stock, reduces our ability to produce future goods. But this is not considered in our national product accounts, and neither is the reduction in the quality of air that we breathe nor the purity of our river waters.

Paradoxically, many of these "economic bads" will engender a higher GNP in the future. Cigarette smoking results in more cancer, thereby increasing GNP in the medical service sector! Crime results in the production of more police protection, household locks, legal services, and detention centers. All of these contribute to GNP. Air pollution results in increased purchases of air purifiers, house paints, and window washers. GNP rises even higher! Water pollution results in a greater cost of producing pure water. Automobile production and the move to suburban communities result in more congestion which will eventually lead to the construction of more highways. GNP will leap forward again!

Production of many goods generates harmful side effects. Such production either reduces the availability of a current good (for example, clean air, good health, noncongested environment) or our ability to produce future goods (for example, depletion of natural resources). GNP does not count these negative side effects. Thus it tends to overstate our "real ouput" of desired goods.

Could we estimate the gross national disproduct? It would be difficult because there are no market prices to register the approximate value that we place on these "economic bads." But increasingly many economists think we should try to account for some of them. For example, Arthur Burns, an economist and the chairman of the Board of Governors of the Federal Reserve System, has expressed a desire to see GNP adjusted "to account for the depreciation of our environment." Dr. Burns went on to indicate that if there was a proper recording of both the pluses and minuses of current production, our output and growth might be substantially lower than most people think. Revision of our methods of counting national output is clearly an exciting and potentially fertile field for tomorrow's economists.

Exclusion of Leisure and Human Costs

Simon Kuznets, the "inventor" of the GNP, indicated that the failure to include human cost fully was one of the grave omissions of national income accounting (see Outstanding Economist, page 105). GNP excludes leisure, a good that is valuable to each of us. One country might derive a $6000 per capita GNP with an average work week of 30 hours. Another might obtain the same per capita GNP by working 50 hours per week. In terms of total output, the first country has the greater production because it "produced" more leisure. Yet, GNP does not reflect this fact.

In addition, the human costs associated with the physical and mental strain of a job are excluded. These factors also serve to make longitudinal GNP comparisons less meaningful. On average, jobs today may be less physically strenuous, less exhaustive, but perhaps more monotonous than 30 years ago. Again, GNP fails to fully consider a relevant cost because there was not a market transaction.

The Problem of New and Changing Goods

GNP comparisons over time are made even more complex by the fact that new goods are always being introduced and the quality of existing goods changes. How meaningful is a comparison of per capita income (or production) between 1900 and 1970? In 1900 there were no airlines, television sets, commercial radios, automatic dishwashers or clothes dryers, automobiles, rock and roll stereo records, electric typewriters, refreshing airconditioners, or cartons of Coca Cola. On the other hand, there were plenty of open spaces, trees, noncongested (but rough) horse and coach roads, pure water rivers, hiking trails, cheap lands, areas with low crime rates, and wild blackberry bushes.

The bundles of goods available during the two time periods are vastly different. It does not really make any sense to talk about what it would have cost in 1900 to consume the typical bundle of goods consumed in 1970. One could not have purchased the typical 1970 "middle income bundle of goods" in 1900 even if he were a billionaire. Neither does it make much sense to talk about the current cost of consuming the typical 1900 bundle of goods. Yet, as we have already indicated, comparisons of money GNP are meaningless without the ability to adjust for price changes (or the cost of purchasing the typical bundle). When the *available* bundle of goods differs widely between two points in time or two countries, comparative GNP statistics lose much of their meaning.

As Exhibit 6-6 shows, the per capita real GNP in 1930 was less than two-fifths the 1974 level. Does this mean that, on average, Americans produced 2.5 times as many goods in 1974 as 1930? The answer is no. A lot of goods were available in 1930 that were not available in 1974, and vice versa. It would be impossible for us to have produced 2.5 times the *1930 output* in 1974. Similarly, it would have been impossible in 1930, to have produced two-fifths of the 1974 output. Our productive capacity has increased remarkably. But as to whether the 1974 productive capacity is two, three, or four times the 1930 level, GNP cannot give a definitive answer.

The introduction of new goods and changes in quality of current commodities present a problem even when comparing GNP between two periods that are separated by as little as a decade. There have been tremendous changes in the convenience packaging and prepreparation of foods since 1960. Heart transplants are an "invention" of the last decade. The quality of medical and dental surgery has changed significantly. Cable television has brought Monday night football (which a colleague of mine argues has done more to improve human welfare than any other change in the last decade) and other television programs to previously unserved areas. And perhaps most significantly, oral contraceptives have changed the "alternatives" available to an entire generation of women (and men) since the early 1960s.

The closer together the time periods under consideration, the more meaningful will be the comparisons of real GNP. But ours is a dynamic world. Change is the one

Exhibit 6-6   Per Capita Real GNP— 1930–1974

In 1974 per capital real GNP was 65 percent greater than in 1950, 2.25 times the 1940 level, and more than two and a half times the 1930 value. How meaningful are these numbers?

Year	Per capita real GNP (in 1974 dollars)
1930	2542
1940	2925
1950	3983
1960	4597
1970	5991
1974	6590

SOURCE: Derived from U.S. Department of Commerce data.

constant. Differences in the availability and quality of goods add to the shortcomings of GNP as a device to measure economic output at two different points in time or between two different countries.

WHAT THE GNP DOES *NOT* MEASURE

The GNP means many things to many people. To some, it serves as a proxy for what is wrong with the United States. To others, the clear majority, it means something nearly the opposite, though adherents of this view are often not quite sure what it does mean. One can sometimes learn a great deal about a thing by first understanding its limitations. GNP is like that.

GNP does not measure welfare, happiness, or even social progress. These subjective concepts are all influenced by many factors other than economic goods. Until recently, popular opinion often associated a rising GNP with progress and improvement in the quality of life. This is unfortunate because GNP was never intended to be an index of social progress.

GNP does not say anything about the usefulness of an activity. If individuals, corporations, or the government purchase the item, it counts as "product." A dollar spent for the schooling of an orphan child counts no more or no less than the alcoholic's dollar spent on another bottle of cheap wine. A dollar spent on advertising counts as much as a dollar spent on a kidney machine to preserve life. A dollar spent on a ticket to a football game counts as much as a dollar spent for admission to a concert by the Boston Symphony Orchestra. GNP makes no distinction. The only test is in whether someone wants the "good" or service enough to pay for it.

THE GREAT CONTRIBUTION OF GNP

What then does GNP measure? The great contribution of GNP (measured in constant prices) is its precision, despite all of its limitations, as an indicator of short-term changes in productive activity.

If short-term business fluctuations cannot be identified accurately, policies cannot be adopted that would reduce or eliminate their most harmful effects. GNP is the instrument that allows us to identify these short-run fluctuations. This contribution alone is sufficiently important to rank the GNP, in Professor Boulding's words, "as one of the great inventions of the twentieth century, probably almost as significant as the automobile. . . ."

OTHER RELATED INCOME MEASURES

While GNP and NNP are the most often quoted indices of economic performance, economists sometimes refer to three other related concepts. Exhibit 6-7 shows how each of them is derived. Remember the net national product measures the total flow of production that is available for consumption plus the net additions to the capital stock.

OUTSTANDING ECONOMIST: Simon Kuznets

This third recipient of the Nobel Prize in Economics and professor emeritus at Harvard is best known for his contribution to national income accounting. Born in czarist Russia, Professor Kuznets migrated to the United States in 1922. Five years later he had completed B.A., M.A., and doctoral degrees at Columbia University. In 1927, he became part of the National Bureau of Economic Research, where he began to pursue methods of measuring national economic performance. His monumental work, *National Income and Its Composition: 1919 to 1938*, was published in 1941.[3] In this book Professor Kuznets developed the concepts and outlined measurement procedures that led to our present-day national accounting techniques. More than any other person, he is the "father of the GNP." Without his contribution modern stabilization policy would be like a ship without a compass.

Professor Kuznets, a past president of the American Economic Association, recognized both the strengths and limitations of his measurement procedures. Writing in 1946, he stated "it (national income) gauges the net positive contribution to consumers' satisfaction in the form of commodities and services; the burdens of work and discomfort are ignored. . . . Working hours have been progressively shortened, and many of the heavier jobs, demanding stamina and endurance, are now performed by machinery. On the other hand, it is claimed that the monotony and dissatisfaction to the individual as an individual due to greater specialization and repetition of a few motions have increased, and that so has the nervous tension. . . . This aspect of economic activity . . . warns us against too easy an acceptance of the thesis that a high national income is the sole consideration in theory or the dominant motive in fact in a nation's economy."[4] Even the father of the GNP warns against excessive reliance on this single indicator of economic performance.

It measures the producton of goods and services of the economy, *valued at market prices.* But these prices include indirect business taxes which boost market prices but do not represent a cost of utilizing a factor of production. When economists subtract these indirect taxes from NNP, the resulting figure is called **national income.** Thus, national income represents net output valued at factor cost. National income can be derived in two ways. As Exhibit 6-7 shows it is NNP minus indirect business taxes. But it is also the income payments to all factors of production. Thus, the sum of employee compensation, interest, self-employment income, rents, and corporate profits also yields national income.

While national income represents the earnings of all resource owners, it is not the same as personal income. **Personal income** is the total of all income received by individuals—income with which they consume, save, and pay taxes. It differs from national income in two respects. First, some income is earned but not *directly* received.

[3] Simon Kuznets, *National Income and Its Composition: 1919 to 1938.* New York: National Bureau of Economic Research, 1941.

[4] Simon Kuznets, *National Income: A Summary of Findings.* New York: National Bureau of Economic Research, 1946, pp 127–128.

Exhibit 6-7 Five Indicators of Economic Performance

Gross National Product and Four Related Concepts—1973.

Economic indicator	Billions of Dollars
Gross national product	1397
Subtract: Depreciation	120
Net national product	1277
Subtract: Indirect business taxes	127
Business transfers	8
National income	1142
Subtract: Corporate profits	105
Social Security contributions	101
Add: Government transfer payments	135
Net interest paid	42
Dividends	33
Business transfer payments	5
Personal income	1151
Subtract: Personal taxes	171
Disposable income	980

SOURCE: *Survey of Current Business.*

Stockholders do not receive all of the income generated by corporations. Corporate tax takes a share. Additional profits are plowed back into the business, remaining undistributed to the stockholder. Social Security taxes are deducted from the employee's paycheck, forming a component of income earned but not directly received. In order to derive personal income, these factors must be subtracted.

Second, some income is received even though it was not earned during the current period. Government transfer payments, including Social Security and interest payments, are included in this category. By the same token, dividends received add to personal income, regardless of when they were earned. These components need to be added to yield personal income.

As anyone who has ever worked on a job knows, the amount of your paycheck is not equal to your salary. Personal taxes must be deducted. **Disposable income** is the income that is yours to do with as you please. It is simply personal income minus personal taxes.

Thus there are five alternative measures of national product and income—

(1) gross national product,
(2) net national product,
(3) national income,
(4) personal income,
(5) disposable income.

Each of the five measures something different, but they are all closely correlated. Exhibit 6-8 presents a graphic picture of the five income measures since World War II. As the graph illustrates, movement of one of the income measures nearly always

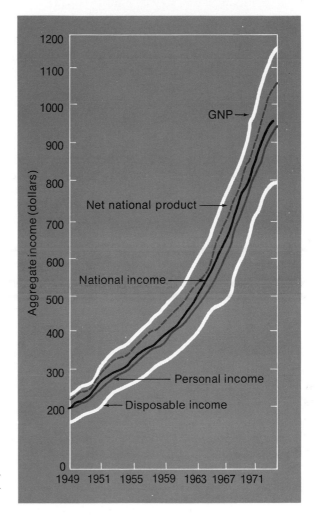

Exhibit 6-8   Five Measures of Productive Activity

GNP and the other four related aggregate income measures tend to move together.

parallels the movement of the other indicators. *Since the five measures move together,* economists often use only GNP or the terms "income," "output," or "aggregate production" when referring to the general movement of all five of the indicators of productive activity.

LOOKING AHEAD

GNP and the related income concepts provide us with a measure of economic performance. In the following chapter we will take a closer look at the movements of prices and real output in the United States and in other countries. We then proceed to analyze two competing theories about why economies are sometimes plagued with unemployment, rising prices, and economic instability.

CHAPTER LEARNING OBJECTIVES

1. Gross national product is a measure of the market value of the final goods and services that were produced during a specific time period.

2. Dollars act as a common denominator for GNP. Production of each "final product" is weighted according to its selling price. Alternatively, GNP could be calculated by adding up the dollar factor cost of producing the "final goods." The two methods will sum to an identical result.

3. When the "expenditure approach" is utilized there are four major components of GNP: **(a)** consumption, **(b)** investment, **(c)** government, and **(d)** net exports.

4. The major components of GNP as calculated by the factor cost approach are **(a)** wages and salaries, **(b)** self-employment income, **(c)** rents, **(d)** interest, **(e)** corporate profits, and **(f)** nonincome expenses—primarily depreciation and indirect business taxes.

5. GNP may increase because of an increase in either output or prices. Price indexes are used to measure the impact of price changes. Real GNP can be derived by adjusting money GNP to account for price changes between periods.

6. GNP is an imperfect measure of current production. It excludes household production. It fails to account for the negative side effects of current production such as air and water pollution, adverse impacts on health, depletion of natural resources, and other factors that do not flow through markets. It imperfectly adjusts for quality changes. The introduction of new goods tends to make GNP comparisons less meaningful when the typical bundle available differs widely.

7. Despite all of its limitations, the "invention" of the GNP is of tremendous importance because it is an accurate tool allowing us to quickly identify short-term economic fluctuations. Without a reliable indicator like the GNP, economic theory would be unable to determine the cause of economic slowdowns and economic policy would be helpless to do anything about them. Elimination of this limitation on both theory and policy is the great contribution of GNP.

8. Economists frequently refer to four other income measures that are related to GNP. The four are net national product, national income, personal income, and disposable income. All of these measures of income tend to move together.

IMPORTANT TERMS TO REMEMBER

Gross national product: The total market value of all "final product" goods and services produced during a period—usually a year.

Consumer price index: An indicator of the general level of prices. It attempts to compare the cost of purchasing the marketbasket bought by a typical consumer during a specific period with the cost of purchasing the same marketbasket during an earlier period.

Money GNP: GNP valued at the current prices of the period.

Real GNP: GNP in current dollars deflated for changes in the price index (PI). Mathematically, real $GNP_2 =$ money $GNP_2 \times PI_1/PI_2$. Thus, if prices have risen between periods 1 and 2, PI_1 divided by PI_2 would deflate the money GNP, since the fraction would be less than one.

Net national product: Gross national product minus a depreciation allowance for the wearing out of machines and buildings during the period.

Disposable income: Income available to individuals after personal taxes. It can either be spent on consumption or saved.

National income: Total income payments to owners of human (labor) and physical capital during a period. It is also equal to NNP minus indirect business taxes.

Personal income: Total income received by individuals which is available for consumption, saving, and payment of personal taxes.

GNP deflator: A price index that reveals the change in the cost of purchasing a market basket of goods that is representative of the gross national product during an earlier base period. Currently, the base year is 1958.

THE ECONOMIC WAY OF THINKING—DISCUSSION QUESTIONS

1. Why does a pound of beef add more to GNP than a pound of wheat? Does it reflect demand or costs? Comment.

2. Explain why the rate of growth in GNP in current dollars can sometimes be a misleading statistic.

3. What is the real GNP? How is it derived? Derive the change in real GNP between 1969 and 1974.

4. Indicate which of the following activities are counted as part of GNP—
   (a) the services of a housewife,
   (b) Frank Murry's purchase of a 1972 Chevrolet,
   (c) Frank Murry's rental payments on a 1972 Chevrolet,
   (d) the purchase of 100 shares of AT&T stock,
   (e) interest on a bond issued by AT&T,
   (f) family lawn services provided by a 16-year-old,
   (g) family lawn services purchased from the neighbor's 16-year-old who has a lawn mowing business,
   (h) a multibillion dollar discovery of natural gas in Oklahoma,
   (i) deterioration of the water quality of Lake Michigan.

5. Why might the GNP be a misleading indicator of changes in output between 1900 and 1975 in the United States? Of differences in output between the United States and Mexico?

6. "The GNP counts the product of steel but not the disproduct of air pollution. It counts the product of auto production, but not the disproduct of 'blight' due to junkyards. It counts the product of cigarette smoking, but not the disproduct of a shorter life expectancy due to cancer. Until we can come up with a more reliable indicator, we cannot tell if economic welfare is progressing or retrogressing." Explain why you either agree or disagree with this view.

7

UNEMPLOYMENT, INFLATION, AND BUSINESS CYCLES

The standard of living in the United States and most other Western nations has improved substantially during the last two centuries. But this progress has not been without periods of high unemployment and rising prices. Why are unemployment rates sometimes high? What makes prices rise rapidly? Why does our economy experience recurring periods of prosperity and economic slowdown? In this chapter we will analyze the historical record and discuss alternative theories about these questions.

Micro- and Macroeconomics

In Chapter 3 we discussed how the forces of supply and demand interact to influence the output level of a *specific* commodity. Analysis that focuses on a single commodity, or at most a single industry, is referred to as microeconomics. As Professor Abba Lerner puts it, "**microeconomics** consists of looking at the economy through a microscope, as it were, to see how the millions of cells in the body economic—the individuals or households as consumers, and the individuals or firms as producers—play their part in the working of the whole organism."[1] We will return to microeconomics in later sections.

The next nine chapters instead will focus on macroeconomics. **Macroeconomics,** like microeconomics, is about markets, prices, and determination of equilibrium, *but* unlike microeconomics, *the markets in macroeconomics are highly aggregated*. For example, in macroeconomics we consider the labor market as a single market, even though we recognize that persons of vastly different skills, training, experience, and education are lumped together in this market. Similarly, in macroeconomics we deal with the market for current goods and services as a single entity, even though this market contains commodities ranging from apples to education, from houses to paper dolls. Macroeconomics deals with the overall picture—what determines the level of aggregate income, output, and employment.

[1] Abba P. Lerner, "Microeconomic Theory," Chapter III in *Perspectives in Economics*, edited by A. A. Brown, E. Neuberger, and M. Palmatier. New York: McGraw-Hill, 1968, p. 29.

SWINGS IN THE ECONOMIC PENDULUM

During the last 40 years, real GNP has grown at a rate of approximately 3.5 percent annually. But the growth rate has not been steady. One of the major objectives of macroeconomics is to determine the cause of fluctuations in aggregate markets, and thereby suggest policy alternatives that would reduce economic instability.

Exhibit 7-1 illustrates the fluctuation in the real GNP during the last 40 years. The annual growth of aggregate real output has exceeded 10 percent for several short periods. In several other years, output as measured by real GNP has actually declined. In 1937 it fell by nearly 5 percent. From 1929 to 1939, a time period referred to as the Great Depression, economic growth came to a complete standstill. Between 1929 and 1933, real GNP actually declined by more than 25 percent! The 1929 level of real GNP was not reached again until 1939. Since the 1930s, growth has been more stable, but there are still economic ups and downs. World War II was characterized by a rapid expansion of GNP which was followed by a decline after the war. The real GNP did not reach its 1944 level again until 1951 though the output of *consumer* goods did increase significantly in the years immediately after the war as the conversion was made to a peacetime economy. The years 1954, 1958, 1960, 1970, and 1974 were characterized by downswings in economic activity. Upswings in real GNP came in 1950, 1955, most of the 1960s, and 1972–1973.

Not only have movements in the aggregate product market been uneven, but so have conditions in the aggregate labor market. A key measure of labor market conditions, the unemployment rate, has fluctuated widely during the last 40 years. In the midst of the Great Depression, one out of every four persons in the labor force was looking for a job but unable to find one. With the expansion associated with the wartime economy of the 1940–1945 period, unemployment rates fell sharply. In 1940, 15 percent of the civilian labor force was unemployed. During the 1943–1945 period the rate fell to less

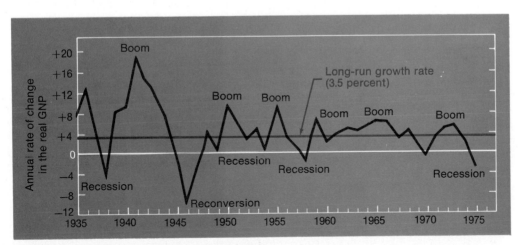

Exhibit 7-1   Instability in the Growth of Real GNP

Note that while fluctuations are present, the periods of positive growth outweigh periods of declining real income. The long-run real GNP in the United States has grown approximately 3.5 percent annually.

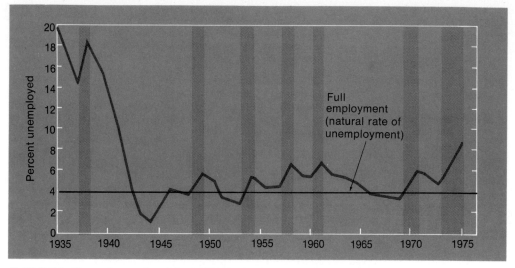

Exhibit 7-2   Unemployment and Instability in the Aggregate Labor Market

Shaded areas represent periods of business recessions as defined by the National Bureau of Economic Research.

than 2 percent (see Exhibit 7-2). Since World War II, the unemployment rate has been more stable, but nevertheless significant unevenness continues. The unemployment rate reached 6 percent in 1949 but fell to 3 percent by 1952. It jumped from 4.3 percent in 1957 to 6.8 percent in 1959. After a slight decline during the 1959–1960 period it again reached 6.7 percent in 1961. During most of the 1960s, the rate declined steadily until it reached a low of near 3 percent in 1968. But it again climbed to near 6 percent in the early 1970s. After a decline to less than 5 percent in 1972–1973, the unemployment rate jumped to nearly 9 percent in 1975. Conditions in the aggregate labor market, like those of the aggregate product market, have been characterized by instability.

A HYPOTHETICAL BUSINESS CYCLE

The historical data show that periods of economic expansion and low unemployment rates have traditionally been followed by economic slowdown and contraction. During the slowdown, real GNP grows at a slower rate, if at all. Unemployment rises. Other Western nations have experienced similar economic ups and downs.

Economists refer to these fluctuations in economic conditions as business cycles. As the term implies, a **business cycle** is a period of up and down motion in aggregate measures of current economic output and income. Exhibit 7-3 illustrates a hypothetical business cycle. When most businesses are operating at capacity level, the real GNP is growing rapidly, and the unemployment rate is low, **boom** conditions exist. Boom conditions result in a high level of economic activity. As aggregate business conditions slow, the economy begins the contraction phase of a business cycle. During the

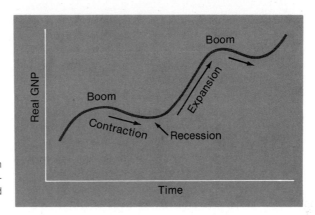

Exhibit 7-3 The Business Cycle

In the past, ups and downs have often characterized aggregate business activity. Despite these fluctuations, an upward trend in real GNP is usually observed.

contraction, the sales of most businesses will fall, real GNP will grow at a slow rate or perhaps decline, and unemployment in the aggregate labor market will rise. When economic activity is low and unemployment is high, these conditions are referred to as a **recession,** or if they are quite serious a **depression.** As we have already seen, depression conditions dominated the 1930s. We experienced recessions in 1949, 1954, 1958, 1960–1961, 1971, and again in 1974–1975. After the recession reaches bottom and economic conditions begin to improve, the economy begins an expansionary stage. During the *expansion* phase, business sales will rise, GNP will grow rapidly, and the unemployment rate will decline. The expansion blossoms into another boom. But the boom will eventually peter out and turn to a contraction, beginning the cycle anew.

Our hypothetical cycle indicates steady and smooth movement from boom to recession and back again to the boom. In the real world, cycles are not nearly so regular or predictable. As demonstrated by Exhibits 7-1 and 7-2, past periods of expansion and contraction have been irregular and they have not exhibited the smooth continuity of our hypothetical cycle. Certain phases of the cycle have sometimes been quite long. The 1930s were characterized by prolonged depression. During the 1950s, the expansionary phases were short and an extended boom was never really attained. In contrast, expansion and prolonged boom characterized the 1960s. Nevertheless, the phases of expansion, boom, contraction, and recession are still present.

Despite the cyclical movements, the trend in real GNP in the United States and most other industrial nations has clearly been upward. During the last 40 years the long-run growth rate in real GNP has been approximately 3.5 percent (see Exhibit 7-1). In some years growth has been greater, and in others less, than the long-run trend. But years of positive growth clearly outweigh the periods of falling real GNP.

THREE DIFFERENT VIEWS OF THE BUSINESS CYCLE

What are the causes of economic instability? Why does the unemployment rate fluctuate up and down? Since economists are not in complete agreement about this question, we would like to outline three alternative theories of economic instability.

1. *Classical View.* Most pre-1930 economists, sometimes referred to as classical economists, thought that economic contraction and high unemployment comprised a temporary phenomenon. They thought that a business recession indicated only a temporary disequilibrium in the labor market. Wages were above the market equilibrium level; therefore there was an excess of supply relative to demand. Eventually, this excess supply would lead to a reduction in wages, resulting in an increase in the quantity demanded of labor. At the lower wage rate employment would increase and expansion of economic activity would result. Lower wages were the solution to a recession.

What caused the disequilibrium wage rate initially? The classical economists had several answers to this question. In a dynamic economy, the demand for both goods and productive factors such as labor is constantly changing. These changes will result in an increase in demand for some types of labor and a decline for others. The wage rate may not adjust instantaneously. Therefore, we should expect some labor markets to be in disequilibrium temporarily.

In addition, inventions and business innovations have an impact on the level of business activity. Technological advances, such as the steam engine, cotton gin, railroad, telephone, internal combustion engine, and similar inventions, have a shock effect on the economy. These inventions can and did result in a vast expansion of important sectors of our economy. They often opened up opportunities in other sectors that had previously been restricted. For example, the railroad expanded not only the transportation industry but also agriculture, commercial trade, and many other sectors of the economy.

Many pre-1930 economists stressed the importance of technological advancements as the source of economic expansion. They thought that economic expansion would increase the demand for labor, thereby causing wages to rise. But they also thought that the higher wage rates would eliminate the excess demand for labor, and unemployment would return to normal levels. Similarly, during a period of economic contraction, wage rates would fall, reducing the *temporarily* high unemployment rates.

For the classical economists, wage flexibility was an automatic pilot that would always assure economic recovery and a return to full employment. They recognized the cyclical nature of economic activity, but wage flexibility would always assure the return to full employment. Recessions were always temporary.

The prolonged depression of the 1930s shook the faith of economists in the classical theory. Wage rates fell, but the economy continued to stagnate. Up to 25 percent of the labor force was unemployed, plants closed down or operated at 50 percent capacity. Businesses went bankrupt. Trade slowed to a standstill. And these depressing economic conditions continued for a decade. Falling wages did not lead to economic recovery! The Great Depression discredited the classical theory among most economists.

2. *Keynesian View.* In 1936 an English economist, John Maynard Keynes, wrote his *General Theory of Employment, Interest and Money.*[2] Professor Keynes became the

---

[2]John Maynard Keynes, *General Theory of Employment, Interest and Money.* 1936. Reprint. New York: Harcourt, 1965.

most influential economist of the twentieth century. His ideas and writings still exert a dominant influence on most economists today.

Keynes attacked the classical idea that falling wage rates would eventually lead the economy back to full employment. He argued that wage reductions lead to falling incomes. Consumers without purchasing power are unable to demand goods and services from producers. In the absence of consumer demand, producers have no incentive to invest in capital equipment or expand their plant capacity. Far from improving matters, falling wages will reduce consumer income and aggregate demand, causing the recession (or depression) to continue.

Declining wages, the automatic mechanism that the classical economists thought would *eventually* restore full employment, was part of the problem, not part of the solution! Unemployment need not be a temporary phenomenon, as envisoned by the classicists, but it could continue indefinitely at a high level. The market mechanism, if left to its own devices, would not necessarily assure full employment.

For the Keynesian, the primary source of economic instability is the instability in the level of private capital investment. When business is good, investors respond by expanding their operations. The increased investment leads to still more expansion and economic boom. Expansionary psychology permeates the economy. But eventually the productive capacity catches up with the demand of consumers, and investment declines or increases at a slower rate. The reduction in the rate of investment reduces consumer income which further reduces the demand for capital. Business conditions worsen because the investment stimulant is absent.

The classical economists thought that investment was *primarily* stimulated by a fall in the interest rate. Lower interest rates made financial capital cheaper and stimulated investment. Keynes posed this question, "Why would a businessman want to invest and expand, if he could not sell his product because of insufficient consumer income to purchase it?" During a business contraction, there would be few new investment opportunities that would be profitable. Businessmen would reduce their capital expenditures, and this reduction in investment would cause the recession to worsen. Even at very low interest rates investors would be unwilling to expand their businesses because there is so little consumer demand for goods.

The solution to the recession, from the Keynesian viewpoint, is straightforward —something must be done to stimulate aggregate demand and in turn investment. This could be done directly by increasing government spending, or indirectly by reducing taxes, thereby stimulating consumer spending. If a recession set in, proper government action could pull the economy back toward expansion. But in the absence of proper policy the recession or depression could last for a long, long time.

3. *The Monetarist View.*   While instability in private investment is the villain of the Keynesian theory, instability in the money supply is the villain of the monetarists. In a modern exchange economy, money plays a very significant role because it is a part of almost every transaction. Consumers buy food, clothing, housing, transportation, and many other commodities with money. Individuals sell labor services and other productive resources for money.

The monetarist view stresses that *changes* in the money supply, induced by improper public policy, exert an important influence on the stability of the economy. When the monetary authorities increase the total supply of money in the economy, they stimulate consumer demand. Consumers with more money will spend more. An increase in the supply of money will cause a higher level of consumer demand, stimulate investment, and lead to an economic boom. But once the economy has approached full employment, further increases in demand will primarily lead to higher prices. Full employment sets a limit on how much the *real* output of an economy can be stimulated by monetary expansion.

While monetary expansion acts as a stimulant to the economy, a reduction in the supply of money is a depressant. A decline of the money stock will cause consumers to reduce their spending. The demand for goods will decline and investors will become pessimistic about future business prospects. A low level of consumer spending and producer investment will result from the reduction in the stock of money.

The major problem of the business cycle, in the view of the monetarists, arises because the monetary planners, historically, have followed an uneven course. They have often expanded the stock of money too rapidly, causing inflation. Then in an effort to fight inflation, they have tended to contract the rate of monetary growth too much, causing the recession. Monetary instability, in the view of the monetarist, is the primary source of economic instability.

Most monetarists, unlike the earlier classicists, recognize that wages and prices are often "sticky," if not completely inflexible, downward. A reduction in the supply of money does *not* lead to a rapid fall in wages and prices. Markets do not adjust instantaneously. Monetarists believe that money does more than simply determine the price level. It exerts a direct impact on economic activity as well.

In contrast to the Keynesian view, the monetarists do not believe that the market is inherently unstable. They believe that economic instability stems primarily from inappropriate monetary policy. The solution to the business cycle, in the monetarist's view, requires that action be taken to halt the stop–go policy of the central monetary planners—particularly the actions of the Federal Reserve System. Monetarists argue that instability would be vastly reduced if we simply expanded the money supply at a constant annual rate—3 percent, for example—regardless of current economic conditions.

THE NORMAL RATE OF UNEMPLOYMENT

Exhibit 7-4 presents data on the unemployment rate for selected Western countries in 1965, 1969, and 1973. The rates vary considerably between countries but one fact is of particular note. No country had a zero unemployment rate. This was true during the last decade and it has always been true for an economy where employees can voluntarily move from job to job.

In a dynamic economy, at any point in time, some industries will be expanding and others contracting. The expanding industries will be seeking to hire additional employees, while the contracting ones will be laying off workers. In addition, some new workers will constantly be entering or re-entering the labor force. Others will be leaving either temporarily or permanently.

Exhibit 7-4   Unemployment Rates—An International Comparison

| | Unemployment rate[a] | | |
Country	1965	1969	1973
United States	4.5	3.5	4.9
Australia	1.3	1.5	2.1
Canada	3.9	4.7	5.6
France	1.8	2.1	3.1
West Germany	0.3	0.8	1.1
Great Britain	2.3	3.7	4.1
Italy	4.0	3.7	3.8
Japan	1.2	1.1	1.3
Sweden	1.2	1.9	2.5

SOURCE: *The Statistical Abstract of the United States—1975.*

[a] The official unemployment figures are adjusted to a common base to permit comparison.

Furthermore, workers already in the labor force are constantly on the move. In the United States in 1973 there were 90 million Americans in the labor force. Approximately one out of every nine workers changed jobs at least once during the year. More than 16 million workers reported themselves as unemployed at some time during the course of the year. More than 6 million experienced temporary unemployment because they quit their last job. There was a constant flow of workers from job to job, from employment to unemployment, and back to employment. Given these dynamic changes that are constantly occurring in the labor market, some unemployment will inevitably result.

Frictional Unemployment

Unemployment that is caused by the constant change in the labor market is called **frictional unemployment.** Frictional unemployment occurs because (1) employers are not fully aware of all available workers and their job qualifications and (2) available workers are not fully aware of the jobs being offered by employers.

The basic cause of frictional unemployment is imperfect information. The number of job vacancies may match up with the number of persons seeking employment. The qualifications of the job seekers may even meet those of firms seeking employees. But frictional unemployment will still occur because it is costly—it takes time—for the qualified employees to identify firms demanding their services, and vice versa.

Employers looking for a new worker will seldom hire the first applicant that walks into their employment office. They will want to find the "best available" worker to fill their opening. It is costly to hire workers who perform poorly. Sometimes it is even costly to terminate their employment. So employers will search—they will expend time and resources trying to screen applicants and choose only those that have the desired qualifications.

Similarly, persons seeking employment will not take the first job available. They too will search among potential alternatives, seeking the best job available as they perceive it. They will undergo search cost (submit to job interviews, contact employment services, and so on) in an effort to find out about available opportunities. As the employees find out about more and more potential job alternatives, the benefits of *additional* job search will diminish. Eventually, the unemployed worker will decide that the benefit of additional job search is not worth the cost and he will choose the "best" of his current alternatives. But all of this takes time and during that time the employee will be contributing to the frictional unemployment of the economy.

Policies that influence the costs and benefits of searching will influence the level of frictional unemployment. If the job seeker's search cost is reduced, he will spend more time searching. For example, higher unemployment benefits would make it less costly to continue looking for a more preferred job. Thus, an increase in unemployment benefits would cause employees to expand their search time, thereby increasing the rate of frictional unemployment. In contrast, an improvement in the flow of information about jobs would reduce the benefits derived from additional search time. Other things constant, improved methods of disseminating job information among unemployed workers would allow workers to shop among job alternatives more quickly. Thus, most economists believe that a national job information data bank would reduce search time and lower frictional unemployment.

Structural Unemployment

Structural unemployment occurs because of changes in the basic characteristics of the economy that prevent the "matching up" of the available employees with the available jobs. Employment openings continue to exist because the unemployed workers do not possess the necessary qualifications to fill them.

There are many causes of structural unemployment. Dynamic changes in demand may change skill requirements necessary for jobs. Some skills may become obsolete, while others are in short supply relative to demand. An influx of younger, less experienced workers, who fail to meet the requirements for the existing job openings, could cause structural unemployment. Dramatic shifts in defense and other government expenditures often promote excess demand and job vacancies in one area, while generating excess supply and unemployment in another location. Institutional factors such as minimum wage legislation might reduce the incentive of business firms to offer on-the-job training that would improve the matchup between the existing job openings and the available employees.

When structural changes result in a declining demand for employees with a specialized skill, temporary unemployment results. Initially, structurally unemployed workers will be reluctant to accept a lower wage in other lines of work. For a time, they are likely to expect conditions to reverse themselves. For example, when the West Coast aerospace industry was severely depressed because of a decline in demand by the government for defense and space services, these workers were not well suited for the available jobs in other industries. It is not easy for an aero engineer to accept the fact that his training will no longer qualify him for a high paying scientific research job.

Eventually many such workers changed careers, undertook retraining, and suffered sharp reductions in income. But this took place only after substantial periods of unemployment had convinced workers that their previous training would no longer qualify them for a high paying job in their current line of work.

The Concept of Full Employment

At any point in time there will be some **normal** or "natural" **rate of unemployment** in a dynamic voluntary exchange economy. This normal unemployment rate results from both frictional and structural factors. The expression "normal rate of unemployment" is not meant to convey the impression that the rate is immutably fixed by nature. On the contrary, the normal unemployment rate reflects both dynamic change and public policy.

By now it should be obvious that some unemployment results because employees take time to shop among job alternatives, while employers shop among the available workers. But other dynamic factors, such as changes in the composition of the labor force, may also influence the normal rate of unemployment. For example, younger workers, in their search to find a desirable permanent occupation, quite reasonably change jobs more often than older employees. An increase in youthful workers, as a percentage of the total labor force, would cause the normal rate of unemployment to rise.

Man-made institutions will also affect the normal unemployment rate. For example, policies that alter the availability of information about jobs, the opportunity cost of continuing to search for a job, and the incentive of employers to offer (and employees accept) on-the-job training will influence the normal unemployment rate. As we proceed, we will take a closer look at public policy in this area.

Therefore, in a dynamic economy, resources, including labor, will not be 100 percent employed. Economists define **full employment** as the level of employment that results when the unemployment rate is normal, considering both frictional and structural factors. Currently, most economists believe that full employment is present when between 95 and 96 percent of the labor force is employed. Full employment implies that, given the current institutional and structural characteristics of the economy, it would be impossible to *maintain* the unemployment rate below its normal rate (for example, below 4 or 5 percent) for extended periods of time.

CYCLICAL UNEMPLOYMENT

Cyclical unemployment results when the sales of most businesses decline, GNP contracts, and there is a decline in demand for labor *in the aggregate*. Previously we saw that when there was a decline in demand in some industries and expansion in others, some frictional unemployment would arise since workers and employers have imperfect information about job openings and potential employees. As Exhibit 7-5 illustrates, imperfect information also helps explain why a decline in the aggregate demand for labor results in unemployment. When the demand for labor declines, some

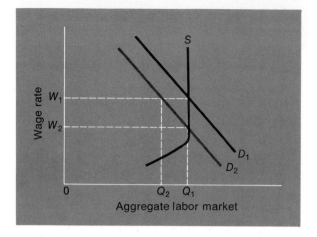

Exhibit 7-5 Unemployment and a Decline in Aggregate Demand

A decline in aggregate demand—the shift from D_1 to D_2— would reduce the level of employment from Q_1 to Q_2 unless the wage rate fell from W_1 to W_2. Workers, because they expect to find jobs at W_1, will not initially accept the lower wage rate. Cyclical unemployment of Q_1 minus Q_2 will result.

workers will be laid off (or fail to be hired) at the existing wage rate. Initially, workers are not sure whether they are being laid off because of a shift in demand away from their previous employer or a general decline in aggregate demand. Not realizing how drastically their job prospects have deteriorated, they will continue unsuccessfully searching for a job at the old wage rate W_1. Unemployment will rise.

If the unemployment were merely frictional, workers would soon be able to find jobs at or near their previous wage rate. But since the unemployment is because of a decline in aggregate demand, the search of many workers for jobs at the old wage will be fruitless. Their duration of unemployment will be longer. As the unemployment continues, eventually workers will reduce their expectations and be willing to take some cut in wages. But all of this takes time. By the time employees reduce their expectations, aggregate demand may have declined even more and the high level of cyclical unemployment may continue or even worsen.

After aggregate demand stops declining, there will be a gradual reduction in cyclical unemployment, as worker expectations about job prospects begin to coincide with reality. The greater the reduction in aggregate demand, the greater will be the reduction in wages necessary to eliminate the cyclical unemployment. Therefore, substantial reductions in aggregate demand will lead to sharp increases in the unemployment rate and long periods of unemployment above the "normal rate."

Macroeconomics is primarily concerned with cyclical unemployment. We will investigate potential sources of cyclical unemployment and consider policy alternatives to reduce it. But that must wait for a later chapter.

ACTUAL AND POTENTIAL GNP

When business conditions are such that cyclical unemployment is present, the economy will not produce up to its full potential. Some resources that could be productively employed will be underutilized because of the low level of aggregate demand. Actual GNP will be less than the potential.

MYTHS OF ECONOMICS
"Unemployed resources would not exist if the economy were operating efficiently."

Nobody likes unemployment. Certainly extended unemployment can be a very painful experience. However, not all unemployment reflects waste and inefficiency. Time spent unemployed and in job searching can sometimes yield a high return to both society and the unemployed worker. Since information is scarce, a person will not be immediately aware of available job opportunities as soon as he begins looking for a job. One acquires information about the available alternatives by shopping. On a matter as important as one's employment, you would certainly expect individuals to spend a significant amount of time shopping, as they attempt to seek out their most preferred job opportunity. Oftentimes, this shopping can be accomplished easiest (cheapest) while unemployed. Thus, job seekers usually do not just take any job that happens to be available. They search, all the while acquiring valuable information, because they believe that the searching will lead to a more preferred job opportunity.

Similarly, employers shop when seeking to purchase labor services. They, too, acquire information about available employees that will help them select employees that are most suited to their needs. The shopping of employees and employers results in some unemployment, but it also communicates information that leads to an efficient matchup between employee characteristics (including the preferences of workers) and job qualifications.

Parallel "unemployment" results in the rental housing market. Dynamic factors are also present in this market. New housing structures are brought onto the market, older structures depreciate and wear out. Households are constantly moving from one community to another. Within the same community, renters will move among housing accommodations, as they seek housing quality, price, and location that best fit their preferences. As in the employment market, information is imperfect. Thus, renters will shop among the available accommodations, seeking the most for their housing expenditures. Similarly, landlords will search among renters, seeking to rent their accommodations to those who value them most highly. "Frictional unemployment" of houses is inevitable. But does it indicate inefficiency? No. It simply results because people are seeking to acquire information that will result in an efficient matchup between housing units and the preferences of renters.

Of course, some unemployment, particularly cyclical unemployment, is indicative of inefficiency. But in a dynamic world, unemployment of labor and other resources results because buyers and sellers are shopping for more preferred alternatives. This shopping, including shopping while unemployed, communicates information to decision-makers that will promote a more efficient matchup between applicants and job openings than would occur if it were absent.

Exhibit 7-6 illustrates the record of the U.S. economy since 1954. During the 1950s the unemployment rate was above the "full employment" level. Excess capacity was present because the level of aggregate demand was insufficient to maintain full employment (that is, approximately a 4 percent unemployment rate). The gap between

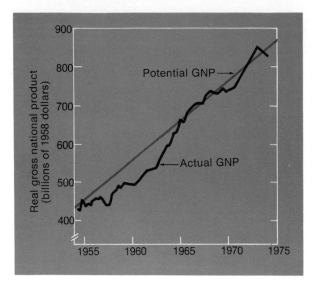

Exhibit 7-6 Actual and Potential GNP

The graph indicates the gap between the actual and potential GNP for the 1954–1974 period. The gap resulted because the resources of the economy were not being fully utilized.

potential and actual GNP was particularly large during the recessions of 1954, 1958, and 1961. During the 1960s the gap narrowed, as the economy approached capacity.

QUESTIONS AND ANSWERS ABOUT INFLATION

When President Ford took office in 1974, he announced that inflation was our number one problem. What do economists know about inflation, its cause, and its cure? Suppose that you were questioning an economist about inflation. What would you be able to learn from him? Let us listen in and find out.[3]

STUDENT: What is inflation?

ECONOMIST: It is a rise in the general price of the goods and services that we purchase. Of course, even when the general level of prices is stable, some prices will be rising and others falling. But during an inflation, the rising prices outweigh those that are falling. Because of the higher prices (on average), a dollar bill will purchase less than it previously would.

STUDENT: How can we measure inflation?

ECONOMIST: The consumer price index is the most common means of measuring inflation. The CPI is an index of what it costs to purchase the typical marketbasket chosen by an urban family of four. As the prices of things bought by the average family rise—food, housing, clothing, entertainment, medical care, recreation, and other items that most of us buy—it will become more expensive to purchase the hypothetical

[3] We will use this question and answer format in several places throughout the text. The teaching experience of the author suggests that it can sometimes help the student pinpoint issues.

typical marketbasket. For example, if it costs 5 percent more this year, in comparison with last, to purchase this typical marketbasket, we would say that the annual rate of inflation was 5 percent. Or perhaps some might say the cost of living has risen 5 percent.

STUDENT: How rapidly have prices risen in the United States?

ECONOMIST: That depends on what time period we are talking about. Prices have not always risen. Prices fell during the early part of the 1930s. As Exhibit 7-7 shows, prices declined, on average, nearly 7 percent each year during the 1929–1933 period. But since that period, prices have risen most of the time. They rose quite rapidly during World War II and again during the Korean War. During the 1968–1973 period prices rose at an annual rate of approximately 5 percent each year. In 1974 alone, the consumer price index rose nearly 11 percent. Clearly, the rate of inflation has accelerated upward during the last decade.

STUDENT: How rapidly have prices risen in other countries?

ECONOMIST: Exhibit 7-8 presents the answer to that question. Beginning in the late 1960s the rate of inflation rose significantly in Western Europe, Canada, Japan, and the United States. Whereas during the 1955–1968 period, most of these countries experienced rising prices of 2 to 4 percent, for the 1969–1974 period their annual inflationary rates jumped to between 5 and 10 percent. As Exhibit 7-8 shows, inflation has been a way of life for some time in South American countries such as Argentina, Brazil, and Chile.

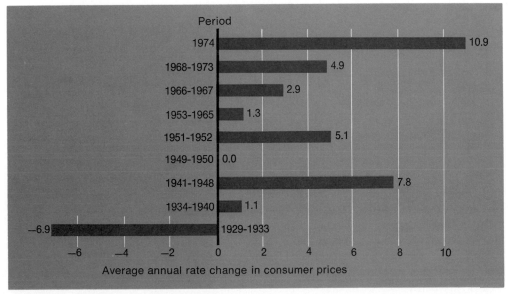

Exhibit 7-7   Inflation in the United States

SOURCE: Bureau of Labor Statistics.

Exhibit 7-8   Worldwide Inflation

Country	Compound annual rate of change in consumer prices	
	1955–1968	1969–1974
Chile	28	225
Argentina	27	32
Brazil	38	21
Columbia	10	15
Ecuador	2	11
Peru	9	9
France	5	7
West Germany	2	6
Italy	3	8
Japan	4	10
Switzerland	2	7
United Kingdom	3	9
Canada	2	5
United States	2	6

SOURCE: International Monetary Fund.

The Gainers and Losers from Inflation

STUDENT: Who does inflation help and who does it hurt?

ECONOMIST: It is useful to think of inflation as a tax on money and future contractual money receipts. Inflation reduces the purchasing power of money, just as a tax on cash balances would. If you held an average cash balance of $500 during the year and the annual rate of inflation was 10 percent, at the end of the year your $500 would purchase approximately the same amount of goods and services as $450 at the beginning of the year. The purchasing power of your cash balances has been reduced just as surely as if prices had been stable and the government had levied a $50 tax on your average bank balance.

Inflation also acts as a tax on future money income such as pensions, life insurance policies, and receipts from outstanding loans. If decision-makers do not consider inflation at the time they agree to a contract, debtors will gain at the expense of lenders. This happens because the purchasing power of dollars used to pay back the lenders has depreciated. Suppose that you loan $1000 to a friend at an 8 percent interest rate. Since you thought prices would be stable during the year, you expected to receive $1080 in terms of the current purchasing power 12 months after you extended the loan. But suppose that prices rose 20 percent during the year. When you receive the $1080 at the end of the year, you find that it will purchase less than the original $1000 that you loaned. Specifically, the $1080 would purchase the same amount of goods and services as $899.64 before prices rose by 20 percent. You were hurt by inflation because you were a lender. Your friend, a debtor, was helped because inflation permitted him to pay you back with dollars that had depreciated in purchasing power.

STUDENT: If inflation helps the indebted, wouldn't it redistribute income from rich lenders to poor debtors?

ECONOMIST: Not necessarily. Don't forget, you have to have reasonably good credit before you can borrow money. This limits the ability of persons in the lowest income brackets to acquire debt. Most studies in this area suggest that unanticipated inflation results in a moderate redistribution from both low (less than $5000) and high (more than $50,000) income recipients to those in the middle income groupings.

The more important redistributional effect of unanticipated inflation is between age groupings. Persons under 35 years of age are more likely to be debtors. Inflation helps them pay back their housing mortgages, car loans, and other outstanding debts. In contrast, those over 50 years of age are more likely to have savings, paid-up life insurance policies, bonds, and other forms of fixed future income. Inflation eats away at the purchasing power of these savings. Thus it tends to redistribute income from the old to the young.

One other point. Households are net lenders and the government is the largest debtor. Therefore, unanticipated inflation tends to transfer wealth from households to the government.

STUDENT: You keep talking about unanticipated inflation. What is it and why is it important?

ECONOMIST: **Unanticipated inflation** is a change in the level of prices that decision-makers did not foresee. If both borrowers and lenders anticipate inflation, they will adjust their behavior to account for it. For example, in comparison with the expectation of stable prices, lenders will demand and borrowers will grant a higher interest rate on outstanding loans because both expect the value of the dollar to depreciate. Suppose that a borrower and lender would agree to a 5 percent interest rate if they anticipate stable prices during the course of the loan. However, when both expect prices to rise 10 percent annually, instead they agree to a 15 percent interest rate. The higher interest rate compensates the lenders for the expected decline in the purchasing power of the dollar during the course of the loan.

When inflation is fully and accurately anticipated, it does not benefit debtors at the expense of lenders. Debtors gain at the expense of creditors only if the actual rate of inflation exceeds the expected rate, at the time the two agreed to the terms of the transaction.

STUDENT: Doesn't inflation cheat us all by eating away at our paychecks?

ECONOMIST: Let's not forget that inflation also influences the size of those paychecks. Money earnings would not have gone up at an annual rate of 8 percent during the 1969–1973 period if the inflationary rate had not been 5 percent. It is wrong to argue that if it were not for the inflation, we all would have been able to buy 5 percent more goods and services during that period.

The rate of inflation directly affects money earnings and the price of things that we buy. However, its impact on our real standard of living is more indirect and complex. It is not obvious that moderate rates of inflation, at least initially, cheat us at all. That is, it is not obvious that our real standard of living is reduced.

ONLY TWO MEN IN WASHINGTON FULLY UNDERSTAND THE CAUSES OF INFLATION —

UNFORTUNATELY, THEY DISAGREE —

The Small Society by Brickman, © Washington Star Syndicate, Inc.

What's Bad about Inflation

STUDENT: If our salaries go up as fast as prices, maybe inflation isn't so bad after all. Is there any need to be concerned about it?

ECONOMIST: Merely because money income initially tends to rise with prices, it doesn't follow that there is no need to be concerned about inflation, particularly high rates of inflation. Three negative aspects of inflation are particularly important.

1. *Price Changes Can Change the Intent of a Long-Term Contract.* Since the rate of inflation varies, it can not be predicted with certainty. Most market exchanges, including long-term contracts, are made in *money* terms. If unanticipated inflation takes place, it can change the intended terms of long-term contracts, such as mortgages, life insurance policies, pensions, bonds, and other arrangements that involve a debt–lender relationship.

2. *Rapid Price Changes Cause Uncertainty.* If you are not sure whether prices are going to increase, decrease, or remain the same, any contract that has a time dimension becomes hazardous because of uncertainty. The builder does not know if he should tack on a charge of 2, 5, or 10 percent to his contract because inflation will increase his cost by some amount during the time period necessary for construction. Union workers do not know whether to accept a contract calling for a 5 percent wage increase for the next two years. Inflation could partially or completely negate the increase. If price changes are unpredictable, if prices go up 10 percent then level off for a year or two, then increase by 5, 10, or 15 percent again in the future, no one knows what to expect. Long-term money exchanges will be based on a substantial inflationary premium or else they will be completely avoided. Such uncertainty hampers the ability of an exchange system to function properly.

3. *Inflation Hurts People with Fixed Incomes.* Some people can adjust to inflation much easier than others. It is particularly difficult for the elderly, many of whom live on fixed incomes, to adjust to inflation. If inflation is quite rapid, it could eat away at a lifetime of savings quickly. The distributional effects may be sufficient cause for government planners to be concerned about inflation.

STUDENT: What causes inflation?

ECONOMIST: We need to acquire some additional tools before we can analyze this question in detail, but we can outline a couple of theories. First, economists emphasize the link between aggregate demand and supply. If aggregate demand rises more rapidly than supply, prices will rise. Second, nearly all economists believe that a rapid expansion in the nation's stock of money would cause inflation. The old saying is that prices will rise because "there is too much money chasing too few goods." The hyperinflation experienced by South American countries has been mostly the result of monetary expansion. Later we will analyze several other popular inflation theories—the monopoly power of business and labor, for example. But we need to do more groundwork so these issues can be better understood.

☐ LOOKING AHEAD

STUDENT: What is the major purpose of macroeconomics? What goals do macroeconomists seek to attain?

ECONOMIST: Almost all economists favor the goals of stable prices, stable growth in output, and low unemployment rates. In a dynamic economy, as we have already indicated, we will have some unemployment. Some unemployment is consistent with economic efficiency. But cyclical unemployment that results because of insufficient demand for labor in aggregate is another matter. This component of unemployment is rooted to a decline in the general level of economic activity. If cyclical unemployment can be reduced or eliminated, real gains in economic output are possible. A higher level of GNP, both current and future, is possible. If growth is to be steady rather than characterized by the uncertainty associated with economic booms and recessions, cyclical unemployment must be minimized.

While economists agree on the goals of steady growth, stable prices, and low unemployment, they do not always agree on their causes, how to deal with them, or what can be done about them. In particular, there are two opposing camps of economists, Keynesians and monetarists, who differ as to the root causes of and solutions to both inflation and unemployment. We have touched on their views already but they will be examined in greater detail in subsequent chapters. We will try to pinpoint the source of their differences. Yet three points should be kept in mind.

First, in our effort to highlight the differences between the two views, it may be easy for the student to overlook the points of consensus. We will attempt to highlight points of both agreement and disagreement between the Keynesians and the monetarists.

Second, even though the two theories may offer alternative explanations of an economic phenomenon, they will not always be mutually exclusive. Often *both* Keynesian and monetarists' views will contribute to the explanation of real world events.

Third, and perhaps most important, the majority of economists are neither purebred Keynesians nor purebred monetarists. Most are a mixture of the two. All Keynesians do not agree with each other, and neither do all monetarists. Therefore, our analysis may appear to indicate more polarization among economists than really exists. But hopefully it will present a fair analysis, highlight differences in points of view, and place you, the student, in a position to better analyze and understand the issues involved. Fair enough?

STUDENT: Sounds okay, if the price is right.

CHAPTER LEARNING OBJECTIVES

1. Macroeconomics is concerned with price, output, and equilibrium in highly aggregated markets. Both micro- and macroeconomics utilize the same tools and postulates. The level of aggregation is the distinction between the two.

2. Aggregate labor and product markets have been characterized by instability. GNP has increased much more rapidly during some periods than others. The unemployment rate has varied considerably during the last 40 years, reaching a high of 25 percent in 1935 while attaining a low of less than 2 percent during World War II. Since World War II, the rate has been more stable, but fluctuations continue to occur.

3. Boom, contraction, recession, and expansion are terms used by economists to describe the economic performance of aggregate markets. During an *expansion*, the unemployment rate will decline and output will increase rapidly. *Boom* is the term used to describe the peak level of output of a business cycle. *Contraction* is characterized by increasing unemployment, declining business conditions, and a low rate of growth. When economic activity is at a low level, this condition is referred to as a *recession*, or *depression* if it is quite serious.

4. Classical economists thought that wages and prices would adjust so as to eliminate any temporary unemployment in a market economy. The Great Depression caused economists to question this hypothesis. Today most economists believe that cyclical economic behavior results from either fluctuations in (a) private investment or (b) the supply of money.

5. Even an efficient exchange economy will experience some unemployment. Frictional unemployment results because of imperfect information about available job openings and qualified applicants. Structural unemployment results because there are factors that prevent the "matching up" of available applicants with the available jobs. Currently frictional and structural unemployment in the United States are thought to involve between 4 and 5 percent of the labor force.

6. Cyclical unemployment results because aggregate demand for labor is insufficient to maintain full employment. A primary concern of macroeconomics is how cyclical unemployment can be minimized. If unemployment resulting from deficient aggregate demand could be eliminated, the actual output of the economy would be able to reach its full potential.

7. Inflation is a general rise in prices. The average annual rate of inflation in the United States during the last 40 years has been about 3 percent. The rate was significantly higher during the 1969–1974 period, the Korean War, and World War II. In the mid-1970s, the rate of inflation for almost all Western nations was substantially in excess of the comparable rates during the 1950s and 1960s.

8. Unanticipated inflation can have a harmful effect on an economy because it **(a)** changes the intended terms of trade of long-term contracts, **(b)** increases the uncertainty of exchanges involving time, and **(c)** reduces the purchasing power of persons on fixed incomes.

9. Economists usually agree on the desirability of steady growth, stable prices, and low unemployment rates. But they often disagree about how these goals can be attained.

IMPORTANT TERMS TO REMEMBER

Microeconomics: That part of economics that focuses on the determination of price, output and equilibrium in narrowly defined markets, for example, the market for a specific product or resource.

Macroeconomics: That part of economics that focuses on the economy as a whole or highly aggregated markets such as the market for labor or consumer products.

Recession: The low point of the business cycle, characterized by a high unemployment rate and a slow rate of growth, or even a decline, in the real gross national product. In an effort to be more precise, some economists have defined a recession as two consecutive quarters for which there is a decline in real GNP.

Depression: A prolonged and very severe recession.

Boom: The high point of the business cycle as indicated by a low unemployment rate and rapid growth in the real GNP.

Business cycle: Fluctuations in the general level of economic activity as measured by such variables as the unemployment rate and changes in real GNP.

Normal rate of unemployment: The long-run level of unemployment due to the frictional and structural conditions of labor markets. This rate is affected by both dynamic change and man-made institutional arrangements. Cyclical unemployment is *not* a part of normal unemployment.

Frictional unemployment: Unemployment due to an inability to immediately match up employees with job openings *for which the unemployed workers are qualified.* It results because of scarce information and job search efforts to acquire employment information.

Structural unemployment: Unemployment due to structural changes in the economy that generate job openings for which the unemployed workers are *not* well qualified. The current skills of unemployed workers do not match the job openings.

Cyclical unemployment: Unemployment due to recessionary business conditions and inadequate aggregate demand for labor.

Full employment: The level of employment that would result from the efficient use of the civilian labor force after allowance is made for the normal rate of unemployment that results from dynamic change and the structural characteristics of the economy. For the United States, full employment is thought to exist when between 95 and 96 percent of the labor force is employed.

Unanticipated inflation: A price rise that was not expected by economic decision-makers. Past experience and current conditions are the major determinants of an individual's expectations with regard to future price changes.

THE ECONOMIC WAY OF THINKING—DISCUSSION QUESTIONS

1. Explain why even an efficiently functioning economic system will have some unemployed resources at any point in time.
2. What is the Keynesian explanation of the business cycle? What solution to the business cycle is suggested by the Keynesian theory?
3. Explain the monetarist view of the business cycle. What do the monetarists believe to be the major source of economic instability? What is their solution?
4. "My money wage rose by 6 percent last year, but inflation completely erased these gains. How can I get ahead when inflation continues to wipe out my increases in earnings?" Evaluate. Do you agree with this view?
5. "Inflation is like a tax on cash balances." Explain the meaning of this statement.

6. What are the most harmful effects of inflation? Explain why it is important whether or not inflation is accurately anticipated.

7. What's Wrong with This Way of Thinking?

"The value of today's dollar is only one-third of what it was in 1940. Five years from now it will be worth only 20 cents. We cannot maintain our standard of living when the value of our currency is declining so rapidly."

8
AGGREGATE EQUILIBRIUM AND A SIMPLE KEYNESIAN MODEL

In the last chapter we indicated that the total output and employment level of our economy has sometimes fallen short of its maximum potential. Now we want to develop and examine a model of national income determination that helps explain why this might happen.

John Maynard Keynes (pronounced "canes"), an Englishman, has had more influence on modern macroeconomic analysis than any other economist. The approach, the terminology, and the analysis of Professor Keynes still dominate modern textbooks some 30 years after his death. We will develop the modern theory of national income determination within the Keynesian framework.

The analysis of this chapter is oversimplified. We will develop the Keynesian model in more detail in subsequent chapters. Our major objectives in this chapter are to (a) place the Keynesian analysis in historical perspective, (b) develop a model that will help us begin to understand some of the factors that influence the levels of national income and employment, and (c) illustrate why Keynesians believe that the rate of production of a strictly capitalistic economy will often fall short of the full employment level.

In its developmental stage, Keynesian economics was an attack on the dominant classical view. Understanding the pre-Keynesian views of classical economists will help place the Keynesian analysis in perspective.

KEYNES AND THE VIEWS OF CLASSICAL ECONOMISTS

Before the Great Depression most economists felt that a free market capitalistic economy would provide for full employment of resources. Of course, there would sometimes be *temporary* periods of high unemployment, reflecting the impact of such things as wars, technological change, droughts, and political conditions. But the pricing system would soon adjust to these changes and push the economy back to the full employment level of output.

Two important propositions formed the foundation for the classical view.

1. **Say's Law**—*Supply Creates Its Own Demand.*   The French economist J. B. Say maintained that a general overproduction of goods relative to total demand is impossible because the act of producing the goods will generate an amount of income exactly equal to the value of the goods produced. Purchasing power grows out of production. The farmer's supply of wheat generates his demand for shoes, clothes, automobiles, and other things that he desires. Similarly, the supply of shoes generates the purchasing power with which shoemakers (and their employees) demand wheat, food, clothes, automobiles, and other goods. Of course, classicists admitted, it is possible to produce too much of some goods and not enough of others. But when that is the case, the prices of goods in excess supply will fall, while the prices for products in excess demand will rise. The pricing system will correct such imbalances as might temporarily exist. However, a general overproduction of goods, in aggregate, was an impossibility according to classical economists.

Keynes attacked the classical view, pointing out that there are leakages from and injections into the income–expenditure flow. All of the income received by producers need not be spent on current consumption. Some of the income might be saved (not spent), thereby reducing current demand. Saving constitutes a leakage, reducing the current spending of income recipients.

The classicists answered back that saving is no problem because each and every dollar saved would be channeled into investment. Businesses produce not only current consumption goods, but also machines and other capital goods that will increase the productive capacity of an economy. Saving provides the funds to finance current investment. Without saving, all of the nation's income would be consumed, leaving nothing for investment. As illustrated by Exhibit 8-1, classical economists argued that the interest rate would bring the desires of savers and investors into balance. If there was an excess supply of saving, the interest rate would fall. At the lower interest rate, the quantity saved would decline and the quantity borrowed would expand. Equilibrium would be restored. Correspondingly, an excess demand for investment funds relative to saving would cause the interest rate to rise. The higher interest rates would

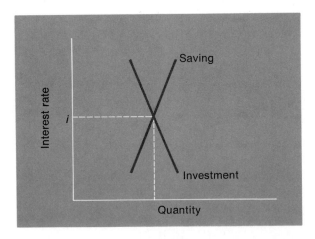

Exhibit 8-1   Classical View of Saving and Investment

Classicists argued that the interest rate would equate saving and investment.

attract additional funds from savers while discouraging borrowing by investors. Thus, the interest rate would see to it that each dollar leaking out of the income–expenditure stream as saving would automatically reappear as investment.

Keynes rejected this view. He stressed that saving and investment are done by different people and for different reasons. Households are the major source of saving. People save for future retirement, a home, a car, a college education, and many other reasons. The decision to save will be far more dependent on income than the interest rate. Keynes went on to stress that investment spending will be primarily determined by technological discoveries, expected future business conditions, innovations, and profitability, rather than the interest rate. If the business outlook is poor, little investment will be undertaken even at low interest rates. Thus, the Keynesian view stresses, there is no reason to believe that the interest rate will bring the plans of savers into balance with the plans of investors *at full employment.*

2. *Flexible Wages and Prices.*   The second major argument used to bolster the classical position was flexible wages and prices. Even if there was a temporary excess supply of most goods, price flexibility would restore equilibrium. If households somehow managed to save more than businesses were willing to invest, prices would decline. At the lower level of prices, households would be able to purchase the total amount of goods produced.

But could the goods be produced profitably at the lower prices? Classicists answered back, "Yes, if resource prices also decline." A general decline in demand for products would lead to a decline in demand for resources, including labor. *Temporary* unemployment might well result. But the competition from the unemployed would leave workers with no choice but to accept the lower wage rates. As wages fall, businesses would hire more labor, eliminating the temporary unemployment. In contrast, an excess demand for labor would cause rising wage rates. As wages rose businesses would hire fewer employees, eliminating the excess demand. Thus, flexible wages (and prices) would assure that unemployment and excess aggregate supply would be only temporary according to the classical view.

Keynes argued that wage–price flexibility, like the interest rate, was an ineffectual mechanism to assure full employment. First, wages and prices tend to be inflexible downward—particularly in the short run. In an economy dominated by large businesses and trade unions, unemployment could continue for a long time before wages and prices would decline very much. But even if wages and prices were flexible, it is doubtful if they could restore equilibrium, at least not very rapidly. As wages decline, income also declines, and a falling income will cause the already too low aggregate demand to decline even more. Lower wages and prices would result in lower money incomes, and a consequent reduction in consumption spending. This would perpetuate or even worsen the already depressed economic conditions.

Neither falling wages (and prices) nor the interest rate can assure that aggregate demand will just equal aggregate supply *at the full employment level of output.* Contrary to the views of classical economists, Keynes argued that prolonged periods of unemployment were possible. A capitalistic market economy fails to provide automatically for full employment.

TOOLS OF MODERN KEYNESIAN ANALYSIS

Why might the income level of a market economy come to rest at less than full employment? According to the Keynesian view, this might happen because the level of spending was insufficient to generate adequate demand for the full employment level of production. The **aggregate demand** for goods and services is the moving force within the Keynesian model.

For a purely private economy, aggregate demand is composed of the demand of households for consumption goods and the demand of businesses for capital goods. Let us take a closer look at these two important components of demand.

Consumption and Saving

When each of us gets a paycheck, what do we usually do with it? Well, most of us spend a great deal of it on housing, food, recreation, medical care, clothes, entertainment, and such things. Household spending on current goods and services is called **consumption.**

Sometimes we may set aside part of our paycheck. That portion we do not use to buy current goods is called saving. **Saving** is the difference between one's current income and the amount spent on current goods and service. It is income not consumed. Sometimes our current spending on goods exceeds our income. When that is the case, we are dissaving. Dissaving is merely negative saving.

Note that both consumption and saving are flow concepts. One's consumption might be $500 per month or $6000 per year. Similarly, saving (without an s) will be the amount saved during a specific time period.

Since current disposable income must be either spent or saved,

$$Disposable\ income = consumption + saving$$

Alternatively, we can rewrite this relationship as

$$Consumption = disposable\ income - saving$$

or

$$Saving = disposable\ income - consumption$$

Several factors influence the consumption decisions of households. If people expect their incomes to rise in the future, they will most likely spend a larger portion of their current income. In contrast, pessimistic future prospects will probably cause households to reduce their current spending. For example, as unemployment rose in the mid-1970s, many employed workers reduced their spending because they were pessimistic about their future employment prospects. Rising prices give consumers an incentive to buy now, before things get higher. Thus, the expectation of future inflation will tend to stimulate *current* spending on goods and services. Higher taxes will reduce the disposable income of households, causing them to spend less on consumption. Correspondingly, a cut in income taxes will serve to stimulate current consumption.

OUTSTANDING ECONOMIST: John Maynard Keynes

Professor Keynes was unquestionably the most influential economist of the twentieth century. He was the son of John Neville Keynes, an eminent economist in his own right. J. M. Keynes established the framework for current macroeconomics, and his ideas form the foundation for modern macroeconomic policy. In the 1930s he advised many political leaders, including President Roosevelt, who was a personal friend of Keynes, on how to escape the Great Depression. The economic advisors of Presidents Kennedy and Johnson encouraged them, and with great success, to adopt Keynesian policies. Twenty-five years after Keynes' death, even a Republican president, Richard Nixon, professed to be a Keynesian.

The ideas of Keynes, like those of other great scholars and philosophers, were not immediately accepted. His writings were often disorganized and confusing. Many critics felt his ideas were an attack on the puritan ethic or on the virtue of saving. Others thought his views were a threat to the market economy. Personally, Keynes believed that his ideas strengthened the case for the private sector by curing its most serious shortcoming, the recession. He praised the virtue of profits. "The engine which drives enterprise," Keynes wrote, "is not thrift but profit." He was unimpressed with Marxian ideas which he found to be "illogical and so dull." Given the environment of the 1930s, conditions were right for the acceptance of his views.

Keynes, the man, is perhaps even more interesting than Keynes, the economist. He earned millions of dollars speculating in the stock market—much of it on behalf of Cambridge University. He was prominent in British social circles. He married a ballerina of the Diaghilev Russian ballet. He enjoyed art, drama, and opera, but also bridge and debate with professional economists and prime ministers. In 1942, King George VI made him a lord.

The influence of Keynes on the economics profession is remarkable. Of course, economists do not always agree with his views on the business cycle or policy prescriptions to cure instability, but almost all economists use the general framework, established by Keynes, to approach macroeconomic problems.

Camera Press

If we are interested in how much most families will consume, one factor stands out above all others. The primary determinant of consumer spending is disposable income. There is a strong positive relation between the amount spent on consumption and the disposable income of households. This relationship between consumption spending and disposable income is called the **consumption function.** It occupies a central position in the Keynesian model of income determination.

Exhibit 8-2 illustrates the disposable income–consumption link for U.S. families in 1973. The consumption spending of low income families exceeded their incomes. They were dissaving. As income increased, the consumption spending of households increased also, though not quite so rapidly as saving. High income families spent a smaller percentage of their disposable income on consumption. More was allocated to saving.

The consumption function suggests that as income rises individuals will increase

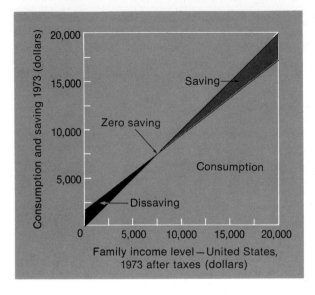

Exhibit 8-2   High Income Families Save More

The percentage of income saved in the short run increases with income level.
SOURCE: U.S. Department of Agriculture.

both their current consumption and saving. Families will use some, but not all, of the additional income for current consumption. By the same token, if income should fall, the consumption function implies that families will not absorb the entire reduction by contracting their current consumption. Saving will be reduced also, cushioning the decline in consumption.

How Large Is Your Propensity to Consume?

Keynes used the expression "propensity to consume" to describe the relationship between an individual's or family's current consumption and income. The propensity to consume can be either an average or marginal concept. The **average propensity to consume** (APC) of your household is your current consumption spending divided by your disposable income.

$$APC = \frac{\text{current consumption}}{\text{current disposable income}}$$

For example, if you had a disposable income of $10,000 and spent $9000 on current consumption items, you would have an APC of 0.9.

As income increases, in the shortrun, your average propensity to consume usually declines. This results because, on a short-term basis, you usually spend a smaller than average portion of your *additional* or marginal income on consumption. A greater share of the *additional* income is allocated to saving. The **marginal propensity to consume** (MPC) of a household is the fraction of additional disposable income that is allocated to consumption. Mathematically,

$$MPC = \frac{\text{additional consumption}}{\text{additional disposable income}}$$

If your income increases by $100, and you therefore increase your current consumption expenditures by $70, your marginal propensity to consume would be 0.7. You spent seven-tenths of the extra $100 on current consumption. The remainder was allocated to saving.

Exhibit 8-3 illustrates both the average and marginal propensity to consume using the family income–consumption data that were shown in Exhibit 8-2. U.S. families with $2500 of income in 1973, spent $3000 on current consumption. Their average propensity to consume—current consumption divided by income—was 1.20. As income rose to $5000, consumption *increased* by $2300, to $5300. Therefore, the marginal propensity to consume between $2500 and $5000 was 0.92 ($2300 divided by $2500). APC at $5000 was 1.06, less than at $2500. As family income expands, a smaller percentage of income is allocated to current consumption. Thus, as Exhibit 8-3 shows, both APC and MPC fall as income increases.

Remember, saving is merely income that is not spent on current consumption. The marginal propensity to save (MPS) is the fraction of additional disposable income that is allocated to saving:

$$\text{MPS} = \frac{\text{additional saving}}{\text{additional disposable income}}$$

Exhibit 8-3 (column 6) also shows the marginal propensity to save for the United States in 1973. As income increased, the proportion of additional income allocated to saving also increased. Since disposable income must be either spent on consumption or saved, MPC plus MPS must equal one.

Thus far we have focused on the positive relationship between consumption spending and disposable income for household data. But there also is a positive relationship between aggregate consumption and income for an entire nation. As disposable income in the United States has risen, consumption (and saving) has increased also. In fact, over time there has been a very close relationship between the two. In recent years

Exhibit 8-3   The Short-Run Average and Marginal Propensity to Consume

Using the family income and consumption data for 1973 (see Exhibit 8-1), the table illustrates how the APC, MPC, and MPS are derived.

Family income (dollars) (1)	Current consumption (dollars) (2)	Additional consumption Δ(2)(dollars) (3)	APC (2) ÷ (1) (4)	MPC (3) ÷ Δ(1) (5)	MPS 1 − MPC (6)
2,500	3,000	—	1.20	—	—
5,000	5,300	2,300	1.06	0.92	0.08
7,500	7,500	2,200	1.00	0.88	0.12
10,000	9,600	2,100	0.96	0.84	0.16
12,500	11,600	2,000	0.93	0.80	0.20
15,000	13,400	1,800	0.89	0.72	0.28
17,500	15,000	1,600	0.86	0.64	0.36
20,000	16,500	1,500	0.83	0.60	0.40

between 92 and 94 percent of the disposable income of U.S. households has been spent on consumption, with the remainder allocated to saving.

Exhibit 8-4 presents a graphic picture of hypothetical aggregate consumption and saving functions. As for real world data, both saving and consumption increase with disposable income. Consumption and disposable income are just equal at $700 billion (Exhibit 8-4a). Of course, saving would be zero at that income level (Exhibit 8-4b). As income rises, consumption increases less rapidly. For example, as income increases from $700 billion to $800 billion, consumption expands to $750 billion. A $100 billion increase in disposable income leads to a $50 billion expansion in consumption. Thus,

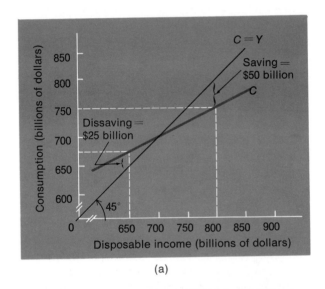

(a)

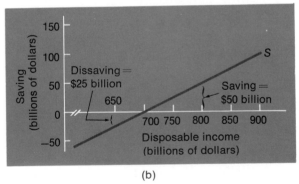

(b)

Exhibit 8-4 The Consumption and Saving Schedules.

Frame (a) pictures the positive relationship between consumption spending and disposable income. The 45 degree line outlines all points for which consumption and disposable income are equal. The vertical distance between the 45 degree line and the consumption function C, indicates the level of saving (or dissaving). Frame (b) shows the saving function alone. Note that the amount of saving at an income level [frame (b)] will always equal the difference between the 45 degree line and the consumption function [frame (a)] for the corresponding level of income.

MPC = 0.50.[1] When disposable income is $800 billion, households will save $50 billion. The saving schedule is merely the difference between the 45 degree line and the consumption function C. When disposable income is less than $700, consumption spending will exceed income (Exhibit 8-4a). Thus households will be dissaving (Exhibit 8-4b). Positive saving will take place when disposable income exceeds $700 billion.

In the absence of government policy, most economists believe that the consumption and saving schedules are quite stable. This stability reflects the important influence of income as a determinant of both consumption and saving.

Investment Demand

Net investment is the addition to the nation's capital goods and business inventories during a period. Additions to capital stock will increase the capacity of the nation to produce goods in the future. Capital goods are not an "end" by themselves, but rather they are a means to produce an end. Machines are produced today so our output of consumer goods can be increased in the future.

Spending on investment goods will increase aggregate demand during the current period. Production of investment goods, like production of consumption goods, requires labor, natural resources, and other factors of production. Additional investment means more employment of both men and machines.

What determines the level of investment? Three factors are particularly important.

1. *Current Sales Relative to the Productive Capabilities of the Existing Capital Stock.* If current sales go up, a firm can usually squeeze a little more output from its existing plant and equipment. It makes sense for firms to maintain some excess capacity. Then they will be able to meet a temporary expansion in demand. But when current sales continue at the higher level for an extended period, pressure will eventually be placed on the firm's existing plant capacity. At some point, it will be profitable to invest, to expand the size of capital stock. Clearly, the relationship between the firm's current sales and existing capital stock is crucial. If current sales are well below productive capacity, there is little incentive to invest. But as current sales approach the capacity limit of the firm's existing plant and equipment, the incentive to invest increases.

2. *Expectations Concerning Future Sales.* Investment decisions, like other choices, must be made with some uncertainty. They will be based on one's future expectations, as well as current business conditions. Businessmen invest in buildings and machines because they expect to be able to sell the products produced at a profit. If business

---

[1]The mathematically inclined student will note that the MPC is simply the slope of the consumption schedule. The slope of any line can be measured by the ratio of the vertical change divided by the horizontal change as the result of a movement from one point to another along the line. The slope of the consumption schedule between any two points is the additional consumption (vertical change) divided by the additional income (horizontal change). Thus, the slope of the line is $\Delta C/\Delta Y$. But this is also the definition of the marginal propensity to the consumer.

expectations are bleak or if businessmen expect the demand for their products to decline, their incentive to invest is sharply reduced. Expectation about future business conditions will exert a powerful influence on investment. Optimism leads to expansion in investment, but business pessimism will cause firms to delay or call off their investment plans.

3. *The Interest Rate.*   The interest rate contributes to the opportunity cost of all investment projects. If the firm must borrow, the interest rate will contribute directly to the cost of an investment project. If the firm uses its own funds, it foregoes interest that could have been earned by loaning the funds to someone else, rather than investing them. A higher interest rate increases the opportunity cost of an investment project, reducing the incentive to undertake it. Lower interest rates will have the opposite effect.

The relationship between the interest rate and investment allows us to anticipate the impact of an important policy tool—control over the money supply. In Chapter 12 we will illustrate how monetary policy can alter the interest rate, at least in the short run, and thereby stimulate additional investment. During normal times, Keynesians would expect investment to be responsive to a change in the interest rate. But they are less confident that this will be true under depressed economic conditions. When an economy is in a recession and future business prospects are bleak, even a sharp decline in the interest rate may not have much impact on investment. Thus, under depressed conditions falling interest rates may not be able to eliminate an excess supply of saving.

EQUILIBRIUM AND THE KEYNESIAN MODEL

We now have the necessary tools to explain the equilibrium levels of output, income, and employment within the Keynesian framework. When an economy is in **equilibrium** there will be a balance of forces such that the existing level of output will be maintained into the future. There is no tendency for output to either expand or decline. Within the Keynesian model, an economy is in equilibrium when the flow of income generated from the goods and services produced gives rise to a level of spending that is just sufficient to purchase the existing level of output. Put another way, in equilibrium, the aggregate income of resource suppliers will just equal the aggregate demand for current goods and services.

There are two closely related methods of approaching aggregate equilibrium—the *aggregate demand–aggregate supply* approach and the *leakage–injection* approach. To begin, we will focus on the former.

Initially, we will make several simplifying assumptions so that the analysis will be more readily understood. First, a closed economy is assumed. The impact of the foreign sector is analyzed in later chapters. Second, at the outset we will focus on the operation of a purely private economy. The impact of government expenditures and taxes will be introduced as we proceed. For a private economy, total spending, that is, aggregate demand, will simply be the sum of the consumption and investment expenditures. Since both taxes and government expenditures are absent, the net national product of the economy will also be equal to disposable income. Third, we will assume that all saving is generated by households, while investment is undertaken in the business sector. In practice, of course, some saving comes from within the business sector. But the major point is that saving is primarily determined by household decisions. Fourth, the analysis of monetary factors and their importance within the Keynesian model will be put off until Chapter 12. Fifth, we will assume that the price level remains constant until full employment is reached. Therefore, changes in total income will lead to both changes in real output and employment as long as the economy has not yet approached its capacity. For the short-run time period, the assumption of stable prices may approximate real world conditions. Our major purpose is to introduce factors that influence movements in supply and demand in highly aggregated markets. As we proceed, each of these simplifying assumptions will be relaxed.

Equilibrium—Tabular Presentation

A pure private economy is composed of two major sectors—household and business. The household sector supplies factors of production such as labor, machines, buildings, and entrepreneurship in exchange for income. The business sector utilizes these factors of production to generate the aggregate output of the economy. Aggregate income and **aggregate supply** (output) are merely opposite sides of the same set of transactions. They will always be equal. Consumers and investors generate the demand for goods and services.

Exhibit 8-5 presents data for hypothetical consumption, saving, and investment schedules. Investment is assumed to be determined by factors such as business expectations and technological change. Thus, it is not dependent on the level of income.[2] The consumption function is, of course, positively related to income. Aggregate equilibrium for the economy will be present when output is $900 billion. At that output level, consumers plan to spend $800 billion for current goods and services, setting aside $100 billion in saving. Businessmen also plan to invest $100 billion. The total planned level of spending $(C + I)$, $900 billion, is just equal to income at that output level.

Exhibit 8-5   Equilibrium Level of Income, Output, and Employment

Possible levels of employment (millions of persons) (1)	Aggregate supply (output and income) (NNP = D + I) (billions of dollars) (2)	Planned consumption (billions of dollars) (3)	Planned saving (billions of dollars) (4)	Planned investment (billions of dollars) (5)	Aggregate demand C + I (billions of dollars) (6)	Tendency of employment, output, and income (7)
60	800	750	50	100	850	Increase
70	850	775	75	100	875	Increase
80	900	800	100	100	900	Equilibrium
90	950	825	125	100	925	Decrease
100	1000	850	150	100	950	Decrease

[2]Net national product is used as the measure of income so that household income received will also be equal to disposable income. Thus, net investment is also utilized rather than gross investment.

When a private economy is in equilibrium the consumption–saving plans of households match perfectly with the investment plans of businessmen. For example, our hypothetical economy is in equilibrium when the total amount that consumers and investors plan to spend on final goods and services is exactly equal to the total value of the final goods and services produced. Consequently, businessmen will have no reason to alter their production rates. Thus, the equilibrium rate of output will be sustained into the future.

But the plans and expectations of business and household decision-makers will sometimes come into conflict. In fact, they will be inconsistent with each other for all income levels other than equilibrium. What would happen if the output of the economy temporarily expanded to $950 billion? Employment would increase from 80 to 90 million. At the higher income level households would plan to save $125 billion, spending $825 billion on consumption. Businessmen would plan to invest $100 billion. Aggregate demand would be $925 billion, $25 billion less than aggregate supply. The spending of consumers and investors is insufficient to purchase the total output produced. Goods will not disappear once they have been produced. The discrepancy will be made up through the accumulation of unwanted and unplanned business inventories. Businessmen are unable to sell as much as they had planned for, and their inventories will rise. The *actual* investment of the business sector will be $125 billion, $100 billion in planned investment and a $25 billion unplanned inventory investment.[3] Because of insufficient consumer demand, the investment plans of businessmen went astray.

But the story does not end here. How will businessmen respond to their now excess inventories? They will cut back production and planned investment next year. Output and income will decline toward the equilibrium level. Employment will decline and unemployment will rise. Given the consumption–saving plans of households, the economy will be unable to maintain the $950 billion income level and the employment level associated with it.

What happens if income is temporarily below equilibrium. Suppose the income level of the economy pictured by Exhibit 8-5 was $850 billion. At that income level, the planned consumption and investment spending would generate an aggregate demand of $875 billion. Businessmen are selling more than they are currently producing. Their inventories will decline below normal levels. Businessmen will respond to this happy state of affairs by expanded output. Production will increase, providing jobs for previously unemployed workers. Income will rise toward the equilibrium level of $900 billion.

In summary, an economy will be able to sustain only the equilibrium level of income. When aggregate income exceeds the equilibrium level, planned aggregate demand will be insufficient to purchase all of the goods and services produced. Unwanted inventories will accumulate, causing businessmen to cut back production and employment. Future income will fall. In contrast, when aggregate income is less than the equilibrium level, planned aggregate demand will exceed the current level of

---

[3]The reader should note the distinction between *planned* investment and *actual* investment. *Actual* investment must always equal *actual* saving. Investment necessitates saving—that is, a reduction in consumption. But *planned* investment will not equal *planned* saving when businessmen find that their inventories are rising or falling in an *un*planned manner.

production. Inventories will diminish, stimulating businessmen to expand output and employment. Future income will rise. The economy will always tend to move toward equilibrium, that level of output for which aggregate demand is just equal to income.

Equilibrium—Graphic Presentation

The Keynesian analysis can readily be envisioned graphically. Exhibit 8-6 shows a graph for which planned aggregate demand, consumption plus investment, is measured on the y axis and total income (NNP) on the x axis. The 45 degree line, extending from the origin, maps out all points that are equidistant from the x and y axes. Therefore, all points on the 45 degree line represent output levels for which aggregate demand and total income are equal.

The 45 degree line can also be thought of as an aggregate supply schedule. The aggregate supply schedule outlines the willingness of producers to offer alternative levels of output. Businessmen will produce (supply) a level of output only if they expect consumers and investors to spend enough to purchase that output level. The 45 degree line outlines all levels of output (income) for which total spending will be sufficient to purchase the output level, thereby inducing businessmen to supply it.

Aggregate demand will equal total income for all points on the 45 degree line. Thus, the 45 degree line maps out all possible equilibrium levels of output. Note that there are many possible equilibrium levels of total income, output, and employment, not just one.

Exhibit 8-7 graphically depicts the consumption and aggregate demand schedule for the data of Exhibit 8-5. Consumption is, of course, positively related to income. As income rises, planned consumption increases, although by a smaller amount than income. Thus the consumption function will be flatter than the 45 degree line. Since investment is determined independent of income, when planned investment ($100

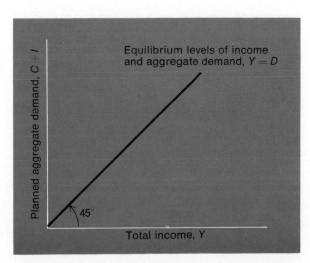

Exhibit 8-6 Aggregate Equilibrium

Total spending (aggregate demand) will equal total income for *all levels* of spending and income along a 45 degree line from the origin.

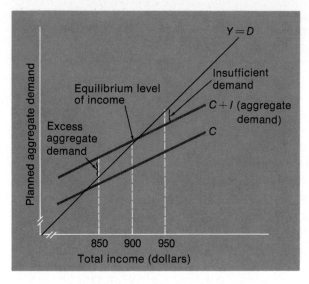

Exhibit 8-7   Graphic Presentation of Equilibrium

Here the data of Exhibit 8-5 are presented graphically. Given the level of aggregate demand, equilibrium income will be $900 billion, where the planned demand of consumers and investors is just equal to total income. At a lower level of income, $850 billion for example, excess demand would cause income to rise. At a higher level, such as $950 billion, aggregate demand would be insufficient to maintain the output level.

billion) is added (vertically) to the consumption schedule, the result yields aggregate demand.

The equilibrium level of total income (NNP) will be at the point where planned aggregate demand is just equal to total income (aggregate supply). Consequently, the equilibrium level of income will be at $900 billion, where the aggregate demand function $(C + I)$ crosses the 45 degree line. Under the conditions that we have outlined no other level of income could be sustained.

Utilizing the graphic analysis, let us consider why total income will move toward the $900 billion equilibrium level. When total income exceeds $900 billion, for example $950 billion, the aggregate demand function lies below the 45 degree line. Remember the $C + I$ line indicates how much people want to spend at each income level. When the $C + I$ line is below the 45 degree line, total spending is less than total income (output). Thus unwanted inventories will accumulate, leading businesses to reduce their future production. Employment will decline. Income will fall back from $950 billion to the equilibrium level of $900 billion.

In contrast, if total income was temporarily below equilibrium, there would be a tendency for income to rise. Suppose income was temporarily at $850. At that income level, the $C + I$ function lies above the 45 degree line. Aggregate demand exceeds total income (output). Businesses are selling more than they are currently producing. Their inventories are falling. They will react to this state of affairs by hiring more workers and expanding production. Income will rise back to the $900 billion equilibrium. Only at the equilibrium level, the point at which the $C + I$ function crosses the 45 degree line, will the plans of consumers and investors sustain the existing income level into the future.

ADDING GOVERNMENT DEMAND

Thus far we have focused on a purely private economy. For a mixed economy, the government, like private consumers and investors, demands resources and contributes to income. Government expenditures contribute to total spending on goods and services, thereby forming the third major component of aggregate demand. Government taxes reduce the amount of income available for consumption spending. Therefore, taxes, like saving, are a withdrawal from the national income stream.

The total aggregate demand for a mixed economy like the United States would be the sum of consumption (C), investment (I), and government (G) spending on goods and services.[4] It is often referred to as $C + I + G$. In equilibrium, aggregate income, often referred to as Y, must still equal aggregate demand. Exhibit 8-8 illustrates the equilibrium level of income for a mixed private–government economy. Planned aggregate demand is equal to total income at income level Y_e. At that level, the total spending of consumers, business investors, and the government is just equal to the income payments to factor suppliers.

If national income were temporarily greater than Y_e, it would tend to fall because of insufficient demand. On the other hand, if income were temporarily less than Y_e, the aggregate demand would exceed income, causing businesses to expand production during the next period. The plans of businessmen, consumers, and government could

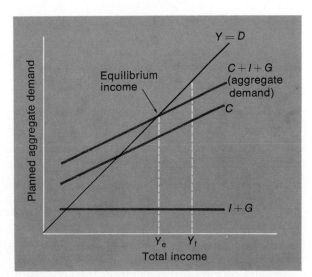

Exhibit 8-8 Equilibrium for a Mixed Economy

Given the current level of aggregate demand, only the income level Y_e could be maintained over time. What if full employment requires an income level greater than Y_e, for example Y_f? Continual unemployment would result unless something happened to change the level of aggregate demand.

[4]This is true for a closed economy, one that does not trade with other nations. We will consider the impact of international trade in a later chapter.

all be realized simultaneously only at income level Y_e, given the current demand. Thus, there will be a tendency for income to converge on Y_e.

What if full employment required a higher income level, such as Y_f. If this were the case, the economy would experience unemployment. Aggregate demand would be insufficient to maintain income level Y_f. Within the Keynesian analysis, aggregate equilibrium need not necessarily coincide with full employment. In fact, for a purely private economy, Keynesians argue that there is no reason to even expect that full employment will be present when the economy is in equilibrium. Therefore, prolonged periods of unemployment are not surprising.

What happens if aggregate demand is so strong that the economy is unable to supply the equilibrium level of income even when all resources are fully employed. Full employment places a ceiling on the production capacity of an economy. Excess aggregate demand at full employment will merely result in rising prices—inflation.

How can aggregate demand be controlled so that it will generate the income level consistent with full employment, but not so great as to cause inflation? This is the $64,000 question of macroeconomics. Introduction of the government sector into the model introduces several policy alternatives that might be used to regulate aggregate demand. To a large extent, the level of government spending is a policy variable. The government might spend more (or less) on such things as highways, defense, education, and cleaning up the environment in order to assure the proper level of aggregate demand. The government's taxing policy can also be utilized to influence demand. In subsequent chapters we will analyze both the potential for and limitations of public policy as a tool with which to control aggregate demand and promote full employment with price stability.

LEAKAGES AND INJECTIONS—ANOTHER WAY OF LOOKING AT EQUILIBRIUM

Thus far we have focused our analysis on the relationship between aggregate demand and total income. But what is aggregate demand? Aggregate demand is simply total income minus the leakages (saving and taxes) from the income stream plus the injections (investment and government expenditures) back into the income stream. Instead of focusing on the aggregate demand–total income relationship, alternatively one could analyze the relationship between leakages and injection. The leakage –injection approach allows us to look at the concept of aggregate equilibrium from another angle.

Investment and government spending contribute to the aggregate demand for goods and services. They are injected into the income stream. In contrast, saving and government taxes are leakages or withdrawals from the current income stream. These leakages will detract from current demand as they will not be spent on the purchase of current goods and services.

In equilibrium the planned leakages (saving and taxes) must be equal to the planned injections (investment and government spending). Any level of income for which leakages and injections are not equal cannot be maintained. When planned injections are in excess of planned leakages, government spending and private investment are

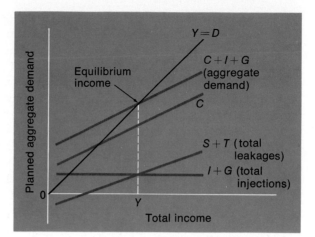

Exhibit 8-9 Two Ways of Looking at Equilibrium

In equilibrium, aggregate demand will be equal to total income. But for this to be true, planned leakages (saving plus taxes) and planned injections (investment plus government spending) must also be equal. They are simply two ways of looking at the same thing.

putting more into the income stream than saving and taxes are taking out. Planned consumption—income minus leakages—would be greater than the current supply of consumer goods. Business inventories would decline, reducing current business investment below planned levels. During the next period, businessmen would expand output in order to build their inventories back up. The flow of money income would grow, expanding employment opportunities.

When planned leakages are in excess of injections, taxes and saving are taking more out of the income stream than investment and government spending are injecting back into it. Production of consumer goods—total output minus investment and government spending—will exceed current consumption demand. Businessmen will accumulate undesired inventories. Their actual investment, including inventories, will exceed their desired level. Firms will respond by cutting their future output. Income and employment will decline.

As Exhibit 8-9 shows, the leakage–injection method is merely another way of looking at aggregate demand relative to income. When aggregate demand is equal to total income, planned injections $(I + G)$ will also be equal to planned leakages $(S + T)$. Thus, the $I + G$ and $S + T$ schedules will cross each other at the same income level where the aggregate demand function crosses the 45 degree line. When there is excess aggregate demand in comparison with income, injections will also exceed leakages. Thus, the income stream will expand. When total income exceeds aggregate demand, leakages will necessarily exceed injections. Income will decline.

PULLING IT TOGETHER

Aggregate demand is the catalyst of the Keynesian model. When aggregate demand changes things happen to income and employment. Until full employment is attained, supply is always accommodative. An increase in aggregate demand will thus lead to an increase in output and real income. The pre-Keynesian view was that "supply creates its own demand." The Keynesian view simply turns it around. Until the full-employment capacity of an economy is reached, "demand creates its own supply."

It is important that the reader understand the concept of equilibrium introduced by the Keynesian model of this chapter. Equilibrium within the Keynesian model is not dependent on full employment. There is no reason to expect that full employment will necessarily be associated with the equilibrium income level. When unemployment is present, falling wages will not restore full employment because wage cuts will only serve to reduce income, thereby reducing aggregate demand. Similarly, the interest rate will not necessarily be able to equate saving and investment. The level of saving will be primarily determined by income, and investment by the prospect for profit. When an economy is slipping into a recession, falling interest rates may fail to bring saving and investment into equality. The negative message of Keynes was "there is no reason to suppose that the unhampered market mechanism will coordinate the millions of individual economic decisions so that the level of aggregate demand will be sufficient to assure the full-employment level of income."

But Government Can Do Something About It

This was the positive side of Keynes. Government spending directly contributes to aggregate demand. Taxation influences disposable income directly, and therefore consumer spending indirectly. If governments want full employment, they must not just sit back and hope that it happens. They can act to assure that aggregate demand is sufficient to secure full employment. In the following chapters, we will analyze in detail precisely how and why governments can use their spending and taxation policies to regulate aggregate demand.

CHAPTER LEARNING OBJECTIVES

1. Classical economists thought that flexible wages (and prices) and the interest rate would eliminate the possibility of prolonged unemployment resulting from overproduction. While temporary unemployment was possible, the classicists believed that a capitalist market economy would automatically generate full employment.

2. Keynes attacked the classical view that a market economy would generate full employment. He stressed two flaws in the classical argument.

(a) Saving and investment are carried out by different people and for different reasons. When conditions are depressed, investment is likely to be far more responsive to business expectations, technological changes, and innovation, than to the interest rate. Similarly, income, rather than the interest rate, will be the primary determinant of saving. Therefore, the interest rate will not assure that saving will equal investment at the full-employment output level.

(b) Wages and prices in the real world tend to be inflexible downward. Therefore, falling wages cannot restore full employment. Even if wages were flexible, falling wages would not restore full employment because declining wage rates would also reduce income, consumption, and aggregate demand.

3. In equilibrium, the planned aggregate demand of the economy will be equal to total income. If planned aggregate demand is temporarily less than income, businesses will be unable to sell as much as they had anticipated (planned). Because they are accumulating undesired inventories, they will reduce future output. Income will decline back to the equilibrium level.

If planned aggregate demand is temporarily in excess of income, businesses will sell more of their products than they anticipate. Their inventories will be depleted below the desired level. In an effort to restore the depleted inventories, they will expand future output, and income will rise back to the equilibrium level.

4. Equilibrium can also be approached from the viewpoint of injections into, and leakages from, the income stream. Investment and government spending are injections into the income stream. They add to aggregate demand. Saving and taxes are withdrawals from the income stream. They diminish aggregate demand. In equilibrium, planned injections must equal planned leakages. If leakages are greater than injections, total income is greater than aggregate demand. Income will decline. In contrast, if injections are greater than the withdrawals, aggregate demand exceeds income, causing income to rise.

5. In the Keynesian model, there are many potential equilibrium levels of income, depending on the level of aggregate demand. Equilibrium may exist at less than full employment.

6. Aggregate demand determines income, output, and employment in the Keynesian model. Until the full-employment capacity is reached, increases in aggregate demand will generate higher levels of real output and employment. Thus, policies that affect aggregate demand can, at least potentially, be utilized to promote full employment with stable prices.

IMPORTANT TERMS TO REMEMBER

Say's law: The view that production creates its own demand. Thus, there cannot be a general oversupply because the total value of goods and services produced (income) will be available to purchase them.

Current consumption: Household spending on consumer goods and services during the current period. Consumption is a "flow" concept.

Consumption function: A fundamental relationship between disposable income and current consumption. As disposable income increases, current consumption expenditures will rise, but by a smaller amount than the increase in income.

Saving: Disposable income that is not spent on consumption.

Average propensity to consume: Current consumption spending divided by current disposable income.

Marginal propensity to consume: *Additional* current consumption divided by *additional* current disposable income.

Planned aggregate demand: The planned level of current spending for goods and services. For a closed economy, it would be the sum of (a) the planned consumption spending of households, (b) the planned investment spending of businesses, and (c) the planned expenditures by government.

Aggregate supply: The total value of current output produced. In the Keynesian model, the aggregate supply of goods and services is always equal to income for all possible levels of income. Therefore, the aggregate supply curve is the 45 degree line.

Equilibrium (macro): Condition that exists when planned aggregate demand is equal to total income (aggregate supply). At this level of income, the planned injections into the income stream will just equal the planned leakages from the income stream. Since there is a balance of forces, the equilibrium income level will be sustained, even if it does not coincide with full employment.

THE ECONOMIC WAY OF THINKING—DISCUSSION QUESTIONS

1. Explain why it may sometimes be impossible for the plans of savers and investors to be fulfilled simultaneously.

2. When is an economy in Keynesian aggregate equilibrium? Explain in your own words why an economy will return to aggregate equilibrium from a position of excess aggregate demand. From a position of insufficient aggregate demand.

3. How will each of the following factors influence the consumption schedule—

   (a) the expectation that consumer prices will rise more rapidly in the future,

   (b) pessimistic future employment conditions,

   (c) a reduction in income taxes,

   (d) an increase in the interest rate,

   (e) a decline in stock prices,

   (f) a redistribution of income from older workers (age 45 and over) to the young (less than 35),

   (g) a redistribution of income from the wealthy to the poor.

4. You have just been appointed to the president's Council of Economic Advisers. Write a short essay explaining to the president the Keynesian view of why a market economy may be unable to generate the full employment level of income. Be sure to explain why equilibrium may result at less than full employment.

5. The early classicists thought that (a) flexible wages and prices and (b) the interest rate would assure that a market economy would reach an equilibrium only at full employment. Why did Keynes disagree? Explain.

9

THE MULTIPLIER, ACCELERATOR, AND A KEYNESIAN VIEW OF THE BUSINESS CYCLE

In the last chapter, we emphasized that when aggregate demand is just equal to income, an economy is in equilibrium. There would not be a tendency for GNP to either increase or decrease from this equilibrium even if unemployment were present. Now we want to analyze factors that cause income to change within the Keynesian model. In particular, we want to investigate the impact that changes in investment, government spending, and saving have on income. Before we focus on these topics, we must develop a new tool that is central to the Keynesian analysis.

THE MULTIPLIER PRINCIPLE

Suppose that there are idle unemployed resources and that a businessman decides to undertake a $1 million investment project. Since investment is a component of aggregate demand, the project would increase demand directly by $1 million. But this does not tell the entire story. The investment project would require plumbers, carpenters, masons, lumber, cement, and many other resources. The suppliers of these resources would have their incomes enlarged by $1 million. What will they do with this additional income? In the last chapter, we showed that consumption and income are closely linked. An increase in current income will result in additional spending on current consumption. We can expect the resource suppliers to expand their current consumption. They will buy more food, clothing, recreation, medical care, and thousands of other items. How will this spending influence the incomes of those who supply these additional consumption products and services? Their incomes will increase also. After setting aside a portion of this additional income, these persons also will spend some of their additional income on current consumption. Their consumption spending will result in still more additional income for other product and service suppliers.

The initial investment sets off a chain reaction that results in both more consumption and more investment spending. Income increases by some multiple of the initial investment. This amplified effect of investment on income is called the **multiplier principle.**

The word "multiplier" is often used to indicate the number by which the initial investment would be multiplied in order to obtain the total amplified increase in income. If the $1 million investment resulted in $4 million of additional income, the multiplier would be 4. Income increased by four times the amount of the initial increase in spending. Similarly, if total income increased by $3 million, the multiplier would be 3.

What Determines the Size of the Multiplier?

The size of the multiplier will be dependent on the marginal propensity to consume. Exhibit 9-1 helps to illustrate this point. Suppose that the MPC for the economy were 3/4, indicating that consumers spend 75 percent of any additional income. Continuing with our previous example, a $1 million investment would initially result in $1 million of additional income in stage 1. Since the MPC is 3/4, consumption would increase by $750,000, contributing that amount to income in stage 2. The recipients of the stage 2 income will spend three-fourths of it on current consumption. Thus, their spending would increase income by $562,500 in stage 3. Exhibit 9-1 continues with the example, illustrating the additions to income through other stages. In total, income would increase by $4 million, given a MPC of 3/4. The multiplier is 4.

If the MPC had been greater, income recipients would have spent a larger share of their additional income on current consumption. Thus, the additional income generated in each stage would have been greater, increasing the size of the multiplier. There is a precise relationship between the multiplier and the MPC. *The multiplier m is*

$$m = \frac{1}{1 - \text{MPC}}$$

Exhibit 9-1   The Multiplier Principle

Expenditure stage	Additional income (dollars)	Additional consumption (dollars)	Marginal propensity to consume
Stage 1	1,000,000	750,000	3/4
Stage 2	750,000	562,500	3/4
Stage 3	562,500	421,875	3/4
Stage 4	421,875	316,406	3/4
Stage 5	316,406	237,305	3/4
All others	949,219	711,914	3/4
Totals	4,000,000	3,000,000	—

**Exhibit 9-2   The Higher the MPC,
the Larger the Multiplier**

MPS	MPC	Multiplier
1/10	9/10	10
1/5	4/5	5
1/4	3/4	4
1/3	2/3	3
1/2	1/2	2
2/3	1/3	1.5

Since income is either consumed or saved, $1 - $ MPC is also the MPS. Therefore, the multiplier is also

$$m = \frac{1}{\text{MPS}}$$

Merely turning the marginal propensity to save upside down yields the multiplier. If households save 1/10 of their additional income, the multiplier would be 10. If MPS were equal to 1/2, the multiplier would be 2. Exhibit 9-2 illustrates the relationship between MPS, MPC, and the multiplier for several alternative values.

While we have used an increase in investment spending to demonstrate the multiplier concept, the general principle applies to all categories of spending—investment, government, and consumption. Any independent shift in the level of government or consumption spending will have the same amplified impact on income as for investment.

The multiplier principle explains why a change in investment, government, or consumer spending can have a strong magnified impact on national income. Relatively small changes in any one of the components of aggregate demand can induce a much larger change in income.

Graphic Illustration of the Multiplier[1]

We have given both a verbal and numerical illustration of the multiplier principle. We can also demonstrate the multiplier graphically within the framework of the Keynesian model. Suppose the economy were initially in equilibrium at income level $1.2 trillion. Exhibit 9-3 illustrates that aggregate demand is just equal to income at $1.2 trillion. What would happen if businessmen suddenly became very optimistic about the future? Perhaps there was a technological breakthrough or some other event that triggered the favorable business expectations. Because of this optimism, businessmen planned to spend an additional $50 billion on investment. This additional investment will cause the aggregate demand function, $C + I_1 + G$, to shift upward $50 billion. At every income level, $50 billion of additional investment is planned, as is indicated by the

---

[1] Appendix B provides mathematically inclined students with an analysis of Keynesian equilibrium and the multiplier illustrated by use of equations.

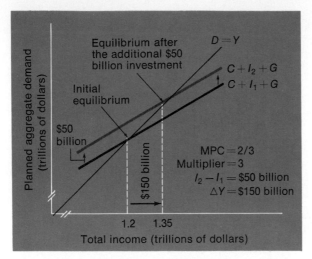

Exhibit 9-3   Graphic Illustration of the Multiplier

When the MPC is $\frac{2}{3}$, a $50 billion *increase* in investment would cause income to expand from $1.2 to $1.35 trillion, an increase of $150 billion. Hence the multiplier is 3.

new $C + I_2 + G$ aggregate demand schedule. A new equilibrium will result where aggregate demand is now equal to income.

How much will equilibrium income increase? This will, of course, depend on the marginal propensity to consume. Graphically, MPC, the fraction of additional income that is consumed, is the slope of the consumption (and for this example, aggregate demand) schedule. The example of Exhibit 9-3 illustrates the multiplier when MPC = 2/3. The $50 billion increase in aggregate demand, induced by the new investment, causes the equilibrium income level to increase by $150 billion to $1.35 trillion. The multiplier is 3. The $50 billion of new investment causes income to increase by three times the amount of the additional investment.

If the MPC were greater than 2/3, the slope of the consumption (and aggregate demand) schedule would have been steeper. The $50 billion of new investment would have had an even larger multiple impact on total income.

The multiplier principle is of great significance because seemingly small shifts in investment, consumption, and government spending will be magnified. There is both a positive and negative side to these amplified effects. On the negative side, the multiplier principle helps explain why shifts in business investment, even when they are small relative to total GNP, can be an important source of economic instability. On the positive side, the principle explains why relatively small changes in government expenditures (or taxes) if properly applied, could exert a substantial expansionary (or contractory) influence on total income and employment.

Reality and the Multiplier Principle

Does the real world conform to the multiplier principle? We will deal with this question in more detail as we go along, but two points should be made now.

1. *It Takes Time for the Multiplier to Work.* Within the model it appears that the multiplier has its impact instantaneously. In the real world, of course, this will not be

the case. The income will be spent over a period of weeks or even months. Thus, there will be some delay before secondary parties receive their additional income. It is usually thought that approximately one-half of the multiplier effect will be felt during the first six months. Thus if the total multiplier is 4, a multiplier effect of approximately 2 should be felt during the first six month period.

2. *Idle Resources Are Necessary Before the Multiplier Can Increase Real Income.* It is important to recognize the distinction between an economy with idle resources, unemployed labor and machines, and one without them. When resources are idle, each round of additional spending generated by the multiplier will expand real output and employment. But when there are no idle resources, the expansion in income will merely be inflationary. The increased spending will result in higher prices, not an expansion in real production.

The Paradox of Thrift

Most of us usually think of saving as a good thing. Long ago Ben Franklin preached the virtues of saving. If you really want something, the way to get it is to save your nickels, dimes, and dollars until you have saved enough to buy it.

The Keynesian model suggests that what is good for the individual household may not always be good for the entire economy. While saving is sometimes the route to fortune for an individual, too much aggregate saving can result in unemployed resources and a decline in national income.

Exhibit 9-4 illustrates what economists call the **paradox of thrift.** Suppose the economy is initially in equilibrium at $1.5 trillion of income. At this income level, the economy is just able to maintain full employment. What would happen if households, upon rereading *Poor Richard's Almanac*, decided they wanted to save more of their income? Suppose the *planned* saving of households increased by $25 billion. Because

Exhibit 9-4 The Paradox of Thrift

Suppose the initial full-employment equilibrium income level were $1.5 trillion, and that consumers suddenly decided to increase their saving by $25 billion. What happens to the equilibrium income level? The equilibrium level of income will fall by $75 billion because the multiplier will amplify the impact of the decline in aggregate demand.

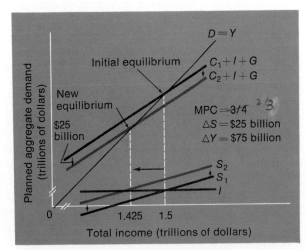

households now planned to save more, the saving schedule would shift upward to S_2, a $25 billion increase. But saving is merely income not consumed. An increase in planned saving means a reduction in planned consumption. Thus, the aggregate demand schedule will shift downward by $25 billion as the result of the thriftiness of individuals.

What happens to the equilibrium level of income? Assuming a marginal propensity to consume of 2/3, income will decline to $1.425 trillion, a $75 billion reduction. Thus the $25 billion reduction in aggregate demand, due to the thriftiness of consumers, is amplified into a $75 billion reduction in equilibrium income. When households in aggregate attempt to save more, their actions cause aggregate demand and the equilibrium level of income to fall!

The sudden increase in the planned thriftiness of consumers leads to several paradoxical conclusions. First, look at the *actual* saving after consumers became more thrifty. The *actual* saving at income level $1.425 trillion was the same as for the initial equilibrium level of income. Even though consumers attempted (planned) to save more, the reduction in income, caused by their efforts to be more thrifty, foiled their efforts. Second, the analysis suggests that what is virtuous for an individual may be folly for an entire nation. From the individual viewpoint, saving adds to wealth. It permits a higher level of future spending. But from society's viewpoint, a dollar saved is a dollar not spent. The reduction in spending could have disastrous consequences leading to declining income, production, and employment. Third, in the real world, efforts to be more thrifty are likely to come at a time when they will be most damaging. If unemployment is increasing, causing more and more workers to fear a layoff, how will they react? A person is unlikely to go on a spending spree today when he thinks he might be unemployed tomorrow. As a recession begins to set in, most people will reduce their spending, attempting to save for the hard times ahead. While this makes sense for the individual, when people in aggregate attempt to save more, it may cause the recession that everyone feared. From society's viewpoint, the remedy of individuals—an increase in thriftiness—becomes part of the problem.

Is thriftiness always folly from the viewpoint of the entire nation? Clearly, the answer is no. If aggregate demand is sufficient to maintain full employment, a reduction in consumption due to increased thriftiness allows more of the national product to be devoted to capital formation. If output were always at the full employment level, increased thriftiness would make it possible for both individuals and the entire economy to invest more. Investment adds to capital stock—the supply of buildings and machines that will help the nation generate future income. High rates of investment can lead to rapid growth in real GNP.

For example, since World War II, countries such as West Germany and Japan have typically invested (and saved) between one-quarter and one-third of their GNP, nearly twice the investment rate of the United States. These high rates of investment have led to rapid growth in real output. The real GNP of both West Germany and Japan has grown nearly twice as rapidly as that of the United States. Without thriftiness, funds would have been unavailable to finance such high levels of capital formation. The real income of these countries would have expanded less rapidly. The conflict between a high level of saving and maximum output is present only when aggregate demand is insufficient to maintain full employment.

BUSINESS PESSIMISM—A SELF-FULFILLING PROPHECY

Popular business publications often poll company executives about their future business plans. "Businessmen expect a banner year," or "Executives predict a recession is around the corner." These and similar headlines often make the covers of media publications.

Why are the expectations of businessmen so important? The Keynesian model, emphasizing the role of planned spending by households, businesses, and the government, yields insight into this question. Suppose that businessmen are pessimistic about the future and *plan* to restrict their rate of annual investment because of this pessimism. Their expectations have a tendency to be self-fulfilling.

Exhibit 9-5 illustrates the point. Suppose the economy were initially at a full-employment income level of $1.5 trillion. Despite the high level of income, something happens to disturb the expectations of businessmen. Maybe the stock market takes a turn for the worse or diplomatic relations with a potential enemy are strained. For whatever reason, businessmen *expect* that the future market for their product will be weak. Thus, they decide to cut back on their current investment by $50 billion. The investment schedule shifts down by this amount (shift from I_1 to I_2, Exhibit 9-5). Aggregate demand will of course also decline by $50 billion. How much will the equilibrium level of income fall? The multiplier principle will magnify the impact of the change in business investment plans. Given a MPC of 3/4, the $50 billion decline in investment will result in a $200 billion reduction of the equilibrium level of income. Declining investment leads to falling income which results in a lower level of consumption, further reducing income. Because of the multiplier principle, the comparatively small reduction in planned investment was amplified. Income fell sharply and depressed economic conditions permeated the economy. As forecasters, the businessmen were on target. The future was not bright. Their prophecy of a future recession was fulfilled.

Economic conditions may, of course, be depressed for reasons other than business

Exhibit 9-5 Business Pessimism and the Multiplier Principle

Suppose that the MPC is ¾ and that businessmen became pessimistic about the future. Because of the multiplier, a $50 billion reduction in planned investment would cause total income to decline by $200 billion. When businessmen *think* economic conditions are going to be bad and therefore cut back on investment, their plans can exert a strong negative impact on total income.

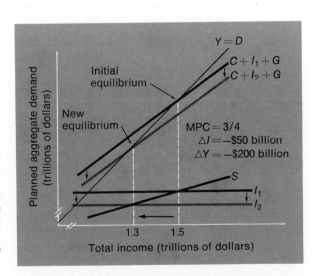

pessimism. But business pessimism will tend to make a bad situation worse. As businessmen adjust their investment plans downward in anticipation of a recession, these adjustments also become a contributing cause of the recession. This is particularly true in light of the multiplier principle.

INVESTMENT INSTABILITY AND THE ACCELERATOR

The multiplier principle emphasizes that changes in investment can generate substantial additional income and consumption. What about a possible link the other way? Could additional consumption induce changes in the level of investment?

According to the **accelerator principle,** rising consumption will induce more investment because a larger capital stock is necessary to produce the additional consumption. The accelerator principle postulates a constant relationship between the economy's capital stock and the level of consumption output. Thus, more consumption necessitates more investment, additions to the nation's capital stock.

The constant capital stock–output relation is thought to be a realistic approximation for many industries of the economy. For example, in the textile industry, a machine is combined with an operator to produce 100 shirts per week. If 200 shirts per week are desired, the number of machines must double. There is a constant relationship between the amount of capital (machines) and weekly output.

If the relationship between the nation's capital stock and current consumption is relatively constant, why does this contribute to economic instability? Exhibit 9-6 will help shed light on that question. Assume that the capital–output ratio is 5, indicating the capital stock of the economy is five times the level of consumption. During stage 1, consumption is constant and investment is just sufficient to replace machines (capital) that are worn out during the period. There is no net investment. But look what happens when stage 2 consumption increases by $5 billion per year. As consumption expands from $100 to $105 billion, a 5 percent increase, the required capital stock increases from $500 to $525 billion. *Net* investment accelerated from zero to $25 billion. For a purely private economy without a foreign sector, total income (NNP) in year 3 increases to $130 billion. A 5 percent increase in consumption causes total income to rise by 30 percent.

As long as consumption continues to *increase* by $5 billion annually, total income continues to grow. But when consumption levels off at $110 billion during stage 3, net investment deaccelerates sharply. The same capital stock is required to produce the constant level of consumption desired during years 4, 5, and 6. Thus, net investment falls to zero in year 5, and total income nosedives. The mere leveling off of consumption during year 5 causes income to fall by $25 billion!

What would happen to total income if there were a reduction in consumption? As stage 4, year 7 illustrates, net investment would be negative (disinvestment) when consumption spending declines. Aggregate income would plunge downward as the nation permitted its capital stock to fall to the level consistent with the reduced rate of consumption. Of course, buildings and machines only wear out so rapidly. Therefore,

Exhibit 9-6   The Accelerator Principle

The accelerator theory postulates a constant relationship between the capital stock and consumption output. The table demonstrates why small *changes* in consumption can induce large changes in investment and total income.

Period	Consumption C (billions of dollars)	Change in C (billions of dollars)	Capital stock ÷ consumption output	Capital stock (billions of dollars)	Net investment (billions of dollars)	NNP = C + I (billions of dollars)
Stage 1 (constant consumption)						
Year 1	100	0	5	500	0	100
Year 2	100	0	5	500	0	100
Stage 2 (increasing consumption)						
Year 3	105	5	5	525	25	130
Year 4	110	5	5	550	25	135
Stage 3 (constant consumption)						
Year 5	110	0	5	550	0	110
Year 6	110	0	5	550	0	110
Stage 4 (declining consumption)						
Year 7	105	−5	5	525	−25	80
Year 8	100	−5	5	500	−25	75

the reduction in the nation's capital stock would most likely be accompanied by substantial excess productive capacity in many industries.

Look at the last two columns of Exhibit 9-6. They illustrate that the relatively small changes in consumption (column 2) induce sharp fluctuations in net investment and total income. Unless consumption grows at a constant and steady rate, net investment will fluctuate substantially. If consumption increases, as was true between years 2 and 3, net investment will shoot up sharply. Income will grow rapidly. But when consumption is expanding, it must continue to grow at the same rate in order for investment to stand still (stage 2). If consumption levels off, investment will decline sharply (stage 3). If consumption should decline, net investment will become negative and total income will really take a plunge (stage 4). The accelerator principle implies that investment will be an extremely volatile component of national income.

In the real world there is not a rigid capital–consumption output ratio for all phases of the business cycle, as postulated by the accelerator principle. But the principle that small changes in consumption can induce large changes in investment, accelerating either a business expansion or contraction, is important.

Because of the accelerator, rising consumption will induce additional investment, causing income to rise rapidly during an upswing. But if consumption merely slows down, investment will decline, causing total income to fall. Thus, according to this theory, private investment will be very volatile, shooting up during an expansion and plummeting during a business slowdown.

A KEYNESIAN VIEW OF THE BUSINESS CYCLE[2]

In the last section we demonstrated how the accelerator principle would result in extreme fluctuations in investment, contributing to economic instability. What would happen if we combined the accelerator and the multiplier? The answer is that the tendency toward economic instability is further magnified.

When GNP is growing, consumption will also expand. The accelerator principle demonstrated that an expansion in consumption would result in a sharp increase in investment, further accelerating GNP. What does the multiplier theory tell us will happen when there is an increase in investment? The higher level of investment will have a multiplier effect, stimulating consumption and GNP still more.

In a sense, the Keynesian view stresses how an upswing feeds on itself. Any type of small impetus—war, new inventions, an increase in consumption, a cut in taxes—might set things off. Then the multiplier and the accelerator interact. Higher incomes lead to additional consumption which induces more investment. The investment, working through the multiplier, reinvigorates consumption, stimulating still more investment! All of this causes businessmen to become very optimistic about the future. They expand investment spending still more to build up inventories in expectation of still greater sales. Stock prices will generally reflect all of this optimism. Everything is up, up!

Can this expansionary phase continue indefinitely? The answer is no. Eventually full employment of both manpower and machines will result. The economy will have reached its capacity—its **full-employment ceiling.** As Exhibit 9-7 illustrates, the economy may temporarily bounce along this full-employment ceiling, but the *growth* in real GNP will have declined and eventually it will level off. Similarly, the growth in the consumption component of GNP will level off.

But according to the accelerator principle, what happens to investment when consumption levels off or grows at a slower rate? Investment declines. According to the multiplier principle, what will be the impact of declining investment on income? Income will fall by a multiple of the reduction in investment. The downswing, too, will

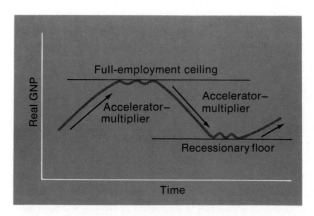

Exhibit 9-7 The Accelerator and the Multiplier

When GNP is expanding, consumption will increase. The multiplier and accelerator will interact, causing GNP to rise rapidly during this phase. However, full employment places a ceiling on growth. When the expansion levels off, business pessimism, the accelerator, and multiplier will combine to plunge the economy downward.

[2] The monetarists have a different theory of the business cycle. See Chapter 13, pages 233–236, for a detailed analysis of their view.

feed itself! Falling income will lead to business pessimism, causing investment to decline even more. People, expecting bad times, may reduce their consumption as they attempt to build up their savings. Falling consumption will further reduce aggregate demand, causing income to plunge downward still more rapidly. Inventories will rise as businesses are unable to sell their goods because of the low level of demand. Production will fall and workers will be laid off. The ranks of unemployed workers will grow. Bankruptcies will become more common. Everything goes bad as the recession sets in.

How far down can the economy go? If the 1930s are any indication, it can plunge a long way. But eventually machines will wear out and the capital stock will decline to a level consistent with current income and consumption. At that point, some investment will be necessary for replacement purposes. With time, inventories will be depleted and businessmen will begin placing new orders which will stimulate production. The gradual upturn in investment and production will generate additional income which will stimulate consumption and start the cycle anew.

Keynesian economists believe that because of this accelerator–multiplier interaction, a market economy, if left to its own direction, is inherently unstable. Both economic expansion and contraction will be magnified and will produce either inflation or recession. External factors such as foreign affairs, population growth or contraction, technological discoveries, the stock market, or business expectations may contribute to the cycle. But the effects of these factors will always be magnified by the multiplier–accelerator interaction. The market, if left to itself, will gyrate between inflationary overexpansion and recessionary unemployment.

INVESTMENT AND THE CYCLE

Private investment is the villain of the accelerator–multiplier theory of the business cycle. The expansion will burst into a boom because investment expands rapidly, stimulating other sectors of the economy. The contraction results in depression because a relatively small reduction in the rate of consumption will bring new investment to a standstill. The theory suggests that volatile investment acts as the moving force behind the business cycle.

Is the evidence consistent with this theory? Exhibit 9-8 illustrates the fluctuating nature of private investment. Periods of declining real GNP have typically been associated with sharp declines in investment. During the depression of 1930–1933, gross investment dropped sharply—more than $10 billion in constant 1958 dollars. This decline alone would have reduced GNP by 5 percent. The multiplier–accelerator interaction suggests that real income would decline by substantially more than the fall in investment. The real world was consistent with the theory. Actually, real income fell by nearly 30 percent between 1929 and 1933. During the 1933–1937 period, investment expanded slowly and the economy began to recover, albeit at a slow rate. But in 1938, investment again tumbled to new lows, plunging the economy deeper into depression. During World War II, the defense effort assured a high level of aggregate demand. Since World War II we have experience six recessions. Each time there has been a sharp decline in private investment (see Exhibit 9-8). By the same token, a sharp upsurge in investment has been associated with the recovery.

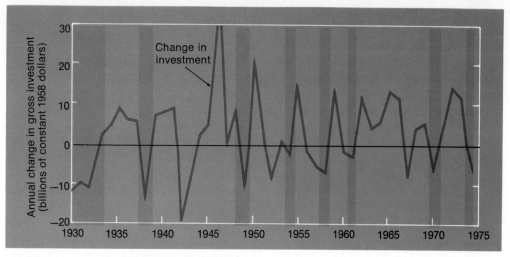

Exhibit 9-8   Investment and the Business Cycle

Investment is usually expanding during a business upswing and declining during a recession. A decline in gross investment was a characteristic of each of the eight recessions during the 1930–1975 period. Shaded areas represent periods of business recessions as defined by the National Bureau of Economic Research.

SOURCE: U.S. Department of Commerce.

The data of Exhibit 9-8 are consistent with the Keynesian view on the importance of the multiplier and accelerator as sources of economic instability. <u>Investment has fluctuated more widely than GNP. Periods of economic contraction have been associated with sharp reductions in the rate of investment. Similarly, rapid expansion in investment has accompanied economic recovery.</u>

⬜ LOOKING AHEAD

The Keynesian model points to a low level of investment, and therefore aggregate demand, as the cause of a recession. Identification of the problem also suggests a solution. If aggregate demand is too low, why not use public policy to prop it up? In the next chapter, we will begin our analysis of policy alternatives that can be utilized to stimulate aggregate demand and minimize the harmful effects of a recession.

Despite the consistency of the evidence with the Keynesian theory of the business cycle, the theory is not accepted by all economists. The monetarists, as we will discuss later, believe that economic fluctuations originate from a different source. Association is not causation. The monetarists believe that changes in investment are the result, not the cause, of changes in real GNP. They believe that economic instability is the result of fluctuations in the supply of money. We will analyze this alternative theory of the business cycle in detail in Chapter 13.

CHAPTER LEARNING OBJECTIVES

1. The multiplier principle notes that independent changes in planned investment, government expenditures, and consumption have a magnified impact on income. Income will increase by some multiple of the initial change in spending. The word multiplier is used to indicate the number by which the initial investment is multiplied in order to obtain the total amplified increase in income. The size of the multiplier increases with the marginal propensity to consume.

2. It takes time for the secondary effects of the multiplier to be felt. It is usually thought that approximately one-half of the multiplier effect will come during the first six months after an independent change in spending.

3. When resources are idle, each round of additional spending generated by the multiplier will expand real output and employment. When there are few idle resources, the increased spending will be inflationary.

4. The Keynesian model suggests that an increase in planned aggregate saving could cause problems. Higher planned saving would mean a reduction in planned consumption. Other things constant, aggregate demand would decline, causing the equilibrium level of income to fall. Since households often try to save more at the beginning of a recessionary period, their actions may push the economy further into a recession and complicate the recovery process.

5. Saving is also necessary for capital accumulation. Thus, *if aggregate demand is sufficient to maintain full employment*, increased saving could facilitate investment, capital accumulation, and a higher level of future income.

6. Economic pessimism often causes businessmen to cut back on their planned investment. Thus, pessimism tends to be self-fulfilling as the reduction in planned investment, magnified by the multiplier, reduces income and tends to trigger the recession that was forecast.

7. Interaction between the multiplier and accelerator serves to enhance the potential for economic instability. During expansion, an increase in investment serves to increase consumption which in turn increases the demand for additional investment. Consumption and investment each feed the other, and the economy booms. But full employment places a ceiling on growth and eventually the expansion will level off. As growth and consumption spending level off, the accelerator principle explains why net investment often declines sharply, plunging the economy toward recession.

8. In the past, private investment has fluctuated more widely than GNP. Periods of economic contraction have been associated with sharp reductions in investment. Similarly, rapid expansion in investment has accompanied economic recovery.

IMPORTANT TERMS TO REMEMBER

Multiplier: The change in the equilibrium level of income brought about by an independent change in investment, consumption, or government spending. Numerically, the multiplier is $1/(1 - MPC)$.

Paradox of thrift: An apparent contradiction between the desire of households to increase saving and their ability to realize a higher rate of saving *in aggregate*. When households *in aggregate* plan to save more, consumption will decline, causing income to fall by the amount of the reduction in consumption times the multiplier. At the lower income level *actual* saving may be no greater (it might even be less) than the level that would have occurred had households not tried to be more thrifty.

Accelerator principle: The proposition that an increase in consumer demand will induce a magnified expansion in investment because a larger capital stock would be necessary to produce the higher level of consumer goods. The principle also implies that when consumption is growing, a mere *slowing down in the rate* of growth in consumer demand would cause gross investment to decline. Thus, the principle suggests that investment will be highly volatile.

Full-employment ceiling: A constraint placed on the *real* income of an economy when idle resources are no longer available.

THE ECONOMIC WAY OF THINKING—DISCUSSION QUESTIONS

1. "The best cure for unemployment and a recession is for everybody, including government, to tighten their belts, cut down on unnecessary spending, and forego luxury items until the recession is over." Do you agree? Why or why not?

2. Explain in your own words how the multiplier and accelerator reinforce each other to generate cyclical business conditions.

3. Explain the paradox of thrift. Was Ben Franklin wrong to sanctify saving? Is saving necessary for investment and economic growth? Should we try to save more or less next year? Why?

4. What is the multiplier principle? What determines the size of the multiplier? Does the multiplier principle make it more or less difficult to stabilize the economy? Explain.

5. "How can the Keynesian model be correct? According to Keynes, falling income, unemployment, and bad times result because people have so much income that they fail to spend enough to buy all of the goods produced. Paradoxically, rising income and good times result because people are reducing their savings and spending more than they are making. This doesn't make sense." Explain why you either agree or disagree with this view.

10
FISCAL POLICY

Fiscal policy means using tax rates and government spending as a means to influence the level of aggregate demand. According to the general Keynesian diagnosis, unemployment results primarily because aggregate demand is deficient. On the other hand, inflation is the result of excess aggregate demand when the economy is already producing at capacity level. Since the government's taxation and expenditure policy —its fiscal policy—can influence aggregate demand, the budget is a most useful weapon for use against our enemies, economic instability and unemployed resources.

Beginning with the 1960s, the popular news media gave wide coverage to fiscal policy. It was often referred to as the New Economics, even though it had been encompassed in economics texts for some 20 years. It was about as new as television. At that time, the desirability of balancing the federal budget annually was widely accepted among business and political leaders. A reluctant President Kennedy, under the constant prodding of Walter Heller, the chairman of his Council of Economic Advisers, finally was convinced of the desirability of a tax cut to stimulate the economy. The major argument of Chairman Heller and other economists was that a tax cut would stimulate consumer spending and increase aggregate demand. Later in 1968, President Johnson pulled another fiscal lever marked "tax increase" in an effort to reduce the inflationary pressures of the economy. Both of these measures were firmly grounded in the Keynesian economic framework. In this chapter we will investigate the logic behind the use of fiscal policy as a tool to keep the economy on a steady course.

PUBLIC POLICY TO DEAL WITH A RECESSION

According to the Keynesian view, market forces will not assure full employment. There might well be a balance of forces between planned aggregate demand and income (supply) even though unemployed resources are present. Exhibit 10-1 presents a graphic picture of an economy experiencing a recession because of insufficient demand. The full employment level of income is $1.32 trillion, but the initial level of aggregate demand $(C + I + G_1)$ results in an actual equilibrium income level of $1.2 trillion— $120 billion below capacity. There is a **recessionary gap** between actual aggregate demand and the level of aggregate demand that is necessary for full employment. The amount by which aggregate demand falls short of the full employment level of income, the recessionary gap, is the *vertical* distance by which the aggregate demand schedule

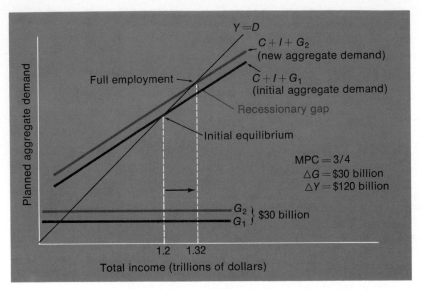

$Y = D$

$C + I + G_2$
(new aggregate demand)

Full employment →

$C + I + G_1$
(initial aggregate demand)

Recessionary gap

Initial equilibrium

$MPC = 3/4$
$\triangle G = \$30$ billion
$\triangle Y = \$120$ billion

$\left.\begin{array}{c} G_2 \\ G_1 \end{array}\right\}$ $30 billion

Planned aggregate demand

1.2   1.32
Total income (trillions of dollars)

Exhibit 10-1   Government Expenditures as a Route to Full-Employment Equilibrium

A $30 billion increase in autonomous government expenditures, *holding taxes constant*, would increase income from $1.2 trillion to the full-employment level of $1.32 trillion—a $120 billion expansion.

falls short of the aggregate supply schedule at the full employment level of income. For the economy pictured by Exhibit 10-1, the recessionary gap would be $30 billion (note: the recessionary gap is *not* the difference between full employment income and actual income).

How could public policy combat the recession, stimulate aggregate demand, and push the economy to its full employment capacity level of output? One way would be to increase government expenditures, while holding taxes constant. If the government increased its demand for such things as education, national defense, recreation areas, office buildings, training programs, and public housing, the aggregate demand for goods and services would rise. Suppose the government spends an *additional* $30 billion on these goods. Aggregate demand would shift upward by $30 billion to $C + I + G_2$. The additional government spending would increase the income of newly employed workers, setting off a multiplier effect. Since the marginal propensity to consume for the economy is 3/4, the multiplier would be 4. Thus, the $30 billion of additional government spending would cause total income to rise by $120 billion, pushing the economy to full employment.

Should the government raise taxes to finance the additional expenditures? From the standpoint of policy effectiveness, it is important that the additional government spending does not merely replace private consumption and investment. If income taxes were raised, this would reduce the disposable income available to households, causing consumption to decline. Higher business taxes would discourage investment. Higher taxes would serve to, at least partially, offset the expansionary effect of the increased level of government expenditures.

If the increased spending is to have a maximum expansionary effect, deficit financing should be used. The government should plan a **budget deficit**—recognizing that its tax revenues will be less than expenditures. Like a private business, the government cannot spend money that it does not have. If taxes are not raised, how will the government finance the higher level of current expenditures? Borrowing is the answer. The government can borrow from individuals, firms, and banks in order to cover its planned deficit. The Treasury can issue bonds, U.S. securities, in order to raise the funds necessary to finance the government's deficit.

A Tax Cut as the Route to Full Employment

As an alternative to increasing government expenditures, a tax cut could be used to stimulate aggregate demand and combat recessionary conditions. Political decision-makers may feel that consumers, rather than the government, can best determine what additional goods to produce as output is expanded. When this is the case, an income tax reduction would be the appropriate tool to lead an underemployed economy back to its full potential.

An income tax cut will increase the disposable income of households. Lower taxes will mean a larger paycheck for millions of consumers. This increase in "take-home pay" will cause consumer spending to rise by an amount equal to the change in disposable income times the MPC. As Exhibit 10-2 illustrates, a $40 billion tax cut would cause the consumption schedule (and aggregate demand) to shift upward by $30 billion, the amount of the tax cut times MPC (3/4). The increased consumer spending will generate more income for shopkeepers, restaurant owners, travel agencies, gasoline stations, automobile dealers, and many others. Because of the multiplier effect, $30 billion of additional consumer spending (stemming from the $40 billion tax cut) will cause income to expand by $120 billion. Thus, a tax cut, like an expansion in government expenditures, can stimulate aggregate demand, and push the economy to the full-employment equilibrium level of income.

Should government expenditures be reduced in order to keep the federal budget in

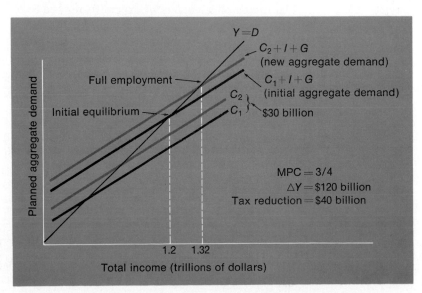

Exhibit 10-2   Tax Reduction as a Route to Full Employment

When the economy is below full-employment equilibrium, a reduction in taxes can also be utilized as a method of stimulating the economy back to full employment.

balance? No. This would be counterproductive. It would reduce aggregate demand and employment, prolonging the recession. Keynesian policy suggests that the government run a budget deficit, financing the tax cut by borrowing.

As we saw in Chapter 8, private investment often declines sharply during a recession. Policy planners may want to combine an income tax cut with a reduction in business taxes designed to stimulate investment. Policy prescriptions, such as a more favorable tax treatment of depreciation, a reduction in corporate income taxes, and/or larger investment tax credits, might be chosen as a means to stimulate private investment. A reduction in business taxes would serve to increase the investment component of aggregate demand, shifting the investment schedule upward. The *additional* investment would, of course, have a multiplier effect—causing income to rise by the expansion in investment times the multiplier.

Is There a Balanced Budget Multiplier?

What happens if the government increases both taxes and expenditures by the same amount, say $30 billion? The knee-jerk reaction is usually to conclude that there would be no net impact on the equilibrium level of income. But let us think the question through. Assume that the MPC of the economy was 3/4, indicating that consumers spend 75 cents out of each *additional* dollar of income received. If government increased expenditures by $30 billion, income would increase by $30 billion times the multiplier of 4. Income would go up by $120 billion, as was illustrated by Exhibit 10-1. If taxes were increased simultaneously by $30 billion, the disposable income of consumers would decline by this amount. But because the MPC is 3/4, consumers would reduce their consumption by only $22.5 billion as the result of the $30 billion reduction in disposable income. This would cause a total reduction in income equal to the $22.5 billion reduction in consumption, times the multiplier (4), or $90 billion. The increased government expenditures add $120 billion to income, while the higher taxes reduce income by only $90 billion. Therefore, a $30 billion increase in both taxes and government expenditures would lead to a $30 billion increase in total income. There would be a balanced budget multiplier of exactly 1. While the tax increase that accompanied the high level of government expenditures certainly dampened the expansionary impact of the increase in G, *within the model*, some expansion resulted even though the budget remained in balance.

The logic for the expansionary effect of the increased balanced budget spending is straightforward. It results because consumers do not reduce their spending by the full amount of their reduction in disposable income. But this analysis is all very mechanical. It follows directly from the assumptions of the model. There are two important reasons why the analysis may overstate the expansionary impact of a higher level of balanced budget spending. First, the increase in government expenditures may provide the consumer with something that he otherwise intended to buy. The government spending may partially be a substitute for the consumer's own spending. If the government expenditure provides him with goods he otherwise would have bought, the consumer may reduce his own expenditures. When this is the case, consumer expenditures will decline, not just because of the higher taxes, but also because of the govern-

OUTSTANDING ECONOMIST: Walter Heller

When President Kennedy took office in January 1961, Walter Heller took over as chairman of the Council of Economic Advisers, a position he held until the end of 1964. Professor Heller has been referred to as the "architect of the prosperity during the sixties." As unemployment hovered near 6 percent in the early 1960s, Heller was convinced that a Keynesian stimulus to aggregate demand was needed. Heller recognized that a tax cut would not be popular in congressional circles since the actual budget was already running a deficit. Nevertheless, he campaigned tirelessly, giving testimony before congressional committees, holding press conferences, lining up academic and public support. Everywhere he went his message was the same. The economy is sluggish. Unemployment is higher than it need be. The answer is a tax cut that will stimulate both private investment and consumption, pushing the economy to full employment. Finally, the 1964 tax cut was enacted and history has recorded the growth and high employment of the decade.

The education of presidents is one of Heller's favorite topics, and well it might be. He has remarked that "President Kennedy was the best economics student I ever had and It's only fair to L.B.J. to say that he was a close second. Their minds were remarkably receptive to new ideas."[1] No previous president relied on economic advisers to the extent that Presidents Kennedy and Johnson did. Yet President Johnson rejected his counsel on one important matter. In early 1966, as inflationary pressures from the Vietnam War and expansionary macropolicy were building, Heller advised the administration to raise taxes immediately. President Johnson delayed until 1967 and the Congress until 1968. By that time, the overheated economy was in a much more difficult state to control. One cannot help but wonder what would have happened had Heller's advice been heeded two years earlier.

A long-time professor of economics at the University of Minnesota, Heller returned to academic life in 1965. But he continues to speak out on national issues and offer counsel to policy-makers. As the unemployment rate soared sharply in 1974–1975, Heller was among the leading critics of the Ford Administration. "They are bewitched by inflation," Heller remarked as he argued for a tax cut and a more expansionary fiscal policy in the face of "the worst recession since the Great Depression." In recent years, he has written on environmental economics and employment discrimination in addition to macropolicy issues. His ability to communicate technical matters in an understandable language has made him a popular figure with the news media.

mental provision of goods. Therefore, the net difference between the increased *G* and reduced *C* due to the tax increase, may overstate the net positive impact on aggregate demand. For example, suppose the government used the $30 billion to buy school lunches, public transportation, and greater retirement benefits. Because of these expenditures, consumers may decide to save more since the government now provides

[1] Walter Heller (interview), *Challenge*, May/June 1973, pp. 32–41. Also see Walter Heller, *New Dimensions of Political Economy* (New York: Norton, 1967).

their school lunches, auto transportation, and retirement insurance policies. Thus, the increase in government spending may be at least partially offset by an increase in current saving (reduction in current consumption) relative to the rate of saving implied by the initial saving–consumption function. Therefore, part of the additional government spending is merely a substitution for private spending.

Second, the balanced budget multiplier may be dampened because of the impact of the higher tax rate on saving and indirectly on private investment. Because of the $30 billion tax increase consumers will save $5 billion less. This reduction in the supply of saving could increase interest rates, making private investment more costly. The level of private investment might therefore fall, further dampening the balanced budget expansionary effect.

What conclusion are we to draw? Within the framework of a model that assumes (a) a MPC of less than 1, (b) no negative (substitution) impact of the *additional* government expenditures on private consumption, and (c) no indirect negative impact on private investment via the interest rate, there is a balanced budget multiplier of unity. But as indicated, this conclusion is drawn cautiously and under restrictive assumptions.

In any case, the important conclusion would seem to be the negative one. Any expansionary impact of fiscal policy is substantially dampened when taxes are raised to finance the higher level of government expenditures.[2]

FISCAL POLICY TO DEAL WITH INFLATION

A wave of business optimism and consumer spending could push aggregate demand beyond the level that is consistent with stable prices. Full employment places a ceiling on the production capacity of the economy. Once full employment is reached, excess demand relative to aggregate supply would cause rising prices. The excessive aggregate demand would be inflationary.

Exhibit 10-3 presents a graphic picture of inflationary pressures that stem from excess demand. When aggregate demand is $C_1 + I_1 + G_1$, an **inflationary gap** AB exists. Specifically, the inflationary gap is the amount by which aggregate demand exceeds income at the level of income that is consistent with both full employment and price stability.

A **restrictive fiscal policy,** higher tax rates and/or a reduction in planned government expenditures, could be used to eliminate the inflationary gap and combat the rising prices. Higher taxes would reduce disposable income, causing consumption to decline. An increase in business taxes would dampen investment. A reduced level of government expenditures would diminish aggregate demand directly. A restrictive fiscal policy could shift the aggregate demand schedule downward to $C_2 + I_2 + G_2$, a level that is consistent with both full employment and price stability.

Higher taxes and a reduction in government expenditures are likely to result in a **budget surplus.** Because of the restrictive fiscal policy, taxation is taking more out

---

[2]Appendix B uses equations to illustrate the concepts of aggregate equilibrium, the multiplier, and the balanced budget multiplier. This would be a good time for the mathematically inclined reader to look into the equation form of the Keynesian model as it is presented in Appendix B.

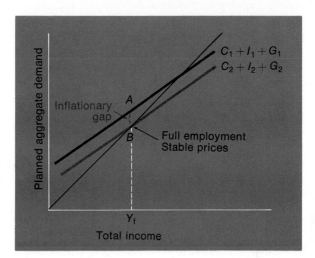

Exhibit 10-3 Restrictive Fiscal Policy to Combat Inflation

Excessive aggregate demand, such as that pictured by $C_1 + I_1 + G_1$, would cause rising prices. Restrictive fiscal policy—a tax increase or a reduction in government spending—is required to eliminate the inflationary gap AB and combat the rising prices.

of the income stream than government expenditures are putting back into it. The Keynesian analysis suggests that this is precisely the proper policy prescription with which to combat inflation generated by excess demand.

THE CENTRAL IDEA OF FISCAL POLICY

Most political figures and budget planners in the 1950s thought of taxes as merely a tool to raise revenues for the financing of government expenditures. The budgetary problem was conceived as one of matching revenues and expenditures.

The Keynesian analysis introduces an entirely new focus. It suggests that the general economic conditions can be altered by budget policy. When economic conditions are slack, a budget deficit, far from being a fiscal sin, is actually a virtue. Expansionary fiscal policy, a planned budget deficit, is called for so the government can put more into the aggregate income stream than it is taking out. Aggregate income will be expanded because of the multiplier effect, and the economy will be pushed toward full employment. Similarly, when the economy is experiencing an economic boom, a balanced budget policy will be insufficient to combat inflation. Greater restraint is needed. The government should follow restrictive fiscal policy, running a budget surplus.

Countercyclical fiscal policy does not recommend that the annual budget be balanced. Rather it calls for a planned budget deficit during an economic slowdown and a surplus in the presence of an inflationary boom. General economic conditions replace the annual balanced budget concept as the proper criteria for determining budget policy.

Planned and Actual Deficits

Not only does the budget policy of the government exert an influence on economic conditions, but economic conditions also influence the revenue and expenditure level of the government. When an economy is at less than full employment, a tax reduction will result in a smaller deficit than may at first appear. The *planned* government deficit, by stimulating income, will also stimulate tax revenues. Thus, despite the reduction in tax rates, tax revenues may decline very little if at all.

There is some evidence that this is what happened as the result of the much heralded 1964 tax cut in the United States. Personal and corporate tax rates were reduced and a planned annual deficit of between $10 and $15 billion was initially expected during the 1964–1966 period. But GNP grew quite rapidly as the result of the tax rate reduction. The total taxes collected at the higher income levels were greater than anticipated. The *actual* government deficits were $1.6 billion in 1965 and $3.8 billion in 1966, much lower than the *planned* deficits for the two years.

How Not to Reduce the Deficit

While a planned deficit can result in a smaller deficit than anticipated, just the opposite can happen when taxes are increased or expenditures reduced in an effort to avoid a budgetary deficit. Exhibit 10-4 illustrates why this is true. Suppose the government is initially running a deficit because total income is at less than the full-employment level. Balanced-budget-minded politicians increase taxes and reduce government expenditures in order to bring the budget into balance. Such a policy will lead to further deteriorating economic conditions. The tax increase will reduce disposable income, causing a decline in consumption and aggregate demand. The reduction in government spending will directly reduce aggregate demand. As demand declines, the $C + I + G$ line will shift down, causing the equilibrium level of income to fall by some multiple of the decline in aggregate demand. At the lower income level, tax revenues will be less than expected even though tax rates have been increased. An *actual* budgetary deficit may still result, even though the policy was designed to avoid it.

There is strong evidence that the 1958–1959 budget policies of the Eisenhower

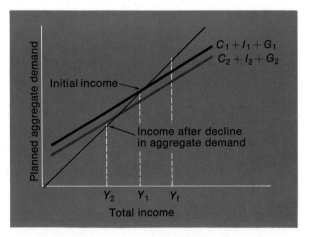

Exhibit 10-4   Trying to Balance the Budget Can Make Things Worse

If an economy is at less than full employment, reduced government expenditures and/or higher tax rates would cause aggregate demand to fall (shift to $C_2 + I_2 + G_2$). Income would decline. At the lower level of income, unemployment would rise and tax revenues would be less than expected. An actual budget deficit is still likely to result.

Administration resulted in precisely this type of unplanned deficit. In 1958 the unemployment rate was 6.8 percent and the economy was performing far below capacity. The Eisenhower Administration *planned* a balanced budget despite the state of the economy at that time. The result was a continuation of the high unemployment rates on through 1961, a slow rate of growth in income, and a $12.9 billion budget deficit. Even though a balanced budget was *planned*, the actual deficit for the 1958–1959 fiscal year was the largest of any single year between World War II and 1968. It was primarily the result of *planning* a balanced budget, when a deficit should have been planned to stimulate income and employment.

THE FULL-EMPLOYMENT BUDGET CONCEPT

The budget is complex and no single indicator can measure its precise impact on the economy. But the most useful summary statistic on the status of fiscal policy is the full-employment budget surplus or deficit. The **full-employment budget** estimate is a measure of the revenues and expenditures of the government as they would appear if the economy were at full employment, the level of activity associated with 4 or 5 percent unemployment.

When government revenue and expenditure estimates are calculated at full employment, the impact of changing economic conditions on the budget can be isolated from changes in a budget surplus or deficit that results from fiscal policy decisions. A full-employment budget deficit is indicative of expansionary fiscal policy. A full-employment budget surplus indicates the government is seeking to restrain the economy.

The *actual* budget deficit can be a misleading indicator of fiscal policy because it will include, not just the impact of the budget on the economy, but also the impact of the economy on the budget. During a recession, income, profits, and sales will decline. Thus, the tax revenues of the government will fall, and a budget deficit will result even though no positive stimulus has been given. As we indicated, the budget deficit of the Eisenhower Administration in 1958 was of this variety.

When unemployment is low (that is, when the economy is at full employment), the actual budget is the full-employment budget. Therefore, we can observe the impact of government fiscal policy unclouded by the effects of recessionary conditions. If the actual budget is in surplus (deficit) under these circumstances, it is indicative of restrictive (expansionary) fiscal policy.

When an economy is slack, a full-employment surplus would certainly not be in order. Similarly, when the unemployment rate is already low, a budget deficit would merely provide stimulus that would only generate rising prices and inflation.

HAS REAL WORLD FISCAL POLICY BEEN STABILIZING?

Planners, like other decision-makers, must make choices without perfect information. It is not always easy to tell what the future will bring. Current economic indicators give us a pretty good picture of where we are today. But the impact of fiscal policy will not be *immediate*. Today's policy decisions may have their major impact 12 to 18 months in the future. Economic forecasting can give us some insight into what the economy will be like in the future, but forecasting is a highly imperfect science. Thus, real world fiscal policy may be substantially at variance with the countercyclical ideal.[3]

While proper fiscal policy can exert a stabilizing influence on both employment and prices, improper policy, or more precisely, improper timing of fiscal policy, can exert a destabilizing influence. The knife that cut the cheese can also cut the finger.

Exhibit 10-5 presents evidence on the stabilizing (?) effects of real world fiscal policy during the last two decades. Data on both the actual and full-employment budget are presented. Since it tends to eliminate the impact of economic conditions on taxes and revenues, the full-employment budget deficit or surplus will be the more precise indicator of real world fiscal policy.

During most of the 1950s fiscal policy was restrictive. Even though the actual budget was in deficit during the 1957–1958 recession, the full-employment budget ran a sizable surplus. In spite of an unemployment rate that approached 7 percent, neither the Eisenhower Administration nor the Democratic Congress took the initiative to follow an expansionary course. The economy had not completely recovered from the 1957–1958 recession before it dipped into another recession in 1960–1961. Again the full-

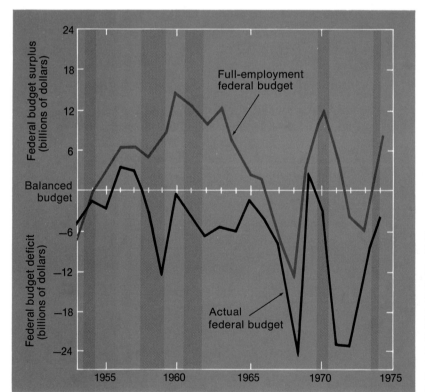

Exhibit 10-5   Real World Fiscal Policy

Both the actual and full-employment budget deficits are shown. Note that the full-employment budget indicates fiscal policy was restrictive prior to, and during, the recessions of 1958, 1961, and 1970. Fiscal policy was highly expansionary during the inflation of the mid and late 1960s. The shaded areas represent periods of recession as defined by the National Bureau of Economic Research.

[3]Chapter 14, pages 255–259, presents a detailed discussion of why macroplanners may do the wrong thing.

employment budget was in surplus during this recession, suggesting that restrictive fiscal policy was actually prolonging the recession and hindering recovery!

The restrictive fiscal policy, as measured by the full-employment budget, continued into the 1960s. It was not until the tax cut of 1964 that fiscal stimulus began to be injected into the economy. However, by 1966 macropolicy and the Vietnam War buildup had pushed the unemployment rate below 4 percent. The economy was operating at its productive capacity. During the 1966–1969 period, as both the actual and full-employment budget reveal, fiscal policy was decidedly expansionary. Fiscal policy was actually intensifying the pressures from aggregate demand, even though the economy was already at full employment. What was the result? Unsurprisingly, from a Keynesian viewpoint, prices which had been relatively stable in the early 1960s began rising at an annual rate in excess of 3 percent. Since the economy was already at full employment, the expansionary fiscal policy of the 1966–1968 period was merely fueling the fires of inflation!

Since 1968 the full-employment budget suggests that fiscal policy has followed a stop–go course. It was restrictive prior to and during the inflationary recession of 1970. An expansionary path was followed, building up to the 1972 elections. After the election, macroplanners pursued a more restrictive course in an effort to combat the inflationary pressure. If the Ford Administration's budget for fiscal year 1975–1976 is indicative, fiscal policy will be more expansionary as the 1976 elections are approached.

Analysis of the record makes it clear that discretionary fiscal policy is not a panacea. A stabilizing course is not easy to follow. Inappropriate fiscal policy can itself be a source of instability. The evidence suggests that the restrictive fiscal policy of the late 1950s and early 1960s actually worsened the recessionary conditions and slowed the recovery. Similarly, the expansionary course of the 1966–1968 period sowed the seeds for the inflation that has haunted the economy into the 1970s. As we continue, we will analyze the problem of proper timing in greater detail.

AUTOMATIC STABILIZERS

There are a few fiscal programs that tend to automatically help stabilize the economy. No discretionary legislative action is needed. Thus, the problem of proper timing is avoided.

Automatic stabilizers, even without legislative action, will tend to contribute to a budget deficit during bad times and a surplus during an economic boom. They will automatically reduce taxes and increase government expenditures, giving the economy a shot in the arm when unemployment is rising and business conditions are slow. On the other hand, automatic stabilizers will serve to increase tax revenues and decrease government spending, helping apply the brakes to an economic boom. Three of these built-in stabilizers deserve specific mention.

1. *Unemployment Compensation.*   When unemployment is high, the receipts from the unemployment compensation tax will decline because of the reduction in employment. Payments will increase because more workers are now eligible to receive benefits. The program will automatically run a deficit during a business slowdown. In contrast,

when the unemployment rate is low, tax receipts from the program will increase because more people are now working. The benefits paid out will decline, because fewer people are unemployed. The program will automatically tend to run a surplus during good times. Thus, without any change in policy, the program has the desired countercyclical effect.

2. *Corporate Profit Tax.* Tax studies show that the corporate profit tax is the most countercyclical of all the automatic stabilizers. This results because corporate profits are highly sensitive to cyclical conditions. During recessionary conditions, corporate profits will decline sharply, and so will corporate tax payments. This sharp decline in tax revenues will tend to enlarge the size of the government deficit. During economic expansion, corporate profits typically increase much more rapidly than wages, income, or consumption. This increase in corporate profits will result in a rapid increase in the "tax take" from the business sector during expansion. Thus, the corporate tax payments go up during expansion and fall rapidly during a contraction even if there is no change in tax policy.

3. *Progressive Income Tax.* During economic expansion, the disposable income of consumers increases less rapidly than total income. This results because, with higher incomes, the progressive income tax pushes more people into the higher tax brackets. Thus tax revenues increase because (a) income is higher and (b) tax rates on marginal income have increased. On the other hand, when income declines, many taxpayers will be assigned lower tax rates, reducing the government's tax take. Thus, progressive taxes are automatically countercyclical.

Research indicates that as much as one-third of the cyclical fluctuations in income are eliminated by automatic stabilizers. But considerable cyclical fluctuation still remains. Discretionary fiscal policy, at least ideally, can supplement the automatic stabilizers, further reducing economic instability.

SPENDING VERSUS TAXING ALTERNATIVES

If fiscal expansion is needed, does it make any difference whether taxes are reduced or government spending increased? Should inflation be dealt with by higher taxes or reduced spending? Should taxes on consumers or businesses be changed? The vehicle chosen to influence aggregate demand may exert an important influence on (a) how rapidly the policy becomes effective and (b) the type of activity that is undertaken.

A reduction in personal income taxes is usually thought to have a more *immediate* impact on current aggregate demand than either a tax reduction designed to stimulate private investment or an increase in government expenditures. Given our withholding system whereby taxes are deducted weekly from an employee's paycheck, a reduction in personal income taxes will almost immediately increase the take-home pay of millions of Americans. This stimulus to private spending will *begin* to have its impact quickly and generally throughout the economy. On the other side of the coin, it takes considerable time to let contracts for increased private investment and government expenditures. The immediate impact, particularly in the case of government spending, is often limited to specific firms or geographic areas. The economy may become "overheated" in some areas, while unemployment persists in other areas.

But the argument for utilizing changes in tax rates or government expenditures often rests on different grounds. Differences of opinion are often based on what an advocate perceives as the proper role of government. Those who favor, on philosophical grounds, an expansion of the public sector relative to the private sector, will tend to favor increased government expenditures to combat unemployment and higher tax rates to limit inflation. Advocates of the private sector will tend to favor lower taxes to combat unemployment and reduced government expenditures to deal with inflation. In later chapters, we will discuss factors that are important to the question of private–public sector activities. But, strictly speaking, maintaining a stable level of aggregate demand is irrelevant to the question of private versus public sector allocation of resources.

The choice of expanding consumption or investment, while unimportant to the maintenance of full employment and stable prices, is relevant from the viewpoint of intergenerational income distribution and future growth. A policy designed primarily to stimulate investment will lead to a greater expansion of capital goods and future capacity to produce. The income of future generations will be favorably affected by the expansion of capital goods (that is, investment) while policies designed to stimulate consumption will have a greater impact on the welfare of the current generation.

▭ LOOKING AHEAD

In this chapter we concentrated on the simple mechanics of fiscal policy. We made several implicit assumptions that call for further investigation. We assumed that the size of the government deficit (or surplus) will not alter the interest rate, thereby indirectly influencing private spending. We still have not considered the importance of money. Neither have we considered the possibility of conflict between good politics and proper stabilization policy. We have made fiscal management look pretty easy. Perhaps some of you are thinking, "If the politicians just knew a little something about economics and were willing to apply that knowledge when making real world policy decisions, the business cycle could be left behind." Perhaps that view is correct, but things are a bit more complicated than our analysis has suggested. In the following chapter, we will discuss the banking system and its importance. As we proceed we will deal with several other issues that add to the complexity of real world fiscal management. But first, let us take a look at something that belongs to each of us, the national debt.

Fact and Fiction about the National Debt

Perspectives in Economics

Keynesian economic analysis suggests that deficit financing can help stimulate an economy to full employment, while a budget surplus is a useful tool to deal with inflation. However, there is no reason to expect that the deficits will just be covered by the surpluses. Over a period of time, fiscal policy designed to stabilize the economy might well result in an increase in the national debt.

For years laymen, politicians, and economists have debated about the burden of the **national debt.** The one side has argued that we are mortgaging the future of our children and grandchildren. Future generations, we have been told, will pay the consequence of our fiscal irresponsibility. The other side retorted, "We owe it to ourselves." Since most of the national debt is held by U.S. citizens in the form of bonds, it represents an asset as well as a future liability. We will pass along not only a tax burden associated with the interest payments on the debt, but we will also bequeath our children and grandchildren a valuable asset—interest-bearing U.S. bonds. The asset will offset the liability of the debt. Has the judge of time declared a winner of this debate? What is fact and what is fiction about the national debt?

1. FACT: The national debt is owned by U.S. citizens, foreigners, U.S. government agencies, and the Federal Reserve System. Exhibit 10-6 gives the breakdown on who owns the debt. The biggest share of it, some 44 percent, is held internally by U.S. citizens and private institutions, such as insurance companies and commercial banks. A little less than 13 percent of the national debt is held by foreigners. The portion owned by foreigners is sometimes referred to as external debt. Approximately 27 percent of the debt is held by agencies of the federal government. For example, surplus Social Security trust funds are often used to purchase U.S. bonds. When the debt is owned by a government agency, it is little more than an accounting transaction indicating that one government agency (for example, Social Security Administration) is making a loan to another (for example, U.S. Treasury). Even the interest payments, in this case, represent little more than an internal government transfer. Approximately one-sixth of the public debt is held by the Federal Reserve System. As we will show in the next chapter, this portion of the debt is an important determinant of the stock of money in the United States.

2. FICTION: The national debt must be paid off. Borrowing is an everyday method of doing business. Many of the nation's largest and most profitable corporations continually have outstanding debts to bondholders. Yet, these corporations, particularly the profitable ones, will have no trouble refinancing the outstanding debt if they so wish. What is necessary is that the borrower have sufficient assets or income to pay both the interest and principal as they come due. As long as General Motors has millions of dollars worth of assets and corporate income, they will have no trouble borrowing a few million and refinancing it, and refinancing it again and again, because lenders know that GM will be able to pay off the loan. Similarly, as long as the U.S. government can raise huge revenues through taxes, lenders can be very sure that the government will be able to return their money plus interest when due. Therefore, there is no date in the future on which the national debt must be repaid.

Exhibit 10-6   Ownership of the National Debt (March 1975)

Ownership of U.S. securities	Dollar value (in billions)	Percent
U.S. government agencies	138.5	27.2
Federal Reserve Banks	81.4	16.0
Domestic investors	224.8	44.1
Foreign investors	65.0	12.7
Totals	509.7	100.0

SOURCE: The Board of Governors of the Federal Reserve System.

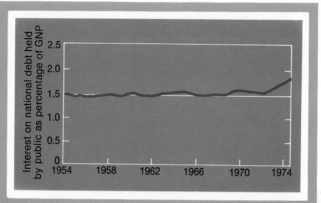

Exhibit 10-7   Interest Payments as a Percentage of Gross National Product

During the last 20 years the interest payments on the portion of the national debt held by the public have comprised between 1.5 and 2.0 percent of GNP. The share has risen in the 1970s.
SOURCE: *Budget of the United States—1976.*

3. FICTION: <u>The national debt has grown so fast, the U.S. government is on the verge of bankruptcy.</u> As we just indicated, what is important is the government's ability to raise revenues to meet its debt obligation. Actually, by this standard the debt has declined in recent years. In 1946, the national debt was 120 percent of the GNP. By 1955 it as only 70 percent of GNP. By 1974, the national debt was only 34 percent of GNP and it is continuing to fall relative to this potential tax base. Exhibit 10-7 presents the interest payments on the debt as a percentage of GNP for the 1954–1974 period. After World War II, interest on the debt declined relative to GNP and since 1954 the debt interest–GNP relationship has varied between 1.5 and 2.0 percent. Approximately 2.0 percent of GNP is currently allocated to interest charges on the debt. During the last two decades, public debt has increased much more slowly than private debt. Exhibit 10-8 shows that

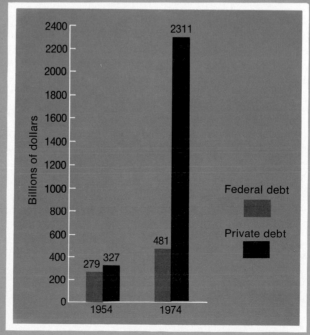

Exhibit 10-8   Private and Public Debt, 1954 and 1974

Private debt has increased much more rapidly than the national debt.
SOURCE: *Budget of the United States—1976.*

between 1954 and 1974, the national debt increased 72 percent, compared to a more than 700 percent increase in private indebtedness! If the growth in the national debt means the federal government is about to go bankrupt, the growth in private debt surely means private borrowers are on the verge of bankruptcy. Of course, neither is the case.

4. FACT: As the result of the national debt future generations will inherit both a higher tax liability and additional bonds. The U.S. debt is a liability to future taxpayers who will pay higher taxes in order to meet the interest payments on the debt. Simultaneously, it is an asset to owners or future owners of U.S. securities who will receive principal and interest payments. For internal debt, both of these parties are U.S. citizens, either current or future.

5. FACT: The true measure of how the debt influences the welfare of future generations would require knowledge on how it influences the future capital stock. The economic welfare of future generations will be determined by how much capital stock—houses, factories, machines, and other productive assets—is bequeathed to them. Understanding this fact is one of the most important steps toward understanding the burden of the debt. How does the debt influence the nation's capital? It depends on a lot of things. When the government borrows, it tends to increase the interest rate and discourage private investment. But when it spends, it often contributes to the future capital stock (for example, hospitals, schools, airplanes, and spaceships).

Even external debt could improve the economic welfare of future generations. If the funds are used to build productive assets yielding future income that is greater than future interest payments, future generations would be helped. Alternatively, if the externally borrowed funds were spent primarily on current consumption, future generations would inherit the liability to the external bondholders, without obtaining an offsetting benefit in the form of a larger capital stock. In this latter case, an expansion in the external debt would impose a burden on future generations.

6. FACT: External debt has increased in recent years. In 1970, only $20 billion of U.S. securities, 5 percent of the total, was held by foreigners. By 1975 the figure had jumped to $65 billion, representing almost 13 percent of the total national debt.

7. FACT: When deficit spending is necessary to push the economy to full employment, it will contribute to the future capital stock and therefore improve the economic welfare of future generations. If there are unemployed resources that could be used to produce houses, factories, and other assets, as well as current consumer goods, a government deficit may help put them to work. When a deficit results in the employment of otherwise idle resources, there can be little doubt that it will help future generations despite the future tax liability. For example, consider the 1930s. Between 1930 and 1934, gross private investment was less than 3 percent of GNP. Once allowance was made for depreciation, the nation's capital stock actually declined. Were future generations helped because the federal government incurred little debt (either with the public or the Federal Reserve) during this period? The answer is clearly no. Future generations would have been made better off if the government had incurred a deficit, while using monetary and fiscal tools to put idle manpower and resources to work. The future capital stock would have been greater, to say nothing of current output during that period.

8. FACT: The tax liability associated with the national debt could act as a disincentive to work, but as long as it is small relative to the GNP, this factor is relatively unimportant. We could certainly imagine a hypothetical case where the interest payments on the debt were so high that they discouraged people from productive work. If, say, 30 percent of the earnings of taxpayers were required just to meet the interest on the debt, this, added to other governmental expenditures, would result in very high tax rates. If one-half or two-thirds of the *additional* earnings of workers went to pay taxes, the incentive to work could be affected. However, as we already indicated, interest payments currently amount to about 2 percent of GNP. In this range, most economists do not believe that they significantly influence tax rates and the incentive to work.

Discussion

1. Can the government or a private corporation have continual debt outstanding? Explain.
2. Do we owe the national debt to ourselves? Does this mean that the size of the debt is of little concern? Why or why not?
3. "The national debt is a mortgage against the future of our children and grandchildren. We are forcing them to pay for our irresponsible and unrestrained spending." Evaluate.

CHAPTER LEARNING OBJECTIVES

1. When an economy's resources are underutilized, an increase in government expenditures, holding taxes constant, will increase aggregate demand and push the economy to a higher level of real income and employment.

2. A tax reduction can also be used to push an economy to full employment. When taxes are reduced, the disposable income of consumers will increase, stimulating consumption. At the higher level of consumption, both real income and employment will expand. Tax reductions can usually influence consumption rapidly as the withholding system can be utilized to alter disposable income almost immediately.

3. Restrictive fiscal policy (higher taxes or reduced government expenditures) can be used to combat inflationary pressure. In the face of inflation, a planned government surplus would be in order.

4. The Keynesian analysis suggests that general economic conditions should be the prime determinant of proper fiscal policy. An annual balanced budget may actually contribute to economic instability. When the economy is slack, budget authorities should plan a deficit. When the economy is experiencing an economic boom, a budget surplus would be in order. Thus the budget can be used to affect the conditions of private aggregate demand.

5. The full-employment budget is a measure of what expenditures and revenues would be if the economy were at full employment. It is a useful summary statistic on the degree to which fiscal policy is expansionary or restrictive because it eliminates the impact of changing economic conditions on the budget, thereby permitting the impact of the budget on the economy to stand out much more clearly.

6. Improper fiscal policy can be destabilizing. A reduction in government spending and/or an increase in taxes could push a slack economy deeper into a recession. Similarly, an increase in government spending and/or a reduction in taxes could cause a full-employment economy to experience inflation. Analysis of the historical record reveals that fiscal policy has, at times, exerted a counterproductive influence.

7. Unemployment compensation, corporate taxes, and the progressive income tax act as automatic stabilizers because they automatically contribute to a budget deficit during slack times and a budget surplus when the economy is at full employment.

8. The burden of the national debt has long been a controversial issue. It is not true that the debt will eventually have to be paid off. Nor is it true that the debt indicates the government is about to go bankrupt. Since World War II the national debt has been declining relative to the GNP. But the share of the debt owned by foreigners has increased rapidly during the 1970s. A true measure of how the debt influences the welfare of future generations would require knowledge on how it influences the future capital stock.

IMPORTANT TERMS TO REMEMBER

Recessionary gap: The amount by which aggregate demand falls short of the full-employment level of income when the nation's resources are not being fully utilized.

Inflationary gap: The amount by which aggregate demand exceeds the full-employment level of income when an economy is experiencing rising prices resulting from excess demand.

Budget deficit: Situation that exists when tax revenues are less than government expenditures.

Budget surplus: Situation that exists when tax revenues are in excess of government expenditures.

Restrictive fiscal policy: A tax rate structure and level of government expenditures such that a full-employment budget surplus would be expected.

Expansionary fiscal policy: A tax structure and level of government expenditures such that a full-employment budget deficit would be expected.

Full-employment budget: An estimate of what government revenues and expenditures would be if the economy were at full employment.

Automatic stabilizers: Built-in features that tend to automatically promote a budget deficit during a recession and budget surplus during an inflationary boom even without any change in policy.

National debt: Interest-bearing U.S. government securities issued by the Treasury and held by private domestic and foreign investors, government agencies, and Federal Reserve Banks. These securities represent loans from these parties to the U.S. Treasury.

THE ECONOMIC WAY OF THINKING—DISCUSSION QUESTIONS

1. Explain what is likely to happen to unemployment, real income, and prices as the result of a tax reduction when the unemployment rate is **(a)** 3.8 percent, **(b)** 5.0 percent, **(c)** 6.7 percent.

2. Suppose that investment tax credits were raised, granting $20 billion of tax relief to the business sector. Indicate the impact of this policy. Use graphic analysis to illustrate how both investment and the equilibrium level of income would be affected.

3. Suppose you are a member of the Council of Economic Advisers. The president has asked you to prepare a statement on "What is the proper fiscal policy for the next 12 months?" Prepare such a statement, indicating **(a)** the current state of the economy (that is, unemployment rate, growth in real income, and rate of inflation) and **(b)** your fiscal policy suggestions. Should the budget be in balance? Present the reasoning behind your suggestions.

4. If an economy were experiencing 6 percent unemployment, while prices were rising at a 2 percent annual rate, indicate your view about proper fiscal policy. Explain your reasons.

5. "In the real world it is wrong to expect that fiscal policy will be symmetrical. Politicians will be glad to run a deficit during bad times to stimulate the economy, but they will surely fail to plan a surplus when it is needed to halt inflationary pressures. Thus, fiscal policy has an inflationary bias." Do you agree with this view? Why or why not?

6. What are automatic stabilizers? Explain the one big advantage of automatic stabilizers.

---

7. What's Wrong with This Way of Thinking?

"Keynesians argue that a budget deficit will stimulate the economy. The historical evidence is highly inconsistent with this view. A $12 billion budget deficit in 1958 was associated with a serious recession, not expansion. We experienced recessions in both 1954 and 1961, despite budget deficits. The federal budget ran a deficit every year from 1931 through 1939. Yet, the economy continued to wallow in the depression. Budget deficits do not stimulate GNP and employment."

11
MONEY AND THE BANKING SYSTEM

The purpose of this chapter is to explain the operation of our banking system and to analyze the determinants of the money supply. Later, we will consider the influence of money on prices, employment, output, and other important economic variables.

To many economists, analysis of national income determination without money is like a football team without a quarterback. The central figure—the moving force—has been excluded. While the majority would assign a somewhat lesser role to money, today almost all economists believe that money, and therefore monetary policy, matters a great deal.

WHAT IS MONEY?

Money makes the world go around. While this is an exaggeration, nonetheless money is an important cog in the wheel that makes trade go around. Without money, everyday exchange would be both tedious and costly. Of course, money today is issued and controlled by governments. But the use of money arose thousands of years ago, not because of government decree, but because money simplifies exchange.

1. *Money Serves as a Medium of Exchange.* If one desires to exchange labor services for a shirt and trousers, he first sells his labor for money then uses the money to buy the shirt and trousers. Similarly, if a farmer wants to exchange a cow for electricity and medical services, he sells the cow for money, which he then uses to buy the electricity and medical services. In a barter economy such simple exchange would necessitate finding a buyer for your goods who was willing to sell precisely those things you wanted to purchase. Exchange would be enormously time-consuming. In an exchange economy with money, money trades in all markets, simplifying exchange and oiling the wheels of trade.

2. *Money Serves as an Accounting Unit.* Consumers will want to compare the prices of widely differing goods and services, so they will be able to make sensible choices. Similarly, cost-conscious businessmen will want to compare the prices of vastly differ-

ent productive resources. Since money is widely used in exchange, it certainly makes sense that we would also use it as the accounting unit, the yardstick by which we compare the value of goods and resources.

3. *Money Is a Store of Value.* It is a financial asset, a form of savings. The big disadvantage of using money to save purchasing power for the future is its low rate of return. Money does not draw interest. But it has the advantage of being a perfectly **liquid asset.** It can be easily and quickly transformed into other goods at a low transaction cost and without an appreciable loss in its nominal value. Thus, most people hold some of their wealth in the form of money, even though it does not pay interest, because it provides purchasing power with which to deal with an uncertain future.

Currency and Demand Deposits—Two Forms of Money

The **money supply** in the United States is composed of currency (paper money and coins in the pockets and billfolds of the public) and demand deposits (funds deposited in checking accounts with commercial banks). As Exhibit 11-1 shows, the total money supply in the United States was $287 billion in mid-1975. Demand deposits account for more than three-fourths of this total.

Demand deposits are freely convertible to currency. Thus, the amount of currency in circulation at any point in time depends solely on the preferences of the public. Currency held in the vaults of commercial banks is not counted as part of the money supply because it is unavailable for spending by the nonbank public. Most of the nation's business, more than 80 percent, is conducted by check. The size of the demand deposit component of the money supply reflects our reliance on checks, rather than cash, as a means of payment.

Exhibit 11-1   Composition of the Money Supply in the United States

Components of the money supply	Total (billions of dollars)	Percentage of total
Amount in circulation, April 1975		
Currency (in circulation)		
Federal Reserve Notes	61	21.3
Coins and other Treasury currency	9	3.1
Demand deposits		
Personal checking accounts	217	75.6
Total money supply	287	100.0

SOURCE: The Board of Governors of the Federal Reserve System.

Near Monies

Several financial assets resemble money in many ways. Time deposits with commercial banks are a highly liquid means of holding purchasing power into the future. Since they pay interest, they are superior to money as a vehicle to store value. While these funds are not legally available on demand, in practice the depositor can usually withdraw his time deposits upon request. But time deposits are not used directly as a means of payment. Checks are not written on savings accounts. Thus, for our purposes they will not be considered part of the money supply, although some economists, who place more emphasis on the store of value function of money, would include them.

The line between money and "near monies" is a fine one. Savings and loan shares and U.S. government securities redeemable within one year are also highly liquid methods of storing value. But they cannot be used directly as a means of payment. Factors that influence individual and business holdings of money, near monies, and other financial assets can, as we will illustrate, exert an important influence on aggregate demand.

Why Is Money Valuable?

Neither currency nor deposits have significant intrinsic value. A dollar bill is just a piece of paper. Bank deposits are nothing more than accounting numbers. Coins do have some intrinsic value as a metal, but considerably less than their value as money.

From what does money derive its value? The confidence of people is important. People are willing to accept money because they are confident that it can be used to purchase real goods and services. This is partly a matter of law. The government has designated currency as "legal tender"—acceptable for payment of debts.

But the major source of money's value is the same as for other commodities. Economic goods are more or less valuable because of their scarcity in supply relative to the amount that people desire. Money is no exception.

The value of a dollar is equivalent to the goods and services that it will buy. When the price level increases, a dollar will buy less. If prices double, the value of money will be halved. The value or purchasing power of money is inversely related to the level of prices.

If the purchasing power of money is to remain stable over time, the supply of money must be controlled. Assuming a constant rate of use, if the supply of money grows more rapidly than the growth in the real output of goods and services, prices will rise. Rapid expansion in the supply of money invariably leads to a decline in its value per unit. This point was dramatically illustrated in Germany after World War I. Money lost its value as the German government printed it by the truckload. During 1923 alone, the number of German marks increased from 2 trillion to 608 trillion! The result—an egg cost 80 billion marks and a loaf of bread 200 billion. Workers picked up their wages in suitcases. Shops closed at lunch hour to change price tags. The value of money was eroded.

THE BUSINESS OF BANKING

We need to understand a few things about the business of banking before we can explain the factors that influence the supply of money. There are nearly 14,000 commercial banks in the United States. About one-third of them are national banks, a bank that is chartered by the federal government. National banks are required to belong to the Federal Reserve System and adhere to its regulations. The remaining two-thirds of all banks are chartered, and regulated by the states. Since many state banks also belong, approximately 40 percent of all commercial banks are members of the Federal Reserve System. FRS member banks hold nearly 80 percent of all banking assets.

Since 1933 almost all commercial banks—state and national—have had their deposits insured with the Federal Deposit Insurance Corporation (FDIC). The FDIC fully insures each account up to $40,000 against losses due to bank failure. Since the establishment of the FDIC, bank failures have become a rare, though not impossible, occurrence.

Banks are in business to make a profit. The major service provided by banks is to hold demand deposits and honor checks drawn upon them. Banks also act as savings institutions paying depositors interest on funds maintained as time deposits (savings accounts). Commercial banks use a sizable share of both demand and time deposits for interest-earning purposes—extending loans and making financial investments.

A look at the consolidated balance sheet of banks that belong to the Federal Reserve System illustrates the major banking functions. Exhibit 11-2 shows that the major liabilities of banks are demand and time deposits. *From the viewpoint of a bank*, these are liabilities because they represent an obligation of the bank to its depositors. Outstanding interest-earning loans comprise the major class of banking assets. In addition, most banks own sizable amounts of interest-earning securities, both government and private.

Exhibit 11-2   The Functions of Commercial Banks

Banks provide services and pay interest to attract demand and time deposits (liabilities). A portion of their assets are held as *reserves* (either cash or deposits with the Fed) to meet their daily obligations toward their depositors. Most of the rest is invested and loaned out, providing interest income for the bank.

CONSOLIDATED BALANCE SHEET OF MEMBER BANKS—JANUARY 1, 1975
(IN BILLIONS OF DOLLARS)

Assets		Liabilities	
Reserves	37.0	Capital accounts	48.0
Loans outstanding	429.1	Demand deposits	249.5
U.S. government securities	38.4	Time deposits	326.8
Other securities	99.5	Other liabilities	91.1
Other assets	111.4		
Total	715.4	Total	715.4

SOURCE: Board of Governors of the Federal Reserve System.

Banking differs from most businesses in that a large portion of its liabilities are payable on demand. But, even though it would be possible for all depositers to come in and demand the money in their checking accounts on the same day, the probability of this is quite remote. Typically, while some individuals will be making withdrawals, others will make deposits. They will tend to balance out, eliminating sudden changes in demand deposits.

Therefore, banks maintain only a fraction of their assets in reserves to meet the requirements of depositors. As Exhibit 11-2 illustrates on average, **reserves**—vault cash and deposits with Federal Reserve—were only about 15 percent as great as the demand deposit obligation of member banks.

FRACTIONAL RESERVE GOLDSMITHING

Economists often like to draw the analogy between the goldsmith of past history and our current banking system. In the past, gold was used as the means of making payments. It was money. During this era, people would store their money with a goldsmith for safekeeping, just as many of us open a checking account for safety reasons. Gold owners received a certificate granting them the right to withdraw their gold any time they wished. If they wanted to buy something, they would go to the goldsmith, withdraw gold, and use it as a means of making payment. Thus, the money supply was equal to the amount of gold in circulation plus the gold deposited with goldsmiths.

The day-to-day deposits of and requests for gold were always only a fraction of the total amount of gold deposited. A major portion of the gold simply lay idle in the goldsmiths' "vaults." Taking notice of this fact, goldsmiths soon began loaning gold to local merchants. The merchants would, after a time, pay back the gold plus an interest payment for its use. What happened to the money supply when a goldsmith extended loans to local merchants? The deposits of persons who initially brought their gold to the goldsmith were not reduced. Depositors could still withdraw their gold any time that they wished (so long as they did not all try to do so at once). The merchants were now able to use the gold that they borrowed from the goldsmith as a means of payment. As the goldsmith lent gold, he increased the amount of gold in circulation, thereby increasing the money supply.

It was inconvenient to make a trip to the goldsmith everytime one wanted to buy something. Since people knew that they were redeemable in gold, the gold certificates, granting the bearer the right to withdraw a stated amount of gold, began circulating as a means of payment. The depositors were pleased with this arrangement, as it eliminated the need for a trip to the goldsmith every time something was exchanged for gold. As long as they had confidence in the goldsmith, sellers were glad to accept the gold certificates as payment.

Since depositors were now able to utilize the gold certificates as money, the daily withdrawals and deposits with goldsmiths declined even more. A local goldsmith would save back maybe 20 percent of the total gold deposited with him so he could meet the current requests to redeem gold certificates that were in circulation. The remaining 80 percent of his gold deposits would be loaned out to business merchants, traders, and other citizens. Therefore, 100 percent of the gold certificates were circulating as money. In addition, another 80 percent of the total deposits, that portion of gold that had been loaned out, was circulating as money. The total money supply, gold certificates plus gold, was now 1.8 times the amount of gold that had been originally deposited with the goldsmith. Since the goldsmith issued loans and only kept a fraction of the total gold deposited with him, he was able to increase the money supply.

As long as the goldsmith held enough reserves to meet the current requests of his depositors, everything went along smoothly. Most gold depositors probably did not even realize that the goldsmith did not have *their* gold and *that of other depositors* precisely designated by name sitting in his "vaults."

Goldsmiths derived income from loaning gold. The more gold they loaned, the greater their total income. Some goldsmiths, trying to increase their income by extending more and more interest-earning loans, depleted the gold in their vaults to imprudently low levels. When an unexpectedly large number of depositors wanted their gold, these greedy goldsmiths were unable to meet their requests. Thus, if a goldsmith was imprudent in extending loans, he might loan out so much gold that he would be unable to meet the current requests of his depositors. Such a goldsmith would lose the confidence of his depositors and the system of fractional reserve goldsmithing would tend to break down.

FRACTIONAL RESERVE BANKING

In principle, our **fractional reserve banking** system is very similar to the early goldsmithing. The early goldsmiths did not have enough gold on hand to pay all of their depositors simultaneously. Neither do our banks have enough cash and other reserves to pay all of their depositors simultaneously (see Exhibit 11-2). The early goldsmiths expanded the money supply by issuing loans. So do our present-day bankers. The amount of gold held in reserve to meet the requirements of depositors limited the ability of the goldsmith to expand the supply of money. The amount of cash and other **required reserves** limit the ability of present-day banks to expand the supply of money.

How Our Friendly Bankers Create Money

How do banks expand the supply of money? In order to better understand this question, let us consider a banking system without a central bank and where only currency acts as reserves against deposits. Initially, we will assume that all banks are required by law to maintain vault currency equal to at least 20 percent of the checking accounts of their depositors.

Suppose that you found $1000 that apparently your long deceased uncle had hidden in the basement of his former house. How much will this newly found $1000 of currency expand the money supply? You take the bills down to the First National Bank, open up a checking account of $1000, and deposit the cash with the banker. First National is now required to keep an additional $200 in vault cash, 20 percent of your deposit. But they received $1000 of additional cash. So after placing $200 in the bank vault, First National has $800 of **excess reserves,** reserves over and above the amount that they are required by law to maintain. Given their current excess reserves, First National can now extend an $800 loan. Suppose that they loan $800 to a local citizen to buy a car. At the time the loan is extended, the money supply will increase by $800 as the bank adds the funds to the checking account of the borrower. No one else has less money. You still have your $1000 checking account, and the borrower has his $800 for a new car.

When he buys his new car, the seller of the automobile accepts a check and heads down to deposit the $800 in his bank, Citizen's State Bank. What happens as the check clears? The temporary excess reserves of the First National Bank will be eliminated as they pay $800 to the Citizen's State Bank. But as Citizen's State Bank receives $800 in currency, they will now have excess reserves. They must keep 20 percent, an additional $160, in reserve against the $800 checking account deposit of the automobile seller. But the remaining $640 could be loaned out. Since Citizen's State, like other banks, is in business to make money, they will be quite happy to "extend a helping hand" to a borrower. As the second bank loans out their excess reserves, the deposits of the persons borrowing the money will increase by $640. Another $640 has now been added to the money supply. You still have your $1000, the automobile seller has an additional $800 in his checking account, and the new borrower has just received an additional $640. Because you found the $1000 stashed away by your uncle, the money supply has increased by $2440.

Of course, the process can continue. Exhibit 11-3 follows the *potential* creation of money resulting from the initial $1000 through several additional stages. In total the money supply can increase by a maximum of $5000, the $1000 initial deposit plus an additional $4000 in demand deposits that can be created by the process of extending new loans.

The multiple by which new reserves increase the stock of money is referred to as the

Exhibit 11-3   Creating Money From New Reserves

When banks are required to maintain 20 percent reserves against demand deposits, the creation of $1000 of new reserves will potentially increase the supply of money by $5000.

Bank	New cash deposits (actual reserves) (dollars)	New required reserves (dollars)	Potential demand deposits created by extending new loans (dollars)
Initial deposit	1000.00	200.00	800.00
Second stage	800.00	160.00	640.00
Third stage	640.00	128.00	512.00
Fourth stage	512.00	102.40	409.60
Fifth stage	409.60	81.92	327.68
Sixth stage	327.68	65.54	262.14
Seventh stage	262.14	52.43	209.71
All others	1048.58	209.71	838.87
Total	5000.00	1000.00	4000.00

deposit expansion multiplier. In our example, the potential deposit expansion multiplier was 5. The amount by which additional reserves can increase the supply of money is determined by the ratio of required reserves to demand deposits. In fact, the deposit expansion multiplier is merely the required reserve ratio turned upside down. For our hypothetical example, the required reserves were 20 percent or 1/5 of total deposits. Thus, the potential deposit expansion multiplier was 5. If only 10 percent reserves were required, the deposit expansion multiplier would be 10, the reciprocal of 1/10.

The lower the percentage reserve requirement, the greater is the potential expansion in the supply of money resulting from the creation of new reserves. This fractional reserve requirement places a ceiling on potential money creation from new reserves.

The Actual Deposit Expansion Multiplier

Will the introduction of the new currency reserves necessarily have a full deposit expansionary multiplier effect? The answer is no. There are two reasons why the actual deposit multiplier may be less than the potential.

First, the deposit expansion multiplier would be reduced if some persons decided to hold the currency rather than depositing it in a bank. For example, suppose that the person who borrowed the $800 in the preceding example spends only $700. He stashes the remaining $100 away for a possible emergency. Then only $700 can possibly end up as a deposit in stage 2 and contribute to the excess reserve necessary for expansion. The potential of new loans in stage 2 and for all subsequent stages will be reduced proportionally. When currency remains in circulation, outside of banks, it will reduce the size of the deposit expansion multiplier.

Second, the deposit multiplier will be less than its maximum when banks fail to utilize all of the new excess reserves to extend loans. However, banks do have a strong incentive to loan out most of their new excess reserves. Idle excess reserves do not draw interest. Banks will want to use most of these excess reserves so they will generate interest income. Exhibit 11-4 shows that this is indeed the case. In recent years excess reserves have comprised only 1 or 2 percent of the total reserves of banks.

Currency leakages and idle excess bank reserves will result in a deposit expansion multiplier that is less than its potential maximum. However, since most people maintain most of their money in bank deposits rather than currency and since banks typically eliminate most of their excess reserves by extending loans, strong forces are present that will lead to multiple expansion.

Exhibit 11-4 Banking and Excess Reserves

Profit-maximizing banks use their excess reserves to extend loans and other forms of credit. Thus, excess reserves are very small, less than 2 percent of the total in recent years.

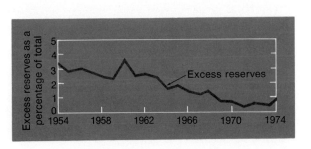

THE FEDERAL RESERVE SYSTEM

The Federal Reserve System is the central monetary authority or "central bank" for the United States. Every major country has a central banking authority. For example, the Bank of England and Bank of France perform central banking functions for their respective countries.

Central banks are charged with the responsibility of carrying out monetary policy. The major purpose of the Federal Reserve System (and other central banks) is to regulate the supply of money and provide a monetary climate that is in the best interest of the entire economy.

The Fed, a term often used when referring to the Federal Reserve System, was created in 1913. Nominally, it is owned by private member commercial banks. As Exhibit 11-5 illustrates, the policies of the Fed and the commercial banking system are determined by the Board of Governors. This powerful board consists of seven members each appointed to 14 year terms by the president with the advice and consent of the Senate. The Board of Governors establishes the rules and regulations by which member banks must abide. For example, it sets the reserve requirements for member banks. It regulates the types of loans that member banks may extend and the composition of their investment portfolios. The Board is the rulemaker, and often the umpire, of the U.S. banking system.

Two important committees assist the Board of Governors in carrying out monetary policy. First, the Open Market Operations Committee, made up of the seven members of the Board of Governors plus five (of 12) of the presidents of Federal Reserve Banks, determines the Fed's policy with respect to the purchase and sales of government bonds. As we shall soon see, this is the Fed's most often used method of controlling the money supply in the United States.

Second, the Federal Advisory Council meets periodically with the Board of Governors to express their views on monetary policy. The Advisory Council is comprised of 12 commercial bankers, one from each of the 12 Federal Reserve District Banks. As the name implies, this council is purely advisory.

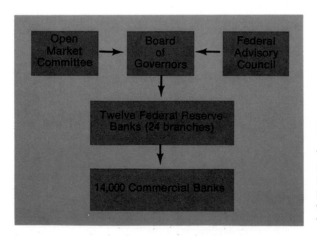

Exhibit 11-5 The Structure of the Federal Reserve System

The Board of Governors of the Federal Reserve System is at the center of the banking system in the United States. The board sets the rules and regulations for the banking system, thereby controlling the supply of money.

OUTSTANDING ECONOMIST: Arthur Burns

Other than the president, many people believe that this cool pipe-smoking economist is the most powerful man in the United States. As the influential chairman of the Board of Governors of the Federal Reserve System, his ideas exert a powerful effect on the money supply, the rate of inflation, and interest rates. Appointed in 1969, Chairman Burns in many ways possesses almost ideal qualifications for his job. Beginning with his association with the National Bureau of Economic Research in the early 1930s, Dr. Burns has long been interested in the causes and cures of business cycles. His work, *Measuring Business Cycles*,[1] coauthored with Wesley Mitchell, has been widely acclaimed by the economics profession. Burns was a professor of economics at Columbia when President Eisenhower tapped him to be the chairman of the Council of Economic Advisers in 1953.

Given the turbulence of the economy in the 1970s, Burns' job is not an easy one. Large budget deficits have increased the demand for loanable funds, thereby causing high interest rates. The Fed has been under considerable pressure to buy more U.S. securities, and expand the money supply in an effort to keep interest rates low. But as the money supply expands more rapidly, inflation results. The alternatives facing the Fed in recent years have not been attractive ones.

In addition to worrying about monetary policy, Burns has expressed concern about the low growth rates of productivity and corporate profits. In Burns' view neither productivity nor profits have kept up with the demands of a competitive world. The pressures of politics have often served to obscure and enlarge the problem. Burns argues for "more vigorous enforcement of the antitrust laws, elimination of barriers to entry in skilled occupations, reduction of barriers to imports from abroad, and modification of minimum-wage laws to improve job opportunities for teenagers." In addition, he suggests that greater incentives "should be provided for enlarging our capacity to produce industrial materials, energy, and othe products in short supply."[2]

Looking toward the expected budget deficits of a recessionary economy in 1975–1976, Burns implies that the Fed will provide more monetary expansion. But at the same time, he cautions against possible disastrous inflationary consequences if monetary expansion is profligate. The betting is that Burns and the Fed will follow a middle course, providing some monetary stimulus, but accepting a slower rate of recovery as the necessary price of avoiding runaway inflation later in the decade.

The Twelve District Banks

The 12 Federal Reserve District Banks operate under the control of the Board of Governors.[3] These district banks handle approximately 85 percent of all check clearing

---

[1] Arthur F. Burns and Wesley C. Mitchell, *Measuring Business Cycles.* New York: National Bureau of Economic Research, 1946.

[2] *U.S. News and World Report*, June 10, 1974, p. 21.

[3] Federal Reserve District Banks are located in Boston, New York, Philadelphia, Cleveland, Richmond, Atlanta, Chicago, St. Louis, Minneapolis, Kansas City, Dallas, and San Francisco. There are also 24 district "branch banks" in 24 other cities.

services of the banking system. Federal Reserve District Banks differ from commercial banks in several important respects.

1. *Federal Reserve Banks Are Not Profit-Making Institutions.* Instead they are an arm of the government. All of their earnings, above minimum expenses, belong to the Treasury.

2. *Unlike Other Banks, Federal Reserve Banks Can Actually Issue Money.* Approximately 85 percent of the currency in circulation was issued by the Fed. Look at the dollar bill in your pocket. Chances are, it has "Federal Reserve Note" engraved on it, indicating it was issued by the FRS. The Fed is the only bank that can issue money.

3. *Federal Reserve Banks Act as a Bankers' Bank.* Private citizens and corporations do *not* bank with Federal Reserve Banks. Commercial bankers and the federal government are the only banking customers of the Fed. Most commercial banks, both members and nonmembers, usually maintain some deposits with the FRS. Deposits with the Fed count as reserves for member commercial banks. The Fed also plays an important role in the clearing of checks through the banking system. Since most banks maintain deposits with the Fed, clearing of checks merely becomes an accounting transaction.

Initially, the Fed was made independent of the executive branch so the Treasury would not use it for political purposes. However, the policies of the Treasury and the Fed are usually closely coordinated. For example, the chairman of the Board of Governors of the Federal Reserve, the Secretary of the Treasury, and the chairman of the President's Council of Economic Advisers meet weekly to discuss and plan macroeconomic policy. In reality, it would be more accurate to think of the Fed and the executive branch as equal partners in the determination of policies designed to promote full employment and stable prices.

HOW THE FED CONTROLS OUR MONEY SUPPLY

The Fed has three major weapons to control the money stock: (1) establishment of reserve requirements for member banks, (2) buying and selling U.S. government securities in the open market, and (3) setting the interest rate at which it will loan funds to commercial banks. We will analyze specifically how each of these tools can be used to regulate the amount of money in circulation.

Reserve Requirements

The FRS requires its members to maintain reserves against the demand deposits of its customers. The reserves of commercial banks are composed of (a) currency held by the bank and (b) deposits of the bank with the Federal Reserve System. A bank can always obtain additional currency by drawing on its deposits with the Federal Reserve. Thus, both cash on hand and the bank's deposits with the Fed can be used to meet the demands of depositors. Therefore, both count as reserves.

Exhibit 11-6   The Required Reserve Ratio of Banks

As of June 1975, banks were required to maintain reserves of $7\frac{1}{2}$ percent against deposits of less than $2 million. This chart shows how the required reserve ratio increases with additional deposits. Note that the required reserves against time deposits are much lower than those for demand deposits.

| | Demand deposits (millions of dollars) | | | | | Time deposits (millions of dollars) | | |
| | | | | | | | Other time | |
	Under 2	2–10	10–100	100–400	Over 400	Saving deposits	Under 5	Over[a] 5
Percentage of required reserves	$7\frac{1}{2}$	10	12	13	$16\frac{1}{2}$	3	3	6

SOURCE: *The Federal Reserve Bulletin.*

[a] Reserve requirements are 3 percent for deposits maturing in 180 days or more in the future.

Exhibit 11-6 indicates the **required reserve ratio**—the percentage of total demand deposits that banks are required to keep in reserve (that is, their cash plus deposits with the Fed). As the demand deposits of a bank increase, the percentage of additional deposits that must be held in reserves also increases.

Why are commercial banks required to maintain assets in the form of reserves? One reason is to prevent imprudent bankers from overextending loans and thereby placing themselves in a poor position to deal with any sudden increase in withdrawals by depositors. The quantity of reserves needed to meet such emergencies is not left totally to the judgment of individual commercial banks. The Fed sets the rules.

But the Fed's control over reserve requirements is important for another reason. By altering them, the Fed can alter the money supply. The law does not prevent commercial banks from holding reserves over and above those required by the Fed. But, as we have noted, profit-seeking commercial banks will prefer to hold interest-bearing assets such as loans, rather than large amounts of excess reserves. Since reserves draw no interest, commercial banks will seek to minimize their excess reserves.

Exhibit 11-7 shows the actual reserve position of banks that belong to the Fed (see also Exhibit 11-4). Unsurprisingly, the actual reserves of these banks are very close to the required level. Since the excess reserves of banks are very small, when the Fed changes the required reserve ratio, banks will respond in a manner that will change the money supply.

If the Fed reduced the required reserve ratio, it would free additional reserves that banks could loan out. Profit-seeking banks will not allow these excess reserves to lie idle. They will extend additional loans. The extension of the new loans will expand the money supply.

What would happen if the Fed increased the reserve requirements? Since banks typically have very few excess reserves, such an increase would mean that banks would have to extend fewer loans in the future. This reduction in loans outstanding would cause a decline in the money supply.

Exhibit 11-7   The Reserves of Banks

In 1974, the actual reserves of banks were only slightly in excess of their required reserves. The required reserves average out at approximately 12 percent against demand and 3 percent against time deposits.

Federal Reserve member bank reserves—December 1974 (millions of dollars)

Total demand deposits	249,504
Total time deposits	326,756
Actual reserves	36,960
Required reserves	36,621
Excess reserves	339

SOURCE: *The Federal Reserve Bulletin.*

Reserve requirements are an important determinant of the money supply because they influence both the availability of excess reserves and the size of the deposit expansion multiplier. Higher reserve requirements will reduce the size of the deposit expansion multiplier and force banks to extend fewer loans. Therefore, an increase in the required reserve ratio will reduce the money supply. On the other hand, a decline in the required reserve ratio will increase the potential deposit expansion multiplier and the availability of excess reserves. Banks will tend to extend additional loans, thereby expanding the money supply.

In recent years, the Fed has seldom changed the required reserves of member banks. Changes that have been made have been marginal. Because of the deposit expansion multiplier, small changes in reserve requirements can cause large changes in the money supply. In addition, the precise magnitude and timing of a change in the money stock that will result from a change in reserve requirements are difficult to predict. For these reasons, the Fed has usually preferred to use other tools in their efforts to control the supply of money.

Open Market Operations

Open market operations, the buying and selling of U.S. securities in the open market, is by far the most important mechanism that the Fed utilizes to control the stock of money. When the Fed enters the market and buys U.S. government securities, it expands the reserves of commercial banks. The sellers of the securities will receive a check drawn on a Federal Reserve Bank. As the check is deposited in a commercial bank, the bank acquires a deposit or credit with the Federal Reserve. The commercial banking system has increased its reserves while the Fed has purchased part of the national debt. Since the deposit with the Fed, like currency, counts as reserves, banks can now extend more loans. The money supply will eventually increase by the amount of the securities purchased by the Fed times the actual deposit expansion multiplier.

Let us consider a hypothetical case. Suppose the FRS purchases $10,000 of U.S.

securities from commercial bank A. Bank A has fewer securities, but it now has additional excess reserves of $10,000. The bank could extend new loans of up to $10,000, while maintaining its initial reserve position. This $10,000 expansion of loans would contribute directly to the money supply. Part of it will eventually be deposited in other banks, and they will also be able to extend additional loans. The creation of the $10,000 of new bank reserves will cause the money supply to increase by some multiple of the amount of U.S. securities purchased by the Fed.

The reserve requirements in effect in the mid-1970s (see Exhibit 11-6) suggest the *potential* deposit multiplier could be 5 or 6. But, of course, as new reserves are injected into the banking system, there is some leakage either because of potential currency reserves circulating as cash or because some banks may be accumulating excess reserves. Exhibit 11-8 shows that the money supply since 1968 has been approximately 2.5 times greater than the potential reserves[4] suggesting that the actual deposit expansion multiplier is near 2.5. Therefore, when the Fed purchases U.S. Securities, injecting additional reserves into the system, *on average*, the money supply tends to increase by approximately $2.50 for each dollar of securities purchased.

Open market operations can, of course, also be used to reduce the money stock, or its rate of increase. If the Fed wants to reduce the money stock, it will sell some of its current holdings of government securities. When the Fed sells securities, the buyer will pay for them with a check drawn on a commercial bank. As the check clears, the reserves of that bank with the Fed will decline. The reserves available to commercial banks are reduced and the money stock will fall.

Since open market operations have been the Fed's primary weapon in recent years, the money stock and the Fed's ownership of U.S. securities have followed similar paths. When the Fed increases its purchases of U.S. securities at a rapid rate, the money stock

Exhibit 11-8   How Big Is the *Actual* Money Deposit Multiplier?

In recent years the *actual* deposit expansion multiplier has been approximately 2.5. Of course, if the reserve requirements were lowered (raised), the deposit expansion multiplier would rise (fall).

Year (December)	Money supply[a]	Total potential reserves[a,b]	Money deposit multiplier
1968	201.5	77.8	2.59
1969	208.6	81.6	2.56
1970	221.2	86.3	2.56
1971	235.2	92.4	2.55
1972	255.7	97.4	2.63
1973	270.4	106.7	2.53
1974	283.1	115.9	2.44

SOURCE: The Board of Governors of the Federal Reserve System.
[a] Billions of dollars.
[b] Economists refer to the total potential reserves as the monetary base.

[4] Currency in circulation plus the actual reserves of commercial banks comprise the total potential reserves. Economists often use the term monetary base when referring to the total potential reserves.

will grow rapidly. A slowdown in the Fed's purchases of government bonds will tend to reduce the rate of monetary expansion.

As we indicated earlier, the Federal Open Market Committee (FOMC), a special committee of the Fed, decides when and how open market operations will be used. They meet every three or four weeks to map out the Fed's future policy concerning the purchase and sale of U.S. securities.

The Discount Rate—The Cost of Borrowing from the Fed

Member banks can borrow from the Federal Reserve, but when they do they must pay interest on the loan. The interest rate that commercial banks pay on loans from the FRS is called the **discount rate.** When the newspapers announced that the discount rate has increased by 0.5 percent, many people think this means their local banker will (must?) now charge them a higher interest rate for a loan.[5] This is not necessarily so. The major source of loan funds of commercial banks is reserves acquired because of holding demand and time deposits. Borrowing from the Fed contributes less than one-half of 1 percent to the available loan funds of commercial banks. Thus an increase in the discount rate does not necessarily cause your friendly banker to raise the rate at which he will lend money to you.

Borrowing from the Fed is not a right. The Fed does not have to loan funds to commercial banks. Therefore, member banks rely on this source primarily to meet a short-run shortage of reserves. They are most likely to turn to the Fed, as a temporary method of meeting their reserve requirements, while they are making other adjustments in their loan and investment portfolio.

An increase in the discount rate makes it more expensive for commercial banks to borrow from the Fed. Borrowing is discouraged and banks are more likely to build up their reserves so as to assure that they will not have to borrow from the Fed. Thus, an increase in the discount rate is restrictive. It will tend to discourage banks from shaving their excess reserves to a low level.

By contrast, a reduction in the discount rate is expansionary. At the lower interest rate, it costs commercial banks less if they have to turn to the Fed to meet a temporary emergency. Thus banks are more likely to reduce their excess reserves to a minimum, extending more loans and increasing the money supply, as the cost of borrowing from the Fed declines.

The general public has a tendency to overestimate the importance of a change in the discount rate. Since it applies to such a small share of total reserves, a 0.5 percent change in the discount rate has something less than a profound impact on the availability of credit and the supply of money. Without completely negating the potential influence of a change in the discount rate, usually the open market operations of the Fed are a much better index of the direction and magnitude of monetary policy.

---

[5] The discount rate is also sometimes confused with the prime interest rate, the rate at which banks will loan money to low risk customers. The two rates are different. A change in the discount rate will not necessarily affect the prime interest rate.

Exhibit 11-9   Summary of the Monetary Tools of the Federal Reserve

Federal Reserve policy	Expansionary monetary policy	Restrictive monetary policy
1. Reserve requirements	Reduce reserve requirements as this will free additional excess reserves and induce banks to extend additional loans that will expand the money supply	Raise reserve requirements as this will reduce the excess reserves of banks causing them to make fewer loans. As the outstanding loans of banks decline, the money stock will be reduced
2. Open market operations	Purchase additional U.S. securities which will expand the money stock directly while increasing the reserves of banks, inducing bankers to extend more loans, indirectly expanding the money stock	Sell U.S. securities, which will reduce both the money stock and excess reserves. The decline in excess reserves will indirectly lead to an additional reduction in the money supply
3. Discount rate	Lower the discount rate which will encourage more borrowing from the Fed by commercial banks. Banks will tend to reduce their reserves and extend more loans because of the lower cost of borrowing from the Fed if they temporarily run short on reserves	Raise the discount rate, thereby discouraging borrowing from the Fed. Banks will tend to extend fewer loans, and build up their reserves so they will not have to borrow from the Fed

Summarizing the Tools of the Fed

Exhibit 11-9 summarizes the monetary tools of the Federal Reserve. If the Fed wants to follow an expansionary policy it could decrease reserve requirements, purchase additional U.S. securities, and/or lower the discount rate. If the Fed wants to reduce the money stock, it would increase the reserve requirements, sell U.S. securities, and/or raise the discount rate. Of course, since the Fed will typically seek only small changes in the money supply (or its rate of increase), it will usually utilize only one or two of these tools to accomplish a desired objective.

THE FED AND THE TREASURY

Many students have a tendency to confuse the Federal Reserve and the U.S. Treasury, probably because both sound like a monetary agency. The Treasury is a budgetary agency. If there is a budgetary deficit, the Treasury will *issue* U.S. securities as a method of financing the deficit. Newly issued U.S. securities are almost always sold to private investors (or invested in government trust funds). Bonds issued by the Treasury to finance a budget deficit are seldom purchased directly by the Fed. In any case, the Treasury is primarily interested in obtaining monetary funds so it can pay Uncle Sam's bills. Except for small nominal amounts, mostly coins, the Treasury does not issue money. Borrowing, the public sale of new U.S. securities, is the primary method used by the Treasury to cover any excess of expenditures relative to tax revenues.

While the Treasury is concerned with the revenues and expenditures of the government, the Fed is primarily concerned with the availability of money and credit for the entire economy. The Fed does not *issue* U.S. securities. It merely utilizes the purchase and sales of government securities issued by the Treasury as a means to control the money supply of the economy. The Fed does not have an obligation to meet the financial responsibilities of the U.S. government. That is the domain of the Treasury. The Fed's responsibility is that of providing a stable monetary framework for the entire economy. Thus, while the two agencies cooperate with each other, they are distinctly different institutions established for different purposes.

DYNAMICS OF MONETARY POLICY

We have discussed the tools available to the Federal Reserve to increase or decrease the money supply. With the passage of time, the money supply, like the GNP, will generally be expanding. In a dynamic setting, therefore, monetary policy might better be gauged by the *rate of change* in the money supply. When economists say that monetary policy is expansionary, they mean that the *rate of growth* of the money stock is high. Similarly, restrictive monetary policy implies a *slow rate of growth or a decline* in the money stock.

CHAPTER LEARNING OBJECTIVES

1. Money is anything that is widely accepted as a medium of exchange. It also acts as a unit of account and provides a means of storing current purchasing power into the future. Without money, exchange would be both costly and tedious.

2. The money supply in the United States is composed of **(a)** currency in the hands of the public and **(b)** demand deposits with commercial banks. Neither has significant intrinsic value. Money derives its value from its scarcity relative to its usefulness.

3. Banking is a business. Commercial banks provide their depositors with safekeeping of money, check clearing services on demand deposits, and interest payments on time deposits. Banks derive most of their income from extension of loans and investments in interest-earning securities.

4. The Federal Reserve System is a central banking authority designed to provide a stable monetary framework for the entire economy. It establishes regulations that determine the supply of money. It issues most of the currency in the United States. It is a banker's bank.

5. The Fed has three major tools with which to control the money supply.

(a) Establishment of the Required Reserve Ratio. Under a fractional reserve banking system, reserve requirements limit the ability of commercial banks to expand the money supply by extending more loans. When the Fed lowers the required reserve ratio, it creates excess reserves and allows banks to extend new loans which will expand the money supply. Raising the ratio would have the opposite effect.

(b) Open Market Operations. The open market operations of the Fed can directly influence both the money supply and available reserves. When the Fed buys U.S. securities, the money supply will expand because bond buyers will acquire money and the reserves of banks will increase as checks drawn on FRS banks are cleared. When the Fed sells securities, the money supply will contract because bond buyers are giving up money in exchange for securities. The reserves available to commercial banks will decline, causing them to issue fewer loans, thereby reducing the money supply.

(c) The Discount Rate. An increase in the discount rate is restrictive because it discourages banks from borrowing from the Fed in order to extend new loans. A reduction in the discount rate is expansionary because it makes it less costly to borrow from the Fed.

6. The Federal Reserve and the U.S. Treasury are two different, distinctive agencies. The Fed is primarily concerned with the money supply and the establishment of a stable monetary climate. The Treasury focuses on budgetary matters—tax revenues, government expenditures, and the financing of government debt.

IMPORTANT TERMS TO REMEMBER

Money supply: Demand (checking) deposits plus currency in the hands of the public.

Liquid asset: An asset that can be easily and quickly converted into cash without loss of value.

Fractional reserve banking: A system that allows banks to keep *less than* 100 percent reserves against their deposits. Required reserves are a fraction of deposits.

Reserves: Vault cash plus deposits of member commercial banks with Federal Reserve Banks.

Required reserves: The minimum amount of reserves that a bank is required by law to keep behind its deposits. Thus, if reserve requirements were 15 percent, banks would be required to keep $150,000 in reserves against each $1 million of deposits.

Required reserve ratio: The reserves that banks are required to hold, expressed as a percentage of their demand and time deposit liabilities.

Excess reserves: Actual reserves that are in excess of the legal requirement.

Deposit expansion multiplier: The multiple by which an increase (decrease) in reserves will increase (decrease) the money supply. It will be inversely related to the required reserve ratio.

Open market operations: Purchases and sales of U.S. government securities (national debt) by the Federal Reserve.

Discount rate: The interest rate that the Federal Reserve charges member banks who borrow funds from it.

THE ECONOMIC WAY OF THINKING—DISCUSSION QUESTIONS

1. Why can banks continue to hold reserves that are only a fraction of the demand deposits of their customers? Is your money safe in a bank? Why or why not?

2. What makes money valuable? Does money perform an economic service? Explain. Could money better perform its function if there were twice as much of it? Why or why not?

3. "People are poor because they don't have very much money. Yet, central bankers keep money scarce. If poor people had more money, poverty could be eliminated." Explain the confusion of this statement.

4. In your own words, explain how the creation of new reserves will cause the supply of money to increase by some multiple of the newly created reserves.

5. How will the following actions affect the money supply:
   (a) a reduction in the discount rate;
   (b) an increase in the reserve requirements;

(c) the Fed purchases $10 million of U.S. securities from a commercial bank;

(d) the U.S. Treasury sells $10 million of newly issued bonds to a commercial bank;

(e) an increase in the discount rate;

(f) the Fed sells $20 million of U.S. securities to a private investor?

6. What is Wrong with This Way of Thinking?

"When the government runs a budget deficit, it simply pays its bills by printing more money. As the newly printed money works its way through the economy, it waters down the paper money already in circulation. Thus it takes more money to buy things. The major source of inflation is newly created paper money issued by the government."

12

MONEY, EMPLOYMENT, INFLATION, AND A MORE COMPLETE KEYNESIAN MODEL

Now that we have an understanding of the banking system and the determinants of the money supply, we can introduce money into the Keynesian model. In this chapter we will present the Keynesian view of monetary policy and how it can be used to influence the level of employment, prices, and output. In a subsequent chapter, the views of the monetarists about money will be discussed and contrasted with the Keynesian position. The relationship between rising prices and unemployment will also be introduced in this chapter. Currently the combination of high unemployment rates and rapidly rising prices is causing many Americans to reflect on our economic future. Might another economic disaster, a depression, be in our future? The controversy in the concluding section of this chapter deals with this issue.

THE DEMAND AND SUPPLY OF MONEY

What factors underlie the **demand for money?** that is, why do people want to maintain part of their wealth in the form of cash and checking account money? Keynes stressed three major reasons. First, the *transactions motive*—money helps each of us carry out everyday purchases. The timing of our income does not match up perfectly with when we want to buy things. So we keep a little cash or money in the bank in order to bridge the gap between everyday expenses and payday. Second, there is the *precautionary motive*. Most of us seek to keep a little money in the bank or stuffed in our billfold just in case some unforeseen contingency should arise—an automobile accident, Junior breaks his arm, or some such thing. Keynes felt that these two motives for holding money balances were primarily determined by the level of income.

Finally, there is the *speculative motive*. Individuals and businesses may want to maintain part of their wealth in the form of money so they will be in a ready position to take advantage of changes in prices, particularly prices of bonds, stocks, and other financial assets. Money is the most liquid form of holding wealth. Unlike land or houses, it can be quickly traded for other assets. Thus, people may want to hold some money so they can quickly respond to a profit-making opportunity.

The speculative demand for money will be closely affected by the existing and expected level of interest rates. When interest rates are high, it is more costly to hold idle money balances (opportunity cost). High interest rates will induce people to hold less money, while low interest rates will have the opposite effect.

Exhibit 12-1a illustrates the negative relationship between the demand for money and the **interest rate.** The supply of money will be determined by the monetary authorities, the Fed in the United States. The money supply will not be affected by interest rates. Hence, as Exhibit 12-1b shows, it is a vertical line.

When the money market is in equilibrium, the quantity of money demanded at the existing interest rate will just equal the quantity supplied. Monetary policy can influence the rate of interest, *at least in the short run.* Suppose the money market was initially in equilibrium, as the public was just willing to hold the existing money stock at the market rate of interest. As Exhibit 12-2 illustrates, an increase in the supply of money would cause the interest rate to fall. The expansionary monetary policy, shift from M to M', creates an excess supply of money. People have larger money balances than they desire to hold at the 10 percent interest rate. The public will attempt to reduce these money balances by purchasing interest-bearing substitutes, primarily bonds. The demand for bonds will increase, causing bond prices to rise. There is a negative relation between bond prices and interest rates. Higher bond prices are the same thing as lower interest rates. Thus, when people reduce their cash balances by purchasing more bonds, the interest rate will fall, reducing the opportunity cost of holding money. Eventually, at the lower rate of interest, 5 percent in the example of Exhibit 12-2, the public will be content to hold the larger supply of money (M').

When open market operations are used to expand the money supply, the impact on interest rates is even more straightforward. How do the open market purchases by the Fed affect the money supply? The Fed buys interest-bearing bonds from the public, bidding up bond prices and lowering interest rates. The public acquires money balances, funds that can be used to extend credit to private investors. This increase in the supply of loanable funds *available to finance private investment* will also place downward pressure on interest rates. Of course, lower interest rates will eventually restore equilibrium in the money market.

What happens to interest rates when the Fed sells bonds to the public, thereby

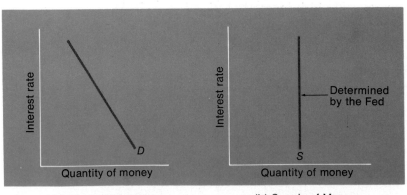

(a) Demand for Money   (b) Supply of Money

Exhibit 12-1   The Demand and Supply of Money

The demand for money will be inversely related to the interest rate [frame (a)]. The supply of money will be determined by the monetary authorities (the Fed) through their open market operations, discount rate policy, and reserve requirements.

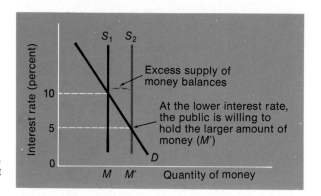

Exhibit 12-2   The Determination of Interest Rate—Keynesian Model

If the demand for money remains fixed, an increase in supply will cause interest rates to decline.

reducing the money stock? The Fed's action increases the supply of bonds, causing lower bond prices (higher interest rates). Temporarily, the reduction in the supply of money will create an excess demand for money balances. The public will attempt to restore their money balances back to the desired level. How can this be done? Sell bonds. Extend fewer loans. Borrow. But all of these actions will place upward pressure on the interest rate. As interest rates rise, the opportunity cost of holding money increases. Eventually, equilibrium will be restored in the money market, as the public will be satisfied with their smaller money balances at a new higher interest rate.

In summary, monetary policy can influence interest rates. Expansionary monetary policy will push interest rates downward. In contrast, a restrictive monetary policy will cause interest rates to rise.[1]

INTEREST RATES AND INVESTMENT

Interest rates exert an influence on the cost of each new investment project. Regardless of whether a businessman produces doorknobs or razorblades, lampposts or refrigerators, or some other product, the interest rate will exert either a direct or indirect impact on the cost of investment. If one has to borrow, there will be a direct interest cost. Even if borrowing is unnecessary, undertaking an investment project will mean foregoing interest income that could have been earned with the same funds. Since the interest rate contributes to the cost of each new investment, we would expect an inverse relationship between the level of investment and the interest rate.

When an entrepreneur considers an investment, he will compare the expected rate of return with the interest rate. If it exceeds the interest rate, the project is profitable. It will be undertaken. In contrast, a profit-seeking entrepreneur would not invest in a project for which the expected rate of return was less than the interest rate.

Exhibit 12-3 pictures the relationship between investment and the interest rate for both a single firm and the entire economy. As a firm undertakes more investment projects, the expected rate of return from each additional investment opportunity will decline. For the firm illustrated by Exhibit 12-3, project A is expected to yield more

[1] Many economists, particularly monetarists, believe that the long-run effect of monetary policy on interest rates is just the opposite of its short-run impact. See Chapter 14, pages 247–251.

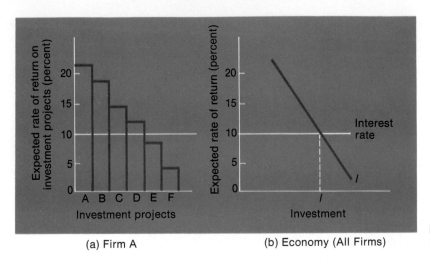

(a) Firm A   (b) Economy (All Firms)

Exhibit 12-3   When Businessmen Invest

If the interest rate were 10 percent, firm A [frame (a)] would undertake investment projects A, B, C, and D. For the entire economy, investment would be I [frame (b)]. There would be a negative relationship between the amount of investment and the interest rate for both individual firms and the economy as a whole.

than a 20 percent rate of return, B about 17 percent, C approximately 15 percent, and so on. If the interest rate were 10 percent, projects A, B, C, and D would be undertaken. If the interest rate fell to 5 percent, E (but not F) would also be carried out. But if the interest rate rose to 16 percent, only projects A and B would be profitable.

As more capital is invested (that is, more projects are undertaken) it will be necessary to include some of the less attractive projects. The rate of return on *additional* investment will decline. This will be true for an individual firm, and in aggregate for the entire economy. Thus, as Exhibit 12-3b shows, there will be a negative relationship between total investment and the interest rate, for an economy.

EXPANSIONARY AND RESTRICTIVE MONETARY POLICY

Since the supply of money can be influenced by the central monetary authorities, it presents planners with another policy variable with which to promote full employment and stabilize prices. If the central monetary planners wanted to follow an **expansionary monetary policy,** they could (a) purchase government bonds, (b) reduce the reserve requirements of banks, and/or (c) reduce the discount rate. All of these changes would tend to increase the supply of money, making credit more readily available to the economy. In contrast, if the monetary authorities sold government bonds, increased bank reserve requirements, and raised the discount rate, the supply of money would tend to decline (or increase at a slower rate). Monetary policy would be **restrictive,** causing interest rates to rise in the short run.

How does monetary policy exert an influence on aggregate demand and income? Economists are not in complete agreement on this issue. In fact, it composes one of the major differences between Keynesians and the monetarists. The Keynesians believe that monetary policy has its major impact indirectly by influencing the interest rate. As we will see later, the monetarists believe there is a more direct link between monetary policy and aggregate demand.

HOW MONETARY POLICY WORKS—THE KEYNESIAN VIEW

Keynesian economists believe that expansionary monetary policy can be used to reduce interest rates. Because of the lower rate, businessmen will undertake a larger number of investment projects. The "easy money" policy can thereby stimulate private investment.

Exhibit 12-4 illustrates the Keynesian view of expansionary monetary policy. The monetary authorities—via open market purchases, for example—expand the supply of money from M to M' (Exhibit 12-4a). At the initial interest rate i_1, the public has more money than it desires to hold. It will attempt to reduce its money balances by buying bonds and other financial assets. The interest rate will decline. What impact will this decline have on private investment? Investment will rise, as businessmen find that more projects are profitable at the lower interest rate. Aggregate investment will increase from I_1 to I_2 (ΔI in Exhibit 12-4b and c). The additional investment, ΔI, will cause aggregate demand to expand (Exhibit 12-4c). By how much will the equilibrium level of income go up? The new investment will have a multiplier effect, causing income to rise by a larger amount than the increase in aggregate demand.

Thus, Keynesian theory suggests that expansionary monetary policy will lower the interest rate and induce additional investment. The expansion in investment will increase aggregate demand and, working via the multiplier, cause aggregate income to

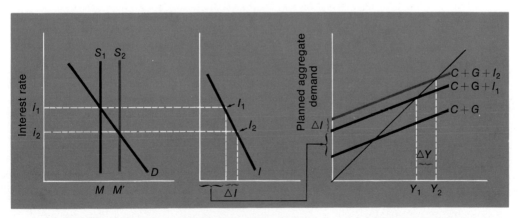

(a) Quantity of Money   (b) Quantity of Investment   (c) Aggregate Income

Exhibit 12-4   How Monetary Policy Can Stimulate Demand

Within the Keynesian model, an increase in the supply of money (shift from S_1 to S_2) would cause the interest rate to decline (from i_1 to i_2), stimulating additional investment (ΔI). Because of the multiplier, the equilibrium level of income would increase by a much larger amount [(ΔY, frame (c)] than investment. Monetary policy works through the interest rate in the Keynesian model.

rise. Expansionary monetary policy provides an additional tool that macroplanners can use to assure sufficient aggregate demand and full employment.

Money and Inflation

Monetary policy also presents planners with another tool to combat inflation. When aggregate demand exceeds full-employment income, prices will tend to rise. The excess demand will be inflationary. Monetary policy can be utilized to reduce aggregate demand to a level that is consistent with full employment and stable prices.

Within the Keynesian framework, the restrictive monetary policy will be transmitted through its impact on the interest rate. Suppose the Federal Reserve decides to sell government bonds. The private purchasers of the bonds will pay for them by giving up deposits (money). The supply of money will be reduced. The smaller supply of money (and larger supply of bonds) will cause bond prices to fall and interest rates to rise. As the rate of interest increases, investors will choose to forego some of their less profitable investment projects. The higher interest rates will increase the opportunity cost of investing in physical capital. Private investment will decline, as some potential investors choose to purchase bonds instead of capital goods. The decline in private investment will reduce both aggregate demand and the inflationary pressure. Restrictive monetary policy can help turn the tide against inflation.

Some industries, construction for example, are much more sensitive to changes in interest rates than others. Higher interest rates increase the monthly payment necessary to finance construction cost. At the higher interest rates (and monthly housing payments), many households will decide to put off housing construction into the future. Thus, restrictive monetary policy may have an uneven impact. Widespread unemployment and little new capital investment may dominate some sectors such as construction, while the inflationary pressures continue in other sectors. Some economists have criticized reliance on monetary policy as an anti-inflationary weapon because of this uneven impact.

COMBINING MONETARY AND FISCAL POLICY

Monetary and fiscal policy are alternative tools that macroplanners can use to help stabilize the economy. Usually macroplanners will want to coordinate the two so they do not work against each other. If stimulus is desired, a budget deficit could be combined with monetary expansion. On the other hand, if restrictive macropolicy is in order, a budget surplus and a slow rate of monetary growth might be planned.

Two Ways of Financing a Deficit

When the government runs a deficit, there are two alternative ways of financing it. First, the Treasury could sell U.S. securities to the public. This action would leave the supply of money unchanged.[2] The demand deposits of private parties would decline, but the Treasury's demand deposits would rise by an offsetting amount. With time, the Treasury will use the newly acquired funds to purchase such things as highways, education, bombs, and airplanes. This method of financing the deficit would reduce the supply of loanable funds available to finance private investment. Higher interest rates would result, dampening the expansionary impact of the budget deficit. But Keynesians believe that aggregate demand, and not the interest rate, is the primary determinant of investment. Thus, the net effect of a budget deficit would be expansionary, even when financed by borrowing from the public.[3]

Alternatively, the budget deficit could be financed by borrowing from the Federal Reserve. When the Treasury borrows from the Fed it is as if the government used printing press money to pay its bills. The budget deficit is financed with newly created money. The action would leave the funds of potential private bondholders undisturbed and available to finance private investment. The monetary expansion would exert downward pressure on the short-run interest rate, further stimulating investment and aggregate demand. This method is really a combination monetary–fiscal action. Clearly, it is more expansionary than when the deficit is financed by selling bonds to the public.

DID MACROPOLICY CAUSE THE INFLATION OF THE 1970s?

The *rate of change* in the national debt, particularly that portion held by the Fed, and the *growth rate* of the money supply reveal a great deal about macropolicy. Budget deficits contribute to the growth of the national debt. Rapid growth in the debt signifies deficit financing and expansionary fiscal policy. When deficits are financed by money creation, the amount of government securities held by the Fed will expand. Rapid growth in the amount of the national debt *held by the Fed* would be indicative of an expansionary monetary policy.

Exhibit 12-5 shows the path of these three indicators of macropolicy for the 1940–1975 period. During World War II both fiscal and monetary policy were highly expansionary as the government sought to finance the war effort. Large budget deficits increased the national debt and much of it was financed by borrowing from the Fed. The amount of U.S. securities held by the Fed increased sharply between 1941 and 1945, leading to a rapid growth in the money supply. Since the wartime economy had reached full employment by 1942, the highly expansionary macropolicy led to rapidly rising prices. Between 1942 and 1947, the consumer price index rose by more than 30 percent.

Between 1949 and 1962 macropolicy was clearly less expansionary. The national debt increased at an annual rate of 1.4 percent. The amount of the debt held by the Fed expanded at a 2.3 percent annual rate, while the money supply grew slightly more rapidly. During this period of relatively restrictive macropolicy, prices rose at an annual rate of 1.5 percent.

---

[2]Be careful not to confuse (a) bond sales by the Treasury to the public and (b) bond sales by the Federal Reserve to the public. The latter, but not the former, will affect the money supply.
[3]Most monetarists disagree with this view. See Chapter 14, pages 260–263.

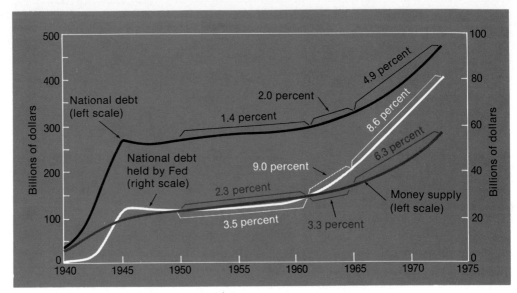

Exhibit 12-5   How Expansionary Has Monetary and Fiscal Policy Been?

The graph shows the changes in money supply, national debt, and the holdings of U.S. securities by the Federal Reserve for 1940–1975. Note that all three have increased more rapidly since 1965, than at any time since World War II. What impact would this have on the price level of a fully employed economy? (Braces indicate the compound annual rates of change for an inclusive period.)

Beginning in the early 1960s, as Exhibit 12-5 shows, macropolicy shifted to a decidedly more expansionary stance. The Fed's holdings of U.S. securities grew at a rate of three to four times more rapidly than during the 1950s. The national debt in total also grew more rapidly. Between 1965 and 1973, the money supply expanded at an annual rate of 6.3 percent, compared to 2.3 percent during the 1949–1961 period. Clearly macropolicies, both fiscal and monetary, were more expansionary than at any time since World War II.

By 1965, the unemployment rate in the United States was approaching 4 percent. What will be the impact of expansionary monetary and fiscal policy when the economy is already operating at capacity? Inflation. Between 1965 and 1968, prices rose at a 3 percent annual rate. As macropolicy became even more expansionary during the late 1960s and into the 1970s, prices rose still more rapidly. During the 1970–1974 period, the average annual rate of inflation was near 7 percent, clipping 40 percent from the purchasing power of a dollar bill in a five year period. While several extenuating circumstances were present, there can be little doubt that the highly expansionary macropolicy of the late 1960s and early 1970s fueled the inflationary fires of the period.

WILL MONETARY POLICY ALWAYS STIMULATE DEMAND?

Within the Keynesian model, theoretically, there are three reasons why expansionary monetary policy *might* sometimes fail to stimulate the economy. Most Keynesians

OUTSTANDING ECONOMIST: Paul Samuelson

Two generations of economists have been brought up on Paul Samuelson. His best-selling introductory text has gone through nine editions and literally millions of students have used it. But as Professor Samuelson noted, "They don't give Nobel Prizes for writing textbooks." The first American to win the Nobel Prize in economics, he was so honored for "raising the level of analysis in economic science." Samuelson's earlier background was in mathematics. His book, *The Foundations of Economic Analysis*,[4] gave precise mathematical meaning to much of economic reasoning. Many graduate students and faculty members have spent months poring over this masterpiece of economics.

Professor Samuelson's interests are wide ranging and his contributions to economics reflect this fact. International trade theory, welfare economics, theory of the firm, theory of public goods, and monetary and fiscal theory have all "felt the brush" of this master artist. His *collected works* have recently been published and they encompass three lengthy volumes.[5]

Professor Samuelson is an avid modern Keynesian. He believes that discretionary fiscal policy can and should be used to reduce unemployment. If that means moderate inflation, so be it. While he accepts the Keynesian view that money exerts an influence on aggregate demand via the interest rate, he has been, perhaps, the most vociferous critic of the monetarists. His confrontations with Milton Friedman, a well-known monetarist, have often enlivened professional meetings.

Professor Samuelson has never held a government position, though he did serve as an advisor to both Presidents Kennedy and Johnson. Many students may be familiar with his *Newsweek* column, in which he often articulates his views on current economic affairs. A professor of economics at Massachusetts Institute of Technology for more than three decades, Samuelson favored the temporary wage–price controls when they were introduced by the Nixon Administration in 1971. Yet he opposes permanent controls, arguing that they would lead "to long lines of black markets and consumer desperation." Samuelson does not believe that we will ever again experience a depression such as that of the 1930s. "It's not in the attitude of the consumer. It's not in the attitude of business. The big change since the 1930s is this: In the last analysis, we will not sit by and do nothing when a chronic slump is developing and threatens to feed upon itself. The government, in a democracy, can step in and turn the tide."[6]

Professor Samuelson is one of the few economists who is well-known and respected by both professional economists and the general public. He has bridged the gap between academia and the real world.

would agree that under normal conditions, none of the three factors would be present. Therefore, typically, expansionary monetary policy will have the stimulating impact on

---

[4] Paul Samuelson, *Foundations of Economic Analysis.* Cambridge, Massachusetts: Harvard Univ. Press, 1947.

[5] Paul Samuelson, *Collected Scientific Papers of Paul Samuelson.* Cambridge, Massachusetts: MIT Press, 1966.

[6] *U.S. News and World Report* (interview), December 14, 1964.

aggregate demand that we previously outlined. Nevertheless, policies to combat abnormal circumstances, particularly depressed economic conditions, are of great importance.

1. *The Liquidity Trap.* Professor Keynes outlined a particular liquidity preference or demand for money schedule that would render monetary policy totally ineffective. Suppose the economy were in a depression and that interest rates were very low. There is little incentive to purchase additional bonds because of their low interest yield. This is particularly true if households think that interest rates may increase in the future. If interest rates should rise, one's current decision to buy a bond yielding a 1 percent rate of return would mean foregoing a bond yielding 2 percent next month. Therefore, households may decide to just stash money away, rather than buying bonds at low interest rates. An increase in the money supply, in this case, will fail to increase the demand for bonds and lower interest rates. Since the expansionary monetary policy does not lower interest rates, it cannot induce new investment, expanding aggregate demand. Monetary policy is rendered ineffective because the **liquidity trap** prevents the interest rate from declining!

Exhibit 12-6 demonstrates the liquidity trap graphically. As the money supply is increased from S_0 to S_1, households simply hold on to (demand) the additional money balances. The demand for money is infinite at the 1 percent interest rate. The expansionary monetary policy therefore is unable to induce new investment and stimulate aggregate demand.

Has the U.S. economy ever been caught in the liquidity trap? Most economists, both Keynesian and non-Keynesian, do not think so. But when interest rates are quite low, as was true during the Great Depression, the demand schedule for money might become quite flat. This would mean that large increases in the supply of money would be necessary to reduce interest rates and induce any specified amount of investment. Monetary policy would not be totally ineffective, but investment and aggregate demand would not be very responsive to a specific change in the stock of money.

2. *Vertical Investment Schedule.* When an economy is in a depression, investors may be very pessimistic about the future. Many plants may be operating below capacity level. Even though an interest reduction lowers their costs, businessmen may still feel

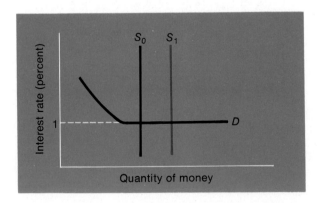

Exhibit 12-6 The Liquidity Trap and Ineffective Monetary Policy

At very low interest rates, the demand for money *might* become perfectly horizontal. Thus, monetary expansion would be unable to reduce the interest rate and stimulate aggregate demand.

the demand is so low that they could not sell additional units even at a lower price. The existing excess capacity and pessimism about the future *may* result in a vertical investment schedule with respect to the interest rate during times of depression.

Exhibit 12-7 illustrates the impact of monetary policy when the investment schedule is vertical. Typically, the expansionary monetary policy will reduce interest rates and induce additional investment. This is illustrated by the shift in the supply of money from S_1 to S_2. The interest rate declines from 3 to 2 percent, and investment increases from I_1 to I_2. But as the money supply continues to increase, the interest rate falls to 1 percent. But no new investment is induced by the decline in interest from 2 to 1 percent. *In this range*, investment is completely unresponsive to changes in the interest rate. Despite the expansionary monetary policy (shift from S_2 to S_3), the level of investment remains constant at I_2. Monetary policy is unable to induce new investment and increase aggregate demand. Fiscal tools (tax cuts and increases in government expenditures) must be utilized if the economy is to be stimulated back to full employment.

3. *Excess Reserve Trap.* Previously, we indicated the major tools that monetary authorities could utilize to increase the supply of money. Almost all of these involve either the creation of excess reserves by banks or a reduction in the cost of obtaining reserves from the Federal Reserve. When the Federal Reserve purchases bonds from banks, the action increases the excess reserves of the banks. The Federal Reserve can also increase excess reserves by lowering the reserve requirements of member banks. But creation of the excess reserves does not influence the money supply unless the banks use the reserves to extend additional loans. If banks extend new loans, this sets off a chain reaction that results in a multiple expansion in the supply of money.

Will the banks use the excess reserves to make new loans? Banks are in business to make money, and they will have a strong incentive to substitute interest-bearing loans

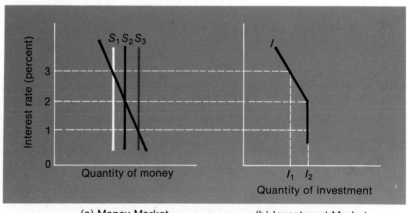

Exhibit 12-7   The Vertical Investment Schedule and Ineffective Monetary Policy

(a) Money Market   (b) Investment Market

At very low interest rates, the investment schedule might become vertical. As the supply of money increases from S_2 to S_3 [frame (a)] the interest rate will decline from 2 to 1 percent. But as the interest rate falls below 2 percent, the level of investment remains constant at I_2. Expansionary monetary policy is ineffective because investment is unresponsive to changes in the interest rate.

for the non-interest bearing excess reserves. Normally, banks will utilize the excess reserves to extend new loans and expand the stock of money. But what if they do not? If the banks refuse to make new loans, the monetary tools of the Federal Reserve will be rendered ineffective because of the **excess reserve trap.**

There is some evidence that banks were reluctant to extend new loans during the Great Depression. Many banks went under in the 1930–1933 period. Others were able to survive only because they had substantial excess reserves. Many bankers were anxious to build up their reserves as they had an opportunity to do so. This factor tended to reduce the ability of the Federal Reserve to directly control the supply of money during this period.

Even in the extreme case of an excess reserve trap, the monetary authorities have one other tool at their disposal. They could purchase bonds directly from the nonbank public and thereby increase the money supply by at least the amount of the bond purchase. Therefore, the excess reserve trap does not render monetary policy completely ineffective, though it may cause the economy to be less responsive to changes in monetary variables.

FULL EMPLOYMENT AND INFLATION IN THE REAL WORLD

Thus far in our analysis of the Keynesian model, we have assumed that the price level remains constant until full employment is reached. Therefore, an increase in aggregate demand would cause both money and real income to grow. However, once full employment is attained, additional demand would result only in higher prices. Money income would increase (because of the rise in prices), but real income would remain constant.

Both theory and evidence suggest that the real world will not conform to this polar view. As full employment is *approached*, prices usually begin to rise. It is not too difficult to see why this is the case. When there is substantial unemployment, there will be excess capacity and unemployed resources in almost all industries and regions of the economy. As aggregate demand increases, almost all of this increase in demand will flow into areas of underemployment and excess capacity. Thus, real output can be increased without bidding up prices. But as the unemployed resources of the economy are reduced and more and more of the industrial subsectors of the economy are pushed to their full-employment capacity, further increases in demand will result primarily in higher prices in these fully employed subsectors. As full employment is approached for the economy as a whole, more and more of the additional stimuli will be channeled into industries and regions which have already attained full employment. Prices will begin rising more rapidly. Real income will expand less rapidly.

Exhibit 12-8 presents this picture graphically. Since excess capacity is present and unemployed resources are available, an increase in aggregate demand from D_1 to D_2 will result in a higher level of real income while prices remain stable. But as the economy begins to approach full employment, bottlenecks develop. Many of the subsectors of the economy are already operating at capacity. When aggregate demand

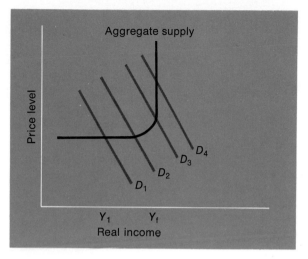

Exhibit 12-8 Inflation, Real Income, and Aggregate Demand

When unemployed resources abound, an increase in aggregate demand (shift from D_1 to D_2) will increase real income without causing inflation. But as the full employment real income level (Y_f) is approached, prices will begin rising as aggregate demand expands (shift from D_2 to D_3). Once full employment is attained, further increases in demand (such as to D_4) would be purely inflationary.

increases from D_2 to D_3, real outcome expands,[7] but prices will also increase as full employment is approached. The expansion in aggregate demand results in both a higher level of real income and rising prices. Once the resources of the economy are fully employed, how would a further expansion in aggregate demand affect prices and real income? As the shift from D_3 to D_4 illustrates, prices would rise but real income would remain unchanged. Having attained full employment, further expansions in aggregate demand would be purely inflationary.

The Conflict Between Full Employment and Stable Prices

The theory that we have just outlined suggests there is a conflict between full employment and stable prices. As an economy moves closer to full employment, the rate of inflation will increase. Historically, the record of the United States and other Western nations is consistent with this view. Periods of high unemployment have been associated with relatively stable or falling prices. Periods of low unemployment have been accompanied by more rapid increases in prices.

An English economist, A. W. Phillips, first discovered there was a consistent negative relation between the unemployment rate and changes in money wages for the United

---

[7] As we will describe later, some economists, particularly monetarists, argue that it will be impossible to *maintain* the higher level of real income that results from the inflationary expansion in aggregate demand (shift from D_2 to D_3, Exhibit 12-8).

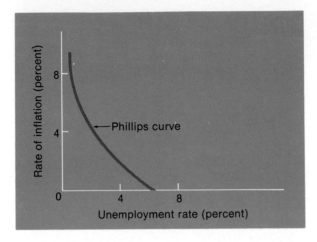

Exhibit 12-9   A Hypothetical Phillips Curve

As the unemployment rate declines, prices usually tend to rise more rapidly.

Kingdom.[8] But since wages are the major component of cost, it is not surprising that others have found a similar relationship between unemployment and changes in prices. The curve indicating the tradeoff between unemployment and inflation (or changes in money wages) has been termed the **Phillips curve,** after its founder.

Exhibit 12-9 demonstrates a hypothetical Phillips curve. When the rate of unemployment is high, say 6 percent, prices will rise slowly. As the unemployment rate falls to 4 percent, prices will rise more rapidly. Additional reductions in the unemployment rate will lead to more and more rapid increases in prices. For example, the unemployment rate might be pushed to 2 percent only if a 5 percent rate of inflation were to be tolerated.

▭ LOOKING AHEAD

During the 1960s most economists argued that the Phillips curve analysis posed a dilemma for policy-makers. It suggests that stable prices and a low unemployment rate are in conflict with each other. Policy-makers cannot have both. But they can trade off less of one, unemployment for example, for more of the other.

While many economists still adhere to the view that the unemployment rate can be reduced if we are willing to tolerate a little inflation, the experience of the 1970s has shaken the faith of others in the simple Phillips curve analysis. Increasingly, monetarists, but also many Keynesians, argue that the Phillips curve is a short-run phenomenon. They do not believe that the unemployment rate can be reduced at the cost of moderate inflation *over extended periods of time.* We will return to this debate and issues related to it as we present the monetarist's position.

Before we move on to consider the views of the monetarists, let us pause to reflect on the future possibility of another Great Depression. Most economists feel that the probability of such an event is remote. But the economic situation of the mid-1970s has shaken the faith of a few. The following debate will highlight the controversy.

[8]A. W. Phillips, "The Relationship Between the Level of Unemployment and the Rate of Change of Money Wage Rates in the United Kingdom," *Economica*, November 1958, pp. 283–299.

Will There Ever Be Another Great Depression? Yes.

Five years ago, this proposition was not particularly controversial. Most professional economists felt that another Great Depression was extremely unlikely, given the potential of fiscal and monetary tools to guide the economy.

What has changed, causing us to reevaluate the picture? In a word, inflation—worldwide, double-digit inflation! Rapid inflation could lead to a major recession because it generates uncertainty. When rapid inflation is not accurately anticipated, it can wipe out the life savings of a long-term lender in just a few years. Similarly, borrowers who are willing to pay high *money* interest rates because they anticipate inflation, may be unable to meet their future obligations if rising wages and prices are halted. Uncertainty about inflation can make contracts, even over moderately short periods, extremely risky.

Inflation, Deflation, and Depressions

The last Great Depression was caused by worldwide deflation and uncertainty. Inappropriate macropolicy produced falling wages and prices. The changing purchasing power of money altered the intent of long-term contracts. Farmers, businessmen, and others who signed long-term contracts (for example, mortgages) in the 1920s were unable later to meet their fixed money commitments in an economy dominated by falling prices and wages. Bankruptcies resulted. Observing these events, fear and uncertainty caused still others to avoid exchanges involving long-term money commitments. Economic exchange came to a standstill!

Do not forget, exchange is a positive-sum game. When people fail to trade because of uncertainty, gains derived from comparative advantage, specialization, and exchange will be lost. When this happens on a large scale, real incomes will decline sharply. The layman would say that the system has broken down. Depression is the result. This is what happened on a worldwide scale in the 1930s.

The next Great Depression will be caused by chronic inflation, not deflation. Inflation, like deflation, can break the back of economic organization. When the price level goes up 15 percent one year, 5 percent the next, and 30 percent the succeeding year, the advantages of money as a vehicle with which to conduct long-term transactions are destroyed. Neither buyer nor seller knows what to expect about the purchasing power of money two, three, or five years into the future. Because of this uncertainty, people will be reluctant to become a party to long-term exchange contracts. Purchases of homes, farms, heavy equipment, life insurance, and other assets usually bought on time, will decline. Uncertainty about the value of money will lead to less saving and less investment (both involve long-term commitments), two ingredients that oil the wheels of economic progress.

Valuable resources will be directed away from production into speculation, protecting oneself against rising prices, and the attainment of individual self-sufficiency (for example, gardening and home building). Businessmen will be more interested in buying and selling (short-term agreements) and less interested in investment and manufacturing. Long-term borrowing will become extremely difficult. Who would want to loan dollars, when they might be paid back with quarters, dimes, or pennies in terms of their purchasing power? Money interest rates, spurred on by both inflation and uncertainty, will go sky high. Speculation could lead businessmen to withhold goods from markets (witness the withholding of agriculture products in 1974) in anticipation

"Can't you sound a note of cautious optimism and still be a leading economist?"

Drawing by Alan Dunn; © 1970 The New Yorker Magazine, Inc.

of further price rises. As the experience of the 1930s demonstrated, a decline in investment, long-term production planning, and long-term exchange agreements will generate depression conditions.

The Evidence of History

Confusion about the relationship between inflation and depression results because a little inflation, initially, stimulates economic activity. But history suggests that high rates of inflation have the opposite effect. In Germany, the great inflation after World War I produced depression and human misery, in addition to a despotic government. Unemployment in 1923 rose to 20 percent, up from 3 percent during the 1919–1921 period. Real output fell by nearly one-third in Germany during the 1921–1923 period.[9]

The slow average growth rate in Argentina, Chile, and Uruguay, countries long plagued by chronic inflation, suggests that rapidly rising prices retard growth. The more rapid growth rate in Brazil appears to be in spite of its rapid inflation. Brazil's most serious recession since World War II, the 1963–1965 period, was accompanied by its

[9]Costantino Bresciani-Turroni, *The Economics of Inflation* (New York: Barnes, 1937) and Karsten Laursen and Jorgen Pedersen, *The German Inflation 1918–1923* (Amsterdam: North Holland Publ., 1964).

highest rates of inflation. Prices increased by 250 percent during the period. When Brazil returned to, what was for it, more moderate rates of inflation (a 20 percent annual rate), real output expanded at a record pace.

But analysis of South American economies understates the negative effects that rapid inflation would have in North America, Japan, and Europe. The latter are much more dependent on complex financial markets and long-term exchange agreements. Barter and self-sufficient agriculture are of less importance. The shock of 20, 30, or 40 percent inflation in the industrial Western nations would be far more serious.

Is Disaster Inevitable?

The answer is, of course, no. Given current conditions, we do know enough to prevent calamity. Nonetheless political factors, even more than economic, make the possibility a real one. Do not forget, the political process is biased against policies that result in short-run identifiable cost (for example, higher unemployment) in order to gain future benefits (for example, a lower rate of inflation) that are difficult to identify now. Halting inflation would lead to higher rates of unemployment in the short run. After an initial bout with inflation, political factors are likely to cause democratic governments to chart a still more expansionary course, further fueling the long-run inflationary fires. A couple of episodes in which we first try to fight inflation and then abruptly expand to fight unemployment could cause inflationary rates to ratchet up to very high levels indeed. Eventually, if not sooner, the situation could get out of hand. This is where the danger lies.

Discussion

1. Do you think rapid inflation could cause a recession in the United States? Why or why not?
2. How do you think macroplanners would respond in the short run (in the long run) to a situation of 15 percent annual inflation and 6 percent unemployment? Why? Would their response help avert a depression? Explain.

Will There Ever Be Another Great Depression? No.

Controversies in Economics

Business ups and downs capable of pushing the unemployment rate to 6 or 7 percent continue to be a threat. But the likelihood of a catastrophic economic decline such as was experienced during the 1930s is nil. The confidence that a major future depression will be averted rests on several grounds.

1. *Knowledge of How to Control the Economy.* In the 1930s Western nations did not understand how to deal with the business cycle. During that period, both politicians and many economists believed the government should always balance its budget. There was an unawareness of the importance of changes in the money supply. As a result antidepression public policy during the 1930s was perverse. Today the environment has changed. We have both the knowledge and the commitment to use the government's expenditure and taxing powers (fiscal policy) and tools for the control of the money supply (monetary policy) in such a way as to assure a level of total spending that would avoid a depression.

2. *The Federal Deposit Insurance Corporation.*   This government agency insures the deposits of commercial and savings banks. It provides the depositor with 100 percent assurance that he will receive the proceeds of his account up to the $40,000 ceiling. Since the FDIC protects the depositor, the possibility of bank runs[10] has been eliminated. Since people know their accounts are safe, they do not panic. Before the FDIC was established in 1933 more than 10,000 banks, one-third of the total, failed between 1922 and 1933. Since that time, annual banking failures have seldom exceeded four or five. The FDIC, more than any other institutional change, has eliminated a major source of monetary and economic instability.

3. *The Increased Importance of Automatic Stabilizers.*   Our economy is now protected by several built-in forces that tend to counter any reduction in the level of spending and income. During a recession, welfare payments and unemployment benefits increase automatically. Social Security assures the maintenance of income for the elderly even during bad times. Government tax revenues from both the progressive income tax and corporate profits tax decline automatically when business conditions are poor. All of these factors serve to cushion the cumulative effects of a declining economy.

4. *The Size of the Government Sector.*   Before the Great Depression, government expenditures, federal, state, and local, accounted for one-tenth of our national income. Today they account for more than one-third. Since these expenditures are not determined by the profit motive, the growth in the public sector provides our economy with a large base of economic activity that is relatively unresponsive to changing economic conditions.

Could Inflation Cause a Depression?

All major depressions in the United States have been associated with monetary restriction, failure to undertake offsetting fiscal action, and deflationary pressure. We now know how to deal with these conditions in a way that will prevent a severe economic contraction.

A few countries, notably Germany, Austria, and Poland, after World War I and Greece during World War II have suffered economic disaster because of hyperinflation. Of course, runaway inflation could cause a depression. But with our knowledge of macroeconomics, we are not going to let it happen. There will be a public outcry to control it long before it reaches rates that would be necessary to cause a major depression.

Expansionary monetary and fiscal policy, which is essential to the continuation of rapid inflation, will be moderated. An economic slowdown may be the price of bringing inflation under control. But this can be handled in a way that will minimize transitional costs. We know about the disruptiveness inherent in a sharp stop–go policy. Thus, when it is necessary to control inflation, we will do so with moderate constraint, avoiding policies that would cause a depression.

The experience of Brazil suggests that an economy can suffer a surprising amount of inflation, while still maintaining rapid economic growth. Between 1948 and 1970, the

---

[10] A bank run is a situation in which all depositors attempt to draw out their deposits at once, because they fear the bank is about to go broke. Under a fractional reserve system, of course, the bank will be unable to pay all of its depositors at once. Thus, bank runs cause bank failures.

average annual rate of inflation in Brazil exceeded 30 percent.[11] It ranged between 10 and 50 percent for 16 out of the 22 years, reaching a high of 92 percent in 1964! But real GNP in Brazil grew at an annual rate of 5.6 percent during this period! This is not to say that inflation did not hamper economic progress in Brazil. Perhaps an even more rapid growth rate would have been attained with more stable prices. But the Brazilian case should lead us to question the view that a 20 to 30 percent rate of inflation would cause economic collapse.

Do We Have Suicidal Tendencies?

The argument that there is a depression in our future is based on the premise that even though we know what to do, we will not do it. It takes a suicidal view of our economy. Macroeconomics tells us the proper pills to take for both economic recession and rising prices. We will take the necessary pills long before a minor illness evolves into an economic disaster.

Discussion

1. Do you think our economy is "depression proof"? Why or why not? What are the major factors that reduce the likelihood of a future depression?
2. Which of the two views about the possibility of a depression do you think is stronger? What are the most basic disagreements between the two positions?

CHAPTER LEARNING OBJECTIVES

1. There will be a negative relationship between the quantity of money demanded and the interest rate. An increase in the supply of money, according to Keynesian theory, will cause people to use their now excess money balances to buy bonds. Bond prices will rise and the interest rate will decline, at least in the short run. On the other hand, restrictive monetary policy will cause the interest rate to rise in the short run.

2. Interest is either a direct or opportunity cost of every capital investment. *Ceteris paribus*, the higher the interest rate, the lower the amount of capital investment. Businessmen will undertake the projects that they expect to be most profitable first. As the interest rate increases, some of the marginal investment projects will be foregone.

3. According to the Keynesian view, expansionary monetary policy will reduce the interest rate, thereby stimulating investment and leading to an increase in aggregate demand. A restrictive monetary policy would increase the interest rate, thereby discouraging investment and reducing aggregate demand. The interest rate is the mechanism that transmits monetary policy in the Keynesian model.

4. There are two ways the Treasury can finance a deficit, borrowing from the public and borrowing from the Fed. The former method will increase the supply of bonds (and reduce the availability of loanable funds to finance private investment), causing the interest rate to rise. In contrast, borrowing from the Fed increases the money supply and exerts downward pressure on interest rates. It is the more expansionary of the two.

5. Both monetary and fiscal policy were considerably more expansionary during the 1965–1974 period than at any time since World War II. Since the economy was operating near

---

[11] See Felipe Pazos, *Chronic Inflation in Latin American Countries* (New York: Praeger, 1972) for an analysis of how inflation has affected South American countries.

capacity at the beginning of the period, the expansionary macropolicy was a major contributing factor to the inflation of the period.

6. In the Keynesian model, monetary policy would be ineffective as a tool to stimulate demand if: **(a)** the economy were in the liquidity trap as evidenced by a perfectly horizontal demand for money schedule, **(b)** investment were insensitive to a decline in the interest rate as evidenced by a completely vertical investment schedule, or **(c)** banks failed to extend loans, expanding the money supply, even though the monetary authorities created excess reserves. Each of these three polar cases is highly atypical in the real world.

7. As an economy approaches full employment, prices usually begin to rise. This may result because, while some sectors are still experiencing unemployment, others are already operating at capacity. Thus, additional demand results in price increases in the fully employed sectors.

8. At least in the short run, past evidence indicates there has been a negative relationship between inflation and the rate of unemployment.

IMPORTANT TERMS TO REMEMBER

Interest rate: The price paid for the use of money or loanable funds for a period of time. It is stated as a percentage of the amount borrowed. For example, an interest rate of 10 percent means that the borrower pays 10 cents annually for each dollar borrowed.

Demand for money: The amount of wealth that people desire to hold in the form of money balances, that is, cash and checking account deposits. It will be inversely related to the interest rate.

Expansionary monetary policy: A policy that results in a rate of change in the supply of money that is in excess of the long-run average rate.

Restrictive monetary policy: A policy that results in a rate of change in the money supply that is less than the long-run average rate.

Liquidity trap: Situation where the demand for money is horizontal with respect to the interest rate. Thus, an increase in the supply of money would not cause the interest rate to decline. Therefore, according to the Keynesian view, monetary policy would be unable to stimulate aggregate demand.

Excess reserve trap: Situation wherein commercial banks would not issue new loans or buy financial assets in response to an increase in their excess reserves.

Phillips curve: A curve that illustrates the relationship between the rate of inflation (or money wages) and the unemployment rate. In the short run, the rate of inflation is usually negatively related to the unemployment rate.

THE ECONOMIC WAY OF THINKING—DISCUSSION QUESTIONS

1. What impact do Keynesians believe that an increase in the supply of money would have on **(a)** interest rates, **(b)** the level of investment, **(c)** aggregate demand, **(d)** employment, and **(e)** prices? Fully explain your answer.

2. Will a government debt be more expansionary if it is financed by borrowing from the Federal Reserve or from the general public? Explain.

3. Was macropolicy expansionary during the recessions of 1954, 1958, and 1970? Did macropolicy cause the inflation of the late 1960s and early 1970s? Has real world macropolicy been a stabilizing influence? Cite empirical evidence to support your view.

4. Suppose that you were just appointed chairman of the Council of Economic Advisers. Prepare a press release outlining your views on unemployment, inflation, and proper macropolicy, both monetary and fiscal, for the next three years.

5. "Macropolicy has been oversold. For years textbooks told us that it would stabilize the economy and eliminate the business cycle. The historical record is inconsistent with this view. It suggests that improper macropolicy caused the Great Depression, the slow rate of growth during the 1950s, and inflations of World War II and the 1970s. Macropolicy, itself, has been the major source of economic instability." Either defend or criticize this view.

6. "The last Great Depression was caused by massive monetary and fiscal contraction. The next Great Depression will be caused by massive macro-expansion." Could expansionary macropolicy cause a depression? Why or why not?

7. What's Wrong with This Way of Thinking?

"Inflation is caused by too much money chasing too few goods. The best way to stop inflation is therefore to expand GNP by, for instance, cutting taxes on business and thus encouraging production. The extra production will provide more goods and stop inflation."

13
THE BUSINESS CYCLE
AND INFLATION—
THE MONETARIST VIEW

In one sense, we are all Keynesians now; in another sense, nobody is any longer a Keynesian. The latter half is at least as important as the first.[1] *[Milton Friedman]*

The ideas of John Maynard Keynes have had a profound impact on almost all economists. His views became widely accepted, dominating the thinking of professional macroeconomists after World War II. During the 1960s, they began to exert a powerful influence on the economic stabilization policies of the United States. Both the 1964 tax cut and 1968 tax increase were solidly based on Keynesian economic reasoning.

While Keynesian views dominated the news media and influenced presidents during the 1960s, the views of monetarists gained increasing support among a new generation of professional economists. What do the monetarists believe? In order to obtain a better perspective on this question, we will begin by noting the intellectual roots of the monetarists.

THE EQUATION OF EXCHANGE

Every purchase is a sale. Usually the buyer receives goods, the seller money. Money is involved in almost every exchange. If we add together the purchases of all *final products and services*, they are equal to the GNP. GNP is merely the sum of the price P times the quantity Q of each "final product" purchased. But when the existing money stock M is multiplied by the number of times V that money is used to buy final products, this too yields the economy's gross national product. Therefore,

$$PQ = \text{GNP} = MV$$

[1]From a speech by Milton Friedman quoted in *Time Magazine*, February 4, 1966.

The V represents **velocity,** or the annual rate at which money changes hands in the purchase of final products. The velocity of money is merely GNP divided by the size of the money stock. For example, in 1973 GNP was 1.29 trillion and the average money stock (currency plus demand deposits) was $270 billion. On the average each dollar was used 4.8 times to purchase a final product or service. Therefore, the velocity of money was 4.8.

THE CLASSICAL VIEW—MONEY DOES NOT MATTER

The **equation of exchange,** $MV = PQ$, is simply an identity or a tautology. The equation is defined in such a way that it must be true. But classical economists built a theory, the quantity theory of money, using the equation. Put crudely, the **quantity theory of money** hypothesizes that V and Q do not change very much. Thus an increase in M, the money supply, would cause an equal proportional increase in prices P. For example, according to the classical view, if the money stock were increased by 5 percent, the price level would rise by 5 percent.

On what did the classical economists base these conclusions? They thought that institutional factors such as the organization of banking and credit, the rapidity of transportation and communication, and the frequency of income payments were the primary determinants of velocity. Since these factors would change very slowly, for all practical purposes the velocity or "turnover" rate of money in the short run was constant. The classicists also thought that flexible wages and prices would assure full employment. Thus, a change in the money supply could not affect real output.

For classical economists, the link between prices and the money supply was straightforward and quite mechanical. An increase in the money stock meant an equal proportional increase in prices. The real income of the economy was determined by other factors such as capital accumulation, technology, and the skill of the labor force. They did not believe that money exerted any independent impact on real production, income, and employment. Money did not matter, in any real sense.

THE EARLY KEYNESIANS—MONEY STILL DOES NOT MATTER MUCH

The Great Depression, of course, completely undermined the simple classical theory and laid the foundation for the Keynesian revolution. The classical theory could not explain widespread unemployment. Wages and prices did not adjust rapidly, as the classicists assumed.

Keynes, in his *General Theory*, gave a plausible explanation of why classical theory might be wrong about money. What if changes in velocity were in an opposite direction from changes in the money stock? If a 5 percent increase in money led to a 5 percent reduction in velocity, money would fail to change anything. Under these conditions, money would exert no direct influence on either real income or the price level.

Early Keynesians felt that the money supply should be ample enough to keep interest rates low and facilitate investment. Since velocity would decline in response to an increase in the money stock, the supply of money could be expanded without causing inflation. Initially, about the only role assigned to monetary policy by the early Keynesians was the provision of credit for expansion. Other than this, money still did not matter.

Lord Keynes himself was *not* an advocate of the extreme position that money did not matter.[2] But he did point out that under unusual conditions, the conditions of the liquidity trap, the interest rate would be unresponsive to a change in the supply of money. In the shadow of the Great Depression, many of his early followers took the unusual to be the typical. Of course, as we have noted, modern Keynesians believe that money does exert an impact on aggregate demand. But, as we will see, they differ with the monetarists about how that impact is transmitted.

THE MODERN MONETARIST—MONEY MATTERS MOST

Like the classicists, the modern monetarists emphasize that money plays a role in each exchange. But, unlike the classicists, the monetarists treat money as not just a medium of exchange, but as a valuable good demanded by households, just as they demand other goods. Money is valuable because it facilitates exchange *and* is an alternative method of holding wealth. Households will make decisions about how much of their wealth they want to tie up (or demand) in the form of houses, cars, clothes, stocks, insurance policies, and money. Money, like other goods, is demanded because it yields a stream of services.[3]

What Determines the Demand for Money?

Since monetarists treat money as a good, in general, factors that influence the demand for any good will influence the **demand for money balances.** Five factors deserve special note.

1. *The Price Level.*   The price level determines the purchasing power of money—how much it will buy. This means that the amount of money necessary to buy any specific bundle of goods (for example, a week's supply of groceries, gas for the car, or lunches for the kids) will increase with the price level. Thus, as the price level rises, the demand for money balances expands.

2. *Income.*   As income increases, households demand more of most goods. Money is no exception. People like to reserve a portion of their money balances for conducting

---

[2] Keynes thought money did matter, even during a recession. He stated, "So long as there is unemployment, employment will change in the same proportion as the quantity of money, and when there is full employment, prices will change in the same proportion as the quantity of money" (*General Theory of Employment, Interest, and Money* [New York: Harcourt, 1936], p. 296).

[3] The student should be careful not to confuse (a) the demand for money with (b) the desire for more income. Of course, all of us would like to have more income, but we may be perfectly satisfied with our holdings of money, given our current wealth position. When we say that people want to hold more (or less) money, we mean that they want to *restructure* their wealth toward larger (smaller) money balances.

OUTSTANDING ECONOMIST: Milton Friedman

Professor Friedman's height is 5 feet 3 inches, but he stands tall among economists. During the 1950s, when economists tended to ignore the importance of money, Friedman almost singlehandedly forced them to reconsider. Today most of the profession adheres to the view that both monetary and fiscal factors are of vital importance to matters of economic stability. Friedman deserves much of the credit for this transformation.

A severe critic of the Fed, Friedman argues that their preoccupation with interest rates has led to one blunder after another. Expansionary monetary policy designed to keep interest rates low has invariably led to inflation and higher interest rates. Restrictive monetary policy designed to deal with inflation then generates recessionary conditions. In the book *A Monetary History of the United States 1867–1960*,[4] Friedman and Anna Schwartz present an impressive case for the view that the Fed's stop-go policies have been the major source of economic instability. The book, already a classic, is a goldmine of monetary and aggregate economic data. Friedman's solution to the problem is to expand the money supply at a steady rate, 4 percent annually, for example.

Friedmanism is almost a religion among many present-day economists. His appearance at professional meetings is sufficient to assure a full auditorium. Always provocative and audacious, he is usually at his best when defending the free market economy, while rebuking the advocates of government intervention. At the heart of Friedmanism is a deep-seated distrust in the ability of government to handle economic affairs. Friedman presents the case for market alternatives to many government programs in *Capitalism and Freedom*.[5] If he were in charge, the minimum wage and other price-fixing legislation would be abolished. Tariffs and other restrictions on international trade would be removed. Regulatory agencies such as the ICC, CAB, FCC, and FTC would be out of business. Social Security and welfare would be replaced with the negative income tax. Educational vouchers would be instituted, granting private education the opportunity to compete on an equal basis with the public schools. The corporate income tax would be abolished, as would all forms of business subsidies. The size of government would be reduced as the sphere of market activity was expanded. Is it any wonder that Friedmanism has little support among bureaucrats and government planners?

Friedman, currently the Paul Snowden Professor of Economics at the University of Chicago, has never held a major government position. Students are perhaps familiar with his stimulating column in *Newsweek*. While he has played the role of critic, his capacity for controversy is matched by his scholarly work. The author of numerous professional books and articles, his work on the consumption function, monetary theory, and economic stability has been widely acclaimed by fellow economists. Fifteen years ago, he was considered something of a heretic by much of the profession. But brilliance and persistence have succeeded in spreading his influence to even Harvard and M.I.T., long-time strongholds of Keynesianism. His fellow economists do not always agree with him, but today he commands the respect of his critics as well as his many followers.

---

[4] Milton Friedman and Anna Schwartz, *A Monetary History of the United States 1867–1960*. Princeton, New Jersey: Princeton Univ. Press, 1971.
[5] Milton Friedman, *Capitalism and Freedom*. Chicago: Univ. of Chicago Press, 1962.

transactions. Since the number and magnitude of one's transactions usually increase with income, high income people usually hold (demand) more money than persons of less means. The demand for money is a positive function of income.

3. *The Price of Closely Related Goods.*   Bonds, stocks, savings accounts, and other liquid forms of holding wealth are close substitutes for money. While most of these assets are not directly exchanged for goods, they can often be easily transformed into money. As the expected rate of return from these forms of holding wealth increases, the opportunity cost of holding money rises. A dollar sitting in one's bank account is a dollar *not* held in an interest-bearing form, bonds for example.

The interest rate is the return derived from the holding of bonds and other financial assets. As the interest rate rises, the opportunity cost of holding money increases—more interest is being sacrificed. Higher interest rates reduce the attractiveness of holding non-interest bearing money. Thus, there will be a negative relationship between the demand for money and the interest rate.

4. *Expected Rate of Inflation.*   As the price of goods (houses, cars, stocks, etc.) rises, the value of a dollar declines. Inflation diminishes the relative value of money, increasing the opportunity cost of holding it. People do not want to hold assets that they expect to decline in value. For example, stockholders want to own stocks that they expect to increase in value, not those that will decline in value. Similarly, when people expect inflation to diminish the value of money, the attractiveness of holding money is reduced. The demand for money will be adversely affected by the **expectation of inflation.** If people think prices are going to rise they will demand (hold) less money.

5. *Institutional Factors.*   How easily can money be borrowed if you run short? How difficult is it to "match up" your current income and expenditures? Does your income arrive in a steady stream, or does it come once a year at harvest time? All of these factors will influence how much money, on the average, a household will demand. But they are primarily determined by institutional factors that influence credit and the timing of one's personal income. In time they will change and exert an influence on the demand for money.

How have changes in institutional factors influenced the demand for money in recent years? Both evidence and logic suggest that they have reduced it. Widespread use

These factors would cause the demand for money balances to:	
Increase	*Decrease*
1. A higher price level	1. A lower price level
2. Expanding real income	2. Falling real income
3. Lower interest rates	3. Higher interest rates
4. Expectation of falling prices	4. Expectation of rising prices
5. Institutional factors that make it more difficult for persons to match up income and spending	5. Institutional factors that make it easier for persons to match up income and spending

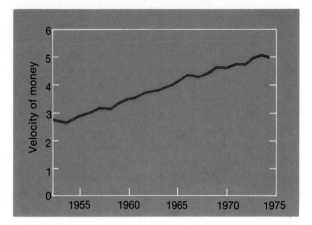

Exhibit 13-1   The Increasing Velocity of Money

The velocity of money (GNP divided by the money stock) has increased from less than 3 in the mid-1950s to more than 5 in 1974. Each dollar is being used more often to purchase things.

of general-purpose credit cards helps households better match up their bills with their receipt of income. Readily available short-term loans have reduced the need to maintain a substantial cash balance for emergencies. The movement away from agriculture means that more families have a steady income every two weeks or once a month, rather than an unpredictable income two or three times a year. This steady income makes planning more predictable. All of these factors have reduced the need for households to maintain large cash balances.

Exhibit 13-1 shows that the velocity of money has climbed from less than 3 in the mid-1950s to almost 5 in the mid-1970s. Today, each dollar turns over much more frequently in the process of purchasing final goods and services. Institutional factors have made it possible to handle a larger volume of transactions today with a smaller bank account than was possible 20 years ago. Credit cards, regular incomes, and readily available short-term loans have reduced the demand for money balances.

The Price of Money

The price of anything is what we must give up in order to acquire it. When we buy most things, we customarily quote their prices in terms of money. How do we acquire money? As anyone who has tried to maintain a balance in his bank account knows, money is acquired by giving up other things—leisure, stereos, television sets, automobiles, and other goods.

The amount of things that must be given up in order to acquire a unit of money will be inversely related to the price level. When prices of goods and services are high, a small marketbasket could be used (or foregone) to acquire a unit of money. In contrast, more things would have to be given up to acquire a unit of money when prices are lower. The price of money is the inverse of the price level.

Exhibit 13-2 shows the demand for money as a function of its price. When the price level rises (its inverse would fall), the quantity demanded of money would increase. Thus the inverse of the price level, the price of money, is negatively related to the amount of money demanded.

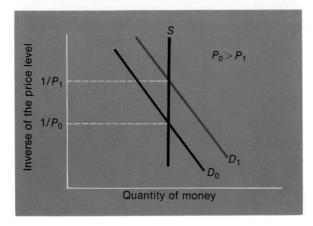

Exhibit 13-2   The Price of Money

The price of money is the inverse of the price level. Other things constant, an increase in demand for money balances would cause prices to fall.

What happens when there is an increase in the demand for money? Perhaps income has increased or the interest rate has declined. Thus people want to hold larger money balances. The demand for money, as Exhibit 13-2 shows, would shift from D_0 to D_1. If the supply of money is held constant, an increase in the demand for money would cause the price of money to rise. But what is the price of money? The inverse of the price level. Thus a higher price of money is the same thing as a decline in the price level. This analysis suggests that when the demand for money expands, other things constant, the price level will fall.

THE IMPACT OF MONEY—THE MONETARIST VIEW

The monetarist believes that the basic aggregate markets—current goods and services, labor resources, loanable funds, and money—are highly interrelated. Supply and demand will work together to determine both prices and output levels.

But unlike the classical economists, monetarists do not believe that prices adjust easily and rapidly. They believe the market process will bring about equilibrium—only slowly, and with the passage of time. Thus a temporary excess supply in some markets and excess demand in others may persist for significant periods of time. From the monetarist's viewpoint, imperfect information and uncertainty about the permanency of changing market conditions play a central role in the adjustment of aggregate markets.

Since money is used so universally in exchange, what happens in the money market is of vital importance. Imbalance in the money market will bring about changes in both production and prices in other markets. Therefore, the actions of the monetary authorities who control the supply of money are central to the establishment of economic stability.

The Transmission Mechanism

One of the most important differences between Keynesians and monetarists involves the mechanism by which monetary policy is transmitted. The Keynesians believe that monetary policy works indirectly through the interest rate. But monetarists believe the link is much more direct.

Monetarists believe that expansionary monetary policy creates an **excess supply of money.** People will adjust by increasing their spending on a wide range of goods, causing aggregate demand to expand. Similarly, monetary restriction would create an **excess demand for money,** causing people to reduce their spending. In their view monetary policy is not dependent on the interest rate for its effectiveness.

Monetary Policy—Two Views of the Transmission Mechanism

1. *Keynesian View*
   Money supply ——→ Interest rate ——→ Investment ——→ Aggregate demand
2. *Monetarist's View*
   Money ————————————————————————→ Aggregate demand

Expanding the Money Supply and Aggregate Demand

What would happen if the Federal Reserve decided to follow a more expansionary policy? For example, suppose that they bought bonds at a record rate, expanding the money supply at an 8 percent annual rate, up from 4 percent. As Exhibit 13-3 shows, their actions would create an excess supply of money balances. People would attempt to

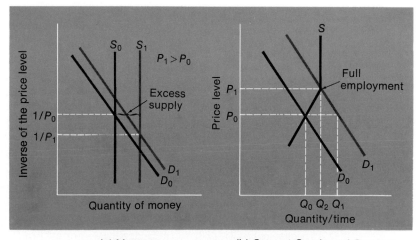

Exhibit 13-3   Money and Expanding Aggregate Demand

(a) Money   (b) Current Goods and Services

An increase in the supply of money [shift from S_0 to S_1, frame (a)] will result in temporary excess holdings of money, causing people to spend more. Aggregate demand will expand from D_0 to D_1 [frame (b)]. Initially, output will expand from Q_0 to Q_1. However, as the long-run full-employment level Q_2 is reached and surpassed *temporarily,* prices will rise from P_0 to P_1, and output will fall back to Q_2. The higher level of income and prices will increase the demand for money (shift from D_0 to D_1), thereby restoring equilibrium in the money market.

adjust, reducing their money holdings. Everybody knows how this can be accomplished. Spend! The aggregate demand for current goods will rise as people spend more on current consumer goods, capital goods, education, and other items.

If there are unemployed resources, the expansionary policy would push the economy to full employment. Real output would expand. But as the economy approaches full employment (Q_2), there will be upward pressure on prices.

In the short run, the full-employment level of output might well be surpassed. Businessmen will not be sure if the higher level of demand *for their product* is temporary or permanent. Their immediate response will be to hire more employees, cut down on maintenance time, and work more overtime. Initially, since they are not sure the higher level of demand is permanent, they will not want to risk driving away potential long-term customers with a price increase. However, an output level such as Q_1 would not be sustainable. Neither workers nor machines would be able to maintain this pace over long periods of time. Eventually, resource constraints would force producers to cut output back to the full-employment level (Q_2) and prices would rise, eliminating the excess demand.

What if an expansionary monetary policy was pursued when unemployment was already at its long-run normal rate? *Temporarily*, output would be pushed beyond the long-run full-employment level and unemployment would fall below its normal rate. But the pace could not be maintained. Soon excess demand in markets would cause prices to rise and output would fall back to the long-run full-employment level. Thus the monetarist view stresses that while expansionary monetary policy can *temporarily* push unemployment below its normal rate, in the long run such a policy would cause inflation without *permanently* reducing the rate of unemployment.

Disaster and a Reduction in the Stock of Money

What would happen if someone, perhaps a mischievous Santa Claus, destroyed half of the U.S. money stock? Suppose we get up one morning and half of the cash in our billfolds and deposits in our banks is gone! Ignore for the sake of analysis, the liability of bankers and the fact that the federal government would take corrective action. Just ask yourself, "What has changed because the money supply has been drastically reduced?" The work force is the same. Our buildings, machines, land, and other productive resources are untouched by the unjolly gent. There are no consumer durables missing. The gold is still in Fort Knox. Only the money, half of it, is gone.

Exhibit 13-4 helps shed some light on the situation. In order to make things simple, let us assume that before the calamity, individuals were holding their desired level of money balances for current needs. The reduction in the supply of money, the shift from S_0 to S_1, would result in an excess demand for money. Individuals would try to at least partially restore their depleted money holdings.

How does one build up his money balances? All poor struggling college students should know the answer. You spend less. With almost everybody spending less, the aggregate demand for current goods and services will fall (shift from D_0 to D_1, Exhibit 13-4b).

If prices and wages were perfectly flexible, as the classicists thought, this would not

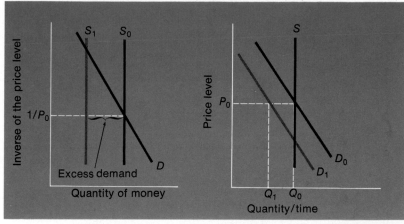

Exhibit 13-4 A Reduction in the Supply of Money

(a) Money   (b) Current Goods and Services

When the stock of money declines, an excess demand for money balances results. Individuals will seek to restore their money balances by spending less. Aggregate demand will decline from D_0 to D_1 and output will fall to Q_1 when prices are inflexible downward. With time, the excess supply in the market for goods and services would cause prices to decline. But this method of restoring equilibrium would be a painful process beset by economic recession or even a depression.

cause any big problem. Both product and resource prices would be cut in half, but real GNP would remain unchanged (that is, it would stay at Q_0). But in the real world, things are not so simple. In the short run, wages and prices tend to be inflexible, particularly downward. When this is the case, the reduced aggregate demand would cause output to fall to Q_1. An excess supply of many products would result. Business inventories would rise. Factories would operate at way below capacity and unemployment would rise. The wicked spirit would have brought about disaster without even touching any of our real assets. With the passage of time, the excess supply would result in declining prices. But recessionary conditions would permeate the economy long before falling prices would be able to restore equilibrium.

Why do prices tend to be inflexible in the short run? Initially, producers and employees will not be sure if the decline in demand for their product is temporary or permanent. They will be reluctant to cut prices substantially or accept lower wages in the short run. Employees, thinking they will soon find a job at or near their old wage rate, will continue unemployed. Therefore, initially a decline in the money supply usually exerts its primary impact on real income rather than prices.

MONEY AND BUSINESS CYCLES

Monetarists believe that instability in the money supply is the major cause of unemployment, deflation, and inflation in a market economy. That is to say, inappropriate monetary policy is the major source of the business cycle. Milton Friedman, the leading spokesman for monetarists, in his presidential address to the American Economic Association in 1967 stated,

> Every major contraction in this country has been either produced by monetary disorder or greatly exacerbated by monetary disorder. Every major inflation has been produced by monetary expansion.

Stabilization of a dynamic economy is not an easy task. The monetarists' argument that inappropriate monetary policy is the major source of economic instability is based on the recognition of just how difficult it is to properly time and apply the appropriate dosage of monetary expansion or restriction. It takes time to institute a policy. It takes time for a policy to have its major impact. By the time a policy is instituted and has its impact, it may be inappropriate.

Monetarists believe that real world macroplanners react primarily to current economic indicators and that this often leads to overreaction and error. Policies designed to fight unemployment are often pursued until they cause inflation. An anti-inflationary macropolicy will be foresaken and reversed as soon as unemployment begins to rise. Expansionary policy "overheats" the economy. The resultant inflation will invariably be followed by restrictive policy, causing a recession. In the view of monetarists, stop–go monetary policy is the major source of economic disturbance.

Government—The Villain of the Monetarists

Instability in the private business sector, particularly the investment sector, was the villain of the Keynesian theory. From the Keynesian viewpoint, the market economy was inherently unstable. Government could play the hero's role by adopting the proper mixture of fiscal and monetary policy.

For the monetarists, the roles are reversed. Inept government monetary policy provides the major source of disturbance. If the planners would just stabilize the growth rate of money, relative stability would dominate. Only minor market disturbances would result if the government would properly fulfill the function of providing for a stable monetary environment.

MONEY, RECESSIONS, AND INFLATION—THE RECORD

The early Keynesians saw the Great Depression as proof of their theory. Likewise, modern monetarists point to the same episode as proof of the potency of monetary policy, even misguided monetary action.

During the early stages of the Great Depression, there was a sharp reduction in the supply of money. The quantity of money declined by one-third between 1929 and 1933. Monetarists attribute the magnitude and length of the Great Depression almost solely to the highly inappropriate monetary policy of the period.

Monetary policy was highly restrictive, 180 degrees from what would have been appropriate to combat recessionary conditions. The monetarists' theory predicts that the restrictive monetary policy would cause a reduction in real income, prices, and employment. As indicated by Exhibit 13-5, this is precisely what happened. Between 1929 and 1933 the money supply declined at an annual rate of 6.5 percent. Real income

Exhibit 13-5   General Relationship between the Money Supply and Economic Indicators

Time period	Average annual rates of change				Period ending unemployment rate
	GNP	Prices (CPI)	Real GNP	Money supply	
1. 1929–1933 Recession	−11.5	−6.1	−7.2	−6.5	24.9
2. 1934–1937 Underemployment expansion	+15.7	+2.7	+11.7	+13.9	14.3
3. 1938 Contraction	−6.7	−1.8	−4.5	−0.1	19.0
4. 1939–1943 Underemployment expansion	+20.1	+4.5	+16.9	+23.0	1.9
5. 1944–1947 Postwar transition	+5.2	+7.3	−1.7	+14.1	3.9
6. 1949–1953 Expansion to full employment	+9.6	+3.3	+5.2	+2.3	2.9
7. 1954–1961 Underemployment	+5.3	+1.5	+3.7	+1.7	6.7
8. 1962–1969 Long expansion	+9.9	+2.8	+5.5	+4.9	3.5
9. 1970–1974 Inflation and unemployment	+9.0	+5.6	+3.6	+6.7	5.4

fell 7.2 percent and prices 6.1 percent. The unemployment rate rose sharply and steadily from 3.2 percent in 1929 to 24.9 percent in 1933.

During the 1934–1937 period, the monetary authorities reversed their course and expanded the supply of money. An increase of 14 percent in the supply of money was associated with a gain of nearly 12 percent in real income, while prices rose only 2.7 percent. Monetarists cite this evidence as proof that expansionary monetary policy works even during depressed economic conditions. In their view, proper monetary expansion could have brought the economy out of the Great Depression even during the post-1934 period.[6]

During the 1930s the monetary authorities (and economists) understood neither the importance nor consequences of their actions. In late 1936 and again in 1937, the Federal Reserve increased the reserve requirements of banks. As would be expected, this had a restrictive impact on the supply of money. In 1938, the money supply again fell, and so did real income. Unemployment rose. With hindsight, from the monetarist's viewpoint, restrictive monetary policy had again unknowingly been used to plunge the economy further into a recession.

During the 1939–1943 period, monetary policy, largely in response to the war effort, was decidedly expansionary (see Exhibit 13-5). The money stock increased at an annual rate of 23 percent. Real income rose 17 percent annually. Prices rose at a 4.5 percent annual rate and the unemployment rate fell to only 1.9 percent in 1943. Rapid

[6] See Milton Friedman and Anna Schwartz, *A Monetary History of the United States 1867–1960*, particularly the chapter on the Great Contraction for a statement of this point of view.

monetary expansion, according to the monetarist, ended the Great Depression and pushed the economy to and beyond normal full employment.

Expansion continued during the 1944–1947 period, but now the economy was operating at capacity. An increase in the money supply of 14 percent was associated with a decline in real income, a 7 percent annual rate of inflation, and an increase in unemployment. This illustrates the limitations of monetary policy. When an economy is operating at capacity, further expansion will exert its primary impact on prices and not on real income.

Since the late 1940s, monetary growth has been more stable. The 1950s were characterized by a slow rate of expansion in the money supply. At the end of the period, the unemployment rate had again risen above 6 percent. More rapid monetary growth dominated the 1960s, and according to the monetarists, pushed the economy back to full employment. At the end of the decade, the expansion had pushed the economy to capacity and inflation was again a problem.

Inflation and Money

Monetarists believe that inflation is almost exclusively a monetary phenomenon. When the supply of money increases more rapidly than the long-run growth of real output, inflation will be the inevitable result. There will usually be a lag of 6 to 24 months between excessive monetary expansion and rising prices, but as surely as night follows day, inflation will follow rapid monetary expansion.

Exhibit 13-6 pictures the relationship between inflation and the rate of growth in the

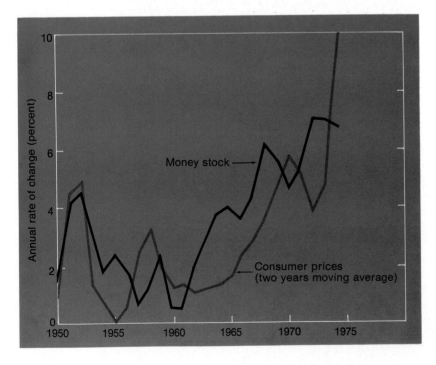

Exhibit 13-6　Changes in the Money Stock and Inflation

money supply since 1950. There does seem to be a pattern between the two. Monetary expansion accompanied inflation during the Korean War. After the war, the money stock grew slowly, about 2 percent annually between 1953 and 1963. While there were fluctuations in the annual rate of inflation, it was usually less than 2 percent during that period.

Beginning in 1963, the Fed stepped up the *rate of expansion* in the money supply to 3 percent, then 4 percent in the mid-1960s, then 5 to 6 percent in the late 1960s. By the early 1970s, monetary expansion was proceeding at a 7 percent rate. Steadily rising prices followed, except for a slight dip in 1971–1972 that probably reflected the suppression of measured inflation by the wage–price controls of that period.

Exhibit 13-7 shows the trend of prices, real GNP, and the money stock for the last decade. Growth in the money supply was at an annual rate of 5.2 percent, compared to 3.3 percent for real GNP. Prices rose at an annual rate of 4.2 percent.

The rate of monetary expansion does appear to be more rapid than would be necessary for the maintenance of stable prices. But is it primarily responsible for the rising prices? Monetarists answer affirmatively. They point out that the use of credit cards and other financial institutional changes have gradually reduced the demand for money. Thus monetary expansion at a slower rate than the growth in real output would

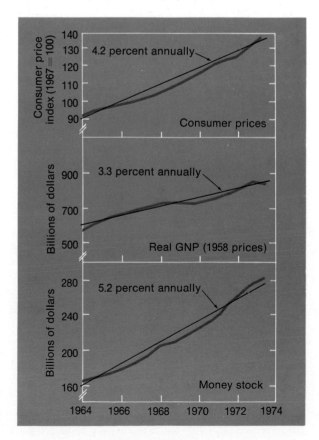

Exhibit 13-7 The Money Stock, Prices, and Output, 1964–1974

be consistent with stable prices. In addition, after two or three years of significant inflation, people begin to expect it. This would also reduce the demand for money balances, further stoking the inflationary fires.

MYTHS OF ECONOMICS
"Inflation is caused by greedy businessmen and union leaders."

Neither logic nor evidence indicates that businessmen and union leaders can cause rising prices, *independent of inflationary governmental policy.* Politicians, seeking a scapegoat for their own inappropriate policies, are anxious to blame big business and unions for inflation. Both business and labor, feeling the need to justify their actions, often blame the other. Thus the myth persists.

Analysts often approach this subject by asking, "Did prices cause wages to rise or was it wages (or other resource costs) pushing up prices?" These are uninteresting questions. Wages and other resource costs are just other names for prices. If resource prices, including labor, are pushing up product prices, the relevant question is, "What is causing resource prices to rise?"

There is evidence that unions are able to gain *higher* wages for their members than would exist in the absence of unionism. But there is no evidence that union wages *rise* more rapidly than other resource (or product) prices, thereby causing inflation. In fact, as we shall see in a moment, the evidence is just the opposite.

Suppose that union members gained a wage increase in both relative and absolute terms. In addition suppose that the demand for union-made products was inelastic. Thus, total consumer expenditures on union-produced goods would expand. The higher level of expenditures on union-made products would necessitate a fall in consumer spending on other products. The demand for other products would decline, offsetting the higher prices of goods produced in unionized sectors. Clearly there would not be generally *rising* prices in both union and nonunion sectors.

What if the demand for union-made products was elastic? In this case higher labor costs and product prices in the unionized sector would cause a sharp decline in the consumption of union-made products. Total spending on union-produced goods would decline. This would imply a decline in the employment of labor and other resources in the union sector. Workers, unable to find jobs in the union sector, would eventually shift to nonunion employment, increasing the supply of labor in the nonunion sector. This supply shift of labor and other resources would result in lower costs and a decline in the price of nonunion goods. Of course, these adjustments will not take place instantaneously. For a period of time, the rising prices might outweigh those that are falling. But, rising prices in the unionized sector would set off forces causing downward pressure on prices in other sectors, *in the absence of expansionary macropolicy.*[7] Certainly, there would be no expectation of continually *rising* prices—that is, inflation.

---

[7] There is a logically consistent scenario that unions (or businesses with monopoly power) *indirectly* cause inflation. It goes as follows. Higher union wages cause unemployment. The market adjustment process will not immediately lead to a reallocation of resources and full employment. The temporary unemployment will cause the macroauthorities to follow an expansionary policy that will cause prices, in general, to rise.

What about the empirical evidence? First, typically, union wages *rise* less rapidly than nonunion wages, at least initially, during an inflationary period. This is because long-term contracts cannot be rapidly adjusted to the rising prices. Relative to nonunion wages, historically, union wage rates have *fallen* during inflationary periods and risen during periods of stable prices.[8] Since they lose ground during an inflation, it hardly seems likely that unions could cause the inflation.

Second, and related to the first, real wages in manufacturing, the most highly unionized sector, actually fell during the 1966–1970 inflationary period, when adjusted for changes in consumer prices. A similar pattern was present during the 1950–1952 and 1955–1957 inflationary periods. How could *falling real wages* in the most highly unionized sectors be pushing prices up? Answer—they did not.

Third, price increases during the inflation of the late 1960s and early 1970s have been more pronounced in the service, medical care, food processing, agriculture, and government sectors. In general, these sectors are not highly unionized.

In summary, while unions could cause the prices of union-made goods and services to be *high*, neither theory nor evidence suggests that they could have caused the continual rising prices of the late 1960s and early 1970s.

What about greedy businessmen? Exhibit 13-8 shows that corporate profits have declined both as a share of GNP and as a percentage of sales during each of the three major inflations since World War II. These declining corporate profits do not suggest that the business sector is the culprit in the inflationary game.

Of course, businessmen raise their prices during inflation, but this is in response to the demand and cost conditions generated by macropolicy. If businessmen can gain by charging higher prices, they will do so, *independent of inflationary conditions.* But when will firms in aggregate be able to gain by

[8]See Albert Rees, "Do Unions Cause Inflation?" *The Journal of Law and Economics.* October 1959.

Exhibit 13-8   Inflation and Changes in Corporate Profits

Inflationary period	Consumer price index (1967 = 100)	Corporate profits as a percentage of GNP	Corporate profits as a percentage of sales (after taxes)
1950–1952			
1950	72.1	13.2	7.1
1952	79.5	11.5	4.3
1955–1957			
1955	80.2	11.8	5.4
1957	84.3	10.3	4.8
1966–1973			
1966	97.2	11.0	5.6
1969	109.8	8.6	4.8
1973	133.1	8.5	4.6

SOURCE: U.S. Department of Commerce.

raising their prices? Only when aggregate demand is such that they can still sell their output even at the higher prices.

What about the monopoly power of big business? The same logic that explained why unions could not cause rising prices applies to big business. If the higher prices in the monopoly business sector result in an increase in total spending in that sector, then demand, and therefore prices, in the nonmonopolized sector would decline. On the other hand, if purchases, in response to the higher prices, decline such that there is a fall in spending on goods produced by big businesses, then fewer resources would be demanded by this sector. This would cause the supply of resources to the nonmonopoly sector to expand, placing downward pressure on costs and prices. Like unions, business monopoly power could cause *high* prices, but not *continually rising* prices.

Unions and big business have lots of faults, but causing inflation is not one of them. The blame for inflation, like the credit for a stable economic environment, belongs to those in charge of monetary and fiscal policy. For some strange reason, the politicians, while glad to take credit for the latter, show reluctance to accept the responsibility for the former.

MONEY AND INFLATION IN OTHER COUNTRIES

There can be little doubt that monetary expansion has been an important source of inflation not only for the United States but also other Western nations.

Exhibit 13-9 shows the rate of monetary expansion in seven Western nations. The growth of the real money supply, the actual money stock adjusted for the nation's growth rate, for each of the seven countries was substantially more rapid during the 1970–1974 period than the long-run trend for the 1955–1969 era. *On the average,* for the seven countries, the real money supply grew three times more rapidly during 1970–1974 than during the earlier period. Unsurprisingly, inflation followed suit. During the last five years, the money supply has grown most rapidly in Italy, Japan, and

Exhibit 13-9 Money and the Worldwide Inflation

Typically, the rate of expansion in the real money supply for Western nations has been approximately three times more rapid during the early 1970s than during the 1955–1969 period. The rising prices of the 1970s have resulted.

Country	*Compound annual rate of change in the real money supply*[a]		*Compound annual rate of change in consumer prices*	
	1955–1969	*1970–1974*	*1955–1969*	*1970–1974*[b]
Canada	1.6	6.5	2.4	6.3
France	3.9	5.7	5.0	8.0
West Germany	2.3	5.5	2.3	5.8
Italy	6.6	16.7	3.2	9.6
Japan	5.1	14.8	4.6	11.0
United Kingdom	1.3	7.8	3.2	10.0
United States	−0.2	3.5	2.5	6.2
Unweighted average (seven nations)	2.8	8.6	3.2	8.1

SOURCES: Beryl W. Sprinkel, *Money and Markets, a Monetarist View* (Homewood, Illinois: Richard D. Irwin, 1971) and Federal Reserve Bank of St. Louis, *Rates of Change in Economic Data for Ten Industrial Countries* (published quarterly).

[a] The real money supply is the actual money supply divided by the real GNP. Thus it is the actual money supply adjusted to reflect a country's growth rate.
[b] Through the third quarter of 1974.

the United Kingdom. Price rises in these countries have been more rapid than for countries with a slower rate of monetary growth.

Of course, association is not causation. Other factors, a slower growth in real output for example, may have contributed to the inflation of the 1970s. But the data for both the United States and other countries are highly consistent with the view that money matters.

☐ LOOKING AHEAD

In this chapter we analyzed monetarists' views about the business cycle and inflation. The following chapter focuses on why monetarists believe that macropolicy will often be inappropriate and what should be done about it.

Inflation: Its Cause and Cure—A Monetarist's View

Perspectives in Economics

COMMITTEE CHAIRMAN: Today we want to discuss this inflation issue. Professor, what causes inflation?

MONETARIST: While the issue is complex, prolonged inflation, such as we have experienced in the 1970s, is the result of expansionary monetary policy. Historically, the long-run supply of goods and services in the United States has increased at an annual rate of approximately 3.5 percent. Some years real output has grown a little more than the 3.5 percent, other years a little less. But we have been unable to exceed this rate of economic growth over extended time periods. When we expand the supply of money at a rate, 7 percent for example, that is in excess of our growth in output, rising prices will result.

CHAIRMAN: But professor, don't you know that the supply conditions for oil have changed? We've experienced crop failures. The energy shortage has retarded our growth. Are you trying to tell us these factors don't cause inflation?

MONETARIST: Let me try to be more specific. Let's analyze the impact that a reduction in the supply of crude oil and agricultural products would have on the general price level. If these factors reduce our long-run growth rate, they would mean a higher rate of inflation, *for any specific rate of monetary expansion*. But we've had crop failures before. Presumably, they are an unpredictable occurrence. A crop failure would tend to cause a slightly higher rate of inflation during that year. Favorable weather next year might generate a larger supply of agricultural products, dampening next year's inflationary rate. Similarly, as the supply conditions for crude oil and other energy sources become more favorable, these factors will retard future price increases. They may cause a little more or a little less inflation for a year or so. They might explain why inflation in 1973 was 10 percent, rather than 7 percent. But they are not the source of the continual inflation experienced by the United States and other Western nations since about 1967. The real growth rate in the United States for the 1967–1974 period was 3.2 percent, only slightly below the long-run average. In contrast, monetary expansion proceeded at nearly a 6 percent annual rate, substantially in excess of the long-run growth in real output. It is too excessive for anything like stable prices.

SENATOR SAM SENIORITY: Some of us have been here a long time. We remember the inflation of World War II, the Korean War, and Vietnam. Isn't war the cause of inflation?

MONETARIST: Senator, wars are often associated with inflation because they are usually financed with budget deficits and monetary expansion. But it is the expansionary macropolicy, not war per se, that causes the inflation. Since 1950, the highest rates of inflation in the world have been experienced by Brazil, Argentina, Chile, and Uruguay. Monetary expansion, not war, was the source of their inflation.

Does Deficit Spending Cause Inflation?

SENATOR AUSTERITY: I'm glad you brought up the subject of deficit financing. I've said for years that these deficits are inflationary. They are bad for the country.

MONETARIST: Senator, one needs to be careful about generalizations. First, it makes a difference how the deficit is financed. If it is financed by borrowing from the public, the demand for loanable funds will increase. Interest rates will rise, which will tend to retard current private investment and consumption. This reduction in private spending will serve to offset the expansionary effect of the deficit. Such deficits have little expansionary impact. In contrast, when the deficit is financed by borrowing from the Federal Reserve, the money supply will expand. The government has more money (cash balances) and no private citizen has less. Since the deficit is essentially financed by creating money, it will neither increase the demand for loanable funds nor the short-run interest rate. Thus, deficits financed by borrowing from the Fed are expansionary. But those financed by borrowing from the general public would have very little, if any, expansionary effect.

Second, one must not forget the state of the economy. If the unemployment rate is high and excess productive capacity is present, even expansionary deficit financing might fail to raise prices. Expanded output, rather than higher prices, might very will be the result of a deficit financed by the Treasury sale of bonds to the Fed.

CHAIRMAN: Let's move on to the policy issue. What's the cure for inflation?

MONETARIST: The higher the rate of inflation, the more difficult it is to deal with. If inflation is to be halted, we must follow a less expansionary macropolicy. This would mean a slower rate of growth in the money supply and tax levies that are sufficient to cover federal expenditures. But a word of caution. Since businessmen, labor leaders, employees, consumers, borrowers, and lenders all expect inflation, restrictive policy will not break the back of inflation without some temporary reduction in output. In order to minimize these short-run hardships, the transition away from excess expansion must be made gradually but firmly.

It needs to be made gradually so that the impact on long-term contracts (for example, union–management wage agreements) will be minimal. Many, if not most, such contracts were negotiated by parties who expected the current inflation to continue or perhaps even accelerate. Macropolicy should not drastically change the terms of these contracts. To do so would lead to hardships, as well as to misuse of our resources.

But firmness is also essential. Once buyers and sellers are convinced that the government is going to really do something about inflation, they will change their expectations. The inflationary premium attached to long-term contracts will decline. Current expectations have been formed through experience. They will not be changed easily. They will not change at all, if people believe that the government is going to fight inflation for 6, 12, or 15 months, and then go on another expansionary binge.

SENATOR DOGOODER: I'm appalled that anyone would be so hardhearted as to suggest a policy designed to increase the unemployment rate. How can you justify such a position?

MONETARIST: Senator, let me begin by saying that alternative policies are available to deal with unemployment (see Chapter 15). Macropolicy is not the only means of reducing it. This is fortunate, because the ability of macropolicy to *permanently* reduce the level of unemployment is extremely limited. We do *not* have the option of using macropolicy to permanently reduce the unemployment rate in the United States to 3 or 4 percent even if we are willing to tolerate (for example, 5 percent) inflation. The inflation–unemployment tradeoff exists only in the short run, not in the long run.

During the mid and late 1960s, we pushed the unemployment rate below its normal level, but not without paying a price. Today's inflation is the result of our past expansionary efforts to deal with unemployment.

Senator, were the macroplanners of the 1960s bighearted because they *temporarily* reduced unemployment at the price of today's 10 percent annual rate of inflation? Would we be bighearted if we again pushed the unemployment rate to 4 percent for 12 to 18 months at a price of 20 percent inflation two or three years from now? There is no obvious answer. There are no free lunches. Water will not run upstream. *Using macropolicy*, we cannot simultaneously fight inflation and follow an expansionary macropolicy to keep unemployment down.

SENATOR DOGOODER: But why can't we continue on the same course, accepting the current rate of inflation?

MONETARIST: We can expand the money supply consistent with the current rate of inflation. Normal unemployment would result. This is a possible alternative, but there are dangers also. Once we have accepted the current rate of inflation, it may be awfully tempting for an incumbent administration to again follow macropolicies that (a) temporarily reduce the unemployment rate at election time and (b) lead to say a 15 percent future inflationary rate. Then we come to accept the 15 percent rate. But where will this process lead us? The risk is that the situation will eventually result in uncertainty, hyperinflation, unemployment, and a breakdown in the economic system. This price should be weighed against the price of a temporary current economic slowdown.

SENATOR SENIORITY: Do we really know enough to control inflation?

MONETARIST: Yes, I think we do. However, once people come to expect inflation, it will be costly to control it. We have failed in the past for political, not economic, reasons. We have deliberately followed overexpansionary policies because they work out so well in the short run. Our ability to manipulate the economy, at least temporarily, may prove to be a mixed blessing.

CHAIRMAN: Why not deal directly with rising wages and prices, particularly those that are rising most rapidly. Are wage–price controls a good idea?

MONETARIST: It's easy to blame inflation on the prices that rise most rapidly. In 1972–1973 the finger was pointed at increasing agricultural prices. By 1974, average farm prices had tumbled by 15 percent, but inflation still continued. In a dynamic economy, relative prices will constantly be changing, reflecting both supply and demand. This fact points out the major shortcoming of the price–wage freeze approach. Changes in relative prices that are essential for economic efficiency are also prevented.

CHAIRMAN: Don't you think you are a bit pessimistic? You have criticized every positive suggestion that has been discussed. You are saying that there is no solution to inflation.

MONETARIST: No, I am saying that there is not a *costless* solution to inflation.

CHAPTER LEARNING OBJECTIVES

1. The early classical economists thought that the velocity of money was constant and that real output was independent of monetary factors. Therefore, an increase in the stock of money meant an equal proportional increase in prices.

2. Many early Keynesians, influenced by the Great Depression, thought that an increase in the supply of money would be completely offset by a reduction in its velocity. Under these conditions, monetary policy would influence neither aggregate demand nor prices. Modern Keynesians, of course, believe that monetary policy, acting through the interest rate, does influence both aggregate demand and the price level.

3. The monetarists emphasize that households and business firms demand money because, like other goods, it yields a stream of services. People demand money by refraining from the purchase of goods. The demand for money is a function of **(a)** the price level, **(b)** income, **(c)**

the price of closely related financial assets, **(d)** the expected rate of inflation, and **(e)** institutional factors.

4. Monetarists believe that there is a direct link between the money market and other basic aggregated markets. Thus, an increase in the supply of money will create an excess supply of money balances. People will attempt to reduce their money balances by spending the excess supply of money in several markets, including the market for goods and services. The increase in the supply of money will therefore lead directly to an increase in aggregate demand. By parallel reasoning, a reduction in the supply of money will lead to a fall in aggregate demand.

5. One of the most important differences between Keynesians and monetarists is the mechanism by which monetary policy is transmitted. Keynesians believe that monetary policy has an indirect impact through the interest rate. The monetarists believe that money has a direct impact on aggregate demand, as people seek to adjust their money balances in response to changes in monetary policy.

6. Monetarists believe that monetary instability is the major source of economic instability. A rapid increase in the stock of money will initially lead to higher real income but eventually inflation will result. Monetary authorities respond to the inflation by reducing the rate of growth in the money stock. After an initial reduction in income, this monetary depressant will eventually reduce the rate of inflation. Historically speaking, the monetarists argue that the major recessions have been the result of monetary contraction and the major inflations the result of overexpansion in the supply of money. The major cause of the business cycle, in the view of monetarists, has been inept monetary policy.

7. Monetarists believe that inflation is almost solely the result of excessive monetary expansion. When the money supply expands more rapidly than real income, an excess supply of money balances inevitably results. People reduce these balances by increasing their spending even when the economy is at full employment. Rising prices result. The inflation of the United States and other Western countries in the 1970s has been associated with greater monetary expansion than was present during the 1950s and 1960s.

8. Contrary to the popular view, there is neither theoretical reason nor empirical evidence indicating that labor unions and businessmen can cause inflation, independent of expansionary macropolicy.

IMPORTANT TERMS TO REMEMBER

Equation of exchange: $MV = PQ$, where M is the money supply, V is the velocity of money, P is the price level, and Q is the quantity of goods and services produced.

Quantity theory of money: Based on the equation of exchange, this theory hypothesizes that a change in the money supply will cause a proportional change in the price level because velocity and real output are unaffected by the quantity of money.

Velocity of money: The average number of times a dollar is used to purchase final goods and services during a year. It is equal to GNP divided by the stock of money.

Demand for money: The average amount of currency and demand deposits that people and business firms desire to hold. Factors such as the price level, interest rate, expected price changes, and income can change the demand for money.

Expected rate of inflation: The rate at which people anticipate that future prices will rise.

Excess demand for money: Situation where the desired money balances of individuals and business firms are less than their actual balances. Thus decision-makers will reduce their spending as they attempt to expand their actual balances.

Excess supply of money: Situation where the actual money balances of individuals and business firms are in excess of their desired level. Thus they will spend more as they attempt to reduce their actual balances to the desired level.

THE ECONOMIC WAY OF THINKING—DISCUSSION QUESTIONS

1. "During the Great Depression monetary policy appeared to be unable to provide much stimulus to the economy" (quote from an economist).
(a) Do you agree with this view? Why or why not?
(b) Was monetary policy impotent or inappropriate during the 1930s? Check the money supply data.
(c) Does the experience of the 1930s indicate that monetary policy exerts little influence on the level of economic activity? Explain.

2. "One never has too much money."
(a) Is this statement true? Explain.
(b) Does the layman sometimes refer to money when wealth would be more descriptive of what he means?

3. "Inappropriate monetary and fiscal policy was the major cause of economic instability during the 1930s and it is the major cause of economic instability in the 1970s." Evaluate this view, presenting empirical evidence to defend your position.

4. The price of a gallon of milk is $1.50 and a pound of butter 90 cents. What is the price of a dollar bill? Is the price of the dollar related to the price of other goods? Explain.

5. Suppose that you had positive information that the prices of all goods were going to double overnight. How would this influence the amount of money that you plan to hold overnight? How would it influence your spending on goods? Explain how the expectation of a general price increase influences the demand for money.

6. "The Federal Reserve can see to it that banks have enough reserves to make loans available to businesses and consumers, but it cannot make people borrow, it cannot make people spend, and it cannot push the economy to prosperity." Would a monetarist agree with this view? Why or why not?

7. "It (inflation) is a hidden tax that no representative or senator needs to vote for. It is collected efficiently, automatically and silently. That is why since time immemorial it has been resorted to by every sovereign who has sought to command a larger share of his nation's output than his subjects would voluntarily spare him." [Milton Friedman, *Newsweek*, August 19, 1974.]
(a) In what sense is inflation a tax? Explain.
(b) Do you agree with this view of Professor Friedman? Why or why not?

8. "We are all causing inflation through our greed. We are all so greedy in competing against each other for goods and services that we are, through this competition, driving up prices." [John Connally, as he became head of the Price Commission.] Evaluate this view. Does greed cause inflation? Explain.

14
PROPER MACROPOLICY—
THE MONETARIST VIEW

The last decade has been a period of extensive debate among professional economists about macroeconomic issues. In the mid-1960s economists, particularly Keynesians, were highly optimistic about our ability to control the business cycle and stabilize prices. However, in the mid-1970s, inflation had reached peacetime highs. Interest rates were at all-time high levels. Unemployment approached 9 percent and real GNP declined temporarily. What went wrong?

Monetarists usually blame most of these problems on improper macropolicy, particularly instability in the growth rate of the money supply. In this chapter we will take a closer look at what monetarists believe monetary policy can accomplish, and what it cannot accomplish. Both economic and political explanations of why macropolicy has often gone astray will be discussed. The chapter concludes with a presentation of the monetarist's view concerning fiscal policy.

TWO THINGS THAT MONETARY POLICY CANNOT DO— THE MONETARIST VIEW

Monetarists believe that monetary policy is far more potent than fiscal policy. In the absence of a change in the money supply, they argue that pure fiscal policy has little effect on output and employment (see Why Fiscal Policy Is Impotent, pages 260–263). Yet, monetarists also believe that discretionary monetary policy is highly limited in what it can accomplish in the long run. Two factors are of prime importance.

1. *Monetary Policy Cannot Permanently Depress Interest Rates.* The interest rate reflects the future burden that borrowers must bear in order to acquire current purchasing power. Similarly, it reflects the future payoff to a lender if he is willing to give up current purchasing power. Both the future burden and payoff will be influenced by changes in the purchasing power of the dollar.

It is useful to think of the interest rate in two senses. First, there is a rate of interest that reflects the real burden to borrowers and real payoffs to lenders. It is often referred to as the real rate of interest. The **real rate of interest** is simply the money rate adjusted for inflation (or deflation). If the money rate of interest were 12 percent and the annual rate of inflation 7 percent, then the real rate would be 5 percent. The real rate of interest is the value of interest in terms of real purchasing power.

Second, of course, there is the money rate of interest. Invariably when people talk about the interest rate being high or low, they are speaking of the money rate even though it tells us little about the real burden of borrowing (for example, is a 10 percent interest rate high when the annual inflation rate is 15 percent?).

Typically, expansionary monetary policy will *temporarily* reduce the money rate of interest because it makes potential loanable funds more readily available. But do not forget the secondary effects. As illustrated by Exhibit 14-1, forces are present that will reverse the initial decline in money interest rates. First, the expansionary monetary policy will also cause an increase in current spending. Aggregate demand and money income will expand. At higher levels of money income, the demand for loanable funds will rise, placing upward pressures on interest rates.

Second, as the economy approaches full employment, prices will begin rising. If the monetary authorities continue the expansionary policy in order to keep interest rates low, inflation will also continue. Eventually, after one or two years, both borrowers and lenders will come to expect the inflation. The demand for loanable funds will increase. A businessman, willing to pay a 5 percent interest rate when he expects stable prices, will also be willing to pay 10 percent when he anticipates prices to rise at a 5 percent annual rate.

Third, the anticipation of inflation will cause the supply of loanable funds to decline. Lenders will insist upon receiving a higher money rate of interest, or otherwise they will transfer their monetary funds into real assets (for example, land or buildings) that tend to increase in value with the inflation.

Thus, inflation and the money interest rate are not strangers. Anticipation of inflation will push the money interest rate upward. Expansionary policy designed to keep interest rates low will also cause prices to rise. As people come to anticipate the

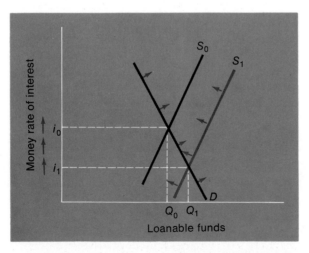

Exhibit 14-1   Interest Rates and Monetary Policy

An expansionary monetary policy *initially* increases the availability (supply) of loanable funds and reduces the interest rate. The quantity of loanable funds available will expand from Q_0 to Q_1 and the interest rate will fall from i_0 to i_1. But with time, a higher level of income, rising prices as full employment is reached, and the expectation of continuing inflation will serve to increase the demand and reduce the supply of loanable funds. Thus, *in the long run*, expansionary monetary policy pressures interest rates up.

rising prices, money interest rates will also rise. If continued, the expansionary policy will raise, not lower, money interest rates. (See Myth, page 250.)

2. *Monetary Policy Cannot Permanently Depress the Unemployment Rate.*   Why not follow a continual expansionary monetary policy, pushing the unemployment rate below its normal level? In the short run this is possible, but in the view of the monetarists, it is not a long-run option.

Suppose the level of prices is currently stable and the authorities increase the annual rate of monetary expansion from 4 to 8 percent. The expansionary policy would cause aggregate demand to increase. *Initially,* producers will not know if the increase in demand for their product is temporary or permanent. Fear of driving away long-term customers will keep sellers from immediately raising their prices. In the short run, they will reduce maintenance time, work more overtime, and seek to hire additional employees in their efforts to meet the current demand. In addition, the price of many products and resources will be influenced by past decisions that were made under the assumption of stable prices. Union contracts, catalog list prices, and other long-term contracts will not be *immediately* affected. However, since the monetary expansion has created an excess supply of money, consumer spending will increase. Initially, the primary impact of the higher level of spending will be on output and employment, not prices.

But as in the case of the interest rate, the intitial reaction is not an accurate indicator of the future. Producers and workers will not be able to keep up the pace. As the strong demand persists, prices will rise. Maintenance and overtime hours will return to normal. As inflation permeates the economy, both buyers and sellers will began to expect it. The expectation of inflation will influence their decisions. Newly negotiated long-term contracts will make an allowance for the rising prices. Lenders will demand and borrowers will offer higher interest rates because both expect the value of the dollar to depreciate while the loan is outstanding. Unions will demand that future wage contracts make allowance for the rising prices. Since product demand conditions are strong, many sellers will consent to the wage demands of employees.

Why will the expectation of future inflation reverse the initial effects of the expansionary policy? Once producers recognize the strong demand for their product, they will raise their prices. The rising prices will serve to *reduce the* **real wages** of workers. Unemployed workers, responding to money wage rates, will initially reduce their job search time. Unemployment will fall below its normal level because *real wages* have declined. But with time, workers (and their representatives) will eventually realize that higher money wages do not necessarily mean higher real wages. Long-term union contracts will begin to reflect the expected rate of inflation. Job search time will return to "normal" as employees begin to make an allowance for the rising prices. Once inflation is fully anticipated, real wages will no longer be depressed by the money illusion of employees. The *temporarily* low real wage rates will rise and the unemployed rate will return to normal, even though the inflation continues.

According to the monetarist's view, macroplanners can reduce the unemployment rate in the short run, but not in the long run. Thus, the unemployment–inflation tradeoff of the Phillips curve is only a temporary phenomenon. Policies that lead to unanticipated inflation will cause real wages to fall and employment to expand. But once the inflation is fully anticipated, the unemployment rate will return to its normal level.

MYTHS OF ECONOMICS
"The high interest rates of the 1970s resulted because the Fed was reducing the rate of monetary expansion. The Fed's tight money policy caused the high interest rates."

Popular weekly news magazines pushed this myth like a huckster selling codliver oil. "When will the Federal Reserve take its foot off the brake and make more money available to panting borrowers?" they asked. Congressmen, who are very adept at getting elected but not so good at telling it like it is, accused Federal Reserve Chairman Arthur Burns of tightening down the monetary screw and driving interest rates to all time highs.

This myth has two fallacies. First, it is wrong about the facts. The Federal Reserve was actually following a policy 180 degrees from what was being charged. As Exhibit 14-2 shows, the supply of money was expanding at an annual rate of 7 percent, approximately twice the rate of the 1950s and 1960s! This rate was double the long-run growth rate in real output for the United States! Far from tightening the monetary screw, the Fed's monetary policy during the 1968–1974 period was more expansionary than at any time since World War II.

Second, money interest rates were high because of the expansionary monetary policy, with a boost from the sharp increase in the Treasury sale of U.S. bonds during the 1969–1972 period. Expansionary monetary policy led to the rising prices of the late 1960s and into the 1970s. After a period of time, both lenders and borrowers adjusted their behavior to the expectation of continued inflation. The money rate of interest was adjusted to include an inflationary premium for the expected decline in the purchasing power of the dollar during the period of the loan. In 1965 when inflation was running at 1.5 percent a year, long-term bond yields were about 4.5 percent. By mid-1970, the inflationary rate was running at a 5 percent annual rate. The prime bond yield rose to 8 percent. Still higher rates of inflation in 1973 and 1974, unsurprisingly, led to still higher interest rates (see Exhibit 14-2). The Fed *was* actually following the policy demanded by its critics, but it was having the opposite effect from what they had anticipated.

The monetary policy of the United Kingdom during the 1965–1974 period also provides a dramatic test of this myth. For the 1965–1969 period, the money supply of the United Kingdom expanded at a 3 percent annual rate. The interest rate on government bonds ranged between 7 and 9 percent. In contrast, between 1970 and 1973 the money supply in the United Kingdom expanded at a 14.0 percent annual rate. This expansionary policy should

Exhibit 14-2   Money, Inflation, and Interest Rates

Period	Annual rate of change in money stock	Annual rate of change in consumer prices	Interest rate, AAA corporate bonds
1950–1963	2.2	1.7	2.6–4.4
1964–1966	4.0	1.5	4.4–5.1
1967–1971	6.0	4.4	5.5–8.1
1972–1974	7.2	6.9	7.2–9.3

SOURCE: *The Federal Reserve Bulletin.*

bring interest rates down—right? Wrong. By mid-1974 prices were rising rapidly and the interest rate on government bonds in the United Kingdom had soared to 16.75 percent.[1]

When money interest rates are high for an extended period of time, you can bet that monetary policy is expansionary. Similarly, interest rates will be lowest when monetary policy is most restrictive. The highest money interest rates in the world are found in countries like Chile, Brazil, and Argentina, where the supply of money has often expanded at annual rates in excess of 30 percent. Low interest rates will be found in countries like Switzerland and the United States (during the 1950s and 1960s), where monetary expansion is moderate, 3 to 5 percent. It is expansionary monetary policy, not restrictive, that causes prolonged high interest rates such as many Western nations experienced during the mid-1970s.

Rising Prices and High Rates of Unemployment

In the 1970s the United States and many other Western economies experienced both high rates of inflation *and* unemployment. These economies were performing in a manner that heretofore many economists had thought impossible. The simple short-run Phillips curve suggests that low, not high, unemployment rates would accompany rapid inflation.

However, once the role of inflationary expectations is understood, these results are no longer puzzling. Exhibit 14-3 illustrates this point within the framework of the

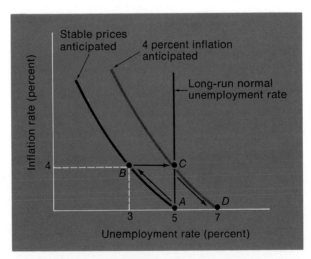

Exhibit 14-3   Losing the Long-Run Battle

In the short run, when stable prices are anticipated, expansionary policy would allow macroplanners to trade off inflation for a lower rate of unemployment (movement from *A* to *B*). But with time, decision-makers will come to anticipate the inflation, the Phillips curve will shift upward, and unemployment will return to its normal level (from *B* to *C*). In the long run, there will not be an inflation–unemployment tradeoff. Once people expect inflation, a return to stable prices (movement from *C* to *D*) would cause temporary above-normal unemployment.

[1]Federal Reserve Bank of St. Louis, *U.S. Balance of Payments Trends*, January 27, 1975.

Phillips curve analysis. Suppose that a 5 percent unemployment rate would result in stable prices if it were both anticipated and attained. At that point, macroplanners begin to follow a short-run expansionary policy that results in 4 percent inflation, while *temporarily* reducing the unemployment rate to 3 percent (point *B*). The expansionary policy is continued and after a couple of years workers begin to expect it as the status quo. They *anticipate* the 4 percent inflation in the foreseeable future. Workers searching for jobs would thus take account of the inflation rate when evaluating employment opportunities. They will no longer continue to respond to the misleading money wage signals. *Once the inflation is fully anticipated*, the unemployment rate will again return to its normal level (movement from *B* to *C*), even though the inflation and monetary expansion continue.

When workers anticipate inflation, what would happen if macroplanners decided to stabilize prices? As Exhibit 14-3 shows, when decision-makers expect 4 percent inflation and the unemployment rate has returned to its normal 5 percent long-run level (point

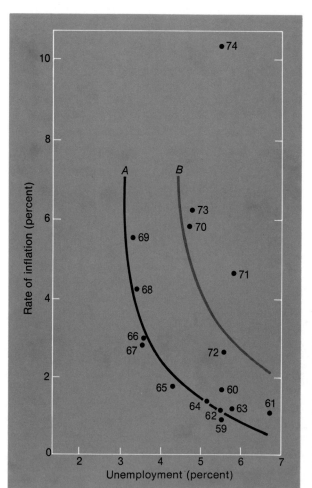

Exhibit 14-4   The Inflation–Unemployment Tradeoff 1959–1974

Between 1959 and 1969, the annual rates of inflation and unemployment map out the Phillips curve *A*. The inflation–unemployment tradeoff during the 1970–1973 period was consistent with Phillips curve *B*, suggesting that the curve shifted after three or four years of significant inflation during the 1966–1969 period.

C), an anti-inflationary policy will cause a *temporary* above-normal unemployment rate (movement from C to D). An anti-inflationary policy would cause the unemployment rate to temporarily increase to, say, 7 percent. The cost of returning to stable prices once the "inflationary psychology" has permeated the economy is an above-normal unemployment rate.

The Shifting of the Real World Phillips Curve.   Today, how long can an inflationary policy be followed before business and union leaders come to anticipate it? Because we have not had much current experience, this question must be answered tentatively. The experience of the late 1960s suggests that significant inflation can take place for about 3 or 4 years before it will be anticipated.

Exhibit 14-4 presents observations on the inflation–unemployment rate for the 1959–1973 period. All observations from 1959 to 1968–1969 were close to Phillips curve A. Each year from 1959 through 1965, prices increased less than 2 percent. Beginning in 1966, prices increased 3 percent or more each year. Despite 3 percent inflation in 1966–1967 and higher rates for 1968–1969, the inflation–unemployment tradeoff remained consistent with Phillips curve A.

But the observations for the 1970–1973 period are substantially to the right and upward from the earlier Phillips curve. After three or four years of continual inflation, business and union leaders began to anticipate it. The real world Phillips curve, just as theory suggests, shifted upward. The 1974 data suggest that the high rate of inflation in the aftermath of the wage–price freeze may have caused the unemployment–inflation tradeoff to further deteriorate.

LIMITED EFFECTIVENESS OF MONETARY POLICY—
THE MONETARIST VIEW

According to the monetarists' theory, government monetary planners can do little to reduce unemployment below its long-run "normal" level. They *can temporarily* reduce it below "normal" by promoting a more rapid inflation than is anticipated. But as the inflationary rate is maintained, workers and employers will eventually expect it and unemployment will return to its long-run normal level. A rate of inflation greater than the currently anticipated rate would be necessary if unemployment were to be pushed back below its "normal" level. Of course, such a policy could only lead to spiraling inflation.

There is a cost of obtaining even the temporarily low unemployment rate. Once workers fully anticipate the inflation, if the planners decide to once again return to stable prices, they can do so only by allowing the unemployment rate to temporarily rise above its normal level.

The planners can do little to change the long-run rate of unemployment. Their efforts to do so, while simultaneously seeking to fight inflation, are likely to promote instability, rather than stability. *In the long run*, the ability of macroplanning to "fine tune" the economy is greatly limited.

This is not to imply that nothing can be done about high unemployment rates. Policies that result in above-equilibrium wages (union restrictions, minimum wage laws, etc.) can be altered. Policies that promote better information about job availability can reduce transitional unemployment. Government-sponsored retraining programs can help structurally unemployed workers gain the skills necessary for employment in today's world. Policies that raise the opportunity cost of remaining unemployed may also be effective in this area. But whatever our policy toward these factors, macropolicy independently can do little to alter the long-run "normal" rate of unemployment in the view of the monetarists.

THREE THINGS MONETARY POLICY CAN DO— THE MONETARIST VIEW

While monetarists do not believe that monetary policy can *permanently* reduce the "normal" unemployment rate, they do believe that money is extremely important. An inappropriate monetary policy can have a destabilizing impact on the economy. What can proper monetary policy accomplish, if it cannot permanently reduce unemployment?

1. *It Can Eliminate Monetary Instability as a Source of Economic Instability.* Milton Friedman in his 1967 AEA presidential address stated:

> The first and most important lesson that history teaches about what monetary policy can do—and it is a lesson of the most profound importance—is that monetary policy can prevent money itself from being a major source of economic disturbance.

Monetary policy should not add to economic instability. Mistakes should be avoided. Planners should not follow an overexpansion policy that will later result in above-normal unemployment rates if and when a policy of stable prices is chosen. The planners certainly should not, as they did during the Great Depression, follow a highly restrictive policy that is bound to disrupt an economy such as ours in which prices are relatively inflexible in a downward direction. Eliminating accelerations and decelerations in the growth of the money supply would be of immense assistance in the battle against economic cycles.

2. *Monetary Policy Can Reduce Uncertainty that Affects Time Dimension Transactions.* The major service of money is that it is extremely important in promoting exchange. Without it trade would slow to a standstill. The welfare of each of us would be drastically reduced because of our inability to experience gains from specialization and voluntary exchange.

If the value of money fluctuates from time to time *in an unexpected manner*, it is less able to perform the function of facilitating exchange. Unfortunately, a great deal of exchange involves long-term contracting. The purchaser of land or a home usually undertakes a future monthly payment *in money terms*. Union wage contracts are long range *in money terms*. Purchasing automobiles, major appliances, furniture, bonds, buildings, equipment, and many other items typically involves the payment of *a designated amount of money in the future*. Exchanges of this type are extremely risky unless the participants have a pretty definite idea about future money wages and their purchasing power. When monetary arrangements are such that people recognize the unpredictable purchasing power of money, long-term contracting becomes much more risky. The number of long-term contractual exchanges will be reduced because of this risk. Economic welfare will decline because money has failed to perform its role of facilitating the exchange process.

3. *Monetary Policy Can Prevent Major Business Swings.*   Monetary policy can help control major disturbances that may result from a war buildup or a transition from a military to peacetime economy. Restrictive monetary policy can help offset government deficits and rapid economic expansion that has, in the past, been associated with military expansion. Inflation can, thereby, be controlled. A more expansionary monetary policy can ease a transition to peacetime by assuring adequate demand even during a sharp contraction in the defense sector. The danger here is overreaction. In such cases, it should be emphasized, the role of monetary policy is transitional. Continual efforts to *maintain* set goals such as below-"normal" unemployment rates will run afoul of the problems we have already described.

WHY MACROPLANNERS MAY DO THE WRONG THING

When discussing the appropriate macropolicy in the classroom, we instructors have a tendency to assume knowledge of factors that may be difficult to ascertain in the real world. The difficulty of identifying the appropriate current policy is sometimes glossed over. The importance of timing is often neglected. We sometimes, unrealistically, assume that a policy will have its total effect instantaneously and in the precise magnitudes indicated by our oversimplified classroom models. The real world is more complex. It takes time for markets to adjust, secondary multiplier effects to work their wonders, and decision-makers to respond to changing incentives. All of these factors complicate the task of the macroplanner. Unfortunately, macroplanners are human beings like the rest of us. They are not omniscient.

The issue of whether or not macroplanners will necessarily do the right thing need not be a source of conflict between Keynesians and monetarists. While Keynesians have, in general, tended to be more optimistic about the possibility of stabilizing macropolicy, this is not a conclusion derived from the Keynesian model. Keynesians and monetarists are both aware of and interested in factors that limit proper macroplanning. There are six major reasons why macroplanners may do the wrong thing.

Recognition Lag

Our knowledge about the future is uncertain. Planners may not immediately recognize the need for a specific policy. The time that elapses between when a policy change is needed and when the need for the change is recognized, is called **recognition lag.** Inflation may be just around the corner, but the macroplanners may not yet see it. The economy may be turning down into a recession, but this information will not appear

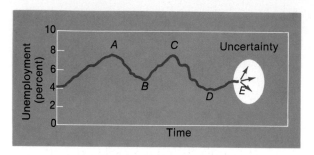

Exhibit 14-5 Uncertainty About Future Unemployment

With hindsight, it is easy to see how proper policy could have smoothed out the cycle. But real world macroplanners always face a point like E. What will happen next? Should macropolicy be expansionary or restrictive?

immediately on an economic radar screen. Forecasting models about the future can help reduce the recognition lag. But presently forecasting is a highly imperfect science.

With hindsight, it is easy to identify past mistakes. There is no one so smart as the Monday morning quarterback. But the coach must make his decision on Saturday, without the knowledge that the opposition is well prepared for the third down and two pass play. Similarly, fiscal planners must make decisions *now* without precise knowledge of what the exact state of the economy will be 6 or 12 months from now.

Exhibit 14-5 demonstrates the problem of uncertainty. At points *A* and *C*, the unemployment rate was over 6 percent, and the need for some fiscal stimulus was straightforward. On hindsight, point *B* turned out to be a cyclical minimum unemployment rate. Mild expansionary fiscal policy properly timed, could have prevented the increase in unemployment upward toward *C*. The most interesting point is *E* because this is where real world macroplanners must make decisions. Will unemployment level off at 4 percent? Will it again decline slightly below that level? If that were the case, further expansionary policy would be inflationary. Will the unemployment rate drift on upward toward the 6 percent level? If so, a macrostimulant is needed *now* to counteract the potential recession. Right now, at time point *E*, we cannot be sure. Therefore, we sometimes unintentionally continue on an off-target course because we are unaware of the need for a change in policy.

Administrative Lag

Even after we recognize the need for a policy change, it takes time to institute the new policy. The time between when we recognize the need for a policy and when the policy is administered is referred to as **administrative lag.** This time period may be anywhere from a few weeks to a couple of years. Given current institutions, a major fiscal policy change usually requires 6 to 18 months. Many factors must be taken care of before, for example, taxes can be reduced (or increased). Committees must meet. Expert witnesses must be heard. Committee chairmen must be pacified. Votes must be rounded up. Logrolling or vote trading may be essential to obtain key support. Both houses of Congress must pass legislation and the president must sign his approval. All of this takes time. The administrative lag is likely to be longer for a tax increase than a tax cut. History indicates that Congress will be reluctant to raise taxes legislatively (for example, 1966–1968 period). Thus the political feasibility of restrictive fiscal policy is highly questionable.

Many economists have advocated that the president be given standby authority to raise or lower taxes by small amounts *without* congressional approval. This would tend to reduce fiscal lag although it might have other destabilizing and adverse effects. Currently, the president does exert some influence on the timing of government expenditures. He can often either speed up or slow down projects that have already been funded. But at present the administrative lag for a major change in fiscal policy is substantial.

Since a change in monetary policy requires only the approval of the Fed's Open Market Committee, which meets monthly, it can usually be instituted somewhat more rapidly. Some argue that this is one of the major advantages of monetary policy.

Impact Lag

In the real world, things do not happen instantaneously. Even after a policy has been instituted, it may be several months before its major impact is felt. Both monetary and fiscal factors exert multiplier effects. These multiplier effects may continue to be felt long after a policy has been instituted. The time between when a policy is operational and when its major impact is felt is called **impact lag.**

A new monetary policy is thought to exert its major influence anywhere from 6 to 30 months after it has been instituted. But the impact lag does not appear to be stable. It varies over the business cycle. An expansionary policy may exert its influence more rapidly than a restrictive one. Our knowledge in this area is far from precise. Economists do not even agree on what past impact lags have been, let alone on what the future ones are likely to be.

One of the major arguments in favor of utilizing changes in tax rates as a fiscal tool is the short impact lag. By changing the amount of taxes withheld from employee paychecks, a change in tax rates can have its initial impact almost immediately. If taxes are cut, less is withheld from the employees income. Disposable income can be increased rapidly. Similarly, an increase in taxes and amount withheld can reduce disposable income quickly. It will still take time for secondary effects to work their way out, but the initial expansionary (or restrictive) impact is rapid.

Changes in government spending take longer. Usually, bidding for contracts has to be announced. Contracts have to be negotiated. Work does not always begin immediately. The impact lag of changes in government spending, in general, exceeds the lag for tax rate adjustments.

Improper Dosage

How many aspirin should be taken for a headache? How much insulin should a diabetic take? Dosage is important in both physical and economic science. But, the proper dosage in economics is particularly difficult to determine.

At the time we are planning the dosage, we are usually unaware of precisely how serious inflationary or recessionary conditions will be 6, 8, or 10 months into the future when the impact of the dosage will be felt. Should taxes be cut 5, 10, or 15 percent? Should government spending be increased $5, $15, or $25 billion? Should the money supply be increased at an annual rate of 4, 5, or 8 percent during the next 10 months? These questions can be easily answered as classroom exercises under restrictive assumptions, but they are difficult to answer in the real world.

If we apply too large a dosage to combat unemployment, we may set off inflation. If we apply too little, the unemployment may continue at an unacceptable level. Similarly, an "overkill" anti-inflationary policy may cause a recession. But a limited policy may fail to halt the inflation. Economists have developed computer simulation models of the U.S. economy, but these models are only as accurate as their postulated relationships. Although they have improved our knowledge of the appropriate dosage necessary to combat various real world situations, their estimates are still subject to an unacceptably wide margin of error. Thus we are still a long way from perfecting our estimates of the probable impact of various policy changes.

Stabilizing Interest Rates and Doing the Wrong Thing

In the past, the Federal Reserve's focus on interest rates has often caused it to follow a counterproductive monetary policy. When the Treasury runs a large deficit, as it did in 1968 and 1971–1973, it will enter the loanable funds market as it sells bonds with which to finance its deficit. The increase in demand for loanable funds will cause interest rates to rise. The Fed, seeking to stabilize interest rates, has typically responded with a more expansionary monetary policy. It was not coincidental that the large government deficits of the late 1960s and early 1970s were accompanied by a rapid growth in the money supply. But what happens as the expansionary policy is continued? Money incomes and prices rise. Inflation persists and eventually both borrowers and lenders come to expect it. All of these factors place upward pressure on the money interest rate, causing it to rise. The Fed's easy money policy to "control" high interest rates results in inflation and actually ends up promoting high interest rates!

Preoccupation with interest rates can cause monetary planners to make mistakes. Restrictive policy when interest rates are low will invariably halt recovery from a recession. Expansionary policy to bring interest rates down during an inflation will invariably cause more inflation and higher interest rates. The suggestions of many opinion leaders[2] and even economists during the inflation and high interest rates of the 1970s indicate that these lessons, particularly the latter one, have not yet been learned.

Overheating the Economy and Winning the Election

Macropolicies are adopted through political procedures. It is inevitable that political considerations will shape real world macropolicy.

Undoubtedly most political figures will ask, "What is the best long-run future policy

---

[2] Some critics, failing to understand the links between monetary expansion, inflation, and higher interest rates, wanted the Fed to follow an even more expansionary policy because they incorrectly perceived that such a policy would reduce the money rate of interest. See Myth, pages 250–251.

for the country?" But, they are human beings and they will also ask another question, "How will the alternative policies influence my probability of winning the next election?" It is foolish to expect that this question will not be considered to some degree by both Republicans and Democrats, liberals and conservatives, politicians and even statesmen.

In a democratic society, macropolicy will be determined by elected representatives and an elected president. Among other things, they will consider their own *personal* welfare. The potential for conflict exists. What is best for the "planners" may not be best for the country.

As complex as our economy is, voters will consider primarily the current state of affairs. Current policies that adversely affect the future, but not the present, will have little impact on election day. Under these circumstances, there are strong incentives for incumbent political entrepreneurs to give prime consideration to the state of the economy at the time of a major election. Potential macroproblems that might arise six months after the election are of less concern.

Political considerations suggest that each incumbent administration will be tempted to follow a pre-election expansionary policy. Since a reduction in the unemployment rate usually precedes an increase in inflation, properly timed macropolicy can have everything looking rosy on election day. If an error is made, better that it be on the side of overexpansion.

Beginning with the Kennedy Administration, incumbent presidents have been well aware of the potency of fiscal and monetary tools. The evidence of the presidential elections of 1964, 1968, 1972 lends support to the "expand at election time" hypothesis. In 1964, taxes were cut immediately preceding the election. Even though the unemployment rate in 1967 was consistently below 4 percent and prices were rising between 2 and 3 percent annually, the Johnson Administration *planned* a large fiscal deficit for both 1967 and 1968. Monetary policy was also highly expansionary during the pre-1968 election period. This policy definitely fueled the fires for the future inflation.

After an on-and-off battle with inflation, the Nixon Administration also pursued a highly expansionary policy during the 12 to 18 months preceding the 1972 election. Price controls limited *measured* inflation before the election. But as they were gradually lifted during the postelection period, to the surprise of few, prices increased at record rates.

Lest the logic of our analysis be misunderstood, it should be noted that our point has not been to criticize recent incumbent administrations. Rather we are suggesting that any utility-maximizing politician (and macroplanner) will consider how his actions will influence his political future. Sometimes there is a conflict between "good politics" and "good macroplanning." Given present institutions and the fact that fiscal and monetary planners also happen to be human beings, we should not be surprised that they are willing to sacrifice some economic stability for political gain.

CONSTANT RATE OF MONETARY GROWTH—THE MONETARIST VIEW OF PROPER POLICY

Discretionary policy, in the view of the monetarists, is likely to be destabilizing. Our knowledge about the magnitude and timing of macropolicy is inadequate. Our forecasting models often yield incorrect predictions. Political factors are almost sure to influence real world policy. All of these factors lead monetarists to conclude that discretionary stabilization policy will end up doing more harm than good. In their view, theory suggests that discretionary policy will often be destabilizing. Examination of past evidence shows that, in fact, it has been.

If discretionary policy is destabilizing because the planners are bound to make mistakes, the solution is straightforward. Eliminate discretionary policy and expand the money supply at a constant, fixed rate. This is precisely what the monetarists advocate. Why not simply increase the stock of money at a fixed rate of, say, 3.5 percent annually? This rate approximates the long-run increase in output for the U.S. economy. It would result in approximately stable prices.

The precise rate of increase in the money stock that would be designated is not too important to the monetarist. Any constant rate in the 3 to 5 percent range would be fine, as long as the constant rate was maintained. If a rate were chosen that was slightly inflationary, everyone would expect it and adjust to it. They could be confident that a change in monetary policy would not result in a major change in the rate of inflation. Uncertainty would be reduced. Long-term money contractual agreements could be arrived at with a minimum of risk and a maximum of confidence.

In addition, if the money supply were increased at a steady rate, it would automatically tend to offset short-term economic fluctuations. If there were an economic disturbance (for example, technological change) that resulted in a rapid short-run growth in output, the money stock would, of course, continue expanding only at the designated constant rate. *Relative to output*, this would mean a slower advancement than had previously been true. Monetary policy would automatically exert a restraining influence on the expansion.

Similarly, during a short-run economic slowdown, the money stock would continue at the constant rate. Because output was increasing at a slower than normal rate, the money supply would now be increasing more rapidly than usual, *relative to output*. Monetary policy would automatically be expansionary.

Would the constant rate rule completely eliminate the business cycle? Probably not. But, if the monetarists are right about discretionary policy acting as a major source of economic disturbance, the constant rate of increase rule would help to smooth out cyclical economic conditions.

THE MONETARIST VIEW OF FISCAL POLICY

Monetarists do not believe that fiscal policy exerts much impact on employment, income and prices, unless it is accompanied by a change in the money supply. They argue that **pure fiscal policy,** fiscal actions that do not alter the supply of money, will be neither expansionary nor restrictive. The following Perspective outlines the monetarist's position on this issue.

Perspectives in Economics

Why Fiscal Policy Is Impotent—An Interview with a Monetarist.

If you, as a student, were to discuss fiscal policy with a professor who was a monetarist, the discussion might go something like this.

STUDENT: I just can't understand why you do not believe that fiscal policy is expansionary. If we cut taxes and increase government expenditures, a budgetary deficit will result. The government is injecting more into the income stream than it is taking out. The impact is bound to be expansionary.

MONETARIST: You have just stated in simple terms the basic fiscal policy argument. The trouble with it is that it only tells half the story. Suppose the government reduces taxes (or increases expenditures) by $10 billion, without borrowing from the Federal Reserve, thereby increasing the supply of money. In order to obtain the $10 billion the government must borrow from private citizens. But when the Treasury enters the loanable funds market and borrows $10 billion, it will drive up the interest rate. Interest rates will continue rising until the combination of reduced private investment and expanded private saving is sufficient to offset the $10 billion deficit. The higher interest rates will curtail both private investment and consumption. After all, if saving increases in response to high interest rates, this is merely another way of saying that current consumption has declined.

What would have happened to the $10 billion if the government had not borrowed it from the private sector? The answer is, it would have been available to finance private investment and consumption. The interest rate would have been lower and the level of private spending higher. Thus, a tax cut (or expansion in government spending) financed by borrowing from the private sector will have little *net* expansionary effect. Government spending (or induced private consumption in the case of a tax reduction) is merely replacing private spending. The left hand loses what the right hand gains.

STUDENT: But won't the initial effect be expansionary?

MONETARIST: This is possible. If the government moves rapidly, fiscal action may initially induce additional spending before the interest rate rises, curtailing private investment. But this lag period is likely to be short and the negative influence of higher interest rates will begin curtailing private spending before there is much opportunity for a multiplier effect.

STUDENT: Throughout this discussion you have assumed that the government sale of bonds will reduce either private investment or consumption. This is not necessarily the case. Savers and investors are different people. There may be an excess supply of private loanable funds that can be utilized to buy the government bonds. If this were the case, the interest rate need not increase.

MONETARIST: The hypothetical case you just outlined would result in economic expansion, but it is highly unlikely in the real world. While savers and investors are different people, their actions have an impact on markets, specifically the market for loanable funds. If there are excess loanable funds available, the interest rate will tend to decline, until the excess supply is eliminated. The lower interest rate would cause both investment and current consumption to rise.

The case you outlined implies the existence of households and institutions that have funds stuffed in pillows and lying in their vaults because they cannot find a borrower at the existing rate. People are getting a zero interest rate, because there are not enough borrowers at the current rate.

In the real world, these excess funds, rather than lying idle, would be offered at a lower, but positive, interest rate. The availability of funds at the lower rate would induce both more private investment and consumption. Except in the extreme case where private savers would continue allowing their funds to lie idle, fiscal actions would merely offset private spending.

STUDENT: Are you saying that monetarists do not believe that a tax cut or an increase in government spending has any expansionary impact?

MONETARIST: Not quite, but you are close. The important point is how the government deficit is financed. If it is financed by the Treasury selling bonds to the Federal Reserve, rather than to private savers, it will be expansionary because the supply of money will increase. The Federal Reserve buys bonds and pays for them with newly created money. Loanable funds available for private investment will not be reduced. The interest rate will not rise. Private investment and consumption will not decline, offsetting the increased private consumption induced by the tax cut. This is basically a description of the 1964 tax cut.

But this is not a pure fiscal action. When the Treasury sells bonds to the Fed, the money supply expands. The economic stimulus comes primarily from monetary policy. The same effect could have been attained by monetary policy alone, even without the tax cut.

In addition, there is one other factor that may result in some expansion from even a pure fiscal action. Since a pure fiscal action will increase the demand for loanable funds and raise the interest rate, it will also increase the opportunity cost of holding money. At the higher interest rate, households and firms have an incentive to conserve on their cash balances. They will use money more intensively, increasing its velocity. This could indirectly exert an expansionary effect, but the precise timing and magnitude of this effect are both questionable and difficult to ascertain.

STUDENT: What about restrictive fiscal policy to combat inflation? Suppose that prices are increasing at a 4 percent annual rate and the government increases taxes in order to combat the inflation. A budget surplus is planned. What happens then?

MONETARIST: The same analysis holds. The important question is what happens to the budget surplus. If the surplus is used by the Treasury to retire bonds held by the Federal Reserve, the money supply will decline. This, of course, would be restrictive. But, if the tax increase does not affect the money supply, it will have little restrictive influence.

Suppose the Treasury uses the budget surplus to buy back government bonds that are held privately. The policy will reduce the demand of loanable funds and lower the interest rate. To say it another way, the Treasury action will increase the current available supply of funds for private investment. A short-run excess supply of loanable funds will result. The interest rate will fall until current investment and consumption have been stimulated sufficiently to eliminate the excess supply of loanable funds. When the action is purely fiscal—that is, when it has no impact on the supply of money—the expansion of private investment and current consumption will offset the restrictive impact of the tax increase. The net impact will exert little influence on inflationary pressures.

STUDENT: If pure fiscal policy neither reduces unemployment nor restrains inflation, why do both economists and government macroplanners talk about a countercyclical tax and spending policy?

MONETARIST: That's easy to answer. Not everybody is a monetarist.

Discussion

1. Can the government cut taxes and run a deficit, while the supply of money and interest rates are constant? If so, how? Explain.
2. "When analyzing fiscal policy, monetarists place the emphasis on how higher

interest rates or prices will *eventually* offset the *immediate* expansionary effect of increased government spending or lower tax rates. Even if this is correct in the long run, the short-run implications of the Keynesian theory remain valid." Explain why you either agree or disagree with this view.

CHAPTER LEARNING OBJECTIVES

1. Monetary policy cannot *permanently* fix interest rates at a low level in order to stimulate investment. Expansionary monetary policy will initially cause interest rates to decline, but eventually this initial reaction will be reversed. Income will expand. As full employment is approached, prices will rise. If the expansionary policy continues, so will the price increases. Private decision-makers will come to anticipate the rising prices. All of these factors will serve to increase interest rates and prevent monetary authorities from maintaining them at a low level.

2. The high interest rates of the mid-1970s reflect inflationary expectations and a sharp increase in the government's demand for loanable funds in the 1969–1972 period. They are the result of expansionary monetary policy and an increase in the sale of U.S. bonds to the public, not tight money policy as the media often charged.

3. Monetary policy cannot *permanently* fix unemployment at a low level. Initially, an expansionary policy will reduce unemployment as aggregate demand increases. But as the unemployment rate is pushed below its "normal" rate, prices will begin to rise. As inflation continues, workers will come to realize that higher money wages do not necessarily mean higher real wages. Once workers fully anticipate the rising prices, unemployment will return to the normal long-run rate, even though the inflation continues.

4. According to the monetarist's theory, macroeconomic policies can do little to reduce the long-run normal rate of unemployment. They can temporarily reduce unemployment by promoting unanticipated inflation. But this can be done only at the expense of rising prices and an above-normal future unemployment rate if there is a return to stable prices.

5. The three most important things that monetary policy can do are **(a)** eliminate monetary instability as a source of economic instability, **(b)** reduce the uncertainty associated with time dimension transactions, and **(c)** prevent major business swings.

6. Both inadequate information and political factors limit our ability to stabilize the economy. Planners may do the wrong thing because of **(a)** recognition lag, **(b)** administrative lag, **(c)** impact lag, **(d)** inability to determine the proper policy dosage, **(e)** preoccupation with attempting to stabilize interest rates, and **(f)** conflicts between good politics and proper economics.

7. In the view of the monetarists, a policy of constant monetary growth would be more stabilizing than discretionary decision-making that inevitably results in a stop–go policy, introducing instability into the economy.

8. Monetarists do not believe that pure fiscal policy exerts much impact on income, employment, and prices. Since a government deficit would have to be financed by borrowing from the private sector, it would cause interest rates to rise and private investment and consumption to fall. These factors would largely negate the expansionary effect. Similarly, a government surplus would cause lower interest rates, stimulating private investment and consumption. Little net restrictive impact would result.

IMPORTANT TERMS TO REMEMBER

Real rate of interest: The money rate of interest minus the rate of inflation.

Real wage rate: The amount of goods and services that can be purchased with the money wages received for labor services. Thus, when prices are rising, real wages will decline unless money wages increase as rapidly as prices.

Pure fiscal policy: A change in taxes or government spending that is not financed by borrowing from Federal Reserve. Thus the policy does not change the supply of money.

Recognition lag: Time between when there is a need for a change in macropolicy and the recognition of that need.

Administrative lag: Time between when the need for a macropolicy change is recognized and when the change is actually instituted.

Impact lag: Time period between when a policy is instituted and when it has its major impact on income, employment, and prices.

THE ECONOMIC WAY OF THINKING—DISCUSSION QUESTIONS

1. "Prices in the U.S. continue to increase at politically intolerable levels despite a monetary policy that last week drove the prime rate to a record 11.8 percent at some banks." [*Newsweek*, July 8, 1974]

   (a) Was it surprising that the monetary policy that drove the prime interest rate to 11.8 percent failed to halt inflation? Explain.

   (b) Why do you think interest rates were so high in 1974? Why did prices rise so much? Explain.

2. "Once the 1976 election comes into view, the dynamics of populist democracy will tend to reactivate the only business cycle left in the modern mixed economy—the political cycle, in which policy is expansionary just before major general elections." [Paul Samuelson, *Newsweek*, August 19, 1974]

   Do you agree with Professor Samuelson? Why or why not?

3. "When unemployment rises as it must when the economy slows, those who are laid off first are the unskilled; efforts to recruit workers from the ghetto are suspended. Social man, therefore, is inclined to trade off inflation for jobs." [David P. Eastburn, President, Federal Reserve Bank of Philadelphia]

   (a) What would be the reaction of a monetarist to the last part of this quote? Is the short-run, long-run distinction important? Explain.

   (b) Are monetarists opposed to trading off inflation for jobs?

   (c) Either defend or criticize Mr. Eastburn's view.

4. "When the money supply is expanded at a fixed rate, it acts as an automatic stabilizer." Explain the logic of this view.

5. Why might political factors make it difficult to attain economic stability? How can these factors be minimized?

6. "In order to achieve the nonperfectionist's goal of high enough output to give us no more than 3 percent unemployment, the price index might have to rise by as much as 4 to 5 percent per year." [Paul Samuelson and Robert Solow, American Economic Association Meetings, December 1959]

   (a) Do you think inflation of 4 or 5 percent would achieve the nonperfectionist's goal of 3 percent unemployment today? Why or why not?

   (b) Would inflation of 15 or 20 percent achieve the goal? If so, could the 3 percent level be maintained? Why or why not? Explain.

7. "Monetary policy will be an effective tool to combat unemployment only if business investment is responsive to a decline in the interest rate."
(a) Would a monetarist agree with this view? What is the monetarist's view of the transmission mechanism of monetary policy?
(b) Does expansionary monetary policy lead to lower interest rates? Explain.

8. "If monetary policy is so effective why didn't it work during the Great Depression. Monetary policy pushed interest rates to low levels, but yet there was little net investment and the economy continued to stagnate."
Use empirical evidence to either criticize or support this view.

15

DEALING WITH UNEMPLOYMENT AND INFLATION

The last decade has taught macroeconomists humility. In the mid-1960s we were sure that we knew how to control things. Admittedly, there would continue to be minor ups and downs, but serious problems of inflation and unemployment were behind us—or so we thought. Most, though certainly not all, economists failed to foresee the possibility of high unemployment and rapidly rising prices. The naive short-run Phillips curve dominated the thinking of many. Currently, economists of all persuasions are questioning the long-run applicability of the Phillips curve analysis. The search for a means to improve the unemployment–inflation tradeoff is underway in earnest.

As economists have become more aware of macropolicy limitations, the interest in micropolicy alternatives designed to shift the Phillips curve inward has grown. We will look at several microbased suggestions. In addition, since a quick solution to inflation is unlikely, we will analyze a policy alternative, indexing, that is designed to reduce its most harmful effects. Part II concludes with a hypothetical interview designed to help the student pull macroeconomics together.

CAN WAGE–PRICE CONTROLS MAKE MACRO-"SOLUTIONS" MORE EFFECTIVE?

> Such controls (wage and price) treat symptoms and not causes. Experience has indicated that they do not work, can never be administered equitably, and are not compatible with a free economy. [1968 presidential candidate Richard M. Nixon]

To many, the solution to inflation is straightforward. If wages and prices are rising too rapidly, why not put a stop to it? Simply freeze them at their current levels.

In mid-1971 the unemployment rate in the United States was near 6 percent. Simultaneously, prices were increasing at an annual rate of 4 percent. In August, President Nixon acted to freeze wages and prices for a 90 day period (Phase I). A more limited freeze followed during the ensuing 12 month period (Phase II).

As the quotation just given indicates, President Nixon completely reversed his

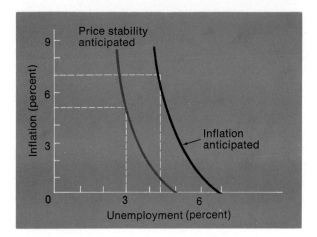

Exhibit 15-1   The Phillips Curve and the Wage–Price Freeze

When they were initially introduced, it was thought that wage–price controls would reduce the anticipation of inflation, thereby shifting the Phillips curve back to the left. Both unemployment and inflation would then be reduced.

position on the merits of **wage–price controls.** In fairness, it should be pointed out that initially the controls were sold as a temporary measure. The idea behind the "freeze" as illustrated by Exhibit 15-1, was to break the existing inflationary psychology. Prices were going up partly because both buyers and sellers anticipated future inflation. Break the inflationary psychology and the short-run Phillips curve would shift to the left—so the reasoning went.

At the time the controls were imposed, there was little empirical evidence, one way or the other, as to their expected macroeffectiveness. In a sense, they were an interesting economic experiment.

Did the Freeze Work?

Most researchers conclude that the wage–price freeze did little to permanently improve the unemployment–inflation tradeoff. Edgar Feige and Douglas Pearce studied the time period both before and after the wage–price freeze. They concluded, "For the controls period as a whole, the results suggest that the consumer price index was unaffected by the imposition of the controls. A similar comparison for wholesale prices indicates that the controls had the effect of increasing the rate of inflation above the rate that would have prevailed in the absence of controls."[1]

Exhibits 15-2 and 15-3 present evidence on the pre- and postfreeze path of prices. During 1969 and 1970, both fiscal and monetary policies were less expansionary than for the immediately preceding years. As Exhibit 15-2 shows, the annual rate of inflation began to decline in mid-1970. In August 1971 prices were rising at a 4 percent annual rate, down from the 6 percent rate of 1970. Real GNP was expanding at a 5 percent rate in 1971 (first three quarters). The recession of 1970 was behind us. Many economists,

---

[1] Edgar Feige and Douglas Pearce, "The Wage–Price Control Experiment—Did It Work," *Challenge*, July/August, 1973. Also, see Feige "Inflation and Unemployment," *American Economic Review*, September 1972.

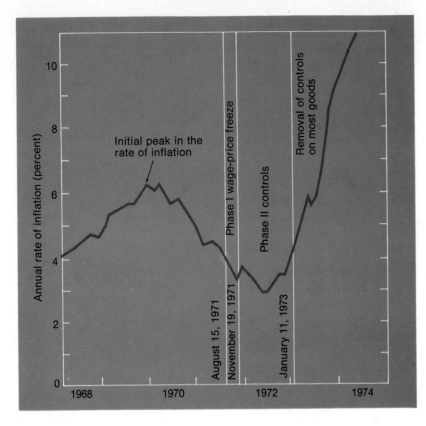

Exhibit 15-2 labels (left to right):
- Initial peak in the rate of inflation
- August 15, 1971
- Phase I wage-price freeze
- November 19, 1971
- Phase II controls
- January 11, 1973
- Removal of controls on most goods

Exhibit 15-2   Was Defeat Snatched from the Jaws of Victory?

The annual rate of inflation (annual rate of change in consumer price index during the 12 previous months) began declining nearly a year before the freeze. The freeze suppressed inflation, but when it was lifted, prices jumped at a record peacetime rate.
SOURCE: *Federal Reserve Bulletin.*

Exhibit 15-3   Prices and the Freeze

While the wage–price freeze suppressed inflation during the freeze, prices soared as soon as it was lifted.

Time period	Annual rate of change		Annual rate of change in the money supply	Federal deficit annual rate (billions of dollars)[a]
	CPI	WPI		
Prefreeze (10 quarters preceding freeze)	5.1	3.5	5.7	6
Freeze (5 quarters—Phases I and II)	3.2	4.5	6.6	26
Postfreeze (5 quarters after freeze)	9.0	18.1	6.4	10
Freeze and postfreeze (10 quarters after freeze was instituted)	6.1	11.1	6.5	18

SOURCE: The Federal Reserve Bank of St. Louis.

[a] Approximated from data of the *Federal Reserve Bulletin.*

particularly monetarists, felt that the gradual restrictive policy of 1969–1970 was stabilizing the economy.

But the unemployment rate was hovering at just under 6 percent. An election was 15 months away. The economy was not recovering rapidly enough to satisfy the political desires of an administration that, as subsequent events have shown, was willing to go to great lengths to assure re-election.

Concurrent with the freeze, the administration reversed its macropolicy of gradual restriction. As Exhibit 15-3 shows, both monetary and fiscal policies were more expansionary during the postfreeze period. President Nixon was bent on getting the unemployment rate down for the 1972 election if at all possible. He would worry about an overheated economy after the election.[2]

During the 18 months of the freeze (Phases I and II) and expansionary macropolicy, consumer prices rose at a slower rate. In contrast, wholesale prices rose even more rapidly during this period. But as both Exhibits 15-2 and 15-3 show, when the freeze was relaxed (and removed entirely from several sectors) after the election, prices skyrocketed. Three factors contributed to the soaring postfreeze prices. First, during the freeze both price and wage increases were delayed. Inflation was being suppressed, not controlled. When the freeze was lifted, both businessmen and resource suppliers raised prices (and wages) to make up for lost ground. Second, the expansionary monetary and fiscal policies were stoking the fires of inflation all during the period. Excess aggregate demand placed upward pressure on prices. Third, since the possibility of stiffened wage–price controls was still in the picture, businessmen had an incentive to tack a premium onto their prices. If prices were to be frozen again, each seller wanted to make sure that his prices would already be at a higher level.

The Pre- and Postfreeze Record

Analysis of pre- and postfreeze 30 month periods yields little evidence that the freeze had a positive lasting impact on the unemployment–inflation tradeoff. Exhibit 15-3 shows that wholesale prices rose three times more rapidly during the postfreeze, compared with the prefreeze rate. Consumer prices also rose more rapidly. At the same time, while unemployment declined slowly in 1972 and 1973, it began to rise again in late 1973. The average unemployment rate for the 30 month postfreeze period was 5.3 percent, compared to 4.6 percent for the 30 months before the freeze. The "controls" experiment certainly suggests that a temporary freeze, coupled with expansionary monetary and fiscal policy, is not a shortcut to stable prices and low unemployment.

A review of the European experience with price controls paints a similar picture. Economists Lloyd Ulman and Robert Flanagan concluded their review of wage–price "freezes" in Western Europe with the following observation. "In none of the variations so far turned up has the incomes (wage–price controls) policy succeeded in its fundamental objective . . . of making full employment consistent with a reasonable degree of price stability." Like the U.S. experience, Ulman and Flanagan found that controlled

[2]One could argue that President Johnson acted similarly in both 1964 and 1968.

periods "were frequently followed by wage and price explosions which sometimes blew up the policies themselves."[3]

The Freeze Was Good Politics

While the freeze did little to actually shift the Phillips curve inward, its attractiveness as a political weapon should not be overlooked. Unless the awareness of voters has increased, it will be tempting for utility (and vote) maximizing future politicians to follow a similar course. The short-run politics of it is beautiful. Suppress price increases, reducing the rate of *measured* inflation. At the same time, follow an expansionary macropolicy to push unemployment to a low level. Adopt the strategy 9 to 24 months before an important election. Things will look great on election day! It worked for the Nixon Administration and it is likely to work, from a political viewpoint, in the future. Of course, the pressures of excess demand will build up, making inflation (and unemployment) more difficult to deal with in the future. But these future costs will be difficult to identify on election day. Later they can be blamed on others—big business, unions, or foreigners, for example. Politically, it worked once, and it is likely to be tried again.

Why Not Try Permanent Controls?

Some economists argue that while temporary controls do little to improve the long-run inflation–unemployment tradeoffs, a permanent wage–price freeze would do the job. During the year and a half that comprehensive controls were in effect, prices rose at a 3 percent annual rate, while unemployment was pushed below 5 percent. By the standards of 1974–1975, that is not a bad record. If administered by political officials who believed in their necessity, perhaps the record might be even better.

The problem with this logic is its failure to recognize how difficult it is to suppress market forces, even when the competition is among the few. A huge bureaucracy would be necessary to enforce permanent controls. During World War II, 60,000 bureaucrats, backed up by 300,000 volunteers, were involved in the price control effort. Even this would fail to repeal market forces.

Bureaucrats could conceivably control the money price of products. But this would not assure their availability. Below-equilibrium prices would be bargains, however the "sold out" sign would often be in front of the counter. Neither could price controls keep sellers from using quality adjustments as a means of rationing goods to panting consumers. Do not forget, there are two ways to raise prices—charge a higher money price or offer a lower quality. With price controls, the latter would be used extensively.

Several consequences of controls are predictable. Shortage would develop, particularly with the passage of time. The quality of products would deteriorate. Favoritism, congestion, tie-in sales, and barter exchange would all become more important in the

[3]Lloyd Ulman and Robert J. Flanagan, *Wage Restraint: A Study of Incomes Policies in Western Europe.* Berkeley: Univ. of California Press, 1971.

rationing process. Blackmarkets would appear. Production and legal market exchange of some commodities would come to a complete standstill.

Some of these events were observed even during the temporary wage–price freeze of 1971–1972. A chicken producer killed 50,000 baby chicks because, with the controls, he could not afford to raise them to fryer stage. Meat cuts began to deteriorate. Hamburger fried away because of its fat content. Shortages of steel pipe, paper, bathroom fixtures, hunting rifles, antifreeze, cutting tools, fertilizer, electric wire and cable, and many other products developed during and immediately after the freeze. Long lines (congestion) were used to ration gasoline.

With permanent controls the gap between the fixed prices and actual market conditions would widen with the passage of time. Dynamic changes in market conditions would not stop merely because Uncle Sam has fixed prices. As cost conditions change and shortages of various products result, undoubtedly the government would respond by setting up a review process whereby some price increases are permitted "under extenuating circumstances." With time, predictably these exceptions would reflect primarily political power and payoffs. Our experience with regulatory agencies such as the ICC, CAB, and the Federal Power Commission gives one little reason to believe that real world government price fixing would pay much heed to market conditions, particularly in the long run (see Perspectives in Economics, pages 375–379).

Economic theory indicates that neither permanent nor temporary price controls can do much to improve the inflation–unemployment tradeoff. They are cosmetic, not real solutions. In the long run, as the 1971–1974 period suggests, such policies would add to uncertainty and lead to supply reductions, aggravating the inflation–unemployment dilemma.

PUBLIC EMPLOYMENT

Restrictive macropolicy to deal with inflation causes the unemployment rate to rise temporarily above its long-run level. To reduce the withdrawal pains, why not have the government provide jobs to the unemployed during this period? The idea is appealing. Rather than waste these unemployed resources, why not put them to work cleaning our streets and beautifying our environment?

The program may temporarily reduce unemployment. But economic theory suggests that we should not expect miracles. Do not forget the secondary effects. The funds to pay for these new public employees will have to come from somewhere. If they come from a larger federal deficit and monetary expansion, they would worsen the problem of inflation. If they come from higher taxes, this would reduce the aggregate demand for other goods. Employment in the private sector, particularly with the passage of time, would decline. The new government employees would be partially replacing persons employed in the private sector.

Would public employment be popular? It is here that the appeal of the policy lies. Persons newly employed in the public sector are readily identifiable. They are easily seen. Persons unemployed because of the secondary effects of the policy, the higher taxes, are not so easily identifiable. Most voters would not trace a lower level of private employment back to the higher taxes necessary to finance the new public employment jobs. The benefits are easily identified while the real costs tend to be concealed. Therefore, even though its real positive impact is questionable, this program would be a political winner.

DEALING WITH YOUTH UNEMPLOYMENT

In recent years efforts to maintain stable prices and a low unemployment rate have been complicated by the influx of youthful workers into the labor force. Unemployment rates among persons 24 and under are between two and four times the comparable rates for older workers. This is not particularly surprising, as one would expect that younger workers would be more likely to transfer from job to job, as they seek to find their most preferred career. In 1956, workers age 24 and under accounted for only 16 percent of the labor force. By 1973 they composed 24 percent of the total. Since there is good reason for youthful workers to do more job shifting, the normal unemployment rate will rise as youthful workers make up a larger share of the total labor force.[4]

As Exhibit 15-4 illustrates, youthful workers comprised more than one-half of all unemployed workers in 1973, compared to only 31 percent in 1956. Unless unemployment among younger labor force participants can be reduced, it will be difficult to push the aggregate unemployment rate below 5 percent.

In recent years unemployment among teenagers and other youthful workers has

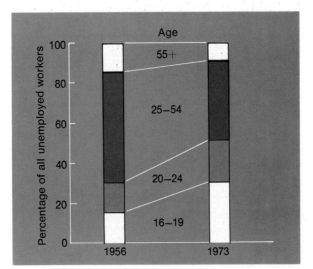

Exhibit 15-4 Youth as a Percentage of All Unemployed Workers

Persons under 25 comprised more than 51 percent of all unemployed workers in 1973 compared to 31 percent in 1956.
SOURCE: *The Manpower Report of the President, 1974.*

[4] A comparison of unemployment rates in 1956 and 1972 illustrates the impact that the relative expansion in the number of youthful workers has had on the aggregate unemployment rate. The unemployment rates for males (and females) over 25 years of age were equal in 1956 and 1972. But the aggregate unemployment rate in 1972 was 5.6 percent, compared to 4.1 percent in 1956. Why? In 1972 youthful workers (and married women) were a much larger share of the labor force. Thus, the aggregate unemployment rate rose 1.5 percent, even though the unemployment rate according to sex for persons 25 and over was identical for the two years.

often exceeded 10 percent. These high rates should be interpreted with caution. Many younger workers are inexperienced. Most have not yet decided upon a career. Many shift back and forth between school and the labor force. It is also important to keep the motivations and attitudes of many youthful workers in mind. Many do not have family responsibilities. It is significant that in 1971, when the unemployment rate for males 16–24 was 16 percent, it was only 6.4 percent for those who were household heads. Many unattached younger workers apparently desire more leisure and vacation opportunities than are available when one holds a permanent full-time job.

Yet many economists believe there is more to it than this. The experience of other countries, notably West Germany and Britain, indicates that high youth unemployment rates can be avoided. Two specific proposals deserve mentioning.

1. *Exemption from Minimum Wage Legislation.*   Many younger workers are searching for a path to a good job in the future. This is why so many choose formal education. But training and skill-building experience can also provide the ticket to future success. Often these attributes are best learned on the job. But they are costly for an employer to provide. The minimum wage law often makes it unfeasible for an employer to both (a) provide training to inexperienced workers and (b) pay the legal minimum wage. Thus there are few (temporarily) low-paid jobs offering a combination of informal (or formal) training and skill-building experience. While we subsidize formal education, this aspect of public policy clearly discriminates against on-the-job training.[5]

2. *Youth Work Scholarships.*   Martin Feldstein, a Harvard economist, has suggested that we provide youthful workers, those under 25 years of age for example, with a **work scholarship**.[6] A wide variety of alternatives are possible. At one extreme, each individual could be provided with a monthly subsidy, in addition to wage benefits from his employer, as long as he was employed. Under this plan it would be up to each worker to choose his most preferable combination of current wage and on-the-job training. A maximum duration, two years for example, could be established for each scholarship. An additional reward for continual employment could be provided.

Another possibility would be to provide the scholarship only for jobs that involved approved training. Jobs that resulted in the development of craft, clerical, operative, and perhaps even managerial skill could be high priority targets. The long-run goal would be to improve the quality of the labor force and promote productivity gains that are essential for real income gains without inflation.

Changing the Types of Jobs Available to Youth

The major thrust of any approach should be to change the types of jobs available to youthful workers. In spite of the talk about the declining work ethic of youthful workers, the evidence does not support the view. The proportion of both teenage males and females in the labor force has crept up in recent years. But most jobs for which they

[5]See pages 445–447 for additional information on the impact of the minimum wage.
[6]The author has greatly benefited from reading Feldstein's excellent article "The Economics of the New Unemployment," *Public Interest*, Fall 1973. It is highly recommended to the reader.

would qualify are dead-end jobs, thanks in no small part to minimum wage legislation. This is 180 degrees from what most young people are looking for. They are looking for jobs that will be stepping stones to more lucrative future opportunities. They want training and skills that will lead to an income earning career. The proportion of young people choosing college demonstrates the fact that many are willing to accept a lower temporary income, while building for a brighter future. Unless we can find a way to provide both jobs and training for youthful workers who do not want to go to college, macropolicy will do little to reduce the extremely high youth unemployment rate.

COULD WE BETTER TARGET GOVERNMENT SPENDING?

Geographically, the unemployed are not evenly distributed throughout the United States. Unemployment rates may be high in West Virginia, but low in Texas. If this is the case, increased government spending on the space industry in Texas will exert little impact on unemployment in West Virginia. Similarly, unemployment is often high in rural areas of the South and certain industrial areas that are hit by sharp shifts in demand. Many economists believe that fiscal policy would be much more effective if it were more carefully targeted. If there is unemployment in rural Mississippi or urban Michigan, channel fiscal stimuli to these areas.

The economics of this argument is probably better than the politics. In the real world, representatives from high employment areas are probably going to be more interested in changing the rules so their areas would qualify for government assistance, rather than merely voting funds to low employment areas. Politicial factors pose a real limit on what we can realistically expect from a targeted public works policy. However, if properly conducted, such a policy might well give us a better inflation–unemployment tradeoff.

DO UNEMPLOYMENT COMPENSATION AND WELFARE BENEFITS INCREASE THE UNEMPLOYMENT RATE?

Public policy has attempted to reduce the hardships of poverty and unemployment by adopting various welfare and unemployment compensation programs. As desirable as these programs are from a humanitarian viewpoint, they have the impact of reducing the opportunity cost of remaining unemployed. One of the fundamental postulates of all economics is that if you reduce the cost of choosing an activity, more people will choose it. Therefore, the conflict between high welfare and low unemployment should not be surprising.

In some states the *net* cost of continuing unemployed is very low (see box). Under these circumstances, some workers will be reluctant to take anything but a very good job, given their skill level. Thus, attractive unemployment and welfare payments will contribute to the number of persons who are unemployed. Economic policy often involves a tradeoff between two desirable economic goals.

What can be done to reduce the conflict? The welfare and unemployment compensa-

Taxes, Unemployment Compensation, and the Incentive to Accept a Job

Consider a worker in Massachusetts in 1971 with a wife and two children. He earns $500 per month or $6000 per year if he experiences no unemployment. She earns $350 per month or $4200 per year if she experiences no unemployment. If he is unemployed for one month, he loses $500 in gross earnings, but less than $100 in net income. How does this occur? A reduction of $500 in annual earnings reduces his federal income tax by $83, his Social Security payroll tax by $26, and his Massachusetts income tax by $25. The total reduction in taxes is $134. Unemployment compensation consists of 50 percent of his wage plus dependents' allowance of $6 per week for each child. Total unemployment compensation is therefore $302. This payment is not part of taxable income. His net income therefore falls from $366 for the month if he is employed (i.e., his $500 gross earnings less $134 in taxes) to the $302 paid as unemployed compensation. The combination of taxes and unemployment compensation imposes an effective marginal tax rate of 87 percent—i.e., the man's net earnings fall by only 13 percent of his gross pay ($64) when he is unemployed for a month. The same very high marginal rate continues for several more months. If he returns to work after one month, his annual net income is only $128 higher than if he returns after three months. Moreover, part of this increase in income would be offset by the cost of transportation to work and other expenses associated with employment. [Martin Feldstein, *The Public Interest*, Fall 1973]

tion programs might be altered, requiring able-bodied persons to accept public employment or any available job if they were to continue receiving benefits.[7] Eligibility requirements might be tightened. The benefits of persons who are unemployed more than a certain time period, or who have a *personal* record of high unemployment, might be reduced, penalizing those persons who take advantage of the system.

In addition, the tax structure could be changed in a manner that would reduce the benefits from continuing unemployment. Currently, unemployment compensation income is not taxed when it is received. If such income were taxed, two things would be accomplished. First, unemployed workers would have a greater incentive to accept available jobs because *both* income received from earnings and unemployment compensation (not just the former) would now be taxable. Second, people with the same annual income would pay the same tax bill. The current system results in lower taxes as the proportion of income received from unemployment compensation increases. Independent of its impact on work incentives only a perverse concept of equity could justify taxing an employed person more than another with the same income who was unemployed.

---

[7] Currently, unemployment legislation in most states requires only that one accepts available employment *in his previous occupation* (for example, Chinese cook, aerospace engineer, etc.).

"And for the jobless, my committee is making a two-million-dollar study on how to survive on welfare."

Grin and Bear It by Lichty & Wagner, © Field Enterprises, Inc., 1975

INDEXING—LEARNING TO LIVE WITH INFLATION

The path back to stable prices is likely to be long and difficult. Quick, easy remedies are extremely scarce. Viable policy alternatives will take time. Recognizing these facts, ideas to reduce the disruptive and harmful effects of inflation have attracted interest.

One such idea is called **indexing.** In its most simplified form, indexing would adjust wages and salaries, pensions, the face value of life insurance policies, interest rates, and even the income tax for changes in the cost of living. Long-term contracts would be negotiated in real terms, in dollars of constant purchasing power. Then, at designated intervals, the money terms of these contracts would be altered to reflect changes in the purchasing power of a dollar bill.

For example, suppose that a new homeowner agreed to a $30,000 mortgage at a 5 percent interest rate—*in dollars of constant purchasing power.* If prices were stable, he would pay the 5 percent annual rate. If prices rose 5 percent, he would pay a 10 percent rate. With 10 percent inflation, interest charges would be 15 percent, and so on. Annual interest changes would be adjusted upward or downward to reflect both inflation and deflation.

Some 50 million Americans already have their incomes explicitly pegged, at least in part, to the consumer price index. For example, union wage contracts with escalator clauses are tied to the CPI. Social Security payments and the pensions of former congressmen are also indexed.

The Indexing Debate

The proponents of indexing emphasize that it would reduce the uncertainty associated with the present, informal indexing. When people are fairly sure that inflation will stay at 10 percent, a 10 percent premium is tacked onto wage increases, interest rates, and prices. But nobody knows what the actual rate of inflation will be in the future. Tying contracts to changes in the CPI would reduce this uncertainty.

Proponents also stress that indexing would cut down the incentive of government to follow inflationary policies. The government gains in two major ways from inflation. First, unanticipated inflation helps debtors. The U.S. government is the largest net debtor in the world. Inflation means that the government, by following policies that promote inflation, will be able to pay back its debtors (U.S. bondholders) with dollars of depreciated purchasing power.

Second, inflation increases tax rates without a formal vote. Since the tax rates are set in money terms, inflation pushes many people into higher tax brackets even when their real earnings are unchanged. For example, if inflation were 7 percent and an individual just kept pace, a person earning $5000 in 1976 would have money earnings of $10,000 in 1986. Under current arrangements, the tax bill of a married person filing a joint return would increase fivefold because of inflation. All along the line, inflation pushes people into higher tax brackets, even though their real income, before taxes, is unchanged.

Indexing would automatically adjust the tax rate structure, *keeping the same rates for incomes of constant purchasing power*. The government tax take would no longer go up (and the taxpayer's disposable income go down) as prices rose. If Congress wanted to take a larger share of our incomes, they would have to formally vote to do so! Proponents argue that this factor alone would put the brakes on government spending that promotes money creation and inflation.

The critics of indexing argue that it would be too complicated. Many persons would find it difficult to understand and adjust to the concept of elastic prices, rather than a dollar with elastic purchasing power. It would be an accounting nuisance, requiring bookkeepers to alter their entries as contracts are altered at various intervals. Clearly indexing is not a perfect substitute for stable prices.

Some critics of indexing have argued that it would build inflation into the system since the prices of previously negotiated long-term contracts would automatically rise with the general price level. This argument is based on less than solid ground. It fails to recognize two important points. First, with indexing, *initially* long-term contracts will not contain an inflation premium since indexing will automatically adjust the terms of these contracts if prices do, in fact, rise. Second, current long-term contracts already include a premium for the expected rate of inflation,[8] and this premium is not to be adjusted downward if prices rise less rapidly than was initially anticipated. If prices did not rise (or if they rose at less than the expected rate), indexing would result in a smaller inflationary premium than with the current method of handling long-term contracting. Actually the present arrangement does more to build inflation into the

---

[8]Readers who do not believe this should ask themselves if purchasers would pay the current interest rates (between 9 and 10 percent) for a 25 year home mortgage loan if they did not anticipate 3 to 5 percent inflation in the future.

system than indexing would. Indexing, unlike the current arrangements, would reduce the inflationary premium implicit in previously negotiated contracts if the actual inflation rate was less than the decision-makers initially anticipated.

Indexing Is a Painkiller, Not a Panacea

The popular news media, *Time*, for example, has criticized the idea of indexing because it has not halted inflation in countries that apply it. This view stems from a misunderstanding of both indexing and inflation. Continuous inflation, of the type experienced by Western nations during the late 1960s and 1970s, is the result of expansionary monetary and fiscal policy. Until this course is altered, inflation will continue, indexing or no indexing. The only solution to inflation is to plot a long-run macropolicy course that is consistent with stable prices, one that is less expansionary.

Indexing is not a substitute for sensible macropolicy. It is not an attempt to solve the inflation problem. The purpose of indexing is to reduce uncertainty and avoid some of the inequities, the windfall gains and losses that accrue to individuals because of unanticipated inflation.

Perhaps it might also reduce the government's incentive to follow an inflationary course. But this is only a secondary objective, not its primary purpose.

Has it worked in other countries? This is hard to answer because it is not easy to tell if uncertainty has been reduced. Beginning in the 1964–1967 period, Brazil, the nation that uses indexing most extensively, applied it to several economic sectors. By 1967, wages, salaries, rents, pensions, savings accounts, long-term private and public debt, tax brackets, and exchange rates were all subject to indexing—the Brazilians call it "monetary correction." Since 1967, Brazil's real GNP has grown at a 9.4 percent rate compared to 5.8 percent for the decade prior to the adoption of indexing. This is consistent with the view that indexing helps cut down uncertainty. However, one observation does not make an experiment.

PULLING IT ALL TOGETHER

In the last 10 chapters we have presented a great deal of material on macroeconomic theory and our experience with macropolicy.[9] About this time, students often have difficulty separating the important issues from the trivial ones. In order to help pull all the material together in a meaningful manner, we will conclude Part II with a hypothetical interview between a student and economists of three different perspectives—Keynesian, monetarist, and a middle-of-the-roader. The economics department at your university is likely to be staffed by economists with views similar to those of our hypothetical participants. Perhaps you can arrange a similar interview in a real-life class setting. After all, both Keynesians and monetarists share common educational goals. They agree on many important aspects of economics. They are likely to be good friends (each thinks the other is a nice guy, even though he is wrong). Why not try it?

---

[9] Appendix C presents the Keynesian and monetarist positions within the framework of the IS–LM model. Advanced students may want to analyze this appendix at this time.

Keynesians, Monetarists, and Middle-of-the-Roaders on Macroeconomics

STUDENT: Why do we experience booms and recessions?

KEYNESIAN: A market system is inherently unstable. A minor disruption will throw it off course. Trends in economic activity tend to be contagious. A reduction in aggregate demand causes business pessimism and a decline in investment, causing demand conditions to worsen still more. A business contraction feeds on itself. Slowdowns turn to recessions that would often result in depressions if the government failed to act. Similarly, during an upswing, an increase in demand leads to optimism and expanding investment. Acting through the multiplier, the additional investment expands demand still more. There is a snowballing effect, pushing the economy upward. Of course, full employment will bring the expansion to a halt and the cycle will eventually begin anew.

MONETARIST: Improper macropolicy, particularly monetary policy, is the major source of economic instability. Every significant recession in the United States has been characterized by monetary restriction. On the other hand, excessive monetary expansion has been far and away the most important source of inflation. The market is not inherently unstable, at least not to the extent that we have actually experienced economic instability. The government itself is the major source of instability.

STUDENT: Can anything be done to reduce economic instability?

KEYNESIAN: We've already accomplished a great deal. Automatic stabilizers, such as unemployment compensation, the progressive income tax, and the corporate profits tax, help to keep the economy on track. Other than this, we need to continue improving our forecasting methods so we can improve our timing of discretionary macropolicy and provide additional stabilization.

MONETARIST: The government can provide a stable macroframework. A monetary rule requiring a continuous expansion in the money supply *at a fixed rate*, 3 percent annually for example, would do much to eliminate both recession and inflation.

STUDENT: Why don't monetarists believe that fiscal policy is very important? What is the logic of their argument?

MONETARIST: A purely expansionary fiscal action, one that does not change the money supply, would necessitate that the Treasury cover its deficit by selling bonds to the public. Thus, the supply of bonds increases, reducing bond prices and driving up interest rates. Interest rates will continue to rise until private investment and consumption have been choked off sufficiently to offset the fiscal action. The funds to finance the deficit (that is, to buy the Treasury bonds) must come from somewhere. The major source of these funds will normally be a reduction in private investment and consumption in response to higher interest rates.

Similarly, a restrictive fiscal policy is likely to have little impact on inflation. An increase in taxes and a government surplus would reduce the supply of bonds. Bond prices will increase and the interest rate will fall. The reduction in interest rates would stimulate private spending, tending to offset the restrictive fiscal action.

STUDENT: What is your reaction to the views of Mr. Monetarist? Where would you disagree with his analysis?

KEYNESIAN: Mr. Monetarist apparently does not understand the fundamental purpose of fiscal action. Expansionary fiscal action is adopted because there is insufficient aggregate demand to attain full employment. Planned saving exceeds planned investment at the full-employment level of output. The fiscal action will directly contribute to aggregate demand and reduce the excess of saving relative to private investment. Throughout his comments Mr. Monetarist was implicitly assuming that planned saving and planned investment were equal. If this were true, his analysis would be essentially correct.

But high unemployment rates and insufficient aggregate demand would indicate planned saving and investment are not equal at the full-employment level of output. This is the signal for expansionary fiscal policy, and under these circumstances, even a pure fiscal action would be expansionary. Similarly, inflation indicates an excess of aggregate demand relative to supply. Restrictive fiscal action, under these circumstances, would eliminate this excess demand.

In considering offsetting reactions to a policy, Mr. Monetarist stopped one step too soon. If an expansionary fiscal policy leads to higher interest rates, the higher interest rates will have two effects on private spending. They might, as Mr. Monetarist describes, cause some reduction in private investment and possibly consumption. But they will also cause households to reduce their holdings of cash, spending more on cars, houses, books, education, and other goods. The velocity of money will increase, because at higher interest rates, it is more costly to maintain idle cash balances.

The negative relationship between the interest rate and money balances has been confirmed by many studies, including several by today's leading monetarists. As the interest rate increases, each unit of money turns over more rapidly. Thus, even if the money supply remains constant, a pure fiscal action will be expansionary, because of its positive impact on velocity.

Similarly, a government surplus will be restrictive, even when the money supply remains unchanged. The restrictive fiscal policy will lead to a fall in interest rates, a decline in velocity, and a reduction in aggregate demand.

The Effectiveness of Monetary Policy

STUDENT: Keynesians sometimes argue that monetary policy has a limited impact on employment and income. Why are they so pessimistic about the impact of monetary policy?

KEYNESIAN: Money is an area where the views of economists in general, and Keynesians in particular, have changed in recent years. Before the 1930s, the classical economists thought that prolonged unemployment was impossible. This position was particularly awkward during the Great Depression.

It was against this background that Keynes developed his theory. He discussed two polar cases for which monetary policy would be totally ineffective. First, if investors are extremely pessimistic, a fall in the interest rate would fail to stimulate investment. At low interest rates, the investment schedule might become perfectly vertical and fail to equate investment with planned saving at a positive interest rate. Second, if pessimism abounded and interest rates were already low, the demand for money schedule might become perfectly horizontal. Therefore, expansionary monetary policy would fail to reduce the interest rates. In both of these cases monetary policy, operating through the interest rate, would be helpless to deal with the depression conditions. As the saying used to go, "You cannot push a string."

Some, I think unfairly, continue to associate this view with Keynesianism. Keynes himself merely suggested these possibilities. He did not say that they were actually present even in the 1930s. Modern Keynesians have long ago integrated money into their models, and indicated its impact on interest rates and investment.

STUDENT: Mr. Monetarist, how would you assess Mr. Keynesian's views on monetary policy?

MONETARIST: I think his historical analysis is on target. During and after the Great Depression, most Keynesians thought monetary policy was ineffective. But recent studies show that monetary policy had a substantial impact even during the 1930s. And, of course, current economic conditions are a far cry from the Great Depression. These two factors have contributed to a substantial shift in the views of almost all economists on the role of money.

Where monetarists and Keynesians still disagree is on the transmission mechanism by which money exerts its impact. Keynesians think that money operates through the interest rate. We monetarists believe that it has a direct impact on aggregate demand. An increase in the supply of money (or its rate of increase) will cause an excess supply of money. Households are holding more money than they desire and they will adjust by spending some of these excess money balances on bonds, but also some of it will be spent on cars, radios, houses, clothes, and lots of other commodities. Aggregate demand will increase directly.

Monetary–Fiscal Consensus

STUDENT: Mr. Middle-of-the-Roader, you have heard the monetarist and Keynesian views on the potency of both monetary and fiscal policy. How do they correspond to your own views?

MIDDLE-OF-THE-ROADER: Well, I think they have tended to stress their differences, while a closer analysis indicates they have much common ground. From a policy viewpoint, what matters most is the stimulating abilities of monetary and fiscal tools. Other issues are secondary. It matters little whether monetary policy is transmitted primarily through the interest rate or directly by influencing the demand for a broad spectrum of goods. What is important is the expansionary and restrictive potential of monetary policy. Similarly, with fiscal policy, it makes little difference if the fiscal policy acts directly through its impact on total spending or indirectly by influencing the velocity of money.

Fiscal and monetary policies are not competitive. They are complementary. If an expansionary effect is needed, the two tools can be utilized to supplement each other. Undoubtedly, greater expansion will result if a loose monetary policy is combined with a tax cut, than if monetary policy is restrictive. Why shouldn't the two be combined to attain the target expansion? This was the strategy of the 1964 tax cut.

Monetarists and Keynesians can debate whether the resulting expansion was primarily the result of one or the other of the tools. But this argument is of less than earth-shaking interest to policy-makers who are quite prepared to utilize fiscal and monetary action in a complementary manner.

The most difficult problem from a policy viewpoint is how to apply proper doses of macropolicy and how to properly time the doses so as to stabilize the economy. In my judgment, in this area the differences between the Keynesians and monetarists are both real and more important.

Is Discretionary Policy the Solution or the Problem?

STUDENT: How do monetarists and Keynesians differ on the use of discretionary tools?

MONETARIST: In general, monetarists are skeptical about the ability of macroplanners to stabilize the economy with discretionary policy. The past record grants us little reason for confidence. On the other hand, there are sound reasons to expect macroplanners to make mistakes. It is not easy to forecast future business conditions, gain the approval of Congress and the president for a needed policy change, and properly time the policy so its *impact* will exert a stabilizing effect. That's too much to ask. Thus, we should expect future, unintended mistakes to result.

In addition, political factors will continue to lead to inappropriate, discretionary macropolicy. Politicians will continue to finance war and other government spending with inflation rather than direct taxation. They will continue to "overheat" the economy at election time, causing postelection inflation. The battle with inflation will inevitably generate rising unemployment. As long as discretionary macropolicy remains in the hands of the politicians, a stop–go, destabilizing policy is the expected outcome, not the surprising occurrence that many Keynesians would have one believe. The solution is to tie the hands of the politicians with rules. This is why monetarists favor a fixed rule for monetary expansion.

STUDENT: How do Keynesians view discretionary policy?

KEYNESIAN: If monetary disturbance were the only source of economic instability, the case for a constant rate of monetary growth would have considerable attractiveness. But unfortunately instability stems from many other sources such as private investment, technology, war, and a consumption spending spree. The monetary rule would eliminate the flexibility of macroplanners to deal with disturbances arising from these other sources.

Admittedly, mistakes have been made in the past. Our knowledge of the future is imperfect. But in recent years, we have improved our knowledge in this area. Utilizing recently developed forecasting models, we will improve on the past record, while maintaining the flexibility to deal with disturbances that originated from nonmonetary sources. At a time when we have reached the pinnacle of our ability to knowledgeably deal with inflation and unemployment, the monetarists want us to adopt a "do-nothing, standby policy."

MIDDLE-OF-THE-ROADER: There is merit in the position of both monetarists and Keynesians on this issue. The monetarists are right in pointing out that the past stabilization record of the macroplanners has been erratic. To argue that they will succeed tomorrow, despite their past failures, is not overwhelmingly persuasive. Similarly, Keynesians are right in noting that disturbances may arise from nonmonetary sources. Disarming macroplanners reduces their ability to deal with such cases.

The views of Keynesians and monetarists on the merits of discretionary macropolicy are based on political as well as economic factors. The monetarists have little faith in political macroplanners. Simultaneously, they believe that the market mechanism will be able to adjust to disturbances of the magnitude that are likely to arise from nonmonetary sources. In contrast, Keynesians have more faith in the future ability of macroplanners to do the right thing and less confidence in the ability of the market mechanism to mitigate future disturbances.

STUDENT: What can be done to improve the unemployment inflation tradeoff?

KEYNESIAN: Greater effort should be expended to limit price rises stemming from monopoly power. In addition, we need to be more selective in channeling expansionary effects into areas of unemployment. This means a greater reliance on tools which are designed to achieve a rather narrow purpose. If there is unemployment in West Virginia, the Great Lakes area, or the Northwest, increased government spending should be channeled to those areas, not to areas of full employment. If electronics workers are unemployed, fiscal action that will stimulate useful production and employment of electronics workers should be designed. In the immediate past, our fiscal and monetary policy has been too broad. We should narrow its focus.

MONETARIST: It will be extremely difficult for macropolicy alone to do much to change the long-run rate of unemployment. Macropolicy can lower it today while simultaneously sowing the seeds for higher future unemployment. Or if appropriately applied, it can smooth out the extremes. But it can do little to change the long-run normal unemployment rate.

We do need to strengthen the competitiveness of both product and labor markets. Often this can be accomplished by simply repealing government grants of special privileges and regulations that currently limit competition.

STUDENT: Are economists pessimistic about our ability to deal with future inflation and unemployment?

MIDDLE-OF-THE-ROADER: The 1960s probably led to an unjustified overoptimism about the ability of macropolicy to maintain both stable prices and high employment. Currently economists of various persuasions are placing more emphasis on a micro-approach to macroproblems. We need to provide more incentives for employers to hire unskilled workers, train them, and offer them opportunity for future advancement. Simultaneously, workers, particularly those with little experience, must face an incentive structure that encourages them to both work and acquire training. Such an approach will improve our productivity and lead to expanding real incomes.

STUDENT: Since monetarists and Keynesians differ about so many things, how does a student know who is right?

MIDDLE-OF-THE-ROADER: I have already indicated that it is easy to exaggerate the differences between the two. Nevertheless there are some important differences.

In a sense both Keynesians and monetarists may be right. Time plays an important role in economics. The immediate impact of a policy often differs from its effect over a longer time period. Many of the differences between Keynesians and monetarists are of this type.

The Keynesian focus is short run—what will happen in the next 3 to 12 months. Often the monetarist's focus is most relevant to the long run—what happens one or two years from now. Consider their differences about the effects of pure fiscal policy. Monetarists stress that a government deficit will cause higher interest rates, reducing private spending. Keynesians tend to de-emphasize this secondary factor. In the short run, Keynesians are probably right as the interest rate does not *immediately* rise in response to the government's increased demand for loanable funds. But after 12 to 24 months, the monetarists are right, as interest rates will eventually rise, dampening private spending.

STUDENT: Are there other areas where the differences may stem primarily from long-run, short-run factors?

MIDDLE-OF-THE-ROADER: Yes, there are several. Keynesians usually stress that expansionary monetary policy will cause interest rates to fall. In the short run they are right. But over a longer period of time, monetarists are right in their view that monetary expansion will cause rising money incomes, higher prices, expectation of inflation, and higher interest rates.

Macropolicy and unemployment are another case. Keynesians emphasize that expansionary macropolicy can reduce unemployment. In the short run this is clearly correct. Neither wages nor prices will rise instantaneously in response to an increase in aggregate demand. Thus macroexpansion has its primary influence on real income and employment, in the short run. But with time, the view that prices and wages will rise as the result of the expansionary policy is probably correct. And with time, decision-makers will begin to anticipate the rising prices. Under those circumstances, the ability of macropolicy to *permanently* reduce the unemployment rate will be limited.

STUDENT: Which is most important, the short run or the long run?

MIDDLE-OF-THE-ROADER: They're both important. Lord Keynes once said "In the long run, we are all dead." This is not really correct. Today's generation is here to experience the consequences of short-run policies followed one, two, or five years ago. If those policies were wrong from a long-run viewpoint, we won't be dead. We'll just be currently ill! But short-run consequences are important also. Sometimes a short-run policy, applied in the right situation, can even help us plot an improved long-run course.

STUDENT: Should I be a Keynesian or a monetarist?

MIDDLE-OF-THE-ROADER: At exam time you might want to consider the views of your instructor. But other than that, the choice is yours.

CHAPTER LEARNING OBJECTIVES

1. The experience of the late 1960s and early 1970s has made economists more aware of the limits of macropolicy.

2. The wage–price controls of the Nixon Administration were an effort to break the anticipation of inflation, and therefore shift the Phillips curve to the left. Current research indicates they were ineffective in this regard.

3. Economists are increasingly seeking to improve the inflation–unemployment tradeoff by focusing on structural problems and how to improve fiscal action. Narrower targeting of government spending, training programs and creation of more productive jobs for the unskilled, relaxation of the minimum wage, particularly for teenages, and revision of welfare and unemployment compensation in a way that would increase the incentive to accept employment are some of the ideas that are currently being considered.

4. Persons under 25 years of age accounted for half of the total unemployment in the mid-1970s. Policies that provide increased incentives for employers to offer (and employees to accept) jobs with training and attractive future earnings opportunities would help to reduce unemployment among youthful workers.

5. Indexing is an idea designed to reduce the uncertainty and inequities associated with long-term contracting. With indexing, long-term contracts would be negotiated in real dollars, dollars of constant purchasing power. The money terms of contracts would be adjusted at various time intervals for changes in the price level. Union contracts with escalator clauses, Social Security payments, and a few life insurance policies are already indexed, at least in part.

6. Most economists (and macroplanners) believe that both monetary and fiscal policies have significant impacts on aggregate demand. Many believe that the key issue is proper timing and dosage, not the mechanism by which the policy exerts its impact. Thus, monetary and fiscal policies are thought of as complementary rather than competitive.

7. Often differences between Keynesians and monetarists are really reflections of the differences between the long- and short-run impact of a policy. The Keynesian analysis often tends to stress the short run, while the monetarist's position may be more descriptive of the long run.

IMPORTANT TERMS TO REMEMBER

Wage-price controls: Legal prohibition preventing business firms and employees from raising prices and wages.

Indexing: Adjusting wages and salaries, interest rates, income tax brackets, and other long-term agreements to the trend of prices. Thus, the terms of long-term contracts are adjusted to reflect changes in the purchasing power of the dollar.

Youth work scholarship: A plan to provide subsidies to younger workers who maintain jobs. Some plans would limit the subsidies to employment that results in on-the-job training.

THE ECONOMIC WAY OF THINKING—DISCUSSION QUESTIONS

1. Do you think that the wage–price controls of the Nixon Administration helped reduce inflation? Might they have made it worse? If so, why? Indicate why you either favor or oppose wage–price controls.

2. The chairman of the Council of Economic Advisers has requested that you write a short position paper on "How to Improve the Unemployment–Inflation Tradeoff." Be specific. Indicate why your recommendations will work. Submit it to your instructor and he will pass it along to the CEA.

3. Explain in your own words the idea of indexing. Do you think it would help stabilize prices? Why or why not? Would it build in inflation? Why or why not?

4. "Unemployment involves the loss of real resources. Inflation results only in a decline in the value of money. Unemployment is the more serious problem because real production suffers when people are unemployed. By contrast, inflation is merely a paper loss." What do you think of this view? Explain why you either agree or disagree.

5. In 1971 the National Urban Coalition recommended that the government provide a more generous level of unemployment benefits as a means of fighting the unemployment problem.
   (a) What impact would higher unemployment benefits have on the opportunity cost for an unemployed worker to reject a job offer.
   (b) Do you think the idea would increase or decrease the rate of unemployment? Why?

6. Indicate the points of agreement and disagreement between the views of Keynesians and monetarists. In areas where they disagree, might they both be right? Explain.

7. What's wrong with This Way of Thinking?

"In 1973 consumer prices rose by 10 percent. The major cause of the inflation was the soaring prices of meats, dairy products, food away from home, and consumer nondurables."

III
MICROECONOMICS

16
DEMAND AND CONSUMER CHOICE

Macroeconomics focuses on aggregate markets—the big picture. In this section we will take a microlook at the highly aggregated markets that we have been discussing. We will break down the aggregate product market into micromarkets for specific products such as sugar, green vegetables, automobiles, houses, gasoline, electricity, and literally thousands of other items.

Microeconomics focuses on how changes in *relative* prices influence consumer decisions. At the microlevel, markets are narrowly defined and highly interrelated. Therefore, changes in one market will affect conditions in related markets. The economic way of thinking, as we stressed in Chapter 3, implies that there will be a negative relationship between the price of a product and the amount demanded by consumers. Our purpose in this chapter is to take a closer look at (a) the interrelationships between markets and (b) the factors that underlie the demand for specific products.

CONSUMER DECISION-MAKING—DECIDING WHAT TO BUY

Exhibit 16-1 shows how consumers allocated their spending among alternative goods in 1950 and 1972. Why did consumers spend more on transportation than medical care, or more on tobacco than religious and welfare activities? Why have consumer expenditures on food declined (as a percentage of the total) while spending on housing has expanded? If we are to answer these questions, we will need to know something about the factors that influence the behavior of consumers.

When analyzing the choices of consumers, economists usually make the following assumptions.

1. *Limited Income Necessitates Choice.* Most of us are all too aware that our desire for goods far exceeds our limited income. We do not have sufficient resources to purchase everything that we would like. So we must make choices, deciding to purchase some goods, while foregoing many, many others for which we lack the necessary purchasing power.

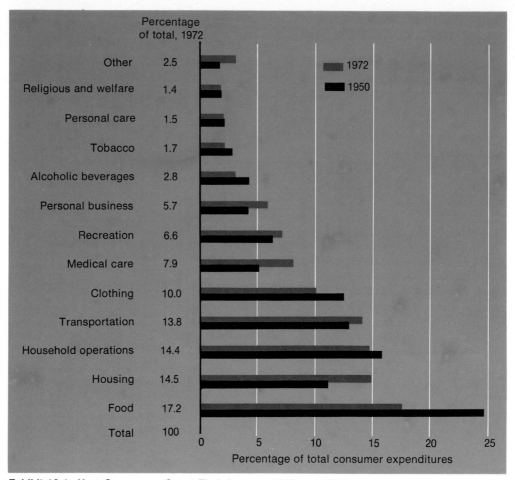

Exhibit 16-1 How Consumers Spent Their Income, 1950 and 1972

SOURCE: *Statistical Abstract of the United States—1975.*

2. Consumers Will Make Decisions Purposefully. The consumption decisions that each of us make will influence our personal welfare. We must bear the consequences of our decisions. A consumer who spends $10 on something that he does not care much for will have $10 less to spend on things that he would really like. Foolish decisions are costly, and thus, it makes sense to avoid them. Consumers will not *knowingly* choose a product when the choice necessitates giving up a higher-valued alternative.

3. The Law of Diminishing Marginal Utility—As the Rate of Consumption Increases per Unit of Time, the Utility Derived from Consuming Additional Units of a Good Will Decline. Utility is a term that economists use to describe the subjective personal benefits that result from an action. The **law of diminishing marginal utility** states that the **marginal** (or additional) **utility** derived from consuming successive units of a product will *eventually* decline as the utilization rate increases.

For example, the law implies that even though you might like ice cream, your marginal satisfaction from an *additional* bowl of ice cream will eventually decline. Ice cream at lunchtime might be great. An additional helping for dinner might be even better. But after you have had it for evening dessert and a midnight snack, ice cream for breakfast will begin to lose some of its attraction. The law of diminishing marginal utility has set in, and thus the marginal utility derived from the consumption of additional units of ice cream will decline.

4. *Goods Can Be Substituted One for Another.* No good is so precious that some of it would not be given up in exchange for more of other goods. For example, consumers will give up some fried chicken in order to have more pizza, hamburger, fish, ham sandwiches, or apple pie. Similarly, books, movies, television, card games, and girl (boy) watching can be substituted for playing football.

5. *Consumers Must Make Decisions without Perfect Information, Even Though Knowledge and Past Experience Will Help Them Become Better Informed.* No man has perfect foresight. Napoleon did not anticipate Waterloo; Julius Caesar did not anticipate the actions of Brutus. Consumers will not always correctly anticipate the consequences of their choices.

But consumer choices are not made in a vacuum. You have a pretty good idea of what to expect when you buy a cup of coffee, 5 gallons of gasoline, or lunch at your favorite diner. Why? Because you have learned from experience—your own and that of others. When you buy a product, your expectations may not be fulfilled precisely (for example, the coffee may be stronger than expected or the gasoline may make your car knock). But even these experiences will help you acquire valuable information that can be used when making future decisions.

INDIVIDUAL DEMAND

Demand is the schedule of the amounts of a product that consumers would be willing to purchase at different prices during a specific time period. The amount of a product purchased will be negatively related to its price. Why? First, as the price of a product falls, it becomes more attractive compared to other products with unchanged prices. Consumers will substitute the cheaper product for goods that are now relatively more expensive. Economists refer to this factor as the substitution effect. Second, when the consumer's money income is constant, a reduction in the price of a product increases his real income. Typically, a consumer will respond by purchasing more of the cheaper product (as well as other products) because he can now better afford to do so. This factor is referred to as the income effect.

Consumer choices, like other decisions, will be influenced by changes in benefits and costs. Thus, it is helpful to think of demand within the general framework of the theory of choice. If a consumer wants to get the most out of his expenditures, how much of each good will he purchase? As more of a good is consumed per unit of time, the law of diminishing marginal utility states that the consumer's marginal benefits per unit of time will decline. A consumer will gain by purchasing more of a product so long as the benefits (marginal utility, MU) from the additional unit exceed their cost (the product price P). In the continuous case, this implies that the consumer will get the most for his money when each product is consumed to the point where the marginal utility from the last unit is just equal to its price.[1]

How will changes in price influence the decisions of consumers? As the price of a product declines, the opportunity cost of consuming it will fall. The lower opportunity cost will induce consumers to buy more of it. But as they increase their rate of consumption, what happens to the marginal utility derived from the product? It falls. Thus, as more of the product is consumed, eventually the benefits (marginal utility) derived from the consumption of still more units will again be less than their cost. Purposeful decision-makers will not choose such units. Thus, a price reduction will induce consumers to purchase more, but the response will be limited because of the law of diminishing marginal utility.

Similarly, if the price of a product rises, consumers will curtail their consumption. Why? The product's opportunity cost has risen, making it a less attractive buy. But as consumption is reduced, the consumer's marginal utility derived from the product will rise. Eventually it will again exceed opportunity cost. Therefore, the individual's reduction in consumption rate will typically be limited.

Exhibit 16-2 illustrates the impact of price on consumption level and marginal utility. In 1973–1974 gasoline prices rose rapidly in the United States. As demand theory would predict, Sam Jones and other consumers reduced their rate of consumption. As gasoline prices rose from 35 cents to 50 cents, Jones' weekly consumption fell from 20 to 18 gallons. Initially, Jones and other consumers eliminated the least valued uses of gasoline. Less valuable trips were discontinued, shopping trips were combined with other business near shopping centers, and television watching was substituted for leisure

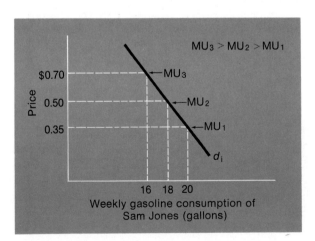

Exhibit 16-2   Gas Prices, Consumption, and Marginal Utility

Individuals will expand their consumption rate of a product as long as MU exceeds price. Higher prices will cause individuals to consume less. But the reduction in consumption will be limited because the MU of the product rises as consumption falls.

---

[1] Thus, the consumer's total utility is at a maximum when his limited income is spent on products such that:

$$P_A/MU_A = P_B/MU_B = \cdots = P_N/MU_N$$

Verbally, this means that the last dollar spent on product A, yields the same utility as if the dollar were spent on product B (or any other product). If this were not true, it would be possible to increase total utility by spending less on products for which the marginal utility from the last dollar expenditure was low, while spending more on products for which the marginal utility from the last dollar expenditure was high.

driving. At the lower consumption level, the marginal utility of gasoline rose, bringing it into line with the higher price.

Still higher gasoline prices would elicit an even greater reduction in consumption. The additional decline in consumption would require consumers to forego still higher valued uses of gasoline. But if the price rose to 70 cents, for example, the response would again be limited, because the marginal utility of gasoline would rise as consumption was reduced.

CONSUMER CHOICE AND MARKET DEMAND

<u>The market demand schedule is the amount demanded by all the individuals in the market area at various prices. Since individual consumers purchase less at higher prices, the amount demanded in a market area will also be negatively related to price.</u>

Exhibit 16-3 illustrates the relationship between individual and market demand for a hypothetical two person market. The individual demand curves for both Sam Jones and Harvey Smith are shown. At 35 cents per gallon, both Jones and Smith consume 20 gallons of gasoline weekly. The amount demanded in the two person market would be 40 gallons. If the price rose to 70 cents per gallon, the amount demanded in the market would fall to 28 gallons, 16 by Jones and 12 by Smith. The market demand is simply the horizontal sum of the individual demand curves.

The market demand curve is merely a reflection of individual demand schedules. Individuals buy less as price increases. Therefore, the total amount demanded in the market will decline as price increases.

WHAT WILL CAUSE THE DEMAND CURVE TO SHIFT?

The demand schedule isolates the impact of price on amount purchased, assuming other factors are held constant. What are these "other factors"? How will they influence demand?

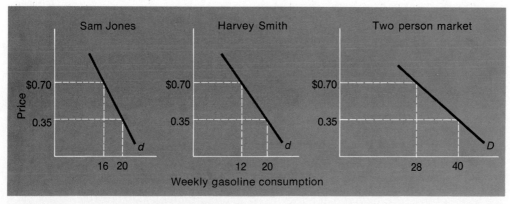

Exhibit 16-3 Individual and Market Demand Curves

The market demand curve is merely the horizontal sum of the individual demand curves. The market demand curve will slope downward to the right because individual demand curves do so.

First, changes in the income of consumers will influence the demand for a product.[2] The demand for most products will be positively related to income. As their income expands, consumers will typically spend more on consumption. The demand for most products will increase. Conversely, a reduction in consumer income usually causes the demand for a product to fall.

Second, changes in the distribution of income will also influence the demand for specific products. If more income were allocated to alcoholics and less to vegetarians, the demand for liquor would increase while the demand for vegetables would fall. Consider another example. Suppose that a law were passed that taxed all inheritances over $50,000 at a 90 percent rate. If the law effectively reduced the income of the sons and daughters of the wealthy, it would also reduce their demand for yachts, around the world cruises, diamonds, and perhaps even a Harvard education. If the revenues from the tax were redistributed to persons with incomes below $5000, the demand for hamburgers, used cars, moderately priced housing, and other commodities that low income families purchase *disproportionately* would increase.

Third, the prices of closely related goods will influence the demand for a product. Related goods may be either substitutes or complements. When two products perform similar functions or fulfill similar needs, they are **substitutes.** There will be a direct relationship between the price of a product and the demand for substitutes. For example, butter and margarine are substitutes. Higher butter prices will increase the demand for margarine, as consumers substitute it for the more expensive butter. Similarly, higher coffee prices would increase the demand for substitutes such as Sanka and tea. A substitute relationship exists between beef and pork, pencils and pens, sugar and saccharin, and so forth.

Other closely related products will be consumed jointly. Goods that "go together" so to speak are called **complements.** For complements, there will be a negative relationship between the price of one and the demand for the other. For example, as the experiences of the 1970s illustrate quite well, higher gasoline prices will cause the demand for automobiles to decline. Gasoline and automobiles are complementary. Similarly, lower prices for portable radios will increase the demand for complementary batteries. Ham and eggs, tents and camping equipment, automatic dishwashers and electricity, these products are complementary to each other.

Fourth, changes in consumer preferences will influence demand. Why might preferences change? In time, human beings change. New information might change their evaluation of a good. How did consumers respond to new information linking cigarette smoking to cancer in the mid-1960s? They smoked fewer cigarettes. Annual per capita consumption, which had been increasing, fell more than 6 percent between 1965 and 1970. When consumers acquired information that cigarettes were also cancer sticks, many of them changed their preferences!

Fifth, changes in population and its composition will influence the demand for products. The demand for products in a market area will be directly related to the number of consumers. Changes in the composition of the population may also exert an impact on demand. If a higher percentage of the population is between 16 and 21 years of age, the demand for movies, stereo equipment and records, sports cars,

---

[2]Do not forget a change in *quantity demanded* is a movement along a demand curve in response to a change in price. But a change in *demand* is a shift in the entire demand curve. Review Chapter 3 if there is confusion on this point.

THUMBNAIL SKETCH—Change in Demand and Change in Quantity Demanded

Changes in these factors will cause the entire demand curve to shift:

(1) consumer income,
(2) the distribution of consumer income,
(3) price of related products (substitutes and complements),
(4) consumer preferences,
(5) population in the market area, and
(6) expectations about the future price of the product.

A change in this factor will cause the quantity demanded (but not demand) to change:

(1) the current price of the product.

and college education will be positively affected. An increase in the number of elderly people will positively affect the demand for medical care, retirement housing, and vacation travel.

Sixth, expectations will influence demand. When consumers expect the future price of a product to rise (fall), their current demand for it will expand (decline). Buy now before the price goes even higher! When the price of sugar soared in 1974, how did shoppers respond? Initially current sales increased, as consumers hoarded the product because they expected its price to continue rising. Conversely, if you thought that the price of a product, automobiles for example, would be 10 percent lower next year, would this influence your current actions? Of course, most consumers would seek to lengthen their auto purchasing decisions into the future so they could buy at next year's bargain prices.

When an economist constructs a demand schedule for a product, it is assumed that factors other than the price of the product are held constant. As Exhibit 16-4 shows, changes in any of these other factors that influence consumer decisions will cause the entire demand curve to shift.

Exhibit 16-4 Price Is Not All That Matters

Other things constant, the demand schedule will slope downward to the right. But changes in income and its distribution, the prices of closely related products, preferences, population, and expectations about future prices will also influence consumer decisions. Changes in these factors would cause the entire demand curve to shift (for example, increase from D_1 to D_2).

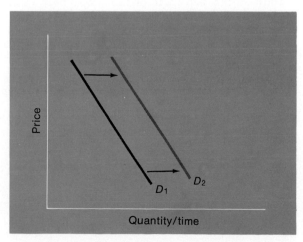

TIME COST AND CONSUMER CHOICE

The monetary price of a good is not always a complete measure of its cost to the consumer. Consumption of most goods requires time as well as money. Time, like money, is scarce to the consumer. A lower time cost, like a lower money price, will make a product more attractive to consumers.[3]

Some commodities are demanded primarily because of their ability to reduce the consumer's time cost. Consumers are often willing to pay higher money prices for such goods. The popularity of automatic dishwashers, electric razors, prepared foods, air travel, and taxi service is based on their low time cost by comparison with substitutes.

What is the cost of a college education? Tuition payments plus the price of books. These items comprise only a small component. The major cost of a college education is the approximate 4000 hours of time cost. If a student values his time at only $2 per hour, the time cost of a college education will be $8000!

Time costs, unlike money prices, will differ between individuals. They will be higher for persons with greater earning power. Other things being equal, high wage consumers will choose fewer time intensive (and more time saving) commodities than persons with a lower time cost. High wage consumers will be overrepresented among air and taxicab passengers, but underrepresented among television watchers, chess players, and long-distance auto travelers. Can you explain why? You should be able to if you understand that both money and time cost will influence the choices of consumers.

ELASTICITY OF DEMAND

If the tuition charges at your school go up 50 percent next year, how many of your classmates will be back? If the price of salt doubles, how much less will you purchase? These are questions about price elasticity of demand.

Price elasticity of demand is defined as the percent change in quantity demanded divided by the percent change in price.[4] This ratio is called the elasticity coefficient. The term elasticity is highly appropriate because it connotes flexibility or responsiveness. If the amount of a good that consumers will choose falls substantially in response to a small rise in price, the demand for the product is elastic. In contrast, if a substantial increase in price induces only a small reduction in quantity demanded, demand is said to be inelastic. The quantity demanded along an elastic demand curve

[3] For a technical treatment of the importance of time as a component of cost from the vantage point of the consumer, see Gary Becker, "A Theory of the Allocation of Time," *Economic Journal*, 1965, pp. 493–517.

[4] The careful student might want to distinguish between (a) the elasticity at a point on the demand curve and (b) the *arc* elasticity *between* two points on the demand curve. The formula for point elasticity is

$$\frac{\text{Change in quantity demanded}}{\text{initial quantity demanded}} \div \frac{\text{change in price}}{\text{initial price}}$$

The formula for arc elasticity is

$$(q_0 - q_1)/(q_0 + q_1) \div (P_0 - P_1)/(P_0 + P_1)$$

where the subscripts 0 and 1 refer to the respective prices and amounts demanded at two alternative points on a specific demand curve. The arc elasticity is really an average elasticity between the two points on the curve.

will be highly sensitive to a change in price. An inelastic demand curve would indicate inflexibility or little consumer response to variation in price.

When the elasticity coefficient is greater than one (ignoring the sign), demand is elastic. An elasticity coefficient of less than one means that demand is inelastic. "Unitary elasticity" is the term used to denote a price elasticity of one. Of course, the sign of the elasticity coefficient will always be negative since a change in price will cause the quantity demanded to change in the opposite direction.

Graphic Representation of Demand Elasticity

Exhibit 16-5 presents a graphic representation of demand curves of varying elasticity. A demand curve that is completely vertical is termed "perfectly inelastic." No demand

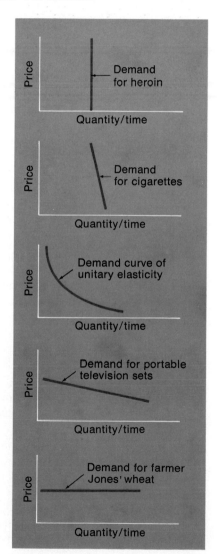

Perfectly inelastic—Despite an increase in price, consumers still purchase the same amount. The price elasticity of demand for heroin by an addict or insulin by a diabetic might be approximated by this curve.

Relatively inelastic—A large percent increase in price results in only a small reduction in sales. The demand for cigarettes has been estimated to be highly inelastic.

Unitary elasticity—The percent change in quantity demanded is equal to the percent change in price. A *curve* of decreasing slope results.

Relatively elastic—A small increase in price leads to a relatively large reduction in purchases. Consumers substitute other products for the more expensive good.

Perfectly elastic—Consumers will buy all of Mr. Jones' wheat at the market price, but he could not sell any above the market price.

Exhibit 16-5   Picturing the Elasticity of Demand

curve will be perfectly inelastic at all prices, although the addict's demand for heroin or the diabetic's demand for insulin might approximate perfect inelasticity over a wide range of prices.

The more inelastic the demand, the steeper is the demand curve over any specific price range. Inspection of the demand for cigarettes, which is inelastic, and the demand for portable television sets, which is relatively elastic, indicates that the inelastic curve tends to be steeper (see Exhibit 16-5). When demand elasticity is constant, a demand curve that is convex to the origin will result.[5] When a demand curve is completely horizontal, an economist would say that it is perfectly elastic. The demand for the wheat of a single wheat farmer, for example, would approximate perfect elasticity.

The Elasticity of Demand in the Real World

Economists have estimated the price elasticity of demand for many products. Exhibit 16-6 presents some of these estimates. They vary a great deal. The demand for several products—salt, toothpicks, matches, light bulbs, and newspapers, for example—is highly inelastic. On the other hand, the demand for fresh tomatoes, Chevrolet automobiles, and fresh green peas is highly elastic. What factors explain this variation? Why is demand for some products, but not others, highly responsive to changes in price?

1. *The Availability of Substitutes.*   This factor is the most important determinant of demand elasticity. When there are good substitutes available for a product, a price rise simply induces consumers to switch to other products. Demand will be elastic. For example, if the price of fountain pens rose, many consumers would switch to pencils, ballpoint pens, and felt tip pens. If the price of Chevrolets increases consumers will substitute Fords, Dodges, and Volkswagons for them.

When there are few good substitutes available, the demand for a product will tend to be inelastic. Medical services are an example. When we are really sick, most of us find witch doctors, faith healers, palm readers, and cod liver oil to be highly imperfect substitutes for a doctor. Unsurprisingly, the demand for physician services is inelastic.

The availability of substitutes is expanded as one narrows the product class. Therefore, the price elasticity will be greater for narrowly defined product classes than for broad ones. For example, as Exhibit 16-6 shows, the price elasticity of Chevrolets, a narrow product class, exceeds that for automobiles in general.

2. *Share of Total Budget Expended on the Product.*   If the expenditures on a product are quite small relative to the consumer's budget, demand will tend to be more inelastic. Compared to one's total budget, expenditures on some commodities are

---

[5]Students often confuse elasticity with the slope of the line. The two are different. Elasticity is the *relative* change in quantity divided by the *relative* change in price. Since it is a relative concept, the elasticity of a straight line demand curve will differ for each point on the line even though the slope of the line is constant.

Exhibit 16-6   The Estimated Price Elasticity of Demand for Selected Products

Inelastic	
Salt	0.1
Matches	0.1
Toothpicks	0.1
Airline travel, short run	0.1
Gasoline, short run	0.2
Gasoline, long run	0.5
Coffee	0.25
Cigarettes	0.35
Legal services	0.5
Physician services	0.6
Taxi	0.4
Tires, short run	0.6
Tires, long run	0.4
Automobiles, long run	0.2
Approximate unitary elasticity	
Housing	0.9
Private education	1.1
China and tableware	1.1
Radio and television receivers	1.2
Elastic	
Fresh tomatoes	4.6
Foreign travel, long run	4.0
Airline travel, long run	2.4
Fresh green peas	2.8
Automobiles, short run	1.2–1.5
Chevrolet automobiles	4.0

SOURCE: Hendrik S. Houthakker and Lester D. Taylor, *Consumer Demand in the United States 1929–1970* (Cambridge, Massachusetts: Harvard Univ. Press, 1966), and U.S. Department of Agriculture.

almost inconsequential. Matches, toothpicks, and salt are good examples. Most consumers spend only one or two dollars per year on each of these items. A doubling of their price would exert little influence on the family budget.

3. *Time and Adjusting to a Price Change.*   It will take time for consumers to respond fully to a change in the price of a product. Typically, product demand will be more elastic with the passage of time. The sharp increase in the price of gasoline in 1973–1974 serves as a good example to illustrate the importance of time. When gasoline prices rose from 35 to 55 cents, did consumers *immediately* quit driving their 350 horsepower, gas guzzling automobiles? No. But when their full-sized cars wore out, did many consumers switch to higher gas milage, compact cars? Yes. In the short run, consumers responded to higher gas prices by reducing speeds, forming car pools, and driving less. But given more time, compact cars were substituted for full-size models,

reducing gasoline consumption even more. Thus, as Exhibit 16-6 shows, the long-run demand for gasoline (0.5) was more elastic than for the short run (0.2).

The demand for a few products, particularly consumer durables, will be more elastic in the short run than in the long run. Such purchases can initially be "lengthened into the future" as prices rise. The old tires can be driven a few more miles or the old washing machine repaired one more time. Thus, higher prices will induce a greater immediate reduction in quantity demanded than will be possible over an extended time period.

Elasticity and Total Expenditures

Price elasticity establishes the relationship between a change in price and the corresponding change in the total expenditures of the product. When demand is inelastic, a change in price will cause total expenditures to change in the same direction. If demand is elastic, price and total expenditures will change in opposite directions. For unitary elasticity, total expenditure will remain constant as price changes.

Let us examine why. When demand is inelastic, the percent change in price exceeds the percent reduction in sales. The price effect dominates. For example, when the price of beef increased from $1.00 to $1.20 per pound (a 20 percent increase) between 1971 and 1973, per capita consumption fell from 120 to 110 pounds (an 8.3 percent reduction). The average person spent $120 (120 pounds at $1 per pound) on beef in 1971. But when the beef price rose to $1.20 per pound in 1973, average expenditures rose to $132.[6] The higher beef prices caused total expenditures to increase because demand was inelastic.

When demand is elastic, the percent decline in quantity demanded will exceed the percent increase in price. The loss of sales will exert a greater influence on total expenditures than the rise in price. Therefore, total revenues will fall. Exhibit 16-7 summarizes the relationship between changes in price and total expenditures for demand curves of varying elasticity.

Exhibit 16-7   Demand Elasticity, Change in Price, and Change in Total Expenditures

Price elasticity of demand	Numerical elasticity coefficient[a]	The impact of a change in price on total expenditures (sales revenues)
Elastic	1 to ∞	Price and total expenditures change in opposite directions
Unitary	1	Total expenditures remain constant as price changes
Inelastic	0 to 1	Price and total expenditures change in the same direction

[a] The sign of the elasticity coefficient will, of course, be negative.

[6] Calculate the elasticity coefficient as an exercise. Is it less than one?

OUTSTANDING ECONOMIST: John Kenneth Galbraith

Prolific, innovative, controversial, arrogant, and nonconventional are all words that have been used to describe Harvard's John Kenneth Galbraith. Professor Galbraith is a philosopher, poet, social critic, political activist, and economic advisor—all at the same time. He was ambassador to India during the Kennedy Administration. He helped Lyndon Johnson plan the war on poverty, before splitting with him over the Vietnam issue. Galbraith was one of George McGovern's earliest supporters and served as a McGovern delegate to the Democratic National Convention in 1972.

Galbraith has been a long-time critic of consumer theory in general and advertising in particular. In his best-selling book, *The Affluent Society*, Galbraith charged, "The fact that wants can be synthesized by advertising, catalyzed by salesmanship, and shaped by discreet manipulations of the persuaders shows that they are not very urgent."[7]

In Galbraith's view, consumers in affluent Western societies are on a never ending merry-go-round. Artificial wants are created so businessmen can sell more goods for profit. While economists typically view production as the means of satisfying wants, Galbraith argues that it is the foundation requiring the creation of wants. Advertising and want creation are simply the arms of production in a modern economy.

The solution to the problem in Galbraith's view is a vast expansion in the role of government.[8] Galbraith favors permanent price controls for sectors of the economy dominated by large corporations, redistribution of income toward greater equality, and socialization of several major industries such as steel, petroleum, and automobiles. Needless to say, he is not exactly the businessman's friend. Reflecting on his experience as a price fixer with the Office of Price Administration during World War II, he once remarked, "I always thought that any businessman who left my office smiling indicated that I made some kind of mistake."

For many years Galbraith was either ignored or treated with scorn by most of his fellow economists. But in the late 1960s, his undisputed popularity among the general populace began to rub off on his professional peers. In 1971 he served as president of the American Economic Association, an honor that many felt was long overdue.

Galbraith's critics charge that he pays no heed to scientific methods. Most economists bask in the sun of theory, testing, computers, and statistics. Galbraith will have none of it. He simply makes the charges, requiring his listeners to either have faith or do their own number grubbing. While his approach is unlikely to transform the methodology of the profession, he has already caused it to reconsider the foundations of economic analysis. That is not a bad accomplishment for a politician, poet, and social reformer.

---

[7]John Kenneth Galbraith, *The Affluent Society*. Boston: Houghton Mifflin, 1958, p. 123.
[8]See J. K. Galbraith, "Conversations with an Inconvenient Economist," *Challenge*, September/October 1973, for a short statement of Galbraith's views on a broad range of issues. Chapter 22, pages 413–417, contains a more complete presentation of the Galbraithian position on a modern industrial economy.

Exhibit 16-8 The Estimated Income Elasticity of Demand for Selected Products

Low income elasticity	
Fuel	0.38
Electricity	0.50
Food	0.51
Tobacco	0.64
Hospital care	0.69
High income elasticity	
Private education	2.46
New cars	2.45
Recreation–amusements	1.57
Alcohol	1.54

SOURCE: Hendrik S. Houthakker and Lester D. Taylor, *Consumer Demand in the United States 1929–1970.* Cambridge, Massachusetts: Harvard Univ. Press, 1966.

HOW DOES INCOME INFLUENCE DEMAND?

As income expands, the demand for most goods will increase. **Income elasticity** indicates the responsiveness of the demand for a product to a change in income. It is defined as the percent change in quantity demanded divided by the percent change in income.

As Exhibit 16-8 shows, the income elasticity coefficients for products vary, although they will normally be positive. Air travel, recreation, motel accommodations, new cars, private education, and swimming pools all have a high income elasticity. In contrast, business travel, fuel, electricity, potatoes, and tobacco have a low income elasticity. A few commodities, such as navy beans, low quality meat cuts, and bus travel, have a negative income elasticity. Economists have termed them inferior goods. As income expands, the demand for inferior goods will decline.

WHY DO CONSUMERS BUY THAT?

Did you ever wonder why a friend spent hard-earned money on something that you would not have even if it were free? Tastes differ, and as we have already shown, they influence demand. What determines preferences? Why do people like one thing, but not another? For the most part, economists have been unconcerned about factors that determine the preferences of consumers. The reason for this view is related to the economist's concept of choice. Choice reveals preferences. An individual chooses an alternative because he expects it to yield greater pleasure than costs. Few economists have concerned themselves with "why" a product or activity yields satisfaction, or why the individual thinks it will yield satisfaction. However, a few points about consumer preferences should be brought out.

First, the *homo sapiens* is a complex creature. He may prefer filet mignon to hash or football games to opera for a variety of reasons, some functional and others purely subjective. Functional reasons are often important: Housing protects us from the elements, food helps to cure hunger pains, and medical care is sometimes essential to the preservation of life. But clearly subjective factors are also important: Diamonds have little functional value, yet many consumers pay high prices for them. Functionally speaking, a diet of navy beans, rice, turnip greens, and milk is as nourishing as the diet of most college students and it would be much cheaper. Yet, such a diet would satisfy the subjective needs of few students. Consumers have different subjective needs, but these needs influence the decisions of each of us.

Second, the decisions of others often exert an influence on individual choices. We may purchase some products because they are fashionable or currently in style. We want to get on the bandwagon. Conversely, other products may be purchased because they are distinctive. They have "snob appeal," setting one apart from the crowd.[9] Swimming pools, sailboats, Cadillacs, expensive jewelry, and similar goods are often purchased because of their ability to distinguish one's consumption pattern. Goods need not be expensive in order to possess snob appeal. One could argue that the attraction of old Army jackets, patched blue jeans, and even "the no-bra look" is related to the distinctiveness that these products bestow upon their consumers.

Third, advertising must exert some influence on the choices of consumers. If it does not, advertisers made a $25 billion mistake in 1973! But *how* does it affect the consumer? Does it simply provide him with valuable information about product quality, price, and availability? Or does it use repetition and misleading information to manipulate the consumer? Economists are not of one opinion. The following discussion analyzes the issue.

Advertising—The Views of Its Critics and Defenders

Controversies in Economics

As Exhibit 16-9 illustrates, advertising expenditures in 1973 amounted to $25 billion, slightly less than 2 percent of GNP. What useful services did these expenditures provide? Could the funds have been better expended in an alternative manner? Advertising has both critics and defenders among economists. The following discussion highlights the viewpoint of both.

What is the Purpose of Advertising?

DEFENDER: The major purpose of advertising is to provide information. Advertising often provides consumers with valuable information on price, quality, and availability (for example, where a good can be purchased). Advertising promotes competition and reduces the consumer's shopping time—his search cost. When improved products are developed, advertising permits the sellers to spread the information quickly, breaking down the competitive advantage of established firms. Newspaper advertising, containing information on bargain prices and product availability, enables shoppers to make

---

[9]See Harvey Leibenstein, "Bandwagon, Snob, and Veblen Effects in the Theory of Consumer Demand," *Quarterly Journal of Economics*, May 1950, and R. Joseph Monsen and Anthony Downs, "Public Goods and Private Status," *The Public Interest*, 1971, for a more complete discussion of bandwagon and snob effects.

Exhibit 16-9   Advertising Expenditures by Medium, 1973

Advertising medium	ESTIMATED EXPENDITURES, 1973	
	Millions of dollars	Percentage of total
Newspaper	8,625	34.3
Radio	1,625	6.5
Television	4,565	18.1
Magazines	1,470	5.9
Direct mail	3,580	14.2
Outdoor	310	1.2
Miscellaneous	4,965	19.8
Total	25,140	100.0

SOURCE: *The Statistical Abstract of the United States—1975.*

more intelligent choices. Classified advertising helps to bring buyers and sellers together in the marketplace.

CRITIC: Of course, certain types of advertising do promote consumer awareness, but noninformative television, radio, and billboard advertising can hardly be defended on these grounds. The purpose of advertising is to convince the consumer to buy, to increase the demand for the advertised product. Rather than simply providing information, persuasive advertising often seeks to create an image for a product that bears little relationship to reality. Secret ingredients that reduce cavities and keep one "extra dry" do little to enlighten consumers. Many television commercials leave the viewer with the image that consumption of product X will make the consumer more distinctive, more popular, more respected, and even more likely to be seduced by members of the opposite sex. In reality, these attributes, particularly the latter, are well beyond the delivery capabilities of the products. These are not efforts to inform the consumer, rather their purpose is to misinform, to "brainwash" the potential buyer.

Does Advertising Mold the Preferences of Consumers?

DEFENDER: If a product does not meet the preferences of consumers, no amount of advertising can induce them to buy it. How much advertising would it take to convince consumers to use candles rather than electric light bulbs, horse-drawn carriages rather than cars, or scrolls rather than books? True, we sometimes like to revert temporarily to past ways of accomplishing things out of a sense of nostalgia. But consistently consumers are going to choose products that are best at removing obstacles that diminish personal satisfaction. Advertising can do little to change their concept of what these obstacles are.

The junkyards of Madison Avenue are full of advertising campaigns that failed to sway the real world consumer. The introduction of the Edsel was accompanied by the most extensive advertising campaign ever undertaken by a major auto producer. Edsel was advertised much more heavily than the Falcon and Mustang, two later models introduced by Ford. The latter two models were successful because they met the preferences of consumers, the Edsel was a failure because it did not.

Much additional evidence exists. Advertising and the promotion of designers failed to convince women to go "maxi" in 1971. The market shares of three heavily advertised detergents—Rinso, Super Suds, and Oxydol—fell from 48 percent in 1948 to 5 percent in 1953, despite the promotional efforts of Madison Avenue. The market shares of three heavily advertised cigarette brands—Camel, Lucky Strike, and Chesterfield—fell from 42 percent in 1956 to 18 percent 10 years later.

Even if businesses could manipulate consumer wants through advertising, it is legitimate to ask why they would want to do so. Why would a businessman incur the necessary expenditures to create new wants, when lots of unsatisfied wants already exist? Why not simply concentrate on trying to satisfy already existing wants? Profit-maximizing business firms can be expected to choose the simplest route to economic gain. And the simplest route, in this case, is to decide to satisfy already existing wants rather than trying to create new ones.

CRITIC: The defenders of consumer sovereignty are fond of pointing out that advertising campaigns do not always convince the consumer to buy the product. Ford heavily advertised the Edsel, but it flopped. From time to time new colas are heralded, but the dominancy of Coke continues. These isolated examples do not prove that producers do not manipulate consumer preferences. They only show that opinion molding is, at this point in time, an imperfect science.

If consumers really wanted a product, advertising would not be necessary to convince them to buy it. You do not have to convince a freezing person of his need for a coat on a cold winter day. When commodities are functional, consumers will choose them independent of advertising. Contrast this with the so-called desire of the consumer for silk shirts, extra dry deodorants, germ-killing mouthwashes, or super-whitener toothpastes. Producers have to convince consumers that they have the desire for such products.

Other actions of producers have promoted artificial desires among consumers. The advertising of almost all products is used to promote the "keep up with the Jones" syndrome. You must get a color television, a swimming pool, or a third car because your neighbor has done so. Such items will make you distinctive this year, and others will surely be promoted to make you distinctive next year.

Does Advertising Distort the Real Preferences of Consumers?

CRITIC: The purpose of advertising is to alter the decisions of consumers. Little of value can be gleaned from the soap, toothpaste, or beer commercials that cover your television screens. Yet, advertising of this variety induces consumers to pay high prices for well-known products, while superior, unadvertised products are often available at lower prices. In general, the choices of consumers are distorted toward widely advertised products.

In addition, as Professor Galbraith has argued, advertising distorts private–public sector choices. In the words of Galbraith, "The engines of mass communication . . . assail the eyes and ears of the community on behalf of more beer but not of more schools. Even in the conventional wisdom it will scarcely be contended that this leads to an equal choice between the two." [10]

---

[10] Galbraith, *The Affluent Society*, p. 205.

DEFENDER: Okay, so advertising alters the choices of consumers. But this alone is indicative of neither a strength nor weakness. There is nothing sacred about the set of choices that would result in the absence of advertising. Inasmuch as advertising provides the consumer with information, there is good reason to believe that it will help him make better choices.

Is Advertising Wasteful?

CRITIC: The major point is the sizable share of advertising expenditures that are noninformative. They do not help the consumer make better choices. As Exhibit 16-9 shows, expenditures for television, radio, and outdoor advertising come to $5.5 billion, approximately one-quarter of the total. For the most part, the advertising of these media, particularly television, is noninformative.

DEFENDER: Exhibit 16-9 also shows that newspaper, magazine, and direct mail account for well over half of all advertising expenditures. By and large, these media provide informative advertising. Thus, the majority of advertising is not of the variety on which critics tend to focus.

In addition, it is misleading to argue that radio and television advertising is wasteful. It does provide the viewer with free programing. The nature of advertising on these media reflect the system that we use to pay for radio and television programing. Elimination of this advertising would simultaneously require an alternative form of program financing—for example, pay television or public television with higher taxation. The issue is not so simple as merely pointing out that advertising on these media is sometimes noninformative, as viewed by the critics.

CRITIC: Often the effects of advertising competitive products tend to cancel each other out. A multimillion dollar advertising campaign by a soap, cigarette, or automobile manufacturer is largely offset by multimillion dollar campaigns waged by rivals. Each firm ends up with about the same share of the market. But the advertising expenditures result in higher costs and therefore higher prices. The consumer pays the bill for this wasteful duplication.

DEFENDER: Firms do not have to advertise. Neither do consumers have to purchase advertised products. When advertising results in higher prices without providing information and other compensating benefits to consumers, it will be unprofitable for the seller. All products yield both subjective and functional benefits. If consumers are willing to pay more for heavily advertised products, these products must yield them sufficient benefits to offset the higher prices. If this were not so, consumers would buy the cheaper, nonadvertised products.

What Can Be Done to Eliminate Some of the Shortcomings of Advertising?

CRITIC: First, legal restrictions against deceptive advertising need to be vigorously enforced. Producers should not be allowed to make claims that are beyond the capabilities of their products. Second, we need to make a careful distinction between informative and noninformative advertising. Commercials that are designed to exploit our senses or lack of knowledge should be prohibited. Perhaps the Federal Trade Commission or some other "watchdog" agency should be granted the power to prohibit noninformative advertising. Advertising need not be wasteful. Let's take steps to assure that it will be informative.

DEFENDER: Unfair and deceptive advertising is already illegal under the Federal Trade Commission Act. It is the dishonesty, not the advertising, that is wrong. Dishonesty should be condemned regardless of whether it is contained in commercial advertising or political speeches. Perhaps current legislation concerning the former should be extended to cover the latter.

Distinguishing between good (informative) and bad (noninformative) advertising is an idea that sounds good, but in reality it would be counterproductive. Somebody, no doubt a government agency, must decide what's good and what's bad. If we could be assured that the agency would be staffed by "regulatory saints," borrowing a phrase from George Stigler, it would make sense to move ahead. But past experience indicates this is not the case. With the passage of time, such a regulatory agency would be controlled by established business firms and the advertising media. Firms that played ball with the dominant political block controlling the agency would be allowed to promote their products unmolested. Less powerful and less political rivals would be hassled. Firms would be required to submit both necessary and unnecessary reports. The additional paperwork would place still another constraint on the entry of new rivals and the survival ability of small businesses. The idea pits well-organized special interest groups (established firms and the advertising media) against the disorganized consumer. Under these circumstances the political process is stacked against the latter. Predictably such a regulatory agency would limit competition, add to cost, and result in higher prices than would exist in its absence.

Discussion Questions

1. What are the major arguments against advertising? What are its major strengths? Do you agree with the critics or defenders of advertising? Explain.
2. What do you think could be done to correct some of the shortcomings of commercial advertising? Might corrective action cause other problems? Explain.

CHAPTER LEARNING OBJECTIVES

1. The demand schedule indicates the amount of a good that consumers would be willing to buy at each potential price. The quantity demanded of a product will be negatively related to its price. A reduction in the price of a product reduces the opportunity cost of consuming it. At the lower price, many consumers will substitute the now cheaper good for other products. In contrast, higher prices would induce consumers to buy less, as they would turn to substitutes that are now *relatively* cheaper.

2. The market demand curve reflects the demand of individuals. It is simply the horizontal sum of the demand curves of individuals in the market area.

3. In addition to price, the demand for a product will be influenced by the **(a)** level of consumer income, **(b)** distribution of income among consumers, **(c)** price of related products (substitutes and complements), **(d)** preferences of consumers, **(e)** population in the market area, and **(f)** consumer expectations about the future price of the product. Changes in any of these six factors will cause the *demand* for the product to change (the entire curve to shift).

4. Time, like money, is scarce to consumers. Consumers will consider both time and money costs when making decisions. Other things constant, a reduction in the time cost of a good will induce consumers to purchase more of it.

5. Price elasticity reveals the responsiveness of the amount purchased to a change in price. When there are good substitutes available and the item forms a sizable component of the consumer's budget, its demand will tend to be more elastic. Typically, the price elasticity of a product will increase with the passage of time.

6. Both functional and subjective factors will influence the demand for a product. Some goods will be chosen because they have "snob appeal." Goods may also have a bandwagon appeal, fulfilling a consumer's desire to be fashionable. Observation suggests that goods are demanded for a variety of reasons.

7. The precise effect of advertising on consumer decisions is difficult to sift out. The magnitude of advertising by profit-seeking business firms is strong evidence that it influences consumer decisions. Advertising often reduces the search time of consumers and helps them make more informed choices. However, a sizable share, though probably substantially less than half, of all advertising expenditures are for largely noninformational messages. Competitive advertising of products is sometimes offsetting. Many economists, though certainly not all, feel that this variety of advertising is wasteful. There is no easy solution. Government regulation, the most often mentioned solution, would also have a cost, both in terms of administrative resources and the potential for abuse.

IMPORTANT TERMS TO REMEMBER

Marginal utility: The additional utility received by a person from the consumption of an additional unit of a good within a given time period.

Law of diminishing marginal utility: A basic economic postulate which states that as the consumption of a commodity increases, eventually the marginal utility derived from consuming more of the commodity (per unit time) will decline. Marginal utility may decline even though total utility continues to increase, albeit at a reduced rate.

Substitutes: Products that are related such that an increase in the price of one will cause an increase in demand for the other (examples: butter and margarine, Chevrolets and Fords).

Complements: Products that are usually consumed jointly. Therefore an increase in the price of one will cause the demand for the other to fall (examples: lamps and light bulbs).

Price elasticity of demand: The percent change in the quantity demanded of a product divided by the percent change in its price.

Income elasticity: The percent change in the quantity demanded of a product divided by the percent change in consumer income. It measures the responsiveness of the demand for a good to a change in income.

THE ECONOMIC WAY OF THINKING—DISCUSSION QUESTIONS

1. What impact did the substantially higher gasoline prices of the mid-1970s have on **(a)** the demand for big cars, **(b)** the demand for small cars, **(c)** the incentive to experiment and develop electric and other nongas-powered cars, **(d)** the demand for gasoline (*Hint:* Be careful.), and **(e)** the demand for Florida vacations?

2. "As the price of beef rose, the demand of consumers began to decline. Economists estimate that a 5 percent rise in beef prices will cause demand to decline by 1 percent." Indicate the two errors in this quote.

3. The following chart presents data on the price of fuel oil, the amount of it demanded, and the demand for insulation. **(a)** Calculate the price elasticity of demand for fuel oil as its price rises from 30 to 50 cents. From 50 to 70 cents. **(b)** Are fuel oil and insulation substitutes or complements? How can you tell?

	FUEL OIL	INSULATION
Price per gallon (cents)	*Quantity demanded (millions of gallons)*	*Quantity demanded (millions of tons)*
30	100	30
50	90	35
70	60	40

4. What are the major factors that influence a product's price elasticity of demand? Explain why these factors are important.

5. Do you think that television advertising—as it is conducted by the automobile industry, for example—is wasteful? If so, what would you propose to do about it? Indicate why your proposal would be better than the current situation.

6. What's Wrong with This Way of Thinking?

"Economics is unable to explain the value of goods in a sensible manner. A quart of water is much cheaper than a quart of oil. Yet, water is essential to both animal and plant life. Without it we could not survive. How can oil be more valuable than water? Yet economics says that it is."

17

COSTS AND PRODUCER DECISIONS

A class in economics would be a success if students gained from it an understanding of the meaning of cost in all its many aspects. [J. M. Clark, 1923]

Consumer choices provided the foundation for market demand analysis. Similarly, the choices of producers will form the underlying foundation for our analysis of production costs and market supply. What factors influence production cost? Why are costs important? Does it ever make sense to sell below costs? We discuss these and related questions in this chapter.

THE BUSINESS FIRM

The business firm is an entity designed to organize raw materials, labor, and machines with the goal of producing goods and/or services. Firms (a) purchase productive resources from households and other firms, (b) transform them into a different commodity, and (c) sell the transformed product or service to consumers.

Economies may differ in the amount of freedom they allow business decision-makers. They may also differ in the incentive structure that is used to induce productive business activity. Nonetheless, every society relies on business firms to organize resources and transform them into products. In Western economies most business firms choose their own price, output level, and productive techniques. In socialist countries government policy will often establish the selling price and constrain the actions of the business firm in various other ways. But the central position of the business firm as the organized productive unit is universal to both.

In capitalist countries most firms are owned privately. The owners, we might call them entrepreneurs, are the individuals who risk their wealth on the success of the business. If the firm is successful and makes profits, these financial gains will go to the owners. Conversely, if things go bad and the firm suffers losses, the owners must bear the consequences. Thus, the wealth position of the entrepreneurial owners will be directly influenced by the success or failure of the firm.

There are three major alternative legal structures under which business firms may be organized—proprietorships, partnerships, and corporations.

Proprietorships

A proprietorship is a business firm that is owned by a single individual who is fully liable for the debts of the firm. Oftentimes the proprietor will work directly for the firm, providing managerial and other labor services, in addition to his ownership responsibilities. Many small businesses, including neighborhood grocery stores, barbershops, and farms, are business proprietorships. They are owned by a single individual. As Exhibit 17-1 shows, proprietorships comprised 78 percent of all business firms in 1971. But because most proprietorships are small, they generated only 11 percent of all business receipts.

Partnerships

A partnership consists of two or more persons acting as co-owners of a business firm. The partners will share both risks and responsibilities in some prearranged manner. There is no difference between a proprietorship and a partnership in terms of owner liability. In both cases, the owners are fully liable for all business debts incurred by the firm. Many law, medical, and accounting firms are organized along partnership lines. This form of business structure accounts for only 8 percent of the total number of firms and 5 percent of all business receipts.

Corporations

Measured in terms of business receipts, the corporate business structure is by far the most important. In 1971, while corporations comprised only 14 percent of all business firms, they accounted for 84 percent of all business receipts. What are the distinctive characteristics of the corporation? What accounts for its attractiveness?

Exhibit 17-1   How Business Firms Are Organized

	TYPES OF BUSINESS FIRMS, 1971		
Business structure	Number (in thousands)	Percentage of all firms	Percentage of all business receipts
Proprietorships	9745	78	11
Partnerships	959	8	5
Corporations	1733	14	84

SOURCE: *The Statistical Abstract of the United States—1975.*

First, the stockholders of the corporation are the legal owners of the firm. Any profits of the firm belong to them. But their liability is strictly limited. They are liable for corporate debts only to the extent of their original investment. If a corporation owes you money, you cannot sue the stockholders directly. You can, of course, sue the corporation. But what if it goes bankrupt? Then you and others to whom the firm owes money will just be out of luck.

Second, the limited liability makes it possible for corporations to attract investment funds from a large number of "owners" who do not participate in the day-to-day management of the firm. The stockholders of many large corporations simply hire managers to operate the firm. Thus, there is often a divorce between corporate owners and managers.

A third characteristic that makes the corporate form attractive is the ease with which ownership can be transferred. If an owner should die, his ownership rights can be sold by his heirs to another without disrupting the business firm. Thus, the corporation acquires a perpetual life. Similarly, if a stockholder becomes unhappy with the way a corporation is run, he too can bail out merely by selling his stock.

In a sense, the managers of a large corporation might be thought of as trained experts hired by the stockholders to run the firm. The decisions of stockholders to buy and sell stock (ownership rights) will mirror the confidence of investors in the management of a firm. If both current and prospective stockholders feel that the managers are doing a good job, the demand for the firm's stock will be strong. Stock prices will reflect this demand. Conversely, when a large number of the current stockholders want to sell their shares because they are dissatisfied with the current management, the demand for the firm's stock will weaken, causing its price to tumble. Falling stock prices will often lead to a shake up in the management of the firm.

CALCULATING ECONOMIC COSTS AND PROFITS

Business firms, regardless of size, will give some attention to profits. But what are profits? Most people, including many businessmen, think of profits as what is left over from their sales revenues after making their payments for raw materials, labor, machines, and similar inputs. The problem with this concept is that it may exclude some of the firm's costs.

The key to the understanding of economic profit is our old friend—opportunity cost. The firm incurs a cost whenever it utilizes a resource, thereby requiring the resource owner to forego his highest valued alternative. These costs might be either explicit or implicit. **Explicit costs** result when the firm makes a monetary payment to resource owners. Money wages, interest, and rental payments are a measure of what the firm gives up in order to employ the services of labor and capital resources. But firms will usually also incur **implicit costs**—costs associated with the use of resources owned by the firm, even though they do not involve a direct money payment. Nonetheless, they are costs, as the resources owned by the firm could be used in other ways if they were not tied up in the productive process.

How do implicit costs influence profits? Consider a corner grocery store owned and operated by Bo Smith. Bo works full time as the manager, chief cashier, and janitor.

He has $25,000 of his own money invested in the store, providing floor space and other necessary equipment. Last year Bo's total sales were $60,000, while he paid his suppliers and employees $50,000. His revenues exceeded his explicit cost by $10,000. Did Bo make a profit last year? His accounting statement may suggest that he did. However, if Bo had not been tied up with his own business, he could have earned $10,000 working for the A&P. Similarly, if he did not have a $25,000 personal investment in the store, he could be drawing 8 percent interest ($2000) on these funds. He is foregoing $10,000 of earnings and $2000 interest in order to operate his grocery store. His total costs, both explicit and implicit, were $62,000. The total revenues of Bo's grocery were less than the opportunity cost of the resources utilized. From the economist's viewpoint, Bo incurred a $2000 loss.

Accounting costs often exclude implicit cost. For example, they always omit the opportunity cost associated with the use of the equity capital of the owners. Thus, accounting costs will understate the opportunity cost of production, while **accounting profits** will overstate the level of economic profits. As Bo's grocery illustrates, a firm's accounting statement might show a profit, even though the firm was actually earning economic losses.

Henceforth, when discussing the costs of the firm, both explicit and implicit cost will be included. When the firm's total revenues exceed its total costs (both explicit and implicit), **economic profits** will arise. Economic profits exist only when the business is earning an excess over and above the opportunity cost of utilizing the assets owned by the firm. Losses result when the earnings of the firm are insufficient to cover both explicit and implicit costs. When the firm's revenues are just equal to its costs, both explicit and implicit, economic profits will be zero. Note that zero economic profits do not imply that the firm is about to go out of business. On the contrary, they indicate that the owners are receiving exactly the market rate of return on their investment (assets owned by the firm).

TOTAL COSTS, AVERAGE COSTS, AND MARGINAL COSTS

The **total cost** of producing a specific output level is the sum of the explicit and implicit costs incurred from the employment of all the necessary factors of production. For example, if a craftsman and his tools are combined with lumber and other raw materials to produce five coffee tables, the craftsman's total cost for the five coffee tables would be (a) the opportunity cost of the craftsman and his tools plus (b) the payment for lumber and materials required to produce the tables.

Exhibit 17-2 demonstrates a hypothetical total cost schedule for the production of coffee tables. If only one table is produced, the cost of the necessary lumber is $30 and the craftsman's opportunity cost is $50. If the craftsman were not producing tables, he could utilize his time in another way, perhaps producing chairs. His evaluation of the highest valued alternative foregone because of the time required to produce one table (that is, his opportunity cost) is $50.

As the craftsman produces additional tables his average production time per table is likely to decline because of "learning by doing" and the opportunity to incorporate mass production techniques when larger outputs are planned and produced. Therefore,

Exhibit 17-2   Factor Costs and Cost Schedules

Output (tables)	Total payments for lumber and materials	Implicit opportunity cost of the craftsman and his tools	Total cost	Average total cost	Marginal cost
1	$30	$50	$80	$80	$80
2	60	90	150	75	70
3	90	120	210	70	60
4	120	148	268	67	58
5	150	175	325	65	57

since it does not take the craftsman twice as long to produce two tables, his opportunity costs at that level will be less than twice the comparable figure for one table. When two tables are produced the craftsman's opportunity cost will be $90 and his total production cost would be $150, including $60 for materials. As additional tables are built, total costs increase. They are always equal to the craftsman's opportunity cost (an implicit cost) plus the payments for the necessary materials (an explicit cost).

The **average total cost** of production is the total cost divided by the total number of units produced. For example, as Exhibit 17-2 shows, the average total cost of producing two coffee tables is $75, the total cost ($150) divided by the level of output (2). When three units are produced, the average total cost is $70—$210 divided by 3. The average total costs for other output levels are also presented.

How much does it cost the carpenter to produce each *additional* table? This question refers to what economists call marginal cost. **Marginal cost** is the change in total cost that results from the production of one additional unit. The carpenter's marginal cost for the first unit was $80. But how much does the second table cost? Right, $70. Total costs go up by $70 as the second table is produced. Marginal costs will decline as more tables are produced. This should not be surprising since the necessary time requirement for the craftsman to build *additional* coffee tables is less. Thus, the craftsman's opportunity cost for each *additional* coffee table will decline, reducing his marginal costs.

RATE OF OUTPUT AND THE FIRM'S COST IN THE SHORT RUN

A firm cannot adjust its output instantaneously. Time plays an important role in the production process. Economists often speak of the **short run** as a time period so short that the firm is unable to alter its present plant size. In the short run the firm is "stuck" with its existing plant and heavy equipment. They are "fixed" for a finite time period.

How long is the short run? That will vary from industry to industry. For some industries substantial changes in plant size can be accomplished in a few months. In other industries, particularly those that utilize assembly lines and mass production techniques (for example, aircraft and automobiles), the short run might be a year or even several years.

As the firm alters its rate of output in the short run, how will per unit cost be affected? Initially, let us look at this question intuitively. In the short run the firm can vary output by utilizing its fixed plant size more (or less) intensively. One can clearly think of two extremes that will result in high costs per unit of output. First, if a plant is underutilized, the average cost per unit of output will be high. A large plant operating substantially below its capacity level will be costly and inefficient. Average costs would decline if the plant were more fully utilized. Second, overutilization can also result in high per unit cost. An overutilized plant will result in congestion, waiting time for machines, and similar costly delays. Thus, both overutilization and underutilization of a firm's fixed plant size will lead to high per unit cost.

Diminishing Returns and Cost Curves

The law of diminishing returns can be utilized to illustrate the validity of our intuitive logic. The **law of diminishing returns** states that as more and more units of a variable factor are applied to a fixed amount of other resources, eventually output will increase by correspondingly smaller amounts. Therefore, measured in terms of their impact on output, the returns to the variable factor will diminish.

The law sounds complicated, but fortunately it is not. It is more or less common sense. Have you ever noticed that as you apply a single resource more intensively, eventually the resource will tend to accomplish less and less? For example, the gain to a student from the tenth hour of cramming for an exam is typically less than for the first or second hour of study time.[1] Similarly, as a farmer applies fertilizer more and more intensively to an acre of land (a fixed factor), eventually the application of additional 100 pound units of fertilizer will expand his wheat yield by successively smaller amounts.

Essentially, the law of diminishing returns is a constraint imposed by nature. If it were not valid, it would be possible to raise all of the world's foodstuff on an acre of land, or even in a flowerpot. Suppose that we did *not* experience diminishing returns when we applied more labor and fertilizer to land. If this were true, would it ever make sense to cultivate any of the less fertile land? Of course not. We would be able to increase output more rapidly by simply applying another unit of labor and fertilizer to the world's most fertile flowerpot! But, of course, this is a fairy tale. The law of diminishing returns does apply.

What does the law of diminishing returns imply about the firm's cost? Since the firm's plant size is fixed in the short run, eventually the law of diminishing returns will apply to the use of the variable factors. Output will expand less and less as the variable factors are applied more intensively to the firm's fixed plant size. Once diminishing returns are confronted, successively larger amounts of the variable factors will be required to expand output by an additional unit. What impact will this have

---

[1] Why does each additional hour of study time improve your grade less than previous ones? What do you study first? The most important material. As you continue studying, more and more time is allocated to less important tasks, the study of less relevant material. Thus, your return from *additional* hours of study will diminish. It is highly recommended that all economics students carry out this experiment for themselves.

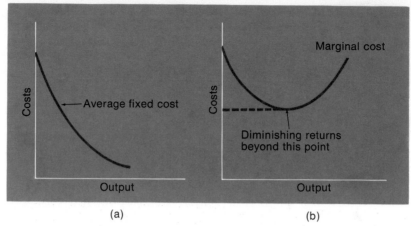

(a)   (b)

Exhibit 17-3   General Characteristics of the Short-Run Average Fixed and Marginal Cost Curves

The average fixed costs will always decline as output expands [frame (a)]. Initially, marginal costs may either decline or remain constant (the dashed line) as the rate of output is increased [frame (b)]. But as diminishing returns set in, marginal costs will rise.

on the firm's marginal costs? Because it takes more and more of the variable factors to expand output, marginal costs will rise. As the plant is used more intensively, the marginal costs of producing additional units will rise higher and higher (see Exhibit 17-3b).

Since the firm utilizes both variable and fixed resources in the short run, costs can also be divided into two components—variable costs and fixed costs. **Variable costs** will change as the firm alters its rate of output. For example, an expansion in output would require more labor and raw materials. Expenditures on these and similar resources will vary with rate of output.

On the other hand, **fixed costs** will remain unchanged as output is altered. The firm's insurance premiums, its property taxes, the opportunity cost of utilizing its fixed assets—these costs will be present whether the firm produces a large or a small rate of output. Neither will they vary with output. They are "fixed" as long as the firm remains in business. Fixed costs can be avoided only if the firm closes down.

How will fixed cost influence the per unit cost of a firm? Remember, the firm's fixed cost will be the same whether the output is 1, 100, or 1000. What will happen to **average fixed cost** (AFC) as output expands? Since average fixed costs are simply fixed costs divided by output, AFC will always decline as output is increased (see Exhibit 17-3a).

Exhibit 17-4 summarizes the general characteristics of the firm's short-run cost curves. When output is small relative to plant size, both the average fixed and average total costs will be high because the existing plant facilities are underutilized. As output expands, both AFC and ATC will decline. Will ATC continue to decline? No. When diminishing returns are confronted, marginal costs will begin to rise. Eventually, they will exceed average total cost. When marginal costs are greater than the average total cost, ATC will increase. It is easy to see why. What happens when an above-average

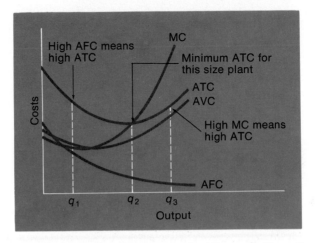

Exhibit 17-4   The Firm's Short-Run Cost Curves

The diagram shows the general shape of the firm's cost curves for a specific plant size. When output is small relative to plant size (for example, q_1), high average fixed costs will cause per unit cost to be high. When a large output (relative to plant size) such as q_3 is produced, per unit cost will be high because of the high cost of producing the marginal units. Thus the short-run ATC curve will be U-shaped. ATC will be minimized at output q_2.

student is added to a class? The class average goes up, right? What then would happen if a unit of above-average cost is added to output? Average total cost will rise. Therefore, the firm's marginal cost curve will cross the ATC curve at its minimum.

Our analysis reveals that the short-run average total cost curve will be U-shaped, as pictured by Exhibit 17-4. Just as our intuition suggests, per unit cost will be high for both an underutilized plant (with a high AFC) and an overutilized plant (with a high MC).

Exhibit 17-5 presents hypothetical numerical short-run cost schedules for Ron's Roller Skate Factory. The average total cost of producing roller skates is very high when output

Exhibit 17-5   Hypothetical Numerical Short-Run Cost Schedules of Ron's Roller Skates, Inc.

(1) Output per day	(2) Total fixed cost	(3) Total variable cost	(4) Total cost (2) + (3)	(5) Average fixed cost (2) ÷ (1)	(6) Average variable cost (3) ÷ (1)	(7) Average total cost (4) ÷ (1)	(8) Marginal cost $\Delta(4) \div \Delta(1)$
0	$50	$0	$50	—	—	—	—
1	50	15	65	$50.00	$15.00	$65.00	$15
2	50	27	77	25.00	13.50	38.50	12
3	50	37	87	16.67	12.33	29.00	10
4	50	45	95	12.50	11.25	23.75	8
5	50	55	105	10.00	11.00	21.00	10
6	50	67	117	8.33	11.17	19.50	12
7	50	82	132	7.14	11.71	18.86	15
8	50	100	150	6.25	12.50	18.75	18
9	50	124	174	5.56	13.78	19.33	24
10	50	154	204	5.00	15.40	20.40	30

is low, primarily because of the high average fixed cost. Initially, marginal costs are less than ATC. When more than four roller skates per day are produced, diminishing returns set in.[2] Rising marginal costs result in increasing average total cost, as the rate of output exceeds eight units per day. The student should observe the data of Exhibit 17-5 carefully to make sure that the relationships among the various cost curves are fully understood. The thumbnail sketch summarizes these relationships.

THUMBNAIL SKETCH—Relationships among the Firm's Costs

(1) Total cost includes both explicit and implicit costs.

(2) Total cost equals fixed cost plus variable cost.

(3) Marginal cost equals change in total cost per unit of output.

(4) Average total cost equals total cost divided by output.

(5) Average fixed cost equals fixed cost divided by output.

(6) Average variable cost equals variable cost divided by output.

(7) Average total cost equals average fixed cost plus average variable cost.

COSTS IN THE LONG RUN

The short-run analysis relates costs to output *for a specific size of plant*. But firms are not committed, forever, to their existing plant. The **long run** is a time period of sufficient length to allow a firm the opportunity to alter its plant size and all other factors of production. All of the resources of the firm are variable in the long-run.

How will the firm's choice of plant size affect production costs? Exhibit 17-6 illustrates the short-run average total cost curves for three alternative plant sizes, ranging from small to large. If these three plant sizes were the only possible choices, which one would be best? That would depend on the rate of output that the firm expected

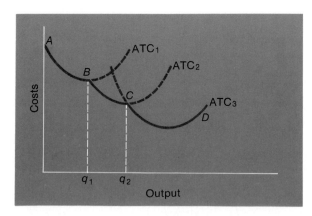

Exhibit 17-6 The Long-Run Average Cost

The short-run average cost curves are shown for three alternative plant sizes. If these three were the only possible plant sizes, the long-run average cost curve would be *ABCD*.

[2]How can you tell this from the data of Exhibit 17-5? (*Hint:* Look at the firm's MC schedule.)

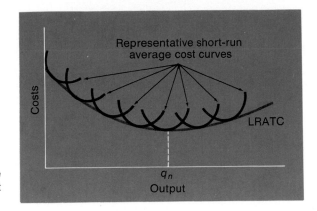

Exhibit 17-7 The Planning Curve

When many alternative plant sizes are possible, the long-run average total cost curve LRATC is mapped out.

to produce. The smallest plant would have the lowest cost if an output rate of less than q_1 were produced. The medium-sized plant would be the least cost method of producing output rates between q_1 and q_2. For any output level above q_2, the largest plant would be cost efficient.

The long-run average cost curve shows the minimum average cost of producing each output level when the firm is free to choose among all possible alternative plant sizes. It would best be thought of as a "planning curve," because it reflects the expected per unit cost of producing alternative rates of output while plants are still in the blueprint stage.

Exhibit 17-6 illustrates the long-run average total cost curve when only three plant sizes are possible. The planning curve $ABCD$ is mapped out. However, given sufficient time, firms can usually choose among many plants of varying size. Exhibit 17-7 presents the long-run planning curve under these circumstances. A smooth planning curve results. Each short-run average cost curve will be tangent to the long-run planning curve. However, the tangency will occur at the least cost output level for the short-run curve only when the long-run curve is parallel to the x axis (for example, q_n, Exhibit 17-7).

No single plant size could produce the alternative output rates at the costs indicated by the planning curve. The long-run average cost curve merely outlines the expected average production costs for each of a large number of plants which differ in size.

Size of Firm and Per Unit Cost

Will larger firms have lower minimum per unit costs than smaller ones? The answer to this question will differ between industries. However, there is a sound basis for *initially* expecting some cost reductions from large scale production methods. Why? Large firms will typically produce a large total volume of output.[3] Volume of output

---

[3]Throughout this section, we will assume that larger plants necessarily plan a larger volume of output than their smaller counterparts. Reality approximates these conditions. Firms will choose large plants because they are planning to produce a large volume.

connotes the total number of units of a product that the firm expects to produce.[4] There are three major reasons why per unit costs will initially decline as firms plan a larger total volume of output.

1. *Adoption of Mass Production Techniques.* Oftentimes large firms will be able to utilize mass production techniques that are economical *only* when large volumes of output are planned. Mass production usually involves large development and setup costs. But once the production methods are established, marginal costs are low. Because of the large setup costs, mass production techniques are uneconomical for small volumes of output. For example, use of molds, dies, and assembly line production methods reduces the per unit cost of automobiles only when the planned volume runs into the millions. In contrast, these methods would result in high per unit costs if they were utilized to produce only a few thousand automobiles. Thus, large plants can often adopt cost-reducing methods that are uneconomical for firms producing a smaller total volume of output.

2. *Specialization.* Large scale operation results in a greater opportunity for specialized use of both labor and machines. Adam Smith noted 200 years ago that the output of a pin factory was much greater when one man draws the wire, another straightens it, a third cuts it, a fourth grinds the point, a fifth makes the head of the pin, and so on.[5] In economics the whole can sometimes be greater than the sum of the parts. Specialization provides the opportunity for persons to become exceptionally proficient at performing small but essential functions. Therefore, when each of them acts as a specialist, more is produced than if they each made the final product from start to finish.

3. *Learning by Doing.* As a firm increases the number of units manufactured, both labor and management will learn from their past mistakes. Improvements in the production process will result. Performance improves one's skills. Baseball players improve by playing and musicians improve by performing. Similarly, workers and management improve their skills as they "practice" productive techniques. This factor has been found to be tremendously important in several areas including the aircraft and automobile industries.

---

[4] Note the distinction between rate and volume of output. *Rate* of output is the number of units produced during a specific period (for example, the next six months). *Volume* is the total number of units produced during all time periods. For example, Boeing might produce two 747 airplanes per month (their rate of output), while planning to produce a volume of 100 747's during the expected life of the model. For additional information on production and costs, see Armen Alchian "Costs," in *International Encyclopedia of the Social Sciences* (New York: Macmillan, 1968, pp. 404–415) and Jack Hirshleifer, "The Firm's Cost Function: A Successful Reconstruction," *Journal of Business,* July 1962.

[5] Smith went on to state: "I have seen a small manufactory of this kind where ten men only were employed, and where some of them consequently performed two or three distinct operations. Those ten persons, therefore, could make among them upwards of forty-eight thousand pins in a day. But if they had all wrought separately and independently, and without any of them having been educated to this peculiar business, they certainly could not each of them have made twenty, perhaps not one pin in a day." (Adam Smith, *The Wealth of Nations,* 1776, pp. 4–5.)

Economies and Diseconomies of Scale

Economic theory does suggest that, at least initially, larger firms will have lower per unit costs. When per unit cost declines as output expands, **economies of scale** are present. The long-run average total cost curve will be falling.

Are diseconomies of scale possible; that is, will the long-run average costs ever be greater for large firms than for small ones? The economic justification for diseconomies of scale is less obvious (and less tenable) than for economies of scale. However, as a firm gets bigger and bigger, bureaucratic inefficiencies *may* result. Code book procedures will tend to replace managerial genius. Problems associated with coordinating activities, conveying information, and carrying out managerial directives may multiply. These factors will combine to cause rising long-term average total cost in some, though certainly not all, industries.

Exhibit 17-8 outlines three different long-run average total cost (LRATC) curves that are observed in the real world. For Exhibit 17-8a both economies and diseconomies of scale are present. Higher per unit costs will result when firms choose a plant size other than the one that minimizes the cost of producing output q, the ideal size of plant for this industry. Both plants that are larger and those that are smaller than

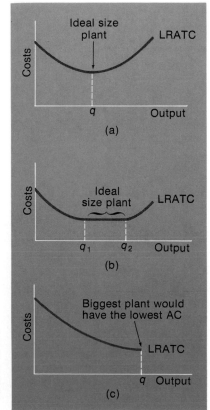

Exhibit 17-8 Three Different Types of Long-Run Average Cost Curves

Frame (a) indicates that for output levels less than q, economies of scale are present. But immediately beyond q, diseconomies of scale dominate. Frame (b) indicates that economies of scale are important until some minimum output level q_1 is obtained. But once the minimum has been attained, there is a wide range of output levels (q_1 to q_2) that are consistent with the minimum ATC for the industry. Frame (c) indicates that economies of scale exist for all relevant output levels. As we will see later, this type of long-run ATC curve has important implications for the structure of the industry.

the ideal size will experience higher per unit cost. A very narrow range of plant sizes would be possible in industries with the LRATC depicted by Exhibit 17-8a. Retail sales and agriculture might approximate these conditions.

Exhibit 17-8b demonstrates the general shape of the long-run average total cost that economists believe to exist in most industries. Initially, economies of scale are important, but once a minimum efficient scale is reached, wide variation in firm size is possible. Firms smaller than the minimum efficient size would have higher per unit costs. But firms many times larger than those of the minimum efficient scale would not gain a cost advantage. This situation is consistent with real world conditions in many industries. For example, small firms can be as efficient as larger ones in such industries as apparel, lumber, shoes, publishing, and many lines of retailing.

Exhibit 17-8c indicates that economies of scale are important for all relevant output levels. The larger the firm size, the lower the per unit cost. The long-run ATC in the telephone service industry approximates the curve of Exhibit 17-8c.

WHAT FACTORS WILL CAUSE THE FIRM'S COST CURVES TO SHIFT?

When outlining the general shapes of a firm's cost curves we assumed that certain other factors remained constant. What are those other factors and how will they affect production costs?

1. *Prices of Resources.* If the price of resources utilized should rise, the firm's cost curves will shift upward. Higher resources prices will increase the cost of producing each alternative output level. For example, what happens to the cost of producing automobiles when the price of steel rises? The production cost of automobiles would rise also.

Conversely, lower resource prices would result in cost reductions. Thus, the cost curves for any specific plant size would shift downward.

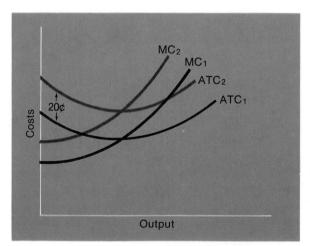

Exhibit 17-9 Taxes and Costs

A 20 cent per gallon tax on gasoline would shift both the firm's average total and marginal cost curves up by the full amount of the tax.

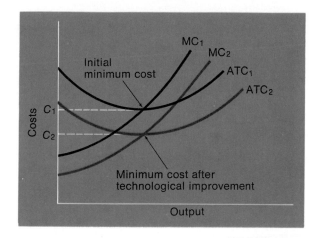

Exhibit 17-10 Egg Production, Costs, and Technological Change

Suppose that an egg producer discovers (or develops) a "super" mineral water that makes it possible to get more eggs from the same number of chickens. Because of this technological improvement, he can now produce various output levels of eggs with less feed, space, water, and labor. His cost will be reduced. The egg producer's ATC and MC curves will shift down.

2. *Taxes.*   Taxes are a component of the firm's cost. Suppose an excise tax of 20 cents was levied on each gallon of gasoline sold by a service station. What would happen to the seller's costs? They would increase. As Exhibit 17-9 shows, the firm's average total and marginal cost curves would shift upward by the amount of the tax.

3. *Technology.*   Oftentimes technological improvements will make it possible to produce a specific output with fewer resources. For example, the printing press drastically reduced the number of man-hours required to print newspapers and books. The spinning wheel reduced the man-hours necessary to weave cotton into cloth. More recently, electronic calculators, computers, and automated machines have served to reduce costs in many industries. As Exhibit 17-10 shows, a technological improvement will shift the firm's cost curves downward, reflecting the reduction in the amount of resources used to produce alternative levels of output.

COSTS AND THE ECONOMIC WAY OF THINKING

When analyzing the firm's costs, economists often present a highly mechanical, some would say unrealistic, view. The role of choice and the human decision-maker tends to be glossed over.

It is important to keep in mind that costs are incurred when choices are made. When the businessman chooses to purchase raw materials, hire a new employee, or renew the lease on his plant, he will incur costs. All of these decisions, like other choices, must be made under conditions of uncertainty. Of course, past experience acts as a useful guide, yielding valuable information to business decision-makers. Thus, they will have a good idea of the costs that will be associated with alternative decisions.

Accounting and Economic Costs

Economic costs represent opportunities that are foregone as the result of choosing an alternative. Think for a moment what the cost curves that we developed in this chapter really are. The firm's short-run marginal cost curve represents the opportunity cost of expanding output, *given the firm's current plant size.* The firm's long-run average total cost curve represents the opportunity cost per unit of output associated with varying plant sizes and rates of output, *given that the alternative plants are still on the drawing boards.*

Opportunity costs are really "expected costs"—what the decision-maker believes he is foregoing. Strictly speaking, the cost curves that we have developed cannot be derived from accounting data. Accounting costs look backward. They yield valuable information about historical costs, costs that were incurred in the past. This information serves as a guide when making current decisions. In contrast, economic (opportunity) costs look forward. They are expectations concerning costs that will be associated with current decisions.

Costs and Supply

Opportunity costs will influence decisions. Economists are interested in cost because they seek to explain the supply decisions of firms. A strictly profit-maximizing firm will compare the expected revenues derived from a decision or a course of action with the expected costs. If the expected revenues exceed costs, the course of action will be chosen since it will add to profits (or reduce losses). For example, when deciding whether to expand the current rate of output, the profit-maximizing decision-makers will compare the expected additional revenues from larger sales with the expected marginal cost. If the former exceeds the latter, output (supply) will be expanded.

Decision-makers will make long-range decisions in precisely the same way. Should the firm enlarge the size of its current plant? Again expected costs and revenues will determine the decision for a profit-maximizing firm. If the firm anticipates that market conditions are such that the expansion in plant facilities will add more to revenues (via increased sales) than costs, it will choose to expand.

How does a firm decide whether or not to enter an industry? *Before entry into the industry,* the firm will compare price with the long-run average per unit cost. If a firm expects market price to exceed its average total cost in the long run, it will gain by entering the industry. On the other hand, if a profit-maximizing entrepreneur expects that the market price of a product will be insufficient to cover even his minimum long-run average total cost, he would refuse to supply the product under such conditions.

Sunk Costs

Opportunity costs are what matter when making decisions. Historical costs associated with past decisions—economists call them **sunk costs**—should exert no direct influence on current choices. Past decisions may have been made wisely or unwisely. The outcome of these choices will provide knowledge that will be relevant to future decisions. But past choices cannot be reversed. Current choices should be based on

MYTHS OF ECONOMICS
"A good business decision-maker will never sell a product for less than its production costs."

This statement contains a grain of truth. A profit-seeking entrepreneur would not undertake a project, knowing that he would be unable to cover his costs. But the view fails to emphasize (a) the time dimension of the production process and (b) the uncertainty associated with business decisions. The production process takes time. Raw materials must be purchased, employees hired, and plants equipped. Retailers must contract with suppliers. As these decisions are made, costs will result. Many of the firm's costs of production will have been incurred long before the product is ready for marketing.

Even a good business decision-maker will not always be able to perceive the future correctly. Market conditions may change in an unexpected manner. At the time the product is ready for sale, buyers may be unwilling to pay a price that will cover the seller's past costs of production. But these past costs are no longer relevant. Current decisions must be made on the basis of current cost and revenue considerations.

Should a grocer refuse to sell oranges that are about to spoil because he cannot cover his wholesale cost? The grocer's current opportunity cost of selling the oranges may be near zero. His alternative may be to throw them in the garbage next week. Almost any price, even one far below his past costs, would be better than letting them spoil.

Consider another example. Should a homeowner who is going to temporarily relocate refuse to rent his house for $200 (if this is the best offer available) because his monthly house payment is $240? Of course not. The house payment will go on, regardless of whether or not he rents the house. If the homeowner can cover his opportunity costs, perhaps a $60 monthly fee for a property management service, he will gain by renting rather than leaving the house vacant.

Past mistakes provide useful lessons for the future. But they cannot be reversed. Bygones are bygones, even if they resulted in a business loss. Only current revenue and cost considerations are relevant to current decisions. There is no need to fret over spilt milk, burnt toast, or yesterday's business losses.

---

their expected costs and benefits. No attention should be paid to past expenses that have already been incurred.

Business decision-makers, if they are to minimize costs, need to recognize the irrelevancy of sunk costs. Let us consider a simple example that emphasizes this point. Suppose the firm of Exhibit 17-5 paid $100,000 to purchase and install a skate-producing machine. The machine is expected to last 10 years. The company's books record the cost of the machine as $10,000 under the heading of depreciation. The machine can be utilized to make only roller skates. Since dismantling and reinstallation costs are high, the machine could not be leased or sold to another firm. It has no scrap value. In other words, there are no alternative uses for the machine. Utilizing raw materials and other factors of production that cost $45,000, the machine's annual production of roller skates will generate $50,000 of revenues for the firm.

Should the firm continue to utilize the machine? If the annual depreciation cost of the machine is considered, the firm loses $5000 annually on the output of the machine. But the depreciation cost is a sunk cost. It was incurred when the machine was installed. The current opportunity cost of the machine is precisely zero. The firm is not giving anything up by continuing to operate it. Since the machine generates $5000 of additional net revenue, the firm should continue using it. Of course, given current market conditions, the firm would not purchase a similar machine or replace the machine when it wears out. But this should not influence the decision of whether to continue operating the current machine. The irrelevancy of sunk cost helps explain why it often makes sense to continue operating older equipment (it has a low opportunity cost) even though it might not be wise to purchase similar equipment again.

⬜ LOOKING AHEAD

In this chapter we outlined several basic principles that will affect the cost of each firm. We will utilize these basic principles as we analyze the price and output decisions of firms under four alternative market structures in the chapters immediately following.

CHAPTER LEARNING OBJECTIVES

1. The business firm is used to organize productive resources, transforming them into goods and services. There are three major alternative business structures—proprietorships, partnerships, and corporations. Proprietorships are the most numerous, but most of the nation's business activity is conducted through corporations.

2. Economists employ the opportunity cost concept when figuring a firm's costs. Therefore, cost would include not only explicit (money) costs, but also implicit costs associated with the use of productive resources that are owned by the firm.

3. Economic profit (loss) results when a firm's sales revenues exceed (are less than) its total costs, both explicit and implicit. Firms that are making the market rate of return on their assets will therefore make zero economic profit. Firms that transform resources into products of greater value than the opportunity cost of the resources utilized, will make economic profit. On the other hand, if the opportunity cost of the resources used exceeds the value of the product, losses will result.

4. Since accounting costs often omit implicit costs, accounting profits usually exceed economic profits.

5. The law of diminishing returns explains why a firm's short-run marginal and average costs will eventually rise as the rate of output expands. When diminishing marginal returns are present, successively larger amounts of the variable input will be required to increase output by one more unit. Thus marginal costs will eventually rise as output expands. Eventually, MC will exceed ATC, causing the latter to rise also.

6. The firm's short-run average total cost curve will tend to be U-shaped. When output is small (relative to plant size) average fixed cost (and therefore ATC) will be high. However, as output expands, AFC (and ATC) will fall. As the firm attempts to produce a larger and larger rate of output using its fixed plant size, eventually diminishing returns will set in and marginal cost will rise quite rapidly as plant capacity is approached. Thus the short-run ATC will also be high for large output levels because marginal costs are high.

7. The ability to plan larger rates (and volumes) of output will often lead to cost reductions. These cost reductions associated with the scale of one's operation result from **(a)** a greater opportunity to employ mass production methods, **(b)** specialized use of resources, and **(c)** learning by doing.

8. The long-run ATC will reflect the production costs for plants of varying size. When larger plants are more economical (that is, they have lower per unit production costs), the long-run ATC will decline. Rising long-run average costs are also possible. Bureaucratic decision-making and other diseconomies of size may (but not necessarily will) cause the long-run average total cost to rise.

9. When analyzing the general shapes of the firm's cost curves, it was assumed that the following factors were held constant: **(a)** resource prices, **(b)** technology, and **(c)** taxes. Changes in any of these factors would cause the cost curves of a firm to shift.

10. When analyzing business decision-making, it is important to keep the opportunity cost principle in mind. Economists are interested in cost primarily because they will affect the decisions of suppliers. Short-run marginal costs represent the supplier's opportunity cost of producing additional units with the existing plant facilities of the firm. The long-run average cost represents the opportunity cost of supplying alternative rates of output, given sufficient time to vary plant size.

11. Sunk costs have already been incurred. Thus they are irrelevant to current business choices, except as a source of information to guide current decision-making.

IMPORTANT TERMS TO REMEMBER

Explicit costs: Money outlays of the firm to purchase the services of productive resources.

Implicit cost: The opportunity cost associated with a firm's use of resources which it owns. These costs will *not* involve a direct money payment. Examples would include wage income and interest foregone by the owner of a firm who also provides labor services and equity capital to the firm.

Accounting profits: The excess of sales revenues minus the expenses of a firm over a designated time period, usually one year. Accounting profits will typically make allowances for changes in the firm's inventories and depreciation of its assets. But no allowance will be made for the opportunity cost of the equity capital of the firm's owners.

Economic profit: The differences between the firm's total revenues and total costs where both explicit and implicit costs form the components of the firm's total costs.

Total costs: The cost, both explicit and implicit, of the resources utilized by the firm. Total costs include an imputed normal rate of return for the firm's equity capital.

Marginal cost: The change in total cost associated with a unit change in output.

Average total cost: Total cost divided by the number of units produced. It is sometimes called per unit cost.

Fixed costs: Costs that do not vary with output. However, the firm will incur fixed costs as long as it continues in business. Examples would include property taxes and the implicit cost associated with the use of assets owned by the firm.

Average fixed cost: Fixed cost divided by the number of units produced. They will always decline as output increases.

Variable costs: Costs that vary with the rate of output. Examples would include wages paid to workers and payments for raw materials.

Average variable cost: Variable costs divided by the number of units produced.

Short run: A time period so short that the firm is unable to vary some of its factors of production. Since substantial time is required to change a firm's plant size, it is often considered a "fixed" factor.

Long run: Time period sufficiently long to allow the firm the opportunity to vary all factors of production.

Law of diminishing returns: The postulate that as more and more units of a variable resource are combined with a fixed amount of other resources, eventually employment of *additional* units of the variable resource will increase output only at a decreasing rate. Once diminishing returns are reached, it will take successively larger amounts of the variable factor to expand output by one unit.

Economies of scale: Reductions in the firm's per unit costs that are associated with the use of large plants to produce large rates (and volumes) of output.

Sunk costs: Costs that have already been incurred as the result of past decisions. They are sometimes referred to as historical costs.

THE ECONOMIC WAY OF THINKING—DISCUSSION QUESTIONS

1. What is economic profit? How might it differ from accounting profit? Explain why firms that are making zero economic profit are likely to continue in business.

2. Which of the following do you think reflect sound economic thinking? Explain your answer.
   (a) "I paid $200 for this economics course. Therefore, I'm going to attend the lectures even if they are useless and boring."
   (b) "Since we own rather than rent, housing doesn't cost us anything."
   (c) "I own 100 shares of stock that I can't afford to sell until the price goes up enough for me to at least get back my original investment."
   (d) "It costs to produce private education, while public schooling is free."

3. Suppose that a firm produces bicycles. Will the firm's accounting statement reflect the opportunity cost of producing bicycles? Why or why not? What costs would an accounting statement reveal? Should current decisions be based on accounting costs? Explain.

4. Explain in your own words why a firm's short-run average total cost will decline initially, but eventually increase as rate of output is expanded.

5. Which of the following are relevant to the firm's decision to increase output: **(a)** short-run average total cost, **(b)** short-run marginal cost, **(c)** long-run average total cost? Justify your answer.

6. Economics students often confuse **(a)** decreasing returns to the variable factor and **(b)** diseconomies of scale. Explain the difference between the two and give one example of each.

7. **What's Wrong with This Way of Thinking?**

   "The American steel industry cannot compete with German and Japanese steel producers. After World War II, these countries rebuilt modern, efficient mills that made use of the latest technology. In contrast, American mills are older and less efficient. Our costs are higher because we are stuck with old facilities."

18

THE FIRM UNDER PURE COMPETITION

In the last chapter we outlined some basic principles that determine the general relationship between output and production costs for any firm. Of course, a firm's output decisions will be influenced by both its costs and revenues. In this and the next three chapters we will illustrate how the structure of an industry affects the revenues and output levels of firms. We will also analyze four models of industrial structure: (1) pure competition, (2) monopolistic competition, (3) oligopoly, and (4) monopoly. These models will help us better understand the role of competitive forces under varying market conditions. This chapter will focus on pure competition.

TWO MEANINGS OF COMPETITION

The word "competition" is often used in two different ways by economists. First, it is used to indicate a rivalry, particularly between alternative sellers for the business of consumers. This usage is highly consistent with the layman's concept of competition. It emphasizes **competition as a process** that induces rival firms to offer the consumer more for his money than is available from other sellers. Rival firms struggle for the approval (dollar votes) of consumers. Of course, each competitor is in business to make a profit. Thus, each will seek to offer consumers more favorable terms of trade than are available elsewhere (assuming the sale would add to profits), but not more favorable than necessary to obtain his business. Competing firms will use a variety of weapons—quality of product, style, convenience of location, advertising, and price—to convince a consumer that they are offering him a better deal. Independent action and rivalry are the essential ingredients of competition in this sense.

But competition, or more precisely pure competition, is also used to describe a model of industrial structure. This dual usage can often be confusing. For example, firms can be competitive in the rivalry sense even though they are noncompetitive in the industrial structure sense. In order to avoid confusion we will use the entire expression "pure competition" when discussing the competitive model of industrial structure.

329

THE ASSUMPTIONS OF THE PURELY COMPETITIVE MODEL

Pure competition presupposes that the following conditions exist in a market.

1. *All Firms in the Market Are Producing a* **Homogeneous Product.** The product of firm A is identical to the product offered by firm B and all other firms. This presupposition rules out advertising, locational preferences, quality differences, and other forms of nonprice competition.

2. *A Large Number of Independent Firms Produce the Product.* The independence of the firms rules out joint actions designed to restrict output and raise prices.

3. *Each Buyer and Seller Is Small Relative to the Total Market.* Therefore no single buyer or seller is able to exert any noticeable impact on the market supply and demand conditions. For example, a wheat farmer selling 5000 bushels annually would not have a noticeable impact on the U.S. wheat market, where 1,800,000,000 bushels are traded annually. His sales are too small to exert a noticeable independent effect.

4. *There Are No Artificial* **Barriers to Entry** *into or Exit from the Market.* Under pure competition, any entrepreneur is free to either produce or fail to produce in the industry. New entrants need not acquire permission from the government or the existing firms before they are free to compete. Neither does control of an essential resource limit market entry.

The purely competitive model, like other theories, abstracts from the real world. Keep in mind that the test of a theory is its ability to yield predictions that are consistent with the real world (see Chapter 1). Theories should not be judged by the realism of their assumptions. Simplified assumptions are made so we can better organize our thoughts. Models, based on simplified assumptions, can often help us better develop the economic way of thinking.

WHY IS PURE COMPETITION IMPORTANT?

In Chapter 3 we discussed how supply and demand jointly determined market price. The model of pure competition is another way of looking at the operation of market forces. The model will help us better understand the relationship between the decision-making of individual firms and the market supply. Consideration of the way in which economic incentives influence the supply decisions of firms within the competitive model will help us better understand the behavior of firms in markets that are less than purely competitive. Stated another way, the competitive model will help us develop an economic way of thinking that has wide applicability.

There are other reasons for its importance. The conditions of the model are approximated in a few important industries, most notably agriculture. The model will help us better understand these industries. In addition, as we will show later, the equilibrium conditions in the competitive model yield results that are identical to ideal static efficiency conditions. Thus many economists use the competitive model as a standard by which to judge other industrial structures.

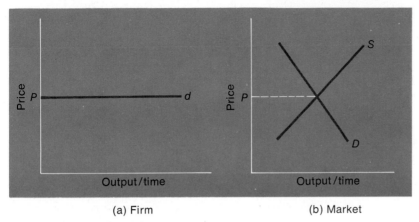

(a) Firm   (b) Market

Exhibit 18-1   The Firm's Demand Curve Under Pure Competition

Here we show that the market forces of supply and demand determine price [frame (b)]. Under pure competition, individual firms have no control over price. Thus the demand for the product of the firm is perfectly elastic [frame (a)].

THE WORKINGS OF THE COMPETITIVE MODEL

Since a competitive firm by itself produces an output that is small relative to the total market, it is unable to influence the market price. The purely competitive firm must accept the market price if it is to sell any of its product. Thus, competitive firms are sometimes called **price takers,** since they must take the market price in order to sell.

Exhibit 18-1 illustrates the relationship between market forces [frame (b)] and the demand curve facing the pure competitor [frame (a)].

If the pure competitor sets his price above the market level, consumers will simply buy from other sellers. Why pay the higher price, when the identical good is available elsewhere at a lower price? For example, if the price of wheat were $4.00 per bushel, farmer Smith would be unable to find buyers for his wheat at $4.50 per bushel. The firm could decrease its price, but since it is small relative to the total market, it can already sell as much as it wants to at the market price. A price reduction would merely reduce revenues. Thus, the purely competitive *firm* confronts a perfectly elastic demand for *its* product.

Deciding How Much to Produce—The Short Run

The firm's output decision is another application of the theory of choice. Decision-makers will simply compare benefits with cost. If a firm produces at all, it will continue expanding output as long as the benefits (additional revenues) from the production of the additional units exceed their marginal costs. This decision-making rule would maximize the firm's profits (or minimize its losses).

How will changes in output influence the firm's costs? In the last chapter, we discovered that the firm's short-run marginal costs will *eventually* increase as output is expanded by working the firm's fixed plant facilities more intensively. The law of diminishing marginal returns assures us that will be the case. *Eventually*, both the firm's short-run marginal and average total costs will rise.

What about the benefits or additional revenues from output expansion? **Marginal revenue** is the change in the firm's total revenue per unit of output. Since the purely competitive firm sells all units at the same price, its marginal revenue will be equal to the market price.

In the short run, the profit-maximizing, purely competitive firm will expand output until price (and marginal revenue) is just equal to marginal cost. Exhibit 18-2 helps explain why. Since the firm can sell as many units as it would like at the market price, sale of one additional unit will increase revenues by the price of the product. As long as price exceeds marginal cost, revenues will increase more than costs as output is expanded. Since profits are merely the difference between total revenues and total costs, profits will expand with output as long as price exceeds MC. For the pure competitor, profits will be at a maximum when $P = MR = MC$. This would be output level q for the firm of Exhibit 18-2.

Why would the firm not expand output beyond q? The cost of producing such units is given by the height of the MC curve. Sale of these units would increase revenues by only P, the product price. Production of units beyond q would add more to cost than to revenue. Therefore, production beyond q, the $P = MC$ output level, would reduce the firm's profits.

A profit-maximizing firm with the cost curves indicated by Exhibit 18-2 would produce exactly q. The total revenue of the firm would be the sales price P multiplied by output sold q. Geometrically the firm's total revenues would be $POqB$. The firm's total cost would be found by multiplying the average total cost by the output level. Geometrically, total costs are represented by $COqA$. The firm's total revenues exceed total costs and the firm is making short-run economic profit (the shaded area).

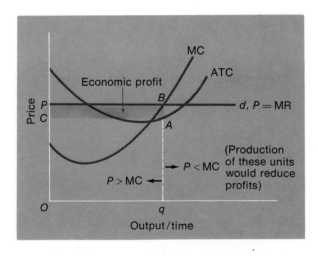

Exhibit 18-2 Profit Maximization and the Purely Competitive Firm

The purely competitive firm would maximize profits by producing the output level q, where $P = $ MC.

Real World Profit Maximizing

In the real world, of course, decisions will be made without perfect certainty. The businessman will not be absolutely certain how a managerial decision will influence cost or output. At the time he must make many production decisions, he cannot be sure what price his product will command in the future. He will, of course, have some expectation about costs and future market price.

The degree of abstraction may make it difficult for the student to associate the model with the real world. We do not mean to imply that businessmen necessarily know anything about the $P = MC$ profit maximization rule. The typical businessman probably does not. Most businessmen indicate that they operate their businesses in a manner that will make them the most money. But if they successfully make decisions so as to maximize profits, the net result would be the same as if they utilized the $P = MC$ rule.

Losses and When to Go Out of Business

Suppose that changes took place in the market which depressed the market price below the firm's average total costs. How would the firm's output and profit levels be altered? If the firm anticipates that the lower market price is temporary, it will continue operating in the short run as long as it is able to cover its variable cost.[1]

Exhibit 18-3 demonstrates that at market price P_1, the firm would minimize its loss

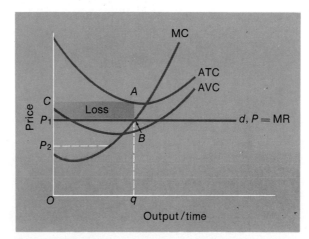

Exhibit 18-3 Operating with Short-Run Losses

In the short run the firm will operate if it (a) can cover its average variable costs and (b) expects the future price to rise so that at least normal profit (that is, zero economic profit) would be possible.

[1] In discussing this issue it is important to keep the opportunity cost concept in mind. The firm's fixed costs are opportunity costs that (a) do not vary with output and (b) cannot be avoided *as long as the firm remains in business*. Fixed costs are *not* (as some economics texts have stated) the original purchase price, less depreciation, on the firm's fixed factors. That figure may bear little relationship to what the firm is currently giving up by continuing in business. Since fixed costs could be avoided by going out of business, the firm would not operate even in the short run if it did not anticipate that market conditions would improve. See Marshall Colberg and James King, "Theory of Production Abandonment," *Rivista Internazionale di Scienze Economiche e Commerciali*, vol. XX, 1973, pp. 961–972.

at output level q, where $P = MC$. At q total revenues ($OqBP_1$) are, however, less than total cost ($OqAC$). The firm confronts short-run economic losses. However, if it shuts down completely, it will still incur fixed costs, *unless it goes out of business.* If the firm anticipates that the market price will increase so that it will be able to cover its ATC in the future, it may not want to sell out. Therefore, it may choose to produce q units in the short run, even though losses are incurred. At price P_1, production of output q is clearly better than shutting down because the firm is able to cover its variable costs and pay some of its fixed costs. If it were to shut down, *but not sell out,* the firm would lose the entire amount of its fixed cost.

If the market price declines below the firm's AVC (for example, below P_2), then the firm would shut down completely as operating losses would supplement losses resulting from the firm's fixed costs. Therefore, even if the firm expects the market price to increase so that it will be able to make "normal" long-run profits in the future, it will still shut down in the short run when the market price falls below AVC.

The Competitive Firm's Supply Curve

The competitive firm will maximize profits (or minimize losses) when it produces the output level where $P = MC$, as long as it is able to cover its variable costs. Therefore, that portion of the firm's short-run marginal cost curve that lies above its average variable cost is the short-run supply curve of the firm.

Exhibit 18-4a illustrates that as the market price increases, the competitive firm will expand output along its MC curve. If the market price were less than P_1, the firm would shut down immediately because it would be unable to cover even its variable costs. However, if the market price is P_1, a price equal to the firm's average variable cost, the firm will supply output q_1 *in the short run.* Economic losses will result, but the firm would incur similar losses if it shut down completely. As the market price increases to P_2, the firm will happily expand output along its marginal cost curve to q_2. At P_2, price is also equal to average costs. The firm is making a "normal rate

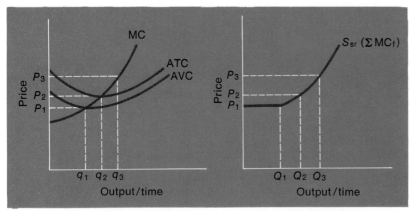

Exhibit 18-4 The Supply Curve for the Firm and the Market

The short-run market supply is merely the sum of the supply produced by all the firms in the market area [frame b)].

(a) Representative Firm   (b) Market

of return" or zero economic profits. Higher prices will induce a still larger short-run output. The firm would supply q_3 units at market price P_3. At this price economic profits would result. At still higher prices, output would be expanded still more. As long as price exceeds AVC, the firm will expand supply along its MC curve, which therefore becomes the firm's short-run supply curve.

The individual firms that produce the good comprise the market. The total amount supplied by the firms is the market supply. Specifically, as pictured by Exhibit 18-4, the horizontal summation of the firm's marginal cost curves will yield the short-run market supply curve. Since the firms will supply a larger quantity at a higher price, the short-run market supply curve will slope upward to the right.

THE FIRM AND COMPETITIVE MARKETS

The market supply curve indicates the willingness of producers to offer the good *at alternative market prices*. The market demand curve indicates the willingness of consumers to purchase the good *at alternative prices*. The market price will coordinate the decisions of producers (suppliers) and consumers (demanders) and bring the two forces into balance. A price will tend to be established so that the quantity demanded by consumers will just equal the quantity supplied by the producers. If there is an excess supply, producers will not be able to sell as much as they would like. Therefore, some producers will decrease price so they will be able to increase their sales. The market price will decline. If there is an excess demand, consumers will not be able to purchase as much as they would like at the existing price. Rather than do without, some consumers will offer higher prices. An excess demand will cause rising prices. The pressures of supply and demand will be in balance, in equilibrium, only at the price where quantity demanded is just equal to quantity supplied.

Adjusting to an Expansion in Demand

Suppose that a purely competitive market were in equilibrium. What would happen if there were an increase in demand? Exhibit 18-5 presents an example. An entrepreneur introduces Icky-Sticky, a fantastic new candy product, into the market. It is sort of a combination between peanut butter and marijuana. Consumers go wild over it. However, since it sticks to one's teeth, the market demand for toothpicks increases from D_1 to D_2. The price of toothpicks rises from P_1 to P_2. What impact will the higher market price have on the output level of toothpick-producing firms? It will increase (from q_1 to q_2, Exhibit 18-5) as the firms expand output along their marginal cost curves. In the short run the toothpick producers will make economic profits. The profits will attract new toothpick producers into the industry and cause the existing firms to expand the scale of their plants.[2] Hence, the market supply will

[2] If the *long-run* average total cost curve results in a unique least cost output level such as was suggested by Exhibit 17-8a, the expansion in long-run supply would be generated entirely by the entry of new firms. However, when the long-run average total cost is such that a wide range of least cost output levels is possible (Exhibit 17-8b), both the entry of new firms and expansion by the established firms will contribute to the increase in supply.

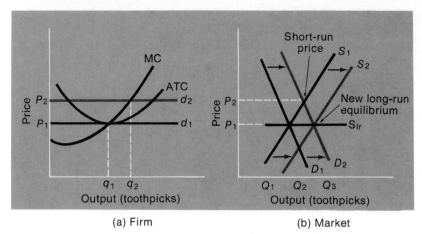

(a) Firm   (b) Market

Exhibit 18-5   How the Market Responds to an Increase in Demand

The introduction of Icky-Sticky candy causes the demand for toothpicks to increase to D_2 [frame (b)]. Toothpick prices rise to P_2, inducing firms to expand output. Toothpick firms make short-run profits [frame (a)], which draw new competitors into the industry. Thus the toothpick supply expands (shifts from S_1 to S_2). If cost conditions are unchanged, the expansion in supply will continue until the market price of toothpicks has declined to its initial level P_1.

increase (shift from S_1 to S_2) and eventually eliminate the short-run profits. If cost conditions are unchanged in the industry, the market price for toothpicks will return to its initial level, even though output has expanded to Q_3.

Adjusting to a Decline in Demand

While economic profits attract new firms into an industry, economic losses will encourage capital and entrepreneurship to move out of the industry and into other areas where the profitability potential is more favorable. Economic losses mean that the owners of capital in the industry are earning less than the market rate of return. The opportunity cost of continuing in the industry exceeds the gain.

Exhibit 18-6 illustrates how market forces react to economic losses. Initially an equilibrium price exists in the industry. The firms are just able to cover their average production costs. Now suppose that there was a reduction in consumer income, causing the market demand for the product to decrease and the market price to decline. At the new lower price, firms in the industry will be unable to cover their costs of production. In the short run they will reduce output along their MC curve. This reduction in output by the individual firms coincides with a reduction in the quantity supplied in the market.

In the face of short-run losses there will be a reduction of even replacement capital into this industry. Some firms will leave the industry. Others will reduce the scale of their operation. These factors will cause the industry supply to decline, shift from

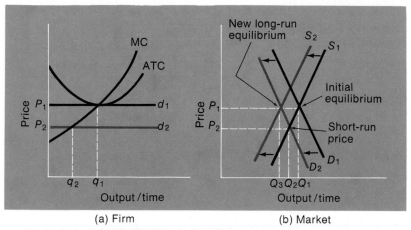

Exhibit 18-6   Impact of a Decline in Demand

A reduction in market demand will cause price to fall and short-run losses to occur. The losses will cause some firms to go out of business and others to reduce their scale. Thus the market supply will fall, causing market price to rise. The supply will continue to decline and price to rise, until the short-run losses have been eliminated (S_2).

S_1 to S_2. What impact will this have on price? Yes, it will rise. In the long run, the market supply will decline until the price rises sufficiently to permit "normal profits" in the industry.

Constant Cost Industries

The long-run market supply curve indicates the minimum price at which firms will supply various market output levels given sufficient time to both adjust plant size (or other fixed factors) and enter or exit from the industry. If factor prices remain unchanged, the long-run market supply curve will be perfectly elastic. In terms of economics it is a **constant cost industry.**

Exhibit 18-5 pictured a constant cost industry. As demand expanded, prices increased *temporarily*. The high prices and profits induced additional production. The short-run market supply continued to expand until the market price returned to its initial level and profits to their normal level. In the long run the larger supply would not require a permanent price increase. Thus, the *long-run* supply curve would be perfectly elastic for constant cost industries.

Increasing Cost Industries

For most industries, economists call them **increasing cost industries,** an expansion in total output will cause the firm's production cost to rise. As the output of an industry increases, the demand for the resources used by the industry will expand. This usually results in higher resource prices, causing the firm's cost curves to shift upward. For example, an increase in demand for housing places upward pressure on the prices of lumber, roofing, window frames, and construction labor, causing the cost of housing to rise. Similarly, an increase in the demand (and market output) for beef may cause the prices of feed grains, hay, and grazing land to rise. Thus, the production costs of beef rise as more of it is produced.

In some industries congestion associated with the use of a factor that is fixed to the industry may generate rising costs as output is increased. For example, an increase in the demand for air travel may lead to additional fuel consumption per flight because planes spend more time circling congested airports. As the demand for lobster increases, additional fishermen will be attracted into the industry. But the increase in the number of fishermen combing lobster beds, typically leads to a reduction in the catch per hour of individual fishermen. Thus, the production cost in the lobster industry will rise as output per man-hour declines.

When an industry experiences increasing costs as total output expands, the long-run supply curve will slope upward. Exhibit 18-7 depicts an increasing cost industry. An expansion in demand causes higher prices and a larger market output. The presence of short-run profits will attract new competitors into the industry, expanding the market output even more. *As the industry expands*, factor prices rise and congestion costs increase. What will happen to the firm's cost curves? Both the average and marginal cost curves will rise (shift to AC_2 and MC_2). This increase in production cost will necessitate a higher long-run price. Hence, the long-run supply curve will slope upward to the right.

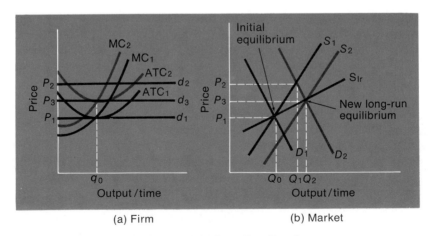

(a) Firm   (b) Market

Exhibit 18-7   Increasing Costs and the Long-Run Supply

Often higher factor prices and industrial congestion will cause costs to rise as the *market* output increases. For such increasing cost industries, the long-run supply [S_{lr}, frame (b)] curve will slope upward to the right.

Decreasing Cost Industries

Conceivably, factor prices could decline as the market output of a product is expanded. Since a reduction in factor prices would lead to a lower long-run competitive market price for the product, economists refer to such industries as **decreasing cost industries.** The long-run (but not the short-run) market supply curve for a decreasing cost industry would slope downward to the right. Since expansion of an industry is far more likely to cause rising (rather than falling) input prices, decreasing cost industries are highly atypical.

THE ROLE OF PROFITS IN THE COMPETITIVE MODEL

In the competitive model, profits and losses are merely signals sent out by consumers to producers. Economic profits will be largest in those areas where consumer wants are greatest *relative* to production cost. Profit-seeking entrepreneurs will guide additional resources into these areas. Supply will increase, driving prices down and eliminating the profits. Free entry and the competitive process will protect the consumer from arbitrarily high prices. In the long run, competitive prices will reflect production costs.

Economic profits result because a firm or entrepreneur increases the value of resources. The successful business decision-maker combines resources into a product that consumers value more than the sum of the resources used to produce it. That is why consumers are willing to pay a price in excess of the good's production costs.

In contrast, losses result when actions of a producer reduce the value of resources. The value of the resources used up by such unsuccessful firms exceeds the price that consumers are willing to pay for their product. Losses and brankruptcy are the market's way of bringing such wasteful activities to a halt.

Producers, like other decision-makers, will of course confront uncertainty and dynamic change. Entrepreneurs, at the time they must make investment decisions, cannot be sure of either future market prices or production costs. They must base their decisions on expectations. But within the framework of the competitive model, the reward–penalty system is clear. Firms that produce efficiently and correctly anticipate products and services for which future demand will be most urgent (relative to production cost), will make economic profit. Those that are inefficient and incorrectly allocate resources into areas of weak future demand will be penalized with losses.

SUPPLY ELASTICITY AND THE ROLE OF TIME

The market supply curve is more elastic in the long run than in the short run because the firm's short-run response is limited by the "fixed" nature of some of its factors. While the short- and long-run distinction offers a convenient two stage analysis, in the real world there will be many intermediate production "runs." Some factors that could not be easily varied in a one week time period, can be varied over a two week period. Expansion of other factors might require a month, and still others, six months.

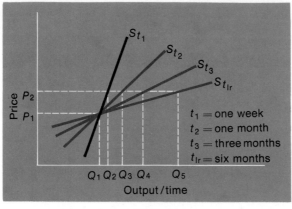

t_1 = one week
t_2 = one month
t_3 = three months
t_{lr} = six months

Market

Exhibit 18-8   Time and the Elasticity of the Supply

The elasticity of the market supply curve usually increases with time.

As the firm has a longer time period to plan output and adjust all of its productive inputs to the desired utilization levels, it will be able to produce any specific rate of output at a lower cost. Because it is less costly to expand output slowly, the expansion of output by firms will increase with the time length of a production run. Therefore the elasticity of the market supply curve will increase with time.

Exhibit 18-8 illustrates the importance of time on the supply response of producers. As the price of a product increases from P_1 to P_2, the *immediate* supply response of the firms will be small because it is costly to expand output hastily. After one week, firms are only willing to expand output from Q_1 to Q_2. After one month, due to cost reductions that are possible because of the longer production planning period, firms would be willing to offer Q_3 units at the price P_2. After three months, the rate of output would expand to Q_4. In the long run, when it is possible to adjust all inputs to the desired utilization levels (a six month time period for example), firms would be willing to supply Q_5 units of output at the market price of P_2. The supply curve for products will typically be more elastic over a long time period than for a shorter period.

MARKET ADJUSTMENTS TO CHANGING PRODUCTION COSTS

We have analyzed the impact that changes in market demand conditions have on both the short- and long-run market price. Oftentimes disequilibrium is the result of changes in production costs. Suppose that a technological advancement makes it possible for the firms of an industry to produce a given output level with fewer inputs. Therefore, costs are reduced. The market price will decline, but in the short run, price will decline less than costs. The firms will make short-run economic profits. But the profits will attract new firms into the industry and the short-run market supply curve will continue shifting to the right until the profits have been eliminated. Price will decline. In long-run equilibrium firms are just able to cover their average (and marginal) costs.

An increase in production costs could be traced out in a similar manner. Higher production costs would cause an increase in the short-run market price, but the immediate increase would not be sufficient to completely cover the higher per unit production cost. Short-run losses would result. Some firms would exit from the industry. This exodus of resources from the industry would continue until the reduction in market supply was sufficient to push the market price upward to the long-run, normal profit equilibrium.

Can you graphically depict the market adjustment process that would result from a reduction (or increase) in production cost? Try it and see. (Remember to assume that demand is unchanged.)

EFFICIENCY AND THE COMPETITIVE MODEL

Economists often seem to be infatuated with the purely competitive model. Sometimes they even hold it up as the standard by which to judge other models. What accounts for the infatuation and special significance of pure competition? Most economists agree that under rather restrictive assumptions, the resource allocation within the purely competitive model is ideal from society's viewpoint. In what sense can we say that it is "ideal"?

1. *Production Costs are Minimized.*   In the long run, the market equilibrium price will equal production costs at their minimum level. Competitive pressures will force firms to operate efficiently and choose a scale of operation that minimizes their long-run average production costs. Inefficient, high cost producers will confront economic losses and be driven from the industry.

2. *Profit-Maximizing Producers will Produce the Goods that Consumers Most Desire.*   The market demand curve for a product reflects the consumer's evaluation of each additional unit of the product. The firm's marginal cost of production reflects the consumer's evaluation of other products which the productive inputs could have been utilized to produce. The consumer's welfare can be increased as long as his evaluation of an additional unit of a commodity (that is, the price that he is willing to pay for the product) exceeds its marginal cost. If the consumer's benefits exceed the producer's costs, potential gains are present. In the purely competitive model in the long run, all potential gains will be realized. Consumers will increase their consumption of all products until their marginal personal benefits are just equal to the market price. Profit-maximizing competitive producers will expand output until marginal costs are just equal to prices. Therefore, in equilibrium, the consumer expected benefits (that is, evaluation of an additional unit of a commodity) will be just equal to the cost of producing the additional unit.

As indicated above, the hypothetical ideal resource allocation of the purely competitive model is true only under very restrictive conditions. As we progress in our analysis, we will focus on cases where the restrictive conditions necessary for the competitive model to allocate resources ideally are unfulfilled.

POSTSCRIPT ON COMPETITION

In this chapter we outlined the mechanics of the purely competitive model. Within the framework of the model, competition (a) induces sellers to produce efficiently and (b) rewards those who produce what consumers desire most urgently (relative to production cost). The purely competitive model is important precisely because it explains in detail why competitive forces are consistent with economic efficiency.

The purely competitive model emphasizes *price* competition. Price alone disciplines the producers of standardized products. In the real world, competition on the basis of product quality, producer reliability and honesty, convenience of location, and quickness of service will also be of tremendous importance. This nonprice competition may be just as intense as the price competition of our hypothetical purely competitive model. The following chapter analyzes market forces under conditions where the pressures of competition, in the rivalry sense, are strong, but the conditions of the purely competitive model are not fully met.

CHAPTER LEARNING OBJECTIVES

1. Competition as a process should not be confused with pure competition, a model of industrial structure. Competition as a process implies rivalry. Rival firms will use quality, style, location, advertising, and price as weapons to convince consumers that they are offering a better deal. On the other hand, pure competition is a model of industrial structure that assumes the presence of a large number of small (relative to the total market) firms, each producing a homogeneous product in a market for which there is complete freedom of entry and exit.

2. Under pure competition, firms are price takers—they face a perfectly elastic demand curve. Profit-maximizing (or loss-minimizing) firms will expand output as long as the additional output *adds* more to revenues than to costs. Therefore the competitive firm will produce at the output level where marginal revenue (and price) equals marginal cost.

3. The firm's short-run marginal cost curve (above its average variable cost) is its supply curve. Under pure competition, the short-run market supply curve is the horizontal sum of the marginal cost curves (when MC is above AVC) for all the firms that comprise the industry.

4. For a short time, a firm may operate even though it is incurring losses. If it anticipates that the "below-average total cost" price is temporary, it will continue to operate if it can cover its average variable costs. A firm that is unable to cover its average variable costs will go out of business immediately.

5. Under pure competition, market prices will be determined by supply and demand. In the short run, firms might make either profits or losses, but in the long run competitive pressures will eliminate economic profits (and losses).

6. When price exceeds average total costs, a firm will make economic profits. Under pure competition, profits will attract new firms into the industry and stimulate the existing firms to expand. The market supply will increase, pushing price down to the level of average total cost. Competitive firms will be unable to make long-run economic profits.

7. Losses exist when the market price is less than the firm's average total cost. Losses will cause firms to exit from the industry or reduce the scale of their operation. The market supply will decline, until price rises sufficiently so that firms can earn normal (that is, zero economic) profits.

8. As the output of an industry expands, in the short-run marginal costs will increase causing the short-run market supply curve to slope upward to the right. If cost conditions in the industry are unchanged as the market output is expanded, the long-run supply curve will be perfectly elastic. However, as the output of an industry expands, usually rising factor prices and industrial congestion will cause the firm's cost curves to shift upward. The long-run market supply curve for such an increasing cost industry will slope upward to the right.

9. Within the framework of the purely competitive model, firms that produce efficiently and correctly anticipate those goods for which future demand will be most urgent (relative to production costs) will make profits. Firms that produce inefficiently and incorrectly allocate resources to the production of goods for which future demand turns out to be weak (relative to production cost), will be penalized with losses.

10. Economists often argue that pure competition leads to ideal economic efficiency because **(a)** average production costs for goods are minimized and **(b)** output is expanded to the level where the consumer's evaluation of an additional unit of a good is just equal to its marginal cost.

IMPORTANT TERMS TO REMEMBER

Pure competition: Model of industrial structure characterized by a large number of small firms producing a homogeneous product in an industry (market area) with complete freedom of entry and exit.

Competition (dynamic process): Connotes rivalry or competitiveness between parties (for example, producers or input suppliers) each of which seeks to deliver a better deal to buyers when quality, price, and product information are all considered. Competing implies a lack of collusion between sellers.

Homogeneous product: Identical products; consumers see no differences in units of the product offered by alternative sellers.

Barriers to entry: Obstacles that limit the freedom of potential rivals to enter an industry.

Marginal revenue: The incremental change in total revenue derived from the sale of one additional unit of a product.

Constant cost industry: Industry for which factor prices and production costs remain constant as market output is expanded. Thus the long-run market supply curve would be horizontal.

Increasing cost industry: Industry for which production costs rise as the industry output is expanded. Thus the long-run market supply is positively related to price.

Decreasing cost industry: Industry for which production costs decline as the industry expands. The market supply would therefore be negatively related to price. Such industries are atypical.

THE ECONOMIC WAY OF THINKING—DISCUSSION QUESTIONS

1. Farmers are often heard to complain about the high cost of machinery, labor, and fertilizer, suggesting that these factors drive down their profit rate. Does it follow that if, say, the price of fertilizer fell by 10 percent, then farming (or any other highly competitive industry with low entry restraints) would be more profitable? Explain.

2. If the firms in a competitive industry are making short-run profits, what will happen to the market price in the long run? Explain.

3. What factors will cause the supply curve for a product to slope upward in the long run? Be specific.

4. A sales tax, collected from the seller, will shift the firm's cost curves upward. Outline the impact of a sales tax within the framework of the competitive model. Use diagrams to indicate both the short-run and long-run impact of the tax. Who bears the burden of the sales tax?

5. What do economists mean when they say that resource allocation is ideal or efficient? Why is it sometimes argued that a purely competitive economy would allocate goods ideally? Explain.

6. "It's wrong to profit from someone else's needs." Do you agree?

    (a) Should a doctor profit from the illness of his patients? The teacher from the ignorance of students? The newscaster from his listener's lack of information about current affairs? The legislator from the needs of his constituents?

    (b) When is it all right to earn a profit?

    (c) What role do profits play in a market economy?

    (d) Do profits and losses actually (ignore the issue of if they should) influence human behavior? Cite evidence that you are familiar with and discuss.

7. The table below presents the expected cost and revenue data for Tom's Tomato Farm. Tom produces tomatoes in a greenhouse and sells them wholesale in a purely competitive market.

    (a) Fill in the firm's marginal cost, average variable cost, average total cost, and profit schedules.

    (b) If Tom is a profit maximizer, how many tomatoes should he produce when the market price is $500 per ton? Indicate his profits.

    (c) Indicate the firm's output level and maximum profit if the market price of tomatoes increases to $550 per ton.

    (d) How many units would Tom's Tomato Farm produce if the price of tomatoes declined to $450? Indicate the firm's profits. Should the firm continue in business? Explain.

Cost and Revenues Schedules—Tom's Tomato Farm, Inc.

Output (tons per month)	Total cost	Price per ton	Marginal cost	Average variable cost	Average total cost	Profits (monthly)
0	$1000	$500	—	—	—	—
1	1200	500	_____	_____	_____	_____
2	1350	500	_____	_____	_____	_____
3	1550	500	_____	_____	_____	_____
4	1900	500	_____	_____	_____	_____
5	2300	500	_____	_____	_____	_____
6	2750	500	_____	_____	_____	_____
7	3250	500	_____	_____	_____	_____
8	3800	500	_____	_____	_____	_____
9	4400	500	_____	_____	_____	_____
10	5150	500	_____	_____	_____	_____

19
MONOPOLISTIC COMPETITION,
PRODUCT DIFFERENTIATION,
AND LOW BARRIERS
TO ENTRY

Under pure competition a firm has no control over prices. If it wants to sell its product, it must take the market price. It is clear that in the real world most firms have some leeway in setting prices. Typically, as a firm increases its price, it will lose some, *but not all*, of its customers. Thus, the *firm* faces a downward sloping demand curve. Such firms are sometimes called **price searchers** because they must search for the price that is most consistent with their overall goal, maximum profits for example.

Even though price searchers can alter their product's price, this does not mean that they are completely free of competitive pressures. Their freedom to raise prices is limited by the existence of both actual and potential producers of similar products. In this chapter we will analyze the behavior of price searchers who produce in markets with complete freedom of entry.

PRODUCT DIFFERENTIATION

Under pure competition, price was all that mattered. Competition in areas other than price was nonexistent. Since each firm offered the same product, consumers did not care which seller they bought from.

In the real world, rival firms typically offer **differentiated products.** Convenience of location, product quality, reputation of the seller, advertising, and other product characteristics will differentiate the good (or service) of one seller from that of his competitors.

Consumers will differ as to the value they place on nonprice product characteristics. But quality factors can make a product more attractive. Products that offer consumers greater convenience, higher quality, or information that reduces their search cost will command higher prices.

For example, consumers often pay higher prices for milk at a convenient local minute mart rather than dealing with the congestion at the supermarket. Many willingly pay higher prices for the repair services of a favorite auto mechanic because they are familiar with his reputation and have confidence in his reliability. When the products offered by rival firms differ from one another, strictly speaking, the purely competitive model is not applicable.

THE HYPOTHETICAL MODEL OF MONOPOLISTIC COMPETITION

How does the market work when sellers offer a similar, but differentiated, product? The model of monopolistic competition will help us answer this question. The distinguishing characteristics of **monopolistic competition** are (1) low barriers to entry, (2) a large number of independent buyers and sellers, (3) small firms relative to the total market, and (4) product differentiation.

Because the products offered by sellers are not identical, monopolistically competitive *firms* face a downward sloping demand curve. A price reduction will permit the firm to attract new customers. Alternatively, a firm can increase its price while sacrificing some reduction in sales. There are no barriers to entry to protect the firm from rivals. Since rivals are offering similar products, monopolistic competitors usually face a highly elastic demand curve.

Despite the term "monopolistic," competitiveness in the usual sense of the word is most descriptive of business conditions under monopolistic competition. Firms will seek to use a variety of weapons such as quality, sales promotion, service, and price to gain the favor of consumers. The threat of rivals, both actual and potential, will always be present to undermine the position of any firm that might become lax or stagnate. There is no business security when barriers to entry are low.

Retailing is perhaps the sector of the U.S. economy that best typifies monopolistic competition. The products and services offered by retail stores differ, although they are clearly competitive. Rivalry is intense. Stores are constantly using a combination of price and quality of service (or merchandise) in their effort to win customers. The *free entry* that typifies most retailing makes it a dynamic sector. Yesterday's novelty can quickly become obsolete as new rivals develop still superior products and marketing methods.

PRICE AND OUTPUT UNDER MONOPOLISTIC COMPETITION

How does a monopolistic competitor decide what price to charge and output to produce? Any firm that maximizes profits will expand output as long as marginal revenue exceeds marginal cost. When a firm faces a downward sloping demand curve, marginal revenue will be less than price because the firm must reduce its price on all units sold in order to increase output. Therefore, the firm's marginal revenue curve will lie inside of its demand curve.

Exhibit 19-1 presents a graphic picture of what happens when a price searcher reduces price in order to increase sales. As the firm reduces its price from P_1 to P_2, sales expand from q_1 to q_2. How do the additional sales influence the firm's total revenues? The impact can be broken into two parts. First, total revenues will increase

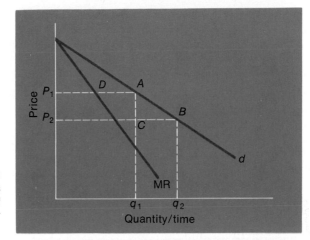

Exhibit 19-1   The Price Searcher's Marginal Revenue Curve

A price searcher must reduce its price on all units in order to expand sales. Thus the marginal revenue from the sale of additional units will be less than their selling price.

by $q_1 q_2 BC$, the *increase* in sales multiplied by the lower product price P_2, because the firm's sales have expanded. But there is also a second effect. The firm must now sell the q_1 units at a lower price, P_2 rather than P_1. The lower sales price for these units will *reduce* total revenues by $P_1 P_2 CA$. The additions to total revenues because of the expanded sales ($q_1 q_2 BC$) are partially offset by the loss of revenues from the price reduction ($P_1 P_2 CA$). The net effect will be an increase in marginal revenue, per unit of output, that is less than the sales price. Therefore, the firm's marginal revenue curve will always lie below its demand curve.[1]

Any firm can increase profits by expanding output as long as marginal revenue exceeds marginal cost. As illustrated by Exhibit 19-2, the profit-maximizing

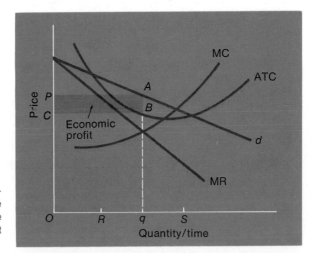

Exhibit 19-2   The Monopolistic Competitor's Price and Output

A monopolistic competitor would maximize profits by producing output q, where MR = MC, and charging price P. The firm is making economic profits. What impact will they have?

[1] For a straight line demand curve, the marginal revenue curve would bisect any line parallel to the x axis. For example, in Exhibit 19-1, the MR curve would divide the line $P_1 A$ into two equal parts—$P_1 D$ and DA.

monopolistically competitive firm would expand output until marginal revenue was just equal to marginal costs. It would charge price *P*. For any output level less than *q*, *R* for example, a price reduction and sales expansion would add more to total revenues than to total costs. At output *R*, marginal revenue exceeds marginal costs. Thus profits would be larger if price were reduced so output could be expanded. On the other hand, if output exceeded *q*, *S* for example, sale of additional units beyond *q* would *add* more to costs (MC) than to revenues (MR). The firm would gain by raising the price back to *P*, even though the price rise would result in the loss of customers. Profits would be maximized by charging price *P* and producing the output level *q*, where MC = MR.

The firm pictured by Exhibit 19-2 is making economic profit. Total revenues *PAqO* exceed the firm's total cost *CBqO* at the profit-maximizing output level. Since entry barriers are low into monopolistically competitive markets, profits will attract rival competitors. Other firms will attempt to duplicate the product (or service) offered by the profit-making firm.

What impact will the entry of new rivals have on the demand for the products of profit-making firms already in the market? These new rivals will draw customers away from the existing firms. As long as monopolistically competitive firms can make economic profits, new competitors will be induced into the market. Eventually, the competition among rivals will shift the demand curve for monopolistic competitors inward and eliminate the economic profits. In the long run, as illustrated by Exhibit 19-3, a monopolistically competitive firm will just be able to cover its production costs. It will produce to the MR = MC output level, but the entry of new competition will force the price down to the average per unit costs.

If losses exist in a monopolistically competitive industry, some of the existing firms in the industry will go out of business over a period of time. As such firms exit from the industry, some of their previous customers will buy from other firms. The demand curve facing the remaining firms in the industry will shift out until the economic losses are eliminated and the long-run, zero profit equilibrium illustrated by Exhibit 19-3 is again restored.

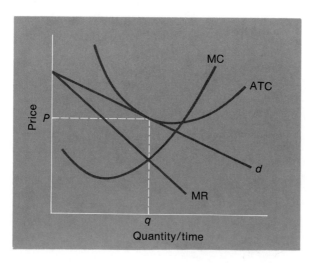

Exhibit 19-3 Monopolistic Competition and Long-Run Normal Profit

Since entry (and exit) is free, competition will eventually drive prices down to the level of average cost.

Under monopolistic competition, profits and losses play precisely the same role as for pure competition. Economic profits will induce new competitors into the market. The increased availability of the product (and similar products) will drive the price down until the profits are eliminated. Conversely, economic losses will cause competitors to exit from a market. The decline in the availability of the product (supply) will allow the price to rise until firms are once again able to cover their average cost.

In the short run a monopolistic competitor may make either economic profits or losses, depending on market conditions. But in the long run, only a normal profit rate (that is, zero economic profits) will be possible because of competitive conditions and freedom of entry.

REAL WORLD MONOPOLISTIC COMPETITORS

Using our hypothetical model, we assumed that firms have perfect knowledge of both their costs and demand conditions. Real world firms will not have such information. They must rely on past experience, market surveys, learning by doing, and other business skills when making price, output, and production decisions.

Could profits be increased if prices were raised or would lower prices lead to larger profits? The real world business decision-maker cannot go into the back room and look at his demand–cost diagram when answering these questions. He must search.

He might raise prices for a time and see what happens to his sales. Or, he might lower prices and see if additional sales will expand revenues more than costs. Note that if maximum profit is the goal of the firm, charging prices that are too high can be just as costly as charging prices that are too low. The successful, astute business decision-maker will search and find that profit-maximizing price (at the $MR = MC$ output level) that our model assumes is common knowledge.

How will real world decision-makers know when demand conditions will permit profits in an industry? Again, past experience, trial and error, and business skill will guide profit-seeking entrepreneurs. Firms will make an entry into a market or introduce a new product only when they expect their action to lead to a profit. If they are right, they will be able temporarily to charge consumers prices that are in excess of their production costs. But economic profits will attract rivals. Other entrepreneurs, observing the success of profitable firms, will not be far behind. Competition will drive prices down to the level of production costs.

Why do losses result in the real world? Since business decisions must be made without perfect information, mistakes will sometimes result. Firms may mistakenly produce a good for which consumers are unwilling to pay a price that will permit the producer to cover his production costs. Losses and bankruptcy are the market's method of bringing such activities to a halt.

PRICE DISCRIMINATION

Throughout this chapter, we have assumed that the price searcher will charge the same price to each customer. Could he gain even more revenues if he were able to discriminate among consumers? This would indeed be possible, if the monopolistic competitor knew which consumers were willing to pay higher prices. Of course, he must also have a way of preventing the customers who are charged lower prices from reselling the product to the potential high price customers.

Suppose a price searcher thought that one group of consumers had a very inelastic demand for his product, while the demand of another group was highly elastic. An *increase* in price would expand the total revenues derived from the former group, while a price *reduction* would increase revenues from the latter. The price searcher could increase his revenues from any specific output by charging the two groups different prices.

Can you think of any examples of **price discrimination?** Remember when airlines offered discount fares to students? Were they trying to help poor college students? Hardly. They offered such discounts because the demand of college students for air travel was quite elastic. The discounts led to greater revenues, and very little expansion in cost, for the airlines. Why do professional journals usually charge individual subscribers lower rates than libraries? They generate more revenue by charging higher prices to subscribers (libraries) with an inelastic demand. Why are women often charged lower prices when attending nightclubs and baseball games? Again, price discrimination apparently leads to greater revenues than costs.

COMPETITION AND THE ECONOMIC WAY OF THINKING

It is useful to think within the framework of a model. Otherwise the interrelationship among numerous variables becomes too complex and the importance of data (facts) is difficult to determine. But models are merely a means to assist us in the economic way of thinking. Sometimes economists are guilty of elevating the importance of models, equilibrium, price competition, and the purely competitive market structure. We should not forget that competition is a means to an end. What can competition, in the rivalry sense, accomplish for us in a dynamic world?

1. *Competitiveness Encourages Resource Movements That Are Efficient.* A world of constant change will be typified by disequilibrium and adjustment. Errors, uncertainty, and time lags are part of the adjustment process. When firms are free to compete, the pursuit of profit will stimulate movements that increase the value of resources. Profit results only when the price of a product exceeds the value of the resources used to produce it. It is a reward to those who increase the value of resources. Losses result when firms produce something that is of less value to consumers than the resources utilized in the production processes. Losses are a penalty imposed on those who reduce the value of resources. Opportunity to compete presents entrepreneurs with both the means and the incentive to adjust resources in a manner that is efficient—that is, to make movements that increase the value of resources.

2. *Competition among Rivals Presents Each with a Strong Incentive to Operate and Manage His Business Efficiently.* If a businessman is a poor manager, he will have high costs. Product quality constant, higher costs will mean lower profits. Both pure and monopolistically competitive firms have a strong incentive to operate their busi-

OUTSTANDING ECONOMIST: Joan Robinson

© Ramsey & Muspratt, Ltd.

Along with Edward Chamberlin, Joan Robinson is given credit for developing the theory of monopolistic competition. In her book *The Economics of Imperfect Competition* (1933) she redefined the market demand curve to account for interdependence between firms.[2] Following Alfred Marshall, she used differences among products to define an industry. Essentially, she viewed each firm as a monopolist facing a downward sloping demand curve that is affected by the behavior of other "monopolists," in the industry. Unlike Chamberlin, she failed to introduce product differentiation and quality competition *within an industry* into her analysis.

Professor Robinson's contribution to economics goes far beyond her role in the development of the theory of monopolistic competition. An Emeritus Professor of Economics at Cambridge University, she was one of a select group of economists who worked with Keynes during the development stage of his *General Theory*. She fully accepts the Keynesian view that the market economy is inherently unstable. Furthermore, she argues that market economies suffer from other serious defects—income inequality, pollution, business concentration, and manipulation of demand.

Professor Robinson has played a prominent role in continuing the Cambridge tradition of dissent from the traditional orthodoxy. Delivering the Richard T. Ely Lecture to the American Economic Association in 1971, she argued that the economics profession faces a second major crisis. Just as pre-Keynesian economists failed to develop a theory of aggregate employment, Professor Robinson charges that current economists have failed to develop a meaningful theory of "what employment should be for." In her view "this primarily concerns the allocation of resources between products, but it is also bound up with the distribution of products between people." She feels that the relative earnings of individuals depends on bargaining power and union influence, not primarily market conditions.

In recent years, she has become a vocal critic of the capitalist system. In many ways, she is something of an English Galbraithian. The *Collected Economic Papers* of Professor Robinson now span four volumes.[3] Her work in economics runs the complete gamut. Capital theory, international trade, Marxian economics, growth theory, and comparative systems are among the many areas that have felt the touch of her pen.

---

nesses efficiently. If new procedures can be utilized or new techniques developed that will reduce costs, businessmen have a strong inducement to adopt them because lower costs will mean higher profits.

3. *Competitiveness Stimulates Product Variety and **Quality Competition**.* Since consumer tastes differ, consumers will prefer to choose from a variety of products and quality levels. Competition is multidimensional. If firms can gain by offering consumers a more (or less) durable product or a different style, they will happily do so.

[2] Joan Robinson, *The Economics of Imperfect Competition.* 1933. Reprint. New York: St. Martin, 1969.
[3] Joan Robinson, *Collected Economic Papers.* 4 vols. New York: Humanities Press, 1960–1972.

How does a businessman decide if he should adjust the quality (or style) of his product? Just like he makes other business decisions. If he believes an improvement in product quality will *increase* his revenues more than costs, he will make the improvement. If higher quality goods can be marketed profitably, competitiveness encourages firms to do so. But, if a reduction in quality reduces costs more than revenues, firms will cater to desires of consumers for cheap low quality products. For example, if people want, as many apparently do, inexpensive, low quality ballpoint pens, they will be produced.

4. *Competition Protects the Consumer from High Prices.*   Why does not A&P raise their prices? Why does not the corner restaurant charge more for food? Competition, the existence of both actual and potential rivals, limits their ability to do so. If a grocery store or restaurant charges high prices (relative to product quality), it will lose customers to rivals. When there is free entry into a market, firms will not be able to gouge the consumer, at least not for long. If they attempt to do so, rival firms are perfectly free to offer consumers a better deal. Competition and free entry to an industry are the consumer's best friends.

CONTRASTING PURE AND MONOPOLISTIC COMPETITION

In many respects monopolistic competition and pure competition are similar. In both cases, firms just cover their production costs in the long run. In both cases, firms are responsive to changing demand conditions. An expansion in demand leads to short-run profits and the entry of additional firms. A reduction in demand causes short-run losses, forcing firms from the market. There are no entry barriers in either case to protect firms from market forces.

But there are also differences. First, the zero profit equilibrium for a monopolistically competitive firm, unlike the pure competitor, will occur at an output level that fails to minimize the firm's long-run average cost. The monopolistic competitor would have lower per unit cost if he produced a larger output. Second, monopolistic competitors will charge a price that exceeds their marginal cost. Pure competitors will not. Third, since monopolistic competitors want consumers to believe that their product is both different and superior, they will often engage in competitive advertising as a means of attracting additional customers. Of course, purely competitive firms will not engage in advertising since they can already sell all they can produce, at the market price.

Many economists argue that monopolistic competition is inefficient because it results in (a) average costs that are in excess of the long-run minimum, (b) product prices that exceed their marginal cost, and (c) wasteful competitive advertising. But not all economists agree. The dissenters argue that this view is mechanistic and unrelated to the real world, that it fails to comprehend the significance of dynamic competition. They stress that monopolistically competitive industries provide consumers with a wider variety of qualities and styles than would result from pure competition. The following debate outlines the major issues involved in the controversy concerning the economic efficiency of monopolistically competitive industries.

Is Monopolistic Competition Inefficient? Yes.

Monopolistically competitive markets are characterized by excess capacity, too many firms, wasteful advertising, and prices that exceed marginal cost. Exhibit 19-4 helps to explain why. In long-run equilibrium, monopolistic competitors will end up at E, producing the output level where MR = MC. Price P_1 will result. Firms would have a lower per unit cost if they produced output q_2. But because of the large number of competitors, demand conditions are such that firms would be unable to realize even the market rate of return, if they sought to operate at the least cost output level q_2.

Consumers do not benefit from the lowest prices that cost conditions would permit. If there were a smaller number of firms in the industry, and each produced at the output level where average total costs are minimum (point A), they would be able to produce the same total output at a lower cost. With a smaller number of firms, demand conditions d_2 would permit each to more fully realize the economies of scale that are present in the industry.

In the absence of regulation, monopolistic competition will be characterized by underutilized firms, each operating at less than ideal capacity. Service stations are a good example. Idle service station operators, utilizing their facilities far below capacity, can often observe a rival, or even rivals, operating a similarly underutilized facility across the street or around the corner. Most cities and highways have far more gasoline stations than are necessary to provide the level of service demanded by consumers. Duplication and waste are the result in this monopolistically competitive industry.

Economic efficiency requires that firms expand output as long as price exceeds marginal cost. Evaluated by this criterion, prices in monopolistic industries are too high and output is too small. Whenever price is greater than marginal cost, consumer benefits from the production of an additional unit are greater than the unit's production cost. Production of such units will lead to a net economic gain. But the monopolistically competitive firm will produce only to where marginal revenue is equal to marginal cost (q_1, Exhibit 19-4). Social gains from the production of marginal units beyond this profit maximum output level will be lost.

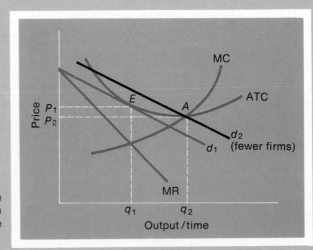

Exhibit 19-4   The Inefficiency of Monopolistic Competition

In equilibrium (point E), prices in monopolistic industries will exceed both marginal cost and the *minimum* average total cost.

In addition, monopolistic competition often leads to self-defeating, wasteful advertising. Firms have an incentive to use advertising to promote artificial distinctions between similar products. Rivals bombard the consumer, telling him that their product is fancier, has greater sex appeal, or brings quicker relief. Firms that do not engage in such advertising can expect their sales to decline.

But what is the net effect when all firms follow this strategy? The advertising effects tend to be offsetting, costs are higher, and higher prices are used to pass the promotional expenses on to the consumer. The consumer receives less for his dollar.

What can be done to eliminate the wasteful effects of monopolistic competition? Consumer protection legislation could be constructed that would reduce artificial distinctions between products. For example, brand name marketing of drugs with the same chemical composition could be prohibited. Government action might be taken to limit the number of firms in industries where excess capacity is particularly acute. Advertising expenditures could be limited in both magnitude and scope in many industries. Noninformational advertising, in particular, might be regulated or prohibited. But there is no way that the uninhibited market mechanism can prevent these wasteful effects. Of course, regulation itself may have certain undesirable characteristics. One will want to weigh these costs against the potential gains that might be obtained from reductions in inefficiency stemming from monopolistically competitive practices.

Controversies in Economics

Is Monopolistic Competition Inefficient? No.

Monopolistically competitive firms make zero economic profits. They seek to offer the consumer a superior bargain, not just through price competition, but also through quality, service, location, information, and other forms of nonprice competition. Why then is the question of inefficiency raised?

Economic theorists are fond of comparing pure and monopolistic competition. Monopolistic competition is usually charged with inefficiency because product price exceeds marginal cost and long-run average costs are not minimized. But the critics fail to stress why this is so. Consumers want variety. They desire differentiated products and are willing to pay for them even when they cost more. Homogeneous products may be ideal to a theorist, but they are not to real world consumers. Consider the home construction industry in the United States. There are a large number of firms producing widely diverse housing structures. It is surely a monopolistically competitive industry. Would we be better off with pure competition and more homogeneous structures? Because of the greater uniformity, housing costs would probably be slightly lower. But the lower cost would be achieved only by giving up individuality and uniqueness of structure. City after city would look like one giant public housing project. In a society where consumers receive utility from product diversity, we cannot say that pure competition is preferable or more efficient than monopolistic competition.

The critics are also fond of arguing that the availability of additional (excess?) capacity is necessarily indicative of waste and inefficiency. Again they inappropriately apply the model to real world conditions. Demand in the real world will be greater at certain times during the day (or week). For example, the appropriate capacity to deal with the demand for gasoline during the evening rush hour will result in some excess capacity during off-peak hours. But this is not evidence of inefficiency. Is it wasteful and inefficient for a house to have two bathrooms? After all, at least one and sometimes both will have excess capacity most of the time. But if the homeowner values the convenience of the additional bathroom more than its cost, two baths, even though they are often underutilized except during peak hours, are perfectly consistent with economic efficiency. Similarly, if consumers value the location, convenience, and noncongested service of a gasoline station more than its cost, the existence of excess capacity during certain hours is not inconsistent with economic efficiency.

The argument that monopolistic competition results in *all firms* operating at less than the least cost output level is incorrect. Often consumers have the option of purchasing from large, cost efficient firms, as well as small, more convenient, less congested ones. For example, large scale supermarkets and discount drug centers, drawing customers from a larger market area, are available in addition to corner drugstores and local minute markets. If consumers want low prices, they will patronize the large scale, optimal capacity producers. But often they will gain by choosing the convenience of the small operator, even though they recognize his prices are necessarily higher.

Critics also often focus on the waste of advertising, particularly noninformational advertising. They point out that the consumer pays the costs of the advertising in the form of higher prices, yet he gets nothing in return. This is not quite true. Advertising often reduces the consumer's search time and provides him with valuable information on prices. If advertising really raises prices, it must provide the consumer with something that is valuable. Otherwise, the consumer will purchase lower priced, nonadvertised goods. When consumers really prefer lower prices and less advertising, firms offering that combination will do quite well. For example, the little-advertised Hershey bar competes effectively with heavily advertised rival candy bars. Similarly, many monopolistic competitors in local market areas will use higher quality service and lower prices to compete with rivals that advertise more heavily.

Competition in the real world is dynamic. Producers discover the desires of consumers by innovating, attempting different designs and styles, and by introducing and promoting new products. Competition cannot be pure under these conditions. Innovative firms, offering unique products, will necessarily face a downward sloping demand curve. But this is not inefficiency. Rather, it is the very essence of competition. Pure and simple, it is entrepreneural action designed to discover and produce those goods (or services) that consumers value most, given their current availability.

The charge that monopolistic competition is inefficient is misdirected. Inefficiency implies that a superior, more efficient alternative exists. The critics have shown us nothing but a *hypothetically* superior alternative that would exist if the world were different (that is, if pure competition or marginal cost pricing were possible in all industries *without reducing the variety of products available*). But the world is not different. In the absence of a "superior" alternative, the charge of inefficiency is a "sham."

Is Planned Obsolescence Good Business?

Perspectives in Economics

Many Americans have the gut feeling that business firms can gain by producing shoddy merchandise that wears out quickly. It is often charged that business firms, over the objections of consumers, produce goods with a short life expectancy so they can sell replacements. Economists have sometimes been at the forefront of those deploring such **planned obsolescence.**

Yet, a solid majority of economists believe that price indexes overstate the measured rate of inflation because they fail to make an adequate allowance for improvements in product quality. This leads to the following question, "If firms have an incentive to produce shoddy, nondurable goods, why has the quality of products, on the average, risen?"

Should a Car Last a Lifetime?

Straight thinking requires us to keep two points in mind. First, production of longer-lasting, higher quality goods will increase costs. There are no free lunches. A car that lasts 15 years will be more expensive than one with a shorter life expectancy. We should expect consumers to trade off lower prices against more durability. At some point, the greater durability will not be worth the price.

Second, "newness," product variability, and style changes are often valued by consumers. For example, operational reliability aside, many consumers would prefer three differently styled, new model cars, lasting five years each to a single car of equal cost which lasts 15 years. *Under these conditions*, production of goods with less than maximum life expectancy is perfectly consistent with consumer tastes.[4]

Suppressing Products

Will a longer-lasting improved product necessarily be introduced into the market as soon as it is discovered? The answer is no. If a firm discovers a new product that would have a decidedly negative impact on the sales of its current product lines, it may initially suppress the newly discovered good. The firm's losses on current lines might outweigh its expected gain from the introduction of the superior product. There is some evidence that major manufacturers of razor blades were slow in introducing longer-lasting blades for just this reason.

Who Gains from Planned Obsolescence?

However, a firm's disincentive to introduce an improved product is not a generalized explanation of planned obsolescence. If superior products are developed by firms with a small share of the current market (or by new entrants), they will use the improvements as a competitive weapon to woo customers away from rivals. Similarly, when the knowledge of how to produce higher quality, more durable products is widespread among producers, rival firms have a strong incentive to heed the wishes of consumers. When consumers are unhappy with the current quality level and desire more durability, a firm that produces longer-lasting products can gain over its rivals.

In contrast, it would be bad business for a firm to design a product that wears out more rapidly than those of its competitors, when consumers do not want such low priced, low quality goods. True, the firm's planned obsolescence might require the consumer to purchase a replacement sooner. But that replacement would almost certainly be bought from a rival who offers a product with the desired life expectancy.

Some consumers may be willing to give up style variation and model changes (rather than more purchasing power) for products with a longer life expectancy. The success

---

[4]Both the author and reader may disagree with such "vulgar taste." However, we should be aware that such disagreements stem from our views about how consumers should behave, not from a defect in the system that caters to those views.

of Volkswagon suggests that this tradeoff is an important consideration to many automobile customers. Other customers may choose even less durability if it is accompanied by a sufficiently lower price. Cheaper, nondurable product lines are evidence of this factor.

Product quality, including durability, is a competitive weapon. If customers really want longer-lasting products, firms have a strong incentive to discover and introduce them, except when the new product would harm the sales of the firm's current product line. When consumers are willing to pay the price for greater durability, catering to their views would allow a firm to gain. However, durability is only one facet of a product that is attractive to consumers. Low prices, newness, and product variation are also preferred by many. Much of our planned obsolescence undoubtedly stems from the choice of consumers to give up some of the former (durability) in order to have more of the latter.

Discussion

1. Suppose that General Electric or Westinghouse discovered how to produce a light bulb that would last 50 years even though its production cost was only twice as much as for current bulbs. What action would they take? Why? What action would a firm that does not currently produce light bulbs take if *it* made the discovery? Explain.

2. Do you think planned obsolescence is bad? Are there any conditions under which it might be desirable? Why or why not?

CHAPTER LEARNING OBJECTIVES

1. Monopolistically competitive firms will face a downward sloping demand curve. They will often use product quality, style, convenience of location, advertising, and price as competitive weapons. Since rivals are free to duplicate the product (or service) of the monopolistic competitor, the demand for his product will be highly elastic.

2. Since a price searcher must reduce price in order to expand sales, his marginal revenue from the sale of additional units will be less than the price. The marginal revenue curve for a price searcher will lie inside of the demand curve.

3. Any firm will maximize profits by expanding output until MR = MC. The monopolistic competitor will sell this profit-maximizing output level for the highest possible price. The vertical height of the demand curve at the output level where MC = MR reveals the price that a profit-maximizing monopolistic competitor would charge.

4. If monopolistic competitors are making economic profits, rival firms will be induced into the market. They will expand the supply of the product (and similar products), enticing some of the customers away from the established firms. The demand curve faced by the firms will shift inward until the profits have been eliminated.

5. Economic losses will cause monopolistic competitors to exit from the market. Thus, the demand for the products (or services) of the remaining firms will rise until the losses have been eliminated.

6. Since entry restraints are low, firms in a monopolistically competitive industry will make only normal profits in the long run. In the short run they might make either economic profits or losses, depending on market conditions.

7. In the real world firms will not have perfect knowledge of either their demand or costs. They will use business experience, research, and trial and error to search for the profit-maximizing price (and output).

8. Firms will make economic profits only if they use resources in a manner that increases their value (that is, the price of the product exceeds the cost of the resources used to produce it). Conversely, losses will result if the actions of the firm reduce the value of the resources used. Free entry grants profit-seeking producers both the opportunity and incentive to increase the value of resources.

9. Traditional economic theory emphasizes that monopolistic competition is inefficient because **(a)** price exceeds marginal cost at the long-run equilibrium output level, **(b)** long-run average cost is not minimized, and **(c)** excessive advertising is sometimes encouraged.

However, other economists have argued that this criticism is misdirected in a dynamic world. Under monopolistic competition, firms have an incentive to **(a)** produce efficiently, **(b)** undertake production if and only if their actions will increase the value of resources used, and **(c)** offer a variety of products.

10. When a new, improved product reduces the demand for the existing product line of the discovering firm, their incentive to introduce the item immediately is reduced. However, product quality, including durability, is a competitive weapon. If consumers are willing to pay the higher costs incurred in production of more durable goods, competitiveness encourages firms to cater to their views. But we should not forget that consumers will rationally trade off durability for price. Much of our planned obsolescence stems from the desire of consumers for lower prices even though durability is sacrificed.

IMPORTANT TERMS TO REMEMBER

Product differentiation: Quality, design, locational, or promotional (advertising) characteristics of a product which cause consumers to distinguish it from similar products produced by other firms.

Monopolistic competition: A situation where there are a large number of independent sellers, each producing a differentiated product in a market with low barriers to entry. Construction, retail sales, and service stations are good examples of monopolistically competitive industries.

Quality competition: Use of such product characteristics as durability, safety, style, design, and reliability as competitive weapons to induce consumers away from rival sellers.

Price searcher: A firm that faces a downward sloping demand curve for its product.

Planned obsolescence: A term used to describe the situation in which firms intentionally produce goods with a relatively short life expectancy. In a sense, all products have some planned life expectancy, but the term is typically used when referring to products that wear out quickly.

Price discrimination: Practice by a seller whereby he charges different prices to different consumers of the same product or service.

THE ECONOMIC WAY OF THINKING—DISCUSSION QUESTIONS

1. Explain in your own words what is meant by product differentiation? What tactics might be used to differentiate one's product?

2. Why do many economists argue that monopolistic competition is inefficient? If there were fewer small firms in a monopolistically competitive industry (for example, retail groceries), would the *average* selling prices in the industry decline? Why or why not? Would convenience, location, and other quality factors change? Why or why not? Do you think monopolistic competition is inefficient? Explain.

3. It is often charged that competitive advertising among monopolistically competitive firms is wasteful.

   (a) Do you think that advertising in the following industries is wasteful: retail grocery sales, retail furniture sales, cigarettes, local restaurants, cosmetics, movie theaters, and retail department stores? Explain.

   (b) Does this advertising result in higher prices?

   (c) Is the advertising valuable to consumers? Explain.

   (d) Why do not more firms compete by eliminating their advertising and charging lower prices?

4. If the firm is a price searcher, why will marginal revenue be less than price?

5. Smith's Quality Furniture, Inc. produces dining room tables. Design and workmanship make their product unique although there are many producers of dining room tables. Their expected cost and demand conditions are indicated below:

   (a) Fill in the marginal revenue, average total cost, and marginal cost schedules for Smith's Quality Furniture. Graph these schedules on a price–quantity diagram.

   (b) If the firm wants to maximize profits, what price should it charge? How large are the firm's expected profits (or losses)?

   (c) If the firm is currently charging $450 per table, what should it do if it wants to maximize profits?

Quantity (per day)	Price	Total revenue	Marginal revenue	Total cost	Average total cost	Marginal cost
0	$510	$0	—	$1000	—	—
1	500	500	_____	1300	_____	_____
2	490	980	_____	1550	_____	_____
3	480	1440	_____	1800	_____	_____
4	470	1880	_____	2070	_____	_____
5	460	2300	_____	2370	_____	_____
6	450	2700	_____	2700	_____	_____
7	440	3080	_____	3070	_____	_____
8	430	3440	_____	3490	_____	_____
9	420	3780	_____	3970	_____	_____
10	410	4100	_____	4520	_____	_____

20

MONOPOLY AND HIGH
BARRIERS TO ENTRY

*Competitive industries have their monopolistic
aspects; monopolized industries have their
competitive aspects. The most that can be said today
is that competition is far too common to justify the
thesis that the competitive system is approaching
extinction, and that monopoly is far too common to
justify its treatment as an occasional exception to
the general rule.[1] [Clair Wilcox]*

In the last two chapters we investigated prices, output, and resource allocation when
there were few restraints on the entry of firms into an industry. In this and the
following chapter we will focus on cases where barriers to entry are high, and the
existing firms have some protection from the competition of new firms. As the
quotation of Professor Wilcox implies, there will be some "competitive" elements
present even when there are only a few producers in a market area. No firm is
completely free from competitive pressures. Yet in many industries, particularly
manufacturing, competitive pressures may be restrained or take a different form than
is suggested by models based on low barriers to entry.

COMPETITION IS GREAT, BUT . . .

Businessmen are often at the forefront as defenders of the competitive, profit-seeking,
enterprise system. Yet, as decision-makers they often face a dilemma. They are in
business to make profits, to increase their wealth. But when barriers to entry are low,
profits attract new competitors into an industry or market area.

The addition of the "new boys on the block" will "spoil the market," driving the
price down and eliminating the economic profits. Businessmen may like the com-

[1]Clair Wilcox, *Competition and Monopoly in American Industry.* Washington, D.C., 1940. Reprint.
Westport, Connecticut: Greenwood Press.

petitive enterprise system in principle, but simultaneously they have a strong incentive to limit competition, to block the efforts of potential rivals. Competition is the enemy of economic profit.

Is it any wonder that business decision-makers look for an alternative? Competition is great for a speech to the Rotary Club, but it is a risky business when one is dealing with his own wealth.

When Are Barriers to Entering a Market High?

What conditions make it possible for a business to at least partially escape the pressures imposed by competition? Why are barriers to market entry high in some industries and low in others? Three factors are of particular importance.

1. *Legal Barriers.* Legal barriers are the oldest and most secure method of protecting a business firm from potential competitors. Kings once granted exclusive business rights to favored citizens or groups. Today, governments continue to establish barriers, restricting the right to buy and sell goods. Exclusive government franchises are granted in transportation, communication, and public utilities in the United States. The post office, a government corporation, is granted exclusive rights to deliver first-class mail. Currently, potential private competitors are eliminated because the government legally prevents them from competing with the federally operated post office. A government franchise is required if you want to compete in the airline, trucking, or communication (for example, operate a radio or television station) industries.

Licensing, a requirement that a person obtain permission from the government before entering a specific occupation or business, often limits entry. In many states, one must obtain a license before he can operate a liquor store, barbershop, taxicab, funeral home, drugstore, and so on. Sometimes these licenses cost little and are merely formalities designed to require certain minimum standards. In other cases they are expensive and designed primarily to limit competition.

2. *Economies of Scale.* In some industries, unless a firm is quite large, both in absolute terms and relative to the market, it will be unable to produce at a low cost. Economies of scale prevent small firms from entering into the market, gradually building a reputation, and eventually becoming large. The existing firms are therefore protected from the entry and gradual growth of potential competitors.

3. *Control over an Essential Resource.* If a single firm has the sole control over a resource that is essential for entry into an industry, it can eliminate potential competitors. The famous DeBeers Company of South Africa is the classic case. Since this company has almost exclusive control over all of the world's diamond mines, it can effectively prevent other firms from entering into the diamond producing industry. Similarly, Alcoa (The Aluminum Company of America) at one time owned almost all of the basic sources of bauxite, the major ore used in the production of aluminum. Alcoa was able effectively to block the entry of all potential competitors until the government intervened in the industry during World War II.

WHAT IS A MONOPOLY?

The word "monopoly," derived from two Greek words, means "single seller." Therefore, a monopolist is the single seller of a product. But this definition is not without ambiguity. Who is a single seller? Harold's Texaco might be the only seller of gasoline on the corner of Meridian and Central Streets in Miami, Florida. Is Harold a monopolist? The question answers itself. Of course not, because there are lots of other gasoline stations in Miami. But if one runs out of gas at Meridian and Central, none of the other stations is a good substitute for Harold's service. Therefore, monopoly must be a question of degree.

No firm produces a product for which there are no substitutes. If other firms offer a similar product to the one for which you are the sole seller, you will have little monopoly power. Harold's service station has little monopoly power because other service stations in the market area offer a very similar product. The A&P retail grocery chain has relatively little monopoly power because in most areas there are several other grocery stores. The Lipton Company is the sole producer of Lipton tea, but its "monopoly power" is greatly limited because of the availability of coffee, orange juice, milk, lemonade, and tea produced by other companies. The availability of good substitutes greatly reduces the monopoly power of a firm.

In most communities there will be only a single telephone company, postal delivery system, and electric company. Admittedly, there are some substitutes available for the services offered by these companies. The telephone company is only one of several forms of communication. But in this case, because of the speed of conversation and the immediacy of response, telephone communication has a tremendous advantage relative to postal services, telegraph, or shouting. Similarly, there are some substitutes for electricity (candles, fuel oil, natural gas, oil lamps), but for some purposes these substitutes are quite inferior.

 We will define a **monopolist** as the single producer of a product for which there are not good substitutes. Even this definition is ambiguous because "good substitutes" is a relative term. Is a letter a good substitute for a phone call? Is a bicycle a good substitute for an automobile? Is a magnifying glass a good substitute for a pair of glasses? Most of us, though possibly not all, would probably answer no to all these questions. Therefore, if a single firm were the sole producer of telephone service, automobiles, or eyeglasses, it would qualify as a monopolist by our definition.

Consider the other extreme. Are Fords, Dodges, Plymouths, and Volkswagens good substitutes for Chevrolets? Are accommodations at other available hotels or motels a good substitute for accommodations at a Holiday Inn? Is synthetic rubber a good substitute for natural rubber? Most of us would probably answer yes to this last set of questions. Therefore, even if a single firm were the sole producer of Chevrolets (but not the others listed), Holiday Inn accommodations, or natural rubber, it would *not* qualify as a monopolist by our definition.

THE HYPOTHETICAL MODEL OF MONOPOLY

Suppose you invented, patented, and produced a microwave device that would lock the hammer of any firearm in the immediate area. This fabulous invention could be used to immobilize potential robbers or hijackers. Since you own the exclusive patent right to it, you are not concerned about a competitive supplier in the foreseeable future. While other products are competitive with your invention, they are poor substitutes. In short, you are a monopolist!

What price would you set for your product? Since you are the only firm in the industry, the industry demand curve will coincide with your demand curve. The demand curve will be downward sloping, indicating that consumers will buy more of your product at a lower price. At high prices, even a monopolist will have few customers. Often a price reduction will expand revenues more than costs. If you want to maximize profits, you should expand output, reducing your price, as long as the increased sales contribute more to *additional* revenues than their production *adds* to cost.

Exhibit 20-1 illustrates the short-run profit-maximizing output level for a monopolist. Output is expanded to Q, where MR = MC. The monopolist, like the monopolistic competitor, will be able to sell the profit-maximizing output Q for a price indicated by the height of his demand curve. At any output smaller than Q, the benefits (marginal revenue) of producing the *additional* units exceed their cost. The monopolist would gain by expanding output. For any output greater than Q, the monopolist's cost of producing *additional* units will be greater than his benefits (marginal revenue). Production of such units would reduce profits.

The profit-maximizing rule for monopolists is identical to that of the monopolistic competitor. But the elasticity of the demand curve faced by the two will differ. A monopolistically competitive firm faces competition from both actual firms producing similar products and potential firms that can easily enter the market. Therefore, the demand curve faced by the monopolistic competitor will usually be highly elastic. In contrast, since there are few good substitutes for his product and high entry barriers grant him some protection from potential rivals, the demand curve of the monopolist will typically be steeper (less elastic) than for monopolistic competitors.

Exhibit 20-1 also depicts the profits of a monopolist. At output Q, the monopolist would charge price P. Price times the number of units sold yields the firm's total revenue (*PAQO*). The firm's total cost would be *CBQO*, the average per unit costs multiplied by the number of units sold. The firm's profits are simply total revenue less total cost, the shaded area of Exhibit 20-1.

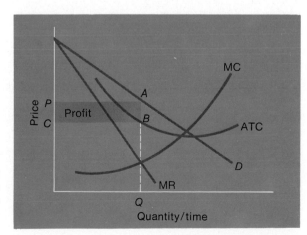

Exhibit 20-1 The Short-Run Price and Output of a Monopolist

The monopolist will reduce price and expand output as long as MR exceeds MC. Output Q would result. When price exceeds average cost at the output level, profits result.

Will market forces eliminate the profits of a monopolist? Perhaps eventually, but eventually may be a long time. The high barriers to market entry insulate the monopolist from competitive pressures. High profits will not induce rival firms to enter the industry, thereby expanding output and reducing price. A monopolist, because entry barriers into the industry are high, is less subject to the discipline of the market.

Does this mean the monopolist can be assured of economic profit? Not necessarily. The monopolist's ability to make profits is limited by the demand for his product. In some cases, even a monopolist may be unable to sell for a profit. For example, there are thousands of clever patented items that are never produced because demand–cost conditions are not favorable enough. Exhibit 20-2 illustrates this possibility. When the average cost curve of the monopolist is always above his demand curve, economic losses will result. Even a monopolist will not want to operate under these conditions. If a monopolist was already in the industry, he would produce output Q (where MR = MC) and charge price P, *operating in the short run* as long as he can cover his variable cost. In the long run, the losses will cause the monopolist to discontinue production.

Thus far we have proceeded as if the monopolist knew exactly what his revenue and cost curves looked like. Of course, in the real world this is not true. A monopolist, like other price searchers, cannot be sure of the demand conditions for his product. Like decision-makers in general, he will have to make choices without the benefit of perfect knowledge. He will have to make decisions on the basis of what he *expects* will happen if he increases price. The revenue and cost curves illustrated in Exhibits 20-1 and 20-2 might better be thought of as *expected* revenues and costs associated with various output levels. If the monopolist expects that the *additional* revenues generated by the production and sale of a unit will exceed the *additional* costs, he will expand output. On the other hand, if he *expects* that an increase in price and reduction in output will lead to a greater decline in costs than revenues, he will reduce output.

The monopolist usually will not calculate or even be aware of what we have called

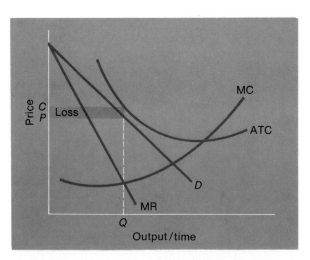

Exhibit 20-2   When a Monopolist Incurs Losses

Even a monopolist will incur short-run losses if his average cost curve lies above his demand curve.

demand, marginal revenue, and cost curves. He may use trial and error as the method of finding the profit maximum price P and output Q. But if he is really maximizing profits, the end result will be the same *as if* he had equated MR and MC.

WHY MONOPOLY IS BAD

> The monopolists, by keeping the market constantly under-stocked, by never fully supplying the effectual demand, sell their commodities much above the natural price, and raise their emoluments, whether they consist of wages or profit, greatly above their natural rate. [Adam Smith, *The Wealth of Nations,* 1776]

Through the ages, economists have had few complimentary things to say about monopoly. Most have considered it a beast, a necessary evil at best. There are three major reasons why economists have taken such a dim view toward monopoly.

First, monopoly severely limits the options available to consumers. If you do not like the food at a local restaurant, you can go to another. If you do not like the wares of a local department store, you can buy good substitutes someplace else. The competition of rivals protects the consumer from the arbitrary behavior of a single seller. But what are your alternatives if you do not like the local telephone service? You can send a letter or deliver your message in person or you can write your congressman and complain. But these are not very satisfactory options to the service of the monopolists. If the monopolist "pushes" you around, often you have no feasible alternative but to accept poor service, rude treatment, or high prices.

In the absence of monopoly, the consumer can either buy a product from firm A or another firm. In the presence of monopoly, his option is to buy from the monopolist or do without. This reduction in the options available to the consumer greatly reduces the consumer's ability to discipline monopolists.

Second, economists have a negative view toward monopoly because it results in allocative inefficiency. Efficiency requires a community to undertake an activity when it generates additional benefits that are in excess of their costs. As applied to monopoly, this would require that the firm expand output as long as price exceeds marginal costs. But a profit-maximizing monopolist will restrict output below this level.

The logic of this criticism is pictured in Exhibit 20-3. The demand is, of course, a measure of how much consumers evaluate additional units of a product. The marginal cost curve represents the opportunity cost of the resources utilized to produce the additional units. Ideally, economic efficiency would require output to be expanded as long as the height of the demand curve exceeds the marginal costs. From the viewpoint of the entire community, output level Q_i would be best.

But the monopolist will produce only Q_m units. If output were expanded beyond Q_m to Q_i, how much would consumers gain? The area under the demand curve, ABQ_iQ_m, reveals the answer. How much does it cost the monopolist to produce these units? CBO_iQ_m reflects his costs. The benefits of producing the units exceed their costs. Yet the monopolist will not produce them since they add less to *his* revenues (assuming he must charge all consumers the same price) than to *his* costs. As Adam

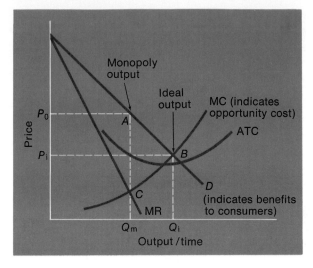

Exhibit 20-3   Understocking the Market

A monopolist would produce only output Q_m, even though Q_i is best for the entire community.

Smith noted 200 years ago (quotation at the beginning of the section), the monopolist understocks the market and charges prices that are too high.

A third shortcoming of monopoly is that profits and losses are no longer able to induce firms to enter into and exit from industries. When barriers to entry are low, profits induce firms to produce goods for which consumers are willing to pay prices (because of their expected benefits) sufficient to cover production costs. Losses constrain firms from the production of goods for which consumers are unwilling to cover production costs. Profits and losses are able to direct factors of production into those activities for which consumers have the highest evaluation.

For the monopolist, profits play no such role because entry barriers are high. The monopolist's profits are merely a premium enjoyed at the expense of the consumer.

WHEN CAN A MONOPOLIZED INDUSTRY BE COMPETITIVE?

In a nutshell, the most serious problems raised by a monopoly would be avoided if the monopolist faced the threat of rivals producing the same product or even close substitute products. The presence of competitors would prevent independent firms from restricting output and raising prices.

Why not break the monopolist up into several rival units, substituting competition for monopoly? If it were not for economies of scale, this would be a very good strategy. Many leading economists believe that there are several industries currently dominated by a few firms (or monopolists) that could be made considerably more competitive, while fully realizing the potential economies associated with large scale production.[2]

Exhibit 20-4 compares competition and monopoly, assuming that economies of scale are unimportant in the industry. Thus the least cost production conditions for purely

[2]Chapters 21 and 22 discuss the potential of policies designed to promote competition in greater detail.

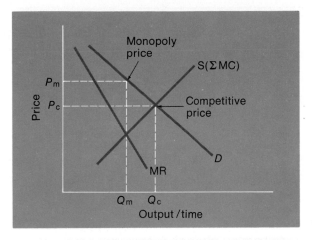

Exhibit 20-4   Comparing Competition and Monopoly

When there is not a cost advantage from large scale production, competition serves to reduce price. For a purely competitive industry, supply and demand would dictate price P_c. The firms would just be able to cover their average (and marginal) costs. If the firms all merged into a monopoly and *cost conditions remained the same*, the monopolist would restrict output to Q_m (where his MC would equal MR). Price would rise to P_m.

competitive firms will not differ from those of a monopolist. When the industry is purely competitive, price will be determined by supply and demand. As Exhibit 20-4 illustrates, under these conditions competition would drive price down to P_c in the long run. An industry output of Q_c would result. The market price would just equal the *marginal* opportunity costs of production.

In contrast, if the industry were monopolized, the profit-maximizing monopolist would equate marginal revenue with marginal cost. This would mean an output level of Q_m, because the industry supply curve would also be the *monopolist's* MC curve. The monopolist would charge P_m, a higher price than would exist in a competitive industry. When economies of scale are unimportant, imposition of competitive conditions on a monopolized industry would result in lower prices, a larger output, and improved economic efficiency.

ECONOMIES OF SCALE AND NATURAL MONOPOLY

Unfortunately, many times it is unrealistic to expect similar cost conditions for pure competition and monopoly. Economies of scale are often the reason why certain industries tend to be monopolized. If economies of scale are important, larger firms will have lower per unit cost than smaller rivals. Sometimes economies of scale may be so important that per unit production cost will be lowest when the entire industry output is produced by a single firm. In the absence of government intervention, the "natural" tendency would then be toward monopoly, because increases in firm size through merger or "survival of the fittest" will lead to lower per unit costs. The largest firm will always tend to eliminate smaller rivals because of the economies of scale.

Exhibit 20-5 graphically depicts the **natural monopoly** case. The long-run average cost in the industry declines and eventually crosses the demand curve. In order to fully take advantage of the economies of scale, given the demand for the product, all of the output of the industry would have to be produced by a single firm. If the firm were an unregulated monopolist, it would produce output Q_m and charge price P_m. The firm would realize economic profits, as average costs are less than price at the profit-maximizing output level. Yet, it would be very difficult for any firm to begin to compete with the natural monopolist because initially, while the new competitor is small, it would have very high costs of production and would be unable to make profits at price P_m. The "natural" monopoly conditions of the industry act as an entry barrier limiting the threat of potential competitors.

Note that when "natural" monopoly exists, a "competitive" market structure would be both high cost and difficult to maintain. Suppose the output of an industry were divided among 10 firms of size Q_c (see Exhibit 20-5). These small firms would have per unit average costs of P_c. Even if they charged a price that was just equal to their average cost, the price would be higher than the monopolistic price P_m. In addition, since firms larger than Q_c would always be at a competitive advantage, there would continue to be a strong tendency for firms to merge and become larger. Imposition of a competitive structure is self-defeating, when monopoly would "naturally" exist because of the economies of scale.

The telephone industry and local public utilities (water, electricity, etc.) approximate natural monopoly conditions. If there were several telephone companies operating in the same area, each with its own lines, transmission equipment, and home phones, costly duplication would result. In such industries a large number of firms would not be feasible.

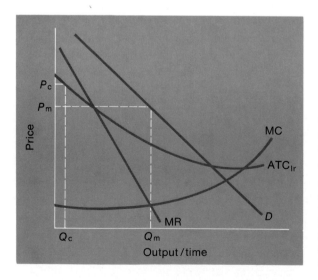

Exhibit 20-5   Monopoly and Competition with Economies of Scale.

When economies of scale are important, efforts to impose a competitive market structure are self-defeating. For an industry with the cost (and demand) curves like those indicated here, prices (and costs) would be lower under monopoly than if there were 10 competitors of size Q_c.

Natural Monopoly—The Policy Alternatives

When monopoly or near monopoly results because of economies of scale, there are really only three feasible policy alternatives. First, the monopolists could be permitted to operate unmolested. We have already pointed out that this option limits consumer choice and results in a higher product price (and smaller output) than is consistent with ideal economic efficiency. Second, government regulation could be imposed on the monopolists; or third, the government could completely take over production in the industry. Government operation is an alternative to private monopoly. Let us take a closer look at the latter two alternatives so that we might better compare them with private monopoly.

REGULATING THE MONOPOLIST

Can government regulation improve on the allocative efficiency of unregulated monopoly? In theory, the answer to this question is clearly yes. Government regulation *can* force the monopolist to reduce his price and, at the lower government imposed price ceiling, the monopolist will voluntarily produce a larger output.

Exhibit 20-6 illustrates why ideal government price regulation will improve resource allocation. The profit-maximizing monopolist would set price at P_0 and produce q_0 output, where $MR = MC$. But at this output level the consumer's evaluation of *additional* units clearly exceeds their opportunity cost. How can the regulating agency improve on the outcome of the unregulated monopolists?

1. *Average Cost Pricing.* If a regulating agency forced the monopolist to reduce price to P_1, the intersection of the firm's AC curve and the market (and firm) demand

Exhibit 20-6 Regulation of a Monopolist

If unregulated, a profit-maximizing monopolist with the costs indicated here would produce Q_0 units and charge P_0. If a regulating agency forced the monopolist to reduce price to P_1, the monopolist would expand output to Q_1. Ideally, we would like to have output expanded to Q_2, where $P = MC$. But regulating agencies usually do not attempt to force prices as low as P_2. Can you explain why?

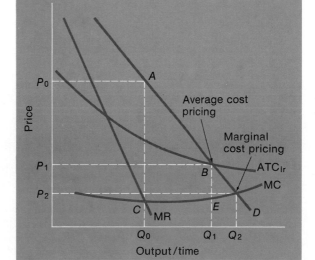

curve, the monopolist would expand output to Q_1. Since the firm cannot charge a price above P_1, it would no longer be possible for it to increase revenues by selling a smaller output at a higher price. Once the price ceiling is instituted, the firm can increase revenues by P_1, but only P_1, for each unit that it sells. The regulated firm's marginal revenue is constant at P_1 for all units sold until output is increased to Q_1. Since the firm's MC is less than P_1 (and therefore MR), the profit-maximizing regulated monopolist would expand output from Q_0 to Q_1. The benefits from the consumption of these units (ABQ_1Q_0) clearly exceed their costs (CEQ_1Q_0). Ignoring the impact on the distribution of income, social welfare has improved as the result of the regulative action. At that output level, revenues are just sufficient to cover costs. The firm is making zero economic profit (that is, "normal" profits).

2. *Marginal Cost Pricing.*   Ideally, since marginal cost is still less than price even at the Q_1 output level, additional welfare gains are possible if output were increased to Q_2. But, if a regulating agency forced the monopolist to reduce its price to P_2 (so price would just equal marginal cost at the output level Q_2), economic losses would result. Even a monopolist, unless he was subsidized, would not undertake production if the regulating agency set the price at P_2 or any price below P_1. Usually problems associated with determining and allocating the necessary subsidy would make this option unfeasible.

"And though in 1969, as in previous years, your company had to contend with spiralling labor costs, exorbitant interest rates, and unconscionable government interference, management was able once more, through a combination of deceptive marketing practices, false advertising, and price fixing, to show a profit which, in all modesty, can only be called excessive."

Drawing by Lorenz; © 1970 The New Yorker Magazine, Inc.

Why Regulation May Go Astray

The regulation solution looks nice on paper. We have made it look simple. But the real world is more complex. Analysis of economic incentives suggests that even the regulated solution will usually be less than ideal. Why?

1. *Lack of Information.*   In discussing ideal regulation solutions, we assumed that we knew what the firm's AC, MC, and demand curves looked like. In reality, of course, this is not the case.

Because estimates of demand and marginal costs will be difficult to obtain, regulating agencies usually use profits (or rate of return) as a gauge to determine whether the regulated price is too high or too low. The regulating agency, guarding the public interest, seeks to impose a "fair" or "normal" rate of return on the firm.

The firm's profits, if properly measured, present a regulating agency with a nice rule of thumb as a guide to establishing the "price equal average cost" solution. If the firm is making profits (that is, an abnormally high rate of return), the price must not be as low as P_1 (Exhibit 20-6). Therefore, it should be lowered. If the firm is incurring losses (less than the fair or normal rate of return), the regulated price must be less than P_1. The firm should be allowed to increase price.

But the actual existence of profits is not easily identified. Accounting profit, even allowing for a normal rate of profit, is of course not the same thing as economic profit. Regulated firms have a definite incentive to adopt reporting techniques and accounting methods that conceal profits. But still, an aggressive regulating agency should, at least initially, be able to move price toward P_1 if it is attempting to establish a "normal" rate of return for the monopolist.

2. *Cost Shifting.*   Monopolists not only have an incentive to conceal profits, but the *owners* of the regulated firm have less incentive to be concerned about costs than the owners of unregulated firms. If costs decrease, the "fair return" rule will force a price reduction. If costs increase, the fair return rule will allow a price increase. The owners of the regulated firm can expect that the long-run profit rate will be pretty much fixed regardless of whether efficient management reduces costs or inefficient management allows costs to increase.

Managers will have a freer hand to pursue personal objectives. They will be more likely to fly first class, entertain lavishly on an expense account, give their relatives and friends good jobs, grant larger wage increases, and hundreds of other such activities that increase the firm's costs, while yielding personal benefits to the managers.

Essentially, the managers are able to capture some of the gains that would otherwise go to consumers in the form of lower prices (or to owners as higher profits). Normally, these activities would be policed by the owners, but since the firm's rate of return is established by the regulating agency, the owners have little incentive to be concerned.

Exhibit 20-7 demonstrates the impact of such activities. If the firm's costs were effectively policed, average cost curve AC_1 would result. But because of production inefficiency, the firm's average cost curve shifts to AC_2. A regulating agency, granting

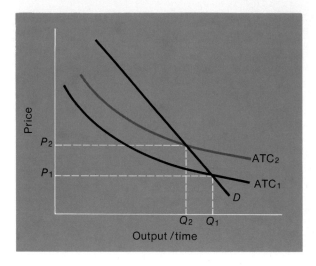

Exhibit 20-7   Cost Shifting and Monopoly Regulation

Managers of a regulated firm have a greater incentive to follow policies that yield personal gain at the expense of higher cost. With time, this may cause the cost curves of the regulated monopolist to rise, resulting in higher prices even though monetary profits are still normal.

the firm a fair return, would then allow a price increase to P_2.[3] While P_2 may still be less than the unregulated profit-maximizing monopolist would charge, some of the gains of the regulatory policy have been lost.[4]

3. *Special Interest Influence.*   The special interest effect suggests a serious practical shortcoming of the regulatory approach. Regulatory agencies exert a life or death grip on the firms that they regulate. These firms will have a strong incentive to assure that "friendly people" serve as regulators. They will invest political and economic resources to this end.

What about consumer interests? Do you know who serves on the ICC or the CAB? Do you know any consumer who voted against a politician because of his appointments to a regulatory commission? These questions answer themselves.

Consumer interests are widely dispersed and disorganized. Consumers cannot be expected to invest time, resources, votes, and political contributions to assure that regulatory commissions represent their views. The firms that are regulated will make such investments.[5] Even though the initial stimulus for a regulating agency might come from consumer interests, economic theory suggests that eventually such agencies are likely to reflect the views of the business and labor interests that they are supposed to regulate.

Does the process really work this way? This is certainly an area where more research

[3] Or the regulating agency might permit the firm to maintain price P_2 because the firm's costs are AC_2 even though AC_1 could be attained with efficient operation.

[4] If the regulating agency did not *immediately* force the monopolist to reduce prices after a cost reduction, the incentive of the monopolist to operate efficiently would be increased since any improvement in operational efficiency would then result in *short-run* (temporary) economic profits. However, during a period of general inflation "regulation lag" may result in economic losses for regulated firms. This would make it extremely difficult for the regulated firm to raise funds for capital expansion. Quality of service, particularly for potential new customers, would probably deteriorate under these conditions.

[5] The special interest influence will be weaker when regulatory commissions are elected rather than appointed. This would allow the voter to separate this issue, which is relatively unimportant to the typical voter, from other issues of greater importance.

is needed. But studies which have been conducted of major regulatory agencies indicate that regulators do typically reflect the interests of those who are regulated (see Perspectives in Economics, pages 375–379, for empirical evidence that relates to this view).

THE GOVERNMENT OPERATED FIRM

Government operated firms, such as the post office, the Tennessee Valley Authority, and local public utilities, present an alternative to both private monopoly and regulation. What can we say about how the socialized firm will operate in the real world? The decision-makers of public owned firms will be influenced by both political and economic factors. With the rise of public choice, economists have recently expressed renewed interest in the socialized firm. Certainly the final chapter on this subject has not been written.

The ideal theoretical solution is straightforward. The socialized firm should (a) operate efficiently and (b) set price equal to marginal cost. When cost conditions are like those illustrated by Exhibit 20-3, the government operated monopoly firm will ideally expand output to Q_i (where $P = MC$) and charge price P_i. The firm will make profits that can be channeled into the public treasury. On the other hand, marginal cost pricing may sometimes result in economic losses, requiring a subsidy for the public operated firm. Exhibit 20-6 illustrates cost conditions that present this possibility. Output should be expanded to Q_2, if the potential marginal welfare gains are to be fully realized. Price P_2 will be charged. The consumer's evaluation of the marginal unit (P_2) will just equal its marginal cost. Since losses result at this price and output, it will be necessary to subsidize the public enterprise.

This analysis is premised on the foundation that the socialized firm will (a) operate efficiently and (b) set the proper price. How realistic are these assumptions? Analyzing the incentives under which the managers of the public sector firm operate will help us better understand this question. Many of the same factors that confront managers of regulated firms with perverse incentives are present, often in a more extreme form, for the government operated firm. Professor Galbraith and others have argued that disperse ownership rights limit the ability of poorly informed stockholders to police management inefficiency. Thus, managers have more freedom to pursue their own objectives at the expense of "owners." The socialized firm presents the polar case of disorganized, uninformed "owners" who are in a weak position to assert their ownership rights. No small group of owners will be able to increase their wealth position if the public enterprise operates more efficiently. Thus, the disorganized owners (voters and taxpayers) will have neither the incentive nor the information to effectively police the managerial decision-making of public enterprises—rewarding efficiency and penalizing inefficiency. Economic theory suggests that higher costs will result.

In addition, the managers and employees of public enterprises often comprise a *special interest group*, particularly if the employees are well organized (for example, unionized) for political action. Should wages and working conditions of public sector employees be raised? Should nice offices, lengthy coffeebreaks, and lucrative fringe benefits be provided to employees? Should attractive positions in the public enterprise be provided to the political faithful? Should management resist pressures to lay off unneeded workers (particularly at election time), abandon unprofitable service areas, and charge users low prices (that is, less than the marginal cost) when the opportunity cost of providing the service is high? On all of these issues, managers and other highly concentrated groups (for example, government employees, specialized users) have a common interest that conflicts with the interests of the disorganized, uninformed taxpayers. Under these circumstances, economic theory suggests that the views of the special interest will usually dominate, even when inefficiency and higher costs result.

Thus, public enterprises can be expected to use at least some of their monopoly power, not to benefit the wide cross section of disorganized taxpayers and consumers, but rather as a cloak for inefficient operation and actions that further the political objectives of those who exercise control over the firm.

THERE ARE NO IDEAL SOLUTIONS

In this chapter, we pointed out why monopoly fails to meet our ideal economic efficiency criteria. Yet, the major alternatives to unregulated natural monopoly also have shortcomings. When economies of scale are the source of the monopoly structure, legislative efforts to make the industry competitive would be self-defeating. Government regulation may result in economic waste, particularly as the regulation becomes institutionalized over a period of time. Government ownership, the other major alternative, will also generate incentives that we can expect to result in economic inefficiency. The world is an imperfect place in which to live. Sometimes none of the alternatives are very attractive.

▭ POSTSCRIPT

There is sometimes a tendency to think of monopoly as the complete absence of rival competitors. Traditional economic theory, because of its emphasis on competition *within* an industry, highlights the market power of the monopolists. But no firm is completely free from competitive pressures. In a dynamic world, changing tastes and technology have a way of *eventually* catching up with even seemingly entrenched monopolists. It is important to stress the economic power derived from monopoly. It is also important to stress factors limiting that power.

Substitutes will exist for the products produced by monopolists. For certain functions, some of the substitutes may be quite attractive. Potential competitors may limit the power of monopolists. High prices will encourage rivals to develop substitutes. For example, the high price of natural rubber spurred the development of synthetic rubber. High rail shipping rates accelerated the development of long distance trucking. Monopolists may charge less than their short-run profit-maximizing price, in order to reduce the incentive of potential rivals to develop competitive products. Of course, competitive factors of this variety are not good alternatives for direct competition within an industry. But they do point out that even a monopolist has rivals, producers who would like to gain by offering consumers a better alternative.

In the following chapter, we will consider the situation where firms may possess some monopoly power, but do not control the entire industry. Before we move on, let us take a closer look at the impact of regulation in an industry, transportation, that many economists believe would be highly competitive in the absence of government regulatory action.

How the Regulators Promote Inefficiency and Protect You from Low Prices—The Case of Transportation

Perspectives in Economics

> What does the consumer owe the ICC? He owes for certain only two things: the support of a compulsory noncompetitive rate structure in the motor trucking industry, which, if not regulated would be a highly competitive industry, and the imposition of a nonviable rigidity upon the railroad industry which is helping to destroy it before our eyes.[6] [George J. Stigler]

In 1887 Congress established the Interstate Commerce Act to deal with the monopoly power of railroads. At that time it was not uncommon for shippers to charge more for short hauls, for which they possessed a monopoly, than for longer hauls served by rival shippers. In addition, special rebates were sometimes given to favorite customers, Standard Oil for example. The act created the Interstate Commerce Commission (ICC), empowering it to regulate rates and prevent discriminatory pricing policies in the rail industry.

With the passage of time, dynamic forces have dramatically changed competitive conditions in the transportation industry. By 1935 highways crisscrossed the country and the rail industry began to feel the competitive pressures of truckers. Still later air freight, offering more rapid service, began to compete with both rails and trucks. Today, trucks, buses, water carriers, airlines, automobiles, pipelines, and railroads all compete for the shipping and transportation dollar. Nonlegal barriers to entry and economies of scale are relatively unimportant for most of these media, particularly in the trucking industries. In the absence of government regulation, most economists believe that today's transportation industry would be highly competitive.

The Life Cycle Hypotheses of Regulatory Agencies

Currently, the transport industry is characterized by detailed government regulation that is usually reserved for monopolists. Why? Analysis of both the economic and political factors that are likely to influence regulatory action will help us answer this question.[7] Regulatory agencies often owe their existence to an outpouring of popular support demanding that something be done about the monopolistic practices of a specific industry. *Initially*, such agencies can be expected to police the actions of the industry with vigor. But with the passage of time, powerful forces are operating to change the nature of the regulatory agency. Individual consumers (and taxpayers) have little incentive to care much about regulatory actions. Often they are lulled into thinking that since there is a regulatory agency, the "public interest" is necessarily represented. In contrast, firms (and employees) in regulated industries will be vitally

[6] Manuel F. Cohen and George J. Stigler, *Can Regulatory Agencies Protect the Consumer?* Washington, D.C.: American Enterprise Institute for Public Policy Research, 1971.
[7] See Dwight R. Lee and Robert F. McNown, *Economics in Our Time: Concepts and Issues* (Chicago: Science Research Associates, 1975), pp. 74–79, for an excellent analysis of this issue.

interested in the structure and composition of regulatory commissions. Favorable actions by the commission could lead to larger profits, higher paying jobs, and insulation from the uncertainties of competition. Thus, firms and employee groups, recognizing their potential gain, will invest both economic and political resources in an effort to influence the actions of regulatory agencies.

How will a vote-maximizing political entrepreneur behave under these conditions? The payoffs from supporting the views of the now apathetic public will be small. Clearly, the "special interest effect" is present. Political entrepreneurs have a strong incentive to support the position of the regulated industry, while milking them for political support, when setting policy and making appointments to regulating agencies.

Does the process really work this way? Many observers believe that it does. Ralph Nader in a *Playboy* interview in October 1968 stated "I originally came to Washington with a great deal of hope that the regulatory agencies would champion the consumers' interest, but it didn't take me very long to become disillusioned. Nobody seriously challenges the fact that the regulatory agencies have made an accommodation with the businesses they are supposed to regulate—and they've done so at the expense of the public."

Senator Proxmire (D., Wisconsin) puts it even stronger in his criticism of the ICC, the granddaddy of regulatory commissions. He states, "The ICC has become a captive of the transportation industry itself. Instead of regulating transportation to avoid monopoly and increased prices, it has established monopolies, reduced competition and ordered high and uneconomical rates to cover the costs of inefficient producers."[8]

The cozy relationship between the "regulators" and regulated industries presents not only the opportunity for political gain but it is also often the route to a high paying job. Of 14 commissioners who have left the ICC since 1958, 12 found jobs representing industries that they once controlled. A Nader report on the subject in 1970 argued that the job switching between the ICC and firms in the transportation industry is so widespread it appears to be a form of "deferred bribery."

What the ICC Does for You

Although it was initially established to prohibit discriminatory pricing policies, the regulatory powers of the ICC have been expanded. Today, its powers in three major areas influence the nature of competition in the ground transportation industry.

1. The ICC limits the number of shippers in interstate commerce.   Shippers, both rail and truck, must obtain a license from the ICC before they are permitted to operate in interstate commerce. Entrants into the shipping industry must not only be willing to undertake the entrepreneural risk, but they must also incur the loss of time and legal effort to convince the ICC that their proposed service is "required by the present or future public convenience and necessity."[9]

Established shippers have the opportunity to present the ICC with counterevidence as to why the entry of a new rival is unnecessary or even harmful. The threat of delay and the fear that protests from established firms will result in costly litigation is enough to deter many potential competitors. Yet, each year the ICC turns down hundreds of qualified companies seeking operating rights for interstate routes. Why? In the words of commission chairman George Stafford, the ICC seeks to assure that

---

[8] Mark Frazier, "Highway Robbery—Via the ICC," *Readers Digest*, January 1974.
[9] U.S. Code 307(a), 1964 ed.

the *existing carriers* "will not have their profits drained by unwarranted or destructive competition."

2. The ICC regulates shipping rates and permits the rail and truck industries to establish price fixing rate bureaus. In practice, shipping rates are established jointly through rate bureaus, associations of carriers designed to set the industry's pricing policy. Such actions would be in violation of antitrust laws in other industries, but ground transportation has been granted a special exemption. Any competitor who wants to cut his price below the schedule established by the rate bureau may ask ICC to hear his case. Typically, it takes six to eight months to obtain a ruling from the ICC. Needless to say, these arrangements strongly discourage price competition in interstate shipping.

3. The ICC often limits the products that carriers can haul, the routes they can travel, and the number of cities along the route that they can serve. All carriers are prohibited from using price reductions as a means to arrange a "return haul." A carrier might be granted a license to haul from St. Louis to Denver, and simultaneously be prohibited from hauling a return shipment from Kansas City. A carrier's assigned route from New Orleans to Chicago might require an intermediate stop in Atlanta. The result—miles of wasteful travel and trucks that are empty nearly 40 percent of the time! The Highway Research Board found that common carriers had full loads in both directions only 50 percent of the time. In contrast, unregulated shippers arrange return hauls more than 80 percent of the time.

Impact on Shipping Costs

It has been estimated that ICC regulations cost consumers between $3.8 and $8.8 billion annually. Most experts believe that regulation inflates truck and rail shipping rates by 20 percent or more. These views are consistent with studies conducted by economists. Richard Farmer found that the average costs per ton-mile of exempt shippers (agricultural commodities are exempted from ICC regulations) were less than half the comparable figures for the general freight carriers regulated by the ICC.[10] Our unregulated experience with poultry, frozen fruits, and vegetables provides additional evidence. In 1956 shipment of these products was exempted from ICC regulation. The Department of Agriculture found that within a year after this deregulation, shipping rates for fresh chicken had fallen 33 percent, while those on frozen chicken declined 36 percent. For frozen fruits and vegetables, rate reductions averaged nearly 20 percent. At the same time, shippers reported the quality of service provided by the nonregulated truckers was "generally superior" to that previously offered by regulated truckers.[11]

Regulating the Airlines

The regulation of air transportation by the Civil Aeronautics Board[12] has followed a similar pattern. The CAB controls entry into the airline industry, grants routes to carriers, and sets rates. Routes are assigned to specific airlines. Any carrier desiring to compete in an interstate route would have to convince the CAB that its services are needed. To say that the CAB has limited entry on major routes would be an understatement. Despite more than 150 requests, the CAB has not granted a single

[10] Richard N. Farmer, "The Case for Unregulated Truck Transportation," *Journal of Farm Economics,* 1964.
[11] *The Economic Report of the President,* 1971.
[12] Many people incorrectly associate the CAB with regulation of air safety, a function that it did perform in the past. However, since 1958, the Federal Aviation Agency has been responsible for air safety rules.

trunk (long-distance) route to a new carrier since 1938! Sixteen firms controlled all interstate trunk routes in 1938. Today, because of mergers, these routes are in the hands of 11 firms.[13]

The combination of controlled entry, a small number of firms servicing each route, and CAB policy has stifled *price* competition in the airline industry. The CAB attempts to establish a rate and route structure which limits airlines to the market rate of return on their capital. Traffic on some routes is heavy and extremely profitable. But airlines are also required to serve other less traveled routes that are unprofitable.

Since CAB policy discourages price competition, quality of service has become a major outlet for competitive behavior in the industry. Airlines compete to provide customers with meals, pretty hostesses, the latest and most modern flight equipment, and the most frequent daily flights from point *A* to point *B*. The result is duplication of routes during prime times, heavy morning and early evening airport congestion, and a tendency toward overcapacity.

How does the consumer fare under this arrangement? Comparison with nonregulated intrastate routes in California presents revealing evidence.[14] The president's Council of Economic Advisers reports, "Competition from intrastate airlines has resulted in fare levels per-mile within California that are approximately 40 percent below those for comparable services in the rest of the Nation."[15] Unsurprisingly, air travel between San Francisco and Los Angeles exceeds that between any two cities in the world.

In recent years, partially stimulated by the existing rate structure, unregulated charter flights entered the air travel market. The CAB moved to head off this competitive pressure. First, it approved discussions between schedule and charter carriers for the purpose of establishing a mutually satisfactory *minimum* price for charter flights. When the two failed to reach an agreement, the CAB announced that affinity group charter flights would not be allowed to operate after December 31, 1975. It now appears that another source of competition in the airline industry will succumb to regulatory policy.[16]

Permitting Competitive Forces to Operate

Most economists favor a policy of deregulation in the transportation industry. In the "age of the truck" ground transportation is almost ideally suited to competition. Industrial organization economists such as Clair Wilcox also believe that, in the absence of regulation, effective competition would also exist in the airline industry.[17] The competitive forces in the California intrastate market lend support to this view.

So as to avoid disruption, the movement toward a competitive transportation industry might best be accomplished gradually. Initially all route restrictions (for

---

[13] See Clair Wilcox, *Public Policies Toward Business*, 4th ed. Homewood, Illinois: Irwin, 1971, pp. 401–404.

[14] With free entry into the California market, 16 new competitors began offering intrastate service between 1946 and 1965. This suggests that there would have been between 110 and 200 new entrants nationally during this time period if the CAB had not limited entry. See D. R. Lee and R. F. McNown, *Economics in Our Time*, Chicago: Science Research Associates, 1975.

[15] *Economic Report of the President—1971*, pp. 128–129.

[16] In recent months the CAB's policy of discouraging charter flight competition has come under intense criticism. As this book goes to press, the CAB approved new rules that would permit additional price competition from charter flights. Trans World Airlines immediately filed a suit seeking to prohibit the CAB from permitting the price reductions on charter flights. Thus, more intense price competition in the airline industry is temporarily stalled pending court action. Potential litigation fees and costly delays certainly do little to encourage meaningful price competition in this industry.

[17] Wilcox, *Public Policies Toward Business*, p. 401.

example, limits on products hauled and routes traveled) might be removed. Congress might require both the CAB and ICC to approve automatically, without delay, all price *reductions* within a reasonable zone (for example, 25 percent of the current rate). The existing exemption of the transportation industry from antitrust legislation, prohibiting collusive practices, should be removed.

During a second phase, other restrictions on competition should be removed. Free entry into interstate trucking should be permitted. The hard-pressed railroads should be permitted to lower their fares substantially on long-distance shipping even if it means that the share of this market held by truckers would decline sharply. Clearly, the truckers will be able to more than hold their current market share on short-distance hauls. With time, all carriers should be permitted to drop unprofitable routes that the ICC and CAB have sometimes forced on them. In the airline industry, charter carriers should be allowed to sell wholesale seats to travel agents (this is currently prohibited). Under this arrangement, travel agents would bear the risk from the purchase of wholesale reservations, but inexpensive organization of charter flights would result. Such an arrangement would almost surely promote lower airfares for long-distance, preplanned travel. Subject to safety regulations, new entrants into the airline industry should automatically be allowed to compete.

In the view of most economists such movements in the direction of free competition would result in lower prices, more efficient usage of our transportation facilities, and improved service on all but sparsely utilized routes.

Discussion

1. Explain why you think regulation either helps or hurts the consumer. How can regulation be improved? Does protecting "competitors" help the consumer? Why or why not? Explain.
2. Current ICC policy is designed to establish a rate structure that prevents "unfair or destructive competitive practices." In reality, the policy has prevented truckers from lowering rates on short hauls (thereby protecting the railroads). At the same time railroads are prevented from lowering rates on long-distance hauls (thereby protecting truckers). Explain why this policy results in economic inefficiency.
3. "If it were not for the ICC and CAB, the transportation industry would be chaotic. Only the powerful would survive. The consumer would be at the mercy of the producer." Evaluate.

CHAPTER LEARNING OBJECTIVES

1. Business firms have an incentive to avoid the discipline of competition. In the presence of competitive pressures and low entry barriers, competition will eliminate economic profit (above-normal profit) in the long run.

2. Legal restrictions, economies of scale, and control of resources are the most common sources of barriers to entry.

3. Monopoly exists when there is a single producer of a product for which there are no good substitutes. A monopolist will maximize profits by expanding output as long as marginal revenue exceeds marginal cost. At this output level, product price will exceed marginal cost.

4. A monopolist might make either profits or losses. If losses occur, the monopolist will go out of business in the long run. If profit results, high barriers to entry shield the monopolist from competitive pressures. Therefore, long-run economic profits are sometimes possible.

5. Even a monopolist is not completely independent of competitive pressures. All products have substitutes of varying degrees. In time, development of substitutes for the product of the monopolist is a threat. Some monopolists may charge prices less than the short-run profit maximum level, in order to discourage *potential* competitors from seeking to develop substitute products.

6. Economists are critical of a monopoly because **(a)** it limits the ability of consumers to "control" the behavior of the producer, **(b)** the unregulated monopolist produces too little output and charges a price in excess of his marginal cost, and **(c)** profits are unable to induce new entry, expanding the supply of the product until price declines to the level of even average production costs.

7. Natural monopoly exists when long-run average costs continue to decline as firm size increases. Thus a larger firm always has lower costs. Production cost would be lowest when a single firm generated the entire output of an industry.

8. In the presence of natural monopoly, there are three policy alternatives—**(a)** private, unregulated monopoly, **(b)** regulated private monopoly, and **(c)** government ownership. Economic theory suggests that each of the three will fail to meet our ideal efficiency conditions. Private monopoly will result in higher prices and less output than would be ideal. Regulation will often fail to meet our ideal efficiency conditions because **(a)** the regulators will not have knowledge of the firm's cost curves and market demand conditions, **(b)** firms have an incentive to conceal their actual cost conditions and take profits in disguised forms, and **(c)** the regulators often end up under the influence of the firms they are supposed to regulate. Under public ownership, managers often can gain by pursuing policies that yield them personal utility and by catering to the views of special interest groups (for example, well-organized employees and specialized customers) who will be able to help them further their political objectives. Such policies can and often do conflict with the efficient operation of the firm.

9. Regulation in industries that would otherwise be competitive can be expected to result in policies that promote economic inefficiency. There is strong evidence that regulatory policy in the transportation area has had this effect.

IMPORTANT TERMS TO REMEMBER

Monopoly: Single seller of a product without good substitutes.

Natural monopoly: An industry for which average production costs continually decline with output. Thus a single firm would be the lowest cost method of producing the output demanded.

THE ECONOMIC WAY OF THINKING—DISCUSSION QUESTIONS

1. Is a monopolist subject to any competitive pressures? Explain. Would an unregulated monopolist have an incentive to operate and produce efficiently? If so, why?

2. Which of the following are monopolists: **(a)** your local newspaper, **(b)** Boston Celtics, **(c)** General Motors, **(d)** U.S. Postal Service, **(e)** Walter Cronkite, **(f)** American Medical Association? Is the definition of an industry and market area important in the determination of a seller's monopoly position? Explain.

3. What are barriers to entry? Give three examples. Why are barriers to entry essential if a firm is going to make profits in the long run.

4. Does a monopolist charge the highest price for which he can sell his product? Does he maximize his average profit per sale? Will a monopolistic firm always be profitable? Why or why not?

5. The retail liquor industry is potentially a competitive industry. But the liquor retailers of a southern state organized a trade association that sets prices for all firms. For all practical purposes, the trade association transformed a competitive industry into a monopoly. Compare the price and output policy for a purely competitive industry with the policy that would be established by a profit-maximizing monopolist or trade association. Who benefits and who is hurt by the formation of the monopoly?

6. Does economic theory indicate that an ideal regulating agency which forced a monopolist to set prices according to either marginal or average cost would be more efficient than an unregulated monopolist? Explain. Does economic theory suggest that a regulating agency *will* follow a proper regulation policy? What are some of the factors that complicate the regulatory function?

7. "The bad economics of competitive textbooks not withstanding, there are no ideal 'real world' solutions to monopoly. All of the potential solutions—unregulated monopoly, regulation, and government operation—have shortcomings." Do you agree or disagree? Discuss.

21
OLIGOPOLY AND THE WORLD OF BIG BUSINESS

Pure monopoly is a rare occurrence in the real world. Most firms must face at least a few rivals that produce similar, or in some cases, identical products. Economists use the term **oligopoly** to describe industries dominated by a small number of firms.

In several important industries, particularly manufacturing industries such as automobiles, steel, cigarettes, and aircraft, the vast majority of output is produced by just four or five firms. In this chapter we will focus on how price and output are determined in oligopolistic industries. Are oligopolists free from competitive pressures? Do they make large profits? In addition, we will present evidence on the competitiveness of the U.S. economy.

CHARACTERISTICS OF OLIGOPOLY

The word oligopoly means "few sellers." In addition to the small number of producers, oligopolistic industries have other characteristics in common.

1. *Large Scale Production (Relative to the Total Market) Is Necessary in Order to Attain a Low per Unit Cost.* In some industries the demand for the product will provide room for only a limited number of firms of efficient size. Using the typewriter industry as an example, Exhibit 21-1 illustrates the importance of economies of scale as a source of oligopoly. It has been estimated that a firm must produce at least 1 million typewriters annually before its per unit production cost will be minimized. But if the selling price of typewriters were just sufficient for firms to cover their costs, the total quantity demanded would be only 4 million. There is only room for three or four firms of cost efficient size in the industry.

2. *A Recognized Mutual Interdependence Exists between Firms in Oligopolistic Industries.* Since the number of sellers is small, each firm must take the potential reactions of rivals into account when making business decisions. The business decisions of a single seller will often exert a substantial impact on product price and profits of rival firms. The welfare of each oligopolistic seller will be mutually interdependent on the policies followed by its major rivals.

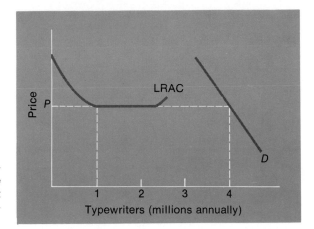

Exhibit 21-1 Economies of Scale and Oligopoly

Oligopoly results in the typewriter industry because firms will not fully realize the cost reductions from large scale output until they produce approximately a quarter of the total market.

3. *Substantial Barriers to Entry Help Protect the Existing Firms from Potential New Competitors.* Large capital requirements, patent rights, control over an essential resource, and government imposed restraints often limit the entry of additional competitors into oligopolistic industries. Without substantial barriers to entry, oligopolistic competition would be similar to monopolistic competition. But entry restraints provide the established firms with a partial shield against competition from new rivals.

4. *Oligopolists May Produce Either a Homogeneous or a Differentiated Product.* While the nature of the product does not help us identify an oligopoly, it will influence the competitive tactics of rival firms. When firms produce identical products there is less opportunity for nonprice competition. On the other hand, rival firms producing differentiated products will be more likely to use style, quality, and advertising as competitive weapons.

PRICE AND OUTPUT DETERMINATION

Because of the close interaction between firms, there is no general theory of oligopoly. However, economics does give signposts that suggest certain behavioral patterns. We can outline the potential range within which prices will lie. We can discuss the factors that will determine whether prices in the industry will be high or low relative to production costs.

Consider an oligopolistic industry where seven or eight rival firms produce the entire market output. Substantial economies of scale are present. The firms produce identical products and have similar production costs. Exhibit 21-2 depicts the market demand conditions and long-run production cost of the individual firms for such an industry.

What price will prevail? We can answer this question under two polar assumptions. First, suppose that each firm sets its price independent of other firms. There is no collusion and each competitor seeks to maximize profits by offering consumers a

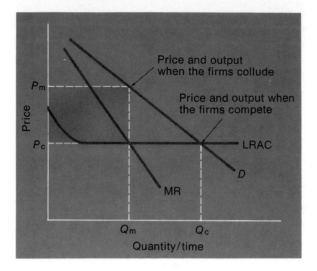

Exhibit 21-2 shows...

Exhibit 21-2 The Range of Price and Output Under Oligopoly

If the oligopolists compete with each other, price cutting would drive the price down to P_c. In contrast, perfect cooperation between firms would lead to a higher price P_m and smaller output (Q_m rather than Q_c).

better deal than is available from rivals. Under these conditions, the market price would be driven down to P_c. Firms would just be able to cover their per unit production costs. What would happen if a *single firm* raised its price? Its customers would switch to rival firms which would now expand to accommodate the new customers. The firm that raised its price would lose out. It would be self-defeating for any one firm to raise its price, independent of the other firms.

What would happen if supply conditions were such that the market price was above P_c? This would permit firms to make short-run profits. The demand curve faced by each *individual firm* would be highly elastic. If one of the sellers shaved his price ever so slightly, say by 1 percent, he could gain numerous customers. At the larger output, his total profits would expand. But what happens when all firms attempt to undercut their rivals? Total output is expanded and price is pushed down to P_c.

When rival oligopolists compete (pricewise) with each other, they will drive the market price down to the level of production cost. Unfortunately, economic theory suggests this polar result will not always come about. There is a strong incentive for the oligopolists to collude, raise price, and restrict output.

We can also determine price under a second polar assumption. Suppose that the oligopolists, recognizing their mutual interdependence, act cooperatively so as to maximize their joint profits. Under federal antitrust laws, collusive action to attain this objective would, of course, be illegal. Nonetheless, let us see what would happen if oligopolists followed this course. Exhibit 21-2 shows the marginal revenue curve that would accompany the market demand D for the product. Under perfect cooperation, the oligopolists would refuse to produce units for which marginal revenue was less than marginal cost. Thus, they would restrict joint output to Q_m, where $MR = MC$. Market price would rise to P_m. With collusion, substantial joint profits (the shaded area of Exhibit 21-2) are attained. Happy days are here again for the oligopolists. The case of perfect cooperation is, of course, identical with the outcome under monopoly.

In the real world neither of these two extremes is likely. Oligopolists will recognize their mutual interdependence and refuse to follow vigorous price competition. But, as we will soon see, there are also obstacles to collusion. Thus, prices in oligopolistic industries will not rise to the monopolistic level. Oligopolistic prices will typically be above the pure competitive, but below the pure monopolistic, level.

IT PAYS TO COLLUDE . . . AND TO CHEAT

> People of the same trade seldom meet together, even for merriment and diversion, but the conversation ends in a conspiracy against the public, or in some contrivance to raise prices. [Adam Smith, *The Wealth of Nations*, 1776]

Collusion is the opposite of competition. It involves joint cooperative actions by sellers to turn the terms of trade in their favor and against buyers. Since oligopolists can profit by colluding to restrict output and raise price, economic theory suggests that they will have a strong incentive to do so.

However, each individual oligopolist also has an incentive to cheat on collusive agreements. Exhibit 21-3 helps to show why. An undetected price cut would enable a firm to attract both customers who (a) would not buy from anyone at the higher price *and* (b) those who would buy from other firms at the higher price. Thus, the demand facing the oligopolistic *firm* will be more elastic than the industry demand curve. As Exhibit 21-3 shows, the price that maximizes the industry's profits (P_i) will be higher than the price that is best for each individual oligopolist (P_f). If a firm can

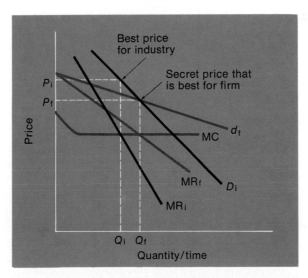

Exhibit 21-3 Gaining from Cheating

The industry demand (D_i) and marginal revenue (MR_i) curves are shown. The joint profits of oligopolists would be maximized at Q_i, where $MR_i = MC$. But the *firm's* demand curve d_f will be much more elastic than D_i. A firm would maximize its profits by cutting its price to P_f and expanding output to q_f, where its $MR_f = MC$. Individual oligopolists can gain by secretly shaving price and cheating on the collusive agreement.

find a way to reduce its price[1] below the collusive agreement, expanded sales will more than make up for the reduction in per unit profit margin.

This leads to a seemingly paradoxical conclusion. Oligopolists have a strong incentive to collude and raise prices. But they also have a strong incentive to cheat secretly on the collusive agreements. Thus oligopolistic agreements tend to be unstable.

When Is Successful Collusion Least (Most) Likely?

Agreements to raise prices are much more likely in some industries than others. The likelihood that oligopolists will be able to conspire successfully (from their viewpoint) will be low when the following conditions exist.

1. *The Number of Oligopolists Is Fairly Large.* Other things constant, it will be more costly to arrive at and maintain collusive agreements as the number of major firms in an industry increases. As the number of firms expands, the likelihood that the objectives of some of them will conflict with those of the industry increases. Each firm will want a bigger slice of the pie. Costs and the existence of unused plant capacity may differ between firms. Aggressive, less mature firms may want to expand their share of total output. These conflicting interests tend to breakdown collusive agreements.

2. *Secret Price Cuts by Rival Firms Are Costly To Detect.* Unless a firm has a way of "policing" the pricing policy of its rivals, it may be the sucker of a collusive agreement. Secret price cutters may rip off a larger share of the market, while the suckers maintain their higher prices and lose out. Sometimes price cutting can be done in ways that are difficult for the other firms to identify, providing better credit terms, faster delivery, and other related services "free" in order to slightly improve the package offered to the consumer.[2]

When firms sell a differentiated product, quality and style improvements can be used as competitive weapons. Price cuts of this variety are particularly attractive to an oligopolist because they cannot be easily and quickly duplicated by his rivals. Competitors can quickly match a reduction in money price, but it will take them time to match a quality improvement. When firms can freely use quality improvements to gain a larger market share, collusive agreements on price are of limited value. When cheating (price cutting) is both profitable and difficult for rivals "to police," it is a good bet that oligopolistic rivals will be induced to cheat.

3. *Entry Barriers Are Low, Creating the Threat of Potential New Rivals to the Established Firms.* Unless potential rivals can be excluded, oligopolists will be unable to make abnormally high profits. Temporarily successful collusion will merely attract

---

[1]Do not forget there are two ways to reduce price. First, money price could be reduced, holding quality constant. Or, second, the money price could be held constant, while upgrading product quality.

[2]See Marshall R. Colberg, Dascomb Forbush, and Gilbert R. Whitaker, *Business Economics* 4th ed. (Homewood, Illinois: Irwin, 1970), for an extensive discussion of the alternative methods by which business firms are able to alter price.

competitors into the industry, eliminating the profits. Even with collusion, long-run profits will not be possible unless entry into the industry can be blocked.

Local markets are sometimes dominated by a few firms. For example, many local communities have only a small number of ready-mix concrete producers, bowling alleys, accounting firms, and furniture stores. But in the absence of government restrictions, entry barriers into these markets are usually low. The threat of potential rivals reduces the gains from collusive behavior under these conditions.

4. *Market Demand Conditions Are Unstable.*   Demand instability may lead to honest differences among oligopolists about what is best for the industry. One firm may want to expand because it anticipates a sharp increase in future demand. A more pessimistic rival may want to hold the line on existing industrial capacity. Differences in expectations about future demand simply add another area of potential conflict among oligopolistic firms. Thus, successful collusion will be more likely when demand is relatively stable.

5. *Vigorous Antitrust Action Increases the Cost of Collusion.*   Under existing antitrust laws, collusive behavior is prohibited. Of course, secret agreements are possible. Simple informal cooperation might be conducted without discussions or collusive agreements. But like other illegal behavior, all such agreements would be nonenforceable. Vigorous antitrust enforcement can discourage firms from undertaking such illegal agreements. As the threat of getting caught increases, participants will be less likely to attempt collusive behavior.

THE KINKED DEMAND CURVE

Prices in oligopolistic industries are often inflexible. Despite changes in input prices, technology, production techniques, and other factors that are bound to influence cost, the prices of the oligopolists will often remain unchanged. The hypothesis of the **kinked demand curve** has been advanced to explain this price inflexibility. The essential idea is that the oligopolist's demand curve will be (a) very *elastic* for a price *increase* because other firms will maintain their prices but (b) very *inelastic* for a price *reduction* because the other firms will respond by reducing their prices also.

The argument makes a certain amount of sense. If an oligopolist does not dominate an industry, why should other firms necessarily duplicate his actions? When other firms do not follow suit, a price increase would mean a substantial loss of sales. But, if a single oligopolist decreases price, he can be almost sure that his rivals will respond. If they do not, their sales will fall sharply. Since a price reduction will be matched by the other firms of the industry, it will lead to few additional sales.

Exhibit 21-4 illustrates the kinked demand curve. Once a price is established, the oligopolist's demand curve is highly elastic in response to a price rise, but quite inelastic for a price reduction. Since the demand curve is kinked at output Q, the marginal revenue curve will be discontinuous. This means that marginal costs could vary substantially at output Q, while continuing to equal marginal revenue. For example, both MC_1 and MC_2 intersect the MR curve at output Q. Therefore, despite

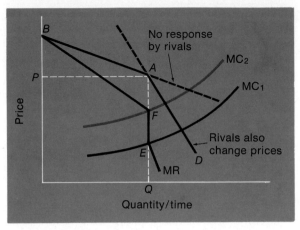

Exhibit 21-4   The Kinked Demand Curve

If an oligopolist increases his price, he will lose many of his customers to rival firms. In contrast, a price reduction, since it will be matched by competitors, will lead to few additional customers. Thus the oligopolist's demand curve is kinked, and the corresponding marginal revenue curve will be discontinuous, as shown. The oligopolist will not change price even if his MC fluctuates between *E* and *F*.

these changes in cost, the profit-maximizing price of the oligopolists would remain at *P*. Prices would be relatively inflexible and only substantial changes in cost conditions would induce a price change.

The kinked demand curve does explain why prices in an oligopolistic industry may be stable, but it is not a general theory. It suffers from a major defect. It does not explain how the price *P*, the initial stable price, is originally established.

Pulling the Theory Together

Uncertainty and imprecision have characterized our analysis of oligopoly. We know that firms can gain if they can successfully agree to restrict output and raise price. But there are also costs of collusion. We have outlined some of the conflicts and difficulties (costs) associated with establishment of perfect cooperation between oligopolistic firms. In some industries, these difficulties are substantial and the market power of the oligopolists will therefore be relatively small. In other industries, oligopolistic cooperation, though probably less than perfect, may permit them to turn the terms of trade in their favor. Analysis of the costs and benefits of collusive behavior helps one better understand when an oligopolist is most (least) likely to be disciplined by competitive pressures and the threat of rivals.

MONOPOLY POWER AND PROFIT—THE EARLY BIRD GETS THE WORM

The theory of oligopoly suggests that when barriers to entry are high, economic profits will not always be driven down to the competitive level. In the last chapter, we saw that under certain conditions an unregulated monopolist could earn economic profit

OUTSTANDING ECONOMIST: George Stigler

George Stigler, a past president of the American Economic Association, has made an outstanding contribution to history of economic thought, production and cost theory, oligopoly theory, utility regulation, information theory, and industrial structure. A long-time professor of economics at the University of Chicago, he is perhaps best known among economists for his cutting humor and defense of competitive markets.

Unlike most other well-known economists, Stigler's numerous publications have dealt almost exclusively with microeconomics. He has long been interested in the role of competition. He believes that competitive forces are strong even in our modern industrial economy. Thus only a moderate amount of antitrust action is necessary to preserve a satisfactory level of competition. Stigler's research suggests that antitrust action, particularly the Sherman Act and more recent antimerger legislation, has helped to preserve competitive markets and reduce business collusion.

Stigler feels that government regulation motivated by the desire to escape competitive forces is a threat to the market economy. He has no illusions about the views of business decision-makers. He once remarked that "Every industry that can afford a spokesman has emphasized both its devotion to the general principle (of competition) and the overriding need for reducing competition within its own market."

Stigler has argued for a reduction in the discretionary power of regulatory agencies such as the ICC, CAB, and SEC. In his words if regulatory commissions have often been "subservient to the industry they purport to regulate, it is inexcusably romantic to assume that all future appointments will be regulatory saints." While admitting this possibility, he notes that "the number of saintly men has not yet risen to the level where the census makes them a separate statistical category."

Professor Stigler had conveniently named his boat "Treatise." Whenever he wants to escape the hassles of a professional economist, he informs his colleagues, "I am going to work on my Treatise." However, his lengthy list of publications and continued research productivity still suggest that he spends much more time in his office than on his "Treatise."

---

even in the long run. Suppose that a well-established firm, such as AT&T or General Motors, is able to use its market power to earn consistent economic profits. Do their current stockholders gain because of their monopoly power? Surprisingly, the answer is no. The ownership value of a share of corporate stock for such corporations long ago began to reflect their market power and profitability. Many of their *present* stockholders paid high prices for their stock because they expected the firms to be highly profitable. In other words, they paid for any above-normal economic profits that these firms might be expected to earn because of their monopoly power.

Do not expect to get rich buying the stock of highly profitable monopolistic or oligopolistic firms. You are already too late. The early bird gets the worm. The owners of the stock at the time these firms initially developed their market position have already captured the gain. The value of their stock increased at that time. But after the firms' future profit prospects are widely recognized, subsequent stockholders fail to gain a high rate of return on their financial investment.

REAL WORLD OLIGOPOLISTS

Which industries are dominated by a small number of firms? How important is oligopoly? Economists have developed a tool, the concentration ratio, that will help us answer these questions.

The **concentration ratio** is the percentage of total industry sales that are accounted for by the four (or sometimes eight) largest firms of an industry. This ratio could vary from near zero to 100, with 100 indicating that the sales of the four largest firms comprised the entire industry.

The concentration ratio could be thought of as a broad indicator of "competitiveness." In general, the higher (lower) the concentration ratio, the more (less) likely that the firms of the industry will be able to collude successfully against the interest of consumers. But it is by no means a perfect measure of competitiveness. Since the sales of foreign producers are omitted, it overstates the degree of concentration in industries for which foreign competition is important. It does not reveal the elasticity

Exhibit 21-5 Percentage of Total Industry Sales Accounted for by the Four Largest Firms (Concentration Ratios) in 1947 and 1970 for Selected Manufacturing Industries

Industry	1947	1970	Change
High concentration (40 or more)			
Motor vehicles and parts	56	80	+24
Blast furnaces and steel mills	50	47	−3
Motors and generators	59	50	−9
Aircraft engines and parts	72	68	−4
Telephone and telegraph	92	94	+2
Cigarettes	90	84	−6
Farm machinery	36	40	+4
Ship building and repairing	43	46	+3
Photographic equipment and supplies	61	75	+14
Malt liquors	21	46	+25
Medium concentration (20–39)			
Petroleum	37	33	−4
Bread, cake, and related products	16	29	+13
Meat packing	41	23	−18
Periodicals	34	28	−6
Machinery tool (metal)	20	24	+4
Gray iron foundries	16	30	+14
Shoes	28	28	0
Low Concentration (less than 20)			
Newspapers	21	16	−5
Valves and pipe fittings	24	14	−10
Wood furniture	7	14	+7
Dresses	4	7	+3

SOURCE: *The American Almanac for 1974*. New York: Grosset & Dunlap, Table No. 1197.

of demand of products. Concentration is less of a problem if there are good substitutes available for a product. For example, the market power of aluminum producers will be partially limited by competition from steel, plastics, copper, and similar products. Concentration ratios tend to conceal such competitiveness between products.

What do concentration ratios reveal about the U.S. economy? Exhibit 21-5 presents concentration data for several manufacturing industries for 1947 and 1970. Several industries, including automobiles, steel, aircraft, telephone and telegraph, malt liquor, and cigarettes, are dominated by a few firms. They are oligopolistic. At the other end of the spectrum, the "big four" accounted for less than 20 percent of the sales of newspapers, valves and pipe fittings, wood furniture, and dresses.

Concentration, Economies of Scale, and Mergers

Why are some industries highly concentrated while others are less so? When the minimum size cost efficient firm is large in relationship to the market demand, concentration typically results. Exhibit 21-6 presents the findings of Joe Bain's classic

Exhibit 21-6   The Importance of Economies of Scale in Selected Industries

Importance of economies of scale	Output of an efficient firm as a percentage of national market	Average share of market of four largest firms (percent)	Four-firm concentration ratio, 1970 (percent)
Very important (10 or more percent)			
Gypsum products	33	21	85
Typewriters	30	20	80
Steel	20	12	48
Cigarettes	20	21	84
Tractors	15	17	67
Soap	15	17	70
Copper	10	23	92
Automobiles	10	25	99
Cement	10	7	30
Fountain pens	10	14	58
Moderately important (3–6 percent)			
Rayon	6	20	78
Farm machinery	6	10	40
Metal containers	3	20	78
Tires	3	18	72
Little importance (less than 2.5 percent)			
Fruit and vegetable canning	0.5	5	21
Meat packing	0.2	6	23
Oil refining	1.75	8	33
Flour milling	0.5	7	28
Liquor distilling	1.75	19	75
Shoes	2.5	7	28

SOURCE: Joe S. Bain, *Barriers to New Competition* (Cambridge, Massachusetts: Harvard Univ. Press, 1956), and *Statistical Abstract of the United States—1974.*

study on the relationship betwen economies of scale and concentration.[3] Bain's study suggests that 10 percent or more of the U.S. market is necessary to realize fully the economies of scale in the production of gypsum products, typewriters, steel, cigarettes, tractors, soap, copper, automobiles, cement, and fountain pens. In most of these industries, the concentration ratio is 50 percent or above. Yet oftentimes the average size of the four largest firms is substantially greater than need be. For example, the four largest auto producers average 25 percent of the market, more than twice the size necessary to realize fully the economies of scale in the industry according to Bain. A similar situation exists in the copper industry.

Economies of scale are clearly not the major source of concentration in several of the industries. For example, Bain found that firms with no more than 2.5 percent of the market have fully realized the economies of scale in the production of shoes, distilled liquors, milled flour, refined oil, meat packing, and fruit and vegetable canning. Yet, the concentration ratio in these industries ranges between 21 and 75. Apparently these industries could be more competitive without the loss of production efficiency.

Many economists believe that mergers, motivated by the pursuit of short-term monopoly profit, have also exerted a vast influence on the structure of American industry. **Horizontal mergers,** the combining of the assets of two or more firms under the same ownership, present firms with an alternative to both competition and collusion. A merger that would allow a single firm to control a substantial share of the output of an industry could be highly profitable, even when there is freedom of entry into the industry. The entry of new competitors will take time. A firm formed via merger that controls a substantial share of the market for a product can often realize oligopolistic profits for a period of time before the entry of new firms drives prices back down to the level of average cost. Of course, if entry barriers can be established to limit or retard the entry of new rivals, the incentive to merge is further strengthened.[4]

There have been two great waves of horizontal mergers. The first occurred between 1887 and 1904 and the second between 1916 and 1929. Many corporations that are now household words—U.S. Steel, General Electric, Standard Oil, General Foods, General Mills, and American Can, for example—are the products of mergers formed during these periods. Mergers led to a dominant firm in manufacturing industries such as steel, sugar refining, agricultural implements, leather, rubber, distilleries, and tin cans. After its initial development, the dominant firm formed via merger lost ground relative to other firms in the industry. This suggests that economies of scale were not the major motivation for the merger.

Economists often argue that competition, with time, will wear away at the market position of a dominant firm unless the firm is more efficient than its competitors. The real world is not inconsistent with this view. Dominant firms in many industries have often had their share of the market reduced as they lost out to smaller competitors with the passage of time. But while competition has served to reduce concentration, horizontal mergers have often promoted it, at least until the 1950s. In 1950 the

[3]Joe S. Bain, *Barriers to New Competition.* Cambridge, Massachusetts: Harvard Univ. Press, 1956.
[4]See George Stigler, "Monopoly and Oligopoly by Merger," *American Economic Review*, vol. XL, 1950, pp. 23–34, for a detailed analysis of this issue.

Celler–Kefauver Act, plugging a hole in the Clayton Act, made it substantially more difficult to use mergers as a means of developing oligopolistic power. Today, mergers involving large firms seldom involve former competitors.

The Stability of Concentration

How has concentration changed? Most research in this area suggests that the level of concentration, on balance, has not changed substantially since the first great wave of mergers at the turn of the century. Of course, there have been some changes within *specific industries*, but as a whole the structure of the U.S. economy is not substantially different than it was 75 years ago. Exhibit 21-5 shows that between 1947 and 1970, the degree of concentration went up in some industries (for example, automobiles and malt liquors), while declining in others (for example, meat packing and petroleum). But the ups and downs tend to balance out. Professor Bain, a leading economist in the field of industrial reorganization, summarizes the current view on concentration as follows:

> Thus we arrive at the conclusion that overall business concentration certainly has not increased since the early 1930s. We have seemed at least temporarily (now for three decades) to have reached some sort of a rough plateau in overall concentration. An ever upward trend is not in evidence.[5]

Where does one draw the line between oligopoly and competition? Economics cannot directly answer this question. But most economists would probably classify industries where the four largest firms produced less than 20 or 25 percent of the market as competitive. On the other hand, industries for which the largest firms produced more than half of the output would be classified as oligopolistic. But do not forget, a lot of other factors are important. Is the industry properly defined? Broadly defined industries will tend to have lower concentration ratios, but fewer good substitutes for the industry's product line. Narrowly defined industries may have higher concentration ratios, but better substitutes may be present. In some industries foreign competition limits the ability of an oligopolist to raise prices above the competitive level. Quality competition, cheating on tacit agreements, and the threat of potential competitors will be important competitive considerations in many industries. Competition is not solely concerned with price; it is multidimensional.

☐ LOOKING AHEAD

If American industry were dominated by monopoly interests, this factor would influence the profit levels of firms, particularly those in highly concentrated industries. Accounting profits in these industries should be in excess of profit levels in competitive industries. During the recent inflationary period, the popularity of profits, particularly in industries where prices rose rapidly, plunged to new lows. Defending profits is somewhat akin to defending radicalism at a Veterans of Foreign Wars convention.

---

[5]Joe S. Bain, *Industrial Organization*, 2nd ed. New York: Wiley, 1968, p. 110.

Yet, economics suggests that profits perform an important function in a market directed economy. The following perspective takes a look at profitability in concentrated industries, while considering the general antagonism that has been directed toward business profits.

Profits and Other Four-Letter Words

In recent years profits have been about as popular as failing grades at the end of the semester. When meat prices were rising, the profits of farmers, meat processors, and food store chains were bounced around by the popular media, usually in an irrelevant way.[6] Many business firms were termed "fast buck artists" and taken to task for "profiteering." As gasoline prices soared, the major oil companies were, of course, chastised for excess profits.[7]

The casual observer could easily have been left with the impression that rising profits were the major source of inflation during the early 1970s. In reality, the opposite was closer to the truth. As Exhibit 21-7 shows, corporate profits as a percentage of national

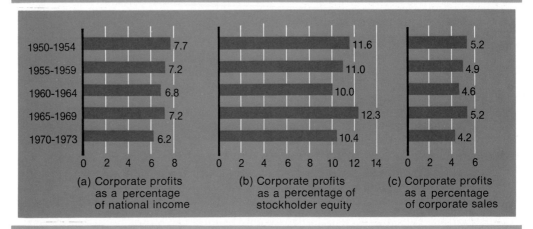

(a) Corporate profits as a percentage of national income

(b) Corporate profits as a percentage of stockholder equity

(c) Corporate profits as a percentage of corporate sales

Exhibit 21-7 How Big Are Profits?

The accounting profits of corporations are usually about 7 percent of national income [frame (a)] and 10 to 11 percent of stockholder equity. On the average, accounting profits comprise less than a nickel of corporate sales revenue [frame (c)].

SOURCE: *Economic Report of the President—1974.*

[6] Accounting profits were used almost exclusively. Even these figures were seldom related to sales, the general rise in prices, or more appropriately the value of the firm's assets (or stockholder equity). A favorite media device was to say that profits, either annual or quarterly, were up by x percent. This statement is irrelevant, since one does not know whether profits were high, normal, or low during the period with which current profits are being compared.

[7] Paradoxically, while the major communications media focused on the profits of others, they themselves were doing quite well. For example, during the first three quarters of 1973, the profits of the major oil companies *rose* 46 percent. During the same period, the profits of the *New York Times* and *Washington Post* rose 93 and 57 percent, respectively. Expressed as a return on stockholder equity, in 1973 no major oil company was able to match the 18.5 percent profit rate of CBS. Since these rates are derived from accounting data, they tell us more about hypocrisy than profit levels.

income [frame (a)] and sales revenues [frame (c)] were lower for the 1970–1973 period than for any comparable period since 1950. Measured as a percentage of stockholder equity (Exhibit 21-7b), corporate profits in 1970–1973 were obviously well below the long-run average. The propaganda of the media aside, rising corporate profits were not the cause of the inflation during the early 1970s (see Myths of Economics, pages 238–240).

Why are profits so unpopular? There are several explanations. First, there is apparently a misconception about the size of profits relative to product prices. Surveys show that young people believe that the after-tax profits of corporations comprise between 25 and 30 percent of sales. As Exhibit 21-7c illustrates, it is actually less than 5 percent.

Second, many believe profits to be an unnecessary premium that the greedy businessman tacks onto the price of consumer goods. Thus, it follows that eliminating profits would have little impact on the functioning of our economy. This view shows a complete misunderstanding of what profits are and the important role they play in our economy. Accounting profits are primarily a return to persons who have invested in machines, buildings, and nonhuman productive resources. Investment in physical capital involves risk. Eliminating profits would eliminate the incentive to invest and provide the tools that make the American worker the most productive in the world. Who would invest in either physical or human capital (for example, education), if such investments did not lead to an increase in future income (that is, profit)? Not much of anyone, that is who.

Concentrated Oligopoly and Profits

Third, others believe that profits stem primarily from monopolistic power. Economic theory lends substance to this view. But do not forget that competition is pervasive. Large firms, even those in highly concentrated industries, are not without their rivals. Thus, the extent to which profits stem from monopolistic power is an empirical question.

We would expect that monopolistic power would be greatest in highly concentrated manufacturing industries. Exhibit 21-8 presents data on profit rates for high, medium, and low concentration industries (two digit) for the 1964–1973 period. Profits as a percentage of stockholder equity were greater for the more concentrated industries. Firms in the automobile, chemical products, tobacco, and instruments industries earned an average profit rate, after taxes, of more than 13 percent on stockholder equity during the 1964–1973 period. None of the less concentrated industries were able to match these profit levels. But the picture was far from uniform. Despite the concentrated nature of the industry, primary metals—steel, aluminum, and related products—earned only 8.3 percent on stockholder equity during the 10 year period. Two other highly concentrated industries, aircraft and electrical machinery, registered below-average profit rates. The average accounting profit rate in highly concentrated industries was 12.3 percent, compared to 11.5 percent for low concentration industries and all manufacturing.

This picture of the relationship between industrial concentration and profitability is consistent with detailed studies conducted by economists. In general, these studies show a weak positive relationship between accounting profits and concentration. For example, Stigler's detailed industry study found that over the 1947–1954 period "the average (profit) rate in the concentrated industries was 8.00 percent, (while) that in

Exhibit 21-8   The Relationship Between the Accounting Profit Rate and the Industry's Concentration Ratio

	Average annual rate of accounting profit, 1964–1973[a] (percent)	Share of total sales by the four largest firms, 1967 (percent)
High concentration (more than 40 percent)		
Aircraft and parts	11.1	69
Tobacco manufactures	14.4	77
Automobiles and other motor vehicles	13.1	79
Instruments and related industries	15.3	49
Primary metals	8.3	42
Chemicals and related products	13.0	42
Electrical machinery	11.4	47
Average profit rate	12.3	—
Medium concentration (20–39 percent)		
Petroleum	11.6	33
Paper and allied products	9.2	26
Leather and leather products	10.3	26
Fabricated metal products	11.0	26
Average profit rate	10.5	—
Low concentration (less than 20 percent)		
Apparel and related products	11.5	19
Printing and publishing	12.5	19
Lumber and wood products	11.1	16
Furniture and fixtures	11.3	19
Food and kindred products	10.9	15
Average profit rate	11.5	—
Total (all manufacturing)	11.5	—

SOURCE: Morris A. Adelman, "Monopoly and Concentration: Comparisons in Time and Space," *Essays in Honour of Marco Fanno*, CEDAM, Padua, 1966; *Economic Report of the President, 1971*, pp. 284–285; and *The American Almanac for 1974*.

[a] Profits after federal income taxes divided by stockholders' equity.

the unconcentrated industries was 7.16 percent."[8] The relationship between concentration and future profitability is even more tenuous. Yale Brozen found that concentration at a specific point in time was not a significant determinant of profits in future periods.

In summary, the data suggest that the average accounting profit rate in concentrated industries is only slightly higher, probably less than 10 percent greater, than for nonconcentrated industries. The odds are only a little better than 50–50 that a more

[8] See Joe S. Bain, "Relation of Profit Rate to Industry Concentration: American Manufacturing 1936–40," *Quarterly Journal of Economics*, August 1951; Yale Brozen, "Concentration and Profits: Does Concentration Matter?" in *The Impact of Large Firms on the U.S. Economy*, edited by J. Fred Weston and Stanley I. Ornstein (Lexington, Massachusetts: Heath, 1973); George Stigler, *Capital and Rates of Return in Manufacturing Industries* (Princeton, New Jersey: Princeton Univ. Press, 1963); and H. M. Mann, "Seller Concentration, Barriers to Entry, and Rates of Return in Thirty Industries, 1950–1960," *Review of Economics and Statistics*, August 1966.

concentrated industry will be more profitable than a less concentrated one. The weak relationship between profitability and concentration implies that competition, efficient management, and changing market conditions are the major determinants of profit rates, even in concentrated industries.

The view that profits are largely an unnecessary "ripoff" is incorrect. They play an important role in a market economy. In general, firms operating efficiently and producing what consumers want will tend to show higher profit rates. Firms that operate inefficiently and insist on producing things that consumers do not want will fare less well. Typically, the latter will show losses—that is, their accounting profits will be insufficient to cover the opportunity cost of their initial investment. The competitive process will assure that long-run profits are not exessive, while rewarding those who efficiently provide products that are in short supply relative to their opportunity cost of production. Rather than focusing on profit rates, consumer advocates would do better to focus on the competitiveness of markets. Competition will take care of the profit rate when markets are competitive.

CHAPTER LEARNING OBJECTIVES

1. Oligopolistic market structure is characterized by **(a)** a small number of firms that produce the entire output of an industry, **(b)** mutual interdependence among firms, and **(c)** high barriers to entry.

2. There is not a general theory of price, output, and equilibrium for oligopolistic markets. If rival oligopolists acted entirely independent of their competitors, they would drive price down to the level of production cost. Alternatively, if they used collusion to obtain perfect cooperation, price would rise to the level that a monopolist would charge. The actual outcome will lie between these two extremes.

3. Collusion is the opposite of competition. Oligopolists have a strong incentive to collude and raise their prices. But the interests of individual firms will conflict with those of the industry. Since the demand curve faced by individual firms will be far more elastic than the industry demand curve, each firm could gain by cutting its price (or raising product quality) a little so it could attract customers from rivals. But when several firms try to do this, the collusive agreement will break down.

4. Oligopolistic firms will be less likely to collude successfully against the interests of consumers when **(a)** the number of rival firms is large, **(b)** it is costly to prohibit competitors from offering secret price cuts (or quality improvements) to customers, **(c)** entry barriers are low, **(d)** market demand conditions tend to be unstable, and **(e)** the threat of antitrust action is present.

5. The kinked demand curve helps explain why oligopolistic prices tend to be inflexible. Under the assumptions of the kinked demand curve (that is, rivals will match price reductions but not increases), a price rise would lead to a sharp reduction in sales. Conversely, a price reduction would attract few new customers. Thus, once a price is established, it will remain inflexible for extended periods of time.

6. Both economies of scale and horizontal mergers have contributed to the concentration of American industry. Analysis of concentration ratios suggests that, on balance, the structure of the U.S. economy has changed little since the end of the first wave of mergers at the turn of the century.

7. Accounting profits are slightly higher in highly concentrated industries than for those that are less concentrated. But the relationship is highly imperfect. This suggests that several other factors (for example, changing market conditions, quality competition, risk, and ability to exclude rivals) are the major determinants of profitability.

IMPORTANT TERMS TO REMEMBER

Oligopoly: A market situation wherein a small number of sellers comprises the entire industry. It is competition among the few.

Collusion: An agreement among firms to avoid various competitive practices, particularly price reductions. It may involve either formal agreements or merely tacit recognition that competitive practices will be self-defeating in the long run. Tacit collusion is difficult to detect. The Sherman Act prohibits collusion and conspiracies to restrain interstate trade.

Kinked demand curve: A demand curve of a firm that is highly elastic when price is *raised*, but inelastic for a price *reduction*. This arises from the assumption that rival firms will match a price reduction, but not a price increase. It is thought to be descriptive of the situation faced by many oligopolistic firms.

Horizontal merger: The combining of the assets of two or more firms *engaged in the production of similar products* under the ownership of a single firm.

Concentration ratio: The total value of the shipments of the four (or sometimes eight) largest firms in an industry divided by the total value of all shipments in the industry. The higher the ratio, the greater is the market dominance of a small number of firms.

THE ECONOMIC WAY OF THINKING—DISCUSSION QUESTIONS

1. Explain why decision-makers for firms in an oligopolistic industry have an incentive to collude. What are the factors that will influence the success or failure of their collusive efforts?
2. "Effective collusion requires firms to agree on both price and quality. A firm can lower price by raising quality or it can raise price by lowering quality, even without changing the actual monetary sale price. Unless a firm can keep its competitor from adjusting quality, the gains from price collusion will be short-lived." Do you agree? Why or why not?
3. "High concentration leads to either overt or tacit collusion. Thus prices in oligopolistic industries will almost surely be rigged against the consumer and to the benefit of the producer." Do you agree? Why or why not?
4. U.S. Steel Corporation supplies between 20 and 30 percent of the total domestic market of steel. McGraw-Hill Book Company supplies nearly 50 percent of the total market for introductory economics texts. Do you think the government should regulate the price of steel and/or introductory economics texts? Discuss the degree of concentration, entry barriers, and "competitiveness" of the two markets. Are concentration ratios always a good index of competitiveness? Why or why not?

5. What's Wrong with This Way of Thinking?

"Firms such as General Motors, AT&T, and General Electric have been using their monopoly power to realize economic profit for years. These high profit rates rebound to the benefit of the current stockholders of these corporations at the expense of the consumers."

6. "Oligopolistic firms have a strong incentive to collude and a strong incentive to break their collusive agreements with rivals." Explain in your own words why this statement is either true or nonsense.

7. Are profits important in a market economy? Why or why not? Can you think of policies designed to reduce profitability that are consistent with economic efficiency? Explain. Do not forget to consider any secondary effects.

22
BUSINESS STRUCTURE, COMPETITION, AND PUBLIC POLICY

In recent years public opinion surveys have shown that the confidence of the American people in both business and government has tumbled to new lows. Business and government are held responsible for many of our current problems—inflation, product shortages, the energy crisis, pollution, and poverty. Some feel that government intervention has changed the nature of our economy. Others argue that the cause–effect relationship is in the other direction, that uncontrolled business power has changed government.

Is concentrated business power a threat to our economy? How strong are competitive forces? How does public policy affect business? What direction should public policy take during the last quarter of the twentieth century? These are vital questions that affect the lives of every one of us. Our answer to them will determine the kind of a world in which we will live for years to come. In this chapter we will discuss several economic considerations that are highly relevant to these issues.

THE TWO FACES OF BUSINESS POWER

There are really two different concerns about the power of business in our society. First, there is the feeling that many segments of our economy are not very competitive. The proponents of this view stress that many of our basic industries are highly concentrated—they are dominated by a few large firms. Under these circumstances many economists question the ability of competition to police the price and output policies of business firms.

But there is also a second concern—the "bigness" of a few hundred large corporations. A. A. Berle and J. K. Galbraith argue that as few as 500 corporate giants dominate our economy. They believe that these firms possess vast economic and political power that affects our very lifestyle. According to this view, these few hundred giant firms determine what kind of cars we drive, jobs we work, and even what type of products we purchase. The following two sections present data that will help the reader place both of these concerns in perspective.

HOW MUCH OF OUR ECONOMY IS COMPETITIVE?

This is a difficult question to answer, but several economists have tried. George Stigler (see Outstanding Economist, page 389) estimated that in 1939, 27 percent of the private sector income came from industries characterized by substantial monopolistic power and high barriers to entry.[1] The remaining 73 percent, Stigler classified as competitive with low barriers to entry. Warren Nutter and Henry Einhorn estimated that in 1958, 16 percent of the nation's output was produced by industries dominated by monopolistic influence, 62 percent in roughly competitive industries, and the remaining 22 percent in the government sector.[2] This study, like Stigler's, suggests that monopolistic influence dominates only 20 to 30 percent of the private economy.

Both of these studies have been criticized by Soloman Fabricant and others. Certainly, forcing all industries into only two classes may cover up a sizable segment of U.S. industry that might more reasonably be designated as intermediate between competition and monopoly. Yet Fabricant concludes "All the doubts that can be raised do not destroy, rather they support, the conclusions that there is no basis for believing that the economy of the United States is largely monopolistic."[3]

Exhibit 22-1 also sheds light on the competitiveness of the U.S. economy. The table breaks national income down by sector and industrial concentration. Agriculture, construction, wholesale and retail trade, and service industries have traditionally been characterized by small firms and low barriers to entry.[4] These sectors plus manufacturing industries with four-firm concentration ratios of less than 20 percent accounted for two-fifths of the total national income in 1972. They comprise roughly one-half of the private sector. This suggests competitive forces still play a highly important role in our economy.

On the other hand, business concentration and regulated sectors are also important. Regulated industries and government generate more than one-third of our national income. Highly concentrated manufacturing industries such as tobacco, chemicals, automobiles, aircraft, primary metals, and electrical equipment accounted for 13 percent of our national income in 1972. Most economists feel that firms in these industries are best able to escape the disciplines of competition. Of course, many of these concentrated industries confront stiff foreign competitors. For example, while General Motors, Ford, Chrysler, and American Motors have a monopoly on *domestic production*, one out of every six U.S. automobile customers purchases from a foreign producer. Similarly, foreign competition is important in other industries such as steel and petroleum. Inability to police quality competition may also result in a strong rivalry even among a limited number of competitors. Thus competitive forces may not be completely absent even in a concentrated industry.

These findings suggest that both competition and industrial concentration are important in the U.S economy. Approximately 40 percent of our national income is

[1] George Stigler, *Five Lectures on Economic Problems*. New York: Longmans, Green, 1949.
[2] G. Warren Nutter and Henry A. Einhorn, *Enterprise Monopoly in the United States: 1899–1958*. New York: Columbia Univ. Press, 1969.
[3] Soloman Fabricant, "Is Monopoly Increasing," *Journal of Economic History*, vol. XIII, 1953.
[4] In 1967 proprietorships, partnerships, and corporations with assets of less than $1 million accounted for 93 percent of the income generated by agriculture, 74 percent for service, 64 percent for construction, and 58 percent for wholesale and retail trade.

Exhibit 22-1   The Competitiveness of the U.S. Economy, 1972

National income originating from:	Billions of dollars	Percentage of total
Low barriers to entry	$373	40
1. Agricultural, forestry, and fisheries	29	
2. Construction	50	
3. Wholesale and retail trade	140	
4. Service	122	
5. Manufacturing (industries with concentration ratios of less than 20 percent)[a]	32	
Median barriers to entry	97	10
1. Manufacturing (industries with concentration ratios between 20 and 40 percent)[a]	97	
High barrier to entry (unregulated)	120	13
1. Manufacturing (industries with concentration ratios greater than 40 percent)[a]	112	
2. Mining	8	
Primarily regulated industries	180	19
1. Transportation, communications, and utility	74	
2. Finance, insurance, and real estate	106	
Government	150	16
All other	15	2
Total	935	100

SOURCE: Derived from the *Economic Report of the President—1974* and *The American Almanac for 1974*, Table No. 527.

[a] The concentration ratios were for two digit industries. The following industries had four firm concentration ratios of greater than 40 percent: tobacco, chemicals, petroleum, stone, clay, and glass products, primary metals, electrical equipment, transportation equipment (aircraft and automobiles), and instruments and related products.

generated from industries that are roughly competitive, in the rivalry sense. Nearly one-fourth of our total output stems from unregulated industries characterized by concentration of varying degrees. Regulated industries and government comprise the remainder.

DOES BIG BUSINESS DOMINATE THE U.S. ECONOMY?

Bigness and lack of competition are not necessarily the same thing. A firm can be big, while functioning in a highly competitive industry. For example, Sears and Montgomery Ward are both big, but they are also in a highly competitive industry—retail sales.

Exhibit 22-2 shows the percentage of the U.S. labor force that is employed by the largest corporations. In 1972, the 100 largest corporate giants employed 10 percent of the labor force. One in five labor force participants was employed by a corporation that ranked in the top 1000. Other measures of corporate power, such as share of total assets or value added, paint a similar picture.

Has the relative size of the largest corporations grown? There is strong evidence that it has. Exhibit 22-3 shows that the value added[5] of the 200 largest manufacturing

[5] Value added is the total value of the firm's sales less the cost of materials and services purchased from resource suppliers and subcontractors. It is a measure of how much the firm's productive efforts added to the value of its product.

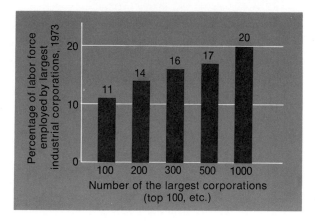

Exhibit 22-2   How Many of Us Work for the Giants?

SOURCE: *Statistical Abstract of the United States—1975.*

corporations has grown relative to both total manufacturing output and GNP during the last 25 years. In 1972 the 200 largest firms generated 43 percent of the value added *in manufacturing,* compared to only 30 percent in 1947. As a share of GNP, the value added of the "200 largest" increased from 7.8 percent in 1947 to 9.5 percent in 1972.

What accounts for this increase in the size of the largest firms relative to the total economy? In a word the answer is mergers, the combining of the assets of previously independent business firms under the ownership of a single firm. Mergers and acquisitions permit firms to expand their size and range of economic activities at a rate far more rapidly than could be accomplished by internal expansion.

As Exhibit 22-4 shows, there has been a rapid increase in the number of mergers among large firms in recent years. During the 1950s the number of large firms (firms with assets of more than $10 million) acquired by another firm was typically less than 50 each year. The figure more than doubled during the 1960s, reaching a peak of more than 200 in 1968.

Conglomerate mergers, the combining of a collection of diverse enterprises under a single management, accounted for the sharp increase in the number of mergers. Several firms developed into industrial giants almost overnight. International

Exhibit 22-3   How Big Are the Giants?

| Year | THE VALUE ADDED OF THE 200 LARGEST INDUSTRIAL CORPORATIONS | |
	Percentage of manufacturing	*Percentage of GNP*
1947	30	7.8
1954	37	9.6
1958	48	9.1
1963	41	9.8
1970	43	9.5
1972	43	9.5

SOURCE: *Statistical Abstract of the United States—1976.*

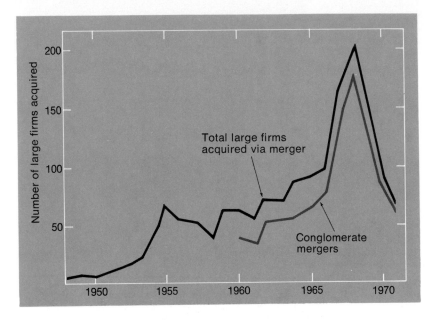

Exhibit 22-4 Trends in the Merger Movement among Large Firms

Large acquired firms include all firms that had $10 million or more of total assets at the time they were acquired. There was a sharp rise in the number of mergers, primarily conglomerate mergers, during the 1960s. Since 1968 the trend appears to have reversed.
SOURCE: *The Statistical Abstract of the United States—1975.*

Telegraph and Telephone (ITT) is a good example.[6] The acquisitions of ITT include Avis, the second largest rental car company; Sheraton Corporation, the largest hotel chain; Continental Baking, the largest manufacturer of bakery products; Educational Service, a leading supplier of educational materials; and Canteen Corporation, a large vending machine company. Other well-known conglomerates include Litton Industries, Gulf and Western, and Radio Corporation of America.

Exhibit 22-5 illustrates the role that mergers have played in the growth of the 200 largest manufacturing corporations *relative to the total economy.* In 1947 the 200 largest firms owned 42.4 percent of the total manufacturing assets. (*Caution:* Keep in mind that manufacturing currently comprises only about one-fourth of our total economy.) By 1968, the comparable figure had risen to 60.9 percent. Mergers were responsible for most of this increase. Internal growth accounted for only one-quarter of the expansion in the *relative* share of assets owned by the 200 manufacturing giants, while mergers supplied three-fourths of their growth. In the absence of mergers, the largest firms would have accounted for 45.3 percent of the total corporate manufacturing assets in 1968, only a slightly larger share than in 1947.

While conglomerate mergers increase the relative size of the largest corporations, it is not obvious that they reduce market competition. Thus, while the economic

[6]At the time of this writing, the Justice Department has filed an antitrust suit against ITT.

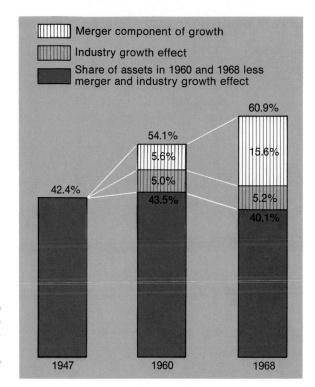

Exhibit 22-5 Share of Assets Acquired by Internal Growth and Merger, 1947–1968, for 200 Largest Manufacturing Corporations, as of 1968

Assets acquired via mergers were the major source of the growth in the share of manufacturing assets held by the largest 200 corporations.

SOURCE: Bureau of Economics, Federal Trade Commission.

concentration of the largest firms has grown, there has *not* been a similar tendency toward greater concentration *within industries* (see Exhibit 21-5). As Exhibit 22-4 illustrates, there is strong evidence that the merger fever of the 1960s is waning. Conglomerates lost much of their glamor as their earnings took a nosedive during the 1970s. In the last few years, the number of large-firm mergers has returned to pre-1960 levels.

ANTITRUST LEGISLATION—THE POLICY OBJECTIVES

The central idea behind antitrust legislation is straightforward. Antitrust legislation seeks to (a) assure that the economy is structured such that competitive rivalry exists among firms in the same industry (or market area) and (b) prohibit business practices that tend to stifle competition. Once these objectives are accomplished, then market forces can be relied on to allocate goods and services.

There are numerous tactics that businessmen might utilize in an effort to avoid the discipline of competition. We have already stressed that collusion and price agreements are potential weapons to turn the terms of trade in favor of the seller. Potential competitors might also decide to divide a market geographically, agreeing not to compete in certain market areas. Supposedly large diversified firms can use **predatory pricing,** a situation whereby the firm *temporarily* reduces its price below cost in certain market areas in order to eliminate the competition of weaker rivals. Once the rivals have been eliminated, the firm will then use its monopoly position to raise prices above costs. A competitor might also use exclusive contracts and reciprocal agreements in an effort to maintain an advantage over its rivals. An **exclusive contract** (or dealership) is an arrangement whereby the manufacturer of a line of products would prohibit retailers from selling any of the products of rival producers. Thus, an established firm, offering many product lines, might use the tactic to limit retail markets to rivals offering only a narrow product line. A **reciprocal agreement** is a situation whereby the buyer of a product requires the seller to purchase another product as a condition of sales. For example, General Motors was charged in 1963 with telling railroads that if they did not buy GM locomotives, then GM would ship its automobiles by other means. All of these business practices involve the use of market power, rather than superior performance, as a vehicle to gain at the expense of rivals. In one form or another, they are all illegal under current antitrust legislation.

MAJOR ANTITRUST LEGISLATION

A society that wants to organize economic activity via competitive markets, rather than detailed regulation or socialized planning, may need to pursue an antitrust policy. The United States, more than most Western countries, has adopted antitrust legislation designed to promote competitive markets. Three major legislative acts—the Sherman Act, Clayton Act, and Federal Trade Commission Act—form the foundation for antitrust policy in the United States.

1. *The Sherman Act.*   This act was passed in 1890, largely in response to a great wave of mergers. The infamous tobacco, sugar, and Standard Oil trusts enraged Congress and the American people into taking action against business concentration. The most important provisions of the act were:

> *Section 1:* Every contract, combination in the form of trust or otherwise, or conspiracy, in restraint of trade or commerce among several states or with foreign nations, is hereby declared illegal.
> *Section 2:* Every person who shall monopolize, or conspire with any other person or persons to monopolize any part of the trade or commerce among the several states, or with foreign nations, shall be guilty of a misdemeanor. . . .

The language of the Sherman Act is vague, subject to interpretation. What does it mean to "attempt to monopolize" or "combine or conspire with another person"? Initially, the courts were hesitant to apply the act to manufacturing corporations. But in 1911, the Supreme Court ruled that Standard Oil and American Tobacco had used "unreasonable" tactics to restrain trade. At the time, the Standard Oil trust controlled 90 percent of the country's refinery capacity. American Tobacco controlled three-fourths of the tobacco manufacturing market. Both of these firms were broken up into several smaller rival firms.

But the Court did not prohibit monopoly per se. It was the tactics used by Standard Oil and American Tobacco that caused the Court to rule against them. In later cases the Supreme Court refused to break up other trusts, U.S. Steel and American Can for example, because they had not followed "unfair or unethical" business practices. But the Sherman Act did not clearly define unfair or unethical business practices. The courts, partially because of its vagueness, were reluctant to apply the legislation. The ineffectiveness of the Sherman Act led to the passage of two other antitrust laws in 1914.

2. *The Clayton Act.*   This act was an effort to spell out and prohibit specific business practices. The following were prohibited by the Clayton Act when they "substantially lessen competition or tend to create a monopoly . . .":

> (1) *price discrimination*—charging purchasers in different markets different prices that are unrelated to transportation costs, (2) *tying contracts*—sale of one item that is conditional upon the buyer purchasing another item, (3) *exclusive dealings*—agreements whereby the seller of a good would be forbidden from selling to a competitor of the purchaser, (4) *interlocking stockholding*—one firm purchasing the stock of a competing firm, (5) *interlocking director-ates*—the same individual serving on the board of directors of competing firms.

While the Clayton Act was more specific than the Sherman Act, it still suffered from vagueness since these actions were illegal only when they "substantially lessen competition." Interpreting this ambiguous phrase still remains with the courts.

3. *The Federal Trade Commission Act.*   This act declared that "unfair methods of competition in commerce are hereby declared unlawful." The Federal Trade Commission (FTC), composed of five members appointed by the president to seven year terms, was established to decide exactly what "unfair" meant. However, in a 1919 Supreme Court decision, it held that the courts, and not the FTC, had the ultimate responsibility to interpret the law. Today, the FTC is primarily concerned with enforcing consumer protection legislation and the Robinson-Patman Act, prohibiting deceptive advertising, a power it acquired in 1938, and investigating the structure and conduct of industry.

When a complaint is filed with the FTC, usually by a third party, it will investigate. If there is a violation, the commission will initially attempt to settle the dispute by negotiation between the parties. Failing this a hearing will be conducted before one of the commission's examiners. The decision of the hearing examiner may be appealed to the full commission, and the FTC's decision may later be appealed to the U.S. Court of Appeals. The great majority of cases brought before the FTC are now settled by mutual consent of the parties involved.

More Recent Antitrust Legislation

During the 1930s two additional laws were passed with the major intention of protecting small businessmen. The Robinson–Patman Act prohibits selling "at unreasonably low prices" when such practices reduce competition. The section of the Clayton Act dealing with price discrimination sought to eliminate predatory prices. The

Robinson–Patman Act went beyond this objective. It sought to protect competitors, not just from stronger rivals who might temporarily sell below cost, but from more efficient rivals who were really producing at a lower cost. Chain stores and mass distributors were the initial targets of the legislation. Economists have often been critical of the Robinson–Patman Act, since it oftentimes eliminates price competition and protects inefficient producers.

The Miller–Tydings Act of 1937 exempted fair trade agreements from prosecution under antitrust legislation. A fair trade agreement permits the manufacturer of a product to prohibit retailers from selling his product below a listed or "fair trade" price. Moreover, in states that have "fair trade legislation," the Miller–Tydings Act permits a manufacturer to tie *all* retailers in the state to a resale price maintenance agreement merely by signing such an agreement with any one retailer. Since such practices would obviously reduce competition, it is not surprising that a study conducted by the Justice Department in 1970 found that brand name merchandise purchased in fair trade states retailed for as much as 37 percent more than identical products in free trade states. Prodded by findings such as these, Congress is currently giving serious consideration to legislation that would repeal fair trade laws.

In 1950 the Celler–Kefauver Act, sometimes referred to as the antimerger act, prohibited a firm from acquiring the assets of a competitor when the transaction lessened competition. Earlier the Clayton Act prohibited mergers through stock acquisition, but the act was unable to prevent business combinations that were formed by asset sale. The Celler–Kefauver Act closed this loophole, further limiting the ability of firms to combine in an effort to escape competitive pressures.

THUMBNAIL SKETCH—Antitrust Legislation

1. Antitrust laws prohibit:

(a) collusion—contracts and conspiracies to restrain trade (Sherman Act, Sec. 1),

(b) monopoly and attempts to monopolize any part of trade or commerce among the several states (Sherman Act, Sec. 2),

(c) persons from serving on the board of directors of competing firms with more than $1 million of assets (Clayton Act, Sec. 8),

(d) unfair and deceptive advertising (Federal Trade Commission Act as amended),

(e) price discrimination where the intent is to injure a competitor (Robinson–Patman).

2. The following practices are also illegal when they substantially lessen competition or tend to create a monopoly:

(a) tying contracts (Clayton Act, Sec. 3),

(b) exclusive dealings (Clayton Act, Sec. 3),

(c) interlocking stockholdings and horizontal mergers (Clayton Act, Sec. 7, as amended),

(d) interlocking directorates (Clayton Act, Sec. 8).

3. Antitrust laws permit resale price maintenance agreements that prohibit retailers from reducing the manufacturer's list price (Miller–Tydings Act).

ALTERNATIVE VIEWS ON ANTITRUST POLICY

While few economists are completely satisfied with all aspects of antitrust policy, most observers believe that it has exerted a positive, though probably not dramatic, influence for competitive markets. The Sherman and Clayton Acts prohibited the most efficient methods of collusion (for example, mergers, interlocking board of directors, and interlocking stockholdings), thereby raising its costs. Since current collusive agreements must be tacit and nonenforceable, rivals are more likely to cheat. Thus the expected benefits have been reduced. Economic theory suggests that this set of forces would reduce the magnitude of anticompetitive collusive business practices. In addition, counterproductive (from the viewpoint of society) competitive tactics—exclusive contracts, price discrimination, and tying contracts, for example—have been made more costly. Prohibiting such practices has probably served to reduce entry barriers into markets.

Antitrust, like most other areas of policy, has its critics. First, many economists do not believe that the existing legislation has been enforced vigorously enough. They argue that greater effort is needed to assure the persistence of competitive markets. The proponents of this position often point out that antitrust has been primarily a holding action. It has prevented large firms from *increasing* their market share, but has been relatively ineffective as a mechanism to *reduce* industrial concentration. The proponents of this view, typically, favor an antitrust policy that would restructure concentrated industries, dividing large firms in such industries into smaller independent units.

Second, other economists argue that antitrust policy places too much emphasis on the number of competitors, while failing to recognize the positive role of dynamic competition even if it leads to concentration. John McGee, of the University of Washington, argues that concentration is neither inefficient nor indicative of a lack of competition. He states his case:

> Take an industry of many independent producers, each of which is efficiently using small scale and simple methods to make the same product. . . . Suppose that a revolution in technology or management techniques now occurs, so that there is room in the market for only one firm using the new and most efficient methods. Whether it occurs quickly through merger or gradually through bankruptcy, an atomistic industry is transformed into a "monopoly," albeit one selling the same product at a lower price than before. If expected long-run price should rise, resort can still be had to the old and less efficient ways, which were compatible with . . . small firms. It would be incomplete and misleading to describe that process as a "decline of competition."[7]

McGee believes that an antitrust policy that limits business concentration will often prevent efficient business organization and result in higher product prices. While few economists agree fully with McGee's defense of industrial concentration, many, including the late Joseph Schumpeter, do believe that dynamic forces are an important source of competitive pressure, even in concentrated industries.

[7]John S. McGee, *In Defense of Industrial Concentration*, pp. 21–22. © 1971 by Praeger Publishers, Inc., New York.

A third group of critics argues that antitrust policy is simply incapable of dealing with a modern economy that is already dominated by a few hundred industrial giants. The proponents of this position, typified by Harvard's John Galbraith, argue that competition is a relic from the past. They believe that it is unrealistic to expect that competition could (should?) discipline the industrial sector of a modern economy. Why? Galbraith supplies the answer:

> Were there only a handful of great corporations exercising power over prices, costs, the consumer and over public attitudes, perhaps their dissolution into smaller units and therewith the dissolution of their power might be possible. But a government cannot proclaim half of the economic system illegal. . . .[8]

Since the time of Adam Smith, economists have debated the issues of competition, regulation, and the role of public policy. We will conclude this section by presenting two views on these subjects. The first suggests a policy designed to assure competitive markets. The second presents the Galbraithian view of a modern industrial economy and argues that public policy to promote competition would be both ineffective and counterproductive.

Perspectives in Economics

A Program to Promote Competitive Markets

In general, economists argue that monopoly results in allocative inefficiency, high prices, and nonfunctional profits. Similarly, our experience with real world government regulation and price fixing reveals that it suffers from serious shortcomings. The regulators often do the wrong thing. Bureaucratic inefficiency and the potential for political abuse are ever present. Except for the case of natural monopoly, the abstract case for public policy to maintain and promote competitive markets is, indeed, a strong one.

In 1963 the Supreme Court stated that "Competition is our fundamental national policy." At best this is an oversimplification. Our public policy has sometimes promoted competition, sometimes promoted monopoly, and sometimes gone to ridiculous lengths to stifle competitive behavior. Actions speak louder than words. The Supreme Court aside, accuracy requires one to admit that public policy toward competition has been schizophrenic.

How could real world public policy promote competitive markets even in the 1970s? The following seven point plan suggests several alternatives that might be pursued. The initial points could be instituted without a major restructuring of the economy. Most proponents of competition would favor them. Some of the latter points, particularly the last two, involve more radical changes. Many will undoubtedly feel that such drastic measures are unnecessary, at least at this time.

1. Remove tariffs and import restrictions, particularly on goods produced by highly concentrated domestic industries. Foreign competition is a substitute for domestic competition. Domestic producers will be less able to restrict output, raise prices, and take advantage of their market power, when consumers have the option of purchasing

[8]John K. Galbraith, *Economics and the Public Purpose*, Boston: Houghton Mifflin, 1973, p. 216.

from foreign producers. It makes no sense to complain about the lack of competition in industries such as automobiles, steel, tires, electrical equipment, and aluminum, while public policy restricts foreign competitors. If we want to limit the ability of domestic producers to arbitrarily raise their prices above cost, we should certainly permit the market entry of foreign competitors.

2. Remove existing regulatory restrictions that limit entry and prohibit firms from lowering their prices. Independent of possible antitrust violations for predatory pricing, firms should not be prevented from using price as a competitive weapon. Neither should potential entrants be excluded from an industry or a new market area. Our regulatory policies in both ground and air transportation industries have prevented the competitive process from working to the advantage of the consumer. Public policy has turned a potentially competitive transportation industry into a maze of entry restraints, inefficient travel routes, and bureaucratic red tape. The result—researchers on the subject estimate that freight and passenger prices on most routes, particularly main line routes, are 10 to 50 percent above what would exist in the presence of competition.[9] Regulatory policies limiting competition in the transportation industry cost American consumers $5 to $15 billion annually in the form of higher prices on everything from groceries to vacations. Anticompetitive public policy in these areas should be discontinued.

3. Reduce government imposed paperwork and regulations that add to the complexity of operating a small business. Businesses of all sizes are required to submit numerous forms to the government. More and more of the businessman's time and resources are required to fill out government applications, statistical questionnaires, and forms on taxes (income, sales, payroll, and Social Security), occupational safety, sanitation and health, manpower training, equal employment opportunity compliance, environmental protection, and inventory estimation among others. Many of these reports are required quarterly. Since there are economies of scale in dealing with these government imposed administrative matters, large firms, employing their own team of accountants and lawyers, can handle them at a lower cost per unit. Thus smaller firms are placed at a disadvantage, not because they are less efficient at producing, but because they are less efficient at performing paperwork calisthenics.

After holding hearings in only four cities, the chairman of the Senate subcommittee on government regulations, Senator Thomas J. McIntyre, concluded that "federal-form pollution . . . is strangling small businessmen across the country." Senator McIntyre estimates that the government imposed paperwork costs business $36 billion annually. Of course, these costs will be passed on to the consumer in the form of higher prices.

Much of this administrative burden could and should be lifted from the back of the small businessman, allowing him to better compete with large firms. For example, firms with less than 50 employees might be exempt from all but necessary annual tax reports. Competition will effectively police the business practices of small firms without the imposition of unnecessary paperwork. The greater threat is that current administrative duties imposed by public policy, may prevent small businesses from applying the competitive pressure necessary to police their larger counterparts.

4. Public policy should not rescue inefficient big businesses. If a business is small, it can go bankrupt; if it is big, it can get a helping hand from the government. In

[9] For a detailed examination of the regulatory policies in the transportation industry, see pages 375–379.

recent years government action has rescued both Penn Central and Lockheed from bankruptcy. Such lifesaving missions can only reduce the incentive of the stockholders of other large firms to keep a watchful eye on potentially inefficient management. Further, it encourages firms to use mergers and other devices to grow in size, because given current policy, "bigness" acts as an insurance policy against bankruptcy. Keep in mind that bankruptcy does not destroy productive assets. On the contrary, the assets of firms that claim bankruptcy will be sold to someone who will acquire them at a low enough price to permit their profitable operation. A policy that protects big firms from the discipline of the market is a policy that promotes inefficiency, not competition.

5. Application and vigorous enforcement of antitrust legislation against businesses, professional associations, and unions when they collude for the purpose of raising prices and restricting competition. In recent years antitrust policy has adequately dealt with cases of collusion and noncompetitive industrial practices. Deregulation of transportation and a reduction in trade barriers will strengthen competition even more in this area. However, our antitrust policy has virtually ignored the noncompetitive practices of professional associations and labor unions. Publication of suggested prices by local associations of doctors, architects, real estate agents, and other professions is commonplace, even though it would appear to be in violation of current antitrust legislation.[10] In a few cases, practitioners who have been willing to charge less than the "suggested price" have been harrassed. In the absence of collusive agreements via associations, the professions would be highly competitive. Antitrust legislation prohibiting collusion, price fixing, and other noncompetitive practices should be applied to professional associations.

Even though the noncompetitive tactics of labor unions are notorious, the political power of organized labor will make them difficult if not impossible to deal with. Since the Clayton Act, unions have been exempt from antitrust legislation. Removal of this exemption, though politically infeasible, would go a long way toward fragmenting the power of unions and preventing them from establishing occupational entry restraints. Occupational licensing requirements, particularly in the crafts, have been used as a means to restrict entry and protect union workers. Repeal or relaxation of such legislation would promote competition in the skilled occupations.

6. Granting a tax break to small and competitive business. Except in the case of the very small corporation, the corporate income tax applies equally to the big and the small, the competitive and the noncompetitive. It could be used as a device to promote competition and penalize monopolistic power. For example, a 2 percent surtax might be imposed on firms that produce 20 percent or more of the output in concentrated industries. The corporate income tax could be made slightly progressive, increasing the tax burden with increasing size. Such a policy would tend to discourage mergers, particularly those of the conglomerate variety. Decentralization, a friend of competition, would be encouraged. While policies in this area have received little discussion, it is clear that they could be used to promote competition and discourage bigness, while avoiding a direct restructuring of industries.

7. Restructuring basic industries. Many industrial organization economists feel that monopolistic power is primarily a problem in 10 or 15 basic industries, such as

---

[10] A recent Supreme Court decision prohibiting collusive list price agreements among lawyers should open the door for additional legal action in this area.

automobiles, chemicals, and primary metals. One method of attacking concentration in these industries would be to divide the existing firms into a larger number of units. For example, the Chevrolet, Pontiac, Oldsmobile, Buick, and Cadillac divisions of General Motors might each be separated and established as independent firms. Ford and Chrysler might also be restructured so that the automobile industry would be composed of 10 or 15 independent firms. Given the incentive to cheat on collusive agreements, the enforcement of current antitrust legislation, and the presence of foreign competitors, competitive pressures would certainly discipline industries with 10 or 15 independent domestic competitors. Proposals along these lines would be counterproductive if economies of scale are important in an industry. The work of Bain and other industrial organization economists is encouraging in this regard. Their findings suggest that most of our basic industries could be substantially less concentrated without the loss of efficiency associated with large scale production.

Discussion

1. Which of the seven proposals given above do you think are good (bad)? Why?
2. Do you think a policy of promoting competition is superior to detailed regulation and/or government ownership of basic industries? Why or why not?

A Galbraithian View of a Modern Industrial Economy

Perspectives in Economics

Professor Galbraith's view of a modern industrial economy differs substantially from that of traditional economics. He believes that large corporations, precisely because they are large, will possess monopolistic power that will partially free them from the forces of competition. But whereas traditional economics argues that the consequences of monopoly will be restriction of output, Galbraith believes that overexpansion and overdevelopment will result.

While Galbraith is certainly a fluent writer, his major hypotheses are seldom put forth in testable form. Unlike most other economists, Galbraith has shown little interest in presenting empirical evidence to buttress his position. While he has spoken out on a wide range of issues, the following six points summarize his views on a modern industrial economy.

The Essentials of Galbraith

1. A modern industrial economy such as the United States is composed of two major sectors—the market system which is influenced by competition, and the planning system which is characterized by monopolistic power. The market system encompasses agriculture, construction, service, and artistic industries that are not susceptible to large scale production. Firms in this sector are "controlled" by market forces along the lines implied by traditional textbook analysis.

On the other hand, the planning system is composed of the 500 or so largest corporations that dominate manufacturing and technical fields. Technological change is much more rapid in this sector. Growth and rapid development characterize the planning sector. Economies of scale lead to concentration. Competition, if present at all, is among the few.

2. The large firms in the planning sector, particularly those in concentrated industries, are able to use their power to "control" demand, input prices, and government policy.

Therefore, earning average profits, or even a bit above average, will be no problem for them. Advertising and related promotional techniques are used to shape consumer tastes and mold demand to the production decisions of the planning system.[11] Consumers will be made to want, indeed to feel that they must have, the products that the modern corporation wants them to have. Through planning, collusion on fashioning, and "gentlemanly" competition among the giants, the options of the consumer at any point in time can be carefully limited. Only doubleknit suits are available this year, only miniskirts next year, and only maxi's the following year. The planning system sets the limits within which consumers will be permitted to choose.

Similarly, public policy will reflect the requirements of large, capital intensive corporations. The state, like large corporations, will be strongly concerned with stability, employment, and growth. The tax structure will be manipulated to assure an adequate demand for the products of the planning system. The purchasing decisions of the state, particularly the Defense Department, will be used to assure an adequate level of demand in each sector of the planning system. If the automobile, steel, aircraft, or space industries suffer a lapse, the government will alter its tax, spending, or subsidy policies in order to prop them up (for example, emergency loans to Lockheed, tariffs to protect depressed industries). State policy and the welfare of the planning system are intertwined.

3. The technostructure is the real center of power and social planning for an industrial, capitalist system. The true decision-making power of the modern corporation rests not with the stockholder, but with the professional experts—engineers, salesmen, accountants, managers, and technicians. These specialists form what Galbraith calls the "technostructure." In his view, they control the information flow, make the major production decisions, and exert enormous control over both the corporation bureaucracy and the state bureaucracy. They move easily between the two and their training in one reinforces their ability to contol the other.

4. Stockholders would, of course, be the beneficiaries of a profit maximization policy. But for a large corporation, they are powerless to control anything. The individual stockholder, because he often has inadequate information and nearly always has few votes relative to the total, has neither the power nor the incentive to police the actions of management closely. If management provides him with a normal rate of return, he is happy regardless of whether the firm is a profit maximizer.

In addition, the power and size of the modern corporation practically assure an average profit rate in the long run. Their size and industrial barriers to entry insulate the planning firms from new rivals. The lessons of time protect it from "price cutting" competition within the industry. There is an incentive for modern corporate managers to follow a "live and let live" policy. There are enough auto sales for General Motors, Ford, and Chrysler. Sales of steel, cigarettes, and aluminum are sufficient to satisfy the major producers in these industries. An aggressive, competitive policy by a firm would be self-defeating.

5. Firms in the planning sector will be characterized by overdevelopment, not underdevelopment. After a target profit level—for example, the average profit rate of the economy—has been attained, the monopoly power of planning firms will be used to fuel their growth. After the giants of industry have earned a profit rate sufficient to keep their stockholders happy, they will seek "to achieve the greatest possible rate

[11]See Controversies in Economics: Advertising—The Views of Its Critics and Defenders, pages 303–307.

of corporate growth as measured by sales."[12] Growth will enhance their power, community status, and national influence. It will provide the security which is essential for the long-term planning required by highly capital intensive enterprises. Growth, not profit maximization, will be the overwhelming goal of firms in the planning sector.

Of course, if the planning sector is overdeveloped, the implication is that the market sector is underdeveloped. Galbraith sees this inequality as our major economic problem.

> The central problem of the modern economy is unequal development. The least development is where there is the least monopoly and market power; the greatest development is where there is the most.[13]

6. Workers in the market system are exploited. Unequal development between sectors also leads to income inequality. In the planning sector both unions and the state protect employees. In addition, market power permits large corporations to pass the cost of lucrative wage settlements along to the consumer. In contrast, competitive forces will discipline wage settlement in the market sector. Thus, in comparison with the planning sectors, workers in the market sector will either be self-exploited or exploited by small business.

Competition—A Negative Force

Galbraith decidedly rejects proposals to promote competition as both unrealistic and counterproductive. In his view, monopoly power is far too prevalent to expect that market forces could be imposed on large corporations. And even if it were possible, competition would hinder, not help, economic development. Galbraith states his case against antitrust and competition:

> But it will also be evident that the antitrust laws, if they worked as their proponents hope, would only make problems worse. Their purpose is to stimulate competition, lower prices, otherwise unshackle resource use and promote a more vigorous expansion of the particular industry. But the problem of the modern economy is not inferior performance of the planning system—of the monopolistic or oligopolistic sector, to revive the traditional terminology. The problem is the greater development here as compared with the market system. And the greater the power, the greater the development. Where the power is least—where economic organization conforms most closely to the goals envisaged by the antitrust laws—the development is least. If they fulfilled the hopes of their supporters and those they support, the antitrust laws would make development more unequal by stimulating development further in precisely those parts of the economy where it is now greatest.[14]

The Galbraithian Solution—Regulation and Government Ownership

In order to correct the situation, Galbraith favors more regulation, encouragement of monopoly, and greater socialization in the market (that is, competitive) sector, and

---

[12] J. K. Galbraith, *The New Industrial State*, 2nd ed. Boston: Houghton Mifflin, 1972, p. 171. This hypothesis originated as Galbraith acknowledges, with William J. Baumol.
[13] Galbraith, *Economics and the Public Purpose*, p. 276.
[14] Galbraith, *Economics and the Public Purpose*, pp. 216–217.

government control over wages and prices, particularly in the planned (that is, big business) sector. Specifically, in *Economics and the Public Purpose*, Galbraith advocates—

(a) an antitrust exemption for small businessmen who form combinations and collude to fix price and output,

(b) encouragement of trade unionism in the market sector,

(c) an extension and major increase in the minimum wage,

(d) subsidization of the educational, capital, and technological needs of the market sector,

(e) legislation to encourage the development of white collar unionism in the planned sector,

(f) permanent wage and price controls with the purpose of pushing prices up in the market sector and promoting greater wage equality between the technostructure and other workers in the planned sector, and

(g) socialization of the housing, transportation, and medical industries.[15]

In general, Galbraith suggests that we substitute detailed government planning for market forces.

Testing the Galbraithian View

From the viewpoint of positive economics, Galbraith's hypotheses are of more interest than the policy conclusions that he derives from them. Several economists have attempted to subject various aspects of his view to empirical testing. In certain areas the difference between the orthodox and Galbraithian view is not as great as it first appears. For example, both information costs and individual incentives within the framework of group (stockholder) decision-making suggest that the managers of a large corporation will have some discretion to pursue their own personal objectives.[16] Here the difference between Galbraith and the traditional view is one of degree. Additional empirical work will help to narrow the gap.

Galbraith's views on the overdevelopment of the oligopolistic, or planning as he refers to it, sector are difficult to subject to direct test. But some research has been conducted in this area. Edwin Mansfield has done more empirical work on the subject of technological change than any other economist. After an extensive study of the relationship between industrial structure and technological progressiveness, Mansfield concludes:

> Thus, contrary to the allegations of Galbraith and others, there is little evidence that industrial giants are needed in most countries to insure rapid technological change, and rapid utilization of new techniques.[17]

Galbraith argues that the oligopolistic ("planning") sector will trade off higher profits for more rapid growth and development. Thus, *for any given profit rate*, firms in the

---

[15] Galbraith, *Economics and the Public Purpose*, pp. 252–285.

[16] See Armen Alchian and Harold Demsetz, "Production, Information Cost, and Economic Organization," *American Economic Review*, December 1972, and Eirik Furubotn and Svetozar Pejovich, "Property Rights and Economic Theory: A Survey of Recent Literature," *Journal of Economic Literature*, December 1972, for a presentation of this view.

[17] E. Mansfield, *Economics, Principles, Problems and Decisions*, New York: W. W. Norton, 1974, pp. 521–522. Also, see Mansfield, *Technological Change*, New York: W. W. Norton, 1971.

oligopolistic sector should experience a more rapid sales growth than smaller firms in more competitive markets. A recent study by Harold Demsetz analyzed the relationship between profits and growth according to firm size and competitiveness of the industry. Demsetz concludes, "None of these experiments yield results consistent with the Galbraith–Baumol sales maximization hypothesis."[18]

Unquestionably Galbraith's ideas have aroused considerable interest among professional economists. With time, more and more of his positions will be subject to empirical testing. Will the Galbraithian view stand up under the illumination of scientific testing? This is an exciting question. Economics is a youthful, dynamic science. Perhaps some of you will become professional economists and contribute to research efforts seeking answers to many of the very important questions that Professor Galbraith has raised.

Discussion

1. Do you agree that competition exerts little influence on large corporations in what Galbraith calls the "planning sector"? Buttress your case with empirical evidence.
2. What parts of the Galbraithian position do you think are correct? Which do you think are incorrect? Can you think of economic experiments that could be used to test various parts of the Galbraithian view? Explain.
3. What do you think would be the major impact of Galbraith's policy suggestions? Which of them do you favor (oppose)? Why?

CHAPTER LEARNING OBJECTIVES

1. It is not easy to classify each industry into boxes entitled "competitive" and "noncompetitive." But empirical research on industrial structure suggests that roughly 40 percent of our economy is highly competitive in the rivalry sense. Another 25 percent of our output is generated by unregulated firms in medium or high concentration industries. The remaining 35 percent of output stems from government and the regulated private sector.

2. The largest 1000 firms employ 20 percent of the civilian labor force and generate one-fifth to one-quarter of the total GNP. The size of the largest firms has grown more rapidly than the rest of the economy during the last 25 years. This growth in the *relative* size of big firms is primarily the result of mergers, particularly conglomerate mergers.

3. Antitrust legislation seeks to **(a)** maintain a competitive structure in the unregulated private sector and **(b)** prohibit business practices that are thought to stifle competition.

4. The Sherman, Clayton, and Federal Trade Commission Acts form the foundation of antitrust policy in the United States. The Sherman Act prohibits conspiracies to restrain trade and/or monopolize an industry. The Clayton Act prohibits specific business practices such as price discrimination, tying contracts, exclusive dealings, and mergers and acquisitions (as amended) when they "substantially lessen competition or tend to create a monopoly." As it has evolved through the years, the Federal Trade Commission is primarily concerned with enforcing consumer protection legislation, prohibiting deceptive advertising, and investigating industrial structure.

5. Most economists believe that antitrust policy in the United States has promoted competition and reduced industrial concentration, although its effect has probably been small.

[18] See H. Demsetz, "Where is the New Industrial State," *Economic Inquiry*, March 1974.

6. Government policy in the area of competition is often contradictory. The purpose of antitrust legislation is to promote competition. However, economic policy on tariffs and other trade barriers, industrial regulation, occupational licensing, and small business regulation has often been inconsistent with the objective of competitive markets.

IMPORTANT TERMS TO REMEMBER

Conglomerate merger: The merging under one ownership of two or more firms that produce unrelated products.

Predatory pricing: Price reductions by a dominant firm in an industry which are motivated by the intention of damaging or eliminating weaker rivals so that prices can be raised above the level of cost in a later period.

Exclusive contract: An agreement between manufacturer and retailer that prohibits the retailer from carrying the product lines of firms that are rivals of the manufacturer. Such contracts are illegal under the Clayton Act when they "lessen competition."

Reciprocal agreement: An agreement between firms A and B whereby A refuses to purchase product X from B unless B purchases product Y from A. The practice is illegal under the Clayton Act.

THE ECONOMIC WAY OF THINKING—DISCUSSION QUESTIONS

1. "Big business dominates the U.S. economy. Big business uses its power to decide what products we purchase, what jobs we work at, what kind of homes we live in, and even what political candidates we vote for." Evaluate.

2. Does public policy consistently promote competitive markets? Why or why not?

3. Do you think that competition can be counted on to discipline the industrial business firms of a modern economy? Explain.

4. Suppose that the government uses licensing to limit the number of firms in the retail liquor industry. Thus, ignoring the cost of a license, firms in the industry make substantial economic profit.
   (a) Analyze the price, costs, and profits of firms when the limited number of licenses (good for five years) are auctioned off to the highest bidders. Assume that ownership of the licenses is widespread, so there is no problem of collusion.
   (b) Analyze the price, costs, and profits of firms when the limited number of licenses are granted "free" to persons approved by a committee appointed by the legislature (or governor).
   (c) When choosing between these two, state legislatures have almost exclusively chosen (b). Can you explain why?

5. Currently, antimerger policy does not restrict conglomerate mergers between large firms if they do not reduce competition in a specific market. Do you think such mergers should be prohibited? Why or why not?

6. "Efficiency requires large scale production. Yet big businesses will mean monopoly power, high prices, and market inefficiency. We must chose between production efficiency and monopoly." Evaluate this view.

IV
FACTOR
MARKETS
AND
INCOME
DISTRIBUTION

23

THE SUPPLY AND DEMAND
OF PRODUCTIVE RESOURCES

In Part III we investigated how markets (a) allocate goods and services among competing consumers and (b) determine which consumer goods will be produced. We will now turn to an analysis of the forces that determine the mix of inputs (resources) used to produce goods and services and the distribution of output among resource suppliers.

Resources are demanded because they contribute to the production of goods and services. Since they must be bid away from their alternative uses, costs are incurred when inputs are employed. Profit-seeking firms will attempt to utilize resources to make products that can be sold for revenues in excess of the firm's resource costs. Conversely, resource owners are willing to supply their services only because they obtain income for them. When choosing among alternative employment opportunities, utility-maximizing resource suppliers will seek out those options that they personally believe to be most advantageous.

Can market forces regulate the actions of profit-seeking resource purchasers and income-seeking resource suppliers? What factors will determine the availability of resources? Why do resource prices often vary? In this chapter we will take a close-up look at resource markets and attempt to answer these questions.

HUMAN AND NONHUMAN RESOURCES

Broadly speaking, there are two different types of productive inputs—nonhuman and human resources. Economists oftentimes differentiate between physical capital, land, and natural resources, when discussing **nonhuman resources.** This distinction is one of degree. Capital consists of man-made goods that are used to produce other goods. Obviously, tools, machines, and buildings are part of the capital stock. Just as man can increase the supply of machines, so too he can use wise land clearing and soil conservation practices to upgrade both the quantity and quality of land. Similarly, the supply of natural resources can be increased (within limits) by the application of more resources to discovery and development.

Increasing the available stock of nonhuman resources involves the sacrifice of current production. Resources that are used to produce machines, upgrade the quality of land, or discover natural resources could be used to produce current goods and services directly. Why take the roundabout path? The answer is that sometimes indirect methods of producing goods will be less costly over the long haul. Robinson Crusoe found that he could catch more fish by taking some time off from hand fishing to build a net. While his initial investment in the net reduced his current catch, once the net was completed he was able to more than make up for his earlier loss of output.

Additions to capital stock, whether they are fishing nets or complex machines, will involve current sacrifices. Capital intensive methods of production will be adapted only when decision-makers expect the benefits of a larger future output to more than offset the current reduction in production.

Current resources can also be used to increase the future productivity of **human resources.** Investment in such things as education, training, health, skill-building experience, and migration to areas where jobs are more readily available involves current sacrifice in order to increase future productivity (and income). Economists refer to such activities as **investment in human capital.**[1]

Decisions to invest in human capital involve all of the basic ingredients of other investment decisions. Consider the decision of whether or not to go to college. As many readers will be able to testify, an investment in a college education requires one to sacrifice current earnings as well as direct expenses for such things as tuition and books. The investment is expected to lead to a better job, *considering both monetary and nonmonetary factors,* and other benefits associated with a college education. The rational investor will weigh the current cost against the expected future benefits. College will be chosen only if the latter are preferred to the former.

Some may find it offensive to refer to human beings as though they were machines. Nothing moral or ethical is implied in the term human capital. Man is, of course, not a factor of production. He is the human being. But the effort, skill, ability, and ingenuity of man are productive resources. They can be used to improve man's welfare, to lessen his burden. It is these productive resources that we will refer to as human resources (or capital).

Human resources differ from nonhuman resources in two important respects. First, human capital is embodied with the individual. Choices concerning the use of human resources will be vitally affected by working conditions, job prestige, and similar nonpecuniary factors. While monetary factors will influence human capital decisions, individuals will have some tradeoff between money income and better working conditions. Second, human resources cannot be bought and sold in nonslave societies. The *services* of human resources are bought and sold daily. But the right to quit, to sell one's services to another employer or use them in an alternative manner, is always present.

The Theory of Factor Prices

In competitive markets, the price of resources, like the price of products, will be determined by supply and demand. In order to elaborate on the theory of price for

[1]The contributions of T. W. Schultz and Gary Becker to the literature on human capital have been particularly significant. See B. F. Kiker, ed., *Investment in Human Capital* (Columbia South Carolina: Univ. of South Carolina Press, 1971), for an excellent accumulation of readings in this area.

resource markets, we need to develop a theory for each of these determining factors. Let us begin by focusing on the demand for resources, both human and nonhuman.

THE DEMAND FOR RESOURCES

Producers employ laborers, machines, raw materials, and the other resources required to produce the goods and services that firms hope to sell for a profit. The demand for a resource exists because there is a demand for goods that the resource helps to produce. Thus, the demand for each resource is a **derived demand**—derived from the consumer's demand for products.

For example, a service station hires mechanics because customers demand repair service, not because the service station owner receives benefits from just having mechanics around. If customers did not demand repair services, mechanics would not be employed for long. Similarly, the demand for such inputs as carpenters, plumbers, lumber, and glass windows is derived from the demand of consumers for houses and other consumer products that these resources help to make.

Anything that increases the demand for a consumer good will simultaneously increase the demand for factors required to make it. Most resources contribute to the production of numerous goods. For example, glass is used to produce windows, automobiles, dishes, light bulbs, and mirrors, among other things. The total demand for a resource will be the sum of the derived demand for it in each of its uses. Consequently, changes in resource price must be traced through to the product market when studying the demand for factors of production.

How will firms respond to an increase in the price of a resource? In the long run, the higher price of the input will lead to two distinct adjustments that will assure a negative relationship between price and the amount of a resource demanded. First, firms will seek to reduce their utilization of the now more expensive input by substituting other resources for it. Second, the increase in the price of the resource will lead to both higher costs and product prices. Consumers will buy less of the higher priced product, leading to a decline in the demand for resources used to make it. Let us look at both of these factors a little closer.

1. *Substitution in Production.*   Firms will want to use the input combination that minimizes their costs. When the price of a resource goes up, cost-conscious firms will seek to use lower cost substitutes. The degree to which such substitution can take place will vary. Resources that are good substitutes may exist even though they are not currently being used. Sometimes the style and dimensions of a product can be altered in a manner that will conserve on the use of a more expensive input.

Consider the reaction of producers to an increase in the price of glass. Some contractors would vary both the number and dimensions of windows, substituting wood, brick, and steel for glass. Many patio furniture manufacturers would use plastics and metals more intensively. Container producers would often turn to plastics and aluminum, substituting these resources for glass. The presence of good substitutes in production assures not only that quantity demanded will be negatively related to price, but also that the demand for the resource will be highly elastic.

2. *Substitution in Consumption.*   An increase in the price of a resource will lead to higher prices for products that the input helps to produce. The higher product prices will grant consumers an incentive to turn to substitute goods, reducing the consumption of the more expensive product. But when less of that product is produced, producer demand for resources (including the one that rose in price) will decline. For example, higher glass prices will cause many consumers to switch to plastic, melamine, and potteryware. The reduction in the sales of glass dishware, will, of course, reduce the quantity demanded of glass and other resources used in the production of glassware.

Other things constant, the more elastic the demand for the product, the more elastic the demand for the resource. Substitution in consumption reinforces the impact of substitution in production. Together they serve to retard the use of resources that rise in price, while stimulating the use of inputs for which price has declined. In short, these two effects—substitution in production plus substitution in consumption—combine to explain why the quantity demanded of a resource will be negatively related to its price.

Time and the Demand for Resources

It will take time for producers to adjust fully to a change in the price of a resource. Typically, a producer will be unable to *immediately* alter his production process or the design of his product in order to conserve on the use of a more expensive input or better utilize an input whose price has declined. Similarly, consumers may be *unable to immediately* alter their consumption patterns in response to price changes. Thus, the short-run demand for resources is typically less elastic than for the long run.

Exhibit 23-1 illustrates the importance of time, using steel as an example. Initially, higher steel prices may lead to only a small reduction in usage. But if the high price of steel persists, automobile manufacturers will alter their designs, moving toward lighter weight cars that require less steel. Construction firms will design buildings that

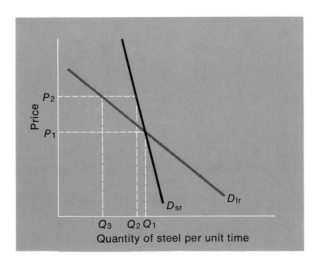

Exhibit 23-1   Time and the Demand Elasticity of Resources

An increase in the price of steel will lead to a much larger reduction in consumption in the long run than for the short run. Typically, the demand for resources will be more inelastic in the short run.

permit more substitution of plastics, wood, aluminum, glass, and other resources for steel. With the passage of time, products using steel will increase in price, encouraging consumers to cut back on their use. But these adjustments will not take place instantaneously. Therefore, in the short run the demand (D) for steel, like that for most other products, will be more inelastic than in the long run.

THE FIRM'S HIRING DECISION

How does a producer decide whether to employ additional units of a resource? This decision, like other choices, will be based on a benefit–cost comparison. The profit-maximizing firm will hire additional units of a resource, skilled labor for example, as long as the additional unit of the input adds more to revenue (the firm's benefit) than it adds to costs. If the price of the resource, a cost to the firm, is less than the additional revenues that it generates, the firm will increase profits by employing the resource. Profits will be maximized by continuing to hire each productive resource so long as the marginal revenue generated by each unit of the resource exceeds its cost. Similarly, a profit-maximizing firm would never hire a unit of resource when its costs exceed the additional revenue that it generates for the firm.

The change in the firm's total revenue brought about by the employment of one extra unit of a resource is called **marginal revenue product** (MRP). The marginal revenue product of each resource is determined by two things—(a) the amount by which employment of an additional unit of the resource causes output to increase, and (b) the marginal revenue of the product produced. The former is called **marginal physical product,** the increase in "physical" units of output that result because the employment of a resource is increased by one unit.

Exhibit 23-2 helps to illustrate the major factors that will influence the firm's hiring

Exhibit 23-2 The Short-Run Demand Schedule of a Firm

SunKissed Inc. sells and installs swimming pools in a competitive industry. The firm receives $1000 for the installation of each pool. Given the firm's current fixed capital, column 2 shows how total output changes as additional units of labor are hired. The marginal revenue product schedule of labor (column 6) would be the firm's short-run demand curve for that input.

(1) Units of the variable factor (skilled labor)	(2) Total output— physical product (pools/month)	(3) Marginal physical product $\left[\dfrac{\text{change in (2)}}{\text{change in (1)}}\right]$	(4) Product installation price	(5) Total revenue (2) × (4)	(6) Marginal revenue product (3) × (4)
0	0		$1000	$ 0	
1	4.0	4.0	1000	4000	$4000
2	8.0	4.0	1000	8,000	4000
3	11.0	3.0	1000	11,000	3000
4	13.0	2.0	1000	13,000	2000
5	14.5	1.5	1000	14,500	1500
6	15.5	1.0	1000	15,500	1000
7	16.0	0.5	1000	16,000	500

decision. SunKissed Inc. installs prefabricated swimming pools for $1000 per pool. Given the fixed quantity of heavy equipment owned by the firm, column 2 relates the firm's expected monthly output to the level of employment. One laborer could install four pools per month, two laborers eight pools, and so on. Column 3 presents the marginal physical product schedule for labor. Column 6, the marginal revenue product schedule, shows how the employment of each *additional* unit of labor affects total revenues.

Since SunKissed sells its service competitively, the marginal revenue product of labor is simply MPP (column 3) times the installation price (column 4) of a pool. What if the firm is not a perfect competitor? Then the marginal revenue of the product will be less than its price. The marginal revenue product of a resource would therefore be equal to its marginal physical product times the marginal revenue of the manufactured product.

How much labor will SunKissed employ? If the monthly wage rate were $2500, it would be profitable to hire three workers. If the wage rate were less than $2000, say $1800, four workers would be employed. At a wage rate of $1400 per month five units of labor would be hired. Profit-maximizing firms will compare the cost of a resource with its MRP when making hiring decisions. Employment of a resource will be expanded so long as the MRP exceeds resource costs.

Marginal Productivity and Demand

If the firm is unable to influence the price of a resource, the marginal cost of employing additional units is simply the resource price. Additionally, if we assume that resources are perfectly divisible, then the firm would expand the employment of each resource until its marginal revenue product was just equal to the price of the resource ($P_i = MRP_i$). Each resource would be paid exactly what it was worth *to the firm*.

As Exhibit 23-3 shows, the marginal productivity approach can be used to illustrate

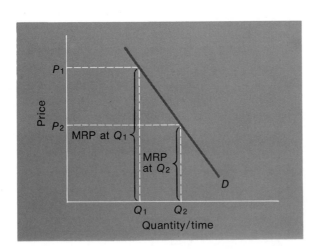

Exhibit 23-3   Marginal Productivity and Demand

Other things constant, an increase in the employment level will cause the MRP of a resource to decline. The larger quantity of the resource can be employed only at a lower price.

the negative relationship between quantity demanded and resource price. As the employment level of a resource increases, other things constant, the law of diminishing returns will assure that its marginal physical product (and MRP) will decline. As the MRP of the resource falls, firms will hire the larger quantity of the resource only at a lower price.

The marginal productivity theory is really a theory about the demand for resources. The central proposition of the theory is that a profit-maximizing employer will never pay more for a unit of input, whether it is skilled labor, a machine, or an acre of land, than the input is worth to him. However, pursuit of profit will induce employers to hire additional units of each resource so long as their marginal productivity generates revenues that are in excess of costs. Thus, resource prices will tend to reflect, albeit in a somewhat rough manner in the real world, the marginal productivity of the resource.

Some observers, noting that under pure competition the price of each resource is just equal to the value of what it produces (that is, input price equals marginal physical product of the input multiplied by the price of the product), have argued that competitive markets are "just" or "equitable" because each resource gets paid exactly what it is worth. But there is a major defect in this line of reasoning. There is no way that the "marginal productivity" of any factor can be determined independent of the contribution of other factors. The productivity of each factor is dependent on the quantity of other resources with which it works. For example, a man with a lawnmower can mow more grass than the same man with a pair of scissors. A student working with a textbook, classnotes, and tutor can learn more economics than the same student without these "tools." The quantity and quality of tools with which we are working vitally affect our productivity. Meaningful statements about the productivity of labor (or any other resource) can be made only after one considers the quantity of related resources with which it is working. But when a product is jointly produced it is impossible to disaggregate it into shares produced by each resource. Thus, in the real world, the productive contribution of an input cannot be isolated.

THE SUPPLY OF RESOURCES IN THE SHORT RUN

In the immediate short-run time period, the *total supply* of specific resources, both human and nonhuman, will be virtually fixed. However, resources usually have alternative uses—they can typically be used to help produce a variety of products. The utility maximization postulate implies that resource owners will use their factors of production in a manner that leads to the greatest net advantage to themselves. Of course, both monetary and nonpecuniary considerations will influence their decisions.

In the short run, changes in price incentives will lead resource owners to *shift* factors of production toward uses for which compensation has risen and away from areas where resource prices have fallen. Thus, the quantity supplied *to a specific use* will be directly related to price.

The elasticity of supply to a particular use will be dependent on **resource mobility.** Resources that can be easily transferred from one use to another in response to changing price incentives are said to be highly mobile. The supply of such factors to any specific use will be elastic. Factors that do not move easily between specific uses are said to be immobile and will have a highly inelastic short-run supply.

What can we say about resource mobility in the real world? First, let us consider the mobility of labor. When labor skills can be easily and quickly transferred, human capital is highly mobile. Within skill categories (for example, plumber, store manager, accountant, secretary, and so on) labor will be highly mobile *within the same geographic area*. Movements between geographic areas and from one skill category to another are more costly to accomplish. Thus labor will be less mobile for movements of this variety.

What about the mobility of land? Land is highly mobile between uses *when location does not matter*. For example, the same land can often be used to raise either corn, wheat, soybeans, or oats. Thus the supply of land allocated to the production of each of these commodities will be highly responsive to changes in their relative prices. Undeveloped land on the outskirts of cities is particularly mobile between uses. In addition to its value in agriculture, such land might be quickly subdivided and used for a housing development or shopping center.

But in cases where location is important, land is almost totally immobile. Land in sparsely populated Nevada cannot be transferred to Manhattan Island. Neither can land in the suburbs be transferred to the central city. Thus, since land is totally immobile physically, supply is unresponsive to *changes in price that reflect the desirability of a location.*

Typically, machines are highly immobile between uses. A machine developed to produce airplane wings is seldom of much use in the production of automobiles, appliances, and other products. Steel mills cannot easily be converted to produce aluminum. Of course there are some exceptions. Trucks can typically be used to haul a variety of products. Building space can often be converted from one use to another. But in the short run, immobility and inelasticity of supply are characteristic of much of our physical capital.

THE SUPPLY OF RESOURCES IN THE LONG RUN

In the long run, the supply of resources is not fixed. Machines will wear out, human skills will depreciate, and even the fertility of land will decline with use and erosion. These factors serve to reduce the supply of resources. But through investment, the supply of productive resources can be expanded. Current resources can be used (invested) to expand the stock of machines, buildings, and durable assets. Or alternatively, they might be used to train, educate, and develop the skills of future labor force participants. With time the supply of both physical and human resources will be altered by investment and depreciation.

Utility maximization suggests that price incentives will influence the investment decisions of both firms and individuals. Considering both monetary and nonmonetary factors, investors will choose those alternatives that they believe to be most advantageous. Higher resource prices will induce utility-maximizing investors to supply a larger amount of the resource. In contrast, other things constant, lower resource prices will reduce the incentive to invest and expand the future supply. Thus, the long-run quantity supplied of a resource will be positively related to its price.

The theory of long-run resource supply is general. The expected payoff from an investment alternative will influence the decisions of investors in both physical and human capital. For example, if the price of aluminum rises and that of steel falls, the payoff from investment in the former will increase relative to the latter. Investment capital will flow toward the production of aluminum, thus increasing the long-run quantity supplied of that resource. In contrast, declining investment in the steel industry will have a negative effect on amount supplied.

The process works exactly the same way for human resources. Higher prices for the services of human resources will lead to additional investment and an expansion in the long-run supply. Lower prices will have the opposite effect. There is much evidence to support this theory. For example, higher salaries for physical and space scientists associated with the expanding space program of the early 1960s induced an expanding number of college students to enter these fields. Similarly, attractive earning opportunities in accounting and law led to an increase in investment and quantity supplied in these areas during the 1965–1975 period. On the other hand, when governmental space efforts tapered off in the late 1960s, the salaries and employment opportunities in physics, aerospace engineering, and astronomy declined. As college enrollments in these areas in the early 1970s attest, human capital investment declined accordingly.

Considering both monetary and nonmonetary factors, investors will not knowingly invest in areas of low return when higher returns are available elsewhere. Of course, since human capital is embodied with the individual, nonpecuniary considerations will typically be more important for human than physical capital. Nonetheless, expected monetary payoffs will influence investment decisions in both areas.

Time will play an important role in the determination of the elasticity of the long-run supply curve. It takes time to construct new machines or discover and develop additional natural resources. Similarly, investment in both time and resources will be required to train, educate, and upgrade the skills of future labor force participants. Current investment in physical and human capital will increase the availability of these resources only with the passage of time.

Additional investment can expand the availability of some resources quickly. For example, it would not take long to train additional bus drivers. Thus, in the absence of entry restraints, the quantity supplied of bus drivers will expand quickly in response to higher wages. But the gestation period between expansion in investment and an increase in quantity supplied will be substantially larger for some resources. It takes a long time to train doctors, dentists, lawyers, and pharmacists. Higher earnings in these occupations may exert only a small impact on their *current* availability. Additional investment will go into these areas, but it will typically be several years before there is any substantial increase in the quantity supplied in response to higher earnings for these resources.

Since investment will have an impact on quantity supplied only after the passage of time, the short-run supply of a resource will be more inelastic than in the long run. This is particularly true when there is a lengthy gestation period between an increase in investment and an actual expansion in the availability of a resource. Using nurses as an example, Exhibit 23-4 illustrates the relationship between the short- and long-run supply of resources. An increase in the price (wage rate) of nursing services will induce some immediate increase in quantity supplied. Trained nurses may choose

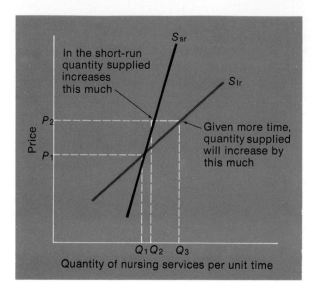

Exhibit 23-4 Time and the Elasticity of Supply for Resources

The supply of nursing services (and other resources that require a substantial gestation period between current investment and the expansion in the future quantity supplied) will be far more inelastic in the short run than in the long run.

to work more hours. Nurses not in the labor force may be drawn back into nursing. Overtime, the more attractive employment opportunities in nursing will cause the level of investment in human capital in this area to expand (for example, more student nurses). However, since most nursing programs take two to four years, it will be several years before the additional investment will begin to have its impact on supply. In the long run the quantity supplied of nurses may be quite elastic, but in the short run it is likely to be highly inelastic.

SUPPLY, DEMAND, AND RESOURCE PRICES

The theories of both supply and demand for resources have been analyzed. This is all we need to develop the theory of resource pricing in competitive markets. When factor prices are free to vary, resource prices will bring the choices of buyers and sellers into line with each other. The forces of supply and demand operate precisely the same in resource markets as was true for product markets. Pressures are present that will push resource prices toward equilibrium, where quantity supplied and quantity demanded are equal. An above-equilibrium price will generate an excess supply, unsold resource services. Inability to sell their services at the above-equilibrium price will induce some resource owners to reduce their price, pushing the market price toward equilibrium. When a resource price is below equilibrium, excess demand will be present. Rather than do without the resource, employers will bid up the price, eliminating the excess supply.

Resource markets, like product markets, work like a process. Complete adjustment does not take place instantaneously—it takes time. For example, at a higher level of demand, initially the price of a resource would rise sharply. But at the higher price, *with time*, the quantity supplied of the resource would expand. If it were a natural resource, individuals and firms would now put forth a greater effort to develop and

OUTSTANDING ECONOMIST: Gary Becker

This innovative economist is perhaps best known for his ingenious application of economics to several areas that many had earlier thought to be noneconomic by nature. Before his pioneering book, *The Economics of Discrimination* (1957),[2] the research of economists in this area was scanty. Apparently many felt that something as irrational as prejudice was beyond the realm of a rational science like economics. Becker's book showed otherwise. He developed a general theory that could be used to analyze (and measure) the impact of discrimination in several areas on the status of minorities and women. His work laid the foundation for the outpouring of research on the economics of discrimination that took place during the 1960s and 1970s.

Later Becker applied economic analysis to such seemingly noneconomic subjects as crime prevention, family development, an individual's allocation of time, and even the selection of a marriage partner. His imaginative work earned him the J. B. Clark Award (1967) granted by the American Economic Association to the "outstanding economist under 40."

The human capital approach underlies much of Becker's research. His widely acclaimed book *Human Capital* (1964)[3] is already a classic. This work developed a theoretical foundation for human investment decisions in education, on-the-job training, migration, and health. Becker looks at the individual as a "firm" that will seek to invest in human resources if it is "profitable" to do so. Considering both monetary and nonmonetary factors, the human capital decisions of these profit (or utility) maximizing individuals will be based on the attractiveness (rate of return) of alternative investment opportunities. High rates of return will attract human capital investment into an area, while low rates of return will repel it.

Becker has estimated the rate of return for both a high school and college education. His work, plus that of others, suggests that, *on average*, human capital investments are highly profitable, yielding rates of return between 11 and 15 percent. A professor of economics at the University of Chicago, Becker also taught at Columbia University for several years.

discover the now more valuable productive factor. If it were physical capital, a building or machine, current suppliers would have greater incentive to work intensively to expand production. New suppliers would be drawn into the market, providing more of the physical capital resource which increased in price. Higher prices for human capital resources will also lead to an expansion in the quantity supplied. With time, more people would acquire the necessary training, education, and experience to develop the skills that now command a higher price.

Depending on the nature of the resource, a substantial time period may be necessary before its availability can be increased very much. But the nature of the process is straightforward. An increase in the demand for a resource will cause its price to rise. If the short-run supply is quite inelastic, as it will be for resources that take a substantial

[2]Gary Becker, *The Economics of Discrimination*. Chicago: Univ. of Chicago Press, 1957.
[3]Gary Becker, *Human Capital*. New York: Columbia Univ. Press, 1964.

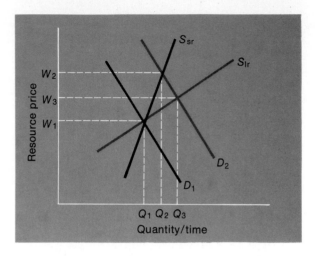

Exhibit 23-5   Adjusting to Dynamic Change

An increase in demand for a resource will typically cause price to rise more in the short run than in the long run. Can you explain why?

time period to develop or create, then prices will initially rise sharply. But with time, resource suppliers, motivated by the higher prices, will increase the availability of the resource, moderating the price rise. Others will move to supply substitute resources. Because of these forces, as Exhibit 23-5 illustrates, the long-run price increase will be less than for the short run.

Similarly, when dynamic change leads to a reduction in demand, the price of the resource will fall more in the short run than over a longer period of time. At the lower price, some resource suppliers will use their talents in other areas. The incentive for potential new suppliers to offer the resource has been reduced by the fall in price. With time, the quantity supplied of the resource will become more elastic, moderating the long-run decline in price. Those with the poorest alternatives (that is, lowest opportunity cost) will continue to provide the resource at the lower prices. Those with better alternatives will move to other areas.

This process of dynamic change and adjustment by resource suppliers is of vital importance to the efficient operation of an economy and the income of its participants. In the following chapter we will take a closer look at the operation of labor markets and factors that influence the earnings of individuals.

CHAPTER LEARNING OBJECTIVES

1. There are two broad classes of productive resources—physical and human capital. Both are durable in the sense that they will last into the future, thereby enhancing future productive capabilities. Both yield income to their owners. Investment can expand the future supply of both.

2. The demand for resources is derived from the demand for products which the resources help to produce. The quantity demanded of a resource will be negatively related to its price. If the price of a resource increases, less of it will be used for two reasons. First, producers will substitute other resources for the now more expensive input (substitution in production). Second, the higher input price will lead to higher prices for products that the resource helps to make, causing consumers to reduce their purchases of these goods (substitution in consumption).

3. The short-run market demand curve will be more inelastic than the long-run curve. It will take time for producers to adjust their production process so as to use more of less expensive resources and less of the more expensive resources.

4. Profit-maximizing firms will hire additional units of a resource so long as the marginal revenue product of the resource exceeds its hiring cost, usually the price of the input. If resources were perfectly divisible, firms would expand their utilization of each until the marginal revenue product of the resource was just equal to its price.

5. Resource owners will use their factors of production in the manner that they consider most advantageous to themselves. In the short run, higher resource prices will induce resource owners to shift factors of production toward uses for which compensation has risen and away from areas where resource prices have fallen. Thus, there will be a positive relationship between amount supplied and resource price even in the short run.

6. Many resources will be relatively immobile in the short run. The more immobile a resource, the more inelastic its short-run supply. In the long run, investment and depreciation will alter resource supply. Since investment can expand the supply of a resource with the passage of time, the long-run supply will be more elastic than in the short run.

7. The prices of resources will be determined by supply and demand. The demand for a resource will reflect the demand for products which it helps make. The supply of resources will reflect the human and physical capital investment decisions of individuals and firms.

8. Changing resource prices will influence the decisions of both users and suppliers. Higher resource prices give users a greater incentive to turn to substitutes and stimulate potential suppliers to provide more of the resource. Since these responses take time, when the demand for a resource expands, the short-run price will usually rise more than in the long run. Similarly, when there is a fall in resource demand, the changing incentives confronting users and suppliers explain why the short-run price will decline more than for the long run.

IMPORTANT TERMS TO REMEMBER

Nonhuman resources: Durable, long-lasting nonhuman inputs that can be used to produce both current and future output. Machines, buildings, land, and raw materials are examples. Investment can increase the supply of nonhuman resources.

Human resources: The long-lasting abilities, skills, and health of human beings which can be used to produce both current and future output. Investment in such things as training and education can increase the supply of human resources.

Investment in human capital: Expenditures on training, education, and skill development designed to improve the productivity of an individual.

Derived demand: Demand for an item which is based on the demand for products which the item helps to produce. The demand for resources will always be a derived demand.

Marginal physical product: The change in total output that results from the employment of one *additional* unit of a factor of production—a man-day of skilled labor, for example.

Marginal revenue product: The change in the total revenue of a firm that results from the employment of one additional unit of a factor of production. The marginal revenue product of an input will be equal to its marginal physical product multiplied by the marginal revenue of the good or service produced.

Resource mobility: Refers to the ease with which factors of production are able to move among alternative uses. Resources than can easily be transferred to a different use or location are said to be highly mobile. In contrast, when a resource has few alternative uses it is immobile. For example, the skills of a trained rodeo rider would be highly immobile since they could not be easily transferred to other lines of work.

THE ECONOMIC WAY OF THINKING—DISCUSSION QUESTIONS

1. What is meant by the expression "invest in human capital"? In what sense is the decision to invest in human capital like the decision to invest in physical capital? Is human capital investment risky? Explain.

2. **(a)** "Firms will hire a resource only if they can make money by doing so."

   (b) "In a market economy, each resource will tend to be paid according to its marginal product. Highly productive resources will command high prices, while less productive resources will get less."

   Are (a) and (b) both correct? Are they inconsistent with each other? Explain.

3. Use the information of Exhibit 23-2 to answer the following:

   (a) How many skilled laborers would SunKissed hire at a monthly wage of $1200, if it seeks to maximize profits?

   (b) If the firm's fixed costs were $7000, indicate the firm's maximum profit.

   (c) Suppose that there was a decline in demand for pools, reducing the market price for installation service to $750. At this demand level, how many employees would SunKissed hire at $1200 per month in the short run? Would SunKissed stay in business at the lower market price? Explain.

4. Are productivity gains the major source of higher wages? If so, how does one account for the rising real wages of barbers, who by and large have used the same technique for half a century? (*Hint:* Do not forget opportunity cost and supply.)

5. "However desirable they might be from an equity viewpoint, programs designed to reduce wage differentials, will necessarily reduce the incentive of people to act efficiently and use their productive abilities in those areas where demand is greatest relative to supply." Do you agree or disagree? Why?

24
EARNINGS AND THE JOB MARKET

The wages of U.S. workers are the highest in the world. In addition, they have been increasing. The compensation for a day of work by the average labor force participant will buy far more today than was true 30 years ago. Individual wages vary widely. An unskilled laborer may earn at or near the $2.30 minimum wage. Lawyers and doctors often earn $50 per hour. Dentists and even economists might receive $25 per hour.

Why do some earn more than others? Why are the earnings, measured in terms of their purchasing power, so high for Americans? Can high wages be legislated? We will proceed to analyze these questions.

WHY DO EARNINGS DIFFER?

The earnings of paired individuals in the same occupation or with the same amount of education very often differ substantially. The earnings of persons with the same family background also vary widely. For example, one researcher found that the average earnings differential between brothers was $5600 compared to $6200 for males paired randomly.[1] In addition the earnings of persons with the same I.Q., or level of training, or amount of experience, typically differ. How do economists explain these variations? Several factors combine to determine the earning power of an individual. Some of them appear to be almost by chance. Others are clearly the result of planned conscious decisions of individuals. In the last chapter, we analyzed how the market forces of supply and demand operate to determine resource prices. The subject of earnings differentials can be usefully approached within the framework of this model.

The necessary conditions for earnings equality will help us better understand why earnings differ. If (a) all individuals were homogeneous, (2) all jobs equally attractive, and (3) workers were perfectly mobile between jobs, the earnings of all employees in a competitive economy would be precisely equal. If higher wages existed in any area of the economy, the supply of workers to such an area would expand until the wage differential was eliminated. Similarly, low wages in any area would cause workers

[1] Christopher Jencks, *Inequality*. New York: Basic Books, 1972, p. 220.

to exit until wages in that area returned to parity. Real world earnings differentials exist because the three conditions necessary for earnings equality are not present.

Earnings Differentials Due to Nonhomogeneous Labor

Clearly, all workers are not the same. They differ in several important respects that will influence both the supply of and demand for their services.

1. *Worker Productivity.* The demand for high productivity employees will be greater than for those who are less productive. Persons who can operate a machine more skillfully, hit a baseball more consistently, or sell life insurance policies with greater regularity will have a higher marginal product than their less skillful counterparts. Because they are more productive, their services will command a higher wage from employers.

Workers can increase their productivity by investment in human capital. Formal education, vocational training, skill-building experience, proper health care to maintain physical fitness—all of these factors can serve to enhance worker productivity. Of course, native ability and motivation will influence the rate at which an individual can transform educational and training experience into greater productivity. Most of us would not be able to hit a baseball with the skill of Reggie Jackson even if we practiced every day from the time we were old enough to walk. Similarly, individuals will differ in the amount of valuable skills that they develop from a year of education, vocational school, or on-the-job training. Thus, we should not expect a rigid relationship to exist between years of training (or education) and the skill level of individuals.

In general, more able persons appear to receive more education and training. Unsurprisingly, greater investment in human capital does lead to higher average annual earnings, *once the person enters the labor force full time.* As Exhibit 24-1 shows, persons with more education do have higher earnings. Similarly, economic research has shown that a positive relation exists between training and earnings.

2. *Specialized Skills.* Investment in human capital and development of specialized skills can protect high wage workers from the competition of others willing to offer their services at a lower price. Few persons could develop the specialized skills of a Johnny Carson or Billie Jean King. Similarly, skill (and human capital) factors also serve to limit the supply in occupations such as heart surgeons, trial lawyers, engineers, and business entrepreneurs. As Exhibit 24-2 illustrates, when the demand for a specialized resource is great relative to its supply, the resource will be able to command a high wage. In 1973 the earnings of engineers were $17,970, more than twice the figure for laborers. Since engineers possess specialized skills that have been developed by both formal education (usually between 16 and 18 years) and experience, laborers are unable to compete directly in the engineering market. In contrast, the training and skill requirements for laborers are possessed by many. Since the supply of laborers is large relative to the demand, their earnings are substantially less.

It is important to keep in mind that wages are determined by demand *relative to supply.* Other things constant, a skilled specialist will command a higher wage than

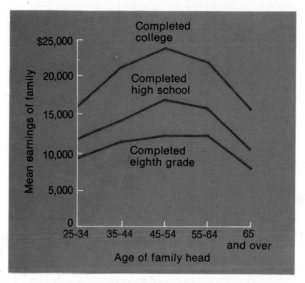

Exhibit 24-1 Education and Earnings, 1973

Investment in education does lead to a higher income level. The mean earnings of families headed by a college graduate exceed those for families headed by a high school graduate. In turn, the earnings of families headed by high school graduates are greater than those for families headed by persons who have completed only the eighth grade.

SOURCE: U.S. Department of Commerce, *Consumer Population Reports—P-60 Series.*

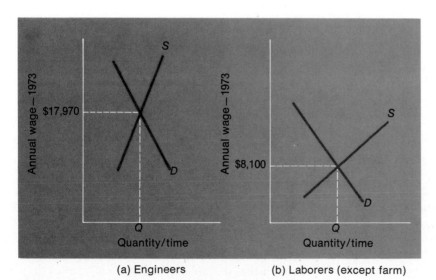

Exhibit 24-2 Supply, Demand, and Wage Differentials

The mean years of education of engineers is 16.5 compared to 10.4 for laborers. Because of their specialized skills, high wage engineers are protected from direct competition with laborers and other persons who do not possess such skills.

SOURCE: Earnings data are from the U.S. Department of Commerce, *Current Population Reports— P-60 Series.*

one with less skill. But high skill will not guarantee high wages in the absence of demand. For example, expert harness makers and blacksmiths typically command low wages today even though their supply is small. Why? Demand for the services of even expert specialists in these areas is low.

3. *Worker Preferences.* This very important source of earnings differentials is sometimes overlooked. People have different objectives in life. Some want to make a lot of money. Many are willing to work long hours, complete agonizing training and educational experiences, and sacrifice social and family life in order to make money. Others may be "workaholics" because they enjoy their job. Still others may be satisfied with enough money to get by, preferring to spend more time with their family, the Boy Scouts, the television, or the local tavern manager.

Nothing in economics indicates that one set of worker preferences is more desirable than another, any more than it suggests that people should eat more vegetables and less meat. But economics does indicate that these factors will contribute to differences in wages and earnings. Other things constant, persons who are more highly motivated toward monetary objectives will be more likely to do the things necessary to command higher wage rates.

4. *Race and Sex.* Discrimination on the basis of race or sex will contribute to earnings differences between individuals. Nonemployment discrimination may limit the opportunity of minority groups (and women) to acquire human capital (for example, quality education or specialized training) that will enhance both their productivity and earnings. Employment discrimination may directly limit their earning power. Chapter 27 deals with this topic in detail.

Earnings Differentials Due to Nonhomogeneous Jobs

When evaluating employment alternatives, individuals will consider working conditions as well as wage rates. Is a job dangerous? Does it offer the opportunity to acquire experience and training that will enhance future earnings? Is the work strenuous and nerve wracking? Are the working hours, job location, and means of transportation convenient? All of these factors add up to what economists call the **nonpecuniary job characteristics.** Workers will be willing to trade off higher wage rates for more favorable nonpecuniary job characteristics. Examples of this are numerous. Because of the dangers involved, aerial window washers (that is, the ones hanging from windows 20 stories up) earn higher wages than other window washers. Sales jobs involving a lot of out-of-town travel typically pay more than similar jobs without such inconvenience. The earnings of economists in academics are typically lower than in business because most of us prefer the more independent work environment and intellectual stimulation offered by colleges and universities.

Substantial wage differentials exist for similar work between (a) large and small firms and (b) urban and rural areas. Nonpecuniary factors, coupled with locational preferences, help to explain these differentials. Large firms must typically draw their labor force from a wider geographic area, causing longer average travel time to and from work. Congestion problems will be more severe. All of these factors serve to make employment with large firms less desirable. Thus, they must pay higher wage rates in order to attract the desired size of labor force. Similarly, the lower wages in rural areas probably, at least partially, reflect the employee's willingness to trade off higher wages for a job closer to his preferred living area. All of these differences in the nonpecuniary characteristics of jobs will contribute to earnings differences between individuals.

Immobility of Labor

It is costly to move to a new location or train for a new occupation in order to acquire a job. Such movements will not take place instantaneously. In the real world labor, like other resources, fails to possess perfect mobility. Thus some wage differentials will result from an incomplete adjustment to dynamic change.

Since the demand for labor resources is a derived demand, it will be affected by dynamic changes in product markets. An expansion in the demand for a product will cause a rise in the demand for specialized labor to produce the product. Since resources are often highly immobile (that is, the supply is inelastic) in the short run, the expansion in demand may cause the wages of the specialized labor to rise sharply. This is what happened in the provision of medical services in the late 1960s. An expansion in demand triggered a rapid increase in the earnings of doctors, nurses, and other medical personnel.

A decline in product demand has the opposite effect. The tapering off of the space program in the late 1960s depressed the wages of engineers, physicists, and space scientists. Demand shifts in the product market will favor those in expanding industries, while working against those in contracting industries.

Man-made barriers may also limit the mobility of labor. Licensing requirements limit the mobility of labor into many occupations—physicians, taxicab drivers, architects, and undertakers among them. Unions may also follow policies that limit labor mobility and alter the free market forces of supply and demand. Chapter 25 analyzes the impact of unions on wage rates.

THUMBNAIL SKETCH—Sources of Earnings Differentials

I. Differences in workers:

(a) productivity (for example, skills, human capital, native ability, motivation),

(b) specialized skills (primarily human capital plus native ability),

(c) worker preferences (tradeoff between money earnings and other things), and

(d) race and sex—discrimination.

II. Differences in jobs (nonpecuniary job characteristics such as convenience of working hours, job safety, job location, and working conditions).

III. Immobility of resources:

(a) temporary disequilibrium resulting from dynamic change, and

(b) man-made restrictions (for example, occupational licensing and union imposed restraints).

Summary on Wage Differentials

As the thumbnail sketch shows, wage differentials stem from many sources. Many of them play an important allocative role, compensating persons for (a) investments that increase their productivity and (b) unfavorable working conditions that reduce personal utility. Other wage differentials, at least partially, reflect locational preferences and the desire of individuals for money income (as opposed to other things that yield utility). But still other differentials, such as those related to discrimination and man-made occupational restrictions, are unrelated to worker preferences and are not required to promote efficient production.

PRODUCTIVITY AND THE GENERAL LEVEL OF WAGES

While wage differentials are important, it is also important to understand why the general level of wages will vary between countries and within the same country at different points in time. Real earnings are vastly greater in the United States than in India or China. In addition, the average real earnings per hour in the United States have approximately doubled during the last 25 years. What factors account for these variations in the general level of wages?

Differences in labor productivity—output produced per man-hour—are the major source of variation in real wages. Exhibit 24-3 illustrates the relationship between real wages and output per man-hour since World War II. As the amount produced per man-hour has steadily increased, real wages have expanded. Between 1947 and 1973 output per man-hour doubled. What happened to employee compensation? During the same time period, the hourly compensation of employees, measured in constant 1972 dollars, increased from $1.94 to $3.80. As output per man-hour doubled, real wages likewise doubled.

The close relationship between amount produced and real wages should not be surprising. Do not forget, real income and real output are simply two ways of viewing the same thing. In the long run (and largely even in the short run) expansion in real income is totally dependent on our ability to expand output. Without expansion of output, our money incomes, whatever they may be, will not permit us, in aggregate, to purchase more goods and services.

In the last chapter we showed that the productivity of a resource, including labor, is dependent on the amount of "other resources" with which it works. Contrary to what many believe, physical capital (for example, modern labor-saving machines) is not the enemy of high real wages. In fact, just the opposite is true. Machines make it possible for labor to produce more per man-hour. Are not jobs destroyed in the process? Sometimes *specific jobs* will be eliminated, but this merely releases human resources so they can be used to expand output in other areas. Output (productivity), not jobs, is the source of high real wages.

Improvements in productivity are brought about by a cooperative process. It is not easy to isolate the precise impact that specific factors such as capital accumulation, labor force quality, technology, and economic organization have on productivity and real income. Exhibit 24-4 presents data on the amount of physical and human capital of

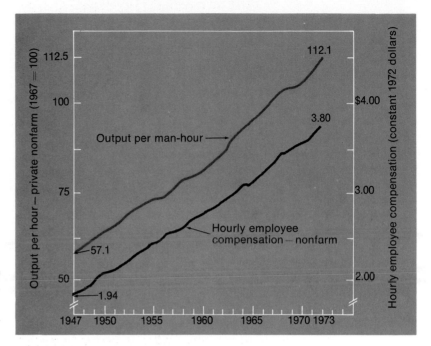

Exhibit 24-3 Productivity and Employee Compensation

As the diagram illustrates, productivity of employees per man-hour is closely related to their earnings.

SOURCE: *Manpower Report of the President—1974,* Tables C-3, G-1, G-2.

Exhibit 24-4 Machines, Education, and Employee Earnings

It is estimated that manufacturing production employees in the mid-1970s, on average, worked with approximately $45,000 of capital equipment, more than three times the amount available in 1949. The schooling data show that the amount of human capital per worker has also risen. Column (3) shows the impact on real wages.

Year	(1) Value of capital per production employee in manufacturing (constant 1972 dollars)	(2) Median years of schooling of persons in the labor force	(3) Average hourly wage in manufacturing (constant 1972 dollars)
1949	$14,075	10.6	$2.41
1959	24,942	12.0	3.14
1963	27,636	12.2	3.36
1970	39,900	12.4	3.62
1973	45,000 (est.)	12.5	3.83

SOURCE: Derived from Tax Foundation, *Facts and Figures of Government Finance—1975,* Table 43. Capital was defined as the total book value of assets less investments in government bonds or securities of other corporations.

U.S. workers for the 1949–1973 period. In 1949 the median years of schooling of persons in the labor force were 10.6. It rose to 12.0 years in 1959 and 12.5 years in 1973. Increasing expenditures on training and skill development also helped to improve the quality of the labor force during the period. Simultaneously, the physical capital per worker was expanded. In 1973, on average, each manufacturing employee worked with machines and capital assets valued at $45,000, more than three times the amount available to workers in 1949. Unsurprisingly, the expansion in both human and physical capital per worker led to both higher output and real wages.

Investment—The United States Versus Other Countries

Since investment is so important to the growth of future output (and real income), observers oftentimes compare investment and growth rates between countries. Ideally, we would like to look at investment in both human and physical capital, including resources utilized to improve the available technology. Investment results in the sacrifice of current consumption in order to allocate more resources to the production of physical capital (for example, machines, discoverable natural resources, and buildings), human capital, and technical knowledge with which to expand future production. Other things constant, countries that allocate more to current investment will build up their stock of valuable productive assets more rapidly and experience a more rapid growth in income.

Unfortunately, comparable international investment data for both human and physical capital have not been developed. Exhibit 24-5 presents United Nations data for gross fixed capital formation (physical capital) as a percentage of domestic production for several nations. During the 1960–1971 period, the share of GNP allocated to investment was considerably lower for the United States than for other major Western nations. Growth in output in the United States lagged accordingly. On the other hand, countries such as Japan, Australia, West Germany, and France that allocate a much

Exhibit 24-5   Investment and Growth Rates—An International Comparison

Country	Gross fixed capital formation as a share of gross domestic product, 1960–71	ANNUAL GROWTH RATE IN REAL GROSS DOMESTIC PRODUCT, 1960–1971	
		Total	Per capita
Japan	33.0	10.7	9.6
Australia	26.5	5.3	3.3
West Germany	25.2	4.7	3.6
France	24.0	5.7	4.7
Sweden	22.5	4.2	3.4
Italy	21.0	5.2	4.4
United Kingdom	18.0	2.8	2.2
United States	14.8	4.3	3.0

SOURCE: *Yearbook of National Accounts Statistics—1972*, vol. III. New York: United Nations, 1974.

larger share of their domestic product to capital formation experienced more rapid growth during the period.

Data such as those of Exhibit 24-5 are causing some experts to express concern about the low rate of capital formation in the United States. John Kendrick of George Washington University, a leading authority in this area, expresses this view:

> I might point out that investment is a smaller portion of gross national product in the United States than in most other industrialized countries. And I believe this is one reason that we have a slower rate of advance in productivity than most other advanced nations.[2]

If more complete data including investment in human capital were available, perhaps the U.S. investment rate would be closer to that of other countries. The more rapid growth rate of other nations may reflect a type of catch-up process and their ability to adopt advanced technology that is already employed by industries in the United States. Nevertheless, several leading economists feel that unless we allocate a larger share of GNP to investment, our growth in real income will continue to lag behind.

MYTHS OF ECONOMICS:
"If we keep allowing machines to replace men, we are going to run out of jobs. Automation is the major cause of unemployment."

Machines will be substituted for men if and only if they reduce production costs. Why has the automatic elevator replaced the operator, the tractor replaced the horse, and the power shovel replaced the ditch digger? Because each is a cheaper method of accomplishing a task, that is why.

The **automation** causes unemployment fallacy stems from a failure to recognize the secondary effects. Suppose someone developed a new toothpaste that actually prevented cavities and sold for half the current price of Colgate. At last, we would have a toothpaste that really worked. But think of the impact that the invention would have on dentists, toothpaste producers, their employees, and even the advertising agencies that give us those marvelous toothpaste commercials. What are these people to do? Jobs have been destroyed. Right?

Wrong! Those are the obvious effects—what is seen as a direct result of the toothpaste invention. What is not seen is the additional jobs that will indirectly be created by the invention. Consumers will now be spending less on toothpaste, dental bills, and pain relievers. Their real income has increased. They will now be able to spend *more* on thousands of products that they would have had to forego had it not been for the new invention. They will increase their spending on clothes, recreation, vacations, swimming pools, education, and many other items. This additional spending—spending that would not have taken place in the absence of the reduced dental cost due to the technological advancement—will generate additional demand and

[2] John Kendrick (interview), "What it Takes to Raise Living Standards in the U.S.," *U.S. News and World Report*, March 24, 1975.

employment in other sectors. True, jobs were eliminated in the toothpaste and dental industries because of a reduction in consumer spendings in these areas. But *new* jobs were created in other industries in which consumers increased their spending as the result of the savings attributable to the new invention. This latter secondary effect often goes unseen, and therefore people believe that jobs have been destroyed.

When the demand for the product is elastic, a cost-saving invention could even generate an increase in employment in the industry affected by the invention. This was essentially what happened in the automobile industry when Henry Ford's mass production techniques reduced the cost (and price) of cars. When the price of automobiles fell 50 percent, consumers bought three times as many. Even though the labor man-hours *per car* decreased by 25 percent between 1920 and 1930, employment in the industry increased from 250,000 to 380,000 during the period, approximately a 50 percent increase.

But even if the demand for automobiles had been inelastic, automation would not have caused long-run unemployment. When demand is inelastic, less will be spent on the lower cost, lower priced commodity, leaving more to be spent on other goods and services. This spending on other products, which would not have resulted in the absence of the new invention, will assure that there is not a net reduction in employment.

Focusing on jobs alone can lead to a fundamental misunderstanding about the importance of machines, automation, and technological improvements. Automation neither creates nor destroys jobs. The real impact of cost-reducing machines and technological improvements is to increase production. Technological advancements make it possible for us to produce as much with fewer resources, thereby releasing valuable resources so production (and consumption) can be expanded in other areas. Since there is a direct link between improved technology and rising output, automation exerts a positive influence on our economic welfare.

HOW IS THE ECONOMIC PIE DIVIDED BETWEEN PHYSICAL AND HUMAN CAPITAL?

We have emphasized that wage rates tend to reflect the availability of tools—physical capital—and the skills and abilities of individual workers—human capital. Wages will tend to be high when physical capital is plentiful, technology advanced, and the work force highly skilled. When the equipment available to the typical worker is primitive and most workers lack education and skills, wages will be low. Both human and physical capital contribute to the productive process.

How is the pie divided between these two broad factors of production in the United States? Exhibit 24-6 provides an answer. In 1974 approximately 83 percent of national income was earned by employees and self-employed proprietors, the major categories that would reflect the earnings of human capital. In recent years, 80 percent or more of our national income has been consistently allocated to human capital. Income earned by physical capital—rents, interest, and corporate profits—currently comprises 17 to 20 percent of the national income.

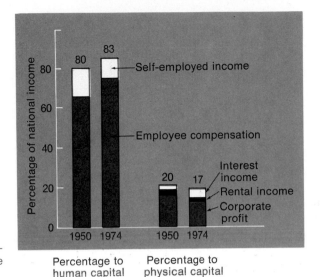

Exhibit 24-6 The Shares of Income Going to Physical and Human Capital

Counting self-employment income, approximately four-fifths of national income is earned by owners of human capital.

CAN HIGHER WAGES BE LEGISLATED?

Higher legal **minimum wages** have often been advanced as a tool to reduce poverty among the working poor. To many, the proposal would appear to be both obvious and simple. If a person in the labor force is poor, why not require employers to pay him above-poverty wages?

Currently, federal legislation requires most employers to pay wage rates of at least $2.30 per hour (the rate was increased to $2.30 in January 1976). What is the impact of minimum wage legislation? Most workers already have hourly earnings in excess of the $2.30 minimum wage. Their wage rates will be influenced only indirectly. Exhibit 24-7 illustrates the effect of the minimum wage on low productivity workers. The direct and obvious effect of the legislation is to increase their wages. What is not so obvious is the indirect, negative impact on the employment opportunities available to low-skilled employees. Employers will substitute machines and highly skilled workers for the now more expensive low-skilled employees. Fewer will be employed at the higher legislated wage.

If other inputs can easily and economically be substituted for the now higher priced low skill workers, the demand for such employees would be highly elastic. The reduction in employment would be substantial. On the other hand, if the demand for low skill employees is inelastic, the employment reduction will be small. As is the case for other inputs, we can expect the demand elasticity to be greater in the long run than in the short run, as firms have time to adjust to the higher wage.

What happens to those employees who would like to work at the minimum wage, but cannot find jobs (excess supply AB of Exhibit 24-7)? Some of them will be pushed, at least temporarily, into the unemployment ranks. With time, many of them, recognizing the difficulties of obtaining permanent and consistent employment at the minimum wage, will turn to other jobs that are not covered by the minimum wage law.

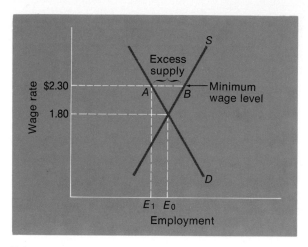

Exhibit 24-7 Employment and the Minimum Wage

If the market wage of a group of employees is $1.80, a $2.30 minimum wage would (a) increase the earnings of persons who are able to maintain employment, while (b) reducing the employment of others (E_0 to E_1), pushing them onto the unemployment roles or into less preferred jobs.

These may be jobs that they had previously evaluated as less attractive than their former employment. Others will continue searching and go through longer periods of unemployment in an effort to gain a job at the minimum wage level.

The minimum wage hits hardest at teenagers and minorities since low skill, inexperienced workers will be overrepresented among these two groups. Before 1956 unemployment among both black and white teenagers was nearly 10 percent. Within two years after the legal minimum wage was increased by 33 percent—from 75 cents to one dollar—unemployment among teenage white males rose to 15 percent. It shot up to nearly 25 percent for blacks.[3] Since that time the minimum wage has remained high relative to the average wage rate. High relative unemployment among teenagers and blacks has also continued.

Keeping the Unskilled, Unskilled

The minimum wage will affect not only employment opportunities but also the *types* of jobs available to those with little human capital. The opportunity to acquire training that will enhance the employee's future productivity (and earning power) increases the attractiveness of a job to workers, particularly young, inexperienced workers. But minimum wage legislation greatly limits the ability of employers to offer such jobs because it prohibits them from paying a temporarily low wage during the training period.[4] Thus the jobs available to low skill employees will tend to be **dead-end jobs**

---

[3] See Marshall Colberg, "Minimum Wage Effects on Florida's Economic Development," *Journal of Law and Enconomics*, October 1960; John M. Peterson, "Research Needs in Minimum Wage Theory," *Southern Economic Journal*, July 1962; and Gene L. Chapin and Douglas K. Adie, "Teenage Unemployment Effects of Federal Minimum Wages," paper presented to the Industrial Relations Research Association, 1970, for evidence of the effect of minimum wages on employment.

[4] Exceptions are made if the employee pays a fee for the training. For example, teacher and nurse training programs often provide their "students" direct on-the-job experience. Paradoxically, it is permissible to pay a negative wage (that is, charge a fee to the employee), but not a low positive wage.

with little opportunity for training and advancement. As Martin Feldstein has pointed out, the minimum wage acts as an institutional barrier limiting the opportunity to acquire on-the-job training.[5] Many leading economists believe that minimum wage legislation is the major reason why there is an almost complete lack of skill-building jobs at the lower end of the wage spectrum.

Helping Poor Southerners

Minimum wage legislation will also influence regional employment opportunities. In addition to support from those who expect that a higher minimum wage rate would reduce poverty, northern industries, Congressmen, and labor unions often promoted such legislation as a means of reducing the competitiveness of southern industries. Since both money wages and the cost of living are usually lower in the South, minimum wage legislation, if enforced, will have a greater impact in that region. Since northern wages are more likely to already be above the minimum, it will have less impact in that region. Northern firms, recognizing this, have often supported minimum wage legislation as a vehicle to increase the costs of southern competitors. Looked at from this perspective, it is not surprising that most of the lobbying and political support for the legislation usually comes from the high wage North and West rather than the lower wage South.

Putting the Minimum Wage in Perspective

It is easy to exaggerate the expected impact of such legislation. Relatively few workers receive wages below the present minimum. Sometimes the structure of employment can be changed to avoid the impact of the minimum wage. But economics does suggest that the antipoverty effectiveness of minimum wage legislation will be mixed. Some low wage workers will maintain their employment and increase their earnings. But others, particularly those at the very bottom of the skill ladder, will both suffer more unemployment and be pushed to less desirable jobs. More importantly, such legislation reduces the ability of many younger labor entrants to acquire training and experience that would act as a ticket to higher (above the legal minimum) wages.

▭ LOOKING AHEAD

Payments to resources are of vital importance because individual incomes will be determined by (a) resource prices and (b) the amount of resources that one owns. In this chapter we considered the role that market forces play in the determination of resource prices. The impact of labor unions is the topic of the following chapter. Issues of inequality—income inequality and inequality of opportunity because of discrimination—compose the latter two chapters of this section.

[5] It is ironic that while we subsidize formal education, we establish barriers that restrict a worker's ability to acquire training. See Martin Feldstein, "The Economics of the New Unemployment," *The Public Interest*, Fall 1973.

CHAPTER LEARNING OBJECTIVES

1. Wage differentials between individuals stem from three major sources—differences in workers, differences in jobs, and lack of labor mobility. Individuals will differ with respect to productivity (skills, human capital, motivation, native ability, and so on), specialized skills, employment preferences, race, and sex. All of these factors will influence either the demand for or supply of labor. In addition, differences in the nonpecuniary job characteristics, dynamic changes in products markets, and man-made restrictions that limit labor mobility will contribute to variation in wages among workers.

2. Productivity is the ultimate source of high wages. U.S. workers have high wages because they have lots of human capital and they work with lots of physical capital.

3. The share of GNP allocated to the formation of physical capital is less for the United States than for most other countries. Many economists believe that this low rate of investment is a major drag on the growth of income in the United States.

4. Approximately 80 percent of national income in the United States is allocated to human capital (labor) and 20 percent to owners of physical capital.

5. Automated production methods will be adopted only if they reduce cost. While automation *might* reduce revenues and employment *in a specific industry*, the lower production cost will increase real income, causing demand in other industries to expand. These secondary effects will cause employment to rise in other industries. Improved technology expands our ability to produce. It is expanded production, not just jobs, that generates improvement in our economic well-being.

6. Minimum wage legislation increases the earnings of some low skill workers, but others are pushed to inferior employment opportunities and experience higher unemployment rates. Minimum wage legislation indirectly reduces the ability of employers to offer (and low skill employees to find) work with on-the-job training and skill-building experience. Thus, the jobs available to low skill workers, even youthful ones, tend to be primarily dead-end jobs.

IMPORTANT TERMS TO REMEMBER

Nonpecuniary job characteristics: Working conditions, prestige, variety, location, employee freedom and responsibilities, and other nonwage characteristics of a job that will influence how employees will evaluate the job.

Automation: Adoption of an alternative, usually less labor intensive, technological method of production as a means to reduce cost. It will be beneficial to adopt a new technology only if it reduces the cost of producing a good or service.

Minimum wage: A legal restriction requiring that all workers in covered industries be paid at least the specified minimum hourly rate of pay.

Dead-end jobs: Jobs that offer the employee little opportunity for advancement or on-the-job training.

THE ECONOMIC WAY OF THINKING—DISCUSSION QUESTIONS

1. What are the major reasons the earnings of individuals differ? Why are wages in some occupations higher than in others? How do wage differentials influence the allocation of resources? How important is this function? Explain.

2. Why are real wages in the United States higher than in other countries? Is the labor force itself responsible for the higher wages of American workers? Explain.

3. What impact does the minimum wage have on the employment and training opportunities of teenagers, blacks, and women with low skills? Explain.

4. "The strength of our economy is threatened by automation. Everywhere we turn machines are replacing men. An economy that does not have jobs for its workers cannot survive."

(a) Evaluate.

(b) Did the refrigerator weaken our economy because it eliminated the job of the iceman? The truck because it eliminated jobs for men with strong backs?

(c) What type of an economy would not have any jobs for its workers? Would you like to live there? Explain.

5. Explain why many northern and western industries and unions, motivated only by self-interest, advocate a higher minimum wage even though its major direct impact is on southern workers and firms.

6. What are the major factors that would normally explain earnings differences between **(a)** lawyers and ministers, **(b)** accountants and elementary schoolteachers, **(c)** business executives and social workers, **(d)** a country lawyer and Wall Street lawyer, **(e)** an experienced skilled craftsman and a 20-year-old high school dropout, **(f)** a fireman and a nightwatchman, and **(g)** upper story and ground floor window washers?

---

7. What's Wrong with This Way of Thinking?

"Higher wages help everybody. The worker is helped because he can now purchase more of the things that he needs. Business is helped because the increase in the worker's purchasing power will expand the demand for products. The taxpayer is helped because the worker will now pay more taxes. Higher wages are the route to economic progress."

---

8. What's Wrong with This Way of Thinking?

"Jobs are the key to economic progress. Unless we can figure out how to produce more jobs, economic progress will be stifled."

25

UNION POWER—A SHIELD
OR A THREAT?

The union monopoly is a threat to the American economy. The stranglehold that union monopolists have on our basic industries is frightening. Something must be done to control the excess power of organized labor.

The union movement has brought dignity and decent wages to the American working man. The blue collar worker who belongs to a union no longer has to live in fear of repressive action by an abrupt supervisor or employer.

Which of these two views is correct? Might they both be on target? Read on and make up your own mind.

Approximately 20 million Americans, one out of every four workers, belong to a labor union (see Exhibit 25-1). A labor union is an organization of employees who have consented to joint bargaining with an employer about wages, grievance procedures, and other conditions of employment. Historically, unions have been controversial. Some believe that the actions of unions are the major source of several economic ills, particularly unemployment and inflation. Others argue that unions are the source of improved economic conditions for the working man, his shield against the beast of employer greed. Who is right? What has been the role of the labor union? How does collective bargaining influence the operation of labor markets? This chapter is addressed to these and similar questions.

WHAT IS A COLLECTIVE BARGAINING CONTRACT?

Each year **collective bargaining contracts** covering wages and working conditions for between 5 and 8 million workers are negotiated. The union negotiators, acting

Exhibit 25-1   Union Membership

Union membership grew quite rapidly between 1930 and 1950. During the 1960s it leveled off at approximately one out of every four workers.

Year	Union membership (in thousands)	Percentage of labor force
1900	791	2.7
1910	2,116	5.6
1920	5,034	12.1
1930	3,632	7.4
1940	8,944	15.9
1950	15,000	22.9
1960	18,117	24.5
1970	20,210	23.5
1972	20,838	24.1

SOURCE: L. Davis et al., *American Economic Growth* (New York: Harper, 1972), and *Statistical Abstract of the United States—1975*.

as agents for a group of employees, bargain with management about the provisions of a labor contract. If the union representatives are able to obtain a contract that they consider acceptable, they will submit it to a vote of the union members. If the members approve the contract, it establishes in detail wage rates, fringe benefits, and working conditions for a future time interval, usually the next two or three years. During that time interval both union and management must abide by the conditions of the contract. While the labor contract is between management and the union, it also applies to nonunion members who are employed by the firm or industry.

Some labor–management contracts will contain a **union shop** provision. A union shop contract requires all workers to join the union after a specified length of employment, usually 30 days. Union proponents argue that since all workers in the bargaining unit enjoy the benefits of collective bargaining, all should be required to join and pay dues. In the absence of a union shop individual workers can reap the gains brought about by the union's actions without incurring the cost.

Opponents of the union shop counter that all employees are not helped by a union. Some unions lack the necessary power to gain wage increases. Some employees may feel that they would be better off if they could bargain for themselves. In addition unions often engage in political activities, either directly or indirectly. These activities may run counter to the views of individual employees. Why should an employee be forced, as a condition of employment, to support activities of which he does not approve? In 1947 Congress passed Section 14-B of the Taft-Hartley Act, which allows states to enact **right-to-work laws** prohibiting union shop contracts. Currently some 20 states have legislation prohibiting contracts that would establish union membership as a condition of employment.

THE STRIKE—A "BIG STICK" OF THE UNION

Typically, management and labor negotiators will begin the bargaining process for a new labor contract several months, or even a year, before the termination of the current agreement. Usually the new contract will be approved before the old contract has terminated. More than 96 percent of all bargaining contracts are approved without a work stoppage. But at the termination of the old labor–management agreement, if the bargaining process has broken down and there is no agreement on a new contract, either side may use its economic power to try to bring the other to terms.

The employer can withhold employment from workers at the expiration of the old contract. This is called a **lockout.** But since the employer can unilaterally announce his terms for continued employment, he will seldom lock out employees. Almost the only occasion for a lockout would be when a union is striking a single member of an employer association, causing that member to lose sales to his competitors. When this is the case, the employers may have an agreement to discontinue work in the entire industry until the labor dispute is settled. In this way, competitors of the firm against which the strike was currently directed, would be using the lockout.

The major source of work stoppages is the strike. A **strike** is composed of two major actions by a union: (1) employees, particularly union employees, refuse to work, and (2) actions are taken to prevent other employees from working for the employer. Both conditions are essential to the strike as we know it today. Without efforts to prevent other employees, often referred to as "scabs" or "strikebreakers," from accepting jobs with the employer, one would have only a mass resignation. Since a strike involves picketing designed to restrict and discourage the hiring of other workers, actions to prevent free entry and exit from a plant, and violence or the threat of violence against workers willing to cross the picket lines, it is more than just a mass resignation.

The purpose of a strike is to impose economic cost on an employer so he will accept the terms proposed by the union. When the strike can be used to disrupt the production process and interfere with the employer's ability to sell goods and services to customers, it is a very powerful weapon. Under such conditions an employer may submit to the wage demands of a union, as a means of avoiding the cost of a strike.

Given its nature, it is not surprising that the "right to strike" has an uneven history. At times it was prohibited as interference with the rights of nonunion workers. In some countries, the Soviet Union for example, strikes are prohibited. In others they are permitted only in certain industries. In the United States, before the passage of legislation in the early 1900s clearly establishing the right to strike, the courts were sometimes willing to intervene and limit certain types of strikes. The role of law enforcement in strikes also has a mixed history. In some areas the police have given nonstrikers willing to continue work, protection to and from their jobs. In other cases they have permitted pickets to block entry and turned their backs on violence that resulted when nonstrikers sought to cross picket lines. Even today, the protection that a nonstriker can expect from the police will vary from location to location.

The United States has established some limitations on the right to strike. Several states limit the right of public employees to strike. The Taft-Hartley Act allows the president to seek a court injunction which will prohibit a strike for 80 days when he believes the strike would create a "national emergency." During the 80 day period, work will continue under the conditions of the old contract. However, if a settlement has not been reached during this "cooling off" period, employees again have the option to use the strike weapon. President Nixon used the 80 day injunction in 1971 when faced with a longshoremen's strike. President Eisenhower applied it during a steel industry strike in 1959.

THE STRIKE AND SERIOUS BARGAINING

A strike can be costly to both the union and management. From the firm's viewpoint a work stoppage may mean that it will be unable to meet the current demand for its product. It may lose customers and they may be difficult to win back once they have turned to competitors during the strike. A strike will be more costly to the employer when (a) the demand for his product is strong, (b) he is unable to stockpile his product, and (c) his fixed costs are high even during the strike. If the firm can stockpile its product in anticipation of a strike, a work stoppage may not have much impact on current sales. For example, automobile producers, particularly during slack times, often have an inventory of new cars that allows them to meet current demand during a 60 or even 90 day strike. In contrast, the shipping revenues of a trucking firm may be completely eliminated by a teamsters' strike. The firm would be unable to deliver its product because of the strike, and potential customers would therefore turn to rail, air, postal, and other forms of shipping. The firm would suffer a permanent loss of sales.

Careful timing can also magnify the cost of a strike. Agricultural unions can threaten farmers with the loss of an entire year's income through the withdrawal of their labor at harvest time. Major League umpires can strengthen their position by striking at World Series time, as they did a few years ago.

Thus, the nature of the product, the level of current demand, and the ability of the firm to continue to meet the requests of its customers during a strike all influence the effectiveness of the strike as a weapon. The more costly a work stoppage would be to a firm, the greater the pressure on it to yield to the demands of the union.

Strikes, particularly if they are long, will also be quite costly to employees. While a carnival attitude often prevails during the early days of a strike, a few paydays without checks will impose an extreme hardship on most families. Strike funds are usually inadequate to deal with a prolonged strike. In recent years welfare benefits have been used to reduce the cost imposed on workers by the strike.[1] Temporary employment in other areas can sometimes be arranged, but as a strike continues, pressures will build on the union to arrive at a settlement.

The strike, or the threat of it, does force both management and labor to bargain seriously. Recognition of the potential cost of a strike to both union and management provides them with an incentive to settle without a work stoppage. Each year, an estimated 120,000 labor contracts are terminated. Thus during the course of a year, 120,000 labor and managment bargaining teams sit across the bargaining table from each other. They deal with the important issues of wages, fringe benefits, grievance

---

[1] The availability of welfare benefits to strikers varies among areas. In 1970, more than $300 million dollars of welfare benefits were distributed to striking workers.

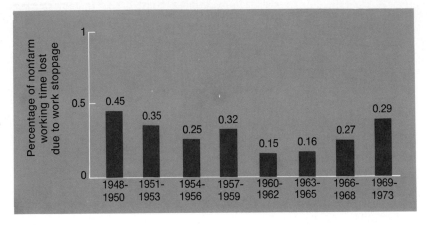

Exhibit 25-2   The Percentage of Work Time Lost Due to Strikes, 1948–1973

Since World War II, approximately 0.3 of 1 percent of nonfarm working time has been lost due to labor disputes.

SOURCE: *Manpower Report of the President—1974.*

procedures, and conditions of employment. More than 96 percent of the time, labor-management contracts are agreed to without the use of the strike. You seldom hear about these contracts because peaceful settlements are back-page news at best. It is strikes that compose the stuff of which headlines are made.

The Bureau of Labor Statistics estimates the amount of working time lost because of strikes. These data, presented in Exhibit 25-2, indicate that during the last 10 years the number of man-hours lost because of strikes was less than three-tenths of one percent of the total working time, far less than work time lost because of absenteeism. The work time loss due to strikes has been declining.

HOW DOES THE "BIG STICK" AFFECT THE PUBLIC?

It is important to place work stoppages in their proper perspective. This is not always an easy task because some strikes have a substantial impact on parties other than the union–management participants. For example, a prolonged strike in the steel industry might cause a loss of work time in auto, construction, and other industries. A teachers' strike might force a working parent to quit his or her job in order to care for the children. A public transit strike in New York can paralyze Fun City. A coal miners' strike can leave Londoners without heat.

Innocent parties, who are unable to influence the labor–management agreement, are often harmed because a vital community service is discontinued. Serious financial losses are sometimes absorbed by wholesalers, retailers, shippers, and secondary manufacturers (and their employees), who are critically dependent on the material or service that has been interrupted by a strike. The public interest is affected. How can one measure the economic loss from such strikes? Should not third parties be protected when strikes involve the public interest? Many would answer the latter question in the affirmative. But how can the public be protected without interfering with the bargaining process? As our economy becomes more and more interdependent, the search for an answer will continue.

GETTING MORE FOR UNION MEMBERS

How can unions influence wages? The collective bargaining setting often gives the appearance that wages are established primarily by institutional factors and the talents of the union–management representatives who sit around the bargaining table. It might appear that market forces play a relative minor role. But as both union and management are well aware, market forces provide the setting in which the bargaining process is conducted. They often serve to tip the balance of power one way or the other.

When the demand for a product is strong, the demand for labor will be high, and the firm will be much more willing to consent to a significant wage increase. At the same time, when demand is weak, the product inventory level of the firm (or industry) is more likely to be high. The firm's current demand for labor will be weakened. It is much less vulnerable to a union work stoppage. Market conditions dictate that wage increases will come much harder under these conditions.

As we have already indicated, collective bargaining agreements cover both wages and fringe benefits (vacation time, sick leave, accident benefits, etc.). Fringe benefits are an indirect component of employee compensation. Thus, when we speak of wage rates, we include both direct money wages and employer-provided fringe benefits.

There are three basic methods that a union may use to increase the wages of its members.

1. *Supply Restrictions.* If a union can successfully reduce the supply of competitive labor, higher wage rates will result automatically. Licensing requirements, long apprenticeship programs, immigration barriers, high initiation fees, refusal to admit new members to the union, and prohibition of nonunion labor from holding jobs are all practices that unions have used to limit the supply of labor to various occupations and jobs. Craft unions, in particular, have often been able to attain higher wages because of their successful effort to limit the entry of competitive labor.

Exhibit 25-3 illustrates the impact of supply restrictions on wage rates. Successful exclusionary tactics will reduce supply, shifting the supply curve from S_0 to S_1. Facing the supply curve S_1, employers will consent to the wage rate W_1. Compared with a free entry market equilibrium, the wage rate has increased from W_0 to W_1, but employment has declined from E_0 to E_1. At the higher wage rate, W_1, an excess supply of employees, AB, will result. The restrictive practices will prevent this excess supply from undercutting the above-equilibrium wage rate. Because of the exclusionary practices, the union is able to obtain higher wages for E_1 employees. Other employees who would be willing to accept work even at wage rate W_0 will now be forced into other lines of employment.

2. *Bargaining Power.* Is it necessary that a union restrict entry? Why cannot they simply use their bargaining power, the strike threat, as a vehicle for raising wages? If they have enough economic power, this will be possible. A strike by even a small percentage of vital employees can sometimes halt the flow of production. For example, a work stoppage by airline mechanics can force major airlines to cancel their flights. Because the mechanics perform an essential function, an airline cannot operate

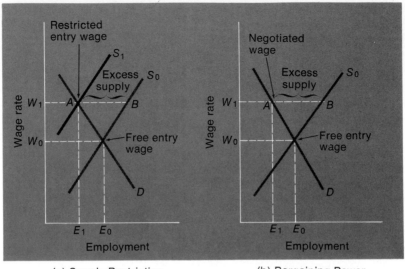

Exhibit 25-3   Supply Restriction, Bargaining Power, and Wage Rates

The impact of higher wages obtained through restricting supply and bargaining power is very similar. As illustrated by frame (a), when union policies reduce the supply of a class of labor, higher wages will result. Similarly, when bargaining power is used to gain higher wages [frame (b)], employment will decline and an excess supply of labor will result.

without their services, even though they constitute *only* 10 percent of all airline employees.

If the union is able to attain an above-free-entry wage rate, the impact on employment is similar to a reduction in supply. As Exhibit 25-3 illustrates, employers will hire fewer workers at the higher wage rate obtained via bargaining power. Employment will decline below the free entry level (from E_0 to E_1), as a result of the rise in wages. An excess supply of labor, AB, will exist, at least temporarily. More employees will seek the high wage union jobs than employers will choose to hire. Nonwage methods of rationing jobs will become more important.

3. *Increase in Demand.*   The demand for union labor is usually determined by factors outside of the union's direct control such as availability of substitute inputs and the demand for the product. But unions can sometimes use their political power to increase the demand for their services. They may be able to induce legislators to pass laws requiring the utilization of certain types or amounts of labor to accomplish a task (for example, unneeded firemen on trains allegedly for safety reasons, a certain number of stage engineers, etc.). Unions often seek the protection of tariffs as a means of increasing the demand for domestic labor. For example, automobile workers strongly support high tariffs on foreign-made automobiles. Garment workers seek a tariff policy that will limit the import of foreign clothing. Such practices will increase the demand for domestic automobiles and clothing, thereby increasing the demand for domestic auto

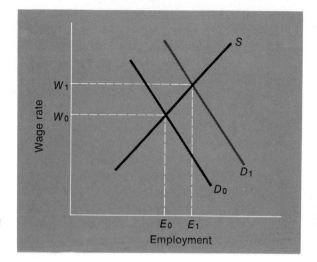

Exhibit 25-4   Rising Demand and Wage Increases

If a union can follow policies that will lead to an increase in demand for its services, wages will rise automatically.

and garment workers. It is not surprising that the management and union representatives of a specific industry often join hands demanding government tariff protection from foreign competition. As Exhibit 25-4 illustrates, successful union actions to increase the demand for the services of their members will result in both higher wages and an expansion in employment.

WHAT GIVES THE UNION MUSCLE?

Not all unions are able to raise the wages of their workers. Some unions are weak, while others are quite powerful. What are the factors that make for a strong union? Why are some unions able to maintain employee wages above free entry level, while others exert negligible impact on wage rates?

The theoretical underpinnings for analyzing the expected strength of a union relate back to Alfred Marshall's discussion of the demand elasticity for factors of production.[2] Simply stated, the demand for the labor of a continually strong union must be inelastic. This will enable the union to obtain large wage increases, while suffering only moderate reductions in employment. In contrast, when the demand for union labor is quite elastic, a substantial rise in wages will mean few, if any, jobs. Marshall listed four conditions as the determinants of the demand elasticity for a factor of production: (1) the availability of substitutes, (2) the elasticity of product demand, (3) the share of the input as a proportion of total cost, and (4) the supply elasticity of substitute inputs.

We now turn to the importance of each of these factors as a determinant of union strength.

1. *The Availability of Good Substitute Inputs.*   When it is difficult to substitute other inputs for the unionized labor, the power of the union is strengthened. This is why

[2] Alfred Marshall, *Principles of Economics*, 8th ed. New York: Macmillan, 1920.

union power to exclude nonunion labor is an important determinant of union strength. Nonunion labor is a good substitute for union labor. Unless a union can prevent nonunion employees from entering an occupation and cutting wages below the union level, they will be unable to raise wages significantly above the free entry level.

Even if a union can successfully restrain competitive nonunion employees, the availability of machines which are good substitutes for labor will greatly reduce the power of a union. Wage increases will induce employers to mechanize, thereby substituting machines for labor. Thus, a substantial wage increase would mean a sharp reduction in employment. Many workers would be laid off.

A comparison of the contrasting experience of elevator operators and airline pilots highlights the importance of substitute inputs. When the elevator operators of many large cities unionized and negotiated substantial wage increases, their gains were short-lived. Employers quickly turned to automated elevators, and the employment of elevator operators fell drastically. But the airline pilots are able to maintain above-free-entry wage rates without much substitution in production. People do not object to riding an automated elevator, but they do not like to ride in an automated airplane. Thus it is very difficult to substitute a machine for an airline pilot. Because a low-cost substitute was available for elevator operators, their union was weak. Since there is currently a lack of low-cost substitutes for airline pilots, the pilots' union is one of the strongest in the United States.

2. *The Elasticity of Product Demand.*   Wages are a component of costs. An increase in the wage of union members will almost surely lead to higher prices for goods produced with union labor. If the product demand is inelastic, the higher product price will exert only a small negative influence on production and employment in the industry. But when product demand is elastic, higher product prices will lead to sharply reduced sales and a substantial cut in employment.

An example will help illustrate the point. Suppose the garment workers in New York City negotiated a 50 percent increase in wages. The higher wage rates make it more costly to produce clothing products in New York. The New York firms must raise their price if they are to cover their cost. But when they do so, their customers turn to good substitutes, namely clothing produced by nonunion labor in the South, Puerto Rico, Japan, and other parts of the world. Sales of New York base firms will fall drastically. Since the demand for their product is highly elastic, New York garment workers would be laid off in droves if they negotiated such a large increase in wages.

The garment industry case points out why unionization of an entire industry is an important determinant of union strength. The demand for the product of a single firm, or even a group of firms in an industry, will almost certainly be quite elastic. When only a portion of an industry is unionized, similar goods produced by the nonunion firms offer consumers a very good substitute. Thus higher wages in the nonunion sector would have a drastic impact on employment.

The real world is consistent with the theory. In the 1920s the United Mine Workers obtained large wage gains in unionized fields. However, these fields soon lost their major share of the market to nonunionized fields, leading to a sharp reduction in the employment of union members. In more recent times unionized employment in the hosiery industry has declined because of the product market competition of nonunion firms. The existence of good substitutes, particularly similar products made by non-union labor, greatly restricts the union's power to raise wages above the open market level.

3. Union Labor as a Share of Production Cost.   If the unionized labor input composes only a small share of total product cost, its demand will tend to be more inelastic. Doubling the plumber's wage would cause only a small increase in the price of houses. Doubling the pilot's wage does not substantially increase the cost of air transportation. Since these inputs comprise only a small share of the total production cost, only a 1 or 2 percent increase in the cost of housing or air travel would result from a doubling or even tripling of the wages of plumbers or airline pilots. Thus a large increase in the price of such inputs would have little impact on product price, output, and employment. This factor has sometimes been referred to as the importance of being unimportant.

4. The Supply Elasticity of Substitute Inputs.   If wage rates in the unionized sector are pushed upward, firms will seek out substitute inputs. The demand for these substitutes will increase. When the supply curve for a substitute input is quite elastic, only a slight price rise will be induced by the higher level of demand. But, if the supply of the substitute input is highly inelastic, the rise in demand for it will cause a substantial price rise. The higher price of the substitute input will discourage firms from attempting to substitute it for the unionized labor input. Thus, a highly inelastic supply of factors of production that are good substitutes for the unionized labor will make the demand for the unionized input more inelastic. The union will be strengthened accordingly.

HOW MUCH MORE DO UNION MEMBERS GET?

Theory suggests that market conditions for the input, substitute inputs, and the elasticity of demand for union-made products place a limit on the ability of a union to raise wages. Even a strong union will have to contend with market forces. The precise impact of unions on the wages of their members is not easy to determine. Many other factors are constantly exerting an independent influence, making it difficult to isolate only the impact of unionization. There have been several studies on the effect of unionism on wages.[3]

H. Gregg Lewis, in a pioneering study published in 1963, estimated that, *on average,* union workers received between 10 and 15 percent higher wages than nonunion workers *with similar productivity characteristics.* Of course, some unions had an even greater impact. Lewis estimated that strong unions such as electricians, plumbers, tool and diemakers, metal craft workers, teamsters, and commercial airline pilots, were able to raise the wages of their members by 25 percent or more. In general, Lewis' evidence indicates that craft unions are stronger than industrial unions. From the viewpoint of

[3]See H. Gregg Lewis, *Unionism and Relative Wages in the United States* (Chicago, Illinois: Univ. of Chicago Press, 1963), for a discussion of many of these studies. Also, see Albert Rees, *The Economics of Trade Unions* (Chicago, Illinois: Univ. of Chicago Press, 1967).

economic theory this is not surprising. Craftsmen usually perform a vital service for which there are few good substitutes.

Unionization appears to have had the least impact on the earnings of cotton textile, footwear, furniture, hosiery, clothing, and retail sales workers. In these areas the power of the union has been substantially limited by the existence of readily available nonunion workers. Even when a union shop exists, the demands of the union must be moderated by the fear of placing the unionized employer at a competitive disadvantage in relation to the nonunion employers of the industry.

The data for Lewis' study were primarily from the 1940s and 1950s. Studies using more recent data suggest that the union–nonunion wage differential may be increasing. Frank Stafford estimated that when the employee characteristics were held constant, the annual earnings of unionized craft and operative workers were 25 percent greater than their nonunion counterparts. Michael Boskin, using 1967 data, placed the union-nonunion differential at between 15 and 25 percent. A still more recent study by Paul

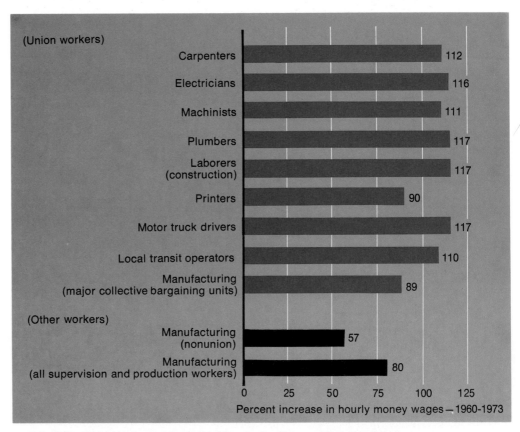

Exhibit 25-5   Changes in Hourly Wage Rate—Union Versus Other Employees

Union wage scales, particularly for craftsmen and truckers, have increased more than for other employees. Nonunion workers in manufacturing lag even further behind. Major collective bargaining units in manufacturing involve contracts covering 1000 or more workers.

SOURCE: *Handbook of Labor Statistics*, U.S. Department of Labor (annual).

Ryscavage estimated that in 1973 the wages of union workers exceeded nonunion workers with *similar productivity characteristics* by more than 25 percent. Ryscavage placed the union–nonunion wage differential at 29 percent for craftsmen, 23 percent for operatives, 44 percent for truck drivers (primarily teamsters), and 36 percent for laborers.[4]

Comparison of *changes* in union and total wage rates is consistent with the view that the union influence on *relative* wages is growing. As Exhibit 25-5 shows, between 1960 and 1973, union wages typically *increased* between 10 and 30 percent more than the wages of employees in general. But do not forget, higher wages for union members do not necessarily mean an increase in the share of income going to *all* workers. The following myth speaks to this issue.

MYTHS OF ECONOMICS
"Unions have increased the share of income going to labor."

Unions have increased the earnings of their members. But there is no evidence that they have had a significant impact on the share of income going to labor (human capital) relative to property owners. Exhibit 25-6 presents data on labor's share of income over the last four decades. Wages and salaries and total employment compensation (including the Social Security contribution of the employer) have increased slightly since World War II. But

Exhibit 25-6   Is Labor's Share Constant?

Time periods are five year averages.

SOURCE: Derived from the national income account estimates of the U.S. Department of Commerce published in the *Survey of Current Business*.

[4] F. P. Stafford, "Concentration and Labor Earnings: Comment," *American Economic Review*, March 1968; M. J. Boskin, "Unions and Relative Wages," *American Economic Review*, June 1972; and P. M. Ryscavage, "Measuring Union–Nonunion Earnings Differences," *Monthly Labor Review*, December 1974.

this is primarily a reflection of the decline in the number of self-employed persons in agriculture and the corresponding increase in the proportion of employed workers.

A major share of the earnings of self-employed, unincorporated business proprietors is clearly a return on their labor services. When the earnings of farmers, salesmen, distributors, lawyers, accountants, and other self-employed proprietors are counted as labor income, a clearer picture of the labor–property owner components of income is presented. This measure of labor's share, employee compensation plus the earnings of self-employed workers, has been amazingly constant. It suggests that between 81 and 83 percent of the national income has gone to labor during each five year period since 1935. The figure was just slightly higher during the depression of 1930–1934. Union membership increased substantially between 1930 and 1950 (see Exhibit 25-1). Yet the data of Exhibit 25-6 do *not* indicate any upward trend in the share of national income going to all workers, including those self-employed, during this period. During the last decade or so, there is increasing evidence that union wages have increased relative to nonunion workers with similar productivity characteristics. But the share of national income going to labor, all employees plus self-employment income, continues to hold steady.[5]

These findings are not surprising in light of economic analysis. If unions are able to use monopoly power, supply restrictions, and muscle to push union wages above the competitive level, who will pay for these benefits? Most laymen and many businessmen who should know better, typically reply, "They will come out of the employer's profits." Analysis of market forces introduces two factors that mediate strongly against this view.

First, do not forget, wages are a resource cost. Higher wages will mean higher costs. *If a product* made by union labor is sold under conditions of competition (either pure or monopolistic), unambiguously the consumer will pay for any above-market wage gains that a union might win for its members. When the firm hiring union labor has some monopoly power, higher costs may partially be absorbed out of profits. But even in this case, higher costs will push the prices of union-made products upward.

Regardless of the competitive conditions in the product market, higher union wages (and costs) will cause the output of products that utilize unionized labor to decline. This factor along with a substitution of capital for labor at the higher wage rate, will cause employment in the unionized sectors to fall. What happens to employees who are unable to find jobs in the unionized sector? They compete for nonunion jobs, increasing supply and depressing nonunion wages.

The major burden (incidence) of any noncompetitive wage gains won by union members will almost surely be with consumers and nonunion employees, not employers. In general, the real wages of nonunion employees will fall because (a) they confront higher prices for unionized products and (b) the supply of labor in the nonunion sector will expand, depressing nonunion wage rates.

[5] Also see Clark Kerr, "Labor's Income Share and the Labor Movement," in *New Concepts in Wage Determination*, edited by G. W. Taylor and Frank C. Pierson (New York: McGraw-Hill, 1957); Sidney Weintraub, "A Law That Can Not Be Repealed," *Challenge*, April 1962; and W. H. Hutt, *The Strike-Threat System* (New Rochelle, New York: Arlington House, 1973).

How important are these factors? Labor economist Gregg Lewis estimates that the real wages of nonunion workers, three-fourths of the labor force, are 3 to 4 percent lower than they would be in the absence of unionism.[6] Both economic theory and the stable share of national income going to labor, *in aggregate*, suggest that the wage gains of union members have been primarily, if not exclusively, at the expense of nonunion workers.

UNIONS AND INFLATION

We pointed out in Chapter 13 that unions, *acting independently*, cannot cause inflation. But many economists believe that they can and do generate conditions that will induce macroplanners to follow an inflationary path. If union power is able to push wage rates above competitive levels in the union sector, employment in that sector will fall (or fail to expand). Unemployment will increase, causing more and more employees who are equipped for employment in the union sector to search for jobs in the nonunion sector. If wages in the nonunion sector were completely flexible downward, they would decline until full employment was attained. But remember, even competitive markets do not adjust instantaneously. The unemployment is likely to persist for a significant period of time.[7]

But how will macroplanners react to the higher unemployment rates? Typically, a more expansionary macropolicy will be chosen. Inflation will result, partially eliminating the union wage gains that are incorporated into long-term union contracts. During the inflation, wages in the nonunion sector will typically rise more rapidly. Thus the expansionary (inflationary) macropolicy will help to retard the union–nonunion wage differential and restore full employment.

However, with the passage of time, union negotiators (and management) will incorporate the inflationary bias of macropolicy into their bargaining strategy. As this happens it will become increasingly difficult for macropolicy to promote full employment, at least without very high rates of inflation, rates that will certainly have other harmful side effects. Thus, even though unions cannot directly cause *continuing* inflation, many leading economists believe that their monopoly power does introduce an inflationary bias into macropolicy.

THE POWER OF BIG LABOR

In an earlier era unions in the United States were quite weak. Employers had several anti-union tactics at their disposal. Employees who were suspected of organizing a

---

[6] H. Gregg Lewis, *Unionism and Relative Wages in the United States*. Chicago, Illinois: Univ. of Chicago Press, 1963.

[7] In addition, when the union–nonunion wage gap widens, workers have an incentive to lengthen their job search time in hopes of finding one of those premium jobs in the union sector. This factor will also lead to a higher unemployment rate.

union could be fired. Prospective workers could be required to sign **yellow-dog contracts,** a contract stating that the employee will not join a union, as a condition of employment. The courts were often willing to grant employers an **injunction,** a court order prohibiting a union from striking. In the 1930s a series of legislative acts, of which the Norris–LaGuardia and Wagner Acts were the most important, prohibited management from utilizing such tactics. The bargaining position of labor was greatly strengthened. During the subsequent two decades, union membership and strength grew rapidly.

Clearly the image of a weak union attempting to gain a fair shake for helpless workers is obsolete in today's setting. In Part III we discussed the monopolistic power of big business. Some economists believe that the market power of big labor poses an even more serious threat. Many labor unions, like business firms with monopoly power, are able to gain higher prices (wages) by restricting supply, usually the supply of nonunion labor. National labor unions, organized along industrial lines, can halt production in an entire industry. Like big business firms, big unions possess a powerful political punch. Union financial and organizational strength has been known to both make and break the careers of political entrepreneurs.

The employer–union setting of collective bargaining strongly suggests that the business firm is the major entity whose interests are in conflict with those of union members. Increasingly, economists are beginning to rethink this view. One can build a strong case that consumers, nonunion members, and taxpayers are the major groups that are most likely to be harmed by the stick of "big labor." We have already pointed out that monopolistic union wages will be passed on to consumers in competitive industries. Otherwise, competitive firms will be unable to survive. In addition, higher wages will reduce employment in the union sector, causing supply to expand and wages to fall in the nonunion sector. Thus, the typical nonunion member receives lower wages and pays higher prices than would result in the absence of the monopoly power of unions.

Since unions represent a well-organized, financially powerful special interest, there is good reason to expect that the political process will be responsive to their requests. Of course, unions have been at the forefront of those promoting civil rights and welfare legislation, expanded Social Security benefits, and higher benefits for the unemployed. Clearly, the benefits (and costs) of these programs are widespread among the general populace. But unions have not hesitated to use their political muscle to gain benefits at the expense of the general populace. Legislation such as the granting of food stamp benefits to strikers, licensing requirements restricting the entry of unapproved (non-union) workers into craft occupations, high tariffs on goods produced by union labor, and high minimum wage rates without any exemption for teenagers bear the "union power" label. In each case the major beneficiaries are union members, while consumers, taxpayers, and nonunion employees bear the brunt of the cost.

Are General Motors and the AFL–CIO too strong? Economics cannot directly answer this question. But it can point out the misleading nature of the view that big labor is needed to offset the power of big business. The power of big labor (and big business) is used at the expense of the disorganized general populace, with business firms merely acting as an intermediary. Using economic efficiency as the criterion, what is good for General Motors, the AFL–CIO, or the Teamsters may not be good for the country.

The Great Contribution of Unions

Wage rates can be observed. Economists have a theory of wage determination and employment. They usually focus on wages and employment when discussing the impact of unions. As we have indicated, the data suggest that many, though probably not all, unions are able to raise the wages of their members. But there is little evidence that unions have been able to significantly influence the share of total income going to wage earners in general. It is also clear that rising production, not union power, is the primary source of the increasing real wages of the modern industrial society.

Yet the union movement continues to be almost sacrosanct in the minds of many workers, particularly blue collar workers. Even workers who belong to weak unions, as indicated by their impact on wage rates, have a strong loyalty to their union. Older workers in particular often spin out stories of how things used to be. Are they wrong? Would the American economy be no different if there were no unions? The focus of economists causes some of them to miss the major contribution of the union movement.

The great contribution of unions in the United States has been their role in defending employees against a sense of powerlessness, unimportance, alienation, and insecurity. The union movement has established a system of on-the-job civil rights and what Summer Slichter has called "industrial jurisprudence" to protect the worker's rights. It provides the worker with a strong line of defense against the whim, arbitrariness, and excesses of a foreman or management representative. Because of the power of the union, even in cases where only a portion of the workers are unionized, management has a greater incentive to treat workers with human dignity and individual self-importance. These worker benefits are, for the most part, nonpecuniary and difficult to measure, but they are undoubtedly extremely important.

In an industrial society it is easy to see how individual employees could acquire a sense of helplessness. After all, what is one employee to General Motors, General Electric, or Boeing? If workers were unorganized, it is also obvious that foremen, supervisors, and personnel officers would possess a great deal of power. In this setting it is not hard to understand the stories about employees being fired because they refused to contribute to the foreman's personal Christmas fund, or because they won half of their supervisor's paycheck in a lunch hour crap game. When the foreman is king and the worker a replaceable cog in the wheel, analysis of economic incentives suggests that management arbitrariness, worker insecurity, and alienation are an expected result.

From its inception the union movement set out to reduce the helplessness of an individual worker. Labor contracts defined a worker's civil rights and provided him with a series of industrial appeal courts. Specifically, a worker could not be fired except for good cause, proven to the satisfaction of his union representative. Actions that the worker considered arbitrary or unfair could be taken to a shop steward, appealed through labor–management channels, and eventually to an objective outside arbitrator. When a union brings a grievance to the attention of management, they listen. In addition they take positive action to assure that foremen and supervisors treat employees fairly. Production at multimillion dollar plants has been brought to a halt because a single worker's civil rights, as specified by the labor contract, were violated.

When employees bargain collectively, management has a strong incentive to avoid indiscretionary incidents.

This is not to say that the worker is always right in disputes involving labor and management. But it is important for worker self-esteem, morale, and human dignity that he is able to have his say, that he is not powerless, and that he can take his case to a neutral third party. Unions have played a vital role in the promotion of these worker rights and in promoting a sense of community among workers. Is it any wonder that some workers, even nonunion employees, think George Meany, Walter Reuther, and John L. Lewis to be of the same stature as presidents?

What about the future of the union movement? Today we hear a lot of talk about worker alienation and meaninglessness of assembly line work. Many authorities tell us that these issues occupy the forefront of the laboring man's current demands. Mechanical, boring production methods are adopted because they are efficient. It will be costly to adopt more meaningful ("dignifying") production techniques. Someone will have to pay for the increased cost. There are no free lunches. But neither is physical production efficiency everything. Each of us has some tradeoff between physical production efficiency and utility derived from certain types of work. Many of today's workers may be seeking a different tradeoff. They may be willing to accept a slower rate of growth in real wages if their job is more self-fulfilling. If this is so, we can expect the union movement to play an important role in inducing management to adopt alternative production methods.

Perspectives in Economics

What Can We Expect from the Rapid Growth of Public Sector Unionsim?

While union membership in general has stagnated over the last decade, public sector unionism has been growing in leaps and bounds. Since 1960 the number of public sector employees belonging to unions has increased from a little over a million to nearly 2.5 million. Between 1966 and 1972 union membership among public employees increased 43.2 percent, compared to a 4.7 percent growth in the private sector. In fact private sector membership in the AFL–CIO actually declined during this period, while public sector AFL–CIO affiliates expanded their membership by 695,000.

This rapid unionization of public sector employees has a number of interesting economic implications. First, public sector unions usually operate under a different set of constraints. In general, strikes by public sector employees such as transit workers, schoolteachers, garbage collectors, policemen, and firemen are prohibited. But this does not mean that they do not occur. The public inconvenience caused by striking government employees is often greater than for a work stoppage in the private sector. If strikes should play a significant role in the bargaining process, the outcry for strong measures to prevent work stoppages that cause public inconvenience is likely to grow.

Second, public sector unionization has often been motivated by the desire for a greater voice in the decision-making process. This has been particularly true in the case of teachers' unions, including college professors. It will be interesting to see if wage demands really do take a second place to concern about administrative practices as the bargaining process evolves over time.

Will public sector unions be strong? Economics theory sheds considerable light on this issue. The wage demands of well-organized public employees clearly present political entrepreneurs with a special interest issue. Government employees will feel very strongly about this issue. A politician's position on the wage demands of the union will be an overriding consideration for government workers. Since the costs of the higher wages are widely dispersed, they will exert only a small influence on the tax bill of the average voter. Clearly, politicians have a strong incentive to cater to the views of the well-organized special interest—that is, unionized government workers—in exchange for their support at election time.

The issue would be almost ideal for the politicians except for the fact that it is rather easy for the voter to relate the wage gains of government workers to higher taxes. Thus, we can expect vote-maximizing politicians to take steps to conceal this relationship. Several alternatives come to mind. Wage increases can be granted in a disguised form—more attractive fringe benefits, more vacation time, longer coffee breaks, less intensive work assignments, a larger travel budget, and similar employee benefits that are difficult for the general public to detect. Or political entrepreneurs might want to appoint a committee of private citizens to bargain with union representatives, thereby "taking public sector wage determination out of politics." This would permit political decision-makers to stack the committee with persons sympathetic with the union position, while maintaining the freedom to criticize the committee's failure to fully represent the taxpayer. Whatever the techniques that might eventually evolve, it is clear that vote-maximizing political entrepreneurs have a strong incentive to (a) cater to the union's demand (after all, they will personally bear little of the financial cost), (b) enlist the political support of the well-organized special interest group (that is, the unionized workers), and (c) take steps to disguise their failure to represent the interest of the disorganized taxpayer.

While the major impact of the expansion in unionization among government employees has probably not been felt, wage rates in the public sector have been increasing rapidly in recent years. Between 1965 and 1973, the mean earnings of public sector employees increased at an annual rate of 7.2 percent, compared to 5.5 percent in the private sector. Empirical research testing the implications of the special interest nature of this issue, as we have outlined it, will make an interesting future research topic.

Discussion

1. Do you think that a state-wide union of public elementary and secondary school-teachers would be strong? Would a union of college professors be strong? Why or why not?
2. Do public and private sector employers have the same incentive to resist union wage demands? Why or why not?

CHAPTER LEARNING OBJECTIVES

1. Approximately one out of every four workers in the United States belongs to a union. Union membership grew rapidly between 1930 and 1950. During the 1960s, it declined slightly as a share of the labor force.

2. Agreement on most collective bargaining contracts is attained without a work stoppage. The strike is a major source of union power. A work stoppage caused by a strike can cause the employer to lose sales, while incurring continuing fixed cost. The threat of a strike, particularly when his inventories are low, is an inducement for the employer to consent to the union's terms.

3. A strike is also costly to employees. Strike funds are usually inadequate to deal with a prolonged strike. Loss of a few paychecks can impose extreme hardship on most families. Recognition of the potential cost of a strike to both union and management provides each with an incentive to bargain seriously in an effort to avoid a work stoppage.

4. Since World War II, approximately three-tenths of 1 percent of the total nonfarm working time has been lost because of work stoppages. When the availability of a good or service to the general public is interrupted, strikes can also impose a high cost on secondary parties.

5. There are three basic methods that a union may use to increase the wages of its members: **(a)** restrict the supply of competitive inputs—including nonunion workers, **(b)** bargaining power enforced by the strike or threat of it, and **(c)** increase the demand for the labor service of the union's members.

6. The strength of a union will vary, depending on the elasticity of demand for its service. The demand for the labor services of a strong union will be inelastic. Thus, the strength of a union will be enhanced if: **(a)** there is an absence of good substitutes for its service; **(b)** the demand for the good it produces is highly inelastic, **(c)** the union labor input is a small share of the total product cost, and **(d)** the supply of any available substitute is highly inelastic. Absence of these conditions will weaken the power of the union.

7. Studies suggest that the earnings of union members exceed those *of similar nonunion members* by between 10 and 25 percent. Research utilizing more recent data tends to place the differential closer to the upper figure. The most powerful unions have been able to attain even larger wage gains for their members. Some weaker unions, unable to restrict the supply of nonunion workers (or products made by them), have had little impact on wages.

8. There is no indication that unions have exerted a significant influence on the share of national income going to labor (human capital) as opposed to physical capital.

9. Many economists believe that union policies introduce an inflationary bias into macropolicy. This view suggests that above-equilibrium union wage rates lead to unemployment, which will induce macroplanners to follow a more expansionary course, thereby causing inflation.

10. Labor unions are no longer a weak sister. The incidence of their economic and political power often falls on consumers, nonunion employees, and taxpayers, rather than on the owners of business firms.

11. Unions in the United States have helped defend employees against a sense of powerlessness, unimportance, alienation, insecurity, and management abruptness. The union movement is primarily responsible for our system of industrial jurisprudence. Many think these nonpecuniary factors are far more important than the impact of unions on wages.

IMPORTANT TERMS TO REMEMBER

Collective bargaining contract: A detailed contract covering wage rates and conditions of employment between (a) a group of employees (a labor union) and (b) an employer.

Union shop: A provision that requires all employees to join the recognized union and pay dues to it within a specific length of time (usually 30 days) after their employment with the firm.

Right-to-work legislation: Legislation that prohibits the union shop. Each state has an option to adopt (or reject) such legislation.

Strike: An action by unionized employees to (a) discontinue working for the employer and (b) prevent other potential workers from offering their services to the employer.

Lockout: Action taken by an employer to deny employment to current employees.

Yellow-dog contract: A contract that requires an employee to promise, as a condition of employment, that he will not join a union. The Norris–LaGuardia Act (1932) declared such contracts illegal.

Injunction: Court order requiring the defendant to refrain from certain practices such as a strike. The Norris–LaGuardia Act made it much more difficult for employers to obtain such an injunction during a labor dispute.

THE ECONOMIC WAY OF THINKING—DISCUSSION QUESTIONS

1. Assume that the primary objective of a union is to raise wages. **(a)** Discuss the conditions that will help the union attain this objective. **(b)** Why might a union be unable to meet its goal?

2. Suppose that Florida migrant farm workers are effectively unionized. What will be the impact of the unionization on **(a)** the price of Florida oranges? **(b)** profits of Florida fruit growers in the short run? in the long run? **(c)** mechanization of the fruit-picking industry? **(d)** the employment of fruit pickers?

3. Unions in the North have been at the forefront of efforts to organize lower wage workers in the South. Union leaders often express their compassion for the low money-wage southern workers. Can you think of a reason, other than compassion, why northern union leaders (and workers) would like to see the higher union scale extended to the South? Explain.

4. "Unions have brought a decent living to the working man. Without unions, employers would still be paying the working man a starvation wage." Analyze.

5. **(a)** "An increase in the price of steel will be passed along in the form of higher prices to the consumers of automobiles, homes, appliances, and other products that utilize steel." Do you agree or disagree?

   (b) "An increase in the price of union craft labor will be passed along in the form of higher prices to the consumers of homes, repair and installation services, appliances, and other products that utilize craft union labor." Do you agree or disagree?

   (c) Are the interests of labor unions primarily in conflict with those of union employers? Explain.

6. "The purpose of a union is to push the wage rate above the competitive level. By their very nature they are monopolists. Therefore, they will necessarily cause resources to be misallocated." Do you agree or disagree? Explain.

26
INEQUALITY, INCOME MOBILITY, AND POVERTY

In the last three chapters, we outlined the major factors that influence the distribution of income. Clearly, income will not be equally distributed in an economy that permits work performance, capital accumulation, individual preferences, and market conditions to play a role in the allocation of resources. How much inequality exists in an economy such as the United States? How has public policy influenced the income distribution? In this chapter we analyze these and other questions related to inequality.

INCOME INEQUALITY IN THE UNITED STATES

Since income represents command over goods and services, it is the most widely used measure of inequality. But if we are interested in identifying real differences in standards of living between people, income is not a perfect indicator. As we proceed, we will point out some of its shortcomings.

Despite the substantial inequality that exists in the United States, the bulk of income is allocated to middle income families, those earning between $8000 and $25,000. In 1972, one-third of all families had earnings of less than $8000. These families received only 12 percent of the total income. At the other extreme, 7 percent of the family units had incomes in excess of $25,000 and they received 18 percent of the total. In between 70 percent of all income was allocated to families with incomes between $8000 and $25,000. Clearly, most income in the United States is generated by persons who are neither rich nor poor.

The precise degree of inequality can be visualized with the aid of something called a Lorenz curve. A **Lorenz curve** outlines the relationship between the cumulative percentage of income recipients, ranked from lowest to highest, and the cumulative percentage of income that they receive. Exhibit 26-1 illustrates the Lorenz curve. If all recipients had the same income, the lowest 20 percent would receive 20 percent of the income, the lowest 40 percent would receive 40 percent, and so on. If there was complete equality, the Lorenz curve would be a 45 degree line. Of course, as we have already seen, income is not distributed equally. The lowest 20 percent of recipients receive less than 20 percent of the income. Thus, the Lorenz curve will bulge out. The greater the difference between the 45 degree line and the actual Lorenz curve, the greater is the degree of inequality.

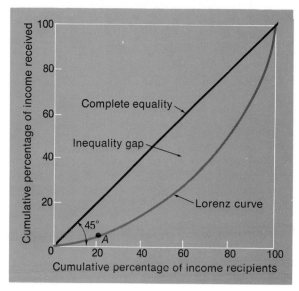

Exhibit 26-1   The Lorenz Curve

The cumulative percentage of *income recipients* is measured on the horizontal axis. The cumulative percentage of *income received* is measured on the vertical axis. A 45° line would indicate perfect equality. Normally, though, the lowest fifth of earners will receive less than one-fifth of the total income. For example, point *A* on the Lorenz curve indicates that the lowest 20 percent of income recipients receive only 5 percent of all income. Thus, the Lorenz curve bulges out, differing from complete equality (the 45° line).

Exhibit 26-2 presents data on the share of income received by each quintile of family income recipients (ranked from lowest to highest) for 1929, 1947, 1960, and 1972. In 1972 the lowest one-fifth of recipients received only 5.4 percent of the total income. The second lowest quintile of income recipients received 11.9 percent of the total. In contrast, a whopping 41.4 percent was allocated to the top 20 percent.

Close observance of the data presented in Exhibit 26-2 reveals that there has been a trend toward greater equality in the distribution of family income. The share of income going to the lowest quintile of recipients has increased from only 3.5 percent in

Exhibit 26-2   Changes in Family Income 1929–1972

The table indicates that during the last four decades there has been a movement toward greater equality of family income, particularly during the 1929–1947 period.

	PERCENTAGE OF TOTAL GROSS INCOME RECEIVED			
Family income class	1929	1947	1960	1972
Lowest fifth	3.5	5.1	4.9	5.4
Second fifth	9.0	11.8	12.2	11.9
Middle fifth	13.8	16.7	17.8	17.5
Fourth fifth	19.3	23.2	24.0	23.9
Highest fifth	54.4	43.3	41.3	41.4
Highest 5 percent	30.0	17.5	15.9	15.9

SOURCE: *The Statistical Abstract of the United States—1975*, Table 619.

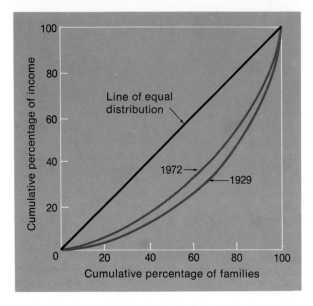

Exhibit 26-3   Inequality in 1929 and 1972

Family income in the early 1970s was considerably more equal than for 1929.

SOURCE: *The Statistical Abstract of the United States—1975.*

1929 to 5.4 percent in 1972. During this period, the share of the top fifth declined from well over 50 percent to just over 40 percent. The share of the top 5 percent of all recipients in 1972 was about half what it was in 1929.

Exhibit 26-3 utilizes the Lorenz curve to present a graphic picture of income inequality in 1929 and 1972. Since there was a movement toward equality, the Lorenz curve for 1972 does not bulge as much as was true in 1929. Most of the movement toward greater equality during the last four decades took place prior to 1947. The inequality gap, the area between the 45 degree line and the actual Lorenz curve, declined by approximately one-fifth between 1929 and 1947. Since 1947 the inequality gap has declined by approximately one-twelfth.

The degree of inequality is sensitive to changes in the business cycle. During hard times the inequality gap usually rises, as low income recipients are more likely to be laid off. During a business upswing the degree of inequality generally declines. The degree of inequality increased during the recession of the late 1950s, declined during the 1960s, and increased slightly again during the 1970–1971 recession.

The Undoubling Effect

We have focused on family income data, excluding single person households. Rising income levels and a movement toward greater equality both generate conditions that make it possible for single young people, the aged, and members of tenuously united families to set up their own households. The number of single person households has increased sharply since World War II. This "undoubling process" leads to an increase in the measured inequality of income *among households*. Oftentimes single person households, established by college students or Social Security recipients for example, will not include a full-time worker. Unsurprisingly, low income recipients are substantially overrepresented in this area.

If household data, including both families and single persons, are utilized, the trend toward greater equality since 1947 would be virtually eliminated. However, since the increase in single person households largely reflects prosperity and equality, it would seem a bit misleading to use these data to argue that there has been no change in the income distribution during the last 25 years.

Taxes and Inequality

Thus far we have concentrated on the distribution of gross income. It is often assumed that there is much less inequality in the distribution of income after taxes. Is this so? It is hard to say precisely how much redistribution does take place. The ultimate burden of taxes is not always obvious. Who pays the corporate income tax? The stockholder, the consumer, or is it perhaps the employees? Who bears the burden of property taxes? Questions like these complicate our ability to estimate the redistributive effects of taxes.

A recent study by Joseph Pechman and Benjamin Okner analyzed the combined effects of federal, state, and local taxes for 1966.[1] They calculated the redistribution effects under alternate assumptions for the progressiveness of various taxes. Their estimates indicate that taxes exert only a moderate influence, reducing the inequality gap by only 0.3 to 4.8 percent.

These findings are consistent with the work of other researchers. Herriot and Miller, utilizing a slightly different methodology, estimated that the combined effect of federal, state, and local taxes was roughly proportionate for recipients with incomes between $4000 and $50,000 in 1968.[2] These recipients accumulate well over 80 percent of all income. Thus, contrary to what many believe, there is little difference between the pre- and post-tax income inequality.

INCOME INEQUALITY IN OTHER COUNTRIES

The distribution of income between countries may differ for a number of reasons. Factors such as the opportunity to acquire skills, income shares going to physical capital and human capital, and redistribution effects of public policy will influence the degree of income inequality. Exhibit 26-4 presents Lorenz curves that compare the inequality of after-tax income for several nations. Since Sweden has a homogeneous population and relies extensively on highly progressive taxes, it is not surprising that income in that country is distributed more equally than for the United States. The pattern of income distribution in the United Kingdom is similar to that in the United States, with perhaps just slightly more equality in the United Kingdom. While data for Canada, France, and West Germany are more fragmentary, the general impression is that the distribution of income in these countries is similar to the U.S. and U.K. data.

The share of income going to the wealthy is much greater in the less developed countries. For example, while the top 5 percent of income recipients receive about 15

[1] Joseph A. Pechman and Benjamin A. Okner, *Who Bears the Tax Burden.* Washington, D.C.: The Brookings Institution, 1974.
[2] Roger A. Herriot and Herman P. Miller, "The Taxes We Pay," *The Conference Board Record*, May 1971.

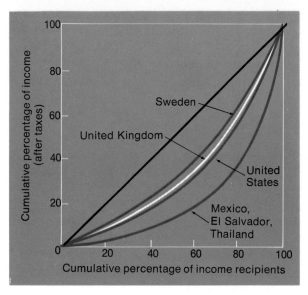

Exhibit 26-4   Income Inequality—An International Comparison (Late 1960s)

After-tax income is distributed more equally in Sweden than in the United States. The degree of inequality in the United Kingdom and the United States is similar, with the income distribution in the former just slightly more equal. Less developed countries such as Mexico, El Salvador, and Thailand are usually characterized by substantial inequality (values for these three countries are approximations).

SOURCE: Joseph A. Pechman and Benjamin A. Okner, *Who Bears the Tax Burden?* (Washington, D.C.: The Brookings Institution, 1974); *Annual Abstract of Statistics, 1969* (United Kingdom); *Statistical Yearbook of Thailand;* and *Statistical Abstract of Sweden, 1968.*

percent of the total in the United States, the comparable figure is between 30 and 40 percent for Mexico, El Salvador, and Thailand. Thus, the overall inequality in the distribution of income in these countries is substantially greater than for the United States.

INEQUALITY AND INCOME INEQUALITY

Some economists argue that money income overstates the variation in the standard of living among income units. The proponents of this view usually stress three major points.

1. *Nonmarket Income Is Excluded.*   Considerable production and consumption of goods take place outside the marketplace. Activities such as unpaid household services, self-provided maintenance and repair services, and other nonmarket output are excluded. How important is nonmonetary "income"? According to Ismail Sirageldin of Johns Hopkins, the nonmonetary "income" component is approximately one-half as great as the monetary income received by the typical family. Since consumption of these self-provided services will vary little among households, inclusion of this nonmonetary factor would reduce the degree of inequality in the standard of living between households (or family) units.

2. *Noncash Transfer "Income" Is Excluded.*   While our data on income do include cash transfer payments received from the government, they exclude items such as

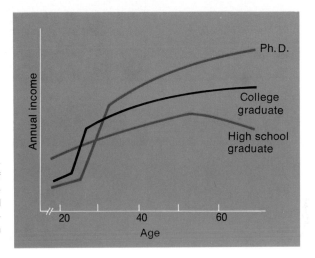

Exhibit 26-5   Shapes of Lifetime Income Streams

Annual incomes will differ partially because of differences in the shapes of lifetime income streams. The typical pattern of lifetime income for a high school graduate, a college graduate, and a person with a doctoral degree are shown here.

subsidized or government provided medical service, food stamps, rent supplements, and public housing. In recent years government expenditures to "help people buy essentials" have increased substantially. In 1968 only $7 billion was spent on in-kind transfer payments. By 1975, these expenditures had increased more than fourfold, to over $33 billion. These in-kind transfers primarily benefit lower income recipients. Of course their impact on equality might, at least partially, be offset by subsidies to airlines or college students and other programs beneficial to high income recipients. But the rapid growth of in-kind transfers to low income recipients suggests that inclusion of these transfers would have reduced measured inequality in recent years.[3]

3. *The Shape of Lifetime Income.*   Annual incomes are not always indicative of one's lifetime income. Exhibit 26-5 illustrates the general pattern of lifetime income for three educational categories. Initially, between ages 18 and 22, the annual incomes of high school graduates who are working full time typically exceed those of students who go on to complete college. Later in life, the opposite is true. Similarly, those who go on for a doctoral degree will, for a while, experience lower incomes than nonstudent college graduates. Variation in annual incomes may tend to overstate the degree of lifetime income inequality. At first glance the future college graduate and doctoral recipient appear to be poor early in life because of their educational activities. Later, high school graduates are the poor ones despite their higher incomes earlier. Even if the value of lifetime incomes were exactly equal, *annual incomes* would still vary because of differences in the patterns of lifetime earnings.

INTERGENERATIONAL INCOME MOBILITY

Income inequality data do not tell us much about the degree of movement between income groupings over time. Are high income and wealth passed along generation after generation? Do the sons and daughters of low income parents have an equal oppor-

[3]Barry M. Blackman, Edward M. Gramlich, and Robert Hartman, *Setting National Priorities—The 1975 Budget* (Washington, D.C.: The Brookings Institution, 1974). Chapter 29, pages 540–544, also provides additional data relating to this point.

tunity to escape poverty and attain high income status? Some observers argue that reducing inequality at the starting line is as important, perhaps even more important, than equalizing incomes. Many Americans, probably most, see nothing wrong with high incomes that reflect hard work, competence, and superior abilities. They are not opposed to income inequality, per se. But they are opposed to inequality that simply reflects inheritance of a socioeconomic position.

For obvious reasons, reliable data on intergenerational income mobility are difficult to obtain. Nevertheless, researchers have recently begun to develop the necessary data to tackle this problem. Christopher Jencks, reporting on a study conducted by the Center for Educational Policy Research at Harvard University, summarizes their findings:

> Among men born into the most affluent fifth of the population, . . . we estimate that less than half will be part of the same elite when they grow up. Of course, it is also true that very few will be in the bottom fifth. Rich parents can at least guarantee their children that much. Yet if we follow families over several generations, even this will not hold true. Affluent families often have at least one relatively indigent grandparent in the background, and poor families, unless they are black or relatively recent immigrants, have often had at least one prosperous grandparent.[4]

Jencks found that one-third of the *children* whose parents were in the upper quintile of income recipients received below-average incomes. On the other hand, one-third with parents in the bottom quintile end up with above-average incomes. Approximately two-fifths of the children with wealthy (poor) grandparents are estimated to end up with below (above) average incomes. These findings indicate that the ideal of equal opportunity is an unrealized goal in America. But they also show that substantial movement takes place between income groupings. Certainly, income status is not solely or even primarily inherited.

How does intergenerational economic mobility in the United States compare with other countries? Again data limitations prevent us from offering a concrete answer to this question. However, the data that are available suggest that there is more upward mobility in the United States than in most other countries. Fox and Miller reported that 30 percent of the sons whose fathers perform manual work (for example, craftsmen, operators, service, and laborers) move up to the so-called white collar occupations (professionals, managers, sales, and clerical).[5] By way of comparison, only 20 to 25 percent of the sons of manual workers in the United Kingdom, Japan, and the Netherlands were able to make such "advancement." In general, more study is needed in this area before we can make more definitive statements about differences in intergenerational income mobility between nations.

Before leaving the topic of income inequality, perhaps one final observation should be made. Economics does not tell us that one income distribution is preferable to

---

[4] From *Inequality: A Reassessment of the Effect of Family and Schooling in America*, by Christopher Jencks et al., p. 216. © 1972 by Basic Books, Inc., Publishers, New York.

[5] T. Fox and S. M. Miller, "Intra-Country Variations: Occupational Stratification and Mobility." *Studies in Comparative International Development*, edited by Irving Louis Horowitz, vol. 1, no. 1. Beverly Hills, California: Sage Publications, 1965.

another, but it does emphasize that incentives matter. Breaking the strong positive relationship between individual productivity and income would drastically reduce the incentive to produce and perform efficiently. Therefore, hardly anyone would advocate complete equality (or extreme inequality). The real problem becomes one of finding an income distribution that is consistent with social cohesiveness and the welfare considerations of a society, while still maintaining a strong incentive for persons to produce.

POVERTY IN THE UNITED STATES

In an affluent society such as the United States, income inequality and poverty are related issues. Poverty is, of course, a relative term. In comparison with the middle income Americans in 1900, even the bottom one-fifth of income recipients are well off today. However, in comparison with the typical American in 1970, they are poor. They own few assets, travel less, and typically live in quarters that most Americans would consider squalid.

Poverty could, of course, be defined strictly in relative terms, the bottom one fifth of all income recipients, for example. But this definition is not very helpful. Defined in this manner, clearly the poor will always be with us.

The most widely used definition of poverty in the United States is the standard developed by the Social Security administration. The cost of an economical and nutritional food plan is developed. Then, since low income families typically spend approximately one-third of their income on food, the cost of the economical food plan is multiplied by three to obtain the poverty income level. Families with less than the poverty income level are defined as poor.

This standard also reflects differences in consumption requirements for families of different size, sex, and age of head, and farm–nonfarm residence. It will automatically increase with the cost of living. As prices rise the cost of purchasing the economy food plan will also rise. The poverty level for a nonfarm family of four was $2973 in 1959 and $4275 in 1972.

How many people are poor? Are the ranks of the poor declining? Using the Social Security definition of poverty, in 1972 there were 24 million poor people, approximately 10 million poor families. Twelve percent of all individuals were classified as poor. Both the number and percentage of people with incomes below the poverty level have been diminishing for several decades. As pictured by Exhibit 26-6, the percentage of poor people declined from 22 percent in 1959, to 17 percent in 1965, to 12 percent in 1972. Though perhaps the pace is slower than many would like, we are winning the war on poverty.

Profiles of the Poor

Two major explanations are often advanced as to the cause of poverty. The first argues that the blame for poverty rests primarily with the personal shortcomings of the poor. According to this view, the poor have often frittered away educational and training opportunities, refused to relocate in order to advance themselves, and typically made

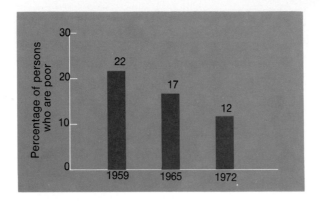

Exhibit 26-6   The Score in the War on Poverty

The percentage of poor families continues to decline.

SOURCE: *Statistical Abstract of the United States—1975.*

shortsighted consumption and employment decisions. In addition their low income status is often directly related to their personal excesses—drinking, drug use, and sexual permissiveness. Thus, unless the poor can be reformed, income redistribution will not solve the poverty problem.[6]

The second view argues that the poor are merely social victims of our society. They are poor because technological change has made their skills obsolete, nature has ravaged their land, or serious illness, injury, or physical handicap has depleted their savings and reduced their earning power. This view also emphasizes that society has failed to provide the poor with adequate schooling, training, and employment opportunity. Minorities in particular have suffered because they have been forced to carry the additional burden of discrimination. Thus, according to this view, poverty is largely the fault of our society.[7]

Which of these two views is correct? While each highlights certain aspects of the poverty problem, both views visualize the poor as a homogeneous population. The data do not confirm this position. Unfortunately from the viewpoint of policy, by and large the poor are a heterogeneous population.

Exhibit 26-7 demonstrates some of the diversity among the 10 million poor households in the United States in 1972. The following seven points stand out.

1. Contrary to what some believe, most—68 percent—of the poor are white. However, the incidence of poverty is nearly three times greater among nonwhites than whites. Thus, nonwhites comprise 11 percent of the total population, but nearly a third of the poor (Exhibit 26-7a).

2. Over half—57 percent—of the poor households are headed by a male (Exhibit 26-7b). But the incidence of poverty is five and one half times greater for female- than male-headed households (Exhibit 26-7c).

3. To a large extent, differences between males and females in the incidence of poverty reflect the presence of children. Ten percent of the females *without children* are poor, compared to 6 percent for males (Exhibit 26-7c).

[6] See E. Banfield, *The Unheavenly City* (Boston: Massachusetts: Little, Brown, 1970), for a presentation of this view.

[7] See Michael Harrington, *The Other America* (Baltimore, Maryland: Penguin Books, 1962), for a complete presentation of this view.

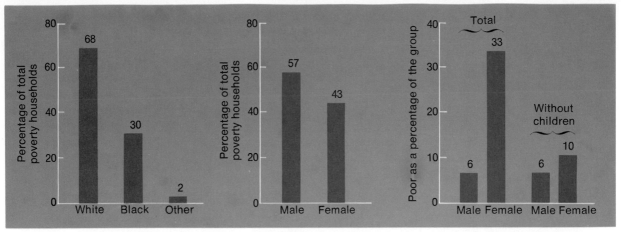

(a) Color of Poverty Population

(b) Sex of Household Head

(c) Incidence of Poverty by Sex of Household Head and Presence of Children

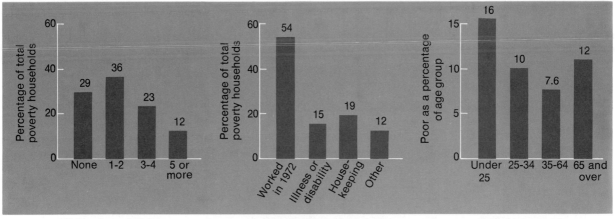

(d) Number of Children in Household

(e) Employment Experience of Household Head—1972

(f) Incidence of Poverty by Age Groupings

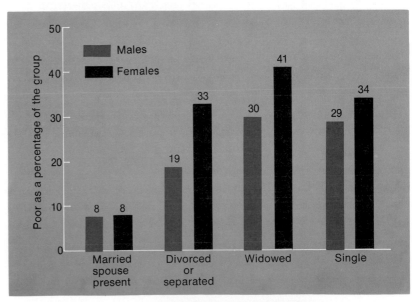

(g) Incidence of Poverty by Sex and Marital Status—1970

Exhibit 26-7 Who Are the Poor?

Profile of the poor—1972.

SOURCE: *Current Population Reports—P-60 Series* and *U.S. Census of Population—1970.*

4. There is substantial variation in family size among the poor (Exhibit 26-7d). While 29 percent of the poor have no children, 35 percent have 3 or more.

5. A surprisingly large number of the poor—54 percent in 1972—worked at some time during the year. Only 15 percent were unable to work because of illness or disability (Exhibit 26-7e).

6. Both the young and the old are overrepresented among those with poverty status income levels. Sixteen percent of the households with a head under 25 years of age and 12 percent with heads age 65 and over were poor in 1972. In contrast only 7.6 percent in the 35–64 age group were classified as poor (Exhibit 26-7f).

7. The incidence of poverty is between two and four times greater among persons divorced, separated, widowed, or single than for members of intact families (Exhibit 26-7g). This suggests that marital problems and death of a marriage partner are sometimes a source of poverty status.

The Temporary Poor and the Vicious Circle Poor

While precise data are difficult to piece together there is good reason to believe that the poor are heterogeneous in another important area—length of time with below-poverty-level income. Annual income in any one year is not always a good indicator of one's long-run standard of living. A sizable portion of those with low current incomes are "temporarily poor." Wives (and husbands) separated or divorced from their spouse, unemployed workers, young married couples, perhaps attending college, and college students who have established their own households are likely to fall into this category. Their current income status places them among the poor, but their future income prospects are much brighter. Similarly, many of the elderly who are classified as poor may have experienced earnings substantially in excess of the poverty level for most of their lifetime.

Consumption patterns indicate that the poverty status of many low income households is temporary. For example, ownership of black and white television sets, telephones, and refrigerators among the poor is similar to that for the general populace. In 1971, 41 percent of the poor (persons with less than $3000 of income) owned automobiles, 52 percent owned washing machines, 16 percent a color television set, and 14 percent an airconditioner.[8] Clearly a sizable number of the poor either have not always been poor or they are confident that they will not be poor in the future.

But another sizable portion of the poor are caught in what is known as the *vicious circle of poverty*. They are poor because they have few skills and little earning power. And since they are poor, they (and their children) have limited access to training, education, and health facilities. In addition, they lack funds to move from depressed areas in search of better jobs. But inadequate education, training, health care, and labor force immobility are precisely the conditions that breed poverty. Thus, perpetual poverty has a cumulative effect. It is easily passed from one generation to another, as the *Economic Report of the President* (1964) has pointed out:

[8]*The Statistical Abstract of the United States—1975*, Table 646.

Poor parents cannot give their children the opportunities for better health and education needed to improve their lot. Lack of motivation, hope, and incentive is a more subtle but no less powerful barrier than lack of financial means. Thus the cruel legacy of poverty is passed from parents to children.

THREE APPROACHES TO POVERTY

The United States has adopted numerous programs with the expressed intent of reducing poverty. In reality, programs designed to help the poor have not always done so. One can build a strong case that some of them, minimum wage legislation for example, have even been counterproductive. In general, there are three alternative ways to attack poverty. The three are not necessarily mutually exclusive.

The Human Capital Approach

The purpose of the **human capital approach** is to increase the productivity of the poor, thereby expanding their earning power. This approach hypothesizes that lack of schooling, training, health care, and geographic mobility is a major cause of low income status. Once the poor (and their children) are provided with the means to acquire the education and skill levels necessary for success in our modern industrial economy, they will be able to escape poverty.

The human capital approach was quite fashionable during the 1960s. It formed the underpinnings for much of the war on poverty of the Johnson Administration. Of course, it was always recognized that it was not the entire answer to the poverty problem because a substantial number of the poor—the aged, disabled, and female household heads with small children—are not in the labor force. Nevertheless, it was widely envisioned that major expenditures on manpower training, education, Job Corps, Youth Corps, and similar programs would reduce the incidence of poverty.

In recent years the human capital approach has lost much of its shine. Several studies have shown that such programs are very expensive relative to the number of people who are actually helped. In addition some observers believe that the premise of the human capital approach is simply wrong. Christopher Jencks, for one, does not believe that programs designed to equalize opportunity and promote skill acquisition among the poor will be very effective. Jencks presents his view:

> Poverty is not primarily hereditary. While children born into poverty have a higher-than-average chance of ending up poor, there is still an enormous amount of economic mobility from one generation to the next. . . . The primary reason some people end up richer than others is not that they have more adequate cognitive skills. . . . There is almost as much economic inequality among those who score high on standardized tests as in the general population.[9]

[9]Jencks, *Inequality*, pp. 7–8.

The Gifts-in-Kind Approach

Some people see the consumption pattern of the poor and provision of basic necessities as the major problem of low income status. They are not bothered by the income distribution as such, but rather by the lack of adequate food, housing, and medical care, particularly among the children of the poor. The advocates of this approach believe that if one merely grants income to the poor, it is likely to be spent on the wrong things. The poor may buy television sets, automobiles, luxury clothes, and still fail to provide adequate food and medical care for themselves and their children. Those who hold this view are more likely to favor the **gift-in-kind approach,** a policy of direct grants (or subsidies) to the poor for food, housing, medical care, and other basic essentials.

If one considers only the preferences of the recipient, a gift in kind would do less to improve welfare than a cash grant of equal magnitude. The recipient might very well value the gift in kind less than other things that he could have purchased with the cash. However, when nonpoverty taxpayers are more concerned with what the poor buy rather than their income status, the gift-in-kind approach could be best from the viewpoint of the entire community.

In recent years this approach has expanded in relative importance. In 1960 the federal government spent $1.1 billion helping people buy essentials such as food, housing, and medical service. But since that time, the Medicare program has been passed, providing medical services to the elderly. The Medicaid program provides similar benefits to low income families. Housing subsidies to both the poor and not so poor have been expanded. In 1974 the food stamp program provided monthly subsidies ranging up to $150 for low income and other qualified families. By 1975 total federal expenditures designed to help people buy essentials totaled $33 billion, a 30-fold increase in 15 years.

The Redistribution of Income Approach

The redistribution approach advocates taxing the earnings of some in order to transfer money income to others. The proponents of this approach argue that direct money transfers will do more to solve the problems of the poor than either training or gifts in kind.

Currently the federal government spends nearly $100 billion on programs that transfer money income from current earners to beneficiaries. Programs such as Social Security, unemployment compensation, agricultural subsidies, and public assistance supply money income directly to the aged, unemployed, poor, and disabled. Some of these programs provide income transfers on the basis of need alone. Others, such as Social Security and unemployment compensation, limit the recipients to those who have made previous contributions.

The continued persistence of poverty, even in the face of large expenditures on redistribution programs, has led several leading economists such as Milton Friedman and James Tobin to suggest that a negative income tax (NIT) be substituted for the current system.

Given that we spend $100 billion on income transfers, why has poverty not been eliminated? The proponents of the NIT reply, "Because the current programs transfer income to people because they are elderly, unemployed, farmers, or veterans, rather than because they are poor. Thus the lion's share of these income transfers go to the nonpoor." They argue that if the NIT were substituted for the current system, poverty could be eliminated even while spending on income transfers was reduced.

How would the **negative income tax** work? To begin with, a base income level is established. This guaranteed income level would reflect family size with larger families receiving higher incomes. As income is earned, the base income supplement would be reduced by a *fraction* of the family's outside income. This fraction of the family's additional income that is allocated to the reduction of the family's income supplement is their **marginal tax rate.** A family would always face a marginal tax rate of less than one—most plans suggest a 33 or 50 percent rate. Thus additional earnings will always increase the family's after-tax income. Monetary incentives to work are maintained.

Exhibit 26-8 illustrates the mechanics of the NIT. This illustrated plan establishes a guaranteed income level of $3200 for a family of four and a marginal tax rate of 33 percent. As outside income rises, the family's disposable income increases by two-thirds of the amount earned. For example, an initial earnings of $1200 would increase the family's disposable income by $800, from $3200 to $4000. The family would receive more supplementary income than it would pay in taxes until income reaches $9600, the break-even point. At the **break-even point** the family's tax bill would just equal the income supplement. Beyond the break-even point, the family would have a positive tax bill.

How much would the NIT cost? That depends on the guaranteed income level and the marginal tax rate. An increase in the base income level, holding the marginal tax rate constant, would increase the number of people receiving income subsidies and the cost of the plan. Costs could be lower by increasing the marginal tax rate, but this would tend to reduce work incentives. Thus, there is a conflict between keeping costs

Exhibit 26-8   The Mechanics of the Negative Income Tax

The graph pictures how a negative income tax with a 33 percent marginal tax rate and a minimum income of $3200 for a family of four would work. If the family had zero earnings during the year, it would receive a $3200 annual subsidy. As earnings rose, the family's after-tax income would increase by 67 cents (and the subsidy would decline by 33 cents) for every dollar of income earned.

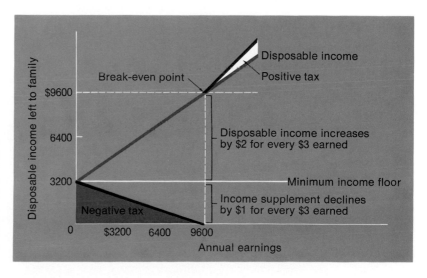

low and maintaining both a high guaranteed income level and a low marginal tax rate in order to provide for work incentives. One cannot accomplish all three objectives simultaneously.

The Brookings Institute has estimated the cost of several alternative NIT plans. Their calculations indicate that the plan outlined by Exhibit 26-8 would cost $19.8 billion, approximately 6 percent of the federal budget. Costs rise rapidly as the minimum guaranteed income is increased. For example, a plan that guarantees $4000 of annual income, while maintaining a 33 percent marginal tax bracket for persons below the break-even point, would cost $33.2 billion.[10] Of course, if the NIT could be substituted for many of the current antipoverty programs, the *net* cost to the taxpayer would be reduced substantially.

A negative income tax would represent a major break from our current approach to poverty. Unsurprisingly it is a highly controversial issue. A limited version of the NIT, the Family Assistance Plan advocated by the Nixon Administration, passed the House of Representatives but later died in the Senate. We can expect to hear more about this approach in the future. The following debate outlines both the merits and demerits of the NIT approach.

Controversies in Economics

The Case for the NIT

The major advantages of the NIT are its ability to concurrently (a) provide income supplements to the poor, (b) maintain work incentives, and (c) avoid the duplication and administrative costs of the present system.

If the objective is to alleviate poverty, we should subsidize people because they are poor, not because they are members of a particular special interest group. This is the major defect of the current system. People are subsidized because they are farmers, female household heads, small businessmen, elderly, or members of various occupations and industries. Others are subsidized if and only if they consume certain items—public housing, medical care, education, or training, for example. While the poor are often over represented among these groups, many of the beneficiaries are not poor and, in some cases, they are quite wealthy.

Since a substantial share of the current welfare dollar benefits those who are not poor, welfare costs are much higher than would be necessary to eliminate poverty. In 1975 the federal government alone spent $130 billion on income maintenance and programs to help people buy essentials.[10]

If these resources had been utilized to help only low income households, the bottom 20 percent of households could have been granted *supplementary* incomes of $9300 each! This would include all families with earnings of $6000 or less. As an alternative with the same resources used to fight poverty in 1975, *supplementary* income grants of $6000 each could have been made to the bottom 20 percent and grants of $3000 made to the second poorest fifth of all households. Our purpose is not to suggest that grants of these magnitudes actually be made, but rather to point out the inefficiency and leakages of the present system. The present system is subsidizing a lot of other people in addition to the poor.

[10]Blechman, Gramlich, and Hartman, *Setting National Priorities—The 1975 Budget.*

The potential advantage of the NIT, relative to the current system, is clear. Without detached regulations and the mirage of diverse and sometimes conflicting programs, more resources could be allocated to the poor at a lower cost to the taxpayer. Welfare administrators, social workers, and the wealthiest welfare recipients of the current system would be hurt. These people do have substantial opportunity though to generate earnings (and production) elsewhere that would be more valuable to society.

The Brookings Institute estimates that the cost of an NIT with a guaranteed income level of $4800 and a marginal tax rate of 33.3 percent would be approximately $50 billion— less than 40 percent of the current federal income transfer expenditures. Further savings in state and local welfare expenditures would be possible.

What impact will the NIT have on work incentives? Recent experimental field studies in New Jersey and elsewhere suggest that the NIT has little impact on the labor force participation of recipients. This is not surprising since under the NIT take-home pay will always increase as an individual's earnings rise. For example, if the marginal tax rate was 33 percent, an individual's disposable income would rise by 67 percent for each *additional* dollar that he earned. Work decisions will be based on the *marginal* cost and *marginal* benefits derived from work. The genius of the NIT is its ability, given the establishment of a low marginal tax rate, to maintain marginal work incentives while providing assistance to people who actually need it.

Since people would always benefit by working additional hours, the need for detailed regulation and costly administration would be eliminated. The program could be incorporated into the current tax system, using spot checks to eliminate cheating, just as we currently do for taxpayers. If some people are lazy and do not want to work, that would be their privilege. But in contrast to the current system, they would always be at an inferior position. There is no need to set up arbitrary definitions of the "deserving" and "undeserving" poor. The need for social workers to act as anything but counselors would be eliminated. The need for a system requiring recipients to fill out multiple forms to qualify for multiple programs would be eliminated.

After a decade of sharp increases in income support, poverty has not been eliminated. Neither has the overall income distribution changed substantially. This suggests that the present system spends a lot of valuable resources and does relatively little to help the poor. It is time to substitute a new concept.

The Case against the NIT

The reality of the negative income tax would almost certainly differ substantially from the vision of many of its well-meaning, but utopian-minded advocates. The NIT would reduce work incentives, tax the industrious, protect the rich, create a vastly enlarged class of welfare recipients, and fail to solve the most serious problem associated with poverty. Let us consider these shortcomings in more detail.

1. *It Would Help the Undeserving.* The NIT assumes that the poor are a homogeneous group and that lack of income is their major problem. For the disabled, blind, elderly, and unfortunate this is true. But unfortunately, the ranks of the poor are not limited to these groups. Many of the poor, perhaps as many as one-half of the adult poor, have low incomes because of drugs, alcoholism, lack of self-discipline —particularly with regard to sexual matters—family instability, and shortsightedness

with regard to both their work and consumption patterns. Additional income will not solve these problems and would most likely contribute to them. The NIT would make it easier to live for the moment, satisfying one's daily desires. The penalty for irresponsibility and lack of any work routine would be reduced. Economics suggests that such behavior would, therefore, be expanded.

2. *It Would Fail to Help Many of the Deserving Poor.*   Children compose approximately 60 percent of the poor. The major problem associated with poverty is how to assure these children an adequate supply of food, housing, and medical care. The surest method of doing so is to provide or subsidize these services for poor people. This is what the current food stamp, Medicaid, and housing supplement programs do. Providing income, rather than goods in kind, would be a less effective means of reducing the hardships borne by the children of the poor. The parent who cannot hold a job because of his or her drinking habit and lack of future orientation will not be likely to use the NIT income supplement for food, housing, and medical care for the children.

3. *Politics Would Assure That the NIT Would Be an Enormously Expensive Additional Welfare Program, Not a Substitute Program.*   Once the NIT were adopted, practical politics would generate an irresistible pressure to guarantee at least the minimum poverty level of income, approximately $4500 for a family of four in the mid-1970s. At this high level, one of the following would have to result. First, the marginal tax rate would be set so high that it would destroy the work incentives of the poor and the near poor. Or second, a marginal rate that would maintain work incentives, 33 percent for example, would require that families with incomes of $10,000 to $14,000 be eligible to receive supplementary payments. Nearly half of all households would be on welfare. The cost of such a program has been estimated at nearly $50 billion, approximately 20 percent of the federal budget.[11]

While many of the advocates of the NIT envision it as a substitute program, political pressures in the opposite direction are overwhelming. Can one seriously imagine that special interest voting blocs—veterans, farmers, the elderly, AFDC recipients, social workers, and welfare administrators—are going to give up their subsidies and positions without serving notice to the politicians? Astute, vote-seeking politicians would respond to their demands, and the NIT, if adopted, would simply be thrown on top of the present bag of welfare measures.

4. *The NIT Would Reduce Income Mobility.*   The tax burden in the United States falls primarily on the back of persons generating current income. The enormous cost of the NIT would increase this burden and make it still more difficult for persons of modest background to accumulate wealth. The positions and power of those who already have substantial wealth would be protected against competition from those with less wealth but greater productive abilities. While the plan would help relieve the guilt complexes of the Kennedys, Rockefellers, Fords, and others who inherited multimillions, society's *currently* most industrious and productive members would bear the cost. There would seem to be a more equitable means of dealing with the guilt feelings of the rich.

The plan simply gives people the wrong incentives. It would encourage irresponsible

---

[11]Blechman, Gramlich, and Hartman, *Setting National Priorities—The 1975 Budget.*

behavior on the part of the undeserving poor, while doing little to assure a proper diet, adequate housing, and medical care for children—the innocents of poverty.

CHAPTER LEARNING OBJECTIVES

1. The bulk of all income (70 percent of the total) is generated by families earning between $8000 and $25,000. Substantial income inequality is present in the United States. The bottom 20 percent of all family income recipients received only 5.4 percent of the total income in 1972. The top 20 percent received slightly more than two-fifths of the total.

2. During the last four decades there has been a trend toward greater equality in the distribution of family income. The share of annual income going to the top 5 percent in 1972 was only about half the percentage they received in 1929. Most of the movement toward equality took place prior to 1947.

3. The impact of federal, state, and local taxes, taken in aggregate, tends to reduce income inequality very little, probably less than 5 percent.

4. In comparison with the United States, greater equality is present in Sweden, while greater inequality exists for less developed countries such as Mexico, El Salvador, and Thailand. The income distribution in the United Kingdom is similar to that for the United States.

5. The distribution of annual income may be a misleading indicator of the variation in living standards between families. Nonmarket income, which is distributed approximately equally, is excluded. Noncash gifts and subsidies in kind, many of which benefit the poor, are excluded. Annual income is an imperfect measure of permanent or expected lifetime income, which will determine a family's standard of living.

6. Poverty is a relative term. The Social Security Administration defines it as three times the budget requirement necessary to purchase an economical food plan. This definition gives poverty meaning in terms of an absolute standard of living adjusted to the size of the family and changes in prices.

7. The poor are not a homogeneous group. Some people are poor through no fault of their own, primarily because of misfortune. Others are poor because they failed to take advantage of opportunities and brought on their own problems. Many are poor because of a combination of bad luck and unsuccessful economic choosing.

8. It is important to distinguish between **(a)** persons who are temporarily poor because their current income understates their lifetime income and **(b)** those who are permanently poor. The latter group is caught up in the vicious circle of poverty. Since they are poor, they cannot afford adequate training, schooling, and medical care for themselves and their children, leaving them with little earning power. Thus they remain poor.

9. There are three basic approaches to the alleviation of poverty. First, the human capital approach stresses that upgrading the skills of the poor will make it possible for them to escape poverty by increasing their earning power. Second, the gift-in-kind approach argues that essential goods (rather than money income) should be provided so society can be assured that adequate food, clothing, and housing will be available to the poor and their children. The redistribution of income approach is based on the premise that the problems of the poor are primarily related to the lack of a *minimum* income level.

10. The negative income tax is a plan to both guarantee a minimum income level and maintain monetary work incentives. The major advantages of the NIT are its **(a)** simplicity, **(b)** ability to allocate income to people because they are poor, rather than their interest group status, and **(c)** provision for a monetary incentive to continue working. The major disadvantages are **(a)** at least some of the recipients may still fail to provide their families with adequate food, housing, and medical services and **(b)** the incentive that it would give people to pursue unreported income, uncounted income in kind, and temporary periods of leisure.

IMPORTANT TERMS TO REMEMBER

Lorenz curve: Graphic device to illustrate visually the degree of income inequality. The cumulative percentage of income recipients, arranged from lowest to highest, is measured on the horizontal axis and the cumulative percentage of the total income they receive is measured on the vertical axis. A 45 degree line would indicate perfect equality. The area or gap between the curve generated by the actual distribution of income and the 45 degree line indicates the inequality gap.

Vicious circle of poverty: The tendency of the poor to remain poor because they do not have the opportunity to invest in schooling, training, health, and other factors that would increase their earning power.

Human capital approach: Programs designed to upgrade the earning power of the poor by providing them the means with which to develop skills and maintain their health.

Gift-in-kind approach: Programs such as food stamps and public housing, which provide the poor with basic goods rather than money income.

Negative income tax: A system of transferring income to the poor. The poor would receive an income supplement that would guarantee a minimum level of income. The supplement would be reduced by some fraction (less than one) as the family earns additional income. An increase in earnings would always cause the disposable income available to the family to rise.

Marginal tax rate: The amount of one's *additional* (marginal) earnings that must be paid directly in taxes or indirectly in the form of a reduction in the level of one's income supplement. Since it establishes the fraction of an *additional* dollar earned that an individual is permitted to keep, it is an important determinant of the incentive to work.

Breakeven point: Under a negative income tax plan, the income level at which one neither pays taxes nor receives supplementary income transfers.

THE ECONOMIC WAY OF THINKING—DISCUSSION QUESTIONS

1. "Welfare is a classic case of conflicting goals. Low welfare payments continue to leave people in poverty. But high welfare payments attract people to welfare roles, reduce work incentives, and cause higher rates of unemployment." [Quoted from the *There is No Free Lunch Newsletter.*]
   (a) Evaluate. (*Hint:* Apply the opportunity cost concept.)
   (b) Can you think of a plan to resolve the dilemma? Explain why or why not.

2. What do you think would be the major impacts of the negative income tax? Do not forget the secondary effects.

3. Explain why the use of household data rather than family income data may be misleading if one seeks to determine whether or not the economic system is evolving toward equality.

4. "As the real value of welfare, charity, and unemployment benefits rises, more and more people can be expected to find the combination of such benefits and leisure more attractive than the best available combination of income and work." [Professor Gordon Tullock, *National Review*, August 3, 1973]

(a) Do you agree or disagree? Why?

(b) If the statement is true, what are the policy implications? Explain your answer and the assumptions on which it is based. Be careful to stick to positive economics.

5. What are the major advantages of the human capital approach to the reduction of poverty? Do you think this approach could do much to alleviate poverty? Why or why not?

6. Senator Snodgrass proposes that Congress spend an additional $20 billion to pay for 50 percent of the housing, food, and clothing expenditures of the poor. State the case both for and against such a proposal.

27
EMPLOYMENT DISCRIMINATION AND THE EARNINGS OF BLACKS AND WOMEN

In the last chapter we focused on several factors that contribute to low incomes. We noted that racial minorities and female-headed households are overrepresented among the poor. Inequality among large *groups* of people (blacks, females, Spanish-Americans, and other racial minorities) raises a different set of issues than inequality among individuals within a group. America was built on the promise, some would say the false promise, of equal opportunity. It was, of course, recognized that individuals have different goals, abilities, and motivations. Inequality between *individuals* would be inevitable, even with equal opportunity. But when an entire race of people has substantially lower incomes than majority whites, this is strong evidence that some are deprived of an equal opportunity because of their race. The American Promise is not being realized.

During the last two decades, both state and federal laws have been passed that were designed to reduce inequality according to race and sex. What has been accomplished? Has public policy influenced the opportunities available to racial minorities and women? We will attempt to answer these questions in this chapter.

WHAT IS EMPLOYMENT DISCRIMINATION?

Employment discrimination is present when minority (female) employees are treated differently than similarly productive whites (males). Employment discrimination may stem from the discriminatory actions of employers, consumers, and/or fellow employees. Employers may object to hiring blacks (females). Economists may say that they have a taste for discrimination. This is a polite way of saying that they are racial bigots or sexists.

Discrimination may also stem from the views of customers. Consumers may fail to patronize retail stores that hire blacks. They may seek to avoid black (or female) lawyers, doctors, dentists, television repairmen, and plumbers.

Fellow employees may also be discriminatory. White males may object to black (or female) supervisors. They may erect employment restrictions, union entry restraints for example, as a means to reduce competition with minorities or females. Fear of retaliation by majority white employees may limit the incentive of even a nondiscriminatory employer to hire minorities or females into certain types of jobs.

Are the lower earnings of blacks (or females) proof of employment discrimination? Economic theory answers, "Only if the earnings differences are unrelated to productivity factors."

We noted earlier that an individual's wage will be related to his stock of human capital—his education, skill level, abilities, and experience. In general, whites have more human capital than blacks. Both the quantity and quality of the education of whites exceed that of blacks. On average, whites also have more skill-building experience. If we want to isolate the importance of current employment discrimination, we should consider these factors. But after we adjust for differences in productivity characteristics, if similar majority and minority employees still have different earnings, it is strong evidence of employment discrimination.

HOW DOES DISCRIMINATION INFLUENCE EARNINGS?

Regardless of the source of employment discrimination, there are two major outlets to express it—wage rates and employment restrictions.

1. *Direct Wage Discrimination.* If wage rates are the primary outlet, the minority will be hired, but only at a lower wage rate than whites of a similar performance level. Since the 1963 Equal Pay Act, it has been illegal to pay employees different wages for the same work. But this act is difficult to enforce because most jobs are at least slightly different from others. In addition, minority employees can be assigned to jobs for which they are overqualified. They can be promoted to higher paying jobs less rapidly than similarly qualified whites. Thus even though they have similar productive abilities, their wages may be less than those of comparable whites.

Exhibit 27-1 illustrates the impact of wage discrimination. When majority employees are preferred to minority and female workers, the demand for the latter two groups will

Exhibit 27-1 The Impact of Direct Wage Discrimination

If there is employment discrimination against blacks or females, the demand for their services will decline, reducing their wage rate from W_W to W_B.

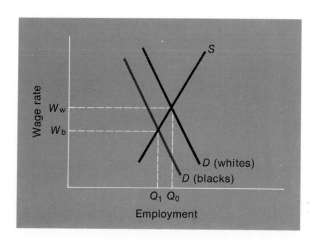

be reduced. The wages of blacks and females will decline relative to those of white males.

Essentially, there is a dual labor market—one market for whites and another for minority employees. Whites are preferred, but the less expensive minority employees are a substitute productive resource. White and minority employees will both be employed, but the whites will be paid a higher wage rate.

2. *Employment Restrictions.* Exclusionary employment practices may also be an outlet for discrimination. Employers, either in response to outside pressure or because of their own views, may designate certain types of jobs as "white only" or "male only." Despite the efforts of labor unions on behalf of workers, the union movement has often been at the forefront of efforts to exclude blacks from some jobs. As early as 1902, W. E. B. DuBois found that 43 national unions had no black members. Many of these unions had a written policy excluding blacks. In recent years, in conflict with public statements of national union leaders, many local unions, particularly craft unions, have maintained procedures that restrict blacks.

The representation of blacks among union electricians, plumbers, pipe fitters, sheet metal workers, and other construction and metal craft trades is substantially below what would be expected, given the educational and skill level of blacks (see Exhibit 27-2). The Justice Department, in a suit filed against the St. Louis Construction and Building Trades Council, found only two black apprentices among 1250 sheet metal workers; no black pipe fitters among more than 1000 union members; one black electrician among the nearly 2000 members of the local Brotherhood of Electrical Workers; no blacks among 1300 union plumbers and apprentices. Yet, one-third of the population of St. Louis is black! A similar pattern exists, even today, in other major cities in both the North and South.

When minority and female workers are excluded from a large number of occupations, they are *crowded* into a smaller number of the remaining jobs (and occupations).

Exhibit 27-2 Black Workers as a Percentage of the Total Labor Force and of Selected Unions

Union	Percent black
Electrical workers	1.9
Iron workers	1.7
Plumbers and pipe fitters	0.8
Sheet metal workers	0.6
Asbestos workers	0.2
Carpenters	2.9
Lithographers	2.0
Stage and motion picture operators	1.9
All unions	9.2
Total labor force	10.1

SOURCE: Equal Opportunity Commission.

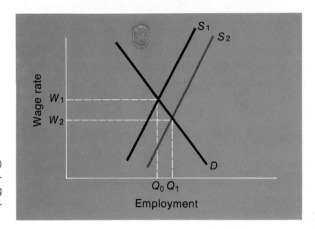

Exhibit 27-3 The Impact of Discriminatory Crowding

The crowding of the minorities (females) into *nonrestricted* occupations will increase their supply from S_1 to S_2, driving the wage rates down in those occupations that are open to minorities.

If entry restraints prevent people from becoming supervisors, foremen, plumbers, electricians, policemen, and firemen, they will be forced to accept other alternatives. Blacks are grossly underrepresented in most construction and metal craft occupations, although the situation has improved in the last few years. Exhibit 27-3 demonstrates the impact of occupational crowding. Since minorities are excluded from some jobs because of discrimination, they will be "pushed" into nonrestricted jobs. This will increase the supply of labor in these areas, and the wages of both majority and minority employees will decline for the nonrestricted jobs. By contrast, the exclusionary practices will result in higher wages for the majority employees holding jobs from which the minority is excluded.

Minority (and female) employees will be concentrated in the low-paying, non-restricted jobs, while majority white workers are protected from minority competition for the higher paying jobs. The impact will be a reduction in the average earnings of minority (and female) workers.

DOES IT PAY TO DISCRIMINATE?

Most people assign the title of "chief discriminator" to the employer. This is because it is the employer who pays lower wages or hires very few minority (or women) employees even if he is only responding to the views of consumers, majority employees, union practices, or even community pressures. Regardless of the source of employment discrimination, the employment decisions rest with the employer.

Undoubtedly many employers have followed discriminatory practices of their own volition. But economic theory suggests that it costs employers to discriminate when they are merely reflecting their own views. If employers can hire equally productive blacks (or women) at lower wages than whites (or males), the profit motive gives them a strong incentive to do so. The discriminator who continues to hire the high wage whites when similar minority employees are available at a lower wage, will have his costs increased. The higher cost will reduce his profits. It does not pay to be a bigot or sexist.

At the same time, a nondiscriminator would refuse to offer whites higher wage rates than equally productive minority or female workers. Any time it is cheaper to hire minority, rather than majority, employees, the nondiscriminator would do so. His equal opportunity policy would serve to reduce his cost and place him at an advantage over a *bigoted* competitor who discriminates.[1]

THE COST OF DISCRIMINATION—THE CASE OF BASEBALL[2]

How can we test to see if low discriminators really obtain an advantage over competitors who discriminate more intensely? In most industries it is a difficult proposition to test because the necessary data are often unavailable. Major league baseball is an interesting case study that sheds some light on the theory.

In the mid-1940s there were no black players in the "big leagues." Simultaneously, a pool of readily available, proven baseball talent existed in the Negro leagues. The services of most of these players could be purchased at a fraction of the cost that would be necessary to obtain comparable white players.

Two inputs, white and/or black players, could be utilized in an effort to win games (an output variable), but the price of an equally productive black player was much cheaper. Once the color line was broken, other things constant, firms had an incentive to substitute the less expensive blacks for the higher priced white players.

There is considerable evidence that baseball executives were aware of the potential. As early as 1944, Bill Veeck tried to buy the sinking franchise of the Philadelphia Phillies and stock the club with stars from the Negro leagues. In his autobiography Veeck states:

> With Satchel Paige, Roy Campanella, Luke Easter, Monte Irvin, and countless others in action and available, I had not the slightest doubt that in 1944, a war year, the Phillies would have leaped from seventh place to the pennant.[3]

Veeck's plan to buy the Phillies was foiled. After a conference with the baseball commissioner, the owners sold the team to someone else for about half the price that Veeck was willing to pay. But four years later Veeck did gain control of the Cleveland Indian franchise. Paced by established players from the Negro leagues such as Paige, Easter, and Larry Doby, the Indians and Yankees dominated the American League in the late 1940s and early 1950s.[4]

Other baseball men were also aware of the potential of black baseball players. John McGraw, in the early days of organized baseball, once tried to play a Negro, referring to him as an Indian. Branch Rickey, the first baseball owner who was willing to break the color line, is reported to have felt that the employment of Negroes was necessary to restore his Brooklyn team that had been ravished by war and old age.

[1] The celebrated AT&T case was based on the logic of this section. The Equal Employment Opportunity Commission argued that AT&T should not be allowed to increase its rates because its discriminatory policies resulted in costs that were higher than necessary.

[2] This section is a digest of an article by James Gwartney and Charles Haworth, "Employer Cost and Discrimination: The Case of Baseball," *Journal of Political Economy*, June 1974.

[3] Bill Veeck, *Veeck as in Wreck*. New York: Putnam, 1962.

[4] Between 1948 and 1956 the Indians won the American League pennant twice and finished second five times.

Is Winning Everything?

Just how large was the potential competitive advantage that could accrue to a "low discriminator"? The ranking of teams according to the cumulative number of blacks on the team each year, "black player years," clearly illustrates the contribution of black players to team success (see Exhibit 27-4). By 1956 the Brooklyn Dodgers had accumulated 37 black player years, 22 of them during the 1952–1956 period. They were followed by New York (N), Cleveland (A), and Boston (N). During the 1947–1956 period, the eight teams with the greatest representation of blacks averaged 17.8 cumulative black player years. The comparable figure for the other eight teams was 1.4. The top eight teams in terms of black player years won 5.6 percent more of their games than did the eight teams with the least representation of black players during the 1952–1956 period.

The evidence is even more impressive for the top five teams. These teams, employing the most black players through 1956, composed five of the top six teams according to won–lost percentage during the 1952–1956 period. They won 58 percent of their games, compared to only 46 percent for the other 11 teams. Only the New York Yankees were able to attain this stature with relatively few black players.

People like to go see a winner. A more detailed analysis also indicates that "lower

Exhibit 27-4   The Cumulative Number of Black Player Years and the Won–Lost Record of Major League Baseball Teams between 1952 and 1956

Team[a]	CUMULATIVE NUMBER OF BLACK PLAYER YEARS		Fraction of games won 1952–1956	Ranking (won–lost percentage) 1952–1956
	1947–1956	1952–1956		
Brooklyn (N)	37	22	0.630	2
New York (N)	25	18	0.527	6
Cleveland (A)	20	12	0.619	3
Boston (N)	18	18	0.548	5
Chicago (A)	14	12	0.571	4
Chicago (N)	12	12	0.439	12
Cincinnati (N)	8	8	0.489	10
Philadelphia (A)	8	8	0.394	14
Pittsburg (N)	3	3	0.351	15
St. Louis (A)	3	3	0.387	16
St. Louis (N)	2	2	0.502	9
New York (A)	2	2	0.638	1
Washington (A)	1	1	0.432	13
Philadelphia (N)	0	0	0.509	8
Boston (A)	0	0	0.516	7
Detroit (A)	0	0	0.440	11
Average (top 8)	17.8	13.8	0.528	7.0
Average (lowest 8)	1.4	1.4	0.472	10.0
Average (top 5)	22.8	16.4	0.579	4.0.

SOURCE: J. D. Gwartney and C. T. Haworth, "Employer Cost and Discrimination, the Case of Baseball," *Journal of Political Economy,* June 1974.

[a] National League teams are denoted by (N) and American League by (A).

discriminators"—teams willing to hire blacks—not only won more games, but they also had higher attendance. Hiring blacks, largely because of their impact on team performance, paid off nicely at the box office. The low discriminating teams gained, while the high discriminators paid a price for their prejudice.

EMPLOYMENT DISCRIMINATION AND THE EARNINGS OF BLACKS

The earnings of black males currently are approximately two-thirds those of whites. The black/white (B/W) earnings ratio for females is near 80 percent. How much of this differential is the result of *current* employment discrimination? This is not an easy question to answer. When isolating the impact of current employment practices, we would like to compare the earnings of whites and blacks who are "similarly situated." Some of the white–black earnings differential reflects productivity factors. On average, whites have approximately two more years of schooling than blacks. Even this figure understates the educational gap between whites and blacks. Blacks often attend schools that are crowded, poorly staffed, and populated primarily by slow learners. Consequently, the scholastic achievement level of blacks is significantly lower than that of whites. In 1965 the monumental study of the U.S. Office of Education estimated that the average black high school graduate had approximately the same scholastic achievement level as a ninth grade white.[5] This factor contributes to the white–black earnings gap. There is little reliable evidence on skill differences according to color. A differential may also exist in this area.

Differences between whites and blacks in educational, achievement, and skill factors may be the result of discriminatory practices in other areas of our economy. There certainly is strong evidence of past (and continuing) discrimination in the quality of public education. But employers should not be held responsible for the discriminatory practices of educational and vocational training institutions.

Economic studies on the relative importance of productive factors indicate that at least half of the white–black earnings differential is attributable to productivity differences.[6] Exhibit 27-5 presents results of estimates made by Joan Haworth, Charles Haworth, and the author, utilizing 1970 U.S. census data. The actual B/W earnings ratios were 66 and 80 percent for males and females, respectively. After adjustment was made for seven "earnings related" variables, the estimated B/W earnings ratio for similar males according to race was between 79 and 83 percent. The adjusted B/W ratio for females was between 90 and 95 percent. However, the seven productivity factors were unable to explain completely the earnings gap between whites and blacks.

---

[5] James Coleman *et al.*, *Equality of Educational Opportunity* (Washington, D.C.: U.S. Office of Education, 1966). Note that scholastic achievement is a culturally bound term. It is intended to measure factors that are important for success in our society. It is *not* indicative of native ability. See B. F. Kiker and W. Pierce Liles, "Earnings, Employment and Racial Discrimination: Additional Evidence," *American Economic Review*, June 1974, for evidence on the importance of scholastic achievement as a factor explaining earnings differences between blacks and whites.

[6] See Gary Becker, *Economics of Discrimination* (Chicago: Univ. of Chicago Press, 1957); David Rasmussen, "Discrimination and the Income of Nonwhite Males," *Journal of Economics and Sociology*, October 1971; and J. Haworth, J. D. Gwartney, and C. T. Haworth, "Earnings, Productivity and Changes in Employment Discrimination During the Sixties," *American Economic Review*, March 1975.

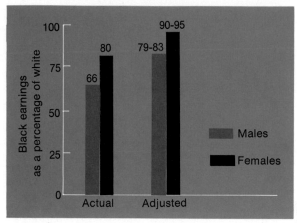

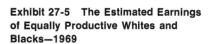

Exhibit 27-5   The Estimated Earnings of Equally Productive Whites and Blacks—1969

Earnings data are adjusted for age, education, region, marital status, hours worked, veteran status, and rural residence.

SOURCE: Derived from the *U.S. Census of Population, 1970—Public Use Sample.*

Can the adjusted earnings differentials, approximately 20 percent for black males and between 5 and 10 percent for black females, be taken as a measure of *current* employment discrimination? If the human capital characteristics of whites and blacks were otherwise identical, the answer would be yes. But there are two reasons why this may not be true. First, due to data limitations, the estimates of Exhibit 27-5 do not consider racial differences in achievement that may result from quality of education and other environmentally related factors. Adjustment for this factor would most likely bring the estimated B/W earnings ratio closer to unity. Second, the past cannot be completely repealed. Past discrimination, inasmuch as it affects current human capital, will continue to exert an influence on current earnings. The on-the-job training and skill-building experience of older blacks in particular may be less than those of whites because of past discriminatory employment practices. For example, the black high school graduate who was channeled into menial, low skill jobs (for example, unskilled laborer, janitor, etc.) by the employment practices of the 1940s or 1950s cannot be expected to possess as much human capital as an otherwise similar white who was given the opportunity to develop craft skills. While current equality of employment opportunity will not equalize the earnings of older blacks and whites where past discrimination has affected human capital, it will generate equality in the earnings of their sons and daughters entering today's labor market. The implications of this analysis are not particularly encouraging. They suggest that complete earnings parity according to race will come only after a couple of decades of equal employment opportunity.

ARE THINGS IMPROVING?

During the 1960s, public policy made a frontal attack on discriminatory employment practices. There was also evidence of moderating racial views within the American society. Was any real progress made toward racial equality? Increasingly, as the returns come in, there are encouraging signs that progress is in fact being made.

Exhibit 27-6 illustrates that the median income of black full-time workers has increased steadily in the South and for females in the North. Between 1962 and 1973,

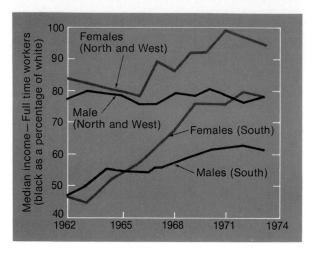

Exhibit 27-6   The Changing Income of Minorities

The income of black full-time workers, except for males in the non-South, has been increasing relative to whites.

SOURCE: U.S. Department of Commerce, Bureau of the Census. The 1962 and 1963 data are for all nonwhite races.

the relative income of black southern males increased from 47 to 61 percent, a 30 percent gain. The B/W earnings ratio of southern females increased from 45 to 78 percent, a whopping 73 percent gain in 12 years. By the early 1970s, black northern females had attained approximate earnings parity with their white counterparts. Only black males in the North have failed to make substantial gains in recent years.[7]

Exhibits 27-7 and 27-8 reveal a great deal about the mechanism that brought about

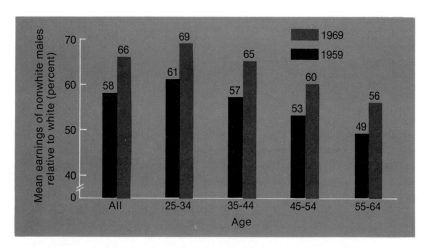

Exhibit 27-7   The Nonwhite/White Earnings Ratio for 1959 and 1969

During the 1960s nonwhite/white earnings increased from 58 to 66 percent. The relative earnings of nonwhites are lowest for the oldest, and highest for the youngest age groups.

SOURCE: Derived from the *U.S. Census of Population—Public Use Sample.* 1960 and 1970.

[7] See R. B. Freeman, "Decline of Labor Market Discrimination and Economic Analysis," *American Economic Review,* May 1973, for additional evidence on changes in employment discrimination over time.

Exhibit 27-8 The Median Years of School of Persons 20 Years Old and Over by Age—1970

	YEARS OF SCHOOLING		
Age	White	Black	Gap
20–21	12.8	12.4	0.4
22–24	12.7	12.3	0.4
25–29	12.6	12.2	0.4
30–34	12.5	12.0	0.5
35–44	12.4	11.2	1.2
45–54	12.3	9.3	3.0
55–64	11.2	7.9	3.3

SOURCE: U.S. Department of Commerce, Bureau of the Census.

the earnings gains of blacks. Exhibit 27-7 presents the relative B/W earnings by age for both 1959 and 1969. One of the interesting facets of this graph is the strong positive relation between relative earnings and youth. <u>The earnings of younger blacks relative to whites are much higher than those of their fathers and grandfathers. For example the B/W earnings ratio for persons 25–34 in 1970 was 69 percent, compared to a ratio of 56 percent for persons 55–64 years of age.</u>

Exhibit 27-8 yields additional insight into why the relative earnings of younger blacks are higher than those of older persons. The white–black educational gap is small, less than one-half year, for persons under 35. But this education gap widens substantially for the older age groupings. It is 1.2 years for persons 35–44 years of age and widens to over three years for persons 55–64.

Taken together, the two exhibits clearly point out that younger blacks are better qualified to compete in the job market with whites of similar age. With the passage of time, the oldest blacks with the poorest relative productivity credentials are exiting from the labor force. They are being replaced by younger blacks, who are more equal to whites in terms of productive abilities. <u>The exit of the least qualified and the entry of the most qualified blacks are improving the relative quality of the black labor force. This mechanism alone is estimated to account for half of the 14 percent increase in the B/W earnings ratio during the 1960s.</u>

But there is additional evidence that indicates the upgrading of the black labor force is being accompanied by improved job opportunities. In the past, discrimination was apparently strongest against the best educated blacks. The intense employment discrimination against the best qualified blacks would reduce the incentive to do well educationally.

Exhibit 27-9 indicates that this is much less the case in the 1970s. The B/W earnings ratio of males is presented for three different educational groupings—less than 10 years of schooling, 11–13, and 14+ years. <u>During the 1960s, the most rapid gains in relative earnings were recorded by males with the most education.</u> The B/W earnings ratio for males with less than 10 years of schooling increased by only 2 percent. Yet the black males with 14+ years of schooling made relative gains of 15 percent in the North and

Exhibit 27-9 The Adjusted Nonwhite/White Earnings Ratio in 1959 and 1969 for Three Education Groupings

Years of schooling and region	ADJUSTED NONWHITE/WHITE EARNINGS[a]		
	1959 (percent)	1969 (percent)	Change (percent)
North			
0–10	83	84	+2
11–13	77	82	+7
14 and over	72	82	+15
South			
0–10	73	74	+2
11–13	65	74	+15
14 and over	61	70	+14

SOURCE: *U.S. Census of Population—Public Use Sample.* 1960 and 1970.

[a] Adjusted for differences in age, education, rural status, regional status, annual hours worked, marital status, and veteran status.

14 percent in the South. More and more, jobs at the top of the employment pyramid are opening up for black Americans. Of course, the promise of equal opportunity has not yet been attained, but there is evidence of progress.

EVERYTHING YOU ALWAYS WANTED TO KNOW ABOUT FEMALE EARNINGS—BUT WERE AFRAID TO ASK

> And the Lord spoke unto Moses, saying, "Speak unto the children of Israel, and say unto them, when a man shall make a special vow, the persons shall be for the Lord by thy valuation. And thy valuation shall be of the males from twenty years old, even unto sixty years old, even thy valuation shall be fifty shekels of silver, after the shekel of the sanctuary. And if it be a female, then thy valuation shall be thirty shekels." [Leviticus 27:1–4]

In 1971 the median earnings of females in the labor force were only 40 percent those of males. The average hourly earnings of females were about two-thirds those of males during the early 1970s. Since data on the earnings of full-time workers have been available, the F/M earnings ratio has hovered near the 60 percent level. Some economists, discovering the quote from Leviticus given above, have wondered aloud if the relative evaluation of females to males has remained at approximately 60 percent since the time of Moses.

The Employment Discrimination Hypothesis

Why are the earnings of women so low compared to those of men? Since productivity characteristics (for example, age, education, achievement) are similar according to sex, most people are prepared to blame the huge earnings differences on discriminatory

OUTSTANDING ECONOMIST: Juanita Kreps

The impressive publication list of Juanita Kreps attests to her ability to compete successfully in a male-dominated occupation. She has authored or co-authored eight books, in addition to numerous articles and mongraphs. Primarily a labor market economist, her research has dealt with a wide variety of topics including automation and unemployment, economics of the aging, minimum wage rates, manpower utilization, and employment discrimination. Her labor economics text, *Contemporary Labor Economics* (co-authored with Richard Perlman and Gerald Somers),[8] is widely used in senior level courses.

She is currently Vice-President and James B. Duke Professor of Economics at Duke University. From 1969 to 1972, Dr. Kreps was Dean of the Women's College and Assistant Provost at Duke. She has served as a consultant to the U.S. Senate Special Committee on Aging and holds a presidential appointment on the National Manpower Commission. She is currently on the boards of directors of the New York Stock Exchange, the J. C. Penny Company, Western Electric, and R. J. Reynolds Industries.

Professor Kreps, the current (1976) president of the Southern Economic Association, is quite interested in employment opportunity for women. In her book, *Sex in the Marketplace: American Women at Work*[9] she asks, "Why do women not opt more often for occupations that are dominated by males, yet include some women in their ranks?"

She speculates on the answer, "The woman who is considering the occupational options may be discouraged from trying to enter a male's field because she accurately perceives employers' reluctance to hire women for these jobs, or because the investment required of her may exceed her estimate of the return, given her expectation of withdrawal from work for a time, and the uncertainty surrounding her subsequent worklife."

Professor Kreps advocates, "It is obvious we have to present some goals to top management: larger numbers of women need to be hired, or promoted. This will have to be done by individual action, on a company by company basis, although in the universities we are getting a large assist from HEW."

She is also optimistic. "I see clearly how many light years ahead my daughters are, beyond where I was when in college." If her daughters continue light years ahead of their mother, their future is bright indeed. Any economist, male or female, would be justly proud of accomplishments comparable to those of Juanita Kreps.

---

employment practices. For example, a Presidential Task Force on Women's Rights and Responsibilities has concluded that discriminatory practices against women are so widespread and pervasive that they have come to be regarded as normal.

Do the data support the employment discrimination hypothesis? We have already pointed out that the earnings of females are only two-thirds as great as those of males of

---

[8] Juanita Kreps, Richard Perlman, and Gerald Somers, *Contemporary Labor Economics*, 3rd ed. Belmont, California: Wadsworth, 1974.

[9] Juanita Kreps, *Sex in the Marketplace: American Women at Work*. Baltimore, Maryland: Johns Hopkins Press, 1971.

similar age, education, and achievement level. Occupational data suggest that females are excluded from the highest paying professional and craft jobs, and crowded into lower paying employment in teaching, clerical, secretarial, and sales fields. Many jobs, particularly those where on-the-job experience and training are an important source of higher earnings, appear to be reserved for males only. There are few female car salesmen, foremen, truck drivers, electricians, or plumbers, not to mention lawyers, doctors, supervisors, accountants, and economists. Women are flagrantly under-represented among union members, particularly unions that have significantly increased wages. All of these factors are consistent with the view that discriminatory employment practices are the major source of earnings differentials according to sex.

Is the Employer Really the Chief Sexist?

Despite the evidence just given, the case that *employment* discrimination is the major source of the 35 percent male–female earnings differential is less than airtight. First, the size of even the adjusted differential mediates against this hypothesis. If an employer could really hire females who are *willing and able to do the same work as his male labor force*, for 35 percent less, he would have a strong incentive to do so. Surely many of the less "sexist" employers, perhaps female employers, would substitute women for the more expensive male employees. Yet there is little evidence that even a 35 percent earnings differential is attracting many profit-seeking, low discriminators into the market.

Second, if employment discrimination is the major source of earnings differences according to sex, we would expect females to seek out self-employment as a method of avoiding the bigoted practices of employers. Since the self-employed female would not discriminate against herself, we would expect a low male–female earnings differential for this group. But research indicates that this is not the case. Females are even more underrepresented among the self-employed than in other areas of the economy. In addition, the female/male earnings ratio for self-employed females is only 41 percent, compared to 58 percent for female employees in the private sector.

The views of female employees should also cause researchers to pause before pointing to the employer as the primary source of the low earnings of females. Malcolm Cohen reports that only 8.1 percent of all working women feel they are discriminated against.[10] One-half of those reporting employment discrimination felt it was slight. In general, women are relatively oblivious to discriminatory practices if they do exist.

The Family Specialization Hypothesis

Despite this evidence against the employment discrimination hypothesis, the fact of large earnings differences according to sex still remains. Is there another theory that might explain this wage gap?

The **family specialization hypothesis** argues that independent of employ-

---

[10] Malcolm S. Cohen, "Sex Differences in Compensation." *Journal of Human Resources*, Fall 1971.

ment discrimination, men and women will look for different things from the labor market. The average woman will carefully evaluate the job location, hours, job pressure, and working conditions as to their effect on her household responsibilities and availability to her children. Will she be home when the children return from school? Will she be worn out and unable to prepare evening meals for the family? Choice theory suggests that she will trade off monetary earnings for working conditions that better fit her other duties.

In addition, the family is more likely to think of the wife as a secondary source of income, one that would enter the labor force only during hard times or in order to meet temporary major expenses (for example, down payment for a home or college education for the children). She will prepare for jobs that would (a) be available wherever the primary earner (the husband) might locate and (b) allow her to reenter the labor force with only a small reduction in earning power. The typical woman would find nursing, teaching, secretarial, and other jobs with easily transportable skills and credentials far more attractive than would males.

In a different light, males give primary consideration to monetary earnings. Since continuous future labor participation is envisioned, males are more willing to train for specialized jobs and accept jobs with lower current earnings, but higher future earnings after one acquires the necessary experience. They are usually more willing to accept jobs with long hours, uncertain schedules, and out of town travel.

Thus, differences in family roles may lead to money earnings differences according to sex.[11] Exhibit 27-10 illustrates the economics of the family specialization hypothesis.

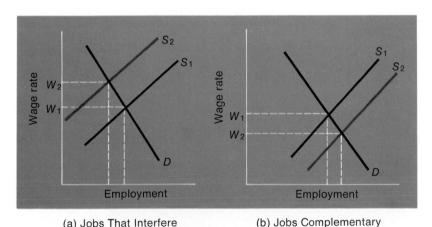

(a) Jobs That Interfere
with Household Duties

(b) Jobs Complementary
with Household Duties

Exhibit 27-10   The Family Specialization Hypothesis

If females specialize in household work, the labor supply in occupations that are complementary with these duties will expand [shift from S_1 to S_2, frame (b)]. It will decline in occupations where the market work responsibilities interfere with the household responsibilities of females [shift from S_1 to S_2, frame (a)]. These shifts would cause an overrepresentation of females in low-paying jobs (b) and an underrepresentation in high wage areas (a).

---

[11] Should there be a different division of household responsibilities? Should both men and women change their views? Positive economics does not grant an answer to these questions.

Since women are attracted to occupations that are highly complementary with their family responsibilities (Exhibit 27-10b), the supply (S_2) in these occupations will be greater than if men and women had the same job preferences (S_1). Wages in these occupations will be depressed and an overrepresentation of women results. Correspondingly, because many females may not compete for jobs that tend to interfere with their household duties, the reduction in supply in these occupations will cause both higher wages and an overrepresentation of males (Exhibit 27-10a).

We have stated the theory. Is there any evidence to support the family specialization view? Since preferences cannot be directly observed the family specialization hypothesis is hard to test. However, our logic suggests preferences will vary in a predictable manner according to marital status. The employment preferences of males and females who have never been married (singles) will be most similar. Single males, like single females, will have to make some provision for personal household services. The importance of wage rates and future opportunity for monetary job rewards should also be similar. In contrast, because of the traditional husband–wife roles, the importance of monetary rewards (relative to other aspects of working conditions) will be substantially different according to sex for persons who are married and living with their spouse. The data are highly consistent with this hypothesis. Utilizing the 1970 census data, the F/M mean annual income ratio for singles was 92 percent. In hourly terms, the income of single females was 95 percent of the comparable figure for single males. While a small differential existed according to sex for singles, a huge gap was present for persons married, with spouse present. Working wives had annual incomes only one-third as great as working husbands. In hourly terms, the F/M income ratio for persons married with spouse present was 56 percent (see Exhibit 27-11).[12]

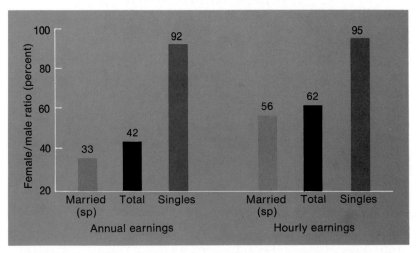

Exhibit 27-11 The Female/Male Earnings According to Marital Status—1970

Both the annual and hourly F/M earnings ratios for all females and those married with spouse present are substantially less than unity. But the earnings of single females are approximately on parity with single males.

SOURCE: Derived from the *U.S. Census of Population, 1970—Public Use Sample.*

[12] Similar results were obtained utilizing 1960 U.S. census data. See James Gwartney and Richard Stroup, "Measurement of Employment Discrimination According to Sex, *Southern Economic Journal*, April 1973.

The "Loser" from Family Specialization

If the family specialization hypothesis is true, does it follow that all women have equal opportunity in employment? The answer to this question is no. First, both employment discrimination against women and family specialization may contribute to the large male–female earnings differential. The two are not mutually exclusive. Second, even if sex discrimination, per se, is of minor importance, employers are likely to use sex as a proxy variable for the employee characteristics possessed *on average* by all women. The personnel manager of a large firm cannot tell the "career oriented" woman who is prepared to make the long-run commitment necessary to become a division manager or company vice-president, from the typical woman who wants a good job for only a year or two. Therefore, the career-oriented woman, even if she is currently single, will have to prove herself. The employment opportunities faced by career-oriented women, those who have employment aspirations similar to those of males, are reduced because employers assume that their objectives are similar to those of other women.

If the family specializing hypothesis were the sole source of earnings differences according to sex, the typical women employee would be trading off higher wages for working conditions that are more suitable to her preferences. This is her choice. But the career-oriented woman wants to opt for higher wages and is willing to make the necessary job commitment. Because she is a woman, she will often be treated as if she did not have such aspirations. Females with job preferences like males are the "big losers," if the family specialization hypothesis is true.

THE FUTURE STATUS OF MINORITIES AND WOMEN

Our analysis suggests several things about the future earnings of blacks and females. First, since younger blacks are better prepared (that is, they have more human capital) for employment, we can expect that they will continue to do better (relative to whites) than their fathers and grandfathers who are exiting from the labor force. This factor will continue to push the B/W earnings ratio slowly upward with the passage of time.

Second, equal employment opportunity will not *immediately* lead to earnings parity. The aggregate earnings of both blacks and women will continue to be depressed because, *in years gone by*, both training and skill-building experience were denied current labor force participants, particularly those in older age groupings. Thus, the movement to earnings parity, for both women and blacks, will be time-consuming. Of course, if equal employment opportunity really did exist, immediate earnings parity according to color (sex) *for similar labor force entrants* would result.

Third, there is strong evidence that discriminatory educational and training barriers have declined in recent years. For example, in 1973, 44 percent of the blacks in the South attended integrated schools, compared to only 1 percent in 1964. Court decisions are slowly breaking down some of the barriers restricting the entry of minorities into apprenticeship programs and craft occupations. In contrast to the situation a few years ago, many of the leading colleges and graduate schools now actively recruit minorities and women. In fact, the charge of preferential treatment is sometimes heard. The impact of these developments should be kept in perspective, lest we build false expectations. Improved educational and training opportunities will have their major impact on earnings *several years into the future*. It takes time to develop competent engineers, doctors, economists, administrators, and craftsmen. Improvement in the opportunity to build human capital is an important development. Merely because it does not lead to immediate earnings parity should not deter us from continued efforts to promote equal opportunity.

Fourth, inasmuch as earnings differences according to sex reflect family specialization, equal employment opportunity will not result in earnings parity. While changes in preferences are difficult to detect, opinion polls suggest that our perception of proper family roles is changing. Nevertheless, the debate among women concerning the Equal Rights Amendment to the Constitution reveals that many women (and men), perhaps even a majority, continue to favor differential family roles. These preferences will influence the types of jobs sought by women and their earnings in the future. Thus, from the viewpoint of positive economics, the problem becomes one of how to assure equal opportunity for career-oriented women. Clearly, job quotas are not the answer as they would often result in preferential treatment. Strict enforcement of legislation prohibiting the denial of either training or employment because of sex would help to assure equal opportunity for career-oriented women. In the past, law and medical schools in particular have often discriminated against women because they argued, with some justification, that they would not permanently remain in the labor force and fully utilize the training. Incentives in this area could be altered granting a lesser subsidy (most of this training is subsidized) to both men and women who fail to remain in the labor force a specified length of time.

As long as groups differ with regard to preferences and productivity characteristics, providing equal employment opportunity to all—blacks and whites, men and women, career-oriented women and family-centered women—will not be an easy task. *Under these circumstances*, employment policies that impose *identical outcomes*, for example, quotas or equalization of mean earnings paid by a firm, will favor some groups (particularly less productive minorities and women), while discriminating against others. They are inconsistent with equal opportunity. Unfortunately, the pathway to equal opportunity according to color and sex is not a simple one. But recognition of its complexity will better prepare us to pursue it.

CHAPTER LEARNING OBJECTIVES

   1. Employment discrimination exists when a group is either **(a)** paid less than other groups of similar productivity or **(b)** excluded from jobs available to other groups of similar productivity.
   2. Employment discrimination may stem from the views of employers, consumers, and/or fellow employees.
   3. Employment discrimination will directly reduce the earnings of a group if they are paid less than the majority group for similar work. Exclusion of a group from some employment opportunities will indirectly reduce their earnings because they will be crowded into a smaller set of occupations. This crowding will reduce wage rates in these occupations.
   4. Economic theory suggests that, in the absence of consumer or fellow employee discrimination, it costs an employer to discriminate. The employer could reduce his costs by substituting equally productive blacks (or females) for high wage whites (or males).

5. The earnings of black males were approximately two-thirds those of whites in the early 1970s. For females the B/W earnings ratio was 80 percent. At least one-half of these differentials reflect productivity differences, rather than current employment discrimination.

6. The relative earnings of younger blacks are higher than those of the older age groupings. The best educated blacks have made the most rapid gains in recent years. The earnings of black females have increased more rapidly than whites. The earnings of black and white females are currently near parity in the North.

7. The male–female earnings gap is much greater than the gap between whites and blacks. The hourly earnings of females are only two-thirds those of males with similar productivity characteristics. The earning gap according to sex probably reflects both employment discrimination and family specialization.

IMPORTANT TERMS TO REMEMBER

Employment discrimination: Unequal treatment of race, sex, or religious groups that restricts their employment and earnings opportunities compared to others of similar productivity. Employment discrimination may stem from the prejudices of employers, consumers, and/or fellow employees.

Family specialization hypothesis: The theory that differences in family roles, independent of employment discrimination, contribute to differences in earnings according to sex. It is usually assumed that females tend to specialize in household duties and child care services, while males specialize in providing the family with monetary income.

THE ECONOMIC WAY OF THINKING—DISCUSSION QUESTIONS

1. In early 1974 a government agency released a report stating that only 10 percent of the business executives making over $25,000 were 10 pounds or more overweight. By contrast, 40 percent of the executives making between $10,000 and $25,000 were 10 or more pounds overweight. The report concluded that fat people were one of the nation's largest and most oppressed minorities. [Heard on CBS radio, January 2, 1974.]

(a) What additional evidence would you want before deciding if fat people were, in fact, discriminated against?

(b) Should it be illegal to discriminate against fat people? Why or why not?

2. "Females are the most oppressed group in the United States. On an average, their earnings are less than those of both white and black males. Until sex discrimination in employment is eliminated, females will be relegated to second class citizenship."

(a) Explain why you either agree or disagree with this view.

(b) Discuss similarities and differences between the economic status of females and that of minority groups.

3. The earnings of black males employed by the federal government are approximately 80 percent those of whites with similar education and experience. What are the possible explanations of this differential?

4. "During the 1960s the earnings of black males increased more rapidly than whites, pushing the B/W earnings ratio from 0.58 up to 0.66."

"During the 1960s the earnings gap between white and black males continued to expand. In 1960 black males made $2171 less than their white counterparts. By 1970, this white–black dollar gap had increased to $2857." Explain how both of these seemingly paradoxical statements could (they were) be true.

5. How does the representation of females in sociology, home economics, music, fashion design, and English at your university compare with their representation in economics, business administration, chemistry, engineering, law, and medicine? If there are differences in representation according to sex, how will they influence relative earnings? Explain your answer carefully.

6. If *current* discrimination against blacks was completely eliminated, would earnings parity immediately be attained? Explain. Answer the same question for women.

V
PUBLIC
CHOICE

28

PROBLEM AREAS FOR THE MARKET

The market coordinates the self-interest of individuals, inducing them to produce a diverse menu of housing structures and food products, convenient shopping centers, completely planned communities with their own police and fire protection, beautiful golf courses, and even the fairyland entertainment center that we call Disney World. The market is a computer that must surely be one of the seven wonders of the world.

Personal self-interest working within the framework of a market economy has led to stripped mountainsides, destruction of scenic beauty, pollution of meandering brooks and rivers, air that is a menace to our health, and junkyards that blot our landscape. Unless we alter the market behavior of firms and individuals, we will suffer the continuation of an environmental disaster.

Do you believe that the same person could adhere to both of these views? These statements are paraphrased from a lecture given by a professor of economics. He believes both. This chapter will help explain why they are not inconsistent.

We have emphasized how the pricing system coordinates the decisions of buyers and sellers. When competitive markets are present, product prices tend to move toward their cost of production. In the long run, a good will be supplied if, *and only if,* consumers value it enough to cover the cost of the resources used to produce it. Competition is a great regulator that harmonizes the interests of resource suppliers, producers, and consumers.

But the pricing system sometimes suffers from "market failure," an expression used by economists to describe conditions under which even a smoothly operating market system will result in allocative inefficiency. We have already shown that the presence of monopoly in product and/or labor markets hampers the ability of a pricing system to guide resources into their highest valued uses. In this chapter we investigate other situations under which market failure will be present.

Despite the dreadful sound of the term market failure, the reader should keep in mind that it merely implies a failure to attain *ideal* efficiency conditions. Alternative forms of economic organization may also have defects. Market failure creates an opportunity for government intervention to improve the situation. However, sometimes circumstances suggest that public sector action will not be corrective. Sometimes there may even be good reason to expect that it will be counterproductive. After analyzing market failure, Chapters 29 and 30 focus on the operation of the public sector. The purpose of these three chapters is straightforward—we want to provide the reader the tools with which to compare the strengths and weaknesses of both market action and public sector intervention.

MARKET FAILURE: EXTERNAL COST

The genius of a market exchange system lies in its ability to bring personal and social welfare into harmony. Individuals produce and exchange goods because they derive personal gain from doing so. When only the consenting parties are affected, it is expected that they will gain from the exchange without harm to anyone else and thus the general welfare will also be promoted. Adam Smith's invisible hand is able to perform its magic.

But what about cases where externalities are present? Economic action sometimes imposes an unwanted **external cost** on nonconsenting secondary parties. The steel mill that belches smoke into the air imposes an external cost on surrounding residents who prefer clear air. The junkyard creates an eyesore, making life less enjoyable for passersby. Similarly, the actions of litterbugs, drinking drivers, speeders, muggers, and robbers impose unwanted costs on others.

What is so bad about external costs? When external costs are present, the market may incorrectly register the social (or total) cost of an action. **Social costs** include both (a) the private costs borne by the consenting parties and (b) any external cost imposed on nonconsenting secondary parties. When external costs are present, individuals, motivated by self-interest, may undertake action that generates a net loss to the community. The harm done to the secondary parties may exceed the net private gain. Private interests and economic efficiency may conflict.

Exhibit 28-1 presents a hypothetical example concerning the establishment of a mobile home park in a residential area that highlights the potential conflict. The trading partners—the park owner and those who rent his space—gain. But their actions generate congestion and noise (external costs). The harm to the neighboring residents exceeds the private benefits to the park owner and the renters. Social costs exceed social benefits. But since the residents do not have noise or noncongestion rights, the market fails to register their views. The park owner and renters have an incentive to undertake the project even though it will reduce the community's social welfare.

Why not simply prohibit activities that result in external cost? After all why should we allow nonconsenting parties to be harmed? This approach has a certain appeal, but closer inspection indicates that it is often an unsatisfactory solution. Automobile

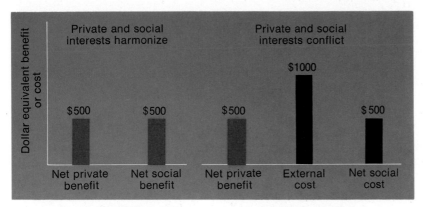

Exhibit 28-1   External Cost and Market Failure

Jones has 10 acres of land. If he plants it in wheat and eventually sells it to the miller, both he and the miller gain [frame (a)]. There are no external costs imposed. But when external costs are present [frame (b)] a market exchange may reduce total welfare, even though the consenting parties gain. For example, suppose Jones decides to use his 10 acres for a mobile home park. Both Jones and his customers gain because he establishes the trailer park. Suppose their joint net monthly gain is $500. But Jones' neighbors are harmed because the trailer park is jammed with noisy kids and is poorly kept. Overall monthly costs of $1000 are imposed on Jones' nonconsenting neighbors. The $500 gain that accrues to Jones and his customers (the net private benefit) is less than the cost imposed in the neighbors. The action reduces the welfare of the community.

exhaust imposes an external cost on bicyclists, and everyone who breathes. Dogs are notorious for using the neighbor's lawn for bone burying and relief purposes. Motorboats are noisy and scare the fish, much to the disgust of fishermen. Yet few would argue that we do away with cars, dogs, and motorboats. From a social viewpoint, prohibition is often a less desirable alternative than putting up with the inconvenience of the external costs. The gains from the activity are often substantially in excess of the costs imposed on those who are harmed.

External Costs and the Ideal Output

Externalities may result from the actions of either consumers or producers. When the actions of producers impose an external cost on others, the cost curves of firms, reflecting only private costs, are not accurate indicators of the true cost of production.

Exhibit 28-2 illustrates the impact of external costs on the socially desirable price and output. Suppose that there are a large number of firms producing wood pulp, which will later be used to make paper. The production of wood pulp pollutes the atmosphere. If left to their own devices, the pulp firms have little incentive to adopt either production techniques that result in less smoke or a control device that would reduce the harmful effects of their smoke discharge. These alternatives would only increase their private

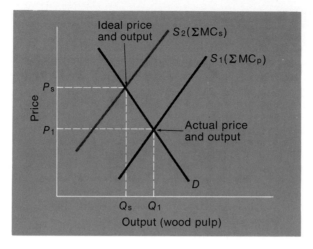

Exhibit 28-2   Adding External Cost

When external costs are present, output will be expanded too far. The actual market price will be less than the social opportunity cost of producing the good.

production cost. Since there is no charge for emission of smoke into the atmosphere, the firms can freely utilize this scarce resource.

Although the discharge of smoke is a "free" good to the producer, it does involve a cost to others. Smoke causes a rapid deterioration to the exterior of buildings; paint cracks and does not last long. Excessive smoke creates smog and has a negative effect on health. The discharge of smoke into the atmosphere is not a free resource to the community at large. But even though this is the case, the producer has only humanitarian concerns to counterbalance his private interest. In most cases we can expect self-interest to dominante.

The pulp firms, if left to their own discretion, will expand output as long as their marginal private costs are less than price. Supply curve S_1 (Exhibit 28-2), the sum of the private MC curves, will result. The market price and output of pulp would be P_1 and Q_1, respectively.

This output level results in the waste of some of the community's valuable resources. If the external cost imposed on the residents of areas with pulp mills were considered, supply S_2 would result. This supply curve reflects both the private and external costs. Ideally, wood pulp should be priced at P_s and output Q_s should be produced. At that price and output, the value of the last unit of pulp would just equal its cost to the community ($P = MC_s$).

The opportunity cost (counting the external cost) of producing units beyond Q_s exceeds their value. From the viewpoint of efficiency, the market price, which does not reflect the external cost, is too low. Thus, too much wood pulp (and not enough of other low pollution goods) is produced. An excess amount of pollution is the by-product.

External Costs and Property Rights

External costs arise because the property rights of resource owners are not clearly defined and enforced. Although property rights are often associated with selfishness, they would be more properly viewed as a device by which individuals *prevent* others from selfishly ignoring the cost of their actions. If property rights were not defined and enforced, spillover external costs would be common. The existence of property rights provides individuals with legal protection against the actions of parties who might damage, abuse, or steal their property.

Property owners often *sell* the right to use their property in a manner that will reduce its value. Rental car firms sell individuals the right to use their automobiles even though the use reduces the resale value of the car. Housing is often rented even though normal use by the renter will impose a maintenance and upkeep cost on the home-owner. However, since property rights are clearly defined in these cases, the market exchange system forces the person who uses the property to fully consider the costs of his actions.

In contrast, when property rights are nonexistent or poorly enforced, the incentive to use a resource wisely is removed. This is precisely the problem with air and water usage. Such resources are **common property.** Since no one has ownership rights, all individuals (and firms) are free to use them as intensively as they wish. Why is this bad? Since common property resources are "free" (to users but not to society), users will fail to consider the costs that their actions impose on others. In fact, it would be silly for any *single user* of our commonly owned air and water resources to incur control costs voluntarily in order to reduce the pollutants that *he* puts into the air (or water). The general level of pollution would be virtually unaffected by *his* actions. But when *all* users fail to consider how their actions affect air and water quality, the result is overutilization, excessive pollution, and economic inefficiency.

The technological nature of some commodities makes it costly or nearly impossible for the government to establish property rights in a manner that will assure that private parties bear the entire cost or reap all of the benefits of an activity. Exclusive ownership can easily be granted for commodities such as apples, cabbages, waterbeds, cars, and airline tickets. But how do you assign property rights to salmon or whales that travel thousands of miles each year? Similarly, who owns the oil pool that is located under the property of hundreds of different landowners? In the absence of clearly assigned property rights, spillover costs and overutilization are inevitable. Salmon and whales are on the verge of extinction because no single individual (or small group) has an incentive to reduce his current catch so that his future catch will be larger. Each person tries to catch all that he can now, for if he does not, someone else will. The same principle applies to the oil pool rights. In the absence of regulation, each oil well operator has an incentive to draw the oil *from a common pool* as rapidly as possible. But when they all do so, the commonly owned oil is drawn out too rapidly.

Efficiency and Taxing the Polluter

Some economists have suggested that a tax be levied on activities that generate external costs. Using pollution control as an example, Exhibit 28-3 illustrates the logic of this argument. Since pollution controls are costly, the firm's production cost will be lower if it can freely emit waste into the air. The marginal benefit curve reveals the cost savings that accrue to the firm when it thus freely utilizes the atmosphere. However, as the damage cost curve shows, the cost imposed on secondary parties increases with the

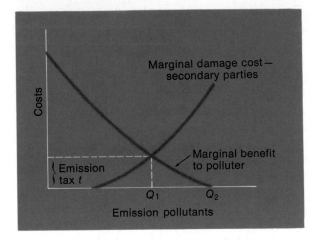

Exhibit 28-3   Taxing the Polluter

In the absence of government action, the firm depicted here emits too much pollution. An emission tax *t* would correct the situation.

level of pollution emission. In the absence of a tax (or other legal restraints), the firm's pollution emission level would be Q_2. When pollution emission rises above Q_1, the damage cost imposed on secondary parties exceeds the marginal benefits derived by the firm and its customers. Clearly, Q_2 emission level is inefficient.

Would society gain by prohibiting the firm from putting any pollutants into the air? Surprisingly, the answer is no. Note that the total gain of the firm and its customers (area under the marginal benefit curve) from emission level Q_2 exceeds the harm (the area under the marginal damage cost curve) imposed on secondary parties. Economic efficiency suggests that emission level Q_1 would be best considering the views of both the polluter and secondary parties that are affected by the pollution. This level would result if the public authorities imposed an emission tax *t* on the firm. Confronted with the tax, the firm would take steps to reduce its pollution emission to Q_1, where marginal benefits equal marginal costs. The revenues generated by the tax could be used to compensate the secondary parties harmed by the pollutants or to finance a wide range of projects including technical research on alternative methods of improving air quality.

At least in theory, the tax solution would help to promote efficient resource allocation. Several economic incentives are changed in a highly desirable manner. First, the emissions tax would increase the cost of producing pollution intensive goods, causing the supply in these industries to decline. If the tax is properly set, the ideal price and output conditions illustrated by Exhibit 28-2 would be approximated. Second, the emission tax would give firms an economic incentive to utilize production methods (and technology) that would result in less pollution. Third, since pollution control would lower the tax bill of firms, a market for control devices would exist. Entrepreneurs would be enticed to develop low cost control devices that could be marketed to firms who would now have a strong incentive to reduce their level of emissions.

Like all emission control plans, the pollution tax scheme has its drawbacks. While the technology is available to measure the pollutants emitted into the air, it is the damages that are important. Unfortunately, the damages imposed on secondary parties are not easily measured. Clearly they will vary between areas. Emission of additional units of sulfur oxides into the environment in Four Corners, Wyoming will be far less damaging than similar emissions in New York City or St. Louis. An emission tax rate might be directly tied to the population of an area. Thus, densely populated areas would have higher emissions taxes, encouraging high pollution firms to locate where there would be fewer people to be harmed. If the tax rate were set by a regulating agency, the possibility for favoritism and graft would clearly be present. With time, political power might very well replace economic efficiency as the major consideration in the establishment of a pollution tax structure. Unfortunately, there is not an easy, ideal solution to the pollution problem.

MARKET FAILURE: EXTERNAL BENEFITS AND OPPORTUNITIES MISSED

Spillover effects are not always harmful. Sometimes the actions of an individual (or firm) will generate **external benefits,** gains that accrue to nonparticipating (and nonpaying) secondary parties. When external benefits are present, the personal gains of the consenting parties will understate the total social gain, including that of secondary parties. Activities with greater social benefits than costs may not be undertaken because no decision-maker is able to capture the gains fully. Considering only personal net gains, decision-makers will allow potential social gains to go unrealized. Socially gainful opportunities will be missed.

Usually the reason external gains cannot be captured is that it is costly (or impossible) to withhold the benefit to secondary parties while still making it available to oneself. For example, my neighbors benefit when my son keeps our yard neatly trimmed and sprays our lot to inhibit mosquitoes and other insects. Similarly, they benefit from my flu shot and my children's measles shots which help reduce the incidence of communicable diseases in the neighborhood. But there is no way that I can charge for these services.

Why do I care if others benefit from my actions? Most of us usually do not, and external benefits become important only when one's inability to capture these potential gains causes him to forego a socially beneficial activity. Exhibit 28-4 illustrates this point. Education adds to the productivity of the student, permitting him to enjoy higher future earnings. In addition, at least certain types of education will reduce the future cost of welfare, generate a more intelligent populace, and perhaps even lower the crime rate. Thus, some of the benefits from education, particularly elementary and secondary education, will accrue to the citizenry in general. The private market demand curve will understate the total social benefits of education. In the absence of government intervention, as shown in Exhibit 28-4, Q_1 units of education would result from market forces. But, when the external benefits MB are added to the private benefits, the social gain from additional units of education exceeds the cost until output level Q_s is produced. Social welfare could be improved if output were expanded beyond Q_1 to Q_s. But since educational consumers cannot capture these external gains, they fail to purchase units beyond Q_1. The free market output will be too small. A subsidy would be required if the ideal output level Q_s were to be achieved.

The analysis of the preceding section suggested that external costs may result in activities being undertaken even though social benefits are less than cost. The activity is carried too far. In contrast, when external benefits are present, decision-makers lack

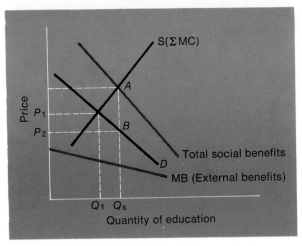

Exhibit 28-4   Adding External Benefits

The demand curve, indicating only private benefits, understates the social benefits of education. At output Q_1, the social benefit of an additional unit of education exceeds its cost. Ideally, output should be expanded to Q_s, where the social benefit of the marginal unit of education is just equal to its cost. A public subsidy of AB, per unit of education, would lead to this output level.

the incentive to carry the activity far enough. Potential gains are present, but they may go unrealized because the pricing mechanism does not make it possible for a decision-maker to appropriate or capture the gain that he bestows on others.

Should activities that generate external benefits be subsidized? Theoretically, subsidization could often result in greater social welfare. But as with the tax solution for external cost, the administrative mechanics of subsidy schemes would often be complex and costly. How does one know how large the marginal external benefits are? Would the subsidy schemes be used for political purposes in conflict with economic efficiency? Which goods should be subsidized? For example, pretty girls generate external benefits because they are pleasing to the eye. Should the government subsidize makeup kits, silicone implants, and miniskirts in order to encourage beautiful women? Should rose gardens, vaccination programs, and/or education be subsidized? If so, by how much? Administrative feasibility usually makes the neat theoretical subsidy scheme much less attractive in the real world.

The Ingenuity of the Market

When substantial potential gains are present one should not underestimate the ingenuity of market participants. Some ingenious schemes have been devised by entrepreneurs seeking to capture previously unrealized external benefits. The shopping center is, at least partially, an effort to secure benefits that result from the location of several complementary stores close together. Community housing developments make it possible to capture benefits that arise when houses are located near a country club, golf course, and/or public park. If consumers are willing to pay for these amenities, developers who provide such services will be able to capture their value in the form of higher prices on the sale of surrounding lots. Thus, market forces can sometimes devise efficient arrangements to deal with external benefits.

MARKET FAILURE: PUBLIC GOODS

Public goods compose the polar case of commodities whose consumption results in spillover benefits to secondary parties. In the original formulation by Paul Samuelson, there were two distinctive characteristics of public goods. First, the availability of a public good to one person simultaneously made it equally available to all others. Public goods must therefore be consumed jointly by all. Second, because of this joint consumption, it was impossible to exclude nonpayers from receiving public goods.[1]

Examples of pure public goods are not numerous. National defense would appear to qualify. The defense system that protects you simultaneously provides similar protection to all other citizens. Our legal and monetary systems are also public goods. The laws and individual rights that are available to one citizen are also provided for others. Similarly, the policies of the Federal Reserve are provided equally to all citizens. The quality of the atmosphere, rivers, and waterways may also be classified as a public good.

Riding Free Is Good for You, but Not for Society

Since nonpaying consumers cannot be excluded (at least not at a reasonable cost), the market mechanism will fail to provide a sufficient amount of public goods. If public goods were provided via the market, each of us would have an incentive to become a **free rider,** one who receives the benefits of a good, even though he fails to contribute to its cost. Why contribute to the cost of supplying a public good? Your actions are going to have a negligible impact on the supply of clean air, pure water, national defense, and legal justice. The sensible path will lead you to do nothing. As long as you travel that path alone you ride along free and easy. But when everyone else joins you, the total lack of action will lead to an insufficient amount of public goods.

Suppose that national defense were provided entirely through the market. Would you voluntarily help pay for it? Your contribution would have negligible impact on the total supply of defense available to each of us, even if you made a *large personal* contribution. Many citizens, even though they might value defense highly, would become free riders and few funds would be available to finance the necessary supply. If the military–industrial complex were dependent on market forces, it would be small indeed!

When producers are unable to restrict consumption of the good to paying customers only, self-interest dictates that consumers understate their true preferences. They will not buy a good which is available to them without cost. Since public goods and near public goods must be consumed jointly by several persons, the harmony between private and social interest breaks down.

Perhaps another hypothetical example will serve to clarify this important point. Suppose that you invented an air-purifying machine that would simply draw in dirty

---

[1]Note that public and private goods are determined by the characteristics of the good. For private goods, the consumption benefits of the good are derived entirely by the individual consumer. The benefits are private. In contrast, the consumption of a public good by a single party makes the benefits of the good equally available to others. Whether or not the good is produced in the public or private sector of the economy is *not* the determining factor of how the good is classified.

Exhibit 28-5   Everybody Rides Free—And Loses

Personal ranking of alternative plans for the purchase of the air-purifying machine (a public good)	Potential personal alternative
Option 1	Others pay the purchasing price of the machine. I contribute nothing and have fresh air. I'm a free rider.
Option 2	Jointly the community purchases the machine. I pay my share.
Option 3	Because others fail to pay their share, the community fails to purchase the machine. I also fail to contribute.
Option 4	Because others fail to contribute, the community has insufficient funds to purchase the machine. I pay my share and still have dirty air.

air, remove the gases and dirt, and pump the clean air back into the atmosphere. One of these machines could purify the air within a 3 mile radius. Ten or fifteen of the machines, strategically placed, could purify the air of a large city such as New York or Chicago. How could you market these machines? Assuming no government action, you would have a difficult time privately marketing even such a marvelous invention because each individual would prefer to be a free rider.

Exhibit 28-5 presents a *personal* payoff matrix from the machine for a typical individual—Mr. Smith. Personally, the best outcome for Smith is option 1. Others pay the price of the air purifying machine, and Smith contributes nothing. He obtains the benefits, but does not have to pay for them. Since others cannot provide fresh air for themselves without *equally* providing it for Smith, they have no way of assuring that Smith will voluntarily help pay for the machine if he benefits. Smith has a strong incentive to become a free rider. However when everyone, or almost everyone, tries to ride free, the community will fail to purchase the machine because of insufficient funds. Option 3 will result.

While option 1 is not an alternative available to *all* persons of the community, 2 is. If others have preferences like Smith, they would prefer 2 over 3. Government action that taxed persons and provided the machine would be preferred. But when government action is absent, and each person follows his own personal interest, the community ends up with option 3, a less preferred situation than option 2.

Near Public Goods

While few commodities are pure public goods, a much larger set of goods are jointly consumed even though it is feasible to exclude nonpaying customers. For example, such goods as radio and television broadcasts, national parks, interstate highways, movies, and football games are jointly consumed. Assuming that there is not a congestion problem, additional consumption of these "near public goods," *once they are produced*, would be costless to society.

OUTSTANDING ECONOMIST: Allen Kneese

Currently a professor of economics at the University of New Mexico, Kneese is one of the leading authorities on environmental economics and pollution control. He is the author (or co-author) of numerous articles and nearly a dozen books in this area. His latest book, *Pollution, Prices, and Public Policy* (with Charles Schultze),[2] provides a detailed analysis of alternative pollution control strategies.

Kneese received his doctoral degree from Indiana University in 1956. He has spent much of his professional career with Resources for the Future, a Washington-based research and consulting firm. He was the director of their Quality of the Environment Program from 1967 until 1974.

Kneese has applied the theory of external cost and public goods to a wide range of environmental problems. In the policy area, in general, he tends to favor an emission charge (or tax) control strategy over more direct regulation such as uniform standards.

Kneese recognizes that formulating an efficient control strategy is not an easy task. Control of auto exhaust, a major source of pollution in many urban areas, presents several special problems. The current approach forces automobile manufacturers to meet certain uniform emission standards on all *new cars* produced. This strategy is highly inefficient for two reasons. First, it forces automobile consumers in sparsely populated areas to pay for the emission control systems on new cars even though pollution is often not a problem in these areas. Second, the uniform standards approach fails to provide individuals with a personal incentive to keep the control devices operational and their automobiles well tuned in order to reduce exhaust emissions.

In his widely used introductory level book, *The Economics of Environmental Policy* (co-authored with Myrick Freeman and Robert Haveman),[3] Kneese suggested that we control auto emissions with the use of a "smog tax" rather than national uniform standards. Under the smog tax plan, automobiles would be checked periodically and rated according to their emission level. The smog tax would then be levied, *according to the emissions rating of the vehicle*, when gasoline was purchased. High polluters would pay a higher tax than automobiles with a lower emission level.

The smog tax approach would permit regional variation so that drivers in areas in which pollution is not a problem would not be forced to pay for something that yields little benefit. Unlike the current system, the tax approach would give individuals a personal incentive to adopt effective pollution control devices (on both new and used cars), keep them in good working order, and keep the motor in tune. If policy planners are interested in adopting effective, efficient control strategies, they would do well to listen to the ingenious ideas of Professor Kneese and other economists who understand the necessity of bringing private and social interests into harmony.

---

[2] Allen V. Kneese and Charles L. Schultze, *Pollution, Prices, and Public Policy*. Washington, D.C.: The Brookings Institution, 1975.

[3] A. Myrick Freeman, III, Robert Haveman, and Allen V. Kneese, *The Economics of Environmental Policy*. New York: Wiley, 1973.

Should nonpaying customers be excluded when the marginal cost of providing the good to them is zero? Many economists argue that near public goods such as highways, national parks, and television programming should be provided freely to consumers, at the expense of the taxpayer. Why exclude people from the consumption of these near public goods when their use fails to add to the cost? The argument has a certain appeal.

But one needs to be careful. Television programs, highways, parks, and other public goods are scarce. Consumption of other products must be foregone in order to produce such goods. It is usually impossible to charge some customers while simultaneously making the good available free to others. However, if a zero price is charged, how does one determine if consumers really value additional units enough to cover their opportunity cost? How can an intense minority communicate its views as to what types of near public goods should be produced? Taxes will be necessary in order to cover the costs of making near public goods freely available. Will such taxing devices lead to inefficiency? All of these questions reduce the attractiveness of public sector provisions of jointly consumed commodities when exclusion is possible.

MARKET FAILURE: POOR INFORMATION

In the real world, market choices, like other decisions, are made with imperfect information. Consumers will not have perfect knowledge about the quality of a product, the price of alternative products, or side effects that may result. They may make incorrect decisions, decisions that they will later regret, because they do not possess good information.

The reality of imperfect information is, of course, not the fault of the market. As a matter of fact, the market provides the consumer with a strong incentive to acquire information that will help him make satisfying long-run decisions. Consumers have to bear the consequences of their mistakes, so they certainly will seek to avoid the deliberate purchase of "lemon" products.

Getting Your Money's Worth

The consumer's information problem is minimal if the item is purchased regularly. Consider the problem of purchasing a brand of soap. There is little cost associated with trying out brands. Since soap is a product that is regularly purchased, trial and error is an economical method for a consumer to determine the brand that is most suitable to his personal needs. It is a **repeat purchase item.** The consumer can use his past experience to good advantage when buying repeat purchase items such as soap, toothpaste, most food products, lawn service, and gasoline.

What incentive does the producer have to supply accurate information, helping the customer to make a satisfying long-run choice? Is there a conflict between consumer and producer interest? The answers to these questions are critically affected by the seller's dependence on return customers. If there is a strong adverse effect on a businessman's *future* sales when many of his *current* customers feel they have been "gypped," he will attempt to provide information that will help his customers make correct choices. One hears few customer complaints about the quality of products or services offered by local grocery stores, clothing stores, banks, community restaurants, and national magazines. The future success of businessmen who sell such repeat purchase products is sorely dependent on the future purchases of satisfied customers. There is a harmony of interest, as both the buyer and seller will be better off if the customer is satisfied with the product that he purchases.

Let the Customer Beware

Major problems of conflicting interest, inadequate information, and unhappy customers arise when goods are either:

(a) difficult to evaluate on inspection and seldom repeatedly purchased from the same producer, or

(b) potentially capable of serious and lasting harmful side effects that cannot be detected by a layman.

Human nature being what it is, under these conditions we would expect some unscrupulous producers to sell low quality, defective, and even harmful goods.

Since customers typically are unable to tell the difference between high quality and low quality goods under these conditions, their ability to police quality and price is weakened. The businessman has a strong incentive to cut costs by reducing quality. The consumer gets less for his dollar and, since the seller is not dependent on repeat customers, he may survive and even prosper in the marketplace. These two conditions, because they increase the probability of customer dissatisfaction stemming from poor information and unexpected defective quality, serve to weaken the case for the unhampered market mechanism. Consider the consumer's information problem when he purchases a used car. Most consumers are incapable of determining the operational condition of a car with any degree of certainty. One can judge how it looks and perhaps how it sounds, but most of us are relatively ignorant about the mechanical operation of cars. Since such an item is not purchased very often, past experiences with dealers or brands of automobiles will be of limited assistance. The probability of making an incorrect decision is high.

The consequences of an incorrect decision in some cases can be drastic. Sometimes the information available may be difficult to understand and evaluate without the benefit of special training. The utilization of various types of drugs is a good example. Consumers prefer "safer" drugs, and presumably they would be willing to pay higher prices for such drugs. But the informational problem is precisely the identification of those drugs that are safe. Trial and error does not offer a reasonable alternative when the side effects may be (a) severe, (b) irreversible, and (c) identifiable only in the future. The cost of making an incorrect decision is too high.

One should keep in mind that merely because an individual does not have all the information he would like, it does not necessarily follow that a better (less costly) alternative exists. Information is scarce and therefore costly. Arrangements that would supply better information may not be desirable because of their cost. However, there are definite benefits obtained from improving the information available to consumers. In general, most economists support legislation requiring accurate labeling and requirements to make certain information public (for example, statements indicating the annual interest rate for credit purchases or the listing of ingredients contained). Such information adds very little to the costs of production, while providing useful knowledge to the consumer.

However, public sector action in this area, as in others, has the potential for abuse. For example, regulatory action that keeps potentially dangerous drugs off the market may also limit the availability of other valuable, even lifesaving, products. Some economists feel that regulation agencies are sure to be too cautious in limiting the marketing of products. Dwight Lee and Robert McNown argue that the Federal Drug Administration has followed this course:

> This regulatory agency (FDA) is not protecting the consumer or the industry that it regulates; it is protecting itself. The FDA knows that if it lets one drug out that deforms or kills, the public, the press, and a whole host of congressmen will be on their back. But the FDA also knows that it can tie a lifesaving drug up for years in bureaucratic red tape and get little or no adverse reaction. The blame for those that die and suffer needlessly will not be placed on the FDA.[4]

☐ LOOKING AHEAD

In this chapter we focused on the failures of the market. Chapter 29 utilizes economic analysis to help us better understand the workings of the public sector. Finally, in Chapter 30 we will discuss some of the expected shortcomings of public sector action. Awareness of both the strengths and weaknesses of alternative forms of economic organization will help each of us make more intelligent choices in this important area.

Perspectives in Economics

An Emissions Charge Strategy to Control Pollution

> If you do not succeed in connecting the notion of right with that of personal interest, which is the only immutable point in the human heart, what means will you have of governing the world except by fear? [Alexis de Toqueville, 1835]

As the scene opens, a student announcer is interviewing Professor Marr Ketter on the nightly question-and-answer show for the campus television station.

STUDENT: Professor Ketter, you are well-known for your views favoring market allocation of resources. Yet you recommend that government put an artificial price on pollution emissions. Why do you advocate this particular interference with market behavior?

PROFESSOR KETTER: The market for a private good such as ice cream cones works well because there is a harmony between private property rights and social interests. Ice cream producers must pay for the resources that they use, and they can easily withhold their product from nonpaying customers. They will get ahead (that is, make

---

[4]D. R. Lee and R. F. McNown, *Economics in Our Time: Concepts and Issues*, p. 82. © 1975, Science Research Associates, Inc., Chicago. Reprinted by permission of the publisher.

economic profit) only if they use resources efficiently and produce what consumers want.

In contrast, when *common* property rights exist for a scarce resource, the resource will invariably be overutilized. This is not a recent discovery. Centuries ago the pastures of the English Commons were commonly owned. Grazing was a public good. Under these circumstances, each cattle owner permitted his stock to graze the pasture intensively today, because even though his conservation practices would improve tomorrow's pasture grass, *he* could capture only a small share of such benefits. But when all followed this practice, overgrazing caused declining growth of the pastures. These consequences eventually led to the enclosure movement.

The same principle is operational today with regard to our commonly owned atmosphere and waterways. Individuals must pay the full cost of pollution control, while the benefits of improved air quality accrue to everyone. Since the conservation practices of *any one individual* will exert a negligible impact upon air quality, the personal incentive to control is lacking. When each of us follow our personal interests, air and water resources are overused, just as the commonly owned pastures were overgrazed.

The problem is one of bringing private (and corporate) interests into harmony with social interests. In economic terms, this means that resource prices should reflect opportunity cost. A system of emission charges would accomplish this task.

STUDENT: It does seem unreasonable that something as valuable as air should be treated as "free." But how would you decide on the right price?

PROFESSOR KETTER: Finding the social cost of pollution from various sources, so that emission charges can be set properly is, of course, the difficult part of this control strategy. The fact of the matter is, if establishing the damages from pollution were easy, we would not have a serious pollution problem. Individuals have long been permitted to collect for damages imposed by others. In the case of pollution, the crucial problem has been to prove the source and size of the damage. If I accidentally bend the fender of my neighbor's car, it is easy for him to collect the proper damages. In contrast, if I damage his lungs or his house with air pollution, it is typically impossible for him to collect, because it is exceedingly difficult for him to establish in court that he sustained damages which were attributable to my actions.

There are many ways to approach the problem of determining the social cost of pollution from particular sources. However, there is no easy, cheap, and fully effective approach. All lead to *estimates* of true damages. Some costs may be synthesized through materials damage studies. Estimates can be made by questioning the people involved. A more promising way is to estimate costs indirectly, by determining differences in what people will pay to locate their businesses or residences in a less polluted area. This requires that the other important determinants of property values be accounted for. A major advantage of the latter method is that people will have expressed their willingness to trade off cleaner air for dollars (representing other goods and services) in a setting where expressing other than their true feelings is costly to them. Also, the researcher need not ferret out all the types of damage sustained, or the reasoning used by the people involved. It is enough to know the resulting price differentials, so long as factors other than pollution can be accounted for.[5]

[5] The various methods of estimating pollution costs are discussed with actual examples, in R. Ridker, *Economic Costs of Air Pollution* (New York: Praeger, 1967). An application of the property value methodology, used to calculate emission charges, is given in E. B. Asmus and R. Stroup, "Air Pollution Control Economics: The Case of a Montana Smelter's SO$_2$ Emissions," (Montana Agricultural Experiment Station, Res. Rep. No. 24, 1972).

STUDENT: That still seems like a very difficult job. Aren't other control strategies simpler?

PROFESSOR KETTER: That is true. However, *any* rational strategy depends heavily on the control authority's knowledge of how highly people value alternative levels of air quality. To assign an authority the task and power to use our (society's) resources to clean up our air, without telling them how much cleaner air is worth to us would be absurd. It would be like giving a signed blank check to a stranger and telling him to purchase some groceries for you. Without knowing about how much you are willing to give up to get various kinds and qualities of goods, he could not possibly be expected to do a decent job of allocating your money (resources). In a similar fashion, a control authority, trying to use society's resources to buy cleaner air, must make some estimate of what the public is willing to give up to get less pollution of various kinds, at various times, in various locations.

STUDENT: Today, people are concerned with equity, not just efficiency. As a practical matter, theory aside, can emissions charges be fair and equitable, not favoring the special interests who are big polluters?

PROFESSOR KETTER: One big advantage of the emissions charge strategy is that major elements of the decision can be made centrally, in a situation where all sides of the question can most easily be heard. Even though the emission charge can be tailored to each emission source, the impact of various dosage levels of pollution on individuals can be estimated nationally. Then for an actual or proposed pollution source, atmospheric scientists can estimate the frequency and location of the various dosages just as they do now. This information, combined with site-specific data on the location of people (and valuable resources that might be damaged by pollution), can yield an estimate of total damage from a pollution source. An important result of this procedure is that the best expertise nationally can be brought to bear in an efficient manner, without having to consider the individual problems at each pollution source, as must be the case if emission regulations are to be set. Control costs can be ignored because it is left to polluters to decide the optimal amount of control. Weather conditions and wind patterns may be handled separately, and usually are much less controversial.

Policies could also be set nationally for "special situations" such as wilderness areas affected by pollution. There is a large arbitrary element, nearly inescapable at this point, in any such policy since we currently have no good way of assessing the value of even precisely known degradations of wilderness. The same would hold for locations with unique scenic attractions. Nevertheless, decisions must be made on just what we are willing to give up to retain or regain these valuable items. Once this is done, and the physical relationships are established, these elements of the emissions charge can be calculated. Prior to this being done, no rational decisions can be made with any strategy.

In short, the emissions charge strategy is implemented by forcing polluters to pay the estimated social damages due to their emissions. Polluters are forced to stop treating air (or waterways) as a public good. Lower emission levels would mean lower charges to be paid. The revenue produced in this way would be available for distribution to, or used on behalf of those affected by actual emissions. The full social costs for goods and services would be borne by those who gain from producing and using the goods and services. We should expect, among other things, a change in consumption and production patterns, away from newly expensive pollution intensive goods from which the implicit subsidy of unpriced resources use has been removed. Also, new and cheaper means to control pollution, along with less-polluting production technologies will most likely be sought and eagerly adopted. With the emissions charge strategy in use, the greed of producers and consumers dictates these changes, regardless of how little or how much "public spirited" the individuals might be.

In a word, the emissions charge strategy is *practical.*

STUDENT: You say that this method would be practical. But going back to the problem of information—doesn't this strategy require impossibly large amounts of data on damages, compared to other methods?

PROFESSOR KETTER: This alleged weakness is perhaps the greatest strength of the emissions charge strategy. No other strategy can be effective with less information. Only the cost-of-pollution side of the cost–benefit analysis usually is required to set proper charges. The control authority need not know the control alternatives available, or their costs, to do a good job. No rational strategy could be instituted with less information. Other methods, such as direct regulation of emissions, would require authorities to gather information on both control costs *and* damages, since the tradeoff decisions between damage costs and control costs are made by the authority itself.

STUDENT: But wouldn't this strategy allow pollution to exceed currently established air standards?

PROFESSOR KETTER: If applied in its pure form, this strategy would result in more pollution where control costs are so high that estimated benefits of control are not worth it (and polluters would compensate society on that basis); it would result in *less* pollution when control is cheap enough that extra control could be exercised at a cost that is *less* than the value of reduced damages. However, if current standards are judged to be correctly set, then the same information needed to set them (damage costs *and* control costs) are more than enough to allow the authority to set emission charges just high enough to attain "standard" pollution levels. The advantage of using charges is that in treating all polluters alike—charging them the same amount per unit of damage—each polluter is free to control in his own way, to his own extent, so that the standard is met at a minimum cost. Some high-cost-of-control polluters will control less (and pay the authority more) while those who can find cheap control methods will control more (and pay the authority less).

STUDENT: What about complexity of administration? Isn't that a real problem here?

PROFESSOR KETTER: In general this strategy is quite simple to administer. The administrators have less discretion than they would in alternative strategies. The direct regulation of emissions, now used extensively, really comes down to an endless series of negotiations between control authorities and polluters on the target level of environmental quality, the allocation of emissions between sources, acceptable means of control, the granting of variances, and the proper treatment of violators. Typically the diffused interests of the general public are poorly represented in these negotiations, most of which occur out of the public's eye. In contrast, the producer and consumer interests that benefit from "free air" subsidies are well represented.

STUDENT: This all sounds pretty reasonable, except that it still looks to me like emission charges would not eliminate pollution. Some polluters could still pay to pollute, if control is expensive for them.

PROFESSOR KETTER: Those who advocate that we eliminate all pollution fail to understand the idea of economic efficiency. If the personal gains to the individuals of a society from *some* pollution exceed the cost of the pollution, it is not worth it to eliminate that pollution. An emission charge system would improve our air and water quality. Substantial improvement could be made at a reasonably modest cost. But at some point, it will become extremely costly to make additional improvement. By way of analogy, cleaning up the environment is like squeezing water from a wet towel. Initially, a lot of water can be squeezed from the towel with very little effort. But as more and more of the water has already been squeezed out, it becomes increasingly difficult to squeeze out still more units of water. So it is with the environment. At some point, the benefits of a clearer environment will simply be less that their cost.

STUDENT: Touché, Professor. We are out of time. Thank you for sharing your ideas with us tonight.

Exit student, with relieved expression.

Exit Professor, absentmindedly leaving his pipe, for which he returns.

CHAPTER LEARNING OBJECTIVES

1. When externalities are present the market may fail to confront decision-makers with the proper incentives. Since decision-makers are not forced to consider external cost, they may find it personally advantageous to undertake an economic activity even though it generates a net loss to the community. In contrast, when external benefits are present, decision-makers may fail to undertake economic action that would generate a social gain.

2. Prohibition of activities that result in external cost is not an ideal solution, as it would often eliminate activities for which the gains are substantially in excess of the costs imposed on secondary parties.

3. When external costs result from the activities of a business firm, the firm's costs will understate the social cost of producing goods. Under competition, too much of such goods will be produced. Theoretically, a corrective excise tax could be applied, inducing firms to charge higher prices and produce a smaller output. In reality, administrative complexities reduce the attractiveness of this approach.

4. When external benefits are present, the market demand curve will understate the social gains from conducting the activity. Consumption and production of goods that generate external benefits will tend to be less than the socially ideal amount.

5. When it is costly or impossible to withhold a public good from persons who will not help pay for it, the market system breaks down because everyone has an incentive to become a free rider. But when everyone attempts to ride free, units of the good will not get produced even though the social evaluation of such goods might far exceed their cost.

6. If persons can be excluded from the benefit of a near public good at a low cost, the market mechanism can be used to allocate the good. But some consumers, who positively evaluate the good, will be excluded by the pricing mechanism, even though it would cost nothing to allow them to consume it, *once the good has been produced.*

7. The market provides an incentive for consumers to acquire information. When a business is dependent on repeat customers, it has a strong incentive to promote customer satisfaction. But when goods are either **(a)** difficult to evaluate on inspection and seldom purchased repeatedly from the same producer or **(b)** have potentially serious and lasting harmful effects, consumer trial and error becomes an unsatisfactory means of determining quality. The interests of the consumer and producer are in conflict.

8. Externalities, public goods, conflicting buyer–seller interests for the provision of information, and monopoly all result in market failure. These market deficiencies create an opportunity for public sector action to promote economic efficiency. Of course, alternative forms of economic organization, including public sector action, may also be defective.

IMPORTANT TERMS TO REMEMBER

External costs: An action of an individual or group that harms the welfare of nonconsenting secondary parties. Litterbugs, drunken drivers, and polluters provide examples.

External benefits: Group or individual action that favorably influences the welfare of nonpaying secondary parties.

Social costs: The sum of (a) the private or personal costs that are incurred by a decision-maker and (b) any external costs of the action that are imposed on nonconsenting secondary parties. If there are no external costs, private and social costs will be equal.

Common property: Property that can be used by all citizens as intensively as they desire. No one has the right to exclude another from using such property.

Free rider: One who receives the benefit of a good without contributing toward its costs. Public goods and commodities that generate external benefits present persons with the opportunity of becoming free riders.

Repeat purchase item: An item purchased often by the same buyer.

THE ECONOMIC WAY OF THINKING—DISCUSSION QUESTIONS

1. Explain why external cost may be a cause of economic inefficiency? Why is it important to define property rights clearly? Explain.

2. Devise a tax plan that would **(a)** reduce the extent of automobile pollution, **(b)** provide an incentive for entrepreneurs to develop new products that would limit pollution, and **(c)** permit continued auto travel for those willing to bear the total social costs. Explain how your plan will influence incentives and why it will work.

3. "When goods generate external benefits the market is unable to produce an adequate supply. This is why the government must provide such goods as police and fire protection, education, parks, and shots against communicable diseases."

(a) Do you agree? Explain.

(b) Does governmental provision necessarily assure "an adequate supply"?

(c) Goods such as golf courses, shopping centers, country clubs, neckties, and charity also generate some spillover external benefits. Do you think the government should provide these goods in order to assure "an adequate supply"?

4. Religious influence reduces crime, lessening the demand for police protection. Churches often perform various charitable functions. Do you think churches should be subsidized? Why or why not? Do you think more funds would be allocated for religious purposes if churches were subsidized? Do you think more funds would be allocated to charitable purposes—helping the poor, neglected, unfortunate, and unlucky—if charity were subsidized? Why or why not?

5. Which of the following list of goods are most likely to generate a lot of customers who are later unhappy with the products: **(a)** light bulbs, **(b)** food at a local restaurant, **(c)** food at a restaurant along an interstate highway, **(d)** auto repair service, **(e)** a used car, **(f)** plumbing services, **(g)** a used automatic dishwasher, **(h)** a used sofa, **(i)** television repair service? Explain your answer.

6. What are public goods? Why does a decentralized pricing system have trouble producing an adequate amount of public goods?

7. What's Wrong with This Way of Thinking?

"Corporations are the major beneficiaries of our lax pollution control policy. Their costs are reduced because we permit them to freely use a valuable resource—clean water and air—in order to produce goods. These lower costs are simply added to the profits of the polluting firms."

29

PUBLIC CHOICE AND GAINING FROM GOVERNMENT

What can an economist say about how the public sector allocates goods and resources? Traditionally, economists have been content to focus on how the market works and what ideal public policy could do to improve economic efficiency. The actual operation of the public sector was virtually ignored. However, this neglect has become less and less satisfactory. Each day millions of economic decisions are made in the public sector. Approximately one-third of our national income is channeled through the various government units. In addition, the legal framework establishes the "rules of the game" for the market sector. The government's role in defining property rights, enforcing contracts, fixing prices, and regulating business and labor practices has a tremendous impact on the operation of an economy.

This chapter and the following one analyze how the political process handles various classes of economic issues. When studying collective decision-making, we seek to better understand the link between individual preferences and political outcomes. The political process is simply an alternative method of making economic decisions. Like the market, it is likely to have defects. Thus, when evaluating the cost and benefits of allocating a specific activity via a voting mechanism, one must compare the likelihood of achieving efficiency through collective action with the expected outcome from market allocation.

Most political decisions in Western countries are made legislatively. Thus, we will focus on a system where voters choose legislators, who in turn institute public policy. Let us see what the tools of economics reveal about the political process.

VOTERS AND THE DEMAND FOR POLITICAL ACTION

How does a voter indicate his demand for political goods? In a legislative system, he must work through a representative. The impact of the voter on the quantity and price of political goods is indirectly felt through his influence on the composition of governmental decision-makers.

How does the voter decide whom to support? Many factors will undoubtedly influence his decision. The personal characteristics of a candidate will be important. Is the candidate self-confident and handsome? Does he or she appear to be honest? Does he or she present a good television image? All these factors and others are likely to exert an influence on whether a voter will support a candidate.

In addition to the candidate's personal characteristics, his views on various issues will also be an important determinant of voter support. When a voter agrees with a candidate on a specific issue, the candidate's views yield him utility (benefits); if he disagrees, the candidate's position imposes costs on him. The magnitude of these benefits and costs will be directly related to the importance of the issue to the specific voter.

Supporting the Candidate That Is Best for Me

According to economic theory, other things constant, each voter will support the candidate that offers him the greatest expected net subjective benefits. Factors other than one's expected direct economic gain will influence the voter's expected benefits, but personal gain will certainly be an important component. The greater the perceived net personal economic gain from a candidate's platform, the more likely that the individual voter will favor the candidate. The greater the perceived net economic cost imposed on a voter by a candidate's positions, the less inclined the voter will be to favor the candidate.

Thus, economics implies that dairy farmers are more likely to prefer candidates that support high prices for dairy products. Support of oil depletion allowance makes a candidate more attractive to oilmen. Increased welfare benefits will be inclined to make one more preferable to welfare recipients. And, of course, support of higher teachers' salaries and expanded research funds adds to a politician's score with college professors and other educators.

While each of us may have a streak of altruism and concern for the public interest, the opportunity for personal gain influences our evaluation of both political and market alternatives. The greater the expected personal gain, the more likely it is that personal interests will dominate. Of course, it is also likely that one's view of the "public interest" may be conveniently altered to be consistent with one's opportunities for private gain.

The Rational Ignorance Effect and the Choices of John Doe, Voter

When decisions are made collectively, the direct link between the choice of an individual and the outcome of the issue is broken. The choice of a single voter is seldom decisive when the size of the group is large. Recognizing that the outcome will typically be the same, regardless of their position, individual voters have little incentive to seek out information that will help them cast a more intelligent vote. Typically, they will rely on information that is freely supplied to them by others (candidates, political parties, news media, friends, and interest groups). As we pointed out earlier, economists refer the voters' lack of incentive to acquire information as the "rational igno-rance effect."[1]

The low probability that one's vote will make any difference also explains why many citizens fail to vote. In the 1974 congressional elections only slightly more than one-third of the eligible populace took the time to register and vote. Voter turnouts for minor elections are often even lower. These findings should not surprise us, as they are precisely what we would expect because the *personal* payoffs from voting are low.[2]

How does the rational ignorance effect influence the decision-making of voters? Lacking incentive to acquire information, the typical voter will consider only a subset of issues about which he feels strongest. The views of alternative candidates on these issues of "vital personal importance" will influence the voter's decision. But there will be another entire set of issues that will simply be ignored by most voters. For example, the views of political entrepreneurs on such things as Japanese fishing rights, appoint-ments to the ICC, allocation of licenses to operate television stations, and thousands of similar issues will be inconsequential to most citizens. Typically, they will fail to influence the choices of most voters.

Thus, in the final analysis, most voters will be rationally uninformed on many —probably most—issues. Therefore, each voter will evaluate political suppliers on the basis of a small subset of issues that he perceives to be of substantial personal impor-tance.

SUPPLY, PROFITS, AND THE POLITICAL ENTREPRENEUR

The market entrepreneur is a dynamic force in the private sector. The entrepreneur seeks gain by undertaking projects where the potential for profit is present. Within the framework of the competitive market process, entrepreneurs seeking profit will move to produce commodities that are intensely desired relative to their supply.

Similarly, the **political entrepreneur** (politician) is a dynamic force behind collective decision-making. The political entrepreneur will seek to offer voters a bundle of political goods that will enhance his likelihood of winning elections. While altruistic motives may influence his actions, it is clear that personal gain will also be a factor. He may seek to use the political mechanism as a vehicle to attain private power, fame, and even fortune. After all, a lot of people who spend their entire lives in public service end up with a net worth of several hundred thousand—or even a million—dollars.

The political entrepreneur, in a manner similar to the market entrepreneur, is characterized by an alertness for political goods that are intensely desired in relation-ship to their current supply. The excess demand for a political alternative creates a

---

[1]The rational ignorance effect applies to private group decision-making as well. For example, as we previously discussed, a small shareholder of a large corporation has little incentive to track down the information necessary to determine the extent that corporate managers are acting in his interest. Like the rationally ignorant political voter, the individual shareholder recognizes that his choices will exert little influence on the shape of events at annual stockholder meetings.

[2]Since the probability that a single vote will be decisive is almost zero, one may wonder why even a third to a half of our citizens vote. The puzzle is probably explained by the fact that many citizens—maybe even most—receive personal utility from the act of voting.

profit potential for the political entrepreneur. By moving to supply (or offer to supply) the good, the political entrepreneur can gain votes.

Support for additional political goods that are currently in excess demand by his constituents will enhance the victory prospects of the political entrepreneur. At the same time, support of political alternatives that are already in excess supply would diminish the entrepreneur's chances of winning. The successful political entrepreneur, like his market counterpart, will be responsive to the views of his constituents.

Because persons differ in their tastes, economic interests, income, and other similar variables, voters will seldom agree on the ideal consumption level and allocation of costs for politically provided goods. Unanimity is not a characteristic of the political process. When satisfying the demand of one group of constituents, a political entrepreneur simultaneously will be acting against the wishes of another group. His actions will yield subjective benefits to those who favor his position, but will impose subjective costs on those who are opposed.

A politician cannot satisfy both those for and against a given position. He must choose. The problem of the would-be legislator is to establish a working majority (or plurality) that believes he can obtain more political goods for them than any of the alternative candidates.

This does not mean that a utility-maximizing politician will always favor the viewpoint of the majority of his constitutents on a specific issue. In some cases a candidate may gain more votes among an intense minority of persons who favor his position than he will lose among a dispassionate majority that is opposed to his views.

MONEY, POLITICAL ADVERTISING, AND THE SUCCESSFUL POLITICIAN

Votes win elections. But the rational uninformed voters must be convinced to "want" a candidate. What is required to win the support of voters? One's position on issues, as we have stressed, is important. But candidates must draw their strengths to the attention of voters. Money, manpower, and expertise will be required to promote the candidate among the voting populace.

Professor Galbraith and others have stressed the role of product advertising and the mass media in affecting consumer preferences. Since voters have little incentive to acquire information, the "problem" of media control over the political consumer will be even more acute than for market decisions. The image of a political entrepreneur will be primarily determined by his ability to acquire the resources necessary to utilize mass media promotional devices to promote his positive attributes. Candidates without the financial resources to provide television and other media advertising free to rationally ignorant voters are seriously handicapped.[3] Similarly, candidates who are unacceptable to the major communications media face a serious disadvantage.

These factors highlight the importance of a free press—representing a diversity of views—if the political process is to work. When the media is slanted, giving favorable coverage to those with whom it is in agreement and showing opponents in an unfavor-

---

[3]Political expenditures on advertising and other persuasion techniques indicate that candidates are fully aware of their importance. The average contested candidate for the U.S. Senate or House of Representatives expends between 70 and 80 percent of his campaign resources in this area.

The Small Society, © Washington Star Syndicate, Inc.

able light, issues will not be fairly debated. Voters, having little incentive to inform themselves, will tend to be led by the opinion-makers. Under such circumstances the brand of political candidate bought by consumers will tend to reflect the opinions of the media.

Being Right and Losing

What does our analysis suggest about the motivation of political decision-makers? Are we suggesting that they are highly selfish, that they consider only their own pocket-books, while ignoring the public interest? The answer is no. Man, when he acts in the political sphere, may genuinely want to help his fellow citizens. Factors other than personal political gain, narrowly defined, will influence the actions of many political suppliers. On certain issues, one may feel strongly that one's position is best for the country, even though it may not currently be popular. The national interest as perceived by the political supplier may conflict with the position that would be most favorable to his re-election prospects. Some politicians may opt for the national interest, even when it means political defeat. None of this is inconsistent with an economic view of political choosing.

Being Successful Means Being Political

However, the existence of political suicide does not change the fact that most prefer political life. There is a strong incentive for political suppliers to stake out positions that will enhance their vote total in the next election. A politician who refuses to give primary consideration to electoral gain, increases his risk of replacement by a more astute (and less public minded) political entrepreneur who will. Competition—the competition of vote-maximizing political candidates—presents even the most public-spirited politician with a strong incentive to base his decisions primarily on political considerations. Just as neglect of economic profit is the route to market oblivion, neglect of potential votes is the route to political oblivion.

THE OPPORTUNITY COST OF GOVERNMENT

Public sector allocation means foregoing or limiting market activity either directly through regulation or indirectly through taxation of private activity. The reduction in the level of private sector output associated with a public sector action comprises the opportunity cost of the activity. Using economic efficiency as our allocative criterion, this cost should be compared with the benefits of the public sector action. When the benefits of the public sector activity exceed their opportunity cost, the *potential* for gain is present.

Other things constant, the greater the net benefits derived from public sector action, the greater is the incentive to organize the activity collectively. In contrast, when the costs of public sector action are large relative to the benefits, the incentive for government organization is reduced accordingly.

In a sense, what we are saying is simple—we will tend to use government when there is a net advantage of doing so. But, as we have already indicated, government is merely an institution created by individuals. Thus, we will be interested in not only the social but also personal perceived costs and benefits to political participants. These personal incentives will determine the extent of government action.

What kinds of activities will voters demand and political entrepreneurs supply? Is government organization efficient? Why do democratic governments often produce national defense, but seldom produce wheat, cattle, or shoes? Let us see what economic theory has to say about these things and similar questions. Keep in mind that our focus is on what we would *expect government to do*. As we will analyze in detail in Chapter 30, this may sometimes conflict with what government *should do, using economic efficiency as a criterion*.

MARKET FAILURE AND GAINING FROM GOVERNMENT

Opportunity for personal gain is a powerful motivator. In the marketplace, the search for gain by each party leads to bilateral trade. The pursuit of gain can also motivate people to organize activities in the public sector. At the most basic level, market failure presents government with the opportunity to undertake action that would result in total benefits in excess of their total cost. Public sector action to correct market failure could ideally produce results that would make all affected parties better off. Everyone is a potential winner! Pursuit of this potential gain gives citizens an incentive to turn to government when market failure is present.

Externalities, public goods, monopoly power, and poor information are the major sources of market failure. The greater the net social losses resulting from market failure, the greater is the incentive for government action. Much government action that we take for granted stems from this source.

Public sector legislation against crime is an example. Of course, there are moral reasons why a society would want to prohibit crimes such as robbery, arson, and murder. However, let us look at this from strictly an economic viewpoint. As Exhibit 29-1 illustrates, in the absence of any laws against robbery, individuals would consider only the personal cost incurred in carrying out a robbery (for example, gun, getaway

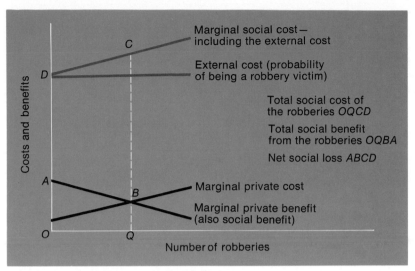

Marginal social cost — including the external cost

External cost (probability of being a robbery victim)

Total social cost of the robberies *OQCD*

Total social benefit from the robberies *OQBA*

Net social loss *ABCD*

Marginal private cost

Marginal private benefit (also social benefit)

Exhibit 29-1   Robbery as an External Cost

Consider a society with no legal restraints against robbery. Potential robbers would consider only their private benefits and costs. The external costs imposed on non-consenting secondary parties (the victims) would be ignored. A nonintervention policy would result in an enormous social loss. Large social gains would be possible from government action to penalize robbers and restrain their activities.

car, threat of retaliation by victim, etc.) relative to the personal financial gain expected from conducting the robbery. Considering only these private costs and benefits, *Q* robberies would be conducted in the absence of legal restraints. However, in addition to the robber's cost of pulling off a job, there would be an enormous cost imposed on victims and potential victims. Counting these external costs imposed on secondary parties, the total social cost of *Q* robberies (*OQCD*) would be far in excess of the social benefits (*OQBA*), including those that occur to robbers. Thus large social gains would be possible from public policy that apprehended and prosecuted robbers, reducing the incidence of this crime.

The lawless town of the Old West makes great television but not many of us would want to live in such a society. In the absence of legal restraints and public policy to reduce such crimes as robbery, the lives and property of citizens would be in constant danger. There would be little incentive to own anything that one could not protect. Chaos would reign.

Almost all individuals, even many of those who occasionally commit crimes, would gain from government action that would make it much more costly for a person to commit such crimes as murder, robbery, kidnapping, rape, arson, and assault. These activities impose such a high external cost on nonconsenting secondary parties that most citizens of the community are quite willing to incur substantial cost in order to obtain the benefits of government action in this area. Government action can lead to personal gain for the citizens of the community.

Exhibit 29-2 presents a hypothetical schedule of voter payoffs from government action against crimes of property and person. Each citizen (in reality perhaps there

Exhibit 29-2   Crime Prevention—Gaining from Government

The table illustrates a hypothetical schedule of personal benefits and costs that are derived from a government legal, judicial, and law enforcement system designed to reduce criminal activity. Typically, we would expect that everybody or almost everybody (including most criminals) would benefit by government action in this area. Taken all together the benefit/cost ratio would be quite high.

Voters	Perceived benefit from government action	Personal tax cost	Net favorable impact
1	$2000	$10	$1990
2	2000	10	1990
3	1500	10	1490
4	1500	10	1490
⋮	⋮	⋮	⋮
999	25	10	15
1000	15	10	5

might be a few who would favor lawlessness) perceives far greater benefits than cost, *in total*, from the government's legal and crime-preventive actions. Few would want to leave crime prevention entirely to the market.

What position would a smart political entrepreneur take on this issue? Obviously, he is going to favor *some* government action in this area. Most voters favor some action, and total social benefits are far in excess of their costs. Thus, it would make no sense at all for a politician to argue that the government should get out of the law enforcement area. It would be political disaster to do so. Given the enormous advantage of public sector action, in terms of voter benefits relative to costs, candidates interested in votes and political contributions will favor a legal, judicial, enforcement, and penal system.

Politicians, from time to time, might debate the merits of terminating government farm price supports, various antipoverty programs, or the minimum wage. But when did you last hear a politician advocate leaving crime prevention to the market? The benefit/cost ratio of government action in this area is huge. Political suppliers have responded to the voters' views.

This is not to say that the *level* and *operation* of our legal system will not be debated. Many citizens may feel that the *marginal* benefits of more crime prevention efforts are less than their *marginal* costs, *given the current level of government activity in this area*. Whether the crime prevention activities of government should be expanded or contracted will be an issue for political discussion. But few would question their personal gain from some government action in this area.

Gaining from Government Provision of Public Goods

As we discussed in Chapter 28, the market fails to allocate public goods efficiently, particularly when it is impossible to exclude nonpaying consumers. National defense is probably the most important public good that approximates these conditions. Most people favor some national defense. But because it is a public good, it would be produced in less than the desired amount, if left to the market. There is no feasible way that a nonpaying citizen could be restricted from the consumption of his neighbor's (in this case all of us are each other's neighbor) national defense. There would be few paying customers because personal consumption of national defense would not depend on personal payment. Everyone has an incentive to become a free rider, but when everybody tries to ride free, little national defense is produced.

Most voters will gain if the government reacts to the market failure, and provides *some* national defense. Exhibit 29-3 presents a hypothetical schedule of the personal costs and benefits that accrue to 10 voters from a governmental defense policy. Eight of the ten receive benefits in excess of their tax cost. Two voters, perhaps pacifists or persons who see little danger from foreign powers, are made worse off by the policy. The public sector action harms this minority. But the net gains of the majority ($3150) far exceeds the net costs imposed on the minority ($150). It would be theoretically possible for the majority to use their net gains to compensate the losers for their $150 loss. Everybody's welfare could have improved. In reality, of course, we seldom compensate people who are adversely affected by governmental policy.

Given the schedule of costs and benefits as outlined by Exhibit 29-3, would the national defense policy be favored by a political entrepreneur? A solid majority favors the action and the net benefits are large relative to net cost. Again, politicians might debate the *level* of national defense. As the defense budget is *increased*, an increasing number of citizens will perceive greater personal costs than benefits. Support for *additional* defense expenditures would decline as spending in this area is expanded, but there would be a strong incentive for some government provision of the good.

Exhibit 29-3   Gaining from Government—But a Minority Loses

The table indicates hypothetical personal benefits and costs from spending $2000 on national defense, a public good. Most voters want more national defense than the market will provide. Thus 8 out of 10 voters favor the defense spending. The benefit/cost ratio is also high, $5000/$2000. Do you think that politicians will favor *some* national defense? Why?

Voters	Benefit from government action	Personal tax cost	Net impact
1	$1000	$200	$800
2	900	200	700
3	900	250	650
4	550	150	400
5	500	200	300
6	400	250	150
7	300	200	100
8	250	200	50
9	150	200	−50
10	50	150	−100
Total (all persons)	$5000	$2000	$3000

Pulling Things Together

Thus far our analysis has been extremely simplified. But the major point is important. Market failure may make it possible for public sector action to create personal benefits for its citizens in excess of their personal cost.[4]

Government action need not be a zero-sum game where one man's gain is another's loss. When a majority of voters favor a political action and the benefits are large relative to cost, vote-seeking political entrepreneurs have a strong incentive to back the proposal. Support of such proposals will enhance one's election prospects. In these instances, there is a harmony between the personal self-interest of political figures and economic efficiency.

There is also a corollary of the point. Lack of market failure reduces the net gains that will accrue to citizens from government intervention. There is little reason to believe that the public sector could provide wheat, oranges, shoes, or beef more efficiently than the market sector. Most voters prefer to have such activities conducted in the private sector because it is more decentralized. Since the opportunity cost of supplying such commodities collectively is large relative to the benefits, most democratic nations will be unlikely to assign such activities to the public sector.

CAN INCOME REDISTRIBUTION PROMOTE SOCIAL GAIN?

Thus far we have focused on public sector action that stems from the opportunity to improve economic efficiency. Often real world policies appear to be motivated by the desire to redistribute income rather than to promote economic efficiency. What does economics tell us about public policy designed to redistribute income rather than enlarge its size?

Some redistribution of income may actually stem from the inability of the market to fully reflect the preferences of the community for antipoverty efforts. The welfare of many citizens may be adversely affected by the hardship and poverty of others. For example, the economic conditions of ill-clothed children, street beggars, and the poor among the elderly may impose a cost on many of their fellow citizens. Private charity results as individuals take action to assist the less fortunate among us.

But private antipoverty efforts, like national defense, have public good characteristics. Consider the views of Carl Citizen. While his welfare would be improved if there were fewer poor people, he recognizes that his *personal* charitable efforts exert little impact on the overall status of the poor. Carl would be quite willing to support and contribute his fair share to a community-wide antipoverty effort. However, since his *personal* contribution exerts a negligible impact on the total level of the voluntary antipoverty efforts, Carl has a strong incentive to become a free rider, to let others help

---

[4] Again it should be noted that both the voter's perceived benefits and costs of assigning an activity to the public sector are subjective though they will often have an objective (direct monetary) component. As these preferences change over time and differ across nations, we would expect to observe differences in activities that are assigned to government, even among democratic nations. Other factors, such as income, its distribution, and technology, are also likely to influence the choice of activities to be assigned to the public sector. Note also that the "total" benefits and costs summed across all voters are dependent on the distribution of income.

the poor. But when everybody acts like Carl, the market will be deficient in the production of public goods such as antipoverty programs and national defense.

Clearly, if there are many voters who have preferences like Carl's, collective action against poverty could improve the general welfare of the community. When everybody is required to contribute, effective antipoverty efforts help not only the poor, but also people like Carl who benefit from a general reduction in the level of poverty.

Self-Interest Redistribution of Income

Collective action to redistribute income may stem from sources other than the public good nature of antipoverty efforts. Pure self-interest may motivate individuals to use the political process as a vehicle to attain personal gain. The simplest theory of **self-interest redistribution** postulates that the bottom 51 percent of the poor will use their political votes to gain income at the expense of the 49 percent who earn the highest incomes. What does our economic analysis of the political process say about this theory? Do the poor oppress the rich?

Exhibit 29-4 helps shed light on the validity of this theory. Consider a hypothetical

Exhibit 29-4   Government and Redistributing Income

Plan A indicates the impact of a strict redistribution of income from the rich to the poor. Under plan A, the four highest income voters are taxed $125 each to provide $100 of benefits to the five lowest income recipients. Plan A is favored 5 to 4. But using majority rule, is this outcome stable? The answer is no. Suppose that the four high income voters, as an alternative to plan A, proposed taxing everyone $20, and redistributing all of the proceeds to voter 5 (plan B). This proposal would impose a net cost of $20 on all voters but 5, who would gain $160. What would be the outcome of a political choice between plans A and B? The four high income voters plus voter 5 would gain more from B than from A. Thus, the strict redistribution of income from the rich to the poor would be greatly reduced. Any majority coalition could redistribute income. Economic theory does *not* suggest that redistribution via the political process will be strictly, or even primarily, from the rich to the poor.

VOTERS	BENEFIT FROM GOVERNMENT ACTION		PERSONAL TAX COST		NET IMPACT	
	Plan A	*Plan B*	*Plan A*	*Plan B*	*Plan A*	*Plan B*
Low income						
1	$100	$ 0	$ 0	$ 20	$ 100	$ −20
2	100	0	0	20	100	−20
3	100	0	0	20	100	−20
4	100	0	0	20	100	−20
5	100	180	0	20	100	160
6	0	0	125	20	−125	−20
7	0	0	125	20	−125	−20
8	0	0	125	20	−125	−20
9	0	0	125	20	−125	−20
High income						
Total	$500	$180	$500	$180	0	0

nine person economy, where redistribution of income is decided by majority vote. Suppose the five poorest voters sought to provide themselves a $100 subsidy each by imposing a tax of $125 on the four rich voters (plan A). No external benefits are present. Therefore, the B/C ratio for the redistribution proposal would be one.

How would the rich react to this scheme? One possibility would be for them to offer one member of the minority a better deal, inducing him to join a new coalition. Suppose the rich voters offered voter 5 a *net* subsidy of $160. Plan B is instituted where everyone is taxed $20 and the proceeds ($180) are distributed to voter 5. The new majority, the rich plus voter 5, could now impose cost on the poor. But even this coalition would tend to be unstable. In order to avoid the cost of plan B, each of the four minority voters would have an incentive to undercut voter 5, forming a new coalition that would further reduce the amount of redistribution.

The analysis of Exhibit 29-4 should lead us to question if the poorest 51 percent of voters will oppress the richest 49 percent. The rich would only need to woo over 1 percent of the middle income voters in order to have a coalition that could oppress the poorest 49 percent of voters!

Two additional factors lead us to further question the real world validity of the redistribution to the poor theory *when decisions are made legislatively*. If voters were strictly self-centered—that is, if there were no external benefits from redistribution to the poor—how attractive would a simple rich–poor transfer scheme be to a political entrepreneur? A strictly self-centered redistribution program would have a benefit/cost ratio of only unity. If the cost imposed on other taxpayers became substantial, the door would be open for opponents of the redistribution to use the issue to gain support and political contributions from the nonpoor. Second, rather than simply redistributing income to the poor, it would make more sense for a vote-maximizing political entrepreneur to focus on all well-organized and clearly defined groups (for example, the elderly, union members, college students, the poorest 10 percent of households, etc.). Such groups would be in a better position to deliver both votes and other political aid to favored candidates. Thus, the political attractiveness of strictly rich–poor transfers would appear to be limited.

ACTUAL INCOME REDISTRIBUTION—WINNERS AND LOSERS

How does reality conform to the theory? In Chapter 5 (see Exhibit 5-9) we pointed out that, *in aggregate*, the tax structure is not progressive. Most of us pay about 30 percent of our income in taxes. Both the poor and the rich pay an even higher percentage. But, both taxes and **cash income transfers** are vehicles for redistribution. As Exhibit 29-5 shows, the poor—households with incomes of less than $4000—are net gainers from the government's distributional policy. They pay a higher percentage of their income in taxes, but they receive back a still larger amount in cash income transfers. As income increases, cash transfers decline as a share of total income. Considering both taxes and cash transfers, the public sector is a moderate force toward greater equality.

However, as Exhibit 29-6 shows, a substantial share of income transfers are to the nonpoor. Approximately 40 percent of the government's *cash* income transfers are to households with incomes in excess of $8000; two-thirds go to those with incomes above

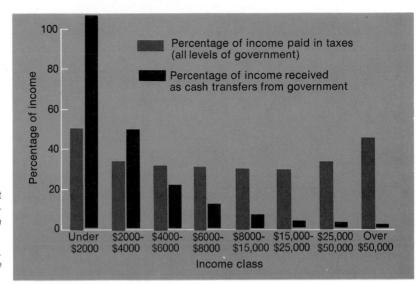

**Exhibit 29-5   Government
Redistribution of Income**

Even though taxes, in aggregate, are not
very progressive, when transfer payments are included, public sector *cash*
redistribution does favor the poor.

SOURCE: Roger A. Herriot and Herman P.
Miller, "The Taxes We Pay," *The Conference
Board Record*, May 1971.

$4000. Thus, as the theory suggests, the redistribution is not just from the rich to the
poor. A sizable share of even cash income redistribution is among *nonpoor* households.

If indirect subsidies and grants of special privilege were considered, the redistribution among the nonpoor would be even greater. Homeowners, oil companies,
industries protected by tariffs, trade and professional associations, investors, and other
interest groups have their incomes enhanced by indirect government aid or tax
concessions. It is difficult to measure precisely how important these indirect redistributional effects are. Many believe that they are more important than cash transfers. Most
of these indirect grants of favors are pretty much independent of income. They are
almost exclusively limited to well-organized and readily identifiable groups. This is the
way our theory suggested the process would work. When both the direct and indirect

**Exhibit 29-6   Redistribution to the
Poor and Nonpoor**

Income class	Percentage of cash transfers received
Less than $2000	12.3
$2000–$4000	20.3
$4000–$6000	16.7
$6000–$8000	12.1
$8000–$15,000	24.5
$15,000–$25,000	10.2
$25,000–$50,000	3.5
Over $50,000	0.4
Total	100.0

SOURCE: Derived from Roger A. Herriot and
Herman P. Miller, "The Taxes We Pay," *The
Conference Board Record, May 1971.*

subsidies are considered, it is not obvious that public policy redistributes income in favor of the poor. It would probably be more accurate to say that redistribution is primarily from the unorganized to the well organized, independent of income grouping.

☐ LOOKING AHEAD

In this chapter, our analysis led us to conclude that government would be highly likely to undertake activities when it could substantially improve on the market. When the personal B/C ratio of voters, in total, was large, government action to help citizens capture this gain would be attractive to political suppliers. As the B/C ratio declines toward unity, other things constant, the incentive for political action will also decline. Thus far, we have focused on government action to either (a) correct market failure or (b) redistribute income. Is there reason to think the government will undertake other functions? Is there ever any incentive for a vote-maximizing political entrepreneur to support proposals that promote inefficiency? These are the topics of Chapter 30.

Perspectives in Economics

Externalities, No-Fault Insurance, and Government Action to Improve on the Market

Insurance is a method of spreading risk and protecting oneself against an unexpected disaster. Automobile insurance protects the insured against personal financial loss resulting from an accident. Before 1971, auto insurance in the United States was based on the fault or liability principle. Under this principle, if a person is at fault in an auto accident, he is liable for any damages that result. Personal liability insurance protects the motorist against this liability. Thus, the insurance company incurs the liability when one of their policyholders is at fault in an accident.

The liability principle results in a conflict situation between parties (or their insurance representatives) involved in an accident. Fault is often not clear-cut: There may be conflicting evidence, and sometimes both parties are at fault. Under the liability principle, valuable resources are allocated to resolving the issue of fault when there is disagreement about issues of fact and law: Witnesses are interrogated, the police investigation is reviewed, and medical reports and physical examinations are required. Depositions, pretrial conferences, and many other steps that take a great deal of time and money are necessary. Many of these procedures will be necessary even when a case does not go to court because there is always the possibility that it might. Resources that are used to determine fault and pay lawyers cannot be used to compensate victims. Thus, accident victims received only 42 to 44 percent of the total auto liability premiums.

Each insurance company has a strong incentive to minimize its liability. If the adversary parties could simply agree on fault and liability, without incurring all of the negotiating and legal costs associated with the determination of fault, a larger share of insurance premiums could be allocated to victims. But what would happen if a single company attempted to follow a more conciliatory policy? If others did not follow suit, the liability of the conciliatory company would increase. Each company, acting independently, has a strong incentive to be hard-nosed and to minimize their company's liability. But when all companies are hard-nosed, the total cost of settling claims increases and the share of premiums paid back to victims remains low.

The problem really comes about because resources employed in the reduction of a company's liability impose an external cost on other companies. What happens when there are external costs associated with an action? It gets carried too far, right? Thus, when all insurance companies pursue their own self-interest, an excessive amount of resources are allocated to actions (for example, interrogation, investigation, medical reports, and legal services) designed to reduce the liability of each company. Individual policyholders are harmed as these costs are passed along in the form of higher insurance rates.

No-fault insurance is an effort to rectify the incorrect market signals that result because of the external cost. There are several alternative forms of no-fault insurance plans, but they all have one thing in common. A policyholder involved in an accident settles *his* claim with *his* insurance company regardless of fault. Other parties involved in the accident must settle *their* claims with *their* company, and thus liability suits to recover clearly defined damages are eliminated. Most no-fault plans do allow leeway for really major suits to continue to be settled according to the liability principle. The liability suit involving several thousand dollars is still permitted, but the fender-bender and accidents involving minor injury are removed from court proceedings and company bargaining procedures.

As of 1975, 24 states had instituted no-fault plans. Many others are considering doing so.[5] What has been the result? Massachusetts, which adopted the no-fault plan in 1971, has experienced two rate reductions since that time. Florida motorists have received rebates since their adoption of no-fault. The plan is also working well in Delaware, Maryland, Oregon, and other states. It appears that government action, modifying the economic incentives facing market participants, has improved the efficiency of the pricing system.

Discussion

1. Generally, insurance companies have favored no-fault insurance, and lawyers have opposed it. Why?
2. Explain, using the theory of external cost, how the plan has cut the expenses of insurance companies and resulted in lower rates for auto insurance customers without any reduction in the funds paid out in claims.

CHAPTER LEARNING OBJECTIVES

1. The public and market sectors are different methods of making economic choices. It is important to understand the advantages and shortcomings of both sectors. Individual preferences and expectations will influence the outcome of democratic political decisions. Using the basic economic postulates of individual behavior, one can develop a theory about how we would expect the public sector to operate.

2. Voters use ballots, political contributions, lobbying, and other political devices to demand public sector action. Other things constant, voters have a strong incentive to support the candidate who offers them the greatest personal gain relative to personal costs. Information is

---

[5] A federal no-fault plan is also pending.

costly. Since group decision-making breaks the link between the choice of the individual and the outcome of the issue, it is rational for voters to remain uninformed on many issues. Thus, each voter typically evaluates candidates on the basis of a small subset of issues that he perceives to be important.

3. The vote-seeking political entrepreneur (politician, legislator, etc.) has a strong incentive to offer additional political goods that are in short supply relative to the demand of voters. He will be attracted by issues with a high benefit/cost ratio for his constitutents.

4. Other things constant, when the benefit/cost ratio from public sector action is quite high, the action is attractive to *both* voters and political entrepreneurs. Such activities will nearly always be conducted by government.

5. Market failure presents government with an opportunity to undertake action that will result in a benefit/cost ratio in excess of unity. Other things constant, the greater the social loss resulting from the market failure, the stronger is the incentive for public sector action.

6. Economic analysis indicates two sources of potential pressure for income redistribution: **(a)** the public good nature of antipoverty efforts and **(b)** self-interest. If self-interest is the major motivation for redistribution, there is little reason to believe that it will necessarily be from the rich to the poor. From the viewpoint of a vote-maximizing entrepreneur, there is incentive to support redistribution from unorganized to well-organized groups. Considerable income redistribution in the United States is of this variety.

IMPORTANT TERMS TO REMEMBER

Political entrepreneur: A legislator or politician who wants the support of voters.

No-fault insurance: An insurance principle whereby each policyholder is compensated by his own insurance company for any damages that he incurs, *regardless of fault.*

Self-interest redistribution: Redistribution motivated solely by the desire of a group to help themselves. Nonrecipients do not gain from observing an improvement in the welfare of the recipients.

Cash income transfers: Direct cash payments to recipients, for example, Social Security, direct welfare, and farm subsidy payments.

THE ECONOMIC WAY OF THINKING—DISCUSSION QUESTIONS

1. "The public sector is more equitable than the market. The rich man's vote counts no more or no less than the vote of the poor man. Everybody is equal when decisions are made through government." Evaluate.

2. Do you think that voters are better informed than consumers? Why or why not?

3. Do you think that promotional advertising exerts more impact on the type of car chosen by the consumer than the type of politician chosen by the voter? Explain the logic underlying your answer.

4. Do you think that the political process works to the advantage of the poor? Explain. Are the poor well organized? Do they make substantial financial campaigns to office seekers? Are they likely to be well informed? Is it surprising that a large amount of the approximately $100 billion of cash income transfer payments in the United States does not go to the poor? Explain.

5. Which of the following public sector actions are designed primarily to correct "market failure": **(a)** laws against fraud, **(b)** truth-in-lending legislation, **(c)** rate regulation in the telephone industry, **(d)** legislation setting emission controls standards, **(e)** subsidization of pure research, **(f)** operation of the post office? Explain your answer.

6. Why do you think so few people vote? Do you think that the people who do not vote are better informed on the candidates (and issues) than those who do? Do you think that public policy would be better if everyone was required to vote? Explain.

30

THE ECONOMICS OF
GOVERNMENT FAILURE

We no longer expect results from government. What was a torrid romance between the people and government for so long has now become a tired middle-aged liaison which we do not quite know how to break off. . . . [Peter Drucker, The Public Interest, Winter 1969]

In Chapter 28 we focused on market failure—reasons why the market mechanism will fail to meet ideal efficiency conditions. In the preceding chapter, we attempted to analyze what economics has to say about how the public sector will work. Now we consider some of the limitations of collective action as a vehicle to promote economic efficiency.

The collective decision-making process is not an ideal mechanism that will automatically correct the inefficiencies of the market. One of the painful lessons of history is that government action often does not turn out as we hoped and planned. Even well-designed programs based on humanitarian principles have been known to go astray and fail to meet their initial objectives.

It is important to understand both the potential advantages and limitations of public sector economic action. During the 1960s many people, including a good number of intellectuals, were quite optimistic about the ability of government to solve several social–economic ills, including poverty, inferior education, economic instability, unemployment, discrimination, and urban decay. Progress was made in some of these areas. But upon reflection, it is obvious that progress, such as it was, did not meet the optimistic expectations of the early 1960s. Some government programs were less effective than had been anticipated, whereas still others were altered in a direction inconsistent with their initial objectives. Sometimes, one program was in direct conflict with another. A frustration developed in many areas.

Many people argued that the system was not working properly. The politicians, the establishment, or the just plain "bad guys" were variously charged with the responsibility for the shortcomings. Did something go wrong? Were the results different from what we should have expected? Perhaps. But economic theory does suggest that the collective decision-making process, like the market, suffers from serious shortcomings that often lead to economic inefficiency.

There is such a thing as "government failure," as well as market failure. **Government failure** results when public policy is undertaken even though it promotes economic inefficiency. In the following sections we will analyze five specific types of government failure.

GOVERNMENT FAILURE: VOTER IGNORANCE AND INEFFICIENT PUBLIC POLICY

It is often difficult for a voter to identify the precise impact of public policy on his well-being. We have already noted that individual voters, recognizing that their views will not decide the issue, will have little incentive to inform themselves on political matters. Because of imperfect voter information, the political process will be biased against proposals with elusive benefits at the expense of easily identifiable costs. Anthony Downs believes that this factor often results in the rejection of beneficial public policy:

> Benefits from many government actions are remote from those who receive them, either in time, space or comprehensibility. Economic aid to a distant nation may prevent a hostile revolution there and save millions of dollars and even the lives of American troops, but because the solution is remote, the average citizen—living in rational ignorance—will not realize he is benefitting at all.[1]

While failure to recognize personal benefits fully may cause voters (and legislators responsive to them) to reject some economically efficient projects, adoption of other proposals that are inefficient will also result from imperfect voter information. The political process will tend to accept counterproductive proposals when the benefits are clearly recognizable while the costs are partially concealed and difficult for voters to identify. In fact, vote-maximizing political entrepreneurs have a strong incentive to package public policy proposals precisely in this way. That is, they will seek to conceal the costs of a political proposal, while fully propagating its benefits among voters who could be expected to gain from the action.

Is the real world consistent with this view? The nature of the subject limits precision, but examples that are consistent with the theory can be cited. For example, consider the area of taxation. Our analysis suggests that taxes that are difficult for voters to identify will be more popular with politicians than direct tax levies. The splitting of payroll taxes (for example, Social Security) suggests that legislators are interested in deceiving voters as to their personal cost of government.[2] Similarly, the continued popularity of deficit spending, money creation, and inflation is consistent with the theory. This method of gaining control over private resources is much more difficult for

[1] Anthony Downs, "Why the Government Budget Is Too Small in a Democracy," *World Politics*, vol. XII, no. 4, p. 551. Copyright © 1960 by Princeton University Press.
[2] See Chapter 5, pages 76–77, for a detailed analysis of this issue.

the voter to understand than a direct tax levy. Thus, it is not surprising the political entrepreneurs continue to follow inflationary policies even while denouncing rising prices and attempting to blame them on unions, businessmen, the Arabs, the wasteful consumption habits of consumers, or any other scapegoat that might be handy.

The point is not that politicians are evil, but rather that perverse incentives will induce vote-maximizing political entrepreneurs to promote economic inefficiency. In the presence of imperfect information the political process is biased (a) toward policies for which costs can be concealed and (b) against policies for which the benefits are elusive.

GOVERNMENT FAILURE: THE SPECIAL INTEREST EFFECT

Many tend to think of government as the great equalizer—a tool to be used to control powerful economic interests. Yet, in reality the relationship often seems to run the other way, from government to the protected power of a strong interest group. Can economic tools help to explain this phenomenon?

A special interest issue is one for which a small number of voters *individually* acquire large gains at the expense of a large number of citizens who *individually* suffer small losses. Exhibit 30-1 illustrates a special interest issue. One voter out of an electorate of 1000 will gain from the passage of issue A, but his net benefits total $998 ($1000 less his $2 share of the cost). The other 999 voters would *each* bear a small cost ($2) if A became law. Since a small minority gains a lot, while the overwhelming share of voters suffer only a little, A is a special interest issue.

The political power of a special interest group cannot be fully understood without recognizing the widespread (and rational) voter ignorance as to (a) the impact of most issues on their personal welfare and (b) the position of their elected representatives on the issues. This lack of knowledge is attributable to the rational ignorance effect and information cost. As a result, voters will be uninformed on most issues. Typically, most of us will decide to vote for or against a political candidate on the basis of just a few issues that are of substantial importance to us. We will ignore numerous other issues that *individually* exert little impact on our well-being.

The hypothetical data of Exhibit 30-1 can be used to illustrate the significance of information cost and voter ignorance. How will issue A affect the voter's evaluation of Senator Supporter? To the 999 voters A is an insignificant issue. Since these voters recognize that A will not affect them very much either way and that it costs more than

Exhibit 30-1   Issue A and Support for a Political Entrepreneur

Number of voters	Individual voter benefit	Individual voter cost	Cost of information necessary to understand impact of politician's position on the voter
1	$1000	$2	$5
999	0	2	5

its worth to track down the necessary information[3] for a rational decision, they ignore A. They will evaluate Senator Supporter on the basis of other issues.

But one voter (0.1 of 1 percent of the electorate) feels very strongly about A. He will know where alternative candidates stand on this issue. Undoubtedly, he will let them know how vitally important it is that A be approved. He may even be able to present politicians with information suggesting that the passage of A will be good for the country.

What position should a vote-maximizing politician take on A and other issues like it? Obviously, he will gain by supporting the special interest minority rather than the uninformed, distinterested majority. Politicians that oppose issue A will lose the minority vote while failing to enhance their image with the disinterested and un-informed majority. Even though A is inefficient from the community's viewpoint (its benefit/cost ratio is $1000/$2000), the political process will lead to its passage.

Special Interests and the Successful Politician

While the analysis just given outlines the general forces that are present when special interest issues are decided by the political process, two other factors serve to enhance their importance. First, money is important in politics. If a politician is going to win the support of voters who have little incentive to study issues, he must provide free information to them. Newspaper ads, printed materials, television spots, and other advertising techniques will be needed to create a positive image. Since special interests feel so strongly on certain issues, they present candidates who support their position with a ready source of campaign contributions.[4] Second, political entrepreneurs can often "package" issues so that most voters will be unaware of the cost that is being imposed on them. The more complex a policy alternative, the more difficult it is for the average voter to identify how he is affected by the issue. Therefore, there is an incentive for legislators to make special interest issues very complex. While the special interest will most assuredly figure out that they stand to gain from such a proposal, the complexity of the issue will make it difficult for the typical voter to determine its actual impact.[5]

Clearly, political suppliers can often reap political gain by supporting special interest legislation, even though such legislation might be economically inefficient. In such instances, the strategy of the politician is clear:

---

[3]If this issue is to influence a voter's evaluation of a political entrepreneur, he must have information on where a politician stands on the issue and how this position will influence his personal welfare.

[4]There is an abundance of evidence documenting the importance of special interest campaign contributions. Senators, congressmen, and presidents have long benefited from the financial assistance of businesses, unions, and other interest groups in a position to be rewarded by public sector decisions. Congressional committee chairmen are, more often than not, well cared for by the industrial and labor interests that stand to benefit from their actions.

Analysis of state government reveals the existence of similar pressures. A study of political contributions in Florida indicated that a lion's share of all political contributions come from special interest groups such as unions and the liquor, insurance, and banking industries. A study in Illinois revealed a similar pattern.

[5]Gordon Tullock, in *Toward a Mathematics of Politics* (Ann Arbor: Univ. of Michigan Press, 1966), emphasizes this point.

(a) support the views of special interest,

(b) clearly articulate one's position among these constituents,

(c) solicit funds from the special interest group,

(d) make it difficult (for example, by advocating a complex policy alternative) for the average voter to clearly understand the consequences of one's position, and,

(e) use the funds obtained from the vested interest[6] to stress the candidate's views on important issues where his position is favored by most voters and promoting those candidate characteristics that are thought to positively influence his election prospects, independent of his position on the issues.

The resources obtained from the special interests will make it possible to run as the "candidate of the people"!

The Real World and the Special Interest Effect

Does the political process really work this way? Does government often benefit well-organized business, labor, and trade groups to the detriment of disorganized interests, such as consumers and taxpayers? Increasingly there is strong evidence that it does. Public policy in some areas appears to be motivated neither by economic efficiency nor a desire for greater equality. For example, consider tariff trade restrictions on such commodities as steel and automobiles.[7] For years economists have pointed out that tariff protection, particularly for an industry that possesses substantial monopoly power, leads to an inefficient allocation of resources. It would be hard to find an issue on which there is more general agreement among economists. But the benefits from the repeal of such legislation are widely dispersed and difficult for consumers to perceive. The costs of the repeal imposed on auto and steel manufacturers and employees are highly concentrated. Despite the fact that political figures argue from time to time that auto and steel prices do not respond to competition, the tariff legislation remains. Politicians obviously perceive that greater political gains are to be obtained by a continuation of the present high tariff policy on these commodities.

The special interest effect also implies that political entrepreneurs can gain by writing tax legislation amendments that yield large benefits to a few while imposing a small personal expense on many. If our theory is correct, we should expect the tax structure of democratic nations to provide at least a few beautiful loopholes, right? What does the evidence indicate?

While the overall federal tax structure gives the appearance that the wealthy carry a heavy share of the load, special tax treatment of certain types of income alters the window dressing. The capital gains tax makes it possible to forestall a tax bill into the future and then pay a rate of no more than 50 percent of one's marginal tax rate. This

---

[6]The alleged campaign reform legislation passed in the aftermath of the Watergate scandal prohibits organizations from contributing more than $5000 to any candidate. However, nothing prohibits special interests from establishing numerous "paper organizations" in order to make multiple $5000 contributions. Of course, from the viewpoint of vote-maximizing political entrepreneurs, such "reform legislation" permits one to put forth the *appearance* of concern about the "power of special interests" and "corruption in politics" without making substantial changes.

[7]The impact of tariffs on economic efficiency is discussed in Chapter 31.

legislation has little impact on most taxpayers but it results in tax savings of thousands, and in some cases, millions of dollars to a minority of taxpayers, particularly the well-to-do.

Tax-free income from municipal bonds, investment tax credits, accelerated depreciation allowances, loopholes in the inheritance tax legislation, and a host of special subsidies each work to the advantage of special interest groups, while imposing a small and difficult to identify cost on most others. Often this legislation promotes various kinds of economic inefficiencies to say nothing of its impact on income distribution. A survey of other democratic nations, including semisocialist countries such as Sweden and Norway, reveals that they too provide a tax structure that is rife with special provisions that benefit the few at the expense of the many. If tax legislation of this variety did not lead to *political* gain for legislators, they would not pass such laws.

Previously, we discussed several other examples of economic inefficiency that appear to stem from the special interest effect. Recall that in Chapter 20 we found that the regulatory policies of the ICC and CAB often support the trucking and airline interests, at the expense of competition and lower consumer prices. Similarly, public policy that benefits unionized public sector employees (see Perspectives in Economics, pages 466–467), farmers, homeowners, and college students, is typically rooted to the special interest effect.

Why do the taxpayers not get together and vote out politicians who support "special interests"? There is some incentive to do this but it is greatly reduced because it is costly to form coalitions, particularly among a loosely knit group.[8] Each taxpayer has a strong incentive to "let the others do it" (that is, to act as a free rider). But when everybody decides to ride free, nothing gets done about the special interest. Also, many, if not most taxpayers will not be opposed to the support of special interests as such. A taxpayer who loses on one special interest issue, subsidies to farmers for example, may be able to utilize his own special interest influence to obtain personal gain on other issues. Therefore he will be reluctant to enter a coalition that sought to eliminate all special interest influence.[9]

GOVERNMENT FAILURE: THE SHORTSIGHTEDNESS EFFECT

The shortsightedness effect results because the complexity of an issue may make it extremely difficult for the voter to anticipate *future* benefits and costs accurately. Thus, voters will tend to rely mostly on current conditions. Candidates and legislators, seeking to win the current election, have a strong incentive to stress public sector action that yields substantial current benefits relative to costs.

Therefore, public sector action will be biased in favor of legislation that offers

---

[8]Sometimes intense publicity will make support of a specific special interest legislation temporarily unpopular. When this is true political entrepreneurs will take extra care to disguise their support of vested interest groups.

[9]While our analysis has concentrated on the special interest effect as a source of public sector inefficiency, it should be noted that not all special interest legislation is inefficient. The total gains that accrue to the special interest (even though they are a minority) may sometimes exceed the total cost imposed on other voters. When this is true, adoption of special interest legislation is consistent with efficiency.

immediate (and easily identifiable) current benefits at the expense of future costs that are complex and difficult to identify. Simultaneously, there is a bias against legislation that involves immediate and easily identifiable cost (for example, higher taxes) while yielding future benefits that are complex and difficult to identify. For issues of this type, government action will tend to be shortsighted.

Short-Term Costs and Government Inaction

Consider the political attractiveness of a proposal to raise current taxes in order to provide future generations with better mass transit. Do you think such a proposal would be a political winner? Due to the necessary capital investment and time required to carry out the project, people would not immediately feel any current benefits. Yet the impact of the higher taxes would be felt now. History has shown that voters are usually reluctant to incur an increase in *current* taxes in order to obtain some uncertain and vague *future* gain. Locally financed mass transit proposals tend to be political losers, at least until a crisis situation develops.[10]

It has been noted that public sector action is "crisis oriented." In recent years we have experienced a welfare crisis, poverty crisis, environmental crisis, energy crisis, and inflation crisis. Given the public sector bias against proposals with current cost but difficult-to-identify future benefits the crisis phenomenon is understandable. The maximizing politician has an incentive to follow a policy of minimum current expenditures until the crisis point is reached, while simultaneously giving lip service to the problem. Economics suggests that democratic decision-making is often inconsistent with sensible *long-range* economic planning.

Short-Term Benefits and Government Action

While proposals with difficult-to-perceive future benefits result in inaction, proposals with immediate benefits, at the expense of complex future costs—costs that will accrue after the next election—will be very attractive to political entrepreneurs. Both office-holders and seekers have a strong incentive to support such proposals and emphasize the immediate voter benefits.

Is there any evidence that the pursuit of short-term political gains has led to inappropriate public sector action? Consider the macroissue of economic instability. Politicians only recently have been completely convinced of their ability to control the "tightness" of labor markets by monetary and fiscal policy. Expansionary monetary and fiscal policy can be utilized to "heat up" the economy and reduce the unemployment rate. If the economy becomes overheated, inflation will shortly follow. The short-sightedness effect would predict that the party in power will tend to follow an expansionary policy in the 12 to 24 months before an election, even if these policies will result in future inflation. As we have already seen, the "stabilization" policies preced-

---

[10]In passing, it might be noted that a federally financed mass transit program would fare better than a locally financed one because its costs could be more fully spread among nonusers. When urban mass transit is financed federally, the issue becomes a "special interest" subsidy to the urban areas undertaking the transit system.

The Small Society, © Washington Star Syndicate, Inc.

ing the presidential elections of 1964, 1968, and 1972 suggest that incumbent political entrepreneurs pressed hard to have the economy looking good on election day. At least in the case of the 1968 and 1972 elections, there can be little doubt that the expansionary macropolicy overheated the economy, causing a postelection problem with inflation. The large deficits that will apparently be incurred in 1975–1976 suggest that similar policies will precede the 1976 presidential election. Within the framework of the shortsightedness effect, these policies are not surprising.

One could argue that our approach to the financing of medical services during the 1960s was, at least initially, quite shortsighted. Given the monopoly power of the American Medical Association, a long-run policy would have emphasized an expansion in the supply of physicians. But it takes time to build additional medical schools, train, and perhaps subsidize capable students. Such a policy would involve some immediate cost, while the benefits would have come in the future. The elderly, in particular, wanted relief from rising medical costs now.

So the political entrepreneurs concentrated on the demand side. The medical subsidies to the elderly did relieve their immediate medical costs, but the process of an increasing demand and nearly fixed supply resulted in sharply higher prices without increasing the quantity of medical services. Medical care was redistributed from others to the elderly, but despite the enormous cost, there was little increase in the quantity of medical care consumed. The process was complicated enough that most voters did not understand it. Political suppliers perceived, and probably correctly, that greater immediate political gain could be derived from a subsidy program that expanded demand, rather than a long-run policy that would increase supply.

The shortsightedness effect is a potential source of conflict between good politics and sound economics. Policies that are efficient from the viewpoint of social benefits and costs will not necessarily be the same policies that will most enhance one's election prospects. Thus we lose out on projects that would have been beneficial and are saddled with many others that are grossly inefficient.

GOVERNMENT FAILURE: LITTLE ENTREPRENEURIAL INCENTIVE FOR INTERNAL EFFICIENCY

Government has often been charged with inaction, duplication, delays, frivolous work, and general inefficiency. The validity of these charges is difficult to document. How does government compare with the private sector? There is certainly a great deal of seemingly meaningless activity that goes on in the private sector as well. But private firms, even those with monopoly power, can gain from actions that improve operational efficiency. There is an incentive to produce efficiently because lower cost will mean larger profits.

In general, there is a lack of a parallel incentive in the public sector. Agency heads, cabinet officers, and others in entrepreneurial positions in the public sector are in a weak position to recoup any personal gain from improved efficiency. Proof of any actual savings would be complex and difficult to communicate to the major beneficiaries of the efficient behavior—the taxpayer. At election time, political candidates and parties had better have something better than efficiency in government if they expect to win.

Inasmuch as political officials are interested in efficiency, they will want to choose *ways that are visible and simple to communicate.* There will be greater political benefits from a well-publicized campaign to save a few dollars by turning off the lights at the White House than can be obtained from a complex government reorganization plan that would save the taxpayers millions of dollars. The latter idea is simply too complex and difficult for voters to identify.

When managerial decision-makers are unable to fully capture the gains of increased efficiency, they have less incentive to be cost conscious. Professor Galbraith and others have argued that the managers of large corporations have a substantial amount of freedom to pursue their own personal objectives since the widely dispersed owners (stockholders) will be unable to police managerial inefficiency effectively. Looked at from this perspective, public sector managers are merely a polar case. Taxpayers would benefit if public sector agencies and bureaus were operated efficiently. But the widely dispersed and uninformed taxpayer–voter is in a very weak position to police the situation effectively. Thus, public sector managers will have a great deal of discretion to pursue personal objectives such as a larger staff, political patronage, more pleasant working conditions, and favors to political allies.

In the private sector bankruptcy and economic losses will eventually halt incompetency. But in the public sector curtailment of failure is much less straightforward. In fact, inability to accomplish an objective is often used as a basis of asking for more funds, a larger staff, and still more resources.

The best proof of inefficiency is the willingness and ability of someone else to do better. But there is usually no opportunity for a private firm to *compete on an equal basis* with a publicly operated firm. Since public firms do not have to outperform potential competitors, we have lost a method of identifying and proving their efficiency. As the result, we have no idea whether the post office, our schools, the TVA, the FBI, the Pentagon, or HEW are operated efficiently. They may be, but none of them have to prove it by superior performance.

It is important to note that the argument of internal inefficiency is not based on the assumption that employees of a bureaucratic government are necessarily lazy or incapable. Rather, the emphasis is on the incentive under which managers and other workers toil. No individual or relatively small group of individuals has much incentive to assure efficiency. There is no small group of persons whose personal wealth would be significantly increased or reduced by changes in the level of efficiency. And if inefficiency is present, there is not a market test to even clearly define and accurately measure it, let alone eliminate it. The incentives are simply all in the wrong direction. Therefore, it is difficult to believe that this does not have some impact on the internal efficiency of governmental operations.

OUTSTANDING ECONOMIST: Kenneth Arrow

In 1972 Arrow along with J. R. Hicks was awarded the Nobel Prize in economics for his "pioneering contributions to general economic equilibrium theory and welfare theory." Arrow has also published widely in several other areas, including capital theory, linear programming, mathematical economics, and economics of discrimination. He is currently a professor of economics at Harvard, after having previously taught at Stanford and the University of Chicago.

In his widely praised book, *Social Choice and Individual Values*,[11] Arrow used symbolic logic and mathematics to show that majority voting could not be counted on to produce consistent collective decisions. The paradox of voting illustrates a possible inconsistency that might result from collective action. Suppose that the preferences of three voters on three possible policy alternatives were

Policy rankings	Linda	Sam	George
Most preferred policy	A	B	C
Second-place option	B	C	A
Least preferred policy	C	A	B

If voters were to make pairwise choices among these policy alternatives, which policy alternative would be chosen? When choosing between policies A and B, a majority (Linda and George) prefer A to B. If voters, having eliminated B, then chose between policies A and C, a majority (Sam and George) would prefer C rather than A. Thus, policy C is the most preferred of the three alternatives. Right? Wrong. What would happen if voters chose between policies B and C. Both Linda and Sam would prefer B rather than C. A majority would favor B rather than C. Therefore, A is preferred to B. C is preferred to A. But B is preferred to C. The order in which the policy options were voted on would influence the final outcome. Given the preferences of voters, no single policy option (similar results could be obtained for candidates) is able to secure a majority over all other alternatives when pairwise comparisons are made.

The "paradox of voting" did not originate with Arrow. But he was the first to place it in the context of generalized economic efficiency. His work caused both economists and political scientists to reevaluate their confidence in the rationality of collective decision-making.

---

[11]K. Arrow, *Social Choice and Individual Values*, 2nd ed. New Haven: Yale Univ. Press, 1970.

GOVERNMENT FAILURE: IMPRECISE REFLECTION OF CONSUMER PREFERENCES

The collective process is likely to be imprecise in reflecting the wishes of "consumers" because they (voters) are usually forced to act through a broker (legislator) who represents a "bundle" of political goods and tax prices. The voter will either get the bundle offered by candidate A or the bundle offered by B. Oftentimes neither of these bundles of political goods is very close to what any specific consumer would like to have. The political consumer loses his freedom to shop around, buying some goods from each of several hundred suppliers. He is stuck with the bundle favored by the majority coalition.

Because our political choices are so all inclusive, very few such choices are made. Circumstances change, new information becomes available, and relative prices change, but the political consumer has little opportunity to respond by making marginal adjustments. Approximately one-third of our economic resources are channeled by the public sector. Yet during a year, each of us make approximately 1000 times as many market as public sector decisions.

What are the implications of the bundle purchasing that dominates the public sector? Suppose that at the beginning of every year, each of us were required to contract with a broker who would make *all* of our market decisions for us. The broker would choose the amount of milk, gas, ice cream, education, mouthwash, and thousands of other items that we would purchase during the year. Suppose additionally that there were lots of different "marketbasket plans" that were offered by brokers. Consumers would, of course, try to choose the plan that was most consistent with their preferences. But once they choose the bundle offered by the broker, they are stuck with his decisions. Such a plan would undoubtedly reduce the ability of consumers to reflect their preferences in the market accurately. Even assuming that brokers (legislators) try their very best to deliver the desired bundle of goods, the consumers would surely be worse off.[12]

In addition to the problem presented by bundle purchase decisions, the political process tends to yield economic uniformity. This uniformity reduces the ability of political goods to best satisfy a broad spectrum of consumer preferences. In the case of public goods, the technical nature of the good requires uniformity, but many goods that are provided in the public sector could easily be rationed only to those willing to pay for them. Education is a clear example. Preferences differ widely about what constitutes a good education. Some parents would like their children to receive an education with a religious emphasis—others do not even want so much as a simple prayer to be uttered in school. Some parents want their children to receive accelerated training in math or reading—others want an extensive athletic program. Within a uniform public school system, there is no way to satisfy all of these groups.[13] This limitation results, not because of the nature of the good, but rather because it is a disadvantage of at least the current institutions for the public provision of the good.

---

[12] See Gordon Tullock, *Private Wants and Public Means* (New York: Basic Books, 1970).

[13] Some may argue that uniform treatment is not a necessary characteristic of government action. See R. Joseph Monsen and Anthony Downs, "Public Goods and Private Status," *Public Interest*, 1971, for an argument that more diversity in the provision of government goods and services would increase the level of public support for these services.

IS AN ECONOMIC ANALYSIS OF THE PUBLIC SECTOR TOO CYNICAL?

We have stressed how economic factors influence the workings of the public sector. Our analysis may differ considerably from that with which one comes in contact in political science courses. Some readers may object that our approach is too cynical, that not enough emphasis has been given to the dedicated public servant who gives the energies of his life to the resolutions of complex public sector issues. Our analysis does not deny the existence of such specimens. We merely emphasize that in a legislative democracy, there are pressures at work that will make it difficult for him to survive without bending.

At the opposite pole, one might argue that the voter is more public spirited than we have indicated. He may be willing to sacrifice his personal welfare for the public good. Perhaps this is so, but then how does one account for the behavior of trade associations, business lobbyists, labor unions, public employee groups, lawyers, doctors, teachers, developers, and hundreds of other organized groups—all attempting to change the rules and regulations of the public sector to their own advantage?

The test of any theory is its consistency with the real world. Certainly, we have not outlined a complete theory of the public sector. Much progress remains to be made. But casual observation of current events should be enough to cause one to question the validity of theories that emphasize only the public interest, equal power, and the humanitarian nature of governmental action. Democratic governments are a creation of the interactions of imperfect human beings. Many economists believe that economic theory has a great deal to say about the types of public sector actions that will result from such human interactions.

PUBLIC SECTOR AND THE MARKET—REVISITED

Most economic texts contain only a brief reference to the major issues discussed in the preceding two chapters. Our purpose has been to analyze how we would *expect* the public sector to handle various classes of economic issues.

In times past, economists have usually been content to stop with what the government should do, regardless of how removed from reality that solution might be. Without rejecting the issue of what government should do, we have pushed on to an analysis of what, in fact, it is likely to do. This approach helps to show the broad relevance of economic tools and their ability to explain real world economic actions.

Throughout, we have argued that there are theoretical reasons that explain why both market forces and public sector action will sometimes break down—why they will not meet ideal efficiency criteria. The deficiencies of one sector or the other will often be much more decisive for certain classes of action. Nobel Prize winner Paul Samuelson has correctly stated, "There are no rules concerning the proper role of government that can be established by a priori reasoning."[14] But this does not mean that economics has

---

[14] P. A. Samuelson, "The Economic Role of Private Activity," in *A Dialogue on the Proper Economic Role of the State*, Selected Paper No. 7, Graduate School of Business, University of Chicago.

nothing to say about the *strength* of the case for the market (or the public sector) for specific classes of activities. Neither does it mean that social scientists have nothing to say about institutional arrangements for conducting economic activity. It merely indicates that each case must be considered independently.

For some activities, the case for government intervention will be stronger than others. For example, if an activity involves substantial external effects, market arrangements will often result in economic inefficiency. Thus, the case for public sector action is strengthened. Similarly, when competitive pressures are weak or there is reason to expect consumers to be poorly informed, market failure is present and the case for the market process is weakened. [See the Thumbnail Sketch for a summary of factors that strengthen (or weaken) the case for market and public sector action.]

The identical analysis holds for the public sector. The case for government action to correct market failures is weakened when there is good reason to believe that special interest influence will eventually, if not immediately, result in inefficient public sector action. Similarly, the loss of a means to identify and weed out public sector inefficiency weakens the case for government action. Sometimes the choice of proper institutions may definitely be a choice among evils. For example, we might expect private sector monopoly if an activity is left to the market, but perverse regulation because of the special interest effect if we turn to the public sector. Unfortunately, the world is an imperfect place to live. But understanding the shortcomings of both the market and public sectors is important if we are going to improve and adapt our current economic institutions.

During a past period, economists implicitly assumed that the private sector operated like the perfectly competitive model said it was supposed to. Reality indicated this was not so. Today, we sometimes implicitly assume that government will operate so as to obtain the ideal efficiency conditions of economists. Again, reality is telling us something different. The application of economics to public choice helps us better understand why public policy sometimes goes astray and how policy sector incentives might be altered to improve the efficiency of government action.

THUMBNAIL SKETCH

These factors weaken the case for market sector allocation:

(1) external costs,
(2) external benefits,
(3) public goods,
(4) monopoly, and
(5) uninformed consumers.

These factors weaken the case for public sector intervention:

(1) voter ignorance and inability to fully recognize costs and benefits,
(2) the expected power of special interests,
(3) the shortsightedness effect,
(4) little incentive for entrepreneurial efficiency, and
(5) imprecision in the reflection of consumer preferences.

Dealing with Special Interests

When the special interest effect is present, the personal welfare of vote-seeking, political entrepreneurs may conflict with economic efficiency. Since taxpayers and consumers are widely dispersed, largely disorganized, and rationally uninformed on political matters, vote-seeking entrepreneurs can often gain by "socking it" to such groups when their welfare conflicts with that of well-organized special interest groups (for example, unions, industrial interests, and trade associations).

Could political institutions be changed to alleviate this problem? While no easy solutions are available, several steps could be taken that would help to bring the personal interests of politicians more into harmony with economic efficiency. The following suggestions would lead in this direction.

1. *Force Legislators to Establish a Budget Constraint—a Maximum Level of Government Spending—as Their First Act During Each Legislative Session.* The current system of appropriations for individual budget items permits legislators to cater to special interests, without ever having to take a clear stand on economy in government.

Individuals must choose within the framework of a fixed budget constraint. More butter means less bread. In contrast, legislators have a third option. They can vote for more butter, passing the tab on to the disorganized taxpayer, while continuing the same level of spending on bread. In general, the system fails to force legislators to make careful choices within the framework of a fixed budget.

This defect, which favors special interest groups, would be corrected if legislative sessions were required to establish a fixed budget constraint at the beginning of each session. Then the issue of additional government spending versus lower taxes could be debated on its merits. In contrast to the current system, a legislator's vote on this single issue—establishment of the size of the government's budget—would provide the voter with a reliable index of the legislator's support of taxpayer interests and government economy.

Once the size of the budget has been decided, then and only then would appropriation decisions be made. Each special interest would then be pitted, not against the taxpayer, but rather against other special interests pursuing government monies. The Defense Department would have to convince legislators that additional Pentagon spending was more meritorious than additional spending on welfare, education, Social Security, college students, and/or subsidies to industrial interests. HEW would have to argue that expanding their appropriation was more important than, for example, additional environmental spending. Special interests could no longer simply rob the taxpayer when they seek additional public sector funds.

2. *Limit the Terms of Congressmen, Senators, and the President.* Many "public servants" are constantly running for re-election. Some have spent their entire adult lifetime as political entrepreneurs. Of necessity, successful professional politicians will consider how their legislative actions will influence their ability to attract political contributions and votes in the future. This behavior strengthens the hand of organized interest groups.

Suppose that Congressmen were permitted to serve only two terms and Senators and the President were limited to one six year term. In addition, suppose that after ten consecutive years as a federal officeholder, political entrepreneurs were required to spend at least four years off the federal payroll. Such a plan would reduce the bias in the current system that favors professional politicians and the special interests who feed their continuous re-election efforts.

3. *Prohibit Campaign Contributions from Organizations.*   The political clout of business groups, unions, and other special interests lies with their ability to provide contributions and political assistance to political entrepreneurs. These resources are often used to create a popular, citizen-oriented image of a politician who in reality thrives on special interest support. Prohibiting organizations from making political contributions would cut off the lifeblood of powerful interest groups.

Currently, organizations are permitted to give up to $5000 to any candidate. However, this limitation is largely cosmetic since there is no limitation on the establishment of "dummy" organizations which would permit the parent interest group to give multiple $5000 contributions to a candidate. Politicians will cater to the views of those upon whom they are dependent. It is too much to expect freedom of action from a legislator who is dependent on special interest political contributions. Perhaps this proposal should be supplemented with a plan (a partial tax credit, for example) to stimulate small political contributions from individuals.

4. *Make More Use of Referendums When Resolving Special Interest Issues.*   When a decision is resolved by referendum, the special interest is much less likely to prevail. A referendum permits each member of the disorganized majority to register his opposition—albeit mild opposition—to a special interest issue, *independent of other issues.* The information necessary to register one's views is reduced, since the voter need not identify the alternative positions of political middlemen (legislators) on the issue. In contrast to legislative decision-making, a referendum virtually eliminates vote trading (so called log rolling: "you support my special issue and I'll support yours") as a weapon to gain passage of legislation favored by interest groups. All of these factors make the referendum an attractive—if seldom used—vehicle with which to attack the power of special interests.[15]

But There is One Big Problem

While the above proposals would serve to limit the influence of interest groups, with the exception of point 4 they have one overriding defect. They would require action by today's political entrepreneurs who are the major beneficiaries of the current system. Unless voter awareness of the economic inefficiency and political corruption that stems from the special interest effect increases substantially, it is unlikely that legislators will take action to reduce the ability (or incentive) of interest groups to continue to use political contributions, organizational power, and bribes in order to obtain support for political action. In short, current political entrepreneurs are unlikely to take up the banner of the disorganized taxpayers and consumers in order to bite the hand that feeds them.

Discussion

1. Explain why you either favor or oppose each of the four suggestions outlined by this perspective. Do you think they would effectively limit the power of interest groups?

[15]See James D. Gwartney and Jonathan Silberman, "Distribution of Costs and Benefits and the Significance of Collective Decision Rules," *Social Science Quarterly*, December 1973 for a more complete analysis of why referendum decision-making limits the power of special interest groups.

2. If the right of political entrepreneurs to run for re-election was limited as point 2 suggests, do you think the quality of public officials would decline? Do you think that career politicians strengthen or weaken democratic government? Explain.
3. Do you think that the first suggestion would decrease or increase the size of government? Would it improve or reduce economic efficiency? Explain.
4. How do you think organized industrial interests, unions, professional associations, and bureaucrats would react to these proposals? Why?

CHAPTER LEARNING OBJECTIVES

1. Economic theory suggests that public sector action, like the market, will sometimes go astray when handling certain classes of economic action. Economic inefficiency will result.

2. When the benefits of public sector action are difficult for voters to perceive, proposals will tend to be rejected even though they would promote the community's welfare (that is, the total benefits from such projects exceed their costs). On the other hand, when the costs of a policy are difficult to perceive, there will be a strong incentive to conduct such projects even though they may be inefficient. Legislators have a strong incentive to "package" public policy in a manner that amplifies the benefits while concealing the costs imposed on voters.

3. There is a strong incentive for political suppliers to support special interest issues, particularly if the issue is complex. The disorganized, largely uninformed majority will fail to understand the issue fully. One will not lose their support. In contrast, one's position on the special interest issue is often the sole determining factor of support, both financial and voting, from the special interest group.

4. The shortsightedness effect is another potential source of conflict and government failure. When the benefits are largely current and the costs are difficult to identify and in the future, there is an incentive to support projects with a benefit/cost ratio, accurately measured, of less than unity. In contrast, if the benefits are in the future and the costs are immediate, there is an incentive for political suppliers to reject projects with an accurately perceived B/C of more than one.

5. The economic incentive for operational efficiency is low for public sector action. No individual or relatively small group of individuals can personally capture gains derived from improved operational efficiency. There is not a force, parallel to bankruptcy in the private sector, that will bring inefficient behavior to a halt.

6. Public sector voters confront a few "bundle" or all-inclusive choices. There is little opportunity for marginal adjustments or diversity in the provision of political goods. Uniformity tends to be the pattern even for goods that are largely private in nature. These factors reduce the ability of the public sector to cater to the views of a diverse populace.

7. Positive economics cannot tell us that an action should be conducted in the public (market) sector. But analysis of how both the private and public sectors operate does shed insight on the strength of the case for conducting an activity in one or the other of the sectors. When market failure is prevalent, the case for public sector action is strengthened. On the other hand, expectation of government failure for a specific economic function reduces the strength of the argument for government intervention. Analysis of both the advantages and shortcomings of economic institutions will help us more clearly develop and choose between the market and public sector alternatives.

IMPORTANT TERMS TO REMEMBER

Government failure: Economic action by the government that is inconsistent with ideal economic efficiency conditions.

The shortsightedness effect: Misallocation of resources that results because public sector action is biased (a) in favor of proposals that yield clearly defined current costs at the expense of difficult to identify future benefits and (b) against proposals with clearly identifiable current costs that would yield future benefits that are less concrete.

THE ECONOMIC WAY OF THINKING—DISCUSSION QUESTIONS

1. "The private interests of political officials and voters can conflict with economic efficiency just as the private interests of a monopolist can conflict with efficiency." Do you agree? Explain.
2. How do you think the following would influence next year's budget of a local police department: **(a)** an increase in prostitution, **(b)** a rise in the number of arrests on drug charges, **(c)** a general rise in the crime rate, **(d)** a reduction in the percentage of crimes solved, **(e)** a reduction in the number of traffic accidents?
3. Do you think that economic activity is conducted more efficiently in the public rather than the private sector? Explain. Do you think that private colleges and universities are more efficient than public ones? Explain.
4. Do political entrepreneurs ever have an incentive to deceive voters about the cost of legislation that they favor? When? Can you give any examples of cases where this has happened?
5. The liquor industry contributes a large share of the political funds for state level contests. Yet its contributions to candidates for national office are minimal. Why do you think this is true? (*Hint:* Who regulates the liquor industry?)

6. What's Wrong with This Way of Thinking?

"Public policy is necessary to protect the average citizen from the power of vested interest groups. In the absence of government intervention, currently regulated industries such as airlines, railroads, and trucking would charge excessive prices, products would be unsafe, and the rich would oppress the poor. Government curbs the power of the special interests."

VI
INTERNATIONAL ECONOMICS

31

GAINING FROM INTERNATIONAL TRADE

We live in a shrinking world. Wheat raised on the flatlands of western Kansas may be processed into bread in a Russian factory. The breakfast of many Americans is rounded out with bananas from Honduras, coffee from Brazil, and hot chocolate made from Nigerian cocoa beans. The volume of world trade, pushed along by improved transportation and communications, has grown rapidly in recent years. In 1973 the total trade between nations was approximately $350 billion, three times the level of a decade ago.

In this chapter, we analyze the impact that foreign trade exerts on the price, consumption, and domestic production of goods. The effects of trade restrictions such as tariffs and quotas are also considered. International trade is an area of economics where fallacies seem to abound. Indirect effects are often ignored. As we progress, several examples of economic nonreasoning are discussed.

THE SIZE OF THE INTERNATIONAL SECTOR

As Exhibit 31-1 shows, the size of the trade sector varies among nations. International trade comprises more than one-fifth of the GNP of the Netherlands, Sweden, Canada, and West Germany. In contrast, only 5 percent of the GNP in the United States results from trade.

However, the size of the international sector relative to GNP may actually understate the importance of trade. Many of the products that we purchase from foreigners would be much more costly if we were solely dependent on our domestic production. We are dependent on foreign producers for several products, including almost all of our coffee and bananas, more than 90 percent of the bauxite we use to make aluminum, all of our chromium, diamonds, and tin, and most of our cobalt, nickel, manganese, and asbestos. The lifestyle of Americans (as well as our trading partners) would be changed if international trade were halted.

Exhibits 31-2 and 31-3 summarize the leading products imported and exported by the United States. Two products, automobiles and petroleum, comprise nearly one-quarter of all U.S. imports. In addition, machinery (both electrical and nonelectrical),

Exhibit 31-1   The Size of the Trade Sector for Selected Countries

Country	International trade as percentage of GNP
Netherlands	44
Sweden	25
Canada	22
West Germany	21
United Kingdom	18
Japan	11
United States	5

SOURCE: U.S. Bureau of Commerce.

meats and fish, iron and steel, and chemicals are among the leading import items. Exhibit 31-3 presents the export side of the picture. In 1973 grains, primarily wheat and corn, were the leading export products of the United States. Chemicals, motor vehicles, electrical equipment, and aircraft were also exported in large quantities.

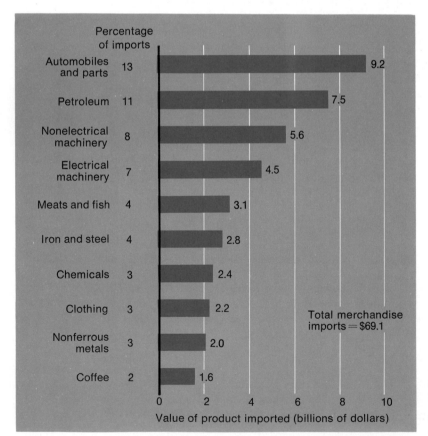

Exhibit 31-2   The Major Import Products of the United States, 1973

SOURCE: *The Statistical Abstract of the United States—1975.*

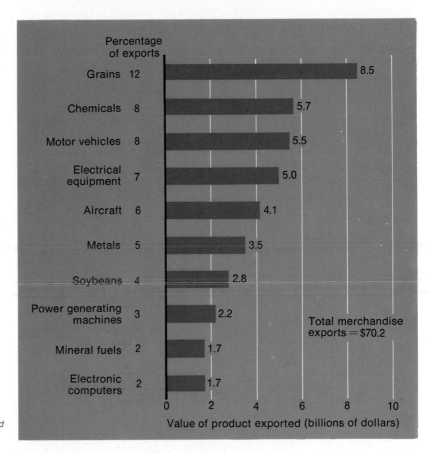

Percentage of exports

		Value of product exported (billions of dollars)
Grains	12	8.5
Chemicals	8	5.7
Motor vehicles	8	5.5
Electrical equipment	7	5.0
Aircraft	6	4.1
Metals	5	3.5
Soybeans	4	2.8
Power generating machines	3	2.2
Mineral fuels	2	1.7
Electronic computers	2	1.7

Total merchandise exports = $70.2

Exhibit 31-3   The Major Export Products of the United States, 1973

SOURCE: *The Statistical Abstract of the United States—1975.*

In recent years the structure of U.S. trade has been changing. Agricultural products (grains, soybeans, and rice) and high technology manufacturing products (for example, aircraft, computers, machine tools) have comprised an increasing share of our total exports. In contrast, foreign producers have supplied an expanding share of our domestic markets in established industries such as automobiles, steel, petroleum, and textiles.

With whom does the United States trade? As Exhibit 31-4 shows, Canada leads the list. In 1973, approximately one-quarter of U.S. imports were from Canadian producers, and more than one-fifth of our exports were to Canada. Japan and the European Economic Community (EEC) are also major trading partners. In 1973 the United States exported $1.1 billion of merchanise, primarily grains, to the Soviet Union. While trade between the two superpowers has been increasing rapidly, it is still a small fraction of the total. Barring an increase in international tension, trade between the two countries will most assuredly grow. The United States is a cost-efficient producer of food products and high technology manufactured goods, in great demand by the Soviet Union. On the other hand, the Soviet Union is rich in raw materials demanded by the United States.

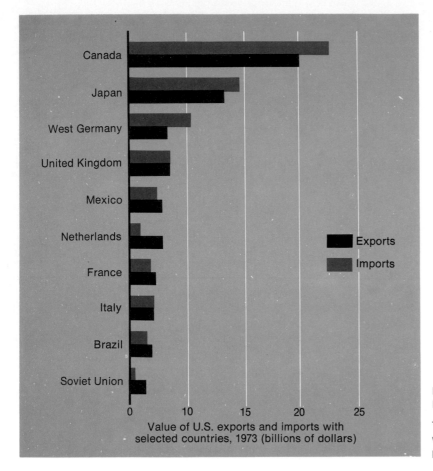

Exhibit 31-4 The Leading Trading Partners of the United States

Two-thirds of all U.S. trade in 1973 was with developed countries, primarily Japan, Canada, and EEC countries.

Value of U.S. exports and imports with selected countries, 1973 (billions of dollars)

WHY DO NATIONS TRADE?

International trade, like other voluntary exchange, results because both the buyer and seller gain from it. If both parties did not expect to gain, there would be no trade. As we explained in Chapter 2, trade permits nations (as well as individuals and regions) to specialize in those things which, comparatively speaking, they do best. Each trading partner can gain by specializing in the production of goods for which he is a low opportunity cost producer, trading them for those products for which he is a high opportunity cost producer.

A doctor may be an excellent typist but he can usually gain by hiring a typist so he can specialize in medical problems. Economists are often proficient computer programmers, yet they usually hire someone to do their programming, so they can specialize in economic research. Even when they are proficient housekeepers, working wives often hire a maid. Why? So they can specialize in work for which they have a comparative advantage. The list is endless. Each of us is constantly trading for items that we could, at some cost, produce. But we trade for them, so that we can specialize in the areas of our greatest comparative advantage.

The principle works exactly the same way for trade between nations. Even when two countries could both produce the same set of products, they will nearly always be able to gain from trade. Each of the nations will have a comparative advantage for at least some of the products. It is easy to see why countries with a warm, rainy climate will have a comparative advantage in the production of bananas and rice. Similarly, cooler northern areas are more suitable for the production of wheat, feed grains, and beef. Under these circumstances, everyone can readily understand why trade and specialization would be mutually advantageous to both parties.

But remember, only comparative advantage is necessary for trade to be mutually profitable. One country might have an absolute advantage (that is, it might use fewer resources to produce each good) over another in the production of goods. But as long as there are differences in relative efficiency in the production of goods, trade between the two countries will lead to mutual gain because it permits each country to apply its resources to the production of those things which it does best.[1]

The Export–Import Link

Confusion about the merit of international trade often results because people forget to consider all the secondary effects. Why are other nations willing to export their goods to the United States? So they can get dollars. Yes, but why do they want dollars? Would foreigners be willing to continue exporting oil, radios, watches, cameras, automobiles, and thousands of other valuable products to us in exchange for pieces of paper? If so, we could all retire except for an occasional workday at the dollar printing press office! But of course, foreigners are not so naive. They trade goods for dollars so they can use the dollars to import U.S. goods and purchase ownership rights to U.S. assets.

Exports and imports are closely linked. Nations export goods to others so they will be able to import foreign products. Exports provide the buying power that makes it possible for a nation to import other goods. As a secondary effect, policies that retard imports will simultaneously retard the ability of foreigners to purchase the export products of a nation.

SUPPLY, DEMAND, AND INTERNATIONAL TRADE

How does international trade affect prices and output levels in domestic markets? Supply and demand analysis will help us answer this question. High transportation costs and the availability of cheaper alternatives elsewhere reduce the attractiveness of some U.S. products to foreigners. These factors may completely eliminate foreign purchases for some commodities. However, foreign consumers will find that many U.S.

---

[1]The reader should be familiar with the law of comparative advantage, initially introduced in Chapter 2. Those who do not thoroughly understand the concept should review Exhibits 2-3 and 2-4, which illustrate the gains from specialization and trade using numerical examples.

products are cheaper even when transportation costs are considered. When this is the case, the demand of foreigners will supplement that of domestic consumers.

For an open economy, the market demand curve for domestic products would be the horizontal sum of the domestic and foreign demand. Exhibit 31-5 illustrates the impact of foreign demand on the domestic wheat market. When the demand of foreigners is added to the domestic demand, it yields the market demand curve D_{f+d} (where the subscripts f and d refer to foreign and domestic, respectively). Price P would bring supply and demand into equilibrium. At the equilibrium market price, foreigners purchase OF units of wheat, while domestic consumers purchase FQ. The competition from foreign consumers resulted in both higher wheat prices and a larger output level.

At first glance it appears that the entry of foreign consumers into the U.S. market helped U.S. wheat producers at the expense of domestic consumers, who must now pay higher wheat prices (or else do without). That view is correct as far as it goes, but it ignores the secondary effects. How will foreigners obtain the purchasing power to import U.S. wheat? Primarily by exporting products for which they are low cost producers to the U.S. market. The domestic supply of those products exported by foreigners in order to pay for the wheat will expand. Their prices will be reduced (compared to the no-trade situation), benefiting the U.S. consumers who appeared to be harmed by the higher wheat prices.

Exhibit 31-6 illustrates this point, using foreign banana imports as an example. The total supply of bananas to the U.S. market is the horizontal sum of (a) the foreign supply to the domestic market plus (b) the supply of domestic producers. Since foreign countries, particularly Honduras, are low opportunity cost producers of bananas, they will be able to supply them to the U.S. market cheaper than most domestic producers. The addition of the imported supply results in both lower prices and a higher consumption level than would be present in the absence of trade.

Relative to the no-trade alternative, international trade and specialization result in lower prices (and higher consumption levels) for imported products and higher prices

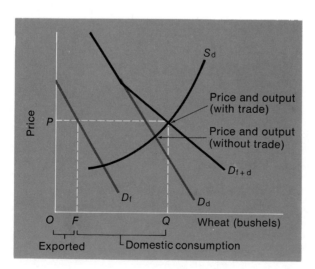

Exhibit 31-5   Exporting to Foreigners

The demand of both foreign and domestic purchasers for U.S. wheat is shown here. The market demand (D_{f+d}) is the horizontal sum of these two components. Total domestic production of the product would be OQ, of which OF would be exported and FQ consumed domestically.

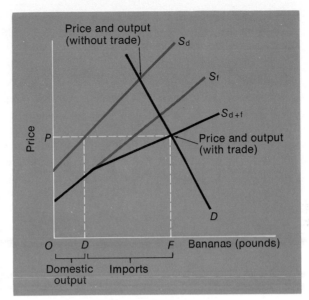

Exhibit 31-6   Importing Cheap Goods

Both the domestic and foreign supply of bananas to the U.S. market are shown here. Since foreign producers have a comparative advantage in the production of bananas, the supply curve of foreigners exceeds that of domestic producers. At price *P*, *OD* would be produced domestically and *DF* imported.

(and lower consumption levels) for exported products. But, as the law of comparative advantage reveals, the net effect is an expansion in the consumption alternatives available to a nation.

TARIFFS AND QUOTAS

While economics suggests that nations would benefit from a free trade policy, in the real world many governments have, in fact, erected trade barriers. Tariffs and quotas are the two most commonly utilized trade-restricting devices. A **tariff** is nothing more than a tax on foreign imports. As Exhibit 31-7 shows, tariff barriers in the United States

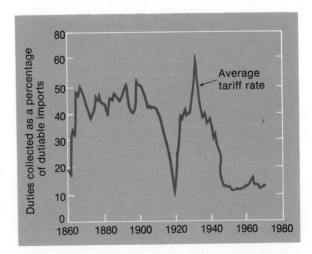

Exhibit 31-7   How High Are U.S. Tariffs?

Tariff rates in the United States fell sharply during the 1930–1950 period. Subsequently, they have leveled off at approximately 10 percent of duty eligible imports.

SOURCE: U.S. Department of Commerce.

have fluctuated. Until the 1940s, tariffs of between 30 and 50 percent of product value were often levied. In recent years the average tariff rate has been approximately 10 percent.

How do tariffs influence the average consumer? When the United States levies a tariff on a product, it becomes more costly for foreign producers to supply the good to the U.S. market. As Exhibit 31-8 shows, the *foreign* supply curve to the U.S. market would shift upward (from S_{f1} to S_{f2}) by the amount of the tariff. The reduction in foreign supply serves to reduce the supply to the domestic market from S_1 to S_2, causing the product price to increase. After the imposition of the tariff, foreigners will supply less to the domestic market. In contrast, domestic producers, since they do not pay the tariff, will actually expand their output in response to the higher market price. In effect the tariff acts as a subsidy to domestic producers, financed by consumers who now face higher prices.

The story does not quite end here. Since foreigners are unable to sell goods for which they are low cost producers in the U.S. market, they will acquire fewer dollars. Foreign demand for U.S. exports, products for which we are low cost producers, with decline because our trade restrictions have diminished the ability of foreigners to acquire the dollars necessary to buy our goods. Potential gains from specialization and trade will go unrealized.

Import quotas, like tariffs, are designed to restrict foreign goods and protect domestic industries. Quotas place a ceiling on the amount of a product that can be imported. In 1972, no fewer than 67 major product categories, ranging from steel to brooms, were subject to import quotas.

Since quotas reduce the foreign supply (and therefore the market supply), the price of quota-protected products will be higher than would result from free trade. In many ways, quotas are more harmful than tariffs. With a quota, additional foreign supply is prohibited regardless of how low priced foreign products are. With the tariff, products will at least be supplied to the domestic market if the cost advantage of foreign producers is sufficient to overcome the tariff.

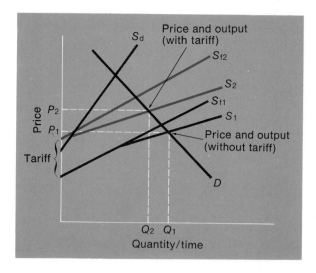

Exhibit 31-8 The Impact of a Tariff

A tariff on imports will reduce the supply available to the domestic market (shift from S_1 to S_2). A higher product price and a smaller consumption level will result.

MYTHS OF ECONOMICS
"Free trade with low-wage countries such as China and India would cause the wages of U.S. workers to fall."

Many Americans believe that trade restrictions are necessary to protect U.S. workers from imported goods produced by cheap foreign labor. How can U.S. labor compete with Indian and Chinese workers receiving 10 cents an hour? The fallacy stems from a misunderstanding of both the source of high wages and the law of comparative advantage.

High *hourly wages* do not necessarily mean high *per unit labor cost*. Labor productivity must also be considered. For example, suppose that a U.S. steel worker received an hourly wage rate of $6. His counterpart in India receives only 50 cents per hour. But, given the capital and production methods used in the two countries, the U.S. worker produces 20 times as many tons of steel per man-hour as the Indian worker. Because of the high productivity per man-hour, per unit labor cost would actually be lower in the United States than in India!

Labor in the United States possesses a high skill level and works with large amounts of capital equipment. These factors contribute to the high productivity and the high hourly wages of American workers. Similarly, low productivity per man-hour is the reason wages are low in countries such as India and China.

But the availability of capital and the high productivity of the U.S. Labor force do not mean that we can produce everything at a lower opportunity cost than foreigners. Low-wage countries are likely to have a comparative advantage in the production of labor intensive products. When other countries can produce wigs, watches, textile goods, sugar, coffee, and miniature radios cheaper than domestic producers, we can gain from specialization and trade. Importation of these products allows us to free labor (and capital) resources so we can export more wheat, feed grains, airplanes, and electrical equipment, products for which we are low cost producers. The net result is a reallocation of U.S. workers away from industries in which they are inefficient (relative to foreign producers) to industries in which they are highly efficient.

If foreigners, even low-wage foreigners, will sell us products cheaper than we ourselves can produce them, we can gain by using our resources to produce other things. Perhaps an extreme example will drive the point home. Suppose that a foreign producer, perhaps a Santa Claus who pays his workers little or nothing, were willing to supply us with winter coats free. Would it make sense to enact a tariff barrier to keep out the free coats? Of course not. Resources that were previously used to produce coats could now be freed to produce other goods. Output and the availability of goods would expand. The real wages of U.S. workers would rise. National defense aside, it makes no more sense to erect trade barriers to keep out low-priced foreign goods than to keep out the free coats of the friendly, foreign Santa Claus.

WHY INDUSTRIES ARE ON THE DOLE

Despite the potential benefits from free trade, in varying degrees, almost all nations have erected trade barriers. Why? Three factors seem to contribute to the explanation of trade barriers. They are

(1) sound arguments for protection of specific industries under certain circumstances,

(2) economic illiteracy that is related to the concealed nature of who is helped and who is harmed by trade restrictions, and

(3) the special interest nature of trade restrictions.

Some Sound Arguments for Restrictions

There are three major, at least partially valid, arguments for protecting certain domestic industries from foreign competitors.

1. *National Defense Argument for Protection.* Certain industries—aircraft, petroleum, and weapons, for example—are vital to national defense. A nation might want to protect such industries from foreign competitors so that a domestic supply of these materials would be available in case of an international conflict. Would we want to be entirely dependent on Arabian or Russian petroleum? Would complete dependence on French aircraft be wise? Most Americans would answer no, even if trade restrictions were required to preserve these domestic industries.

The reasoning of the national defense argument is sound—however, it can be abused. Relatively few industries are really vital to our national defense. Partial reliance on foreign producers during peacetime may not weaken the capacity of certain domestic industries, particularly those that extract raw materials, to supply the nation's needs in case of war. When analyzing the merits of protecting a domestic industry, the costs and benefits of the national defense argument must be weighed carefully.

2. *The Industrial Diversity Argument.* If a domestic economy specializes in the protection of only one or two major products, changes in world demand can exert a drastic influence on domestic economic conditions. Brazil's coffee-dominated economy is an example. Economies that are largely dependent on the revenues from a few major export products or raw materials, will be characterized by instability. Protection of domestic industries would encourage diversity. Clearly this argument would not apply to the U.S. economy, which is already highly diversified.

3. *The* **Infant Industry Argument.** This view states that new domestic industries should be protected from older established foreign competitors. As the new industry matures, so the argument goes, it will be able to stand on its own feet and compete effectively with foreign competitors. The infant industry argument has a long and sometimes notorious history. Alexander Hamilton used it to argue for the protection of early U.S. manufacturing. While it is clearly an argument for *temporary* protection,

once granted, the protection is often difficult to remove. Nearly a century ago this argument was used to gain tariff protection for the early steel industry in the United States. Today, this industry is not only mature, but many believe that competitive pressures are less than vigorous. Yet, public policy has failed to remove the tariff.

Protection and Saving Jobs?

Part of the popularity of trade restrictions stems from their ability to protect or create *easily identifiable jobs.* Whenever foreign competitors begin making inroads into markets that have traditionally been supplied by domestic producers, the outcry for "protection to save jobs" is sure to be raised. Political entrepreneurs will recognize the potential gain from a protectionist policy and respond accordingly.

But the restrictions have a secondary impact on jobs that is usually unnoticed. Because foreigners are unable to sell to us, they will be forced to cut back their purchases from us. Export industries will now contract (or at least fail to expand) because foreigners lack the dollars to pay for our goods. Jobs in export industries are destroyed.

In the long run, trade restrictions can neither create nor destroy jobs, but they can and do promote economic inefficiency. The choice is not whether textiles (or some other product) will be produced in the United States or Japan. The real choice is whether (a) our resources will be used to produce textiles and other products for which we are a high opportunity cost producer or (b) whether they will be used to produce agriculture, high technology manufacturing goods, and other products for which we are a low cost producer. As trade restrictions move resources from high to low productivity areas, they do not create jobs, but they do reduce net output and the availability of goods.

What about industries that are long-time recipients of protection? Of course, immediate removal of trade barriers would harm producers and workers. It would be costly for the protected resources to transfer immediately to other areas and industries. Gradual removal of such barriers would minimize the relocation costs and eliminate the shock effect. The government might also cushion the burden by subsidizing the retraining and relocation costs of displaced workers.

Protection and Representing the Special Interests

Even when trade restrictions promote inefficiency and harm economic welfare, political entrepreneurs may be able to reap political gain from their enactment. Those harmed by a protectionist policy for industry X, will individually bear a small, and difficult to identify, cost. Consumers who will pay higher prices for the products of a protected industry are an unorganized group. Most of them will not relate the higher product prices to the protectionist policy. Similarly, numerous export producers (and their employees) will individually be harmed only a little. The rational ignorance effect implies that those harmed by trade restrictions are likely to be uninformed and disinterested in our trade policy.

In contrast, special interest groups—specific industries, unions, and regions—will be highly concerned with the protection of their industry. They will stand ready to aid political entrepreneurs who support their view, and penalize those who do not. Clearly, vote-seeking politicians will be sensitive to their views. Often there will be a conflict between sound economics and good politics on trade restriction issues. Real world public policy will, of course, reflect the politics of the situation.

INTERNATIONAL TRADE AND THE GREAT OIL CARTEL

Skyrocketing oil prices caused the value of imports for most industrial nations to rise sharply during the mid-1970s. In less than three years, the price of crude oil in the world market increased 400 percent. What caused the world oil price to rocket upward?

A relatively small number of nations, primarily the Middle Eastern countries, Indonesia, and Venezuela, are the major exporters of petroleum. They formed the Organization of Petroleum Exporting Countries (OPEC). In 1973 they agreed to increase the price of crude oil substantially. Essentially, OPEC is an international cartel of petroleum exporters. Exhibit 31-9 illustrates the economic thinking behind OPEC's price fixing behavior. As the price of imported oil rose, industrial nations attempted to reduce their consumption level. However, both the domestic supply and market demand curves for most industrial nations were highly inelastic, particularly in the short run. Industrial nations were neither able to reduce their consumption rate nor expand their domestic production significantly. Therefore, OPEC countries exported almost as much oil at $10 per barrel as they would have at $5. Their oil revenues skyrocketed, as oil prices doubled and then quadrupled with little immediate reduction in the quantity exported. Eventually, perhaps several years from now, the demand of

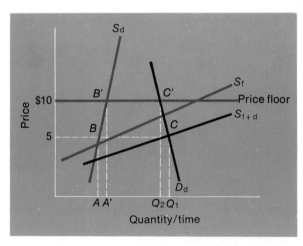

Exhibit 31-9   International Cartels and the Nouveau Riche

The diagram illustrates why foreign producers can *sometimes* gain by forming a cartel. Without collusion, the foreign supply curve for crude oil would be S_f. An equilibrium price of $5 would result. Foreigners would sell AQ_1 units, and their total revenues would be $ABCQ_1$. If an international cartel (*OPEC*, for example) agreed to establish a price floor of $10 per barrel, they could still sell $A'Q_2$ units. Their total revenues would expand to $A'B'C'Q_2$. When a nation's supply and demand curves for the product are highly inelastic, foreign producers can clearly gain from a cartel agreement.

Western nations will become more elastic. If market forces are not stifled by public policy, alternative sources of petroleum and substitute forms of energy will be developed. These forces will weaken the ability of OPEC to maintain the artificially high price of oil.

Are other international cartels likely to be formed? Nations producing coffee, bauxite, and other products have attempted to form export cartels. However, widespread use of such techniques appears unlikely for two reasons. First, unless both the demand of importing countries and their domestic supply are highly inelastic importers will sharply curtail their purchases should exporting nations raise their price. This would dampen the benefits that would accrue to an export cartel. Second, an effective cartel would have to control alternative sources of supply. In the case of petroleum, Nature greatly reduced the difficulty of this task. But for most other products, it would be difficult to keep new entrants from undercutting the cartel price if it is substantially in excess of competitive levels.

▭ LOOKING AHEAD

Trade between nations like trade between individuals usually involves the exchange of goods for money. Yet there is not a common world currency. Chapter 32 deals with the financial arrangements under which international trade is conducted.

CHAPTER LEARNING OBJECTIVES

1. The trade sector comprises approximately 5 percent of the U.S. GNP. Major import items include automobiles, petroleum, machinery, meats, fish, steel, and coffee. The major U.S. exports are grains, chemicals, motor vehicles, electrical equipment, and aircraft.

2. Two-thirds of all U.S. trade is with developed countries, primarily Canada, Japan, and EEC nations.

3. Trade between nations permits each to specialize in the production of those goods for which it has a comparative advantage. Through specialization and trade, aggregate output can be expanded. Mutual gain accrues to the trading partners.

4. Exports and imports are closely linked. The exports of a nation are the primary source of purchasing power used to import goods.

5. Relative to the no-trade alternative, international exchange and specialization will result in lower prices for products that are imported and higher domestic prices for products that are exported. But the net effect will be an expansion in the consumption alternatives available to a nation.

6. Tariffs and quotas restrict trade and reduce the ability of domestic producers to specialize in those areas for which their comparative advantage is greatest. Essentially, they are subsidies to producers (and workers) in protected industries at the expense of **(a)** consumers and **(b)** producers (and workers) in export industries.

7. High wages do not necessarily mean high labor cost. Productivity must also be considered. The law of comparative advantages explains why the United States can benefit from trade —even trade with low-wage countries.

8. National defense, industrial diversity, and the infant industry argument can be used to justify trade restrictions for specific industries under certain conditions. However, it is clear that the power of special interest groups and the obscurity of the harmful effects offer the major explanation for real world protectionist public policy.

IMPORTANT TERMS TO REMEMBER

Tariff: A tax that is levied on goods imported into a country.

Quota: A specific quantity (or value) of a good that is permitted into a country.

Infant industry argument: The argument that specific industries should be protected from foreign competitors until they are "established." Presumably, as the industry matures, protection against foreign competition will be removed.

THE ECONOMIC WAY OF THINKING—DISCUSSION QUESTIONS

1. Suppose that at the time of the Civil War, the United States had been divided into two countries, and that through the years no trade existed between the two. How would the standard of living in the "divided" United States have been affected? Explain.
2. Do you think that the United States could benefit if all barriers to trade among North American nations were eliminated? Would Canada gain? Mexico? Why or why not?
3. **(a)** "Tariffs and import quotas promote economic inefficiency and reduce the real income of a nation. Economic analysis suggests that nations can gain by eliminating trade restrictions."
   (b) "Economic analysis suggests that there is good reason to expect trade restrictions to exist in the real world."
   Could both (a) and (b) be true? Explain.
4. "Tariffs and quotas are necessary to protect the high wages of the American worker." Do you agree or disagree? Why?
5. Suppose that the United States levied a tariff on crude oil that was equal to the import price (approximately $10.50 per barrel in 1975) minus $7.50 per barrel. Thus, an increase in the import price (above $7.50 per barrel) would automatically raise the tariff by an equal amount. What impact would this policy have on **(a)** U.S. consumption of foreign oil, **(b)** the elasticity of demand for foreign oil as seen by foreign producers, and **(c)** the incentive of the international oil cartel (OPEC) to raise their price for oil?

6. What's Wrong with This Economic Experiment?

A researcher hypothesizes that higher tariffs on automobiles will cause total employment in the United States to increase. Automobile tariffs are raised and the following year employment in the U.S. auto industry increases by 100,000, compared to a three year annual average of 50,000 before the higher tariff legislation was passed. The researcher concludes that the higher tariffs on imported automobiles increased total domestic employment by creating approximately 50,000 jobs in the U.S. auto industry.

32
INTERNATIONAL FINANCE
AND BALANCE OF PAYMENTS

As we saw in the previous chapter, exchange between nations, like exchange between individuals, is mutually advantageous to both trading partners. In fact, specialization and trade allow the world to produce a larger output than if each country supplied its own domestic market, refusing to engage in international trade. While the principles of domestic and foreign trade are similar, international trade has additional complications because it involves two different currencies. Farmers in the United States will want dollars—not some foreign currency—when they sell their wheat. Therefore, foreign purchasers must exchange their currency for dollars before they buy U.S. wheat. Similarly, French winemakers will want to be paid in francs, not dollars. Therefore, U.S. consumers will need to exchange dollars for francs when purchasing French wines.

This chapter will analyze how international currencies are linked together and the factors that determine the rates at which different currencies are exchanged one for another. Special attention will be given to problems that arise when a country is spending more abroad than is earned from foreigners. These so called balance of payments problems will lead us to a discussion of different kinds of exchange rate policies and alternative forms of international monetary organization.

FOREIGN EXCHANGE MARKETS

Let us start off by imagining the case of a Californian who needs a pair of sandals. He goes to a shoe store and finds there are three types of sandals: local ones, New York factory-made ones, and Mexican imports. To the consumer, it makes no difference which pair he buys; in each case, he takes the sandals and pays the store owner in dollars. To the store owner, however, there is a drastic difference in the way the producers of the sandals have to be compensated. The local sandals can be either bartered for or paid for with dollars; the New York sandals can be paid for with dollars; but the Mexican sandals must somehow be paid for in pesos because the Mexican manufacturer needs pesos to pay the employees of his firm. Either the store owner will have to go to the bank and change dollars into pesos to send to the Mexican producer, or else the Mexican will have to go to his bank and change the store owner's dollar check into pesos. In either case, there has been an exchange of one currency for another. This illustration exemplifies the creation of a demand for pesos and the simultaneous creation of a supply of dollars in an international foreign exchange market.

While the California store owner and other Americans are demanding pesos with which to purchase Mexican goods, simultaneously many Mexicans who are purchasing U.S. products will be demanding dollars with which to pay American producers. The rate at which pesos are exchanged for dollars is called the **exchange rate** between the two currencies. If it takes 8.0 cents to get one peso, then 8.0 is the dollar-peso exchange rate. Thus an American who wanted to buy 12,500 pesos worth of sandals would have to come up with $1000 ($0.08 multiplied by 12,500) in order to purchase the pesos with which to purchase the sandals. The banks that handle such international exchange transactions typically charge a small percentage for making the transaction.

Exchange rates permit consumers in one country to translate the prices of foreign goods into units of their own currency. When 8 cents exchanges for one Mexican peso, how many dollars would it take to buy a pound of Mexican coffee selling for 25 pesos? The dollar price of the Mexican coffee would simply be 8 cents multiplied by 25, or $2.00.

Fluctuations in exchange rates will alter the prices of a nation's goods to foreign consumers. A **depreciation** in the value of a nation's currency means that more units of the local currency are now required to purchase each unit of a foreign currency. For example, if the number of cents required to purchase a Mexican peso increased from 8 to 10, the dollar has depreciated in value relative to the peso.[1] This depreciation in the value of the dollar would make Mexican goods more expensive to U.S. consumers (and U.S. goods less expensive to Mexican consumers). Thus, it would take $2.50 (rather than only $2.00) to purchase the pound of Mexican coffee if the dollar price of the peso increased from $0.08 to $0.10.

When a nation's currency becomes more valuable relative to a foreign currency, an economist would say that it has appreciated. An **appreciation** would make foreign goods cheaper, since it increases the number of units of a foreign currency that can be purchased with a unit of domestic currency.

Determination of Exchange Rates

Exhibit 32-1 presents data on the exchange rate between the dollar and selected foreign currencies as of March 1975. What determines the exchange rate between two currencies? In order to simplify the analysis, let us assume that the United States and Mexico are the only two countries in the world. The exchange rate between the U.S. dollar and Mexican peso is simply a price. Just as the forces of supply and demand determine other prices, so too will they determine the dollar price of the peso in the absence of government intervention.

[1] At first glance a depreciation looks like an appreciation, since the price of foreign currencies increases *in terms of a nation's domestic currency*. But a little thought reveals that if the dollar price of the peso increases from 8 to 10 cents, the dollar will now buy *fewer* pesos (and Mexican goods). Thus, it has depreciated relative to the peso.

Exhibit 32-1   Foreign Exchange Rates between the U.S. Dollar and Selected Foreign Currency—March 1975.

Foreign currency	Cents required to purchase one unit of the foreign currency
Australian dollar	135.85
Canadian dollar	99.95
French franc	23.80
German mark	43.12
Italian lira	0.16
Japanese yen	0.35
English pound	241.80
Mexican peso	8.00

SOURCE: *The Federal Reserve Bulletin,* April 1975.

When Mexicans purchase goods, services, or financial assets in the United States, they will supply pesos (and demand dollars) on the **foreign exchange market**—a market for the trading of different national currencies. On the other hand, when U.S. residents purchase goods, services, and financial assets in Mexico they will demand pesos (and supply dollars) to the foreign exchange market in order to pay Mexicans for these items.

As Exhibit 32-2 shows, the supply and demand curves for pesos (in terms of dollars) will have their typical shapes. As the price of pesos rises, a dollar will purchase fewer of them. This depreciation in the value of the dollar (relative to the peso) will make Mexican goods more expensive to Americans. Assuming the American demand for Mexican goods is elastic, the higher price of the peso will cause Americans to reduce their expenditures on Mexican goods. Thus, the quantity demanded of pesos will fall as their dollar price rises.

While a higher peso price (in terms of dollars) will tend to reduce the total value of

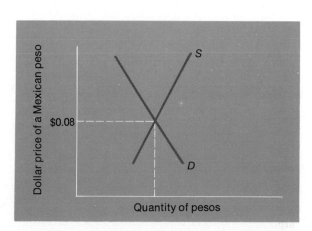

Exhibit 32-2   Equilibrium in the Foreign Exchange Market

In equilibrium, the dollar price of a Mexican peso would bring the demand for pesos into equality with their supply in the foreign exchange market.

Mexican goods, services, and capital assets imported, it will simultaneously make U.S. exports cheaper to Mexicans. For example, a $3000 American automobile will cost Mexican consumers 37,500 pesos when one peso exchanges for 8 cents but it costs only 30,000 pesos when each peso exchanges for 10 cents. If the demand for American automobiles in Mexico is elastic, then the total value of cars purchased by Mexicans from U.S. producers will rise as the dollar depreciates (and the peso appreciates). Thus, an increase in the dollar price of the peso (an appreciation of the peso) will typically cause the quantity of pesos supplied to the foreign exchange market to expand.

In equilibrium, the quantity of pesos demanded by Americans to import goods, services, and assets from Mexico will just equal the quantity supplied by Mexicans to purchase items from the United States. If Mexicans were importing more from the United States than Americans were exporting to Mexico, an excess supply of pesos would result. The excess supply would cause the price of pesos to fall (the dollar to appreciate) making Mexican goods cheaper to U.S. consumers and U.S. goods more expensive to Mexicans. Assuming an elastic demand for foreign goods, the lower price of the peso would restore equilibrium.

On the other hand, when the value of U.S. imports from Mexico exceeds the value of U.S. exports to Mexico, an excess demand for pesos will occur. The price of pesos will then rise (a depreciation of the dollar) making Mexican imports more expensive to U.S. purchasers and U.S. export items cheaper to Mexicans. Again, as long as the demand for exports (and imports) is elastic, freely fluctuating exchange rates will restore equilibrium.

BALANCE OF PAYMENTS AND EXCHANGE MARKETS

Just as countries calculate their gross national product in order to keep tabs on levels of production in their country, so also do most countries calculate their balance of international payments in order to keep track of their transactions with other nations. Rather than adding up the kinds of items we buy and sell and loan to other countries, we simply add up the actual payments between nations and record why those payments were made.

The **balance of payments** account records the flow of payments between one country and all the other countries of the world during a given year. Any transaction, importing foreign goods for example, which supplies the nation's domestic currency (or creates a demand for foreign currency) in the foreign exchange market is recorded as a debit item in the balance of payments account. In contrast, a transaction that gives rise to a demand for the nation's currency (or a supply of foreign currency) on the foreign exchange market, is recorded as a credit. Exports are an example of a credit item.

The balance of payments account attempts to pinpoint the reasons for transactions with foreigners. The U.S. account shows the volume of payments made to foreigners (supplying dollars to the foreign exchange market) for such things as merchandise imports, transportation of goods, services purchased by U.S. tourists abroad, and U.S. investment in other countries. Similarly, they show the flow of payments to the United States by foreigners for items such as merchandise exports, goods transported in U.S. vessels, spending of foreign tourists in the U.S., and foreign investment in the United States.

Exhibit 32-3 summarizes the U.S. balance of payments accounts for 1974. The most important division in the balance of payments account is between the current and capital account.

Exhibit 32-3   U.S. Balance of Payments 1974

DEBITS		CREDITS			
U.S. payments abroad (currency outflow in billions of dollars)		*U.S. receipts from abroad (currency inflow in billions of dollars)*		*Balance*	
Current account		*Current account*			
Merchandise imports	$103.0	Merchandise exports	$ 97.1	Balance of Trade	$−5.9
U.S. military expenditures	5.1	Military sales abroad	3.0		
U.S. travel abroad and transportation of goods on foreign carriers	12.7	Foreign travel in U.S. and foreign transport on U.S. carriers	10.2		
Income on foreign investment in U.S.	16.3	Income on U.S. investments abroad	25.9		
Other services purchased from foreigners	2.4	Other services sold to foreigners	6.4		
Foreign aid (nonmilitary)	7.2				
Import of goods and services	$146.7	Export of goods and services	$142.6	Balance on current account	$−4.1
Capital account		*Capital account*			
U.S. investment abroad and other long-term capital outflow	$ 16.2	Foreign investments in the U.S. and other long-term capital inflow	$ 9.7	Balance on current account and long-term capital	$−10.6
Short-term loans to foreigners and other short-term credit to foreigners	20.1	Short-term loans from foreigners	27.0		
		Errors and omissions	5.1		
Flow of payments on goods, services, and capital	$183.0	Flow of payments on goods, services, and capital	$184.4	Balance on current and capital accounts	$1.4
Transactions in U.S. official reserve assets (gold, SDR's, and convertible currencies)	$ 1.4				
Total outflow of dollars	$184.4	Total inflow of dollars	$184.4	Balance	$0.0

SOURCE: *Survey of Current Business,* March, 1975.

1. *Current Account.*   The balance of payments on current account includes all payments (and gifts) that relate to the purchase or sale of goods and services during the accounting period. The export and import of merchandise goods are by far the largest items on current account. In 1974 the United States imported $103.0 billion of merchandise goods from foreigners. Simultaneously, $97.1 billion of products were exported. The difference between a country's exports and imports is known as the **balance of trade.**

When a nation's imports exceed its exports it is said to have a "deficit in its balance of trade." Although the news media often attaches unfavorable connotations to a trade deficit it is not clear what is so unfavorable about receiving more goods from foreigners than you are sending to them in return. Of course, as our earlier examples about the importation of Mexican sandals revealed, when the United States imports goods, the transaction will result in a flow of dollars to the foreign exchange market. In contrast, U.S. exports will create a demand for dollars on the foreign exchange market. Thus, when the United States is running a deficit in its balance of trade, merchandise imports will be supplying more dollars to the exchange market than will be demanded in order to purchase our exports.

But several factors other than the flow of merchandise goods will affect a nation's balance of payments. As we will soon see, a deficit (or surplus) in a nation's balance of trade will always be offset by other balance of payments transactions.

In addition to the export and import of visible merchandise, service transactions with foreigners will affect the payments balance on current account. For instance, if an American flies from Los Angeles to New York on Air France, the portion of his or her air fare which is returned to France will count as a debit in the United States balance of payments because the transaction caused currency to flow out of the country. Similarly, when a famous movie star insures her legs for one billion dollars with Lloyds of London, that transaction also counts as a debit because dollars flow out of the United States to Great Britain. These and similar items are sometimes referred to as invisible imports (or exports). When Americans purchase services from foreigners, they will contribute to the flow (supply) of dollars to the exchange market. Travel abroad by U.S. citizens or shipment of goods in foreign carriers are important examples of services provided to the United States by foreigners. Since they add to the supply of dollars on the foreign exchange market, they are recorded as a debit in the balance of payments accounts (see Exhibit 32-3).

Similarly, U.S. military expenditures abroad and income paid to foreigners on *their* investments in the United States will cause dollars to flow to foreigners (the exchange market). Thus, they are recorded as debit items in the payments accounts. The handling of foreign aid is a bit more complex. When products are given to foreigners, goods flow abroad but there is not an offsetting inflow of foreign currency—that is, a demand for dollars. Balance of payments accountants handle such transactions as if the U.S. supplied the dollars with which to purchase the direct grants made to foreigners. Thus, foreign aid enters as a debit item.

While service imports cause dollars to flow to the exchange market, invisible exports to foreigners will add to the demand for dollars on the exchange market. When foreigners travel in the United States or ship cargo with American ships, they will demand dollars with which to pay for these services. Similarly, income earned by U.S.

investments abroad will cause dollars to flow from foreigners to Americans. Thus, these items are entered as credits on the current account.

In total, counting direct grants to foreigners, the United States imported $146.7 billion of goods and services in 1974. Simultaneously $142.6 billion of goods and services were exported in 1974. Thus, the U.S. ran a balance of payments deficit on current account of $4.1 billion.

2. *Capital Account.*   In addition to the flow of goods and services, capital movements between countries will affect the demand for and supply of dollars on foreign exchange markets. Suppose that a U.S. businessman purchased a shoe factory in Mexico. The former Mexican owners would want to be paid with pesos. So the U.S. investor would supply dollars (and demand pesos) to the exchange market so he could pay for the factory in pesos. Since U.S. investment abroad creates an outflow of dollars, it is recorded as a debit in the balance of payments accounts. On the other hand, foreign investment in the U.S. will create a demand for dollars on the exchange market. Therefore, it is entered as a credit.

It may seem confusing that the "export" of capital (investment abroad) is a debit item, while the export of goods is a credit. The apparent contradiction is removed when one thinks of investment abroad as the import of a bond or ownership right—a future income stream. Importing ownership of a financial (or real) asset from abroad has the same affect on the balance of payments as importing goods from abroad. Therefore both are recorded as debits. Similarly, in a sense, we are exporting bonds and ownership of capital when foreigners invest in the United States. Thus, these transactions enter as a credit.

As for domestic markets, many international transactions are conducted on credit. When a U.S. banker loans $100,000 to a foreign businessman so he can purchase U.S. exports, in effect, the banker is importing a foreign bond. Since the transaction supplies dollars to the exchange market it is recorded as a debit. On the other hand, when Americans borrow from abroad, they are exporting bonds. Since this transaction would either create a demand for dollars on the part of the foreign banker (in order to supply the loanable funds) or a supply of foreign currency, it is recorded as a credit in the U.S balance of payments account.

DEFICITS, SURPLUSES, AND BALANCE OF PAYMENTS

Since balance of payments accounting is conducted according to the principles of double-entry bookkeeping, the balance of payments must always balance. The total of the debit items must always equal the total of the credit items. The sum of the debit items is the total value of the goods, services, ownership rights, and financial assets that we received from foreigners. But these items must be paid for with credit items—the goods, services, ownership rights, and IOU's that we supply to foreigners. When foreigners supply goods, services, and assets to us, they receive either a payment or loan of equal amount. Thus, every debit item is exactly offset by a credit item. Similarly, when foreigners purchase our exports, they must pay for them. Every good, service, or asset that is exported to foreigners will be exactly offset by the import of either foreign currency (or the return of dollars previously acquired by foreigners) or an IOU. Thus, the balance of payment is always in balance.

What then is all of the discussion often heard in the media about a balance of payments deficit or surplus? The expression "balance of payments deficit" (or surplus) is used to describe at least two different phenomenon. First, it is most commonly used to describe the movement of short-term IOU's (liabilities) among nations. When a country is purchasing more goods, services, and long-term financial assets from foreigners than it is selling to them, it must make up the difference by extending short-term IOU's to foreigners. In other words, the nation is increasing its short-term debt liability to foreigners. This increase in short-term indebtedness is often referred to as a **balance of payments deficit.**

In contrast, when a nation is exporting more goods, services, and long-term assets to foreigners than it is importing, the nation will then acquire short-term liabilities from foreigners. When a nation is extending short-term credit to foreigners, that is, acquiring short-term IOU's, a balance of payments surplus is said to exist.

Exhibit 32-3 shows that the United States purchased $10.6 billion more goods, services (including grants), and long-term assets from foreigners than it sold in 1974. Many commentators would say that the United States ran a balance of payments deficit of $10.6 billion.

The terms deficit and surplus are also used to indicate the relationship between a nation's debits and credits on both its current and capital accounts, *including short-term capital movements.* Thus, when a nation's debits are greater than its credits due to the current and capital accounts for a given year, it is frequently referred to as a **balance of payments deficit.** The opposite situation, where the credits exceeds the debits, is termed a balance of payments surplus. These deficits and surpluses must be offset by changes in the nation's official reserve holdings. For example, if the United States was running a deficit on its current and capital account transaction, it might cover the deficit by transferring official international reserves, such as convertible currencies, gold, or U.S. reserves with the International Monetary Fund to other creditor nations. Thus, a nation's holdings of international reserve balances will decrease as they are used to pay off debt to foreigners (a deficit) and increase as foreigners pay off their debts with official reserves (a "surplus" for the nation receiving the reserve payments). A nation's international reserve account is thus an accommodating account which responds to movements in the current and capital accounts.

TRADING WITH FLEXIBLE EXCHANGE RATES

Flexible exchange rates will nearly always assure equilibrium in the exchange market. When exchange rates are free to fluctuate, if a nation is running a balance of payments deficit on its current and capital accounts, a surplus of its currency will be present on the exchange market. This excess supply will cause the currency to depreciate relative to other currencies. As the currency depreciates, the nation's goods become cheaper to foreigners, and foreign goods become more expensive to domestic consumers. Assuming an elastic demand for goods, services, and assets, the depreciation will lead to an increase in the value of the nation's exports and a decline in the value of its imports, thereby automatically eliminating the balance of payments deficit.

Similarly, if a nation is running a balance of payments surplus, there will be an excess demand for its currency on the foreign exchange market. The excess demand will cause the nation's currency to appreciate. The appreciation will serve to stimulate imports and stifle the nation's exports, thereby acting to restore balance of payments equilibrium.

When exchange rates are free to fluctuate, the market value of a nation's currency will appreciate and depreciate in response to changing market conditions. What are the major factors that will cause exchange rates to change?

1. *Changes in the Value of Exports and Imports.*   If the value of a nation's exports increases relative to its imports, the nation's currency will tend to appreciate. Suppose that the demand for a nation's exports increased because of changing tastes and/or rising incomes abroad. This would lead to both higher prices and expanding sales in export industries. The value of the nation's exports would increase. An increase in the demand for a country's export products will simultaneously generate an expansion in demand for the nation's currency, causing it to appreciate. Of course the appreciation will serve to stimulate imports while discouraging exports, thereby restoring equilibrium in the exchange market.

In contrast, if the domestic demand for foreign imports increases, the nation's currency will tend to depreciate. Exhibit 32-4 illustrates the impact of an increase in the American demand for Volkswagens on the dollar–mark exchange rate. Americans, seeking to purchase more Volkswagens, will also demand more marks with which to pay for them. The demand for marks (and the supply of dollars) will increase, causing the dollar price of the mark to rise. This appreciation in the value of the mark (or what is the same thing, a depreciation in the value of the dollar) will reduce the incentive of Americans to import German goods while increasing the incentive of West Germans to purchase U.S. exports. These two forces will restore equilibrium in the exchange market at a new higher dollar price of the mark.

Exhibit 32-4   Demanding More Volkswagens . . . and Marks

Suppose that high gasoline prices induce U.S. consumers to purchase more Volkswagens. This increase in imports from West Germany will cause the demand for marks to increase. The mark will appreciate relative to the dollar.

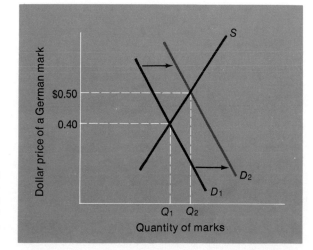

2. *Differential Rates of Inflation.*   Other things constant, domestic inflation will cause a nation's currency to depreciate on the exchange market, while deflation will result in appreciation. Suppose that prices in the United States rose by 10 percent, while our trading partners were experiencing stable prices. The domestic inflation would cause U.S. consumers to increase their demand for imported goods (and foreign currency). In turn, the inflated domestic prices will cause foreigners to reduce their purchases of U.S. goods, thereby reducing the supply of foreign currency to the exchange market. Thus, as Exhibit 32-5 illustrates, the American demand for a foreign currency such as the mark will increase (because German goods are now cheaper), while the supply of marks will decline (because U.S. goods are more expensive to West German consumers). This combination of forces will clearly cause the dollar to depreciate relative to the mark. With time, the depreciation in the dollar will stimulate U.S. exports to West Germany, while discouraging the importation of German products, thereby restoring equilibrium in the exchange market.

What if prices in both West Germany and the United States were rising at a 10 percent annual rate? The prices of imports (and exports) would remain unchanged relative to domestically produced goods. Equal rates of inflation in each of the countries will *not* cause the value of exports to increase relative to imports. Thus, identical rates of inflation will not disturb an equilibrium in the exchange market. Inflation contributes to the depreciation of a nation's currency only when a country's inflation rate is more rapid than that of its trading partners.

3. *Changes in Domestic Interest Rates.*   Short-term financial investments will be quite sensitive to changes in interest rates. International loanable funds will tend to move toward areas where the expected rate of return (after compensation for differences in risk) is highest. An increase in real interest rates—that is, interest rates adjusted for the expected inflationary rate—will attract foreign capital, causing the nation's currency to appreciate on the exchange market. For example, an increase in interest rates in the United States would stimulate British, French, and West German investors to demand dollars (and supply their domestic currency) which they would then loan to U.S.

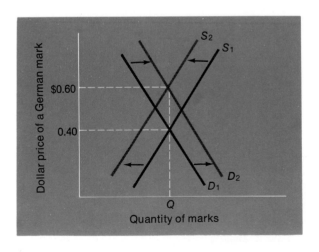

Exhibit 32-5   Inflation with Flexible Exchange Rates

If prices were stable in Germany, while the United States was experiencing domestic inflation, the demand for German products (and marks) would increase, while U.S. exports to West Germany would decline, causing the supply of marks to fall. The dollar would thus depreciate relative to the mark.

borrowers at the now higher interest rate. These capital movements would cause the dollar to appreciate relative to the British pound, French franc, and German mark. A fall in domestic interest rates would, of course, have just the opposite effect—inducing loanable funds to move from the United States and causing the dollar to depreciate relative to other currencies.

4. *Changes in Foreign Interest Rates.*   When interest rates rise in Western European countries, short-term financial investors will exchange dollars for pounds, francs, and marks so they can take advantage of the improved earning opportunity in the European market. Thus high interest rates abroad will increase the demand for foreign currencies, while increasing the supply of dollars. A depreciation of the dollar relative to the currencies of countries experiencing the high interest rates is the result. Lower foreign interest rates will have just the opposite affect, as they will stimulate capital movement toward the United States. The Thumbnail Sketch summarizes the major factors that will cause a nation's currency to appreciate or depreciate when exchange rates are determined by market forces.

THUMBNAIL SKETCH—Currency Appreciation and Depreciation with Freely Fluctuating Exchange Rates

These factors will cause a nation's currency to appreciate:

(1) Increase in exports or decline in imports
(2) Less rapid rate of inflation than trading partners
(3) Higher domestic interest rates
(4) Lower interest rates abroad

These factors will cause a nation's currency to depreciate:

(1) Increase in imports or decline in exports
(2) More rapid inflation than trading partners
(3) Lower domestic interest rates
(4) Higher interest rates abroad

TRADING WITH FIXED EXCHANGE RATES

Between 1944 and 1971 most of the world operated under a system of **fixed exchange rates.** Each nation "pegged" its currency to another currency such as the dollar (or gold) for long periods of time. Fixing the price of a currency in the exchange market, like the fixing of other prices, results in the usual surpluses and shortages.

When a government fixes its exchange rate, it stands ready to buy and sell its currency in order to maintain the fixed price. If a nation is running a balance of payments deficit on its current and capital account, it will have to dip into its international reserves (e.g. holdings of foreign currencies, gold, and special drawing rights with the International Monetary Fund) in order to cover the deficit. But nations that continue to draw down their international reserve balances will soon find them depleted. Once the international reserves are gone, the nation will be unable to supply foreign currencies to customers at the fixed rate.

Suppose that the United States attempted to peg the price of the dollar at 2.5 marks. However, at an exchange rate of 1 dollar equal 2.5 marks, the value of goods, services, and assets imported from West Germany continually exceeded the value of the U.S. exports to Germany. Thus, customers would continually demand more marks to purchase German imports than were being supplied by export of items to Germany. This situation could persist for a while, as the United States drew down its holdings of marks, gold, and other international reserves. But with time, unless corrective action were taken, these reserves would run out and the U.S. monetary authorities would no longer be able to supply 2.5 marks for 1 dollar. The dollar price of the mark must increase (a depreciation of the dollar). This **devaluation** of the dollar—a depreciation of the nation's currency when exchange rates are fixed—would bring the value of German imports into line with the value of exports.

While a surplus nation could continue to maintain fixed exchange rates, it is clearly disadvantageous for it to do so. A balance of payment surplus means that the nation is sending more goods, services, and assets to foreigners than it is receiving in return. Thus it is accumulating foreign currencies in exchange for valuable goods and resources. Does it make sense to continue to do so? Obviously not. If the surplus nation revalued its currency, permitting it to appreciate relative to foreign currencies, it would acquire more goods, services and assets from foreigners, and fewer pieces of paper (foreign currency). Since it is goods and resources, not pieces of paper, that contribute to a nation's well-being, this appreciation makes sense from the viewpoint of a country experiencing a continual surplus in its balance of payments.

FIXED VERSUS FLEXIBLE EXCHANGE RATES

The advocates of fixed exchange rates argue that fluctuating rates add to the uncertainties of international trade—particularly for transactions with a time dimension. Suppose that a U.S. businessman contracts to buy door knobs at 10 marks each. The door knobs are to be delivered and paid for six months from now. Further assume that one mark is currently exchanging for 40 cents. Thus, the businessman anticipates that the dollar price of the door knobs will be $4. But what happens if the mark appreciates to 50 cents by the time the goods are delivered. In this case, the door knobs will cost $5 each, not $4. At the higher price, perhaps the businessman could have purchased them cheaper elsewhere. Of course the dollar might have appreciated rather than the mark. In that case, the U.S. businessman would have had to pay less than $4 per door knob when they were delivered. But the point is that the potential depreciation and appreciation associated with flexible exchange rates adds another dimension to international transactions.

The advocates of flexible exchange rates argue that fluctuations will be minor. Thus they will not be a major deterrent to trade as the opponents charge. In addition, the advocates of flexible rates point out that the trader can avoid the risks associated with changing exchange rates by entering into a future contract now. For example, the businessman who purchases the door knobs, might immediately contract for marks to be delivered six months in the future at a price of $4.05 (typically, the future price will be a little above the current price because of the risk involved). Who might want to sell marks for future delivery at a predetermined price? Perhaps an American exporter who is going to receive marks from a German customer upon his delivery of goods six months from now.

In addition to problems associated with the potential fluctuation of flexible exchange rates, there is a special case for which flexible rates are inappropriate. If the demand for a nation's major exports (or the country's demand for imports) is highly inelastic, flexible rates will be destabilizing. For example, suppose that the world demand for bananas is inelastic. Bananas are the major export product of Honduras. If the currency of Honduras depreciates because of a balance of payments deficit, its exports, primarily bananas, will become cheaper to foreigners. But since the world demand for bananas is so inelastic, the decrease in their price may fail to bring about an increase in expenditures on the export products of Honduras. The depreciation of the Honduran currency may actually make things worse. Thus, it is not a good idea for a country to adopt flexible exchange rates when the demand for its major exports is highly inelastic. While this is an atypical case, developing nations, which export only a few raw material commodities, may find themselves in this position.

While fixed rates may cut down on the uncertainty associated with international exchange, if the fixed rate is not an equilibrium rate, it will be difficult to maintain. Once a nation's exchange rate is pegged, it often takes on an almost sacred meaning. American politicians have often argued that a devaluation (depreciation) of the dollar should be avoided at all cost. Nations have often heightened trade barriers, adopting tariffs and quotas, in order to reduce imports and avoid a depreciation. Paradoxically, defending the fixed rates often leads to restrictions on the flow of trade, which the fixed rates are supposed to help promote by avoiding some of the uncertainties associated with flexible rates.

In addition, policy objectives such as full employment have sometimes been sacrificed at the balance of payments altar. For example, when the unemployment rate is high, an expansionary monetary policy might be the proper prescription to stimulate the economy. However, the expansionary monetary policy would be expected to push *short-run* interest rates downward, causing a flight of capital from the United States and enlarging the nation's balance of payments deficit. Thus, the full employment objective may often conflict with the maintenance of the fixed exchange rates and avoidance of a large balance of payments deficit.

Maintenance of fixed rates in the face of balance of payments deficits is further complicated by the destabilizing role of speculation as the likelihood of a devaluation increases. A student with an eye for making money has probably already seen why balance of payments deficits can quickly generate a crisis under a fixed exchange rate system. Suppose you had one million pesos and it appeared that the peso was going to be devalued. Would you want to hold these pesos while they became less valuable? If your answer is no, you have made the right decision for your own pocketbook, but when you go to sell your pesos for dollars in the foreign exchange market, you will be actually making things worse! That is, the purchase of dollars and the sale of pesos by speculators and others will cause an increase in the supply of pesos and will make it more difficult for international central banks to stabilize the price of the peso. In other words, rational speculators under fixed exchange rates typically help destabilize those exchange rates.

Some economists advocate that we combine the good points of both fixed and flexible exchange rates into a system called **gliding bands.** A gliding band allows an exchange rate to fluctuate according to the forces of supply and demand within a moderate range (say perhaps 5 percent in either direction). If an exchange rate change of greater magnitude appears likely, then and only then will the government step in to support the domestic currency. In this way, stability in exchange rates is maintained while allowing the advantages of flexible exchanges rates to come into play most of the time. These gliding bands have become more and more popular in the last five years; in fact, most countries in the world today use them to one degree or another. Even countries whose exchange rates have been purportedly flexible (like Canada's) have occasionally stepped into the foreign exchange market to support their currency in times of rapid exchange rate change. Under these conditions, flexible exchange rates and fixed exchange rates differ only by the percentage change in an exchange rate which will be allowed before governments step in to stabilize that rate.

CHAPTER LEARNING OBJECTIVES

1. When international trade takes place it is usually necessary to convert one domestic currency into the domestic currency of one's trading partner. Imports of goods, services, and financial assets generate a demand for foreign currency with which to pay for these items. On the other hand, exports of goods, services, and financial assets supply foreign currency to the exchange market as foreigners exchange their currency for dollars with which to purchase our export items.

2. The value of a nation's currency on the exchange market will be in equilibrium when the supply of the currency (generated by imports—the sale of goods, services, and financial assets to foreigners) is just equal to the demand for the currency (generated by exports—the purchasing of goods, services, and financial assets from foreigners).

3. The balance of payments accounts record the flow of payments between a country and other countries. Transactions (for example, imports) which cause currency to flow to foreigners are recorded as debit items. Transactions (for example, exports) which result in an inflow of currency are recorded as credit items. Credit items provide foreign currency, while debit items use it up.

4. Since the total value of goods, services, and assets (debit items) received from foreigners must be paid for with foreign currency provided by the total value of goods, services, and assets (credit items) supplied to foreigners, the balance of payments will always balance. However, it is common to speak of a balance of payments deficit when a country uses up its official reserves (gold, reserves with the International Monetary Fund, and convertible currencies) and/or increases its short-term liabilities to foreigners in order to balance the payments account. In contrast, a balance of payment surplus is often spoken of when a country is increasing its official reserves and/or acquiring liquid liabilities from foreigners.

5. As long as the demand for imports and supply of exports is elastic, flexible exchange rates will assure equilibrium in the exchange market. For example, if there was an excess supply (balance of payments deficit) of dollars to the foreign exchange market, the value of the dollar would depreciate relative to other currencies. This would make foreign goods more expensive to U.S. consumers (and U.S. goods cheaper to foreigners), reducing the value of our imports (and increasing the value of our exports) until equilibrium was restored. On the other hand, an excess demand for dollars would cause the dollar to appreciate, stimulating imports and discouraging exports until equilibrium was restored.

6. With flexible exchange rates, a nation's currency will tend to appreciate when **(a)** exports increase relative to imports, **(b)** the rate of domestic inflation is below that of the nation's trading partners, **(c)** domestic interest rates increase, and/or **(d)** foreign interest rates decline. The opposite of these conditions will cause the nation's currency to depreciate.

7. If the value of the goods, services, and capital assets exported to foreigners is less than the value of the items imported, there will be an excess supply of the country's currency on the foreign exchange market. When this happens under a system of fixed exchange rates, the country must either **(a)** devalue its currency or **(b)** take action to reduce imports and/or expand exports. Often the corrective action designed to maintain fixed exchange rates will interfere with the free flow of trade and/or conflict with macrogoals of full employment and stable prices. Between 1944 and 1971 most countries did pursue a policy of fixed exchange rates.

8. The advocates of fixed exchange rates argue that the stability of such rates will encourage international trade, while erratic fluctuations that may result from flexible exchange rates will make trading riskier, discouraging international exchange. On the other hand, the advocates of flexible rates argue that floating rates will not fluctuate enough to upset trade and that market forces will assure equilibrium in the exchange market while permitting the nation to follow a macropolicy designed to promote full employment with stable prices.

IMPORTANT TERMS TO REMEMBER

Foreign exchange market: Market in which the national currencies of different countries are bought and sold.

Exchange rate: The domestic price of a unit of foreign currency. For example, if it takes 40 cents to purchase one German mark, then the dollar–mark exchange rate is 0.40.

Depreciation: A reduction in the value of a domestic currency relative to foreign currencies. A depreciation reduces the purchasing power of the domestic currency *over foreign goods.*

Appreciation: An increase in the value of a domestic currency relative to foreign currencies. An appreciation will increase the purchasing power of the domestic currency *over foreign goods.*

Balance of payments: A summary of all economic transactions between a country and all other countries for a specific time period —usually a year. The balance of payments account will reflect all payments and liabilities to foreigners (debits) and all payments and obligations (credits) received from foreigners.

Balance of trade: The difference between the merchandise exports and imports of a nation. The balance of trade is only a partial component of a nation's total balance of payments.

Balance of payments deficit: (a) Situation where the nation is importing more goods, services, and *long-term* assets from foreigners than it is exporting to them. Therefore, the nation is adding to its *short-term* indebtedness to foreigners. (b) The term is also used to describe the situation where a nation is depleting its holdings of official international reserves, such as convertible currencies and gold, in order to cover a deficit in the nation's current and capital accounts.

Flexible exchange rates: Exchange rates that are determined by the market forces of supply and demand. They are sometimes called "floating exchange rates."

Fixed exchange rates: A system whereby a government exchanges its currency for foreign currencies at a fixed rate. Government intervention in the foreign exchange and international trade markets is often required to maintain the fixed rate.

Devaluation: An official act that reduces the "fixed" rate at which the government will exchange its domestic currency for foreign currencies (or gold). This depreciation of the fixed exchange rate will typically stimulate exports while discouraging imports.

Gliding bands: A system that would (a) permit market forces to determine the exchange rate as long as it remains within a moderate range (for example, 5 percent) of the "pegged rate" but (b) calls for intervention by the nation's monetary authorities to maintain the fixed bond if the market rate threatens to go outside of the predetermined range.

THE ECONOMIC WAY OF THINKING—DISCUSSION QUESTIONS

1. "We are never going to strengthen the dollar, cure our balance of payments problem, lick our high unemployment, eliminate an ever-worsening inflation, as long as the United States sits idly by as a dumping ground for shoes, television sets, apparel, steel, automobiles, etc." [United Shoe Workers of America]

(a) Would excluding foreign goods from the U.S. market help solve our "ever-worsening inflation"? Explain.

(b) If foreigners were willing to give (dump?) 100,000 pairs of shoes to American consumers do you think it would be bad business to accept them?

(c) Would accepting the shoes "worsen our unemployment and balance of payments problem"? Explain.

2. "If a balance of payments deficit means that we are getting more items from abroad than we are giving to foreigners, then why is it considered to be a bad thing? After all, we are getting more goods than we are sending to foreigners." Comment.

3. Do you think the United States should follow a policy of flexible exchange rates? Why? Under what circumstances would a country prefer fixed exchange rates? Under what circumstances would one prefer flexible rates?

4. Suppose that the exchange rate between the United States and Mexico freely fluctuates in the open market. Indicate which of the following will cause the dollar to appreciate (or depreciate) relative to the peso.

(a) An increase in the quantity of drilling equipment purchased in the United States by Mexican businessmen as the result of a Mexican oil discovery.

(b) An increase in the U.S. purchase of crude oil from Mexico as the result of the development of Mexican oil fields.

(c) Higher interest rates in Mexico inducing U.S. citizens to move their financial investments from U.S. to Mexican banks.

(d) Lower interest rates in the United States inducing Mexican businessmen to borrow dollars, and then exchange them for pesos.

(e) An inflation in the United States while prices are stable in Mexico.

(f) Ten percent inflation in both the United States and Mexico.

(g) An economic boom in Mexico induces Mexicans to buy more U.S. made automobiles, trucks, electric appliances, and television sets.

(h) Attractive investment opportunities induce U.S. businessmen to buy stock in Mexican firms.

5. "A balance of payments deficit will occur only when exchange rates are fixed. Without fixed exchange rates, it would not be necessary for the government to use the official settlement account (for example, short-term liabilities and gold movements) in order to balance the balance of payments account." Do you agree? Explain.

6. What's Wrong with This Way of Thinking?

"The government can change from fixed to flexible exchange rates, but we will continue to run a balance of payments deficit because foreign goods, produced with cheap labor, are simply cheaper than U.S. produced goods."

33
COMPARATIVE ECONOMIC SYSTEMS

How an economy is organized will influence economic outcomes. We have primarily focused our analysis on private property, market-directed economies. The economies of the United States, Canada, Australia, and most of Western Europe fit into this pattern. These economies, as we have pointed out, do not always rely on market forces. The government regulates many private industries. Government ownership and operation of utilities, transportation, communication, and educational facilities is not uncommon, even in Western countries. In addition, taxes and government subsidies are sometimes used to alter market outcomes. Throughout this book we have applied economic tools to help us better understand the incentives and expected results of governmental policy that redirects market forces.

Today, one-third of the world's population lives in the Soviet Union, China, and Eastern Europe. The economies of these countries are organized along socialist lines, in which government ownership and central planning are the dominant economic characteristics.

COMPARING CAPITALISM AND SOCIALISM

Joseph Schumpeter, the renowned Harvard economist, defined **socialism** as:

> . . . an institutional pattern in which the control over means of production and over production itself is vested with a central authority—or, as we may say, in which, as a matter of principle, the economic affairs of society belong to the public and not the private sphere.[1]

As is implicit in Schumpeter's definition, capitalist and socialist economic organizations differ in two important respects—ownership of physical capital and the mechanism for allocating resources.

[1]Joseph A. Schumpeter, *Capitalism, Socialism, and Democracy,* 3rd ed. New York: Harper & Row, 1950 p. 167

Ownership of Physical Capital

Every economic system has a legal framework within which the rights of resource owners are defined. Practically all economic systems guarantee the rights of individuals to sell their own human capital (labor) to the highest bidder. Owners of human capital derive earnings from the sale of labor services in both capitalist and socialist societies.

However, under socialism, the rewards to physical capital (machines, buildings, etc.) used to produce goods and services will accrue to the state. When the state owns the nonhuman productive resources, the earnings generated by physical capital go directly to the state. Alternatively, the state could use taxation to gain at least partial control over earnings that would otherwise accrue to the owners of physical capital.

Under socialism, investment in physical capital will reflect the views of the state, the central planning authority. If the planners want to produce more steel, military defense, or heavy equipment, they can direct investment capital and other resources into these areas. Alternatively, resources can be directed into consumer-oriented industries, if the planners seek to expand output in these sectors. The decisions of the central planners will, therefore, determine the composition of output between consumption and investment industries.

Resource Allocation

Every economy must have a mechanism that will coordinate the economic activity of microunits—business firms, individual resource owners, and consumers. Problems such as the use of resources, the selective production of goods, and the distribution of income must be solved by an allocative mechanism.

Under market-directed **capitalist organization,** economic activity will be coordinated by contractual agreements between private parties who possess property rights to products and resources. There is no central planning mechanism. Market prices direct the actions of decentralized decision-makers. The forces of supply and demand push prices upward or downward in response to the decisions of individual buyers and sellers.

The market is a communication device for pooling the knowledge and actions of market participants. It provides a system of pecuniary and nonpecuniary incentives and penalties which serve to direct the actions of consumers and producers. Producers have an incentive to offer only those goods on which they expect to make a profit. The dollar votes of consumers will direct the efforts of producers. Profit-seeking business firms have an incentive to seek out the least cost method to produce goods and services. They will substitute resources that are relatively cheap (in comparison to their marginal productivity) for factors that are relatively expensive. Finally, the price mechanism will also determine the distribution of income. Those possessing the skills and capital resources valued by the market will receive high incomes, whereas lower incomes will be allocated to persons without such skills and resources.

Under a socialist economic organization, resources will be used and allocated in accordance with a centrally determined and administered scheme. Economic decisions, such as what and how much to produce, how to use resources in production, and

Exhibit 33-1   Contrasting Capitalism and Socialism

	Capitalism	Socialism
Property rights	Nonhuman resources are owned by private parties (for example, individuals or corporations)	Nonhuman resources are owned by the state
Employment	Self-employed or employed by private firms	Employed by the government or government-controlled cooperatives
Investment	Conducted by private parties seeking profits and higher future incomes	Conducted by the government in accordance with the objectives of the planners
Allocation of goods and resources	Determined by market forces	Determined by centralized planning
Income distribution	Determined by market forces that will reward productivity and ownership of economic resources	Determined by central planners who may seek to promote equality or any other desired pattern of income distribution

to whom the product will be distributed, are planned by a central authority. The scope of the economic activity covered by the central plan is wide. It embraces many aspects of economic life of both micro- and macroeconomic units, including volume of output, quantities of raw materials and inputs, techniques of production, prices, wages, location of firms and industries, and labor employment. The central authority is not content with merely making the system operate feasibly or with balancing the supply and demand for the various resources. It also has certain economic objectives that reflect its own set of preferences and value judgments. Economic goals, such as a high rate of capital investment or more equality in the distribution of income, may be pursued. Such objectives may or may not reflect the views of consumers.

Exhibit 33-1 summarizes the distinctive characteristics of capitalist and socialist economic organization. Private property rights and market determination of employment, investment, resource and product allocation, and a market-determined pattern of income distribution are characteristic of capitalism. Government ownership (or control) of physical capital, allocation of capital and consumer goods via central planning, and a distribution of income that reflects the views of the central planners tend to characterize socialist economic organization.

Classifying Real World Economies

In reality all modern economies utilize some combination of capitalist and socialist economic organization. Primarily capitalist economies use government regulation, selective government ownership, and taxation to modify the forces of supply and demand. In socialist countries central planning and administrative control exist side by side with a small but often highly significant market system. When the focus of attention is turned to the developing countries, elements of traditions, customs, and habits are additional factors that affect resource allocation.

Exhibit 33-2 presents a rough classification of several countries according to their reliance on capitalist or socialist economic organization. The United States, Australia,

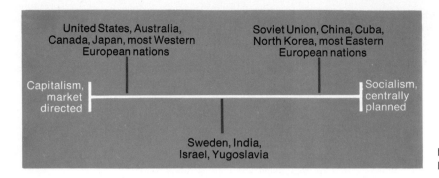

Exhibit 33-2 A Spectrum of Economic Systems

Canada, Japan, and most Western European countries would be classified at the market capitalism end of the spectrum. The Soviet Union, mainland China, and most other communist countries would be at the opposite end. Welfare state economies such as Sweden and Israel would fall between these two extremes.

COMMON CONSTRAINTS AND THE UNIVERSALITY OF ECONOMIC TOOLS

Despite their differences, alternative economic systems face similar constraints. Scarcity of economic goods will confront both individuals and nations with a budgetary problem. No nation will be able to produce as much as its citizens would like to consume. Therefore, regardless of economic organization, choices must be made. The decision to satisfy one desire will of necessity leave many other desires unsatisfied. All economic systems will be constrained by the bonds of scarcity.

In addition, many other economic concepts that have been discussed throughout this book, apply to *all* economic systems. Let us briefly consider a few of them.

1. *Law of Diminishing Marginal Returns.* This law will limit the ability of each nation to generate output from its "fixed" (at least temporarily) supply of land, natural resources, human capital, and man-made physical capital. With the passage of time, the supply of these resources can be expanded. But a nation's ability to expand its resource base will be directly related to its willingness to allocate more of its current production to investment in human and nonhuman capital. This, of course, will necessitate the sacrifice of current consumption. But since the law of diminishing returns applies to all economies, continual expansion in production will require a nation to continually expand its resource base.

2. *Opportunity Cost.* An economy can be organized so that various goods can be provided without charge *to the consumer*. But economic organization cannot eliminate the opportunity costs associated with the provision of goods. Provision of additional medical services, even if provided free, will utilize resources that could have produced other things. Similarly, expansion of the national defense sector will necessitate a contraction of other sectors. Whenever productive resources have alternative uses, as they almost always do, production of goods will be costly, regardless of the form of economic organization utilized.

3. *Comparative Advantage and Efficiency.*   Total production will be greatest when each good is generated by the low opportunity cost producer. Assignment of a productive task to a high opportunity cost producer is inefficient (that is, output will be below its potential level) regardless of whether the activity takes place in a capitalist or socialist economy. If efficient production is a goal, production should be carried out according to the principle of comparative advantage, independent of economic organization.

4. *Law of Diminishing Marginal Utility.*   Consumers in both socialist and capitalist countries will place less value on marginal units of a good as their consumption level of it increases. If the central planners of a country create lots of low-cost housing, but very little private auto transportation, marginal units of the former will decline in value relative to the latter.

Analyzing Alternative Systems

Economic organization is important because it affects the actions of human decision-makers. Changes in the structure of incentives will alter human behavior in both capitalist and socialist countries. For example, in the Soviet Union several years ago, managers of glass plants were rewarded according to the tons of sheet glass produced. Unsurprisingly, most plants produced sheet glass that was so thick one could hardly see through it. The rules were changed so that managers were rewarded according to the square meters of glass produced. Managers reacted in a predictable way. Under the new rules, Soviet firms produced very thin glass that broke quite easily. Incentives matter, even to managers of Soviet firms!

In our analysis of alternative economic systems, we will focus on how economic organization will affect human decision-makers. Marxists often argue that communism will eventually change human beings. They believe that with time man's basic motivations can be altered so he will no longer respond in a predictable way to changes in *personal* costs and benefits. Perhaps this is so, but the Soviet experience and that of other communist countries have produced little evidence to support this view. Therefore, until the conversion of human nature does come, analysis based on the postulate that incentives do affect human decisions is most relevant.

This is not to say that economic considerations are the only thing that matter. Religious, cultural, and political factors can and do influence economic behavior. The economic approach does not deny their importance. Even within the framework of socialism, economic organization may vary substantially. The economies of the Soviet Union and Yugoslavia verify this point. Let us consider these two contrasting socialist economies in more detail.

THE SOVIET ECONOMY[2]

The Soviet economy is a **command economy.** Centralized economic decision-making by planners and detailed directives to production units (for example, firms, collective farms, etc.) are the dominant characteristics of a command economy. The

[2] See Harry Schwartz, *An Introduction to the Soviet Economy* (Columbus, Ohio: Merrill, 1968), particularly Chapter 3, for an excellent and highly readable analysis of the Soviet economy.

Soviet government owns and operates almost all of the industrial sector, foreign trade, transportation and communications, banking and financial institutions, a sizable portion of the agricultural sector, and most of the wholesale and retail network. The state sector of the Soviet economy is the largest economic unit in the world. It employs nearly 100 million workers, both white and blue collar. Even General Motors and American Telephone and Telegraph are small by comparison.[3]

In a sense, the state-operated Soviet economy is akin to a giant corporation, with communist party members acting as stockholders. The party establishes the economic policy objectives, strives to assure their execution, and oversees the bureaucracy necessary to carry out the details of the planning directives. As for Western economies, the basic unit of economic activity is the business firm, which the Soviets call enterprises. But Soviet enterprises, much like individual factories (or units) of a large U.S. corporation, take their orders from the central planning authorities.

How does the giant corporation, the state sector of the Soviet economy, function? The **Gosplan,** the government's central planning agency, drafts the basic economic plan for the entire economy. At present both a five year plan (which focuses on long-range objectives) and an annual plan are constructed by the Gosplan. These operational economic plans are enacted into law by the Soviet government. The basic economic plan is directed to the enterprises. It sets production targets and establishes the resource constraints for each state enterprise. Each enterprise knows how much it is supposed to produce. The resource allotments, the amount of raw materials, labor, machines, and other productive inputs, that the enterprise is permitted to utilize are also contained in the central plan. The problem of the enterprise is to transform its allotted inputs into the target output. The operational targets of the annual plan are used as criteria in evaluating the performance of a firm at the end of the planning period and rewarding it accordingly.

Under Soviet planning, commodities and raw materials are centrally rationed in physical terms. The traditional way of reconciling supply and demand for these materials has been the "method of material balances" approach. For commodities such as petroleum, petrochemicals, iron and steel, coal, timber, and many others, this method means essentially a balance sheet stating all sources of supply (for example, local production, imports, inventories, etc.) and all sources of demand (for example, requirements of local consumers, exports, inventories, etc.). The Gosplan, in planning the final output and input targets, goes through an iterative trial and error process of balancing demand and supply for these products until it reaches the final set of imperative targets. The final set is then used as a basis for physical rationing. Traditionally, an integral part of this method was a system of planners' priorities. Economic sectors such as heavy industry and the military received first priority consideration. Low priority sectors (for example, consumer durables, housing, and agriculture) received residual allocations.

Motivating Soviet Managers

The detailed, centralized planning of the Soviet Union has traditionally been associated with a highly defective incentive–rewards scheme. Enterprise managers' performance

---

[3] The 10 largest firms in the United States employed approximately 3 million workers in 1974.

evaluation and rewards were based on certain measurable output and input targets. Output quality, initiative to invent and innovate, and desire to economize are attributes that typically go unrewarded under Soviet economic organization. Quantity of output is emphasized. Product quality, largely because it is more difficult to measure and control, tends to receive less emphasis. Accordingly, managers and workers have less incentive to innovate and improve quality. Shoddy workmanship is often the result.

The managers of Soviet enterprises are under strong pressure to show a good performance *relative to their output targets*. This raises two important problems. First, the appearance of achievement, rather than actual substance, is amplified. One method of gaining the appearance of high performance is for the manager to arrange beforehand for an easy plan. The planning process requires enterprise managers to submit plan targets. Each enterprise manager has a strong incentive to bargain for a small output target and a generous allocation of productive resources, including labor. Since high level central planners will not know what performance could be expected from an efficiently operated firm, shrewd enterprise managers can often get ahead by understating the true productive capabilities of their enterprise.

Second, a more blatant form of "cheating" on the system is the direct falsifying of reports. The Soviets have established procedures designed to limit such tactics. Nevertheless, they are still prevalent. The system creates a strong incentive for collusion (the Russians call it "familyness") between the controllers and the controlled within the planning process.

Soviet leadership is not unaware of these problems. They recognize that even though operational plans are written into law, they will not be automatically carried out by human decision-makers. They utilize both economic and noneconomic incentives in their efforts to motivate both managers and workers to properly carry out the details of the central plan.

In the past few years numerous changes in the planning organization and incentive structure have been introduced. These changes stem from the so-called economic reforms announced by Premier Kosygin in September 1965. At the outset, the reforms involved the idea that some relaxation of rigid central planning and control of enterprises would increase economic efficiency. Fewer targets would be handed down to enterprises, whose discretionary power is broadened in the areas of labor and capital policies. In addition, incentive–reward schemes would be tied to fulfillment of targets on sales, profits, and return on capital. These changes were to predominate over administrative methods in inducing enterprises to be more productive and efficient.

The implementation of these reforms has meant something different from the original philosophy that seemed to underlie the Kosygin ideas. The emphasis today is placed on finding ways to solve the perennial problems with the retention of central planning and as much central administration as possible. In their current effort to facilitate the enormously difficult task of administering their vastly complex economy, the Soviet planners are resorting to the use of new "scientific" techniques. They use mathematical modeling, electronic data processing methods via computers, input–output analysis, and other research activities. It seems, however, that the only visibly significant outcome is an increase in detailed planning with centralized administrative control being even more entrenched in the system than before.

Many who have analyzed the economic performance of the Soviet Union believe that detailed planning will necessarily result in perverse decision-making and organizational inefficiency. Professor Robert Campbell of Indiana University summarizes this view:

> Waste . . . flows from errors of decision-making—plants located wrongly, production of too much of one commodity and too little of another, misallocation of resources such that one firm has too much capital in relation to labor, and another has too much labor in relationship to capital. But another species of waste represents a kind of slack in the economy—the excessive inventories held by most enterprises, underutilization of capacity, failure to make innovations, managerial inertia that retains labor arrangements that require more labor than would some new plan. The common feature in all these weaknesses is inertia, or willful obstruction on the part of the controllers of the enterprise's activity.[4]

The Private Sector in the Soviet Union

A small but not insignificant private sector exists in the Soviet Union. Soviet law prohibits (a) private persons from acting as a trade middleman and (b) hiring an employee for the purpose of making a profit. However, private market activity does exist in two major areas. First, workers on state and cooperative farms are permitted to grow products on assigned garden plots, and are also allowed to maintain certain animals on their plots. Products raised on these garden plots may be sold in the market, prices for such transactions being set by the fluctuating forces of supply and demand. As Exhibit 33-3 illustrates, these private garden plots account for a major share of the total production for several agricultural products.

The second major source of market activity in the Soviet Union is for professional services. Soviet professionals (for example, doctors and teachers) and artisans (tailors,

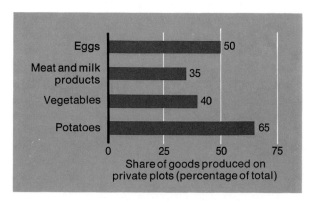

Exhibit 33-3   Private Share of Production for Selected Agricultural Products

A large share of the total output of several agricultural products is produced on the private garden plots allocated to collective and state farm workers.

SOURCE: Douglas B. Diamond and Constance Krueger, "Recent Developments in Output and Productivity in Soviet Agriculture," presented before the Joint Economic Committee, Congress of the United States.

[4] R. W. Campbell, *The Soviet-Type Economies: Performance and Evolution*, 3rd ed., pp. 229–230. Copyright © 1974 by Houghton Mifflin Company, Boston. Reprinted by permission of the publisher.

shoe repairmen, painters, and the like) are permitted to sell their services in a relatively free market. Many of them may also be employed by state enterprise, while providing private services during nonworking hours.

While some market activity does exist, state planning, of course, continues to dominate the Soviet economy. Continued industrialization has led to a greater diversification. The number of enterprises, products, inputs, and production techniques has grown rapidly. All of this serves to increase the complexity of the planning required to control and operate the economy.

The Balance Sheet of the Soviet Economy

When balancing the books on the Soviet economy, several factors stand out. First, the investment rate in the Soviet Union is one of the highest in the world. As Exhibit 33-4 shows, the Soviet Union allocates a much larger share of their GNP to investment (and a much smaller share to consumption) than is true for the United States. Centralized economic organization permits the planners to emphasize industrialization and capital accumulation, even though this may not reflect the views of the citizenry. Of course, current consumption is sacrificed as a result of the planners' emphasis on investment and the growth of physical capital.

Second, the growth rate in the Soviet Union, pushed along by the high rate of capital accumulation has been impressive. Exhibit 33-5 presents data on the growth of real gross domestic product during the 1960–1971 period for countries with varying economic institutions. During that period, real output in the Soviet Union grew at an annual rate of 7.2 percent. Per capita real output expanded 5.9 percent annually. Among major industrial powers, only Japan was able to exceed these rates during the period.

However, the Soviet growth rate needs to be kept in perspective. During the 1950s and into the 1960s, Soviet growth was spurred along by the borrowing of more advanced technology from Western countries, a tactic that was utilized on a grand scale. The emphasis of Soviet planners has clearly been on growth and capital accumulation, even though it necessitates the continued sacrifice of consumption items that Westerners

Exhibit 33-4   The Distribution of U.S. and Soviet GNP by End Use

The Soviet economy, responding to the views of the planners, allocates a much larger share of GNP to investment and defense.

	PERCENT SHARE OF TOTAL GNP	
	United States	Soviet Union
Consumption	72	56
Defense	7	10
Investment	18	33
Government administration	3	1

SOURCE: R. W. Campbell, *The Soviet-Type Economies: Performance and Evolution*, 3rd ed. Boston: Houghton Mifflin, 1974, p. 100.

Exhibit 33-5 The Average Annual Rate of Growth in Real Gross Domestic Product for Selected Countries, 1960–1971

Country	GROWTH RATE 1960–1971 (PERCENT)	
	Total	Per capita
United States	4.3	3.0
Canada	5.4	3.6
West Germany	4.7	3.6
Sweden	4.2	3.4
United Kingdom	2.8	2.2
Australia	5.3	3.3
U.S.S.R.[a]	7.2	5.9
Yugoslavia[a]	6.7	5.6
Japan	10.5	9.4
India	3.5	1.3
Brazil	6.9	4.0

SOURCE: *United Nations Yearbook of National Accounts Statistics—1972.*

[a] Data are for net material product. Therefore they exclude industries such as public administration, defense, and professional services.

would consider essential. Thus, most Soviet economic experts would agree with Campbell who argues that their

> . . . exceptional growth should be attributed more to the ability of Soviet command planning to mobilize resources—to accumulate capital, to educate on a mass scale, to move people from low productivity occupations such as agriculture to high productivity ones such as industry, and to force increases in participation rates—rather than to any special ability to use resources efficiently and increase their productivity.[5]

The distribution of income is also an important consideration in the evaluation of an economy. Most experts believe that the Soviet economy is characterized by less inequality than exists in market-oriented countries although some believe that differences in this area are slight. Accurate data on this question are difficult to obtain. Because of vast differences in the pricing structure between market economies and the Soviet Union, even the available data are subject to alternative interpretations. But some indirect evidence is suggestive. For example, occupational wage differentials are typically smaller in the Soviet Union than for the United States. The prices of products that are purchased primarily by the poor (medical service, clothing, and food) are, relatively speaking, lower in the Soviet Union than for market economies. In contrast, luxury goods such as automobiles and air travel tend to be relatively more expensive in the Soviet Union.

[5] Campbell, *The Soviet-Type Economies: Performance and Evolution*, pp. 106–107.

OUTSTANDING ECONOMIST: Wassily Leontief

This Russian-born economist was awarded the 1973 Nobel Prize for his invention of input–output analysis. Every industry both purchases resources (inputs) from and sells outputs to other industries. Leontief developed the input–output table to show the complex interrelationships between economic sectors. An input–output table lists individual industries both across the top and down the side of a giant accounting sheet. Reading *across* the rows of the table, the total output of each industry is allocated to the industries (listed across the top) that utilize the resource as an input. For example, reading across the row for the steel industry, the amount of steel purchased by the electric power, coal, oil and gas, machinery, and other industries would be presented. The next row would present identical information for another industry, and so on.

Each industry purchases inputs from other industries and the household sector in order to produce output. Glancing down any column of an input–output table, one can identify the amounts of various goods and services that each industry (listed across the top of the table) purchased from the other industries. For example, reading down the column for the steel industry, the amount of resources (inputs) that the steel industry purchased from the electric power, coal, oil and gas, machinery, and other industries—including labor from the household sector—is presented. Thus the input–output table shows (a) the amounts of each input used by an industry and (b) the amount of the industry's output utilized by other industries. The interpretation and manipulation of input–output tables for practical purposes has been made possible by development of a concise mathematical formulation of a so called economic general equilibrium theory.

Input–output analysis is an invaluable planning device for both private firms and governments. It can be used to predict the effect on *specific industries* of an increase in investment tax credits, higher petroleum prices, and other changes that have a differential impact among industries. For example, utilizing input–output analysis, economists were able to predict the industries for which the higher fuel prices of the 1970s would have the greatest impact on prices, outputs, and employments. Many centrally planned economies utilize input–output models. Even the Soviet Union, from which Leontief emigrated in 1925, has given the technique a stamp of approval. The Soviets noted that like the telephone and the telegraph, input–output analysis was discovered by a Russian.

While developing and perfecting the input–output techniques, Leontief spent 44 years on the faculty of Harvard University. In 1946 he was appointed the Henry Lee Professor of Economics. Shortly thereafter he established the Harvard Economic Research Project on the Structure of the American Economy and served as its director for more than 25 years. Disenchanted with the narrow interest of the economics department at Harvard, he recently resigned his position and accepted an appointment at New York University.

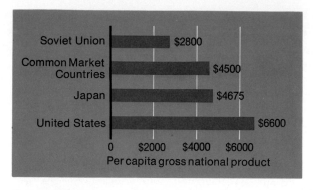

Exhibit 33-6   The Per Capita GNP of the Major Economic Powers in 1974

Common Market countries include Belgium, Denmark, France, West Germany, Ireland, Italy, Netherlands, and the United Kingdom.
SOURCE: Derived from data of *U.S. News and World Report,* January 13, 1975.

While the growth rate of the Soviet economy has been impressive, GNP per capita continues to lag behind Western market-oriented countries. Exhibit 33-6 shows that the per capita GNP of the European Common Market nations, Japan, and the United States is far in excess of that for the Soviet Union. In absolute terms, the Soviet GNP is approximately one-half that of the United States.

Since Soviet planners emphasize investment at the expense of consumption, the real income per capita figures actually overstate the availability of consumer goods in the Soviet Union. Although recent soundings suggest that the planners may begin to pay closer attention to the views of consumers, it is clear that the standard of living for the typical Soviet citizen is far below his Western counterpart.

YUGOSLAVIA—SOCIALISM OR THE MARKET?

The Yugoslavian economy is a hybrid between centralized planning and market direction. Individual Yugoslav citizens are permitted to own and operate small scale enterprises, employing up to a maximum of five workers. In agriculture, peasants can privately own up to 25 acres. In addition, certain business firms—such as law firms, hotels, restaurants, and craft shops—are operated by private entrepreneurs, much as they are in Western countries. But the bulk of economic activity—estimates range from 80 to 90 percent—is conducted by worker managed, socially owned business firms.

Prior to World War II Yugoslavia had a free market, capitalist economy. After the war (and a civil war that followed), communist domination under the leadership of Marshal Jesip Tito resulted. Initially, Tito organized the Yugoslav economy along the Soviet lines. Central planning organs prescribed the quantity and quality of production, determined the methods and techniques of production, allocated inputs, set prices, and decided on the distribution of the national income. Within the framework of a five year plan, all these decisions were translated into output targets and input allocations that were handed down to the socialist managers of individual firms. But Tito was unwilling to accept Soviet domination. In addition, the Yugoslav economy stagnated under detailed central planning. In the early 1950s they moved toward a decentralized economy that permitted market forces to play a significant role in the allocative process.

The Yugoslav Business Firm

In 1952 the government enacted a series of reforms that altered the nature of the socialist business firm. Under the new Yugoslav system, government ownership of the business firm is retained, but management of individual enterprises is turned over to the employers. The employees of each firm elect a Workers' Council, which manages the firm. Each employee has one vote and the Workers' Council is elected by secret ballot. The Council, like managers of Western firms, purchases raw materials and determines the quantity and quality of goods produced, the level of employment, the method of production, and even the price charged for finished products. When the firm's revenues exceed costs, the firm's net profits go, with no strings attached, to the employees (including managers) of the firm. The "employee–owners" divide the firm's profits among themselves in a manner proscribed by the Workers' Council. When a worker retires, leaves his job, or is fired (by a vote of all employees), his ownership rights associated with the business firm expire.

What impact does this form of economic organization have on economic incentives and production methods? Since the income of employees is directly affected by the firm's profit level, they will have an incentive to elect managers who will operate the firm efficiently. In a sense, the employees of the firm are in a parallel position with stockholders in the West. They will seek efficient operation and a high level of profits because they are residual income recipients (in addition to wage recipients). However, unlike stockholders, an *individual* worker in Yugoslavia can neither sell these rights nor can he take them with him when he leaves the firm. Only *current* workers, collectively as a unit, are allowed to own factors of production.

The ramifications of this situation are quite significant. First, this form of economic organization encourages workers to push for an immediate distribution of profits among themselves rather than allocate them to investment or future fringe benefits (for example, fancier offices or a company recreation center). This is a perfectly rational behavior on the part of employees, because present capitalization of future profit-sharing rights cannot be realized through private sale of ownership rights. Unlike stockholders in the West, Yugoslav workers can ill afford to not declare dividends every year. Postponed dividends may be lost forever for those with a likelihood of departing from the firm. In contrast, Western stockholders can always sell their shares whenever they are dissatisfied with the dividend policy of the management.

Consequently, and this is a second major ramification, Yugoslav enterprises are constantly plagued by shortages of funds for both working capital and fixed investment. The workers' tendency to allocate larger shares of the enterprise profits for purposes of wage and salary augmentation, puts a continuous strain on the firm's liquidity. As a result, many enterprises have to resort to heavy borrowing, thereby being forced to operate under perpetual debts.

Third, Yugoslav firms have a strong tendency to substitute capital goods for labor.

The workers' profit-sharing right increases the cost, as seen by current employees, of hiring additional units of labor (that is, additional profit-sharing partners). The share per individual, *ceteris paribus*, will be smaller, the larger the work force of the firm. Consequently, Yugoslav enterprises tend to use highly capital intensive techniques of production. As a result, many laborers—both skilled and unskilled—have been forced to emigrate to other countries in order to find work.

Finally, Yugoslav enterprises have little or no pecuniary incentive to invest their funds in the establishment of new enterprises. Although money invested in new ventures can draw interest, investors have no claim to management rights or dividends. These are reserved exclusively for the workers of the new enterprise. Consequently, the financing of new enterprises comes primarily from governmental authorities, either through direct investment or by guaranteeing bank loans. Here, the gains of the public authority are basically twofold. First, it secures a dominating influence over the firm's management and its policies. Second, it obtains a certain return on its investment through taxation. Taxes levied on the enterprise profits generate a major portion of state revenues in Yugoslavia.

The workers' participation in the decision-making process of the firm is considered in Yugoslavia to be an essential feature of a genuine socialist society. According to the Yugoslavian view, capitalist relations in production and distribution are characterized not only by private ownership but also by separation of labor and management. Since workers are eliminated from the decision-making process, they become disillusioned with the production process and dissatisfied with the income distribution. In contrast, according to this view, the Yugoslavian system of workers' self-management makes it impossible for worker alienation to take place. Finally, the argument goes, profit sharing by workers provides the firm with a strong incentive to become efficient. Since employees have a direct stake in the firm's profits, they will want to avoid waste and other activities that will increase the firm's costs.

A Closer Look at the Yugoslavian Record

The transition of the Yugoslav economy to market socialism was accompanied by remarkable changes elsewhere in the economy. First, there was a shift of labor out of the agricultural sector and into the manufacturing and services sectors. In 1945 approximately 75 percent of the population was rural; in 1974, about 40 percent. At the same time there was a change in exports from agriculture and mining to a highly diversified export pattern. Approximately half of the value of exports in 1974 consisted of manufactured goods. Thus, the Yugoslav economy has moved to the "developed" class of nations, although some regions remain predominantely agricultural in nature.

Second, the growth of real output and income per capita has been remarkable in spite of erratic fluctuations. Before 1952, under centralized command planning, the Yugoslav real output was at a virtual standstill. Between 1952 and 1960, real GNP in Yugoslavia grew at an annual rate of nearly 10 percent. Since that time the annual rate of growth of industrial production has averaged approximately 7 percent. The per capita rise in real income has been closer to 6 percent in recent years. Thus, on balance the Yugoslav economy has been maintaining a relatively high rate of economic growth.

Third, the shift of the Yugoslav economy toward rapid industrial development was accompanied by a problem of unemployment—estimated at around 10 percent in the mid-1970s. Continuous influx of peasants from rural into urban areas created a persistent excess supply of unskilled workers. In addition, semiskilled and skilled workers often could not find employment because of the previously mentioned desire of firms to utilize capital intensive production techniques. Consequently, approximately 1 million Yugoslavs, 5 percent of the total population, have sought jobs in neighboring West European countries.

The dynamics of the Yugoslav economic system are strongly tied with developments in its social and political institutions. Thus, the future shape of the socioeconomic institutions will greatly depend on what happens to the country politically in the aftermath of President Tito's death.

SOCIALISM OR CAPITALISM?

Which form of economic organization is best? Economics alone cannot answer this question. Both philosophical and economical factors must be considered. On the economic side, it is clear that some socialist planned economies have generated impressive growth records. Socialism need not necessarily, as some earlier observers argued, fall victim to its own economic inefficiency. But it is also clear that several market-oriented nations, most notably West Germany, Japan, and Brazil, have in recent years experienced rapid economic growth. Apparently, economic progress is not the sole domain of either capitalism or socialism. While economic data are relevant, the nature of man, freedom, and equality are also important considerations when choosing among alternative forms of economic organization. At the individual level, the choice is yours.

CHAPTER LEARNING OBJECTIVES

1. Under socialism, ownership (or control) of physical capital rests with the state. Central planning replaces market allocation as the method of answering the basic consumption, production, and distribution questions.

2. Basic economic concepts such as diminishing returns, opportunity cost, comparative advantage, and diminishing marginal utility apply to both socialist and capitalist economies. Economic organization can change the incentives faced by decision-makers (for example, managers, workers, etc.), but it does not negate basic economic principles.

3. Central planning is the dominant characteristic of the Soviet economy. The Gosplan, a central planning agency, presents state enterprises with an allocation of inputs and target levels for output. The rewards of managers and workers will be affected by their success at meeting the targets of the central planning authority. Key commodities and raw materials are centrally rationed in physical terms. However, pecuniary as well as nonpecuniary incentives are used to motivate both managers and workers to carry out the directives of the central planners.

4. Central planning in the Soviet Union has stressed industrialization and capital investment. The share of GNP allocated to investment in the Soviet Union is substantially higher than for the United States. Currently there is some evidence that Soviet planners are beginning to place more importance on consumer goods.

5. Stimulated by high investment rates, economic growth in the Soviet Union has been impressive—more rapid than for most Western nations. However, the Soviet per capita GNP is still substantially less than for European Common Market countries, Japan, and the United States.

6. The Yugoslav economy combines socialist and capitalist economic organization. Central planning directs the economy and channels capital investment into designed areas. However, business firms have a great deal of discretionary decision-making authority. Employees of each firm elect a Worker's Council, which manages the firm. The firm is usually free to decide what products it will produce, production techniques to be utilized, the employment level, and even product prices. Profits of the firm are distributed to employees according to their wishes. Despite high rates of unemployment, the growth record of the Yugoslav economy has been impressive.

7. Economics alone does not tell us which form of economic organization is best. However, application of economics can reveal a great deal about how alternative systems will, in reality, operate.

IMPORTANT TERMS TO REMEMBER

Socialism: A system of economic organization whereby (a) the ownership and control of the basic means of production rests with the state and (b) resource allocation is determined by centralized planning rather than market forces.

Command economy: An authoritarian socialist economy that is characterized by centralized planning and detailed directives to productive units. Individual enterprises have little discretionary decision-making power.

Capitalism: An economic system based on private ownership of productive resources and allocation of goods according to the signals provided by free markets.

Gosplan: The central planning agency in the Soviet Union.

THE ECONOMIC WAY OF THINKING—DISCUSSION QUESTIONS

1. Compare and contrast the role of business managers for firms in the United States, the Soviet Union, and Yugoslavia. In which country would managers have the greatest incentive to operate the *firm* efficiently?
2. What do you think are the major advantages of a centrally planned economy? What are the major disadvantages? Explain why you believe that market allocation is either superior or inferior to centralized planning.
3. How does Yugoslav socialism differ from socialism as practiced in the Soviet Union? Which system do you think is better? Why?
4. "Under an authoritarian political system, central planning means the total loss of individual freedom. But democractic socialism would mean manipulation of the economy for the political gain of the planners. Shortsighted policies and the power of special interests will result in both inefficiency and economic favoritism under democratic socialism. The reality of socialism, both authoritarian and democratic, will differ radically from the utopian promise." Explain why you either agree or disagree with this view.

5. "Our system combines the strengths of socialism and the market. The workers own and manage the firm. But consumer preferences, operating through the market, determine what will be produced" (a comment of a Yugoslav planner). Explain why you either agree or disagree with this view.

6. "Socialism means production for use, not for profit. Workers contribute according to their qualifications and they are rewarded according to equalitarian principles. Socialism takes power from the business elite and grants it to the workers who, after all, produce the goods." Analyze this point of view.

7. What's Wrong with This Way of Thinking?

"Central planning makes it possible for an economy to invest more and grow more rapidly. Consumer incomes, stimulated by the high rates of capital accumulation, will also increase rapidly. Thus, the consumer is the major beneficiary of central planning that stresses a rapid rate of capital accumulation."

Appendix A
A GRAPHIC LOOK
AT ECONOMICS

The purpose of this appendix is to illustrate the mechanics of tables (charts) and graphs. Many students—particularly those with an elementary mathematics background—will already be familiar with this material. Thus, they may safely ignore it. This appendix is for those who need to be assured as to their ability to handle graphic economic illustrations.

Economic logic often suggests that two variables will be linked together in a specific way. The relationship between variables can be illustrated with the use of a table, a graph, or a mathematical expression. Understanding these devices—particularly tables and graphs—will help the reader to quickly visualize economic relationships.

It has often been said that a good picture is worth a thousand words, but one must understand the picture if it is to enlighten. Tables and graphs help to create a picture of things; they are visual aids that can concisely communicate valuable information to the understanding reader.

Exhibit A-1 presents a simple table showing the hypothetical relationship between distance traveled and gasoline consumption for two types of automobiles—a Ford-LTD and a Pinto.

Unsurprisingly, gasoline consumption increases with distance traveled for both cars. Using jargon, one would say that there was a positive relationship between distance traveled and gasoline consumption. But this relationship differs for the two cars. The LTD consumes twice as much gasoline per mile as the Pinto.

The information contained in Exhibit A-1 could also be presented graphically. A graph illustrates the relationship between two things, one of which is measured on

Exhibit A-1   The Distance Traveled versus Gas Consumed Relationship

DISTANCE TRAVELED (MILES)	GASOLINE CONSUMED (GALLONS)	
	Ford-LTD	Pinto
10	1.0	0.5
20	2.0	1.0
30	3.0	1.5
40	4.0	2.0
50	5.0	2.5
60	6.0	3.0

the x axis (the horizontal axis), while the other is measured on the y axis (the vertical axis). A line (or curve) on the graph illustrates the relationship between the "x variable" and the "y variable."

Exhibit A-2 graphs the relationship between miles traveled and gasoline consumption for the LTD and the Pinto. Since the x variable and y variable are positively related to each other, the gasoline consumption–distance traveled curve is upward sloping to the right. (In economics "curve" is a general term used to express the relationship between two variables. Even a straight line is often referred to as a curve.)

How much gasoline does the LTD use per mile? The slope or steepness of the line yields the answer. The slope of a line—any line—is the change in the y variable divided by the change in the x variable. Measuring gasoline consumption along the y axis, the graph indicates that an additional gallon of gasoline would be required to travel ten additional miles. A one-unit change in the y variable is associated with a ten-unit change in the x variable for the LTD. The slope of the line (1/10) shows that the LTD consumes one-tenth of a gallon of gasoline for each mile traveled.

Now consider the miles traveled–gasoline consumption relationship for the Pinto. Miles traveled and the gasoline consumption for the Pinto are also positively related. However, the gasoline consumption–distance traveled curve is flatter. For the Pinto, the y variable (gasoline consumed) changes less as the x variable (distance traveled) changes, than was true for the LTD. The slope of the gasoline consumption–distance

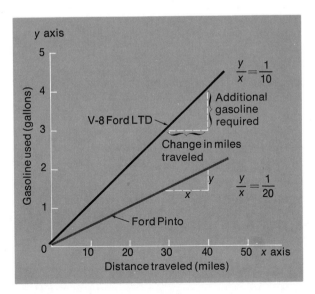

Exhibit A-2 Understanding a Graph

The above graph pictures the relationship between miles traveled, measured on the x axis, and gasoline consumption, measured on the y axis. The black line illustrates the relationship for a Ford LTD. The LTD consumes one-tenth of a gallon of gasoline for every mile traveled, while the Ford Pinto (red line) used only one-twentieth of a gallon per mile. Since both lines slope upward to the right, they illustrate that there is a positive relationship between miles traveled and gasoline consumed for both cars.

traveled curve for the Pinto is 1/20, indicating that the Pinto uses less gasoline per mile than the LTD.

A simple two-dimensional graph, such as the one that helped us visualize the gasoline consumption–miles traveled relationship for the LTD and the Pinto, can also be used to illustrate economic relationships. For example, survey data have shown that high income families, on average, spend more on consumption goods than do families with lower incomes (see Exhibit A-3a). Most of us spend more when we make more. Thus, income and consumer spending are positively related to each other. Exhibit A-3b illustrates the consumer expenditure–income curve for U.S. families in 1973.

Sometimes the x variable and the y variable will be negatively related. A decline in the y variable will be associated with an increase in the x variable. Therefore, a curve picturing the relationship between x and y will slope downward to the right.

Exhibit A-4 illustrates this case. The price of hamburgers is measured on the y axis and the quantity of hamburgers purchases per week is measured on the y axis. When the price of hamburgers is $2 each, only the real hamburger lovers would purchase them. On average, individuals would consume only one hamburger per week. If the price of hamburgers fell to $1, more of us would buy them. Weekly consumption would increase to three. A price reduction to 50 cents would induce consumers to purchase still more hamburgers, and weekly consumption would expand to four. The negative relationship between price and quantity of hamburgers purchased generates a curve that slopes downward to the right.

By now you should be getting a pretty good feel for how to read a graph. Graphs

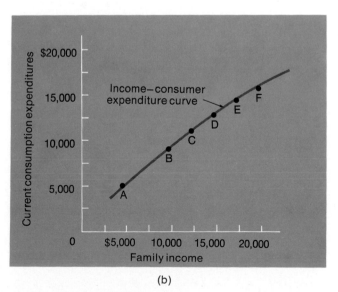

Family income	Current consumption expenditure
(A) $ 5,000	$ 5,300
(B) 10,000	9,600
(C) 12,500	11,600
(D) 15,000	13,400
(E) 17,500	15,000
(F) 20,000	16,500

(a)

(b)

Exhibit A-3 Picturing Family Income and Consumer Expenditures—1973

(a) The table presents data on the relationship between family income and consumer expenditures. (b) Here the same data is presented graphically, illustrating the positive relationship between the two variables.

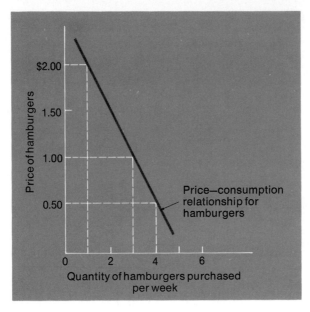

Exhibit A-4 Picturing the Price–Consumption Relationship for Hamburgers

People will buy fewer hamburgers as their price rises. This graph illustrates the negative relationship between price and quantity of hamburgers purchased. Note that the price–consumption curve slopes to the right.

are not a substitute for economic thinking. One cannot communicate anything with a graph that could not be communicated verbally. But graphs can often be used to present ideas quickly and concisely. Do not let your knees knock over graphs. They look much more complex than they really are.

If you think that you will have any trouble reading graphs, try drawing (graphing) the relationship between several things with which you are familiar. If you work, try graphing the relationship between your hours worked (x axis) and weekly earnings (y axis). What does the slope of the earnings–hours worked curve represent? Can you graph the relationship between the price of gasoline and your expenditures on gasoline? Graphing these simple relationships will increase your confidence in your ability to picture more meaningful economic relationships.

Appendix B
ANALYZING
THE EQUILIBRIUM LEVEL
OF INCOME WITH EQUATIONS

Chapters 8, 9, and 10 use logic and graphic aids to develop the concepts of equilibrium aggregate income, the multiplier, and fiscal policy. Most students are best able to understand these tools when they are presented in this manner. However, professional economists often use mathematics to study and communicate these same ideas.

This appendix uses elementary algebra to develop, in greater detail, some of the aggregate income models that we have already discussed. For the beginning student in economics, an exposure to one of two algebraic models has at least two advantages. First, a better understanding of almost any problem can be gained by looking at it with the precision of mathematics. Second, such exposure will make the transition to intermediate or upper level economics courses much easier.

THE EQUILIBRIUM LEVEL OF INCOME

Before beginning, it is important to remind ourselves of a few basic concepts. All the relationships expressed by straight lines earlier in the text can also be expressed by equations which mean the same thing. The relationship between consumption C and disposable income Y_d shown in Exhibit B-1 (see also Exhibit 8-4) can also be communicated by the equation

$$C = C_0 + \text{MPC} \cdot Y_d \qquad (1)$$

The meaning of this equation is that total consumption equals autonomous consumption C_0 plus the marginal propensity to consume (MPC) multiplied by disposable income. The amount of consumption C_0 that takes place when disposable income equals zero can be interpreted as consumption that is not explained by variations in Y_d. The MPC, which is the proportion of a change in disposable income going to changes in consumption, is constant because the graphical function is linear. Of course, the MPC is simply the slope of the line that represents the consumption function.

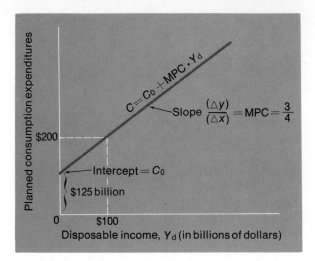

Exhibit B-1   The Consumption Function in Graphic and Equation Form

A consumption function with a y intercept of \$125 billion and MPC of $\frac{3}{4}$ is shown above. The equation form of this function is $C = 125 + \frac{3}{4}y_{d}$.

Example 1: If consumption is \$125 billion when disposable income is zero and if consumption equals \$200 billion when disposable income is \$100 billion (see Exhibit B-1), what is the linear consumption function? In this case $C_0 = \$125$ billion and the MPC is equal to the change in consumption (\$75 billion) divided by the change in disposable income (\$100 billion):

$$\text{MPC} = \tfrac{75}{100} = \tfrac{3}{4}$$

Thus, the function is:

$$C = 125 + \tfrac{3}{4} Y_{d}$$

The other equations necessary for our model are also restatements of concepts already introduced. Gross national product Y in equilibrium is equal to planned consumption expenditures C, plus planned gross investment I, plus planned government expenditures G.

$$Y = C + I + G \tag{2}$$

In addition, a simplification of the definition of disposable income is also useful; Y_{d} is equal to equilibrium GNP minus total taxes T:

$$Y_{d} = Y - T \tag{3}$$

Given these equations, we can easily solve for equilibrium GNP by substituting equations (1) and (3) into equation (2):

$$Y = C + I + G$$
$$Y = C_0 + \text{MPC} \cdot Y_{d} + I + G \tag{4}$$
$$Y = C_0 + \text{MPC} \cdot (Y - T) + I + G \tag{5}$$

Given constant values for C_0, I, G, T, and the MPC, we then can compute equilibrium Y since we have one equation with one unknown variable.

Example 2: Equilibrium occurs when planned aggregate spending $(C + I + G)$ equals the value of output Y. Given that $C_0 = \$125$ billion, $I = \$100$ billion, $G = \$300$ billion, $T = \$300$ billion, and MPC $= \frac{3}{4}$, calculate the equilibrium level of the GNP:

$$Y = C + I + G$$
$$Y = C_0 + \text{MPC} \cdot Y_d + 100 + 300$$
$$Y = 125 + \tfrac{3}{4}(Y - T) + 400$$
$$Y = 525 + \tfrac{3}{4}(Y - 300)$$
$$Y = 525 + \tfrac{3}{4}Y - 225$$
$$Y - \tfrac{3}{4}Y = 300$$
$$\tfrac{1}{4}Y = 300$$
$$Y = \$1200 \text{ billion} \quad \text{(aggregate demand)}$$

THE MULTIPLIER

The concept of the multiplier can also be illustrated mathematically. We learned in Chapter 9 that the multiplier is equal to $1/(1 - \text{MPC})$. Given an MPC of $\frac{3}{4}$, a change in government expenditures (or investment) should generate a fourfold increase in equilibrium income.

Exhibit 10-1 presents a graphic illustration of the impact of a $30 billion increase in government expenditures when the MPC is equal to $\frac{3}{4}$. Example 3 illustrates the same point using equations.

Example 3: If government expenditures (or investment) are increased in Example 2 by $30 billion, will the equilibrium level of GNP increase by $120 billion as the multiplier of 4 implies? A $30 billion dollar increase in government expenditures, holding taxes constant, implies:

$$Y = C + I + G$$
$$Y = C_0 + \text{MPC} \cdot (Y - T) + I + G$$
$$Y = 125 + \tfrac{3}{4}(Y - 300) + 100 + 330$$
$$Y = 125 + \tfrac{3}{4}Y - 225 + 430$$
$$Y = 330 + \tfrac{3}{4}Y$$
$$Y - \tfrac{3}{4}Y = 330$$
$$\tfrac{1}{4}Y = 330$$
$$Y = \$1320 \text{ billion} \quad \text{(new equilibrium)}$$

Thus we can show mathematically what Exhibit 10-1 illustrates graphically—that the $30 billion autonomous increase in government expenditures causes equilibrium income to rise by $120 billion (from $1200 billion to $1320 billion). A multiplier of 4 results when MPC = $3/4$.

An important sidelight of this example is that the multiplier due to changes in taxation is lower than that due to identical changes in investment or government expenditure. The reason for this is that changes in taxation are not totally converted into changes in expenditure. A reduction in tax payments for instance, will eventually cause both an increase in consumption, *and an increase in saving*. As can be seen from equation (2), only the increase in consumption actually impacts the GNP. Thus, a tax reduction that is larger than the increase in government expenditures would be necessary to exert the same expansionary impact on equilibrium income.

Exhibit 10-2 shows that when MPC = $3/4$, a $40 billion tax cut would be necessary to accomplish the same expansionary impact on income as a $30 billion increase in government expenditures. Example 4 illustrates this point algebraically.

Example 4: If taxation in Example 2 is decreased by $40 billion (from $300 to $260 billion), while government expenditures remain constant, by how much will equilibrium income rise?

$$Y = C + I + G$$
$$Y = C_0 + \text{MPC} \cdot (Y - T) + I + G$$
$$Y = 125 + \tfrac{3}{4}(Y - 260) + 100 + 300$$
$$Y = 525 + \tfrac{3}{4}Y - 195$$
$$Y - \tfrac{3}{4}Y = 330$$
$$\tfrac{1}{4}Y = 330$$
$$Y = \$1320 \text{ billion} \quad \text{(new equilibrium)}$$

THE BALANCED BUDGET MULTIPLIER

An interesting implication of Examples 3 and 4 is that a simultaneous increase in government expenditures and taxes of an equal amount will cause the equilibrium GNP to rise by the amount of the increase in G (and T). Thus a multiplier of one results from a balanced budget increase in government expenditures and taxation. This phenomenon, referred to as the "balanced budget multiplier," is illustrated by Example 5.

Example 5: If both taxation and government expenditures in Example 2 are increased by $30 billion, what will happen to the GNP?

$$Y = C + I + G$$
$$Y = C_0 + \text{MPC}\,(Y - T) + I + G$$

Now assume that both G and T are increased by \$30 billion.

$Y = 125 + \frac{3}{4}(Y - 330) + 100 + 330$

$Y = 125 + \frac{3}{4}Y - 247.5 + 430$

$Y = 307.5 + \frac{3}{4}Y$

$\frac{1}{4}Y = 307.5$

$Y = \$1230$ billion   (new equilibrium)

Thus, a \$30 billion increase in both government expenditures and taxes will cause the GNP to increase by \$30 billion. The balanced budget multiplier resulting from an increase in government expenditures is exactly 1. However, as we have already discussed, the balanced budget multiplier holds only under restrictive assumptions. See pages 168–170 for qualifications to the concept of the balanced budget multiplier.

Appendix C
ANALYZING
AGGREGATE EQUILIBRIUM
WITH THE IS–LM MODEL

The interaction effects of changes in income, interest rates, and monetary and fiscal policy are difficult to illustrate within the framework of the simple Keynesian model that we developed in Chapters 8–12. Economists have developed a slightly more complex tool—the IS–LM model—in order to more fully incorporate the money and loanable funds (bond) markets into the traditional Keynesian analysis. The IS–LM model will permit us to view the simultaneous impact of monetary and fiscal forces on the equilibrium level of income. In addition, the model will help to further clarify some of the points involved in the controversy between Keynesians and monetarists.

The IS–LM model, first developed by Nobel laureate J. R. Hicks, emphasizes that aggregate equilibrium requires two conditions. First, injections into the income flow must equal leakages from it. Second, the desired demand for money must equal the actual money supply. In the absence of either of these conditions, disequilibrium will be present.

The IS Curve. The IS curve shows the various combinations of national income and interest rates for which leakages will be equated with injections. Remember, saving and tax collections will increase with income. Similarly injections will expand as the interest rate falls thereby stimulating private investment.

Exhibit C-1a outlines the IS curve for various combinations of interest rates and income levels. The IS curve will slope downward because as income increases, expanding both saving and taxes, a lower interest rate will be necessary to stimulate the injections (investment and government spending) required to maintain the balance between leakages and injections at the higher income level. Similarly, a reduction in income must be accompanied by an increase in the rate of interest, thereby causing a reduction in injections of sufficient magnitude to offset the decline in withdrawals caused by the fall in income.

Thus, the IS curve, representing all combinations of interest rates and income levels for which leakages are equated with injections, must slope downward because income and the interest rate must vary in opposite directions in order to maintain the equality of leakages and injections.

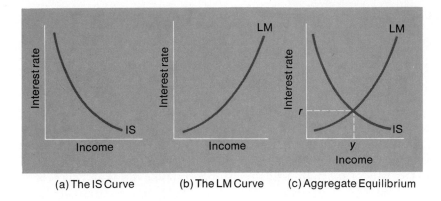

(a) The IS Curve   (b) The LM Curve   (c) Aggregate Equilibrium

Exhibit C-1   The IS–LM Equilibrium Model

The IS curve (a) shows all levels of income and interest rates for which leakages are equal to injections. It slopes downward since lower interest rates will be necessary to induce the additional injections (investment) that are required to offset the larger leakages that will be associated with higher levels of income. The LM curve (b) shows all levels of income and rates of interest for which the *desired* money balances will equal the *actual* money supply. It slopes upward to the right since higher interest rates will be necessary to reduce desired money balances which will increase as output expands. (c) Where the IS curve intersects the LM curve, an income level and an interest rate are established that will equate both (a) the leakages from and injections into the flow of income and (b) the desired and actual money balances in the money market.

The LM Curve.   The LM curve shows the combinations of interest rates and income levels that are consistent with equilibrium in the monetary sector. Households and businesses will desire to hold larger money balances as income increases, thereby expanding their demand for money in order to conduct transactions. In contrast, higher interest rates will increase the opportunity cost of holding money balances thereby causing the level of desired money balances to decline.

Equilibrium in the monetary sector requires that the desired demand for money be just equal to the actual (constant) supply of money. As income increases, the demand for money will expand. Thus, the interest rate must rise in order to keep the desired level of money balances equal to the unchanged supply. Similarly, a fall in income will require a reduction in the interest rate so that households and businesses will continue to desire to hold the unchanged money supply at the lower level of income.

As Exhibit C-1b shows, the LM curve that outlines all combinations of interest rates and income levels for which the desired demand for money is just equal to the supply will slope upward. This is so because maintaining equilibrium in the monetary sector requires income and the rate of interest to vary in the same direction.

Aggregate Equilibrium.   Aggregate equilibrium requires equilibrium in both the commodities (real) sector (injections equal leakages) and the monetary sector. As Exhibit C-1c shows, this will take place at the income level and interest rate combination where the IS and LM curves intersect.

FISCAL AND MONETARY POLICY

The impact of fiscal and monetary policy can be demonstrated by the IS–LM model. Let us begin by considering the Keynesian view of monetary policy.

Monetary Policy. Each LM curve is constructed for a specific supply of money. A change in the money supply caused by open market operations or other actions of the Federal Reserve will clearly shift the LM curve. Expansionary monetary policy will create an excess supply of money at the initial level of income. In the Keynesian view, this excess supply of money will flow into the loanable funds market (that is, it will be used to buy bonds) expanding the supply of borrowable funds and depressing the interest rate. At the new lower rate of interest r_2, investment is stimulated and output expands. As output expands, additional transaction balances are demanded, causing the interest rate to increase slightly (to r_3) from its initial point of decline. Therefore, as Exhibit C-2 illustrates, the expansionary monetary policy shifts the LM curve to the right, resulting in a new equilibrium at a lower interest rate r_3 and higher income level y_2.

A restrictive monetary policy would, of course, have the opposite effect on the LM curve. A reduction in the supply of money would shift the LM curve to the left, causing the equilibrium interest rate to rise and income to fall.

Fiscal Policy. While monetary policy impacts the LM curve, fiscal policy affects the IS curve. What would happen if the government, seeking to follow an expansionary fiscal policy, held taxes constant and increased government expenditures by $30 billion? (This illustration parallels that of Chapter 10, Exhibit 10-1.) Clearly, the higher level of government expenditures would increase injections. At any particular interest rate, a higher level of income could now be attained while still maintaining equilibrium between leakages and injections. Specifically, as Exhibit C-3 shows, the IS curve would shift to the right by the initial increase in injections ($30 billion) times the multiplier (4 as the MPC is assumed to be $3/4$).

At what income level will equilibrium in both the monetary and real sectors be

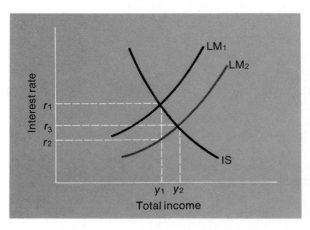

Exhibit C-2   Monetary Policy—The Keynesian View

The Keynesian view stresses that an expansion in the supply of money will shift the LM curve to the right reducing the interest rate (initially to r_2), which will stimulate investment and increase aggregate income. The expansion in income will dampen the initial sharp reduction in the interest rate, and a new equilibrium will eventually be restored at interest rate r_3 and a higher level of income y_2.

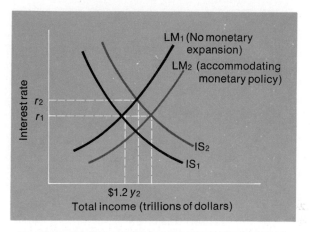

Exhibit C-3: Fiscal Policy—
IS–LM Model

A $30 billion increase in government expenditures will cause the IS curve to shift to the right—to expand by the amount of the increased spending ($30 billion) times the multiplier. As Exhibit 10-1 illustrates, income will increase by $120 billion (assuming the MPC is 3/4) if the interest rate remains constant. However, this will require that expansionary monetary policy shift the LM curve to LM_2.

What if the money supply is held constant—thereby maintaining LM_1? Then the Treasury will have to expand its borrowing in order to finance the higher level of government expenditures. The Treasury's increased borrowing will drive up the interest rate from r_1 to r_2. Therefore, the equilibrium level of income will increase only to y_2, less than the $120 billion indicated by the simple Keynesian model of Exhibit 10-1.

restored? The answer depends on how the higher level of government expenditures is financed. If the Federal Reserve expands the supply of money so as to keep the interest rate constant at r_1, the LM curve would shift to the right, and a full multiplier effect would result. Equilibrium would be restored at interest rate r_1 and an income level of $1.32 trillion. As this analysis shows, our earlier illustration of this case in Exhibit 10-1 implicitly assumed that there was not any offsetting reduction in private spending associated with a rise in the interest rate.

What if the $30 billion expansion in government expenditures were accomplished without any monetary expansion? For example, suppose the Treasury finances its deficit by borrowing from the general public and the Federal Reserve keeps the supply of money constant. In that case, the LM curve will remain unchanged. The Treasury borrowing will increase the demand for loanable funds, driving up the interest rate. As shown by Exhibit C-3, without the monetary expansion the new equilibrium will occur at income y_2 and interest rate r_2. The expansionary *pure fiscal* action does not have a full multiplier effect. It is partially offset by a reduction in private spending that was displaced as the result of the rise in the interest rate.

KEYNESIANS, MONETARISTS, AND THE IS–LM MODEL

We are now in a position to point out two important sources of conflict between Keynesians and monetarists. First, Keynesians believe that the LM curve is highly

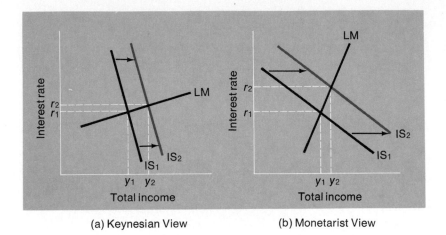

(a) Keynesian View   (b) Monetarist View

Exhibit C-4   The Keynesian and Monetarist Views of Fiscal Policy

(a) Keynesians believe that the LM curve is highly elastic. Thus, expansionary fiscal policy, shifting the IS curve to the right, is highly potent because it results in only a marginal rise in the interest rate. In contrast, (b) monetarists believe that fiscal policy will be impotent because the LM curve is highly inelastic.

elastic. Therefore, as Exhibit C-4a shows, when fiscal policy shifts the IS curve to the right, its major impact is on income, not the interest rate. In contrast, monetarists believe that the LM curve is nearly vertical (Exhibit C-4b). Thus, the major impact of fiscal policy is on the interest rate, not income. An expansionary purely fiscal action, according to the monetarists, is rendered ineffective because it will simply drive up the interest rate causing private investment and consumption to decline.

What forces determine the slope of the LM curve? The relationship between the interest rate and the demand for money gives the LM curve its slope. In the Keynesian view, the demand for money is interest elastic. Thus, as expanding income increases the demand for money, only a small rise in the interest rate will be necessary to induce decision-makers to use their money balances more intensively (increase the velocity of money). The monetarists' case arises when the demand for money is relatively unresponsive to the interest rate. Thus, a large increase in the interest rate will be necessary to keep the overall demand for money in equilibrium with the constant supply when income rises.

Turning to monetary policy, Keynesians and monetarists differ as to both the general slope of the IS curve and the mechanism by which monetary policy is transmitted. Exhibit C-5a outlines the Keynesian view. If investment is highly inelastic with respect to the interest rate the IS curve will be quite steep. Keynesians believe this to be the case. Thus, when expansionary monetary policy, *transmitted through the interest rate*, shifts the LM curve to the right, its primary effect is to lower the interest rate while exerting only a small impact on income. As a result, many though certainly not all, Keynesians believe that monetary policy is relatively impotent because the IS curve is highly inelastic.

Exhibit C-5b outlines the monetarists' view. Since they believe that monetary policy

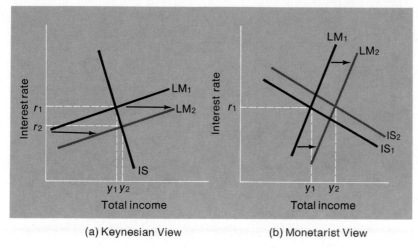

(a) Keynesian View   (b) Monetarist View

Exhibit C-5   The Keynesian and Monetarist Views of Monetary Policy

(a) Keynesians, arguing that investment is relatively unresponsive to the interest rate, believe that the IS curve is highly inelastic. Thus, monetary policy is not very potent. (b) Present-day monetarists argue that expansionary monetary policy will not only shift the LM curve outward, but that the excess supply of money, created by the expansionary policy, will result in a direct increase in spending, shifting the IS curve to the right (to IS_2). Monetarists believe that monetary policy is highly potent since it impacts both the LM and IS curves.

exerts a direct impact on spending as well as an indirect effect via the interest rate, monetarists argue that expansionary monetary policy causes both the LM and IS curves to shift to the right. According to this view, expansionary monetary policy creates an excess supply of money. Households and businesses act to reduce this excess supply by *directly* spending more on both consumption and investment goods. This direct spending is stimulated by an increase in wealth which occurs when the money supply is increased. The size of this effect depends upon the particular definition of wealth incorporated into the model.[1] In addition to the wealth effect, Meiselman has suggested that money exerts a direct effect independent of wealth.[2] Since they believe that monetary policy impacts both the LM and IS curves, it is easy to see why monetarists feel the monetary policy is a highly potent macrotool.

[1] For a lucid discussion of the issues involved in choosing a particular definition of wealth see B. P. Pesek and T. R. Saving, *Money, Wealth, and Economic Theory* (New York: Macmillan, 1967).
[2] David I. Meiselman, "Discussion," in *Controlling Monetary Aggregates.* Federal Reserve Bank of Boston, 1969.

SUGGESTIONS
FOR ADDITIONAL
READING

SUGGESTIONS FOR ADDITIONAL READING

Chapter 1   The Economic Approach

Bastiat, Frederic. "What is Seen and What is Not Seen." In *Selected Essays on Political Economy*. Princeton, New Jersey: Van Nostrand Reinhold, 1964.

Boulding, Kenneth E. *Economics as a Science*. New York: McGraw-Hill, 1970.

Hough, Robbin R. *What Economists Do*. New York: Harper & Row, 1972.

Snider, Delbert. *Economic Essentials*. Pacific Palisades. California: Goodyear Publ. Co., 1972.

Chapter 2   Some Tools of the Economist

Heyne, Paul T. *The Economic Way of Thinking*. Chicago: Science Research Associates, 1973 (Chaps. 5 and 7).

Knight, Frank. *The Economic Organization*. New York: Harper & Row, 1962 (Chap. 1).

Mundell, Robert A. *Man and Economics*. New York: McGraw-Hill, 1968 (Chap. 1).

Chapter 3   Market Decisions and the Market Process

Heyne, Paul T. *The Economic Way of Thinking*. Chicago: Science Research Associates, 1973 (Chaps. 1–4).

Lee, Dwight R., and McNown, Robert F. *Economics in Our Time: Concepts and Issues*. Chicago: Science Research Associates, 1975 (Chaps. 1–3).

Mishan, E. J. *21 Popular Economic Fallacies*, 2nd ed. New York: Praeger, 1973. (Chap. 1: "Rent Controls are Necessary During a Housing Shortage.")

Rogers, Augustus J., III. *Choice: An Introductory to Economics*. Englewood Cliffs, New Jersey: Prentice-Hall, 1971.

Chapter 4   A Bird's-Eye View of the Public Sector

Buchanan, James M., and Flowers, Marilyn. *The Public Finances: An Introductory Textbook*. Homewood, Illinois: Richard D. Irwin, Inc., 1975 (Chaps. 1–6).

Friedman, Milton. "The Market v. the Bureaucrat." *National Review*, May 19, 1970.

Haveman, Robert H. *The Economics of the Public Sector*. New York: Wiley, 1970.

Lee, Dwight R., and McNown, Robert F. *Economics in Our Time: Concepts and Issues*. Chicago: Science Research Associates, 1975 (Chaps. 5–8).

Chapter 5   Taxes and Government Spending

Adelman, Morris A., *et al. No Time to Confuse*. San Francisco: Institute for Contemporary Studies, 1975.

Blechman, B. M., Gramligh, E. M., and Hartman, R. W. *Setting National Priorities—The 1975 Budget*. Washington, D.C.: The Brookings Institution, 1974.

Herriot, R. A., and Miller, H. P. "The Taxes We Pay." *The Conference Board Record*, May 1971.

Leftwich, R. H., and Sharp, A. M. *Economics of Social Issues*. Dallas: Business Publications, Inc., 1974 (Chap. 11).

Miller, R. L. *The Economics of Energy: What Went Wrong?* Glenn Ridge, New Jersey: Thomas Horton and Company, 1974.

Mitchell, Edward J. *U.S. Energy Policy: A Primer*. Washington, D.C.: American Enterprise Institute, 1974.

Pechman, J. A., and Okner, B. A. *Who Bears the Tax Burden?* Washington, D.C.: The Brookings Institution, 1974.

Policy Study Group of M.I.T. Energy Laboratory, "Energy Self-Sufficiency: An Economic Evaluation." *Technology Review*, May 1974, pp. 22–58.

Chapter 6 Taking the Nation's Economic Pulse

Berle, A. A., Jr. "What the GNP Doesn't Tell Us." *Saturday Review*, August 31, 1968.

Boulding, Kenneth E. "Fun and Games with the GNP—The Role of Misleading Indicators in Social Policy." In *The Environmental Crisis*, edited by Harold W. Helfrich, Jr. New Haven: Yale Univ. Press, 1970.

Stewart, Kenneth. "National Income Accounting and Economic Welfare: The Concepts of GNP and MEW." *Review*, Federal Reserve Bank of St. Louis, April 1974.

U.S. Department of Commerce, *The Economic Accounts of the United States: Retrospect and Prospect*. Washington, D.C., 1971.

Chapter 7 Unemployment, Inflation, and Business Cycles

Bach, G. L. "Inflation: Who Gains and Who Loses? *Challenge*. July/August 1974.
  Economic Report of the President, Washington, D.C. Published annually.

Friedman, Milton. "More on Living with Inflation." *Newsweek*, October 29, 1973.

Gordon, Robert Aaron. *Economic Instability and Growth: The American Record*. New York: Harper & Row, 1974.

Samuelson, Paul. "Inflation Fallacies." *Newsweek*, July 29, 1974.

Chapter 8 Aggregate Equilibrium and a Simple Keynesian Model

Hanson, Alvin. *A Guide to Keynes*. New York: McGraw-Hill, 1953.

Peterson, Wallace C. *Income, Employment, and Economic Growth*, 3rd ed. New York: Norton, 1974 (Chaps. 4–8).

Stewart, Michael. *Keynes and After*. Baltimore: Penguin Books, 1967.

Chapter 9 The Multiplier, Accelerator, and a Keynesian View of the Business Cycle

Collery, Arnold. *National Income and Employment Analysis*, 2nd ed. New York: Wiley, 1970 (Chaps. 3 and 4).

Lekachman, Robert. *The Age of Keynes*. New York: Random House, 1966.

Okun, Arthur M., ed. *The Battle Against Unemployment*. New York: Norton, 1972 (Parts 2 and 3).

Chapter 10   Fiscal Policy

Canterbery, E. R. *Economics on a New Frontier.* Belmont, California: Wadsworth, 1968 (Chaps. 1–4).

Heller, Walter. "Let's Tailor the Policies to Fit the Problems." *Challenge,* May/June 1973.
———. *New Dimensions of Political Economy.* New York: Norton, 1967.

Okun, Arthur M. *The Political Economy of Prosperity.* New York: Norton, 1970.

Chapter 11   Money and The Banking System

Bernstein, Peter L. *A Primer on Money, Banking, and Gold.* New York: Random House, 1965.

Board of Governors of the Federal Reserve System. *The Federal Reserve System: Purposes and Function,* 5th ed. Washington, D.C., 1963, pp. 107–111.

Klein, John J. *Money and the Economy,* 2nd ed. New York: Harcourt, 1970 (Chaps. 5–8).

Chapter 12   Money, Unemployment, Inflation, and a More Complete Keynesian Model

Bach, G. L. *Making Monetary and Fiscal Policy.* Washington, D.C.: The Brookings Institute, 1971.

Friedman, Milton. "Why the American Economy is Depression Proof." In *Dollars and Deficits.* Englewood Cliffs, New Jersey: Prentice-Hall, 1968.

Samuelson, Paul. "Another Great Depression?" *Newsweek,* October 28, 1974.

Wallich, H. C., and Wallich, M. I. "What Have We Learned About Inflation?" *Challenge,* March/April 1973.

Chapter 13   The Business Cycle and Inflation—The Monetarist View

Andersen, Leonall C. "The State of the Monetarist Debate." *Review,* The Federal Reserve Bank of St. Louis, September 1973.

Friedman, Milton. "Facing Inflation." *Challenge,* November/December 1973.

Friedman, Milton, and Heller, Walter. *Monetary Versus Fiscal Policy.* New York: Norton, 1969.

Reynolds, Alan. "Unions: Scapegoat for Inflation." *National Review,* December 31, 1971.

Chapter 14   Proper Macropolicy—The Monetarist View

Baird, Charles. *Macroeconomics—An Integration of Monetary, Search, and Income Theories.* Chicago: Science Research Associates, 1973.

Ireland, Thomas R. *Monetarism,* New Rochelle, New York: Arlington House, 1974.

Meigs, A. James. *Money Matters.* New York: Harper & Row, 1972.

Phelps, E. S., *et al. Micro Foundations of Employment and Inflation Theory.* New York: Norton, 1970.

Sprinkel, Beryl W. *Money and Markets—A Monetarist View,* Homewood, Illinois: Richard D. Irwin, Inc., 1971.

Chapter 15   Dealing with Unemployment and Inflation

Faltermayer, Edmund. "A Better Way to Deal with Unemployment." *Fortune,* June 1973.

Feige, Edgar L., and Pearce, Douglas K. "The Wage-Price Control Experiment—Did It Work?" *Challenge,* July/August 1973.

Feldstein, Martin. "The Economics of the New Unemployment." *The Public Interest*, Fall 1973.

Friedman, Milton. "Using Escalators to Help Fight Inflation." *Fortune*, July 1974.

Miller, R. L., and Williams, R. M. *Unemployment and Inflation*. St. Paul, Minnesota: West Publ. Co., 1974.

Chapter 16 Consumer Demand

Galbraith, J. K. *The Affluent Society*. Boston: Houghton, 1958.

————. (interview). "Conversation with an Inconvenient Economist." *Challenge*, December/October 1973.

Leibenstein, Harvey. "Bandwagon, Snob, and Veblen Effects in the Theory of Consumers' Demand." *Quarterly Journal of Economics*, May 1950.

Telser, L. G. "Some Aspects of the Economics of Advertising." *The Journal of Business*, April 1968.

Trivoli, G. W. "Has the Consumer Really Lost His Sovereignty?" *Akron Business and Economic Review*, Winter 1970.

Chapter 17 Costs and Producers Choice

Alchian, A. A. "Costs," *International Encyclopedia of the Social Sciences*. New York: Macmillan, 1968.

Buchanan, J. M. *Costs and Choice*. Chicago: Markham Publ. Co., 1968.

Colberg, M. R., Forbush, D. R., and Whitaker, G. R. *Business Economics, Principles and Cases*, 5th ed. Homewood, Illinois: Richard D. Irwin, Inc., 1975 (Chaps. 6 and 7).

Chapter 18 Competition

Dewey, Donald. *Microeconomics*. New York: Oxford Univ. Press, 1975 (Chaps. 8 and 9).

Hayek, F. A. "The Meaning of Competition." In *Individualism and Economic Order*. Chicago: Univ. of Chicago Press, 1948.

Kirzner, Israel. *Competition and Entrepreneurship*. Chicago: Univ. of Chicago Press, 1973 (Chaps. 1 and 3).

Manfield, Edwin. *Microeconomics: Theory and Applications*. New York: Norton, 1970 (Chap. 8).

Chapter 19 Monopolistic Competition

Chamberlin, E. H. *The Theory of Monopolistic Competition*, 7th ed. Cambridge, Massachusetts: Harvard Univ. Press, 1956.

Leftwich, Richard H. *The Price System and Resource Allocation*, 5th ed. Hinsdale, Illinois: Dryden Press, 1973 (Chap. 13).

Watson, Donald S., ed. *Price Theory in Action*, 2nd ed. Boston: Houghton Mifflin Company, 1969, Part 6.

Chapter 20 Monopoly

Adams, Walter, ed. *The Structure of American Industry*, 4th ed. New York: Macmillan, 1971 (Chap. 11).

Dewey, Donald. *Microeconomics*, New York: Oxford Univ. Press, 1975 (Chaps. 6 and 7).

Engmon, Lewis A. (Chairman, FTC). An address presented to the Financial Analysis Federation in Detroit on October 6, 1974. Reprinted in *U.S. News and World Report,* November 4, 1974.

Lee, Dwight R., and McNown, Robert F. *Economics in Our Time: Concepts and Issues.* Chicago: Science Research Associates, 1975 (Chap. 6).

Stigler, G. T. "Monopoly and Oligopoly by Merger." *American Economic Review—Proceedings,* vol. XL, 1950, pp. 23–34.

Chapter 21 Oligopoly

Adelman, M. A. "Two Faces of Economic Concentration." *The Public Interest,* Fall 1970, pp. 117–126.

Bain, J. S. *American Economic Review,* vol. XLIV (1954), pp. 15–39.

Leonard, William N. *Business Size, Market Power, and Public Policy.* New York: Thomas Y. Crowell Co., 1969.

Scherer, F. M. *Industrial Pricing—Theory and Evidence,* Chicago: Rand McNally, 1970.

Chapter 22 Business Organization, Competition, and Concentration

Adams, Walter. *The Structure of American Industry,* 4th ed. New York: Macmillan, 1971 (Chap. 13).

Demsetz, Harold. "Where is the New Industrial State?" *Economic Inquiry,* March 1974.

Galbraith, J. K. *Economics and the Public Purpose.* Boston: Houghton Mifflin, 1973.

McGee, J. S. *In Defense of Industrial Competition.* New York: Praeger, 1971.

Simons, H. C. *Economic Policy for a Free Society.* Chicago: Univ. of Chicago Press, 1948 (Chaps. 2 and 3).

Chapter 23 The Supply and Demand of Productive Resources

Fabricant, Solomon. *A Primer on Productivity.* New York: Random House, 1969.

Fleisher, Belton M. *Labor Economics—Theory and Evidence,* Englewood Cliffs, New Jersey: Prentice Hall, 1970.

Freeman, Richard B. *Labor Economics,* Englewood Cliffs, New Jersey: Prentice Hall, 1972 (Chaps. 1–5).

Kiker, B. F., ed. *Investment in Human Capital.* Columbia, South Carolina: Univ. of South Carolina Press, 1971.

Terborgh, George. *The Automation Hysteria,* New York: Norton, 1966.

Chapter 24 Earnings and the Job Market

Jencks, Christopher, *et al. Inequality.* New York: Basic Books, 1972.

Knight, Frank H. *The Economic Organization.* New York: Harper & Row, 1965, pp. 96–121.

Okun, Arthur M. *Equality and Efficiency—The Big Tradeoff.* Washington, D.C.: The Brookings Institution, 1975.

Perlman, Richard. *The Economics of Education.* New York: McGraw-Hill, 1973.

Chapter 25 Union Power—A Shield or a Threat?

Barbash, Jack. "The Changing Structure of Collective Bargaining." *Challenge,* September/ October 1973.

Hutt, W. H. *The Strike-Threat System*, New Rochelle, New York: Arlington House, 1973.

Kennedy, Thomas. "Freedom to Strike is in the Public Interest." *Harvard Business Review*, July/August 1970.

Marshall, Ray, and Perlman, Richard, *An Anthology of Labor Economics: Readings and Commentary*. New York: Wiley, 1972.

Rees, Albert. *The Economics of Trade Unions*. Chicago, Univ. of Chicago Press, 1967.

Chapter 26 Inequality, Income Mobility, and Poverty

Banfield, Edward C. *The Unheavenly City*. Boston: Little, Brown, 1970 (Chaps. 5–7).

Harrington, Michael. *The Other America*. Baltimore: Penguin Books, 1962.

Kristol, Irving. "Taxes, Poverty, and Equality." *The Public Interest*, Fall 1974.

McGuire, Joseph W., and Pichler, Joseph A. *Inequality: The Poor and the Rich in America*. Belmont, California: Wadsworth, 1969.

Lee, Dwight R., and McNown, Robert F., *Economics in our Time: Concepts and Issues*. Chicago: Science Research Associates, 1975 (Chaps. 12 and 13).

Tuckman, Howard P. *The Economics of the Rich*. New York: Random House, 1973.

Chapter 27 Employment Discrimination and the Earnings of Blacks and Women

Freeman, Richard B. "Decline of Labor Market Discrimination and Economic Analysis." *American Economic Review*, May 1973.

Gwartney, James, and Stroup, Richard. "Measurement of Employment Discrimination According to Sex." *Southern Economic Journal*, April 1973.

Kain, John F., ed. *Race and Poverty*. Englewood Cliffs, New Jersey: Prentice-Hall, 1969.

Kreps, Juanita M. *Sex in the Marketplace: American Women at Work*. Baltimore: Johns Hopkins Press, 1971.

Chapter 28 Problem Areas for the Market

Colberg, M. R., Forbush, D. R., and Whitaker, G. R. *Business Economics, Principles and Cases*, 5th ed. Homewood, Illinois: Richard D. Irwin, Inc., 1974 (Chap. 9).

Freeman, A. Myrick, III, Haveman, Robert, and Kneese, Allen V. *The Economics of Environmental Policy*. New York: Wiley, 1973.

Friedman, Milton. *Capitalism and Freedom*. Chicago: Univ. of Chicago Press, 1962 (Chap. II).

Haveman, Robert H., and Margolis, Julius, eds. *Public Expenditures and Policy Analysis*, Chicago: Markham Publ. Co., 1970.

McKean, Roland. *Public Spending*. New York: McGraw-Hill, 1968.

Chapter 29 Public Choice and Gaining from Government

Buchanan, James. *The Bases for Collective Action*. New York: General Learning Press, 1971.

Davis, Lance, and North, Douglas. *Institutional Change and American Economic Growth*. London and New York: Cambridge Univ. Press, 1971.

Olson, Mancur. *The Logic of Collective Action*, Cambridge, Massachusetts: Harvard Univ. Press, 1965.

Scott, Andrew M. *Competition in American Politics—An Economic Model*. New York: Holt, Rinehart and Winston, 1970.

Chapter 30   The Economics of Government Failure

Downs, Anthony. *An Economic Theory of Democracy.* New York: Harper & Row, 1958.
Drucker, Peter F. "The Sickness of Government." *The Public Interest,* Winter 1969.
McKean, Roland. "Government and the Consumer." *Southern Economic Journal,* April 1973.
Tullock, Gordon. *Private Wants, Public Means.* New York: Basic Books, 1970.

Chapter 31   Gaining From International Trade

Adams, Walter. "The New Protectionism." *Challenge,* May/June 1973.
Bastiat, Frederic. "Petition of the Candlemakers." In *Economic Sophisms.* New York: Putnam, 1922.
Pen, Jan. *A Primer on International Trade.* New York: Random House, 1967.

Chapter 32   International Finance and Balance of Payments

Kindleberger, Charles P. (interview). "Why World Bankers are Worried." *Challenge,* October/November 1974.
Stevens, Robert W. *A Primer on the Dollar in the World Economy.* New York: Random House, 1972.
Wallich, Henry C. "Interim Arrangements for World Money." *Challenge,* September/October 1974.

Chapter 33   Comparative Economic Systems

Campbell, Robert W. *The Soviet-Type Economies: Performance and Evolution,* 3rd ed. Boston: Houghton Mifflin, 1974.
Macesich, George. *Yugoslavia—The Theory and Practice of Development Planning.* Charlottesville: Univ. Press of Virginia, 1964.
Pejovich, Svetozar. *The Market-Planned Economy of Yugoslavia.* Minneapolis: Univ. of Minnesota Press, 1966.
Schumpeter, Joseph A. *Capitalism, Socialism and Democracy,* 3rd ed. New York: Harper & Row, 1950.
Schwartz, Harry. *An Introduction to the Soviet Economy.* Columbus, Ohio: Charles E. Merrill Publ. Co., 1968.

HINTS
FOR ANSWERING
DISCUSSION
QUESTIONS

HINTS FOR ANSWERING DISCUSSION QUESTIONS

CHAPTER 1

4. Would the researcher have gotten about the same response if he had asked the same question with regard to the need for more automobiles? clothing? ice cream? color television sets? Can more resources be simultaneously allocated to the production of all these products?

6. The disagreement is positive since one can test to determine whether or not minimum wage laws (a) raise the average earnings of unskilled workers or (b) cause the unemployment rate among the unskilled and youthful to increase.

CHAPTER 2

2. Even though the productivity of painters has changed only slightly, rising productivity in *other areas* has led to higher wages in *other occupations*, thereby increasing the opportunity cost of being a house painter. Since persons would not supply house painting services unless they were able to cover their opportunity costs, the higher wages for house painters were necessary to attract them from competitive (alternative) lines of work.

4. Which women—the college educated or those with only an eighth grade education—are likely to be foregoing the highest earnings when they do not engage in market work?

CHAPTER 3

1. Prices perform two major functions: (a) they ration goods to those willing to pay the highest prices and (b) they provide the incentive for producers to supply the goods. Market prices will be determined by the conflicting forces of supply and demand. Of course, governments may set prices, but when they do so nonprice factors such as shortages, waiting lines, quality deterioration, and black markets will play a more significant role in the determination of supply and the rationing of the existing supply to demanders.

3. (a) and (b); (c) and (d) would affect the supply of beef, rather than the demand; (e) is a change in quantity demanded, not a change in demand.

6. Would the amount of calculators supplied *in 1970* have been greater if their price had been $50 rather than $150? Would the amount supplied in 1975 have been greater if their price had been $150 rather than $50? What happened to the supply of calculators between 1970 and 1975? (*Answer:* It increased.)

CHAPTER 4

2. When it is unnecessary to pay in order to be served, potential customers have a strong incentive to attempt to ride free. But when nonpaying customers diminish (and in some cases eliminate) the sales revenues of potential sellers, they thereby reduce (or eliminate) the seller's incentive to supply the good.

5. Economics usually takes preferences as given, regardless of whether they are determined by physical wants, religion, or philosophy. As long as changes in personal costs and benefits influence choices in a predictable manner, theories for both market and public sector action can be derived and tested against reality. Development and testing of theory are the essential ingredients of a positive science.

6. The antimissile system is a public good *for the residents of Washington, D.C.* In the strict sense of the term, none of the others are public goods since each of them could be provided to some consumers (paying customers, for example) without providing them to others.

CHAPTER 5

4. While breaking the payroll tax into an employer's and employee's share affects neither the employer's hiring costs nor the employee's real wages, it does make it more difficult for employees to identify that they bear the primary burden of the entire tax (including the share levied on the employer). Vote-seeking political entrepreneurs will want to conceal this tax burden from employees. Thus, levying at least part of the tax on the employer is good politics.

6. It does not make sense to speak of either annual consumption or future output without reference to price. Whether our annual consumption of oil during the next 30 years increases fourfold, tenfold, or not at all depends on its price. Similarly, our annual production of oil and related energy sources will be dependent upon their prices. A drawing down of proved reserves (inventories) of energy sources will lead to higher prices, which will discourage consumption while providing the incentive for additional exploration and discoveries. Of course, government price fixing could (and has) negate these positive incentives and assure that we run out of discovered oil (and other energy sources) *at the government decreed price.*

CHAPTER 6

2. When measured in current dollars, a rising GNP may reflect rising prices (inflation), rather than an expansion in output.

4. The GNP does not count (a), (d), (f), and (i). It will count (c), (e), and (g). For (b), if the used car is purchased from a dealer, the dealer's sales commission will count, but not the sales value of the used car. For (h), costs incurred during the discovery period will be counted, but the market value of the discovery will not be counted until it is sold.

CHAPTER 7

1. Is job search ever "profitable" to an unemployed worker? Does it ever lead to an improvement in economic efficiency? Does an unoccupied apartment ever perform a useful function?

4. People usually assume that their money wages would have gone up by the same amount even if there had not been any inflation. This is usually not the case. Inflation is often the source of the rising money wages, while productivity gains are the source of rising *real* wages. When the labor market meters out money wage gains that are in excess of productivity gains, inflation is the major source of the rapid gains in *money* wages.

5. A tax on cash balances—one's average bank deposits, for example—would reduce the purchasing power of the deposits held by an individual. Assuming no inflation an average cash balance of $100 would purchase $100 worth of real goods and services. A 5 percent tax on the average $100 deposit would reduce its real purchasing power to $95 after one year. Similarly, a five percent inflationary rate, just as surely as the tax, would reduce the real purchasing power of the $100 cash deposit to approximately $95 after a year.

CHAPTER 8

3. (a) Increase current consumption, as the expectation of rising future prices will induce consumers to buy now.
(b) Decrease current consumption, as people will attempt to save more for hard times.
(c) Increase current consumption, as the result of an expansion in disposable income.
(d) May have little affect, but the tendency will be toward a reduction in consumption as households have an incentive to save more at the higher interest rate.
(e) Decrease consumption, as falling stock prices will reduce the wealth of consumers.
(f) and **(g)** Increase consumption, as the young and the poor typically have a higher marginal propensity to consume than the elderly and wealthy.
5. Keynes argued that falling wages were (a) unlikely and (b) would be counterproductive because they would reduce aggregate demand. Similarly, the interest rate would fail to equate planned saving and investment since saving is primarily a function of income (not the interest rate) and investment is determined primarily by business expectations and the absence of unused productive capacity.

CHAPTER 9

1. How would such actions affect aggregate demand? the equilibrium level of income?
4. The concept that a change in one of the components of aggregate demand, investment, for example, will lead to a far greater change in the equilibrium level of income. Since the multiplier equals $1/(1 - \text{MPC})$, its size is determined by the marginal propensity to consume. The multiplier principle makes it more difficult to stabilize the economy, since relatively small changes in aggregate demand have a much greater impact on equilibrium income.

CHAPTER 10

1. (a) A tax cut would be primarily inflationary, exerting little impact on real income and employment, as the economy is already at capacity.
(c) A tax cut would lead to an expansion in aggregate demand, real income, and employment, while exerting little impact on prices since excess capacity is present.
7. Were the budget deficits referred to by the quote full employment deficits designed to stimulate the economy? Were they the result of or the cause of the recessions to which the quote refers?

CHAPTER 11

2. Money is valuable because of its scarcity relative to the availability of goods and services. The use of money facilitates (reduces the cost of) exchange transactions. Money also serves as a store of value and a unit of account. Doubling the supply of money, holding output constant, would simply lead to a fall in its purchasing power without enhancing the services that it performs. In fact, *fluctuations* in the supply of money would add uncertainty as to its future value and reduce the ability of money to serve as a store of value, accurate unit of account, and medium of exchange for time dimension transactions.

5. (b), (e), and (f) will reduce the money supply; (a) and (c) will increase it. Counting the Treasury's deposits (or the deposits of persons who receive the Treasury's spending) as part of the money supply, (d) will leave the money supply unchanged.

6. Is printing more paper money the typical way that the U.S. government affects the money supply? Is an increase in the money supply always inflationary?

CHAPTER 12

1. (a) Decrease interest rates, (b) stimulate the level of investment, (c) increase aggregate demand because of the expansion in investment, (d) increase employment, and (e) increase prices only if the economy is at or near full employment.

2. Does borrowing from the public reduce the money holdings of the public before the Treasury spends the proceeds of borrowing? Does Treasury borrowing from the Federal Reserve reduce the public's holdings of money?

7. Inflation is caused by an excess of aggregate demand relative to supply. Expansionary monetary policy, too many dollars chasing too few goods, is only one reason—albeit an important one—for excess demand. Given the conditions described by the quote, is production lagging because of deficient aggregate demand? How would a cut in business taxes affect aggregate demand? If the cut in business taxes enlarges the size of the government deficit, how would borrowing from the public affect aggregate demand? How would borrowing from the Federal Reserve affect aggregate demand?

CHAPTER 13

1. (b) Both Keynesians and monetarists would agree that expansionary monetary policy would be appropriate when economic conditions are depressed. In contrast, monetary policy during the 1929–1933 period and again in 1937–1938 was highly restrictive.

(c) As monetarists often point out, both the entry into the depression (1929–1933) and the relapse in 1938 were accompanied by a *sharp monetary contraction*. In contrast, monetary expansion accompanied the economic expansion of 1934–1937 (see Exhibit 13-5). Monetary policy was highly potent, although it was highly inappropriate, even perverse, during the Great Depression.

4. What must you give up in order to obtain a dollar bill? Would what is given up in order to obtain a dollar change if the prices of all goods, services, and resources doubled?

6. However, the Federal Reserve can buy bonds directly from the public, thereby increasing the money balances of households. According to the monetarist view, this would create an excess supply of money balances for households, inducing them to increase their spending on goods and services as they seek to reduce their money balances.

8. Would competition, per se, drive up prices? Is there any evidence that people were more greedy during the inflation of the late 1960s and early 1970s than during a period of relatively stable prices, the 1950s through the mid-1960s, for example? Was the deflation of the 1929–1933 period the result of a substantial decline in greed?

CHAPTER 14

1. What was happening to the money supply during the period preceding the quote? (See Exhibit 13-5.)

4. When the money supply expands at a fixed rate, it will automatically increase (decrease) *relative to the supply of goods and services* during an economic recession (expansion or boom).

7. (b) Expansionary monetary policy may lead to lower interest rates in the short run, but there is no evidence that it will do so in the long run. In fact, high interest rates, not low, result from rapid *continuous* monetary expansion.

8. Were the low interest rates of the 1930s the result of expansionary monetary policy? Would the expectation of deflation (falling prices) lead to low money interest rates?

CHAPTER 15

4. Unemployment and inflation cannot be considered in isolation from each other. When inflation adds to the uncertainty of time dimension transactions, it discourages investment and long-term planning, thereby distorting resource allocation. The uncertainty associated with inflation can be a source of high unemployment and real economic loss. In the same vein, an inflationary policy that reduces interest rates and real wages, thereby stimulating employment in the short run, can be a source of overexpansion and excess investment. But this overexpansion will often be a source of declining future investment as decision-makers adjust to the inflation. The adjustment process will typically result in above-average rates of unemployment. Thus, the expansionary policy that temporarily reduces unemployment may simultaneously lead to inflation and higher *future rates* of unemployment. As the experience of the 1970s attests, the issue is not so simple that either inflation or unemployment can be preferred to the other.

5. (a) Higher unemployment benefits will reduce the cost of rejecting a job offer.

(b) Unless one is prepared to argue that the demand for leisure and job search time is completely inelastic (that is, perfectly vertical), higher unemployment benefits will necessarily increase the unemployment rate because they will make the combination of leisure, job search, and unemployment cheaper.

7. Boiled down to the basics, this view argues that rising prices (inflation) are caused by rising prices—specifically those prices that rise more rapidly than the average. It is circular reasoning. Even when the price level is stable some prices will be rising (and others falling) more rapidly than the average. Changes in *relative prices* do not cause a general rise in the price level (inflation). Commodities whose prices rise most rapidly (that is, their *relative price* increases) are no more responsible for the inflation than commodities for which the money price fails to decline even though their relative price does so. Arguing that rising prices (either relative or absolute) cause inflation is like arguing that high winds cause hurricanes.

CHAPTER 16

3. (a) 0.21; 1.2. **(b)** Substitutes. Higher fuel oil prices lead to an increase in demand (and consumption) for insulation.

6. Water is usually cheaper than oil because its *marginal utility* at current consumption levels is less than for oil. Since water is so abundant relative to oil, the *additional* benefit derived from a quart of water is less than the *additional* benefit from a quart of oil, even though the *total utility* from all units of water is far greater than the *total utility* from all units of oil. The price of a product, however, will reflect marginal utility, not total utility.

CHAPTER 17

1. The economic profit of a firm is its total revenues minus the opportunity cost of all resources used in the production process. Accounting profit often ignores the opportunity cost of certain resources—particularly the equity capital of the firm and any labor services provided by an owner-manager. Zero economic profit means that the resources owned by the firm are earning their opportunity cost—a rate of return that is as high as the highest valued alternative that is foreeaken. Thus, the firm would not gain by pursuing other lines of business.

7. Would American steel producers be better off without their older facilities? They are free to build modern mills that use the latest technology. When they do not do so, this is strong evidence that their opportunity cost of producing steel is cheaper when they utilize their older, so called less efficient mills. American steel producers cannot blame their current problems on the existence of their older, low opportunity cost facilities.

CHAPTER 18

1. In a highly competitive industry such as farming, lower resource prices might improve the short-run profit rate, but in the long run competition will drive prices down until economic profit is eliminated. Thus, lower resource prices will do little to improve the long-run profitability in such industries.

4.

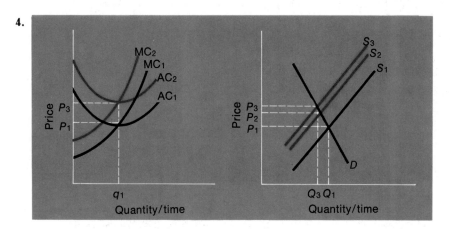

The firm's MC and AC curves will shift upward (to MC_2 and AC_2) by the amount of the tax. The short-run market supply, reflecting the firm's marginal cost, will also shift upward (from S_1 to S_2) by the amount of the tax. In the short run, if the market demand curve is less than perfectly inelastic, the market price will rise to only P_2, an increase that is less than the amount of the tax. Therefore, producers will make short-run losses at price P_2, thereby shouldering part of the burden of the tax. But in the long run firms will exit from the industry, there will be an additional decline in supply (shift to S_3), the price will rise (to P_3), and the profit rate will return to normal. If factor prices remain constant, in the long run the entire burden of the sales taxes will be passed along to consumers. However, since the *industry* output will decline, the demand for the resources used by the industry may fall causing their prices to decline, and thereby placing some of the long-run burden of the tax on the owners of resources used intensively by the industry.

7. (b) 6 or 7 tons; $250 profit.
   (c) 7 or 8 tons; $600 profit.
   (d) 5 or 6 tons; $50 loss; since the firm can cover its variable cost, it should continue in business if it believes that the low ($450) price is temporary.

CHAPTER 19

4. Unless the firm can discriminate among consumers, it must reduce its price on all units, not just the marginal units, in order to expand its sales. Thus, revenue expansion from the additional sales will be at least partially offset by a decline in revenues on other units that must now be sold at a lower price.

5. (b) $440; $10 profit.

(c) Lower price to $440, as a price reduction will *increase* sales revenues more than costs.

CHAPTER 20

4. No; no; no.

5. The formation of the monopoly will result in higher liquor prices and a smaller output. (Show this on a graph.) *Current members* of the retail liquor trade association will gain. However, if they sell their ownership rights to a newcomer, the expected monopoly profits will be capitalized into the value of a retail distributorship. Thus, future purchasers of these ownership rights will have to pay a higher price for them. Liquor consumers will be the major losers from the monopolization of the industry, as they will now confront higher prices.

CHAPTER 21

1. Because they would be able to increase their *joint profits* by raising prices and restricting output until the industry's MR is equal to MC. Collusive efforts are least likely to succeed when there is a large number of firms, entry into the industry cannot be blocked, quality competition is important, demand conditions in the industry are unstable, cost conditions vary among the firms, and the threat of antitrust prosecution is high. Absence of these conditions increases the probability of successful (from the viewpoint of the oligopolists) collusion.

5. Profitability stemming from monopoly power will result in the bidding up of stock prices. Therefore, *current stockholders* will make only the market rate of return on their stock investment even if these firms are making long-run economic profit. *Past stockholders*, who owned shares when the monopoly power was developed would be the major beneficiaries of any market power that these firms might possess. Current stockholders are too late.

CHAPTER 22

4. (a) When the licenses are auctioned off to the highest bidder, their market price will be bid up until it has fully captured any expected economic profit that results from the restrictive entry policy. The firms' average cost curves, including the cost of the license, will shift up until $P = AC$ at the profit-maximizing output level.

(b) When the licenses are granted "free," profit seekers will be willing to make side payments (bribes, political contributions, promises of future jobs, overpayment for services performed, etc.) to political entrepreneurs in order to obtain the valuable licenses. These factors will shift the firms' cost curves upward, at least partially eliminating the economic profit.

(c) Political entrepreneurs prefer (b) because it permits them to at least partially share in the monopoly profits that result from the restrictive policy.

CHAPTER 23

2. Profit-maximizing firms will hire a resource only if they expect its MRP to be greater than (or equal to) its price (resource hiring cost). But they are not unique in this regard. Neither will resource suppliers sell their services unless they expect "to make money by doing so." Trade, including sale of resource services, is not a zero-sum game. With regard to (b), there will be a rough relationship between resource productivity and resource prices, but one should remember that both supply and demand (which will be influenced by the productivity of the resource) operate to determine price. (a) and (b) are not inconsistent with each other.

3. (a) Five.

(b) $1350.

(c) Four; the firm will operate in the short run but it will go out of business in the long run unless the market price rises.

CHAPTER 24

5. Northern and western unions often support a higher minimum wage as a means of increasing the costs of competitive southern firms. Since money wages and the cost of living are lower in the South than the North and West, minimum *money* wage rates will have a greater impact in the South. Rising costs due to a higher minimum wage will reduce the ability of southern firms to compete with their counterparts in the North and West. Thus, industries and union members in the latter two regions can help themselves by pretending to help poor southerners.

8. Jobs are not the key to economic progress. Our economic standard of living will be improved only by production of more goods and services, broadly defined to include such things as leisure, better working conditions, and a cleaner environment in addition to material goods. Improved productivity—that is, greater output per man hour—is the source of such gains. As long as goods are scarce, we will not run out of jobs, although we might have a deficiency in the number of jobs *at a specific wage rate*.

CHAPTER 25

2. If the union is able to raise the wages of the farm workers:

(a) the cost of Florida oranges will rise causing supply to decline and their price to rise in the long run.

(b) profits of the Florida growers will decline in the short run, but in the long run they will return to the normal rate,

(c) mechanization will be encouraged, and

(d) the employment of fruit pickers will decline—particularly in the long run.

3. What impact would higher wages in the South have on the demand for northern union labor?

CHAPTER 26

4. (b) Be careful. The unemployment insurance system reduces the uncertainty associated with loss of one's job. This gain might more than offset reductions in output elsewhere because labor is not fully utilized. *Possible implication:* We should worry less about unemployment when it stems from persons extending their job search time because the cost of continued search has been reduced.

CHAPTER 27

1. **(a)** Before attributing the differential entirely to employment discrimination, one would want to adjust for possible differences between fat and nonfat people with regard to such earnings influencing characteristics as health, education, physical fitness, work experience, marital status, and achievement.

3. Current employment discrimination, past discrimination that has impacted current productivity, and differences in human capital factors such as education (quality as well as quantity), training, *skill-building* experience, and health could all be contributing factors to the wage differentials on the basis of color.

CHAPTER 28

5. Unhappy customers would be most likely for (c), (d), (e), (f), (g) and (i). Light bulbs (a) and food at a local restaurant (b) will be primarily purchased by well informed repeat customers. The quality of the used sofa (h), in contrast to used cars and dishwashers, could be reasonably evaluated by inspection. Thus, fewer unhappy customers would be expected for (a), (b), and (h).

7. When lax pollution control results in lower costs for all firms in an industry, competitive forces will reduce the prices of their products. Thus, the consumers of pollution intensive goods pay lower prices than if production cost fully reflected the opportunity cost of producing such goods. Since profits reflect competitiveness (or lack of same), there is no reason to expect that high pollution firms will make greater (or lesser) profits than other firms. However, differential enforcement could affect the profit rates of firms. If the government vigorously enforces pollution standards against firm A but not firm B, the latter would gain a competitive advantage relative to the former.

CHAPTER 29

1. Do the poor have as much influence on the political process as the rich? Are the poor more likely than the rich to vote? To give political contributions? To lobby?

5. All of the actions, with the possible exception of the operation of the postal service, would appear to stem from "market failure."

CHAPTER 30

5. The regulatory and taxation policy toward the liquor industry is usually conducted at the state, rather than the federal, level. Thus, liquor industry interests will be most likely to use lobbying and campaign contributions to influence the action of state level politicians.

6. When the welfare of a special interest group conflicts with that of a widely dispersed disorganized majority, there is good reason to expect that the legislative political process will work to the benefit of the special interest.

CHAPTER 31

3. (a) and (b) are not in conflict. Since trade restrictions are typically a special interest issue, political enterpreneurs can often gain by supporting them even when they promote economic inefficiency.

5. **(a)** The policy would reduce the supply to the domestic market and raise prices, at least initially.

(b) The elasticity of demand facing foreign producers would increase, since a price increase (above $7.50) would automatically raise the tarriff, raising the price to U.S. purchasers by twice the amount of the seller's increase in price.

(c) OPEC's incentive to collude and raise prices would be reduced by the increase in the elasticity of demand (as seen by OPEC).

6. What impact would a decline in sales of automobiles to the United States have on the ability of foreigners to purchase U.S. goods? How would jobs in other U.S. industries be affected?

CHAPTER 32

4. (a) and (g) would cause the dollar to appreciate; (b), (c), (d), (e), and (h) would cause the dollar to depreciate; (f) would leave the exchange rate unchanged.

CHAPTER 33

7. This view ignores the fact that additional current investment necessitates a reduction in current consumption. Thus, while *future* consumers may gain from a high level of capital accumulation, *current* consumers must clearly sacrifice consumption because of the large share of resources allocated to investment.

INDEX

INDEX

Accelerator, 158–160
Accelerator–multiplier interaction, 160–161
Accelerator principle, 158, 163
Accounting profits, 313, 327
Adams, Walter, 634, 635, 637
Adelman, Morris A., 631, 635
Administrative lag, 256, 264
Advertising, 303–307
Aggregate demand, 134
Aggregate supply, 141, 149
Alchian, A. A., 634
Andersen, Leonall C., 633
Antitrust policy
   alternative views on, 409–413
   antitrust legislation, 405–409
Appreciation, 595
Arrow, Kenneth, 61, 557
Automatic stabilizers, 182
Automation, 443, 448
Average fixed cost, 316, 327
Average propensity to consume, 136–137
Average total cost, 313–314, 318–322, 327

Bach, G. L., 632, 633
Bain, Joe, 392, 635
Baird, Charles, 633
Balance of payments, 584, 588, 595
   deficit, 588, 595
   and exchange markets, 584–587
Balance of trade, 586, 595
Balanced budget multiplier, 168, 622
Banfield, Edward C., 636
Banking system, 187–200
Barbash, Jack, 635

Barriers to entry, 330, 343, 361
Bastiat, Frederic, 8, 631, 637
Becker, Gary, 431
Berle, A. A., 400, 632
Bernstein, Peter L., 633
Blechman, B. M., 632
Board of Governors of the Federal Reserve
   System, 633
Boom, 112, 129
Boskin, Michael, 460
Boulding, Kenneth, 91, 631, 632
Break-even point, 484, 488
Buchanan, James, 61, 65, 631, 634, 636
Budget deficit, 166, 182, 261
Budget surplus, 170, 261
Burns, Arthur, 193, 250
Business cycle, 112, 129, 224–243
   economic contraction, 114
   different views of, 113–116
   and Keynesian view, 160
   and money, 233
Business firm, 310–312
   structures of, 311
Business structures, 400–418

Campbell, Robert W., 604, 606, 637
Canterbery, E. R., 633
Capitalism, 597–600, 611, 612
Capitalist organization, 598
Cash income transfers, 542, 546
Chamberlin, E. H., 634
Choice, 4, 14
   consumer choice, 33–36
   costs and benefits, 9–10

Clark, J. M., 310

Classical theory, 114, 225

Clayton Act, 55, 407

Colberg, M. R., 446, 634, 636

Collective bargaining contract, 450, 468

Collective decision-making, 28, 30, 58–67, 531–546

Collery, Arnold, 632

Collusion, 385–387, 398

Command economy, 601, 612

Common property, 515, 529

Comparative advantage, 20–24, 601
  regional specialization, 23
  trade between nations, 24

Competition, 79, 343, 400–418, 511, *see also* Pure competition
  economic way of thinking, 350
  lack of competition, 54–56

Complements, 294, 308

Concentration, 391–393

Concentration ratio, 390, 398

Conglomerate mergers, 403, 418

Constant cost industries, 337, 343

Consumer choice, 289–308

Consumer expenditures, 289–291, 617

Consumer price index, 99, 108, 122, 267, 277

Consumption, 95–97, 134–139, 149
  substitution in, 424

Consumption function, 135, 149, 620

Corporate profit tax, 176, 179

Corporations, 311–312

Cost, 16, 310–327
  economic way of thinking, 323
  in the long run, 318–322
  shift in cost curves, 322–323
  in the short run, 314–318
  and supply, 324

Davis, Lance, 636

Demand, 289–308
  change in quantity demanded, 38–40
  consumer choice and market demand, 293
  elasticity of, 296–300
  individual demand, 291–293
  international trade, 571
  law of demand, 33–36
  marginal productivity and, 426–427
  for political action, 531–533
  for productive resources, 423–427

for public sector action, 63–64
  and resource prices, 430–432
  shifts in, 38–40, 293–295
  time cost and consumer choice, 296

Demand for money, 222, 226, 245

Dead-end jobs, 446, 448

Decreasing cost industry, 339, 343

Deficit spending, 242

Deficits
  and balance of payments, 587
  planned and actual, 171
  two ways of financing, 208

Deflation, 217–221

Demsetz, Harold, 635

Deposit expansion multiplier, 191, 201

Depression, 113, 129, 217–221

Derived demand, 423, 433

Dewey, Donald, 634

Diseconomies of scale, 321

Discount rate, 198, 201

Discretionary policy, 282

Disposable income, 106, 108, 134

Downs, Anthony, 61, 549, 558, 637

Drucker, Peter, 548, 637

Earnings, 435–448
  of blacks and women, 496–500

Earnings differentials due to nonhomogeneous labor, 436–438

Economic approach, 3–15

Economic efficiency, 52–54, 68, 127, 512, 540, 548

Economic good, 3–4, 14

Economic organization, market and public sector, 60, 559–560

Economic profit, 313, 327

Economic systems, 597–601, 611–612

Economic way of thinking, 5–10

Economics
  normative, 10–11, 14
  positive, 10–11,14

Economies of scale, 321, 327, 391–393

Economizing behavior, 7, 14
  three decisions of, 27–29

Efficiency, *see* Economic efficiency

Einhorn, Henry, 401

Elasticity, 35
  graphic representation of demand, 297
  income elasticity, 302

and total expenditures, 300
Employment
 Keynesian view, 203–217, 279–284
 monetarist's view, 233–236, 279–284
Employment discrimination, 490–507
 the cost of, 494–496
 and earnings, 491–493, 496–497
Energy crisis, 81–86
Engmon, Lewis A., 635
Equation of exchange, 224, 245
Equilibrium, 37–38, 51, 140, 149
 graphic presentation, 143–144
 leakages and injections, 146–147
 tabular presentation, 141–142
 time and the adjustment process, 42–44
Equilibrium level of income, 619–623
Excess demand for money, 245
Excess reserve trap, 213–214, 222
Excess reserves, 190, 201
Excess supply of money, 245
Exchange, personal motivation and gain
 from, 26–27
Exchange rate, 582, 595
 appreciation, 582, 595
 depreciation, 582, 595
 determination of, 582–584
 fixed vs. flexible, 592–594
 flexible, 588–591
Exclusive contract, 406, 418
Expansionary monetary policy, 222, 232, 234
Expected rate of inflation, 245
Explicit costs, 312, 327
Exports, 589
Export–import link, 517
Externalities, 56–57, 68, 544–545
 external benefits, 517–518, 529
 external costs, 512–517, 529

Fabricant, Soloman, 401, 635
Factor prices, 422
Faltermayer, Edmund, 633
Family specialization hypothesis, 502–505,
 507
Federal Reserve System, 116, 192, 212, 250
 tools of, 194–199
 and the treasury, 199
Federal Trade Commission, 55, 407
Feige, Edgar, 267, 633
Feldstein, Martin, 273, 275, 447, 634

Fiscal policy, 165–182, 279, 626–627
 automatic stabilizers, 175
 full-employment budget, 173
 and inflation, 170
 the monetarist view of, 260–263
 and recession, 165
 spending vs. taxing alternatives, 176
Fixed costs, 316, 327
Fixed exchange rates, 591–592, 595
Flanagan, Robert, 269
Fleisher, Belton M., 635
Flexible wages and prices, 133, 588–591, 595
Flowers, Marilyn, 631
Forbush, D. R., 634, 636
Foreign exchange, 581–584, 595
Fractional reserve banking, 189, 201
Free rider, 519, 529
Freeman, Myrick, 521, 636
Freeman, Richard B., 635, 636
Friedman, Milton, 5, 224, 227, 482, 631, 632,
 633, 634, 636
Full employment, 119, 129, 167, 232
 and inflation in the real world, 214
 Keynesians, 279–284
 monetarists, 279–284
 and stable prices, 215
Full-employment budget, 182
Full-employment ceiling, 160, 163

Galbraith, John Kenneth, 301, 373, 400, 410,
 413–417, 534, 556, 634, 635
Gift-in-kind approach, 482, 488
Gliding bands, 594, 595
GNP deflator, 99, 108
Gordon, Robert Aaron, 632
Gosplan, 602, 612
Government demand, 145
Government failure, 548–564
 internal efficiency, 555–557
 shortsightedness effect, 553–555
 special interest effect, 550–553
 voter ignorance, 549
Government spending, 70–87
Gramlich, E. M., 632
Great Depression, 73, 111, 112, 131, 214,
 217–221, 226, 234, 280
Gross national product, 91–109, 111–113, 224
 actual and potential, 120
 components of, 96

expenditure approach, 94–96
and human costs, 102
and nonmarket production, 100
problems with GNP as a measuring rod, 94–104
and production of "bads", 101–102
resource cost–income approach, 97
Gwartney, James, 504, 562, 636

Hanson, Alvin, 632
Harrington, Michael, 636
Hartman, R. W., 632
Haveman, Robert, 521, 631, 636
Haworth, Charles, 496
Haworth, Joan, 496
Hayek, F. A., 634
Heller, Walter, 169, 633
Herriot, R. A., 473, 632
Heyne, Paul T., 631
Hicks, J. R., 557
Homogeneous product, 330, 343
Horizontal mergers, 392, 398
Hough, Robbin R., 631
Human capital approach, 481, 488
Human resources, 421–422, 433
Hutt, W. H., 636

Impact lag, 257, 264
Implicit costs, 312, 327
Import quotas, 574
Imports, 589
Improper dosage, 257
Income distribution, 59–60, 470–475, 540–544
Income elasticity, 302, 308
Income mobility, 475–477
Income redistribution, 482–486, 540–544
Increasing cost industries, 337, 343
Indexing, 276, 285
Inequality, 470–475
Infant industry argument, 576–580
Inflation, 122–127, 209, 217–221, 234, 266–284
differential rates of, 590
expectation of, 228
gains and losses, 124, 126–127
general price level, 122–123
indexing, 276
Keynesian view, 213–217, 279–284

monetarist view, 224–244, 279–284
and money, 326
unanticipated, 125, 129
union impact on, 463
Inflationary gap, 170, 182
Injunction, 464, 468
Interest rates, 140, 204, 222, 250, 258
changes in, 590
investment, 205
real and money rate, 247–250
International finance, 581–595
International sector, size of, 567–570
International trade, 567–579
arguments for restrictions, 576–578
and the great oil cartel, 578–579
protection, 577
Investment, 139–140, 158, 161, 442
in human capital, 422, 433
Investment schedule, 212
Ireland, Thomas R., 633

Jencks, Christopher, 476, 481, 635
Job market, 435–448

Kain, John F., 636
Kendrick, John, 443
Kennedy, Thomas, 636
Keynes, John Maynard, 3, 114, 131, 135, 224
Keynesian theory, 114–115, 225, 279–284, 627–629
business cycle, 160–162
and classical economists, 131–133
consumption and saving, 134–139
equilibrium, 140–141
tools of modern Keynesian analysis, 134–140
Kiker, B. F., 635
Kindleberger, Charles P., 637
Kinked demand curve, 387–398
Kirzner, Israel, 634
Klein, John J., 633
Kneese, Allen, 521, 636
Knight, Frank, 631, 635
Kreps, Juanita, 501, 636
Kristol, Irving, 636
Kuznets, Simon, 105

Labor
  immobility of, 439
  power of, 463–464
Law of comparative advantage, 22–30,
  570–571
Law of demand, 33–36, 51
Law of diminishing marginal utility, 59, 290,
  308, 601
Law of diminishing returns, 315, 327, 600
Law of supply, 36, 51
Lee, Dwight, 524, 631, 635, 636
Leftwich, R. H., 632, 634
Leibenstein, Harvey, 634
Lekachman, Robert, 632
Leonard, William N., 635
Leontief, Wassily, 607
Lerner, Abba, 110
Lewis, H. Gregg, 459
Liquid asset, 201
Liquidity trap, 222, 226
Lockout, 452, 468
Long run, 318, 327
  supply of resources, 428–430
Lorenz curve, 470, 488

McGee, John, 409, 635
McGuire, Joseph W., 636
McKean, Roland, 636, 637
McNown, Robert, 524, 631, 635, 636
Macesich, George, 637
Macroeconomics, 110, 129
Macropolicy, 209, 279
  the monetarist view, 247–263
Mansfield, Edwin, 634
Marginal costs, 314, 327
Marginal physical product, 425, 433
Marginal productivity, 426–427
Marginal propensity to consume, 136–137,
  149
Marginal revenue, 332, 343
Marginal revenue product, 425, 433
Marginal tax rate, 483, 488
Marginal utility, 308
Margolis, Julius, 636
Markets
  repealing the laws of supply and demand,
  46–47
  supply and demand in action, 44–46
  time and the adjustment process, 42–44

  two attributes of, 47–49
Market decisions, 32–51
Market failure, 54–58, 511–529
  external benefits, 517–518
  external cost, 512–517
  and gaining from government, 536–540
  poor information, 522–524
  public goods, 519–522
Market mechanism, 28, 30, 32–51
Marshall, Ray, 636
Meigs, A. James, 633
Meiselman, D. I., 629
Mergers, 391–393
Microeconomics, 110, 129
Miller, H. P., 632
Miller, R. L., 632, 634
Minimum wages, 445, 448
Mishan, E. J., 631
Mitchell, Edward J., 632
Monetarism, 115–116, 224–243, 247–263,
  279–284, 627–629
  constant rate of monetary growth, 259–260
  and fiscal policy, 260–263
  and government, 234
  the impact of money, 230
Monetary policy, 140, 234, 247–260
  and aggregate demand, 210
  effectiveness of, 280
  expansionary and restrictive, 206
  and fiscal policy, 208
  and interest rates, 247
  Keynesian view, 207, 626
  monetarist view, 247–260
  and unemployment rate, 249
Money
  and business cycles, 233
  classical view, 225
  definition of, 184
  demand for, 203, 226
  excess demand for, 231
  excess supply of, 231
  forms of, 185
  functions of, 184–185
  and inflation, 208
  Keynesian view, 203–217, 225
  monetarist view, 226
  near monies, 186
  price of, 229
Money supply, 185, 201, 279
  and aggregate demand, 231

Monopolistic competition, 345–358
  and efficiency, 353–357
  hypothetical model of, 346
  price discrimination, 349–350
  price and output under, 346–349
  product differentiation, 345
Monopoly, 360–380
  government regulation, 369–374
  hypothetical model of, 362–365
  natural, 367–369
Multiplier, 151–155, 163, 621
  balanced budget, 168–170, 622
  graphic illustration of, 153
  reality and, 154
Mundell, Robert A., 631

National debt, 177–182
National income, 105, 108
Natural monopoly, 367–369, 380
  economies of scale and, 367–368
Negative income tax, 483–486, 488
Net national product, 98, 108
No-fault insurance, 544–545
Nonhuman resources, 421–422, 433
Nonpecuniary job characteristics, 438, 448
North, Douglas, 636
Nutter, Warren, 401

Okner, Benjamin, 473, 632
Okun, Arthur M., 632, 633, 635
Oligopoly, 382–398
  characteristics of, 382–383
  collusive action, 385–387
  concentration, economies of scale and
    mergers, 391–393
  kinked demand curve, 387
  price and output determination, 383–385
  and the real world, 390–393
Olson, Mancur, 61, 636
Opportunity cost, 16–18, 25, 30, 312, 600
  of government, 536
  and the real world, 17

Paradox of thrift, 155, 163
Partnerships, 311
Pearce, Douglas, 267, 633
Pechman, J. A., 473, 632

Pejovich, Svetozar, 637
Pen, Jan, 637
Perlman, Richard, 635, 636
Personal income, 105, 108
Pesek, B. P., 629
Peterson, Wallace C., 632
Phelps, E. S., 633
Phillips curve, 216, 222, 251–253, 270
Pichler, Joseph, A., 636
Planned obsolescence, 358
Political advertising, 534
Political entrepreneur, 533–535, 546
Political goods, 61, 68
Pollution, 515–517, 524–528
Poverty, 59, 477–487
  three approaches to, 481–486
Predatory pricing, 405, 418
Price
  and market equilibrium, 37–38
  price ceiling, 46–47, 51
  theory of factor prices, 422
Price discrimination, 350, 358
Price elasticity of demand, 308
Price searcher, 358
Price takers, 331
Pricing system, 42–49
Producer decisions, 310–327
Product differentiation, 345, 358
Production, substitution in, 423
Production possibilities curve, 18–20, 30
Productivity and general level of wages, 440
Profit maximizing, 333
Profits, 394–397
Progressive tax, 78, 86, 176, 279
Property rights, 52, 514–515
Proportional tax, 78, 86
Proprietorships, 311
Public choice, *see* Collective decision-making
Public employment, 271
Public goods, 57, 68, 519–522, 538
Public sector, 28, 52–70
  economic theory and public sector
    decisions, 60
  individual decisions and public policy, 61
  and the market, 559–560
  market and collective action, 61–63
Pure competition, 329–343
  adjustments to changes in demand,
    335–337
  assumptions of, 330

contrasted with monopolistic competition, 352–357
and efficiency, 341
firms and markets, 335–339
firm's supply curve, 334–335
market adjustments to changing production costs, 340–341
role of profits, 339–340
Pure fiscal policy, 260, 264

Quality competition, 351–352, 358
Quantity theory of money, 225, 245
Quotas, 573–574, 580

Rational ignorance effect, 64, 68, 532
Rationing, 47–49
Real GNP, 108
Real rate of interest, 247, 264
Real wages, 249, 264
Recession, 113, 129, 234
Recessionary gap, 165, 182
Reciprocal agreement, 406, 418
Recognition lag, 255, 264
Rees, Albert, 636
Regressive tax, 78, 86
Rent controls, 48
Required reserve ratio, 195, 201
Required reserves, 189, 194–196, 201
Reserves, 188, 201
Resource allocation, 52–58, 350, 598–599
Resource mobility, 433
Resources, 4, 14
    demand for, 423–425
    human and nonhuman, 421
    supply of, 427–430
Restrictive fiscal policy, 170, 182
Restrictive monetary policy, 222
Reynolds, Alan, 633
Right-to-work laws, 451, 468
Robinson, Joan, 351
Rogers, Augustus J., 631
Ryscavage, Paul, 461

Samuelson, Paul, 5, 211, 519, 559, 632, 633
Saving, T. R., 629
Saving, 134, 149
Say, J. B., 132

Say's law, 132, 149
Scarcity, 3–5, 14, 38
    and poverty, 5
    and rationing, 32–33
Scherer, F. M., 635
Schultze, Charles, 521
Schumpeter, Joseph A., 597, 637
Schwartz, Anna, 227
Schwartz, Harry, 637
Scott, Andrew M., 636
Secondary effects, 8, 14
Self-interest redistribution, 541–542, 546
Sharp, A. M., 632
Sherman Antitrust Act, 55, 406
Short run, 314, 327, 331–332
    supply of resources in the, 427–428
Shortage, 38, 51, 270
Shortsightedness effect, 553–555, 564
Simons, H. C., 635
Sirageldin, Ismail, 474
Smith, Adam, 32, 365, 410
Snider, Delbert, 631
Social costs, 512, 529
Socialism, 597–600, 611, 612
Soviet economy, 601–608
    balance sheet, 605
    private sector, 604
Special interest effect, 65–66, 68, 550–553, 561–563
Specialization
    personal motivation and gain from, 26–27
    and work alienation, 25
Sprinkel, Beryl W., 633
Stafford, Frank, 460
Stevens, Robert W., 637
Stewart, Kenneth, 632
Stewart, Michael, 632
Stigler, George J., 375, 389, 401, 635
Strike, 452–454, 468
Stroup, Richard, 504, 636
Substitutes, 294, 308
Sunk costs, 324, 327
Supply
    and international trade, 571
    law of supply, 36
    and the political entrepreneur, 533
    of productive resources, 427–430
    of public sector action, 63–64
    repealing the laws of supply and demand, 46–47

and resource prices, 430–432
shifts in, 40–42
Surplus, 38, 51
and balance of payments, 587

Tariffs, 573–574, 580
Tax incidence, 86
Taxes, 70–87, 148
concept of incidence, 75–77
corporate income, 77
income, 75
indirect business taxes, 97
and inequality, 473
negative income tax, 483–486
payroll, 76
progressive, 78
proportional, 78
regressive, 78
sales and excise taxes, 75
sources of tax revenues, 74
Technology, 20, 30
Telser, L. G., 634
Terborgh, George, 635
Tobin, James, 482
Treasury, 199
Trivoli, G. W., 634
Tuckman, Howard P., 636
Tullock, Gordon, 61, 64, 65, 558, 637

Ulman, Lloyd, 269
Unemployment, 110–130, 133, 266–284
cyclical, 119, 129
dealing with youth, 272
frictional, 117, 129
natural rate of, 119
normal rate of, 129

structural, 118, 129
types of, 116–120
welfare and unemployment compensation,
274
Unemployment compensation, 175, 274, 279
Union shop, 451, 468
Unions, 450–468
collective bargaining contracts, 450
contribution of, 465
determinants of union strength, 457–459
and inflation, 463
methods of gaining wage increases,
455–457
United States
income inequality, 470–473
poverty in, 477–487
Utility, 7, 14, 290

Variable costs, 316, 327
Velocity of money, 225, 245, 280

Wage–price controls, 266–267, 285
Wages, 440
Wallich, H. C., 633, 637
Wallich, M. I., 633
Watson, Donald S., 634
Welfare benefits, 274
Whitaker, G. R., 634, 636
Wilcox, Clair, 360
Williams, R. M., 634
Work scholarship, 273, 285

Yellow-dog contracts, 464, 468
Yugoslavia, 608–611
business firm, 609

GENERAL BUSINESS AND ECONOMIC INDICATORS

Employment, Wages, and Productivity   Prices

Year	Population	Civilian labor force	Unemployment	Unemployment as percent of civilian labor force	Average gross hourly earnings, Total non-agricultural private sector	Index of output per man-hour, Total private sector	Compensation per man-hour, Total private sector	Index of industrial production	Consumer price index	Wholesale price index	Implicit price index (GNP deflator)
	Millions of persons			Percent	Dollars	1967 = 100		1967 = 100	1967 = 100		1958 = 100
1929	121.9	49.2	1.6	3.2	—	—	—	21.6	51.3	49.1	50.6
1930	123.2	49.8	4.3	8.7	—	—	—	18.0	50.0	44.6	49.3
1931	124.1	50.4	8.0	15.9	—	—	—	14.9	45.6	37.6	44.8
1932	124.9	51.0	12.1	23.6	—	—	—	11.6	40.9	33.6	40.2
1933	125.7	51.6	12.8	24.9	—	—	—	13.7	38.8	34.0	39.3
1934	126.5	52.2	11.3	21.7	—	—	—	15.0	40.1	38.6	42.2
1935	127.4	52.9	10.6	20.1	—	—	—	17.3	41.1	41.3	42.6
1936	128.2	53.4	9.0	16.9	—	—	—	20.4	41.5	41.7	42.7
1937	129.0	54.0	7.7	14.3	—	—	—	22.3	43.0	44.5	44.5
1938	130.0	54.6	10.4	19.0	—	—	—	17.6	42.2	40.5	43.9
1939	131.0	55.2	9.5	17.2	—	—	—	21.7	41.6	39.8	43.2
1940	132.1	55.6	8.1	14.6	—	—	—	25.4	42.0	40.5	43.9
1941	133.4	55.9	5.6	9.9	—	—	—	31.6	44.1	45.1	47.2
1942	134.9	56.4	2.7	4.7	—	—	—	36.3	48.8	50.9	53.0
1943	136.7	55.5	1.1	1.9	—	—	—	44.0	51.8	53.3	56.8
1944	138.4	54.6	0.7	1.2	—	—	—	47.4	52.7	53.6	58.2
1945	140.0	53.9	1.0	1.9	—	—	—	40.6	53.9	54.6	59.7
1946	141.4	57.5	2.3	3.9	—	—	—	35.0	58.5	62.3	66.7
1947	144.1	59.4	2.3	3.9	1.131	51.3	36.2	39.4	66.9	76.5	74.6
1948	146.6	60.6	2.3	3.8	1.225	53.6	39.5	41.0	72.1	82.8	79.6
1949	149.2	61.3	3.6	5.9	1.275	55.3	40.1	38.8	71.4	78.7	79.1
1950	151.7	62.2	3.3	5.3	1.335	59.7	42.8	44.9	72.1	81.8	80.2
1951	154.3	62.0	2.1	3.3	1.45	61.5	46.9	48.7	77.8	91.1	85.6
1952	157.0	62.1	1.9	3.0	1.52	62.7	49.8	50.6	79.5	88.6	87.5
1953	159.6	63.0	1.8	2.9	1.61	65.3	52.9	54.8	80.1	87.4	88.3
1954	162.4	63.6	3.5	5.5	1.65	66.9	54.5	51.9	80.5	87.6	89.6
1955	165.3	65.0	2.9	4.4	1.71	69.9	55.9	58.5	80.2	87.8	90.0
1956	168.2	66.6	2.8	4.1	1.80	70.0	59.5	61.1	81.4	90.7	94.0
1957	171.3	66.9	2.9	4.3	1.89	72.0	63.3	61.9	84.3	93.3	97.5
1958	174.1	67.6	4.6	6.8	1.95	74.3	66.0	57.9	86.6	94.6	100.0
1959	177.1	68.4	3.7	5.5	2.02	76.9	69.0	64.8	87.3	94.8	101.7
1960	180.7	69.6	3.9	5.5	2.09	78.2	71.7	66.2	88.7	94.9	103.3
1961	183.8	70.5	4.7	6.7	2.14	80.9	74.4	66.7	89.6	94.5	104.6
1962	186.7	70.6	3.9	5.5	2.22	84.7	77.7	72.2	90.6	94.8	105.8
1963	189.4	71.8	4.1	5.7	2.28	87.7	80.8	76.5	91.7	94.5	107.2
1964	192.1	73.1	3.8	5.2	2.36	91.1	84.9	81.7	92.9	94.7	108.9
1965	194.6	74.5	3.4	4.5	2.45	94.2	88.4	89.2	94.5	96.6	110.9
1966	197.0	75.8	2.9	3.8	2.56	98.0	94.5	97.9	97.2	99.8	114.0
1967	199.1	77.3	3.0	3.8	2.68	100.0	100.0	100.0	100.0	100.0	117.6
1968	201.2	78.7	2.8	3.6	2.85	102.9	107.6	105.7	104.2	102.5	122.3
1969	202.7	80.7	2.8	3.5	3.04	103.3	115.8	110.7	109.8	106.5	128.2
1970	204.9	82.7	4.1	4.9	3.22	104.4	124.6	106.6	116.3	110.4	135.2
1971	207.0	84.1	5.0	5.9	3.43	108.7	133.3	106.8	121.3	133.9	141.6
1972	208.8	86.5	4.8	5.6	3.65	111.8	140.2	115.2	125.3	119.1	146.1
1973	210.4	88.7	4.3	4.9	3.89	114.8	151.0	125.5	133.1	134.7	153.9
1974	211.2	91.0	5.1	5.6	4.22	111.7	164.1	122.5	147.7	160.1	170.2